Fodor's

UTAH

WELCOME TO UTAH

From mountain-biking on slickrock to hiking past dinosaur fossils, Utah has thrilling adventures for everyone. The world-class ski resorts of the Wasatch Mountains are a haven for those seeking perfect powder, and national parks such as Arches and Zion offer colorful geology lessons with natural arches, hoodoos, and mesas in brilliant ocher and red. History lovers can ponder petroglyphs made by the earliest inhabitants or explore the Mormons' pioneer past in Salt Lake City. At the end of the day's activities, a hot tub and plush bed await.

TOP REASONS TO GO

★ **National Parks:** Spectacular Zion, Bryce Canyon, Arches, Capitol Reef, and Canyonlands.

★ **Outdoor Fun:** Rafting the Colorado River, fishing at Flaming Gorge, and more.

★ **Sundance:** The resort is an artist's dream, the indie film festival a must-do.

★ **Skiing:** Superb snow, varied runs, and swanky resorts like Deer Valley and Snowbird.

★ **Frontier History:** The Pony Express Trail, Wild West towns, and the Golden Spike.

★ **Salt Lake City:** Remarkable Temple Square, plus renowned museums and gorgeous vistas.

12
TOP EXPERIENCES

Utah offers terrific experiences that should be on every traveler's list. Here are Fodor's top picks for a memorable trip.

1 Winter Sports

The "greatest snow on Earth," plentiful sunshine, and beautiful panoramas make Utah a fabulous winter playground. Deer Valley Resort *(above)* in Park City draws crowds with its groomed ski trails for families as well as experts. *(Ch. 2, 3, 4)*

2 Scenic Drives

Mirror Lake Scenic Byway *(above)* through the Uinta Mountains is one of the state's unforgettable drives. Highway 12 is another stunner. *(Ch. 5, 6, 7, 8, 9, 10, 11)*

3 Bryce Canyon National Park

Drive the main park road for breathtaking views into the canyon. For a closer look, accessible hikes take you into the amphitheater to see limestone spires, called hoodoos. *(Ch. 8)*

4 Sundance

A ski resort and year-round artistic retreat, Sundance is best known for the annual independent film festival founded by Robert Redford and based in nearby Park City. *(Ch. 3)*

5 Dinosaur Tracking

Utah is a treasure chest of dinosaur remains. See tantalizing footprints at several museums, including the Natural History Museum of Utah *(above)* in Salt Lake City. *(Ch. 2, 5, 9, 12)*

6 Delicate Arch

Recognize this arch? Utah's calling card is this well-known rock formation in Arches National Park. Get up close on a moderate 3-mile hike and marvel at its scale. *(Ch. 10)*

7 Water Sports

Skiing grabs the headlines but fly fishing, boating, and river rafting, especially on the mighty Colorado River *(above)*, make this a year-round destination. *(Ch. 5, 12)*

8 Salt Lake City

At the foot of the Wasatch Mountains, Utah's capital has a stunning setting, Mormon culture, cosmopolitan dining, and easy access to outdoor activities. *(Ch. 2)*

9 Zion National Park

Angels Landing Trail *(below)*, with its exhilarating overlooks, and the Narrows Trail, set in a river between dramatic 2,000-foot cliffs, make Zion one of America's top parks. *(Ch. 7)*

10 Moab

This countercultural frontier town is a hub of artsy activity and a great base for Arches National Park. It's a must for biking, rock-climbing, and rafting as well. *(Ch. 12)*

11 Great Salt Lake

The best place to explore one of the earth's saltiest locales is Antelope Island, home to scores of bison *(above)* and a pit stop for migrating birds. *(Ch. 2)*

12 Two-wheeled Fun

Mountain-bike trails, such as the world-famous Slickrock Trail near Moab and the White Rim Trail *(above)*, are unparalleled. *(Ch. 5, 11, 12)*

CONTENTS

1 EXPERIENCE UTAH 13
  What's Where 14
  Utah Planner 18
  Utah Outdoor Adventures 20
  If You Like 26
  Great Itineraries 28
  Utah's Five Glorious National
  Parks, 6 Days 28
  The Best of Salt Lake City and
  Northern Utah, 4 Days 30
  A Brief History of Mormonism 32
  Utah with Kids 33
  Which National Park
  Should I Visit? 34

2 SALT LAKE CITY 35
  Orientation and Planning 37
  Exploring 42
  Sports and the Outdoors 59
  Where to Eat 62
  Best Bets for Salt Lake
  City Dining 64
  Where to Stay 73
  Best Bets for Salt Lake
  City Lodging 74
  Nightlife and Performing Arts 78
  Shopping 81
  Side Trips from Salt Lake City 82

3 PARK CITY AND THE SOUTHERN
  WASATCH 95
  Orientation and Planning 96
  Park City and the Wasatch Back . . 100
  South of Salt Lake City 123

4 NORTH OF SALT LAKE CITY . . 137
  Orientation and Planning 138
  Ogden City and Valley 143
  The Golden Spike Empire 154
  Cache Valley 159

  Bear Lake Country 167

5 DINOSAURLAND AND
  EASTERN UTAH 171
  Orientation and Planning 173
  Northeast–Central Utah
  (Castle Country) 176
  The Uinta Basin (Dinosaurland) . . . 181

6 CAPITOL REEF NATIONAL
  PARK 195
  Welcome to Capitol Reef
  National Park 196
  Capitol Reef Planner 198
  Exploring 201
  Sports and the Outdoors 203
  Where to Eat 207
  Where to Stay 207

7 ZION NATIONAL PARK 209
  Welcome to Zion National Park . . . 210
  Zion Planner 212
  Exploring 216
  Sports and the Outdoors 219
  Where to Eat 223
  Where to Stay 224

8 BRYCE CANYON NATIONAL
  PARK 225
  Welcome to Bryce Canyon
  National Park 226
  Bryce Canyon Planner 228
  Exploring 231
  Sports and the Outdoors 234
  Where to Eat 238
  Where to Stay 239

9 SOUTHWESTERN UTAH 241
  Orientation and Planning 242
  Utah's Dixie 246

CONTENTS

Along U.S. 89—Utah's Heritage
Highway 259

Grand Staircase–Escalante
National Monument 264

10 ARCHES NATIONAL PARK. . . . 273

Welcome to Arches National
Park. 274

Arches Planner. 276

Exploring. 279

Sports and the Outdoors. 282

Where to Eat 287

**11 CANYONLANDS NATIONAL
PARK 289**

Welcome to Canyonlands
National Park 290

Canyonlands Planner. 292

Exploring. 295

Sports and the Outdoors. 298

**12 MOAB AND SOUTHEASTERN
UTAH 305**

Orientation and Planning. 306

Moab. 310

Southeastern Utah 325

TRAVEL SMART UTAH. 337

INDEX. 351

ABOUT OUR WRITERS 360

Park City and the Southern
Wasatch 98

Park City and the Wasatch Back . . 102

Park City 104

South of Salt Lake City. 124

North of Salt Lake City. 140

Northern Utah 155

Logan 162

Dinosaurland and Eastern Utah. . . 177

Central Bryce Canyon 236

Southwestern Utah. 244

Utah's Dixie. 247

St. George. 252

U.S. 89 and Grand Staircase–
Escalante 260

Devils Garden Trail. 286

Island in the Sky. 301

Needles. 302

Moab and Southeastern Utah 309

Moab. 313

Southeastern Utah 327

MAPS

Exploring Salt Lake City 44–45

Temple Square 46

Downtown Salt Lake City. 48

Capitol Hill and the Avenues. 52

East Side and the University
of Utah 54

Where to Eat and Stay in
Salt Lake City 66–67

ABOUT THIS GUIDE

Fodor's Recommendations

Everything in this guide is worth doing—we don't cover what isn't—but exceptional sights, hotels, and restaurants are recognized with additional accolades. **Fodor's Choice★** indicates our top recommendations; and **Best Bets** call attention to notable hotels and restaurants in various categories. Care to nominate a new place? Visit Fodors.com/contact-us.

Trip Costs

We list prices wherever possible to help you budget well. Hotel and restaurant price categories from **$** to **$$$$** are noted alongside each recommendation. For hotels, we include the lowest cost of a standard double room in high season. For restaurants, we cite the average price of a main course at dinner or, if dinner isn't served, at lunch. For attractions, we always list adult admission fees; discounts are usually available for children, students, and senior citizens.

Hotels

Our local writers vet every hotel to recommend the best overnights in each price category, from budget to expensive. Unless otherwise specified, you can expect private bath, phone, and TV in your room. For expanded hotel reviews, facilities, and deals, visit Fodors.com.

Top Picks	Hotels &
★ **Fodor's** Choice	**Restaurants**
	🏨 Hotel
Listings	⤴ Number of
✉ Address	rooms
✉ Branch address	❑ Meal plans
☎ Telephone	✗ Restaurant
📠 Fax	⌺ Reservations
⊕ Website	🏛 Dress code
✉ E-mail	▭ No credit cards
▦ Admission fee	[$] Price
◷ Open/closed	
times	**Other**
Ⓜ Subway	⇨ See also
⊹ Directions or	☞ Take note
Map coordinates	⅃ Golf facilities

Restaurants

Unless we state otherwise, restaurants are open for lunch and dinner daily. We mention dress code only when there's a specific requirement and reservations only when they're essential or not accepted. To make restaurant reservations, visit Fodors.com.

Credit Cards

The hotels and restaurants in this guide typically accept credit cards. If not, we'll say so.

EUGENE FODOR

Hungarian-born Eugene Fodor (1905–91) began his travel career as an interpreter on a French cruise ship. The experience inspired him to write *On the Continent* (1936), the first guidebook to receive annual updates and discuss a country's way of life as well as its sights. Fodor later joined the U.S. Army and worked for the OSS in World War II. After the war, he kept up his intelligence work while expanding his guidebook series. During the Cold War, many guides were written by fellow agents who understood the value of insider information. Today's guides continue Fodor's legacy by providing travelers with timely coverage, insider tips, and cultural context.

EXPERIENCE
UTAH

WHAT'S WHERE

The following numbers refer to chapters in the book.

2 Salt Lake City. Though it is the home of the Mormon Church, Utah's capital city is surprisingly progressive, and is an ideal launch pad for your Utah adventure. The region played host to the 2002 Winter Olympics, but has more to offer than religious and sporting sights. Don't miss the new museums, walkable downtown shopping at Gateway and City Creek, and an emerging dining scene.

3 Park City and the Southern Wasatch. Miners tunneled throughout the beautiful Wasatch Range to build the local economy, but modern-day prospectors look skyward to winter snow and summer sunshine to drive the economy in this primo spot. Three world-class resorts, historic Main Street, and the Sundance Film Festival are just a few reasons to escape to the mountains less than an hour from Salt Lake City Airport. The bucolic college town of Provo, home to America's "driest" university (Brigham Young University) lies at the other end of the excitement spectrum.

4 North of Salt Lake City. Much of northern Utah is within the boundaries of the Wasatch-Cache National Forest, with breathtaking landscapes, miles of trails, and the turquoise waters of Bear Lake. Busy tourists invariably skip this region for the national parks in the south, so come here to escape crowds. Ogden and Logan offer services, restaurants, and universities.

5 Dinosaurland and Eastern Utah. Imagine high Western skies and an endless range, and you have a vision of eastern Utah. The Uinta Range of the Rocky Mountains is a land of craggy peaks and remote ranches, where fertile farms and grazing lands mingle with red-rock deserts. Mirror Lake, Flaming Gorge, and the Dinosaurland National Monument deliver entirely unique experiences.

6 Capitol Reef National Park. Formed by cataclysmic forces that have pushed and compressed the earth, this otherworldly landscape is marked by oversize, unique sandstone formations, some layered with plant and animal fossils. It is best known for its 100-mile long geological feature, the Waterpocket Fold. Loa, Teasdale, and Torrey have become hot spots for artists and wanderers.

GREAT SALT LAKE DESERT

GREAT SALT LAKE DESERT

NEVADA
UTAH

DEEP CREEK RANGE

30

80

6

21

257

0   50 mi

0   50 km

Minersville

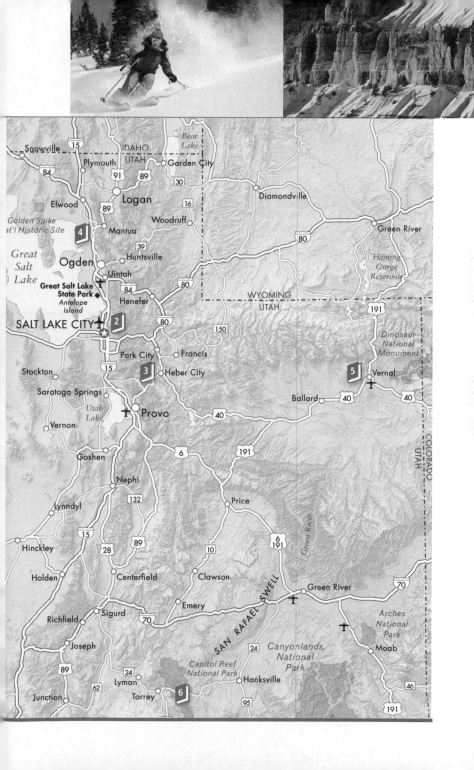

WHAT'S WHERE

7 Zion National Park. Known for its sheer 2,000-foot cliffs and river-carved canyons, Zion deserves to be on every Las Vegas and/or Grand Canyon agenda. There is no match for the soaring perspective on trails like Angels Landing and the Narrows, but you don't have to hike to see why the park is so special: the roadways leading through Zion provide ample viewing opportunities.

8 Bryce Canyon National Park. The bizarrely shaped, bright red-orange rocks that are this park's signature formation are known as hoodoos. If you can hit the trails at sunrise or sunset, your reward will be amazing colors; the sun's light at either end of the day intensifies the rocks' deep orange and crimson hues. See every vista in the park from the 18-mile Main Road, then retreat to historic Bryce Lodge for dinner or a ranger talk.

9 Southwestern Utah. You can play golf year-round in the retirement community of St. George, but the region's best attractions are not man-made. Venture onto trails, view an active dinosaur excavation site, or lose yourself in the mostly road-free, expansive Grand Staircase–Escalante National Monument.

10 Arches National Park. The largest collection of natural sandstone arches in the world—more than 2,000—are within this park, but the landscapes framed by the graceful structures leave just as lasting an impression. The desert here is a rich tapestry of red, purple, and chocolate hues. Look carefully for hardy wildlife and desert flowers—true survivor tales under year-round sunshine.

11 Canyonlands National Park. This might be the most difficult park to truly fathom without putting on your hiking boots. Canyonlands is best enjoyed on a hike, mountain bike, or raft. You'll wish you were a high-flying bald eagle or red-tail hawk to appreciate the precipice of adjacent Dead Horse Point and the wishbone canyons carved by the Colorado and Green rivers.

12 Moab and Southeastern Utah. Home to the world-famous Slick Rock mountain bike trail—and some of America's best river rafting—Moab is a countercultural retreat with quirky and original boutiques, restaurants, bars, and locals. The perfect base for Arches and Canyonlands National Parks, this area's sagebrush flats, slot canyons, broad mesas, and snow-capped peaks leave a lasting impression.

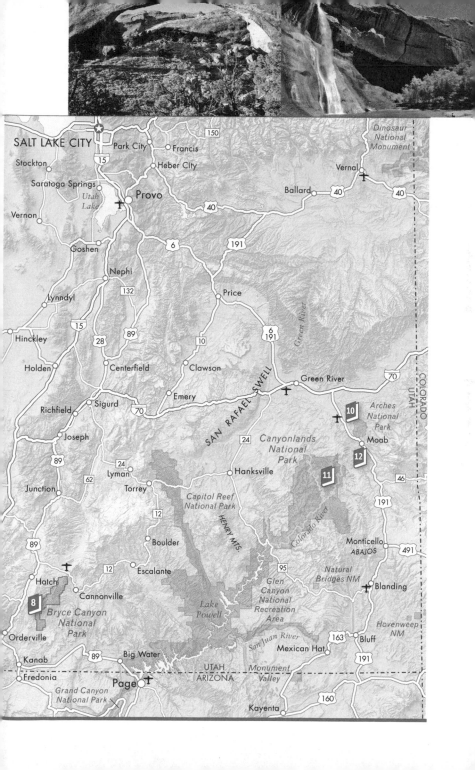

UTAH PLANNER

When to Go

Home to both inhospitable desert and soaring mountain peaks renowned for their powdery snow, Utah is a bipolar state with something to experience year-round. You can golf, bike, fish, and swim year-round in St. George—but you can also ski from as early as November to as late as July 4 at Snowbird Ski Resort just outside Salt Lake City. The national parks are best visited in spring and fall to avoid millions (literally) of other visitors, but they're located at high elevations, so be prepared for shoulder season rain or snow. Fall color displays can be found in nearly every canyon in the state. Cottonwood trees turning brilliant gold along river bottoms with a backdrop of red rock make particularly good photographs.

Given the glut of tourists in southern Utah parks in the summer, plan ahead to ensure that you have lodging—even the growing number of RV parks and campgrounds fill to capacity in July and August.

Getting Here

AIR TRAVEL

Salt Lake City International Airport is the efficient gateway to the state for many visitors, and as a hub for Delta and Southwest, you can get here direct from most of the United States plus several cities in Canada and Mexico. If you're concentrating your time in the southern national parks, consider Las Vegas or St. George airports to avoid the five-hour drive from Utah's capital to Zion.

CAR TRAVEL

The automobile rules this expansive state, and it's the only way to connect the national parks with the services, hotels, and restaurants you'll need to enjoy your visit. Three interstates cover the main approaches to the state: I–15 connects Yellowstone (5 hours north of Salt Lake City), Utah's capital, Bryce, Zion, St. George, Las Vegas, and, ultimately, Los Angeles; I–70 connects east–west travelers from Denver (via Moab and Canyon country); and I–80 delivers you from northern California and Reno across the Bonneville Salt Flats and the Great Basin.

Driving Times

FROM–TO	MILES	HOURS
Las Vegas–St. George	119	2
Salt Lake City–St. George	300	4½
St. George–Zion	41	1
Yellowstone–Salt Lake City	320	5
Salt Lake City–Moab	235	4
Las Vegas–Zion	165	3
Zion to Bryce	115	2
Canyonlands to Salt Lake City	244	4

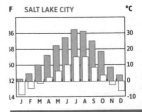

SALT LAKE CITY

1

Getting Around

North to south, Utah's I–15 spine is longer than the drive from New York to Montreal, so Utah's pristine beauty requires motorized transportation (car, motorcycle, or RV) for access. In summer, winding mountain roads and long dry basins are either a boon (convertibles, motorcycles) or bane (some roads were clearly not built with RVs in mind). In winter, high elevations and serious storms make a sturdy car the best option. Storms occasionally shut down highway passes and/or resort access, so be flexible.

About the only places you can do without a car are Salt Lake City and Park City. You can enjoy three world-class ski resorts in Park City without a car (grab a taxi or shuttle from the airport and ride the town's public transportation), but it's harder to get to resorts like Alta, Snowbasin, or Snowbird without a car.

The Predominant Religion

The population of Utah was estimated to be 2.9 million in 2013. About 50% of Salt Lake City's residents belong to the Church of Jesus Christ of Latter-day Saints (LDS), but statewide the number is closer to 70% of Utah's population.

For all the misconceptions about the Mormon faith, you may scarcely notice any evidence of it as you explore Utah. It's true that Mormons generally don't smoke, or drink coffee, tea, or alcohol—but tobacco, caffeinated drinks, and liquor tend to be widely available in stores. Members of the LDS faith generally observe Sunday as a day of rest, so plan ahead, as many stores, restaurants, and other services may be closed—including all liquor stores. You will see many non-LDS houses of worship in Utah, including a major Catholic cathedral, a mosque, and a synagogue in Salt Lake City. Mormon missionaries are famed for their proselytizing, but outside of the state's temples you likely won't encounter one, as they tend to spend their time in residential areas. Finally, Mormons tend to be very friendly, family-oriented, and have a great deal of civic activism and pride—all of which make Utah a very hospitable and enjoyable place to visit.

Mark Your Calendar

Utah has a few annual events that are worth planning your trip around, so mark your calendars and make reservations early.

■ **Sundance Film Festival** takes place annually over 11 days at the end of January (Jan. 21–Jan. 31, 2016). Park City and its crowds get the limelight, but you can catch films (and their stars) in Salt Lake City and Ogden as well.

■ The largest outdoor recreation trade show in the country, the **Outdoor Retailer Expo,** makes winter (Jan. 20–23, 2016) and summer (August 5–9, 2015) stops in Salt Lake City. It's closed to the public, but could affect your plans because it often rents every hotel room in the valley.

■ Utah's **Pioneer Day** celebrations mark Brigham Young's arrival on July 24, 1847. Statewide, you will find fireworks, rodeos, parades, and fairs that often dwarf Independence Day celebrations.

■ **Ski season** traditionally begins Thanksgiving week at many resorts. Plan to ski in November, March, or April to avoid the biggest crowds. Prices spike and accommodations fill around major holidays like President's Day.

UTAH OUTDOOR ADVENTURES

BIKING

Cycling buffs have long known that Utah's open roads are frequented by Tour de France stars, including locals Levi Leipheimer and David Zabriskie, and since 2010 the Larry H. Miller Tour of Utah has been one of America's premier multi-day stage races. Add to that Moab's Slick Rock, Porcupine, and White Rim trails for mountain bikers, and Utah is one of the top three destinations for cycling in the United States.

Rent a Bike

Thanks to the popularity of the sport here, it's usually easy to find a place that rents bicycles if you'd prefer to leave yours at home. Shops often rent a variety of bikes from entry-level to high-end, though the latter come at a premium. Bike shops are also a good bet for information on local rides and group tours.

Rules of the Road

On the road, watch for trucks, and stay as close as possible to the right side of the road, in single file. If you're nervous about cars, hop on the **Legacy Park Trail** near Salt Lake City Airport and ride 15 miles north on a perfectly flat, paved trail that skirts Great Salt Lake. If you're downstate, the rural roads outside St. George, Cedar City, and Moab offer miles of varied topography with relatively little traffic to affect the experience. On the trail, ride within your limits and keep your eyes peeled for hikers and horses (both of which have the right of way), as well as dogs. Always wear a helmet and carry plenty of water.

Best Rides

Antelope Island State Park. It's cheaper to enter Antelope on two wheels, and much more enjoyable, but only strong riders should brave the 7-mile causeway, especially in the heat of summer. Once you reach the island, however, there are miles of rolling and empty trails.

Bonneville Shoreline Trail. Partway up and along the Wasatch Front on the northeast side of Salt Lake City, this hiking and mountain biking trail offers expansive views of the entire Salt Lake Valley, plus points west and south. Its level of difficulty is easy to moderate, with challenging stretches near the University of Utah Hospital.

Flaming Gorge National Recreation Area. Because it mixes high-desert vegetation— blooming sage, rabbit brush, cactus, and wildflowers—and red-rock terrain with a cool climate, Flaming Gorge is an ideal destination for road and trail biking. The 3-mile round-trip Bear Canyon–Bootleg ride begins south of the dam off U.S. 191 at the Firefighters' Memorial Campground and runs west to an overlook of the reservoir.

Klondike Bluffs Trail. This trail offers the less-experienced mountain biker a relatively easy introduction to the sport. The climb to Klondike Bluffs is not difficult, and the reward is a fantastic view into Arches National Park. Access is off U.S. 191, 15 miles north of Moab—not the main park entrance.

Mid-Mountain Trail. Midway up the slopes (about 8,000 feet above sea level), this trail connects Deer Valley, Park City, and Canyons ski resorts. It's moderate enough for experienced kids to handle, although the descents to the valley floor vary widely. This trail is one of the reasons that the **International Mountain Biking Association** bestowed its first-ever "Gold Level Ride Center" status on Park City.

Slick Rock Trail. America's most famous mountain-biking trail is a 12-mile loop

through sagebrush and sand, over slick granite rock and across undulations that can only be described as moonlike. It's well marked, popular, and incredibly challenging, but not particularly scary. Don't be afraid to walk up or down a few of the crazier inclines and always wear a helmet. This trail is not recommended for kids under 12.

FISHING

Trout do not live in ugly places. And, so it is in the American West, where you'll discover unbridled beauty, towering pines, rippling mountain streams, and bottomless pools. It is here that blue-ribbon trout streams remain much as they were when Native American tribes, French fur trappers, and a few thousand miners, muleskinners, and sodbusters first placed a muddy footprint along their banks.

Make the Most of Your Time

Early-day settlers had one advantage that you won't: time. If you're going to make best use of that limited vacation in which fishing is a preferred activity, you should consider hiring a guide. You could spend days locating a great fishing spot, learning the water currents and fish behavior, and determining what flies, lures, or bait the fish are following. A good guide will cut through the clutter, get you into fish, and turn your excursion into an adventure complete with a full creel.

If you're not inclined to fork over the $250-plus that most quality guides charge per day for two anglers and a boat, your best bet is a stop at a reputable fly shop. They'll shorten your learning curve, tell you where the fish are, what they're biting on, and whether you should be "skittering" your dry-fly on top of the water or "dead-drifting" a nymph. ■TIP→ Famed

fisherman Lee Wolff wrote, "Catching fish is a sport. Eating fish is not a sport." Consequently, you'll find most fishermen catch and release in an effort to maintain productive fisheries and protect native species.

What to Bring

If you're comfortable with your fishing gear, bring it along, though most guides loan or rent equipment. Bring a rod and reel, waders, vest, hat, sunglasses, net, tackle, hemostats, and sunscreen. Always buy a fishing license.

When to Go

The season is always a concern when fishing. Spring run-offs can cloud the waters. Summer droughts may reduce stream flows. Fall weather can be unpredictable in the West. But, as many fishing guides will attest, the best time to come and wet a line is whenever you can make it.

Best Fishing

Flaming Gorge. For some of the finest river fishing, try the Green River below Flaming Gorge Dam, where rainbow and brown trout are plentiful and big. Fed by cold water from the bottom of the lake, this stretch has been identified as one of the best trout fisheries in the world.

Lake Powell. Formed by the construction of Glen Canyon Dam, this popular recreational attraction in southern Utah is home to a wide variety of fish, including bass—striped, smallmouth, and largemouth—as well as bluegill and channel catfish. Ask the locals about night fishing for stripers.

Provo River. One of Utah's world-class fly-fishing rivers, the Provo is divided into three sections, starting in the High Uintas Wilderness about 90 minutes east of Salt Lake City and ending in Utah Lake in Provo. Brown and rainbow trout are the big draw here.

HIKING

You can conjure up some of the longest, most challenging backcountry hikes in America in countless locations in Utah, but hiking doesn't have to be that difficult. Don sturdy boots, pack water, lean on the hardworking park rangers for guidance, and head out for a few hours. Your heart, lungs, and soul will thank you. Trailheads depart from most cities, too, including worthy treks from downtown Salt Lake City, Ogden, Park City, and Moab.

Safety

There are several hazards to hiking, but a little preparedness goes a long way. Know your limits, and make sure the terrain you are about to embark on does not exceed your abilities. It's a good idea to check the elevation change on a trail before you set out—a 1-mile trail might sound easy, until you realize how steep it is—and be careful not to get caught on exposed trails at elevation during afternoon storms (rain or snow) any time of year. Dress appropriately, bringing layers to address changing weather conditions, and always carry enough drinking water. Also, make sure someone knows where you are going and when to expect your return. Don't be so sure your mobile phone will rescue you from the wilderness either. Much of rural Utah is a black hole for cellular coverage.

When to Go

You will be rewarded with pristine vistas ranging from deserts to canyons to tree-lined mountain ranges any time of year. Spring in Utah, however, brings an explosion of wildflowers and color (Alta Ski Resort and Mirror Lake are two destinations near Salt Lake City to walk in May or June). Fall brings a turning of cottonwood and cypress leaves that rivals autumn in the Shenandoah mountains. Summer's heat makes many desert locales unbearable, but the shade and breeze of Utah's canyons have offered respite for centuries. The hardiest outdoor types will even gear up in the dead of winter with snowshoes.

Best Hikes

Angels Landing Trail, Zion National Park. A 5-mile round-trip hike, with 1,500 feet of elevation gain, including a series of steps known as "Walter's Wiggles," this is the one trail in Zion no healthy hiker should miss. If you're afraid of heights, stop short at Scout's Lookout for the breathtaking view and head back down the trail.

City Creek Canyon. Depart from your downtown Salt Lake City hotel, pass Temple Square and Memory Grove Park and five minutes later you're on a tree-lined, paved 5.8-mile path where bikes (on odd days only in summer) and moose are likely to be your only companions.

Fiery Furnace Walk, Arches National Park. You need to reserve this one as soon as you know when you'll be in the park because the two- to three-hour walk through narrow sandstone canyons is only offered via ranger-led tour (twice daily from mid-March to October). The landscape is unforgettable and the rangers illuminate the geologic history and reassure nervous hikers.

Hickman Bridge Trail, Capitol Reef National Park. Just 2 miles long, this trail is a perfect introduction to Capital Reef. You'll walk past a great natural bridge as well as Fremont culture ruins.

Mount Timpanogas. One hour south of Salt Lake Valley, "Timp" is one of the tallest and most striking of the Wasatch Mountains. Access to Timpanogas Cave is via a 3-mile round-trip hike led by park rangers

daily in summer. Be aware that outside temperatures can reach triple digits, even at 6,700 feet—but inside the caves it's 45°F year-round.

The Narrows Trail, Zion National Park. Experience the thrill of walking in the Virgin River, peering up at millennia-old rock canyons, hanging gardens, and sandstone grottoes. To see the Narrows you must wade—and occasionally swim—upstream through chilly water and over uneven, slippery rocks, but the views are breathtaking.

HORSEBACK RIDING

Horseback-riding options in Utah run the gamut from hour-long rides on a well-worn trail to multiday excursions out into the wilderness. A short trek is a great way to get acquainted with the landscape—and with horseback riding if you're a beginner. Longer horse-pack trips are great ways to visit the backcountry, because horses can travel distances and carry supplies that hikers can't. Although horsemanship isn't required for most trips, it is helpful, and even an experienced rider can expect to be a little sore for the first few days. June through August is the peak period for horse-packing trips; before signing up with an outfitter, inquire about the skills they expect. ■TIP→ **Most horseback-riding outfitters have a weight limit of 250 pounds, and children must be at least seven years old.**

What to Wear
Because this is the West, jeans and cowboy boots are still the preferred attire for horseback riding, although hiking boots and Gore-Tex have long since become fashionable, especially in colder months and at higher altitudes. Long pants are a must either way. And as with most Utah

activities, layering is key; plan to have some kind of fleece or heavier outer layer no matter what time of year it is, because the mountains will be cooler the higher you go. Generally, outfitters provide most or all of the gear you'll need for extended trips, including a pack animal to carry it all for you and plenty of food for the sometimes surprisingly lavish dinners that they whip up in the middle of nowhere.

Best Horseback Rides
Bryce Canyon National Park. The park's namesake claimed it was a "Hell of a place to lose a cow," but failed to say anything about how great a place it is to explore on horseback. Sign up for a guided tour at Ruby's Horseback Adventures near the park entrance. Let the animals do the work as you descend and emerge hundreds of feet into the Bryce Amphitheatre to see the orange-pink spires and hoodoos that are unrivaled on this planet.

Capitol Reef National Park. Much of this park is accessible only on foot or horseback, which promises an experience of wide-open Western spaces that hark back to the time of cowboys. Indeed, some of the trails may have been used by herdsmen and Native Americans. Sandstone, canyons, mesa, buttes—they're all here. Check at the visitor center for details of horseback riding outfitters and opportunities for an unforgettable experience.

Zion Ponderosa Ranch Resort. Just east of Zion National Park at the site of a former pioneer logging camp, this multipursuit resort offers plenty of things to do after time spent in the saddle meandering along the multitude of pioneer-era trails. Horseback-riding options run from beginner to experienced (and even include a cattle round-up), and when you're not in the saddle you can ride an ATV, rent

a Harley-Davidson motorcycle, or learn how to rappel and rock climb on the only man-made climbing wall in the Zion National Park area.

RAFTING

Rafting combines a sea of emotions ranging from the calming effects of flat waters surrounded by backcountry beauty and wildlife to the thrill and excitement of charging a raging torrent of foam.

For the inexperienced, the young, and the aged, dozens of tour companies throughout the West offer relatively tame floats—ranging from one hour to one day and starting at around $40—that are ideal for anyone from 4 years old to 90. Others fulfill the needs of the adventure tourist content only with chills, potential spills, and the occasional wall of water striking them smack-dab in the chest.

How to Choose a Guide

Seasoned outfitters know their routes and their waters as well as you know the road between home and work. Beginners and novices are encouraged to use guides, and many offer luxurious multiday trips in which they do everything, including searing your steak in a beach barbecue, setting up your tent, and rolling out your sleeping bag.

Select an outfitter based on recommendations from the local chamber of commerce, experience level, websites, and word of mouth. The International Scale of River Difficulty is a widely accepted rating system that ranges from Class I (the easiest) to Class VI (the most difficult—think Niagara Falls). When in doubt, ask your guide about the rating on your route before you book. Remember, ratings can vary greatly throughout the season due to run-off and weather events.

What to Wear

Wear a swimsuit or shorts and sandals and bring along sunscreen and sunglasses. Outfitters must supply a life jacket for each passenger and ensure it's worn. Midsummer is ideal for rafting in the West, although many outfitters will stretch the season, particularly on calmer routes.

Best River Runs

Cataract Canyon. It begins below Moab and takes three to five days as you wind your way to Lake Powell. Expect a smooth ride for the first day or two, before you dive into the rapids. This multiday adventure offers broad beaches, Native American ruins, deep-color canyon walls, and waves as high as 20 feet.

Colorado River, Moab. The Grand Poobah of river rafting in Utah. There are numerous outfitters in the Moab area with a wide assortment of half-, full-, and multiday trips on the river. Even though it is the same river, it meanders in part and rages in others.

Green River. Before it meets up with the Colorado River, the Green River offers plenty of stunning scenery and fast water through canyons such as Desolation and Gray. Desolation Canyon is a favorite family trip, with wildlife sightings, hikes, and beaches. Sign on with an outfitter in the town of Green River.

Weber River. You may see more kayakers than rafters on the Weber, but there are stretches that offer Class II rapids that are commercially run. For a one-day excursion, this is a great side trip from Salt Lake City or Park City.

Westwater Canyon. This short stretch of river can be negotiated in two to three hours, but with notable rapids like Funnel, Sock-it-to-me, and Skull Rapid, it's an action-packed ride.

SKIING AND SNOWBOARDING

Utah's "greatest snow on Earth" can be a revelation for skiers and snowboarders familiar only with the slopes of other regions. In Utah the snow builds up quickly, leaving a solid base at each resort that hangs tough all season, only to be layered with thick, fluffy powder that holds an edge, ready to be groomed into rippling corduroy or left in giddy stashes along the sides and through the trees. Moguls and half-pipe-studded terrain parks are the norm, not the special attractions, here. The added bonus of Utah terrain is that it has something for everyone, often within the same resort—many have various beginner, intermediate, advanced, and expert slopes.

What to Wear

Skiing Utah means preparing for all kinds of weather, because the high altitudes can start a day off sunny and bright but kick in a blizzard by afternoon. Layers help, as well as plenty of polypropylene to wick away sweat in the sun and a water-resistant outer layer to keep off the powdery wetness that's sure to accumulate, especially if you're a beginner snowboarder. Spring skiing in April or May often means short-sleeved T-shirts and 70-degree days. **Must-haves:** plenty of sunscreen, because the sun is closer than you think, and a helmet, because the trees are, too.

Best Slopes

Alta and Snowbird resorts. These Little Cottonwood Canyon neighbors, within 40 minutes of downtown Salt Lake City, are regularly ranked the top ski resorts in the United States. Seasons with 500 to 600 and more inches of Utah's famous powder are at the root of the accolades. A joint pass lets you ski both mountains on one ticket, but snowboarders are still not allowed at Alta. Snowbird has the longest season in the nation, occasionally staying open through July 4 weekend.

Brian Head Ski Resort. The closest Utah ski resort to the Las Vegas airport, it's worth checking out for the novelty of skiing in southern Utah. The red-orange rocks of Cedar Breaks National Monument form a backdrop to many trails, which tend to focus on beginner and intermediate skiers and snowboarders. Experts can ski off the 11,000-foot summit.

Deer Valley, Park City, Canyons resorts. The three Park City resorts are known for their great groomed trails, fine dining, and accommodations. Deer Valley is one of three resorts in America that doesn't allow snowboarders, but Park City and Canyons cater to both skiers and riders. The skiing is excellent, but for many it's the whole experience—including the mid-day feast at Silver Lake Lodge and farm-to-table dining at The Farm—that keeps them coming back.

Snowbasin and Powder Mountain resorts. An hour north of Salt Lake City, Ogden-area residents will tell you the best skiing is at this pair of resorts. Powder Mountain has more skiable terrain than any Utah resort and Snowbasin was good enough to host the Olympic downhill and slalom during the 2002 Winter Games. These two are often cheaper and less crowded than the Salt Lake City and Park City resorts.

Utah Olympic Park. At the site of the 2002 Olympic bobsled, luge, and ski-jumping events in Park City, you can take recreational ski-jumping lessons or strap in behind a professional driver for a bobsled ride down the actual Olympic course.

IF YOU LIKE

Dinosaur Fossils

The context of dinosaur skeletons in urban museums never quite fits, but when you see giant rib fossils protruding from the ground in central Utah, your lessons in Jurassic history will snap into focus.

Cleveland-Lloyd Dinosaur Quarry. On the way to Moab (via 30 miles of dirt road), lies a dense concentration of at least 46 allosaurus remains. It's a mystery to scientists why so many bones, but not intact skeletons, are clustered here.

Dinosaur National Monument. Near the Wyoming and Colorado borders, you will find an exposed hillside with 65-million-year-old fossils, plus hiking trails and campsites.

Natural History Museum of Utah. The stunning copper-clad exterior of this museum blends into the hills east of Salt Lake City. Inside, find a massive gallery with more than 30 reconstructions of dinosaur skeletons. You can also watch paleontologists working on fossils in a glassed-in lab.

St. George Dinosaur Discovery Site at Johnson Farm. At the very southern end of the state, a local optometrist found dozens of dinosaur tracks in 2000 and turned his family farm into a museum.

Scenic Drives

Cowboy poets and country artists sing the praises of the wide-open spaces of the West, but Utah's size can create challenges for time-pressed visitors. Take these routes and the miles will fly by—except for all the times you'll want to stop to take photographs.

Highway 89. If you've had enough of Interstate 15, Highway 89 is a 502-mile scenic alternative from Bear Lake on the Idaho border to Glen Canyon on the Arizona line. Other bodies of water that

are accessible from Highway 89 include Great Salt Lake and Utah Lake. Take Highway 89 not to save time, but to see historic sites like the Pony Express and Oregon trails, charming old downtowns, and Utah's agricultural heart including orchards, farms, and ranches.

Provo River Canyon. The gateway to Robert Redford's Sundance Resort, this drive from Provo to Park City parallels rushing rapids during snow melt and soothing gurgles the rest of the year. Parley's, Emigration, Big and Little Cottonwood, Mill Creek, and Ogden are six other canyons from the Wasatch front equally worth driving. Because of their proximity to Utah's population base, all have trailheads, services, and restaurants.

Scenic Byway 12. Grand Staircase-Escalante covers 2 million acres of southern Utah, much of it linked to this All-American road between Torrey (Capitol Reef National Park) and Bryce Canyon National Park. Pause to see red rock, slickrock, canyons, forest, waterfalls, and an abundance of desert wildlife including deer, elk, and birds of prey.

Trail of the Ancients. The heart of country once home to the Anasazi people, Hovenweep, Natural Bridges, and Four Corners National Monuments are your landmarks in this most remote corner of southeast Utah. Expect very little traffic and burning heat as you pass miles and miles of rock formations, petroglyphs, and mountain ranges. Fill up on gas, water, and food when you can—services are spread pretty thin here.

Exceptional Eats

Predominantly Mormon Utah liberalized its liquor laws when it welcomed the world for the 2002 Winter Olympic Games and when restaurateurs realized they could profit, the dining scene exploded. Although many small towns offer little more than diners, with a little assistance, you can find award-winning food and drink.

Canyon cuisine. Not every canyon has a great restaurant, but Emigration (Ruth's Diner), Mill Creek (Log Haven), Provo (Tree House at Sundance Resort), and Big Cottonwood (Silver Fork Lodge) have outposts for a delicious meal before or after you hit a trailhead. All offer respite from the summer heat, but may close during big snowstorms in winter.

Park City. It figures that the wealthy playground of Park City would attract hot chefs, but this is much more than a ski town—it's also heaven on earth in the summer with great deals. Time your trip to hit the summer Savor the Summit, when more than 30 restaurants set up a mile-long table along Main Street (which isn't flat, by the way!) or the Food and Wine Classic.

Rural kitchens. Although you likely came to Utah to escape the city, you probably wouldn't mind splurging for a well-cooked meal in the middle of Utah's rural expanse. Boulder's Hell's Backbone Grill and Brigham City's Maddox Ranch are two that fit the bill.

Salt Lake City. When did Utah become home to world-class chefs and mixologists? Surprise! Bowman Brown and Viet Pham's Forage restaurant has earned James Beard recognition, while Copper Onion, Pago, and Red Iguana earn high marks for their food. You'll also find great restaurants from across the global spectrum, including Indian (Kathmandu), Middle Eastern (Mazza), and Mediterranean (Layla Grill and Mezze)—and several microbreweries.

Small Towns
Leave behind the more densely populated Wasatch front and discover a plethora of small towns with Main Street diners, well-maintained museums, and plentiful parks.

National Park Gateways. Zion National Park's gateway town is Springdale, an artsy community with traditional bed-and-breakfasts, eateries, and the incomparable backdrop of the canyon. Moab fuels visitors to Arches and Canyonlands with granola and outfits them with gear shops galore, but it also offers arts and theater by a community of out-of-state transplants who never left. En route to Capitol Reef are Torrey and Boulder; Hell's Backbone Grill, one of the best restaurants in Utah, is well worth a stop.

Mountain Hideaways. Park City's legacy as a silver mining town pervades an authentic, steep-sloped Main Street that would thrive even without the ski resorts and the Sundance Film Festival. Nearby communities Heber and Midway offer mountain-fed trout-filled streams amidst ranches and farms.

Highway Detours. On your way to the southern parks, don't miss the frontier capital of the Utah territory, Fillmore. Also on Interstate 15, Cedar City is home to Southern Utah University. St. George is a booming retirement community with golf courses, resorts, and shopping.

Go North, Young Man. Utah's rural north is often overlooked, but Logan is a postcard-quality college town in the gorgeous Cache valley. Bear Lake straddles the Idaho border and while its water is stunningly blue, the nickname "Caribbean of the Rockies" is a bit hyperbolic. Peaches and raspberries are harvested in the late summer, making it the ideal time to visit both towns.

GREAT ITINERARIES

UTAH'S FIVE GLORIOUS NATIONAL PARKS, 6 DAYS

Days 1 and 2: Zion National Park
(2½-hour drive from Las Vegas)

Start early from Las Vegas and within two hours you'll be across the most barren stretches of desert and marveling at the bends in the Virgin River gorge. Just past St. George, Utah, on I–15, take the Route 9 exit to **Zion National Park.** Spend your afternoon in the park—if it's April to October, the National Park Service bus system does the driving for you on Zion Canyon Scenic Drive (in fact, when the bus is running, cars are not allowed to enter the canyon).

For a nice introductory walk, try the short and easy (read family-friendly) **Weeping Rock Trail.** It won't take very long, even if you linger with your camera, so follow it with a stroll along the **Emerald Pools Trail** in Zion Canyon itself, where you might come across wild turkeys and ravens looking for handouts. Before leaving the park, talk to the rangers to decide which of Zion's two iconic hikes is right for you the next day—the 1,488-foot elevation gain to Angel's Landing or river wading along the improbably steep canyon called the Narrows. Overnight at **Zion Lodge** inside the park (book well in advance or call for last-minute cancellations), but venture into the bustling gateway town of **Springdale** for dinner and a peak into an art gallery or boutique. Try the **Switchback Grille** or **Bit & Spur** for tasty Southwestern food.

Next day start at dawn to beat the crowds and heat if you're ascending Angel's Landing (allow three to four hours). If you're headed up the Narrows (enquire locally about where to rent gear), you'll be walking in the river, so you might want to wait an extra hour or two for the sun. Either way, pack a lunch and take your time—there's no sense rushing one of the highlights of the U.S. National Park system. Work your way back to your hotel and set a date with your hot tub, or get a head start on Day 3 by driving the Zion-Mount Carmel Highway and staying just outside the park at **Zion Ponderosa Ranch Resort.**

Day 3: Bryce Canyon National Park
(2-hour drive from Zion National Park)

It's a long 70 miles from Zion to Bryce via Route 9 (the Zion-Mount Carmel Highway), particularly as traffic must be escorted through a 1.1-mile-long tunnel. Canyon Overlook is a great stopping point, providing views of massive rock formations such as East and West Temples. When you emerge, you are in slickrock country, where huge petrified sandstone dunes have been etched by ancient waters. Stay on Route 9 for 23 miles and then turn north onto U.S. 89 and follow the signs to the entrance of **Bryce Canyon National Park.** Allow up to two hours for the trip from Springdale to Bryce Canyon.

Unless you fall in love with the hoodoos, Bryce Canyon can be enjoyed in one day. Central to your tour is the 18-mile main park road, from which numerous scenic turnouts provide vistas of bright red-orange rock (we recommend starting with the view at **Sunrise Point**). You'll notice that the air is a little cooler here than it was at Zion, so get out and enjoy it. Trails most worth checking out include the **Bristlecone Loop Trail** and the **Navajo Loop Trail,** both of which you can easily fit into a day trip and will get you into the heart of the park with minimum effort. Listen for

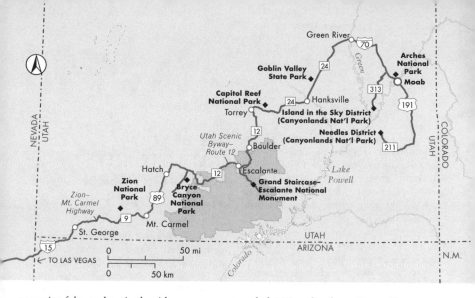

peregrine falcons deep in the side canyons, and keep an eye out for a species of prairie dog that only lives in these parts. If you can't stay in the park (camping or **Bryce Canyon Lodge** are your options), overnight at **Ruby's Inn**, near the junction of Routes 12 and 63.

Day 4: Capitol Reef
(3-hour drive from Bryce Canyon National Park)

If you can, get up early to see sunrise paint Bryce's hoodoos, then head out on the spectacular Utah Scenic Byway–Route 12. If the views don't take your breath away, the narrow, winding road with little margin for error will. Route 12 winds over and through **Grand Staircase–Escalante National Monument.** The views from the narrow hogback are nothing short of incredible. Remember that Capitol Reef is your goal, but Calf Creek Recreation Area, Boulder, Torrey, and Fruita each offer opportunities to stretch your legs, take a walk, and find an off-the-beaten-path gem. Boulder's **Hell's Backbone Grill,** for example, may be the best remote restaurant you'll find in the West and you don't want to bypass Fruita's bountiful orchards in the late summer and fall.

At the intersection of Routes 12 and 24, turn east onto Route 24. You have

traveled 112 miles from Bryce Canyon to reach **Capitol Reef National Park.** The crowds are smaller here than at other national parks in the state, and the scenery is stunning. Assuming it's still daylight when you arrive, hike the 1-mile **Hickman Bridge Trail,** stop in at the visitor center, open until 4:30 (later in the summer), and view pioneer and Native American exhibits, talk with rangers about geography or geology, or watch a film. Nearby **Torrey** is your best bet for lodging, and be sure to eat at the seasonal **Cafe Diablo,** serving some of Utah's finest Southwestern cuisine from mid-April to mid-October.

Days 5-6: Moab, Arches, and Canyonlands National Parks
(2½ hours from Capitol Reef to Canyonlands)

Explore Capitol Reef more the next morning. When you leave, travel east and north for 75 miles on Route 24. If you want a break after about an hour, stop at the small **Goblin Valley State Park.** Youngsters love to run around the sandstone formations known as "goblins." Continue on Route 24 to I–70 and turn east toward Colorado.

Take Exit 182 south onto U.S. 191, proceeding about 19 miles to Island in the Sky Road. Make sure you have water, food, and gas, as **Canyonlands National Park** offers no services. Be sure to follow the drive out to Grand View Point to look down on the convergence of the Colorado and Green rivers. Along the way, **Mesa Arch** is a half-mile walk and offers a sneak preview of what to expect at Arches. More ambitious individuals should hike the mysterious crater at **Upheaval Dome,** which is a steeper 1-mile round-trip hike. A few hours in the park here are sufficient, so backtrack to U.S. 191 and turn right for the final 12-mile drive into **Moab.** Along the way, you'll pass the entrance to **Arches National Park,** which holds the world's largest concentration of natural rock windows or "arches."

You can easily devote three days to the Moab area, but build your itinerary around hikes to **Delicate Arch** and **Landscape Arch.** If you made a reservation in advance, the guided hike in the Fiery Furnace, a maze of sandstone canyons and fins, is considered one of the most spectacular hikes in the park.

Adventurous types, note that you can raft the Colorado River here or bike the Slick Rock Trail. Either is well worth a half-day or daylong excursion. Other options from Moab include exploring the Needles district of Canyonlands (about 90 minutes south), viewing petroglyphs on Route 279 (Potash Road) and driving along the Colorado River north of town to Fisher Towers.

You've now enjoyed five national parks and hundreds of miles of scenic drives in southern Utah. It's 4½ hours back to Salt Lake City or about two hours to Grand Junction, Colorado; if Las Vegas is your hub, it's a 6½-hour drive from Moab.

THE BEST OF SALT LAKE CITY AND NORTHERN UTAH, 4 DAYS

Day 1: Salt Lake City

Many people begin their explorations of northern Utah from the comfortable hospitality of downtown **Salt Lake City.** Grab the TRAX light rail (now accessible from Terminal One at Salt Lake City Airport) to **Temple Square** and begin a walking tour of the city. The temple is off-limits unless you belong to the LDS Church, but its grounds and the rest of the complex make for interesting wandering. Immediately south is **City Creek Center,** the city's first upscale shopping district. To the west are **Gateway Mall** and the entertainment district, where you can have lunch in one of the outdoor plazas. The **Discovery Gateway** children's museum and **Clark Planetarium** are best bets here, as well as the Olympic Tribute Plaza. Complete your walk by crossing Pioneer Park, heading east through Gallivan Plaza (you may catch live music midday or evenings) as far as **Salt Lake City Main Library**—a modern architectural gem that includes a soaring roof that you can ascend for one of the best views of the city. **Salt Lake Roasting Company,** in the library promenade, is a good place for a drink or snack. There's ample downtown lodging to choose from. Pamper yourself at the **Grand America Hotel** or ask for a goldfish for your room at **Hotel Monaco.** Dining and drinking options are varied. Sample the microbrews from **Squatters Pub Brewery,** then fill up on America's best Mexican food at **Red Iguana** or check out **Copper Onion** for Continental cuisine.

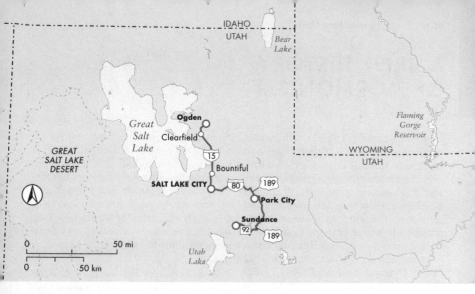

Days 2 and 3: Park City
(40-minute drive from Salt Lake City)

Salt Lake's majesty lies in the hills surrounding it, so tackle them today. **Park City** is 25 miles to the east along I–80 and you can easily spend the entire day wandering its historic Main Street, where the discovery of silver in 1868 led to a boom era of prospectors, mine workers, and schemers. You can still see in the storefronts that dozens of saloons and a red-light district once flourished here in defiance of the Mormon Church. The **Park City Museum** is the perfect place to discover the town's colorful history, and the **Park Silly Sunday Market** (June to September) portrays its modern-day fun side. For lunch or dinner, **Wasatch Brew Pub** is at the top of Main Street, **Zoom** is at the bottom, and **High West Distillery** is just off Main on Park Avenue. You can't go wrong with any of them for a meal. If it's winter, hit the slopes; if it's summer hit the trails, where you might just encounter a moose. Either season, stop at **Utah Olympic Park** where you will often glimpse America's next gold medal hopefuls training in any of a half-dozen disciplines including ski jumping, bobsled, or luge. If you have time and love roller coaster thrills, ride the bobsled course from top to bottom with a trained driver.

Indulge in the spa, lounge, or restaurant at Deer Valley's **Stein Ericksen Lodge,** or opt for the equally refined (but no less expensive) **Waldorf Astoria Park City.** The **Newpark Resort** is a more affordable option near the outlet mall.

Day 4: Sundance Resort or Ogden
(1-hour drive from Park City to Sundance or Odgen)

You can easily spend several more days in Park City, but its environs are beckoning. There's fly-fishing and rafting on the Provo River, balloon rides and hot springs. Robert Redford's **Sundance Resort** is a year-round destination for artists, filmmakers, and musicians—not just tourists and skiers. It's about an hour south of Park City through the gorgeous Provo River canyon. Dine at the **Foundry Grill** or **Tree Room** and keep your eyes open for Mr. Redford. Railroad buffs may prefer to make the hour drive north to **Ogden** where **Union Station** has welcomed trains on the transcontinental route since it opened in 1924. Historic 25th Street has a multitude of restaurants. From there, head west to **Promontory,** Utah, to see where the golden spike was hammered in to connect east and west in 1869.

A BRIEF HISTORY OF MORMONISM

From its beginnings in 1830 with just six members, the Church of Jesus Christ of Latter-day Saints (LDS) has evolved into one of the fastest-growing religions in the world. There are more than 10 million members in more than 160 countries and territories. The faith has drawn increased attention in recent years, with the presidential candidacy of Mitt Romney, and a huge increase in tourism since the 2002 Winter Olympics and the 2006–11 HBO show *Big Love*.

In the Beginning

The church is considered a uniquely "American" faith, as it was conceived and founded in New York by Joseph Smith, who said God the Father and his son, Jesus Christ, came to him in a vision when he was a young boy. Smith said he also saw a resurrected entity named Moroni, who led him to metal plates that were engraved with the religious history of an ancient American civilization. In 1827 Smith translated this record into the Book of Mormon.

Persecution and Settlement in Utah

Not long after the creation of the church, religious persecution forced Smith and his followers to flee New York, and they traveled first to Ohio and then to Missouri before settling in Nauvoo, Illinois, in 1839. But even here the fledgling faith was ostracized. Smith was killed by a mob in June 1844 in Carthage, Illinois. To escape the oppression, Brigham Young, who ascended to the church's leadership following Smith's death, led a pilgrimage to Utah, the first group arriving in the Salt Lake Valley on July 24, 1847. Here, under Young's guidance, Mormonism quickly grew and flourished.

In keeping with the Latter Day Saints' emphasis on proselytizing, Young laid plans to both colonize Utah and spread the church's word farther afield. This work led to the founding of small towns not only throughout the territory but also from southern Canada to Mexico. Today Mormons continue that work through its young people, many of whom take time out from college or careers to spend two years on a mission at home or abroad.

Beliefs

Latter-day Saints believe that they are guided by divine revelations received from God by the religion's president, who is viewed as a modern-day prophet in the same sense as other biblical leaders. The Book of Mormon is viewed as divinely inspired scripture, and is used side-by-side with the Holy Bible. Families are highly valued in the faith, and marriages performed in Mormon temples are thought to continue through eternity.

Though Mormons were originally polygamists, this practice was abolished in order to gain statehood for the territory in the 1890s. Excommunication is the religious consequence for those continuing polygamy, and since 2001 Utah authorities have begun to prosecute polygamists. High-profile cases have included that of Tom Green, who publicized his five-wife family on national talk shows, and Warren Jeffs, who led the cultlike community of Hilldale, Utah (on the Arizona border).

Under Mormon guidance Utah is a conservative state. Despite conventional wisdom that church and government should be separate, Utah's civic bodies are overwhelmingly filled by church members who often simultaneously hold leadership positions in their local church units (called wards).

UTAH WITH KIDS

Utah families tend to be larger than anywhere else in America, so it's no surprise that this is such a great place to travel with kids. Indoor and outdoor recreation opportunities abound, touching upon perennial kid delights such as dinosaurs, trains, planes, sports, and camping. From Dinosaurland and Bear Lake in the far northeast of the state to the slot canyons of the south, the only argument will be how to fit it all in. Furthermore, virtually no site, restaurant, or destination is off-limits to kids, so don't hesitate about including them in your itinerary.

City Diversions

In and around **Salt Lake City,** start with two very kid-friendly museums in **Gateway Mall.** The **Discovery Gateway** children's museum has a Life Flight helicopter, television news set, pint-size village, construction site, and much more—best suited to children under the age of 11. The **Clark Planetarium** opens kids' eyes to the universe and natural phenomena through its interactive exhibits and 3-D and IMAX theaters. The Leonardo, an inspirational museum combining science, art, and technology, is on its own a good reason to bring kids to Utah, and the **Natural History Museum of Utah, Red Butte Garden, Tracy Aviary,** and **Hogle Zoo** are also year-round destinations within the city limits—bundle up in the winter and have any one of them virtually to yourself. See bison in a natural setting on **Antelope Island** (if visiting in October, don't miss the annual roundup of the animals).

In **Ogden,** you can fly like a bird in the wind tunnel, learn to surf, swim in a wave pool, or rock-climb indoors at the state-of-the-art **Salomon Center at the Junction.** Young children will enjoy the models and playground at the **George S. Eccles Dinosaur Park.** Older kids can kayak a man-made course on the **Ogden River** and catch the Raptors who are, along with Salt Lake's Bees and Ogden's Owlz, a fun, inexpensive, entertaining minor-league baseball team.

Natural Wonders

Utah's outdoor attractions provide plenty of outlets for kids' energies. Hikes offer larger-than-life rewards that can even lure kids away from video games. Each of Utah's five national parks has special youth-oriented programming and a **Junior Ranger program** that provides them with an interactive booklet of activities and tasks to complete so that they have fun while learning about environmental responsibility.

In **Arches,** hardy kids over the age of 6 can likely make the 3-mile round-trip hike to **Delicate Arch.** Make **Sand Arch** a destination for littler ones—it's right off the road and offers a massive "sandbox" of soft red sand. In **Zion** kids 10 and up can trek up the Virgin River toward the **Narrows.** At **Bryce** or Zion you can go **horseback riding** to places where little legs might fail you.

There are **dinosaur excavation** sites near **Vernal, St. George,** and **Price.** Stargazing and scorpion hunting are nighttime programs offered by park rangers at **Goblin Valley State Park. Moab** has kid-friendly bike trails, and you might find that your BMX-riding teen is more comfortable on the **Slick Rock Trail** than you are.

Finally, if you have swimmers, great places to cool off in hot summers include **Lake Powell, Bear Lake,** and glacier-fed rivers and creeks that fill national forest land across the eastern half of the state.

WHICH NATIONAL PARK SHOULD I VISIT?

Plan on taking a whole week to enjoy the highlights of all five of Utah's national parks, but if time is a luxury and you have to narrow your choices, we've set out the particular appeal of each park to help you decide. If you dislike crowds, visit any of them in winter, but bundle up, as snowflakes could be your only companions.

Arches National Park
If 3 miles is your hiking limit, Arches and specifically the trek to Delicate Arch is your destination. On the way out to Utah's most famous arch (the one on the license plates), it's a steady uphill and if you don't go early enough, the sun can be blistering. You need to persevere, however, because when you round a bend after crossing a somewhat narrow ledge and you see the arch for the very first time, every step is redeemed. It's a just reward for everyone in the family, from kids to senior citizens. **Also:** there are multiple short hikes in this park that will reward you with arches to photograph, to walk up to and to pass through.

Bryce Canyon National Park
For families with young children, Bryce is small and manageable—and what kid doesn't like a hoodoo? They're fanciful, inexplicable, and on a human scale. Plus, if your little ones aren't ready for full-on hiking, Bryce Canyon is a great choice because many of the vistas are just steps from the 18-mile road that runs the length of the park. **Also:** Bryce Canyon Lodge and the Best Western Ruby's Inn are kid-friendly places to stay on the grassy plateau at the park entrance. Spotting wildlife is always a thrill, so watch for deer, elk, eagles, and more.

Canyonlands National Park
Great views and stunning geological formations characterize all of Utah's national parks so the thing that sets Canyonlands apart is its opportunities for epic adventures. Raft through Desolation Canyon, hike the Needles district, or bike the 100-mile White Rim trail for an adventure that few seasoned national park visitors can claim. **Also:** if you like the massive scale of, say, the Grand Canyon, you'll love Grand View Point and the perspective of miles and miles (and millions of years) of nature's relentless handiwork.

Capitol Reef National Park
If you find the crowds at America's iconic Western parks daunting and seek the blue roads instead, this is the park for you. Most Utah visitors miss it. Capitol Gorge and the remarkable 100-mile-long geological wonder of the Waterpocket Fold offer incomparable glimpses into the Earth's crust. **Also:** the adjacent towns of Torrey, Boulder, and Fruita don't get the attention that Moab does, and if you like them as much as we do, you'll want to keep it that way and not tell anyone either!

Zion National Park
Last alphabetically, but first in the hearts of many who visit Utah, Zion has the wow factor, and we think it should definitely belong on any southern Utah itinerary. For a one-of-a-kind outlook on more than 1,500 vertical feet, look up from the Narrows or down from Angel's Landing—there are few places like either in the world. From the valley floor to the slickrock, Zion is really three parks in one, with some challenges for serious hikers. You'll leave feeling that you got your money's worth. **Also:** Springdale is a delightful town at the park's main point of entry.

SALT LAKE CITY

Updated by
Caitlin Martz

Nestled at the foot of the rugged Wasatch Mountains and extending to the south shore of the Great Salt Lake, Salt Lake City is a small, navigable city at the heart of a metropolitan area with more than 1 million residents. The Salt Lake valley offers one of the most striking landscapes of any American city, and its proximity to wilderness lures residents and visitors alike all year long. Fall and spring are heavenly. Canyon breezes turn hot summer afternoons into enjoyable evenings, and snowy winter days are moderated with temperatures warmer than those at most ski destinations.

The city has emerged as the economic and cultural center of the vast Great Basin, between the Rocky Mountains and California's Sierra Nevada. Salt Lake City will always be known as the center of the Mormon universe, but the 2002 Winter Olympics changed the character of the city forever. More than a million people now call the Wasatch Front home, including many transplants who came to ski or hike and have never left. As a reflection of this growth, ever-widening rings of suburbia have sprouted, and smog can be a serious problem, but Salt Lake is working hard to remain a small, personable city.

Since Brigham Young led his first party of pioneers here in 1847, Salt Lake City has been synonymous with the Mormon Church, which is formally called the Church of Jesus Christ of Latter-day Saints (LDS). The valley appealed to Young because, at the time, it was under the control of Mexico rather than the U.S. government, which the Mormons blamed for much of their persecution. The area had few permanent settlements, an adequate supply of water and building materials, and a protected location, with the Wasatch Mountains to the east and a vast desert to the west. Still, on July 24, 1847, when Young gazed across the somewhat desolate valley and reportedly announced, "This is the right place," his followers understandably had mixed feelings. They saw no familiar forests or lush pasture, just a dry valley and a salty lake.

Within hours of arriving, Young and his followers began planting crops and diverting water for irrigation. Within days Young drew up plans for Salt Lake City, which was to be the hub of the Mormons' promised land, a vast empire stretching from the Rockies to the Southern California coast. Although the area that eventually became the state of Utah was smaller than Young planned, Salt Lake City quickly outstripped his original vision. Missionaries throughout Scandinavia and the British Isles converted thousands, who flocked to the city to live near their church president—a living prophet, according to Mormon doctrine—and worship in the newly built temple.

In the 1860s income from railroads and mines created a class of industrialists who built mansions near downtown and whose businesses brought thousands of workers—mainly from Europe and few of whom were Mormon—to Utah Territory. By the time Utah became a state, in 1896, Salt Lake had become a thriving city. Although the majority of the city was Mormon, it claimed a healthy mix of Protestant, Catholic, and Jewish citizens.

Today the city is an important center for business, medicine, education, and culture. The LDS Church still has its headquarters in Temple Square as well as the Tabernacle, home to the world-famous Mormon Tabernacle Choir. Several high-rise hotels, office buildings, and downtown condominiums mark the skyline; restaurants serve a world of tastes; fashionable retail enclaves are appearing all around town; and nightlife is improving.

Increased commitment to the arts from the public and private sectors has created a varied cultural scene that you'd expect in a city twice Salt Lake's size. When it comes to sports, the community takes great pride in two major-league franchises—basketball's Utah Jazz and soccer's Real Salt Lake—and the passion for University of Utah and Brigham Young University athletics rivals that for Harvard-Yale and Michigan-Ohio State.

The city's greatest sports legacy, however, will always be the 2002 Olympic Winter Games, for which Mitt Romney tackled a corruption-ridden organizing committee, inspired thousands of volunteers, and produced a memorable competition that showcased the Rocky Mountain secret.

Near Salt Lake City, the Wasatch Mountains and Antelope Island have superb hiking, mountain biking, skiing, and wildlife watching. Park City has a rich mining history and world-class skiing resorts. Five national parks are within a half-day's drive, and American history buffs will enjoy well-preserved sections of the Pony Express Trail, the site of the Golden Spike railroad junction, and the Bonneville Salt Flats.

ORIENTATION AND PLANNING

GETTING ORIENTED

Salt Lake City proper is a modest sprawling city of about 190,000 people. Most visitors will concentrate their time in the downtown (marked by the Mormon Temple, from which all addresses emanate), east side, and adjacent canyons and mountains. Locals live as far as 10 or 15 miles from the city's walkable center, and suburbs have created an almost uninterrupted residential metropolis from Ogden (30 miles to the north) to Provo (40 miles south).

Temple Square. Temple Square is the hub of Mormonism, with the Salt Lake Temple and Tabernacle, but it's also the cultural hub of this intermountain region, with museums and restaurants. An emphasis on green spaces by past and present city planners means you won't experience the claustrophobic feeling found in many big cities.

Downtown Salt Lake. The heart of Salt Lake's social, religious, and political institutions is within a few blocks of Temple Square, downtown.

TOP REASONS TO GO

Downtown: The Mormon Church is centered here in a beautifully landscaped four-square-block compound called Temple Square, but downtown visitors will also enjoy the massive new commercial and shopping complex, City Creek, walkable surrounding streets that house restaurants, bars (yes, they have them here), theaters, EnergySolutions Arena, and plenty more.

Wasatch Front Mountains: Leave city life and enter cool canyons replete with fascinating topography, flora, and fauna.

Olympic Legacy: The "Light the Fire Within" theme of the 2002 Winter Games is still seen everywhere. They helped put Salt Lake City on the tourist map, and still there are plenty of ways to experience the excitement of the games.

Inland Sea: Explore the Great Salt Lake by car or on foot or bicycle. If you're here in the summer, take a float off the beaches at Antelope Island—the water is so salty, it's impossible to sink!

Pow-pow-powder: Schuss the "greatest snow on earth" within an hour of the airport at seven resorts.

The city's best outdoor gathering places are all here. The $1.5 billion City Creek Center opened in 2012, introducing high-profile shopping (an Apple store, Tiffany & Co., Nordstrom, and more) to an open-air setting and bringing the once-buried City Creek waters back to the surface. Gallivan Center hosts midday and evening concerts throughout the summer and an outdoor skating rink in winter. There's a farmers' market in Pioneer Park every Saturday in summer, and City Creek Canyon offers walks, runs, and bike rides near downtown hotels. The main library marks the east end of downtown.

Capitol Hill and the Avenues. Just a few blocks (and one significant hill) up from Temple Square is the state capitol, which was designed to resemble the nation's Capitol in Washington, D.C., in part to prove the Utah Territory's loyalty as it emerged from its polygamous roots in the late 19th century. On all four sides of the capitol are residential areas known for historic houses, hidden bistros, and the charm that makes this one of the most livable cities in America.

East Side and the University of Utah. Look for the U on the hillside, and you'll find one of the leading centers of academia, research, and athletics in the West. Nobel Prize–winner Mario Capecchi put the university's science department on the map, and the football team did the same for school sports when it won the 2008 Sugar Bowl. Many of the school's staff and faculty live in the east-side neighborhoods of Federal Heights, Harvard-Yale, and Sugarhouse, which are full of 80- to 100-year-old homes, trees, and thriving restaurants and boutiques.

Great Salt Lake. Salt Lake International Airport lies at the southern tip of Great Salt Lake, the remnants of the ancient Bonneville Lake that covered much of the northern half of Utah. With no place for the mountain stream-fed waters to go, the lake has a salinity level far higher than the Earth's oceans, creating a unique water world that revolves around brine shrimp. Explore the lake through Great Salt Lake State Park, about 13 miles west of the airport, or Antelope Island (where you're more likely to encounter bison and birds than antelope), reached by a causeway 37 miles north of the airport.

Wasatch Front. The foothills of the Wasatch Range of the Rocky Mountains form the northern and eastern city limits. Several canyons bring water and cool breezes to the desert, and are the best way to enjoy the wilderness in summer. Trailheads for hikes can be reached from downtown via City Creek Canyon, on the east side in Emigration Canyon and Mill Creek Canyon, and near the city's southern limits in Big and Little Cottonwood canyons. Four of the nation's top ski resorts, Snowbird, Alta, Solitude, and Brighton, are a short drive up Big and Little Cottonwood, with summer and winter activities galore.

PLANNING

WHEN TO GO

Spring and fall are the best times to visit Salt Lake City, as cooler afternoons give way to idyllic breezy evenings. Summertime high temperatures average more than 90° (June–August), with a few days above 100° each month. Winters bring snow, but abundant sunshine tends to melt it quickly in the valley. If your plans are taking you to Park City or the Cottonwood Canyons, follow weather forecasts closely, because a fluffy 6-inch snowfall in the city will often be accompanied by 3 to 5 feet "up the hill." Check weather forecasts closely if you have allergies. Extreme heat or cold without any wind often brings about "inversions" of polluted air that sometimes linger for longer than a week and prompt "red" alert warnings against activity in the valley. Escape to the mountains on these days. Most years, ski season kicks off by mid-November and ends in early April. (During a heavy snow year Snowbird Ski Resort will stay open on weekends as late as July 4.) Expect heavier crowds at the airport and higher rates at hotels and resorts that serve the ski slopes on wintry weekends, particularly around holidays such as Christmas, Martin Luther King Jr. Day, and Presidents' Day. City accommodations are cheaper than those elsewhere in the country much of the rest of the year, but occasional large conventions significantly affect tourist travel to Salt Lake City. The largest is the Outdoor Retailers Show, which books nearly every hotel room in the city and surrounding suburbs during its weeklong winter and summer shows.

July 24 is celebrated statewide as Pioneer Day, and it's a bigger deal than July 4 or any other holiday except Christmas. You may be able to catch one of the nation's largest parades if you're here on July 24, but also expect closed streets (because of the parade and a marathon), fireworks, and many closed businesses.

FESTIVALS AND EVENTS

Gallery Stroll. Local artists and art galleries enjoy one evening each month (the third Friday of the month, except for December when it's the first Friday) sharing their artwork with the public in the Gallery Stroll. Stop at any gallery on the stroll to obtain a self-guiding map. Artists and art lovers chat over wine and snacks at each stop. ☏ *801/870–0956* ⊕ *www.gallerystroll.org* ✉ *Free.*

Phillips Gallery. A possible starting point is Phillips Gallery. ✉ *444 E. 200 S, Downtown* ☏ *801/364–8284.*

Fodor'sChoice ★ **Sundance Film Festival.** Even casual movie buffs should make plans to attend Robert Redford's Sundance Film Festival at least once in a lifetime. Each January the crowds and the paparazzi tend to congregate in Park City, but savvy moviegoers catch top picks in three venues in downtown Salt Lake City. With a theme of "discovering and developing independent artists," the festival has more than 100 screenings in Salt Lake City at the Tower Theatre, Broadway Center Theatre, and Rose Wagner Performing Arts Center. Ticket registration begins in September, or check the box office for unsold day-of-show tickets, if available, at the Trolley Corners box office. ☏ *435/776–7878* ⊕ *www.sundance.org/festival.*

FAMILY **Utah Arts Festival.** If you're in town in late June, check out Utah's premier festival showcasing every form of visual and performance art. If you're downtown, you can't miss it, as the festival takes over two full blocks surrounding the City and County Building and the Salt Lake City main library. Look for original art at the Marketplace, create your own at the Art Yard, sample a wide array of food, and swing to the beat of live music on multiple stages. ✉ *201 E. 400 S, Downtown* ☏ *801/322–2428* ⊕ *www.uaf.org* ✉ *$6–$12.*

GETTING HERE AND AROUND
AIR TRAVEL
Locals say that Salt Lake City International Airport is closer to its downtown than any major airport in the country. It's 7 miles northwest of downtown via I–80, or you can take North Temple, which leads to the city center. A taxi ride from the airport to town costs about $20. The Utah Transit Authority (UTA) opened an aboveground light-rail extension (TRAX green line) in 2013 that ferries riders to and from the airport in less than 30 minutes for $2.50 each way.

Air Information Salt Lake City International Airport ✉ *776 N. Terminal Dr.* ☏ *801/575–2400, 800/595–2442* ⊕ *www.slcairport.com.*

BUS AND RAIL TRAVEL
Finding your way around Salt Lake City is easy, largely because the city is laid out on an orthogonal grid. However, the city blocks are longer than in many other cities, so distances can be deceiving. Salt Lake has a very workable public transportation system. A Free Fare Zone for travel by bus covers a roughly 36-square-block area downtown and on Capitol Hill. A light-rail system, called TRAX, moves passengers quickly around the city and to the suburbs south of Salt Lake. There are 41 stations, originating from Salt Lake Central Station, where you can connect to FrontRunner (inter-county light rail), Amtrak, and buses. The Blue Line runs north–south from downtown to the suburb of Draper, serving the downtown landmarks (Temple Square, EnergySolutions Arena, Gallivan Center, Smith's Ballpark—home of the AAA baseball team—Fashion Place Mall) and Rio Tinto Stadium (home of Real Salt Lake soccer) in Sandy. The Red line extends eastward to the University of Utah and

The Mormon Influence

Clearly, Salt Lake City exists, and thrives today, because of the settling of the Church of Jesus Christ of Latter-day Saints. Mormon influence began with the city's founding, on July 24, 1847 (still recognized as a state holiday), is reflected in the physical layout of its streets, and continues in nearly every institution.

Under the church's guidance, Utah has evolved into a conservative state where the good of the church is placed above most other concerns. The Utah legislature is overwhelmingly Mormon, Republican, and conservative. In 2012, nearly 73% of the state voted for presidential candidate Mitt Romney, and national Republican candidates regularly pull 70% of the state's votes. It is estimated that 70%

of Utah's population belongs to the LDS faith, and the church controls or operates the number-one television and radio stations (KSL), the number-two newspaper (the *Deseret News*), a major university (Brigham Young), and the largest bank (Zions).

Salt Lake City, however, is closer to 50% Mormon and has had Democratic mayors and city-council majorities for several years. The presence of the University of Utah serves as a counterbalance to conservative BYU. The only other Democratic strongholds in the state are in Park City and Moab. Otherwise, virtually all communities have Republican and LDS leadership, which, among other things, often means closed doors for all sorts of services and stores on Sunday.

---

southwest to the suburb of South Jordan. The Green line originates at the airport and loops into downtown before heading west to the suburb of West Valley. More than 20 stations have free park-and-ride lots. One-way tickets are $2.50 and can be purchased on the platform through vending machines. Two children under five can ride free with a paying adult. For $15, up to four people can buy a Group Pass, good for unlimited rides on buses and TRAX. For trips that begin on a bus, you must purchase the day pass at selected UTA Pass outlets. For trips beginning on TRAX, day passes must be purchased at a ticket vending machine.

Bus and Rail Information Utah Transit Authority (UTA) ☏ *801/743-3882, 888/743-3882* ⊕ *www.rideuta.com.*

TAXI TRAVEL

Though taxi fares are low, cabs can be hard to find on the street so it's best to call for one. Yellow Cab and City Cab provide 24-hour service throughout the Salt Lake Valley.

Taxi Contacts City Cab Company ☏ *801/363-5550* ⊕ *www.saltlakecitycab. com.* **Yellow Cab** ☏ *801/521-2100* ⊕ *www.yellowcabutah.com.*

TOURS

Most excursions run by City Sights include lunch at Brigham Young's historic living quarters. The Utah Heritage Foundation offers the most authoritative tours of Salt Lake's historic sights—the Kearns (Governor's) Mansion, McCune Mansion, and Union Pacific Depot—and their regularly scheduled public tours are free. The Utah Heritage Foundation website has downloadable self-guided tours.

Tour Contacts City Sights. A four-hour, 30-mile bus tour of the city includes all the major sights and many interesting lesser-known places you wouldn't neces-sarily find on your own, with a 30-minute organ recital at the Mormon Taber-nacle and a stop for lunch in Brigham Young's Lion House. A 5½-hour tour also includes a Mormon Tabernacle Choir concert or rehearsal. Various other tours out of the city are available. They will pick up from some downtown hotels. ☎ 801/531–1001 ⊕ www.toursofutah.com ✉ 4-hr tour $50, includes entrance fees but not lunch; 5½-hr tour $55 ☉ 4-hr tour Mon.–Sat. 9 am; 5½-hr tour Thurs. at 4 pm or Sun. at 8:30 am. **Utah Heritage Foundation.** Tours led by knowledgeable guides include a walking tour of the Marmalade Historic District. You'll need to book at least two weeks in advance, and the tour will only go ahead if at least 10 people sign up for it. Tours of individual historic buildings, including the Kearns Mansion, McCune Mansion, and the City and County Build-ing are also available. ✉ 485 N. Canyon Rd., Temple Square ☎ 801/533–0858 ⊕ www.utahheritagefoundation.com ✉ Marmalade Historic District Tour $10; scheduled mansion tours free ☉ Marmalade Historic District Tour Apr.–Oct. by arrangement; call for details of mansion tours.

VISITOR INFORMATION

Pick up maps, ask questions, and otherwise plan your stay at the Salt Lake Convention & Visitors Bureau, on the east side of the downtown convention center. The office is open daily 9–5. If you're at the state capitol, make your plans at the Utah Office of Tourism, inside Council Hall across the street. Once a meeting place for politicians in the Utah Territory, Council Hall now offers brochures and books on tourist des-tinations throughout the city and state, and a knowledgeable staff can answer questions. A small store carries Utah books and gifts.

Contacts Salt Lake Convention and Visitors Bureau ✉ 90 S. West Temple, Downtown ☎ 801/534–4900, 800/541–4955 ⊕ www.visitsaltlake.com. **Utah Office of Tourism** ✉ 300 N. State St., Capitol Hill ☎ 801/538–1030, 800/200–1160 ⊕ www.visitutah.com.

EXPLORING

Salt Lake City is a visitor-friendly city with a remarkable assortment of shopping, culture, and arts. Start with a stroll around the city center, devoting as much time to Temple Square, the heart of the Church of Jesus Christ of Latter-day Saints, as you desire. Within blocks, you'll find museums, theaters, historic buildings, and shopping, including the Gateway and Center outdoor malls. Reminders of the 2002 Winter Olympics are scattered throughout.

Then, branch out into the surrounding neighborhoods to capture more of the flavor of the city. Like most Utah municipalities, Salt Lake City is based on a grid plan that was devised by Brigham Young in the 19th century. Most street names have a directional and a numerical desig-nation, which describes their location in relation to one of two axes. Streets with "East" or "West" in their names are east or west of (and parallel to) Main Street, which runs north–south; and "North" and "South" streets run parallel to South Temple Street.

The numbers tell how far the streets are from the axes. (For example, 200 East Street is two blocks east of Main Street.) Addresses typically include two directional references and two numerical references—320 East 200 South Street, for instance, is within the east 300 block of 200 South Street. Generally, in speech and in written addresses, abbreviations shorten these to, for example, 320 E. 200 S or South; the word "street" is never used. Three of Salt Lake's most prominent streets are named after the Mormon Temple: North Temple, South Temple, and West Temple, indicating that the streets run parallel to the north, south, and west borders of Temple Square. Main Street borders the square's east side.

TEMPLE SQUARE

When Mormon pioneer leader Brigham Young first entered the Salt Lake Valley, he chose this spot at the mouth of City Creek Canyon for the headquarters of the Mormon Church, a role it maintains to this day. The buildings in Temple Square range in age from the Tabernacle constructed in the 1860s to the Conference Center constructed in 2000. Perhaps the most striking aspect of the square is the attention to landscaping, which makes the heart of downtown Salt Lake City into a year-round oasis. The church takes particular pride in its Christmas decorations, which make a nighttime downtown stroll, or horse-and-buggy ride, a must on December calendars.

TOP ATTRACTIONS

Fodor's Choice ★ **Salt Lake Temple.** The centerpiece and spiritual capital of the Church of Jesus Christ of Latter-day Saints, the Salt Lake Temple is a sacred pilgrimage destination for members of the faith. Brigham Young chose this spot for a temple as soon as he arrived in the Salt Lake Valley in 1847, but work on the building didn't begin for another six years. Built of blocks of granite hauled by oxen and train from Little Cottonwood Canyon, the Mormon Temple took 40 years to the day to complete. Its walls are 16 feet thick at the base. Enjoy the grounds and the stately structure. Only observant Mormons may enter the temple itself. ⊠ *South Temple and Main St., Temple Square* ☎ *801/240–4872 Visitor Info* ⊕ *www.lds.org* ☉ *Not open to public.*

Tabernacle. The Tabernacle is known as the home of the famous Mormon Tabernacle Choir and its impressive organ with 11,623 pipes. Visitors can tour the dome-shape building and hear organ recitals daily. From Memorial Day through Labor Day, organ recitals are held Monday through Saturday at noon and 2 and Sunday at 2. The rest of the year, recitals are held Monday through Saturday at noon and Sunday at 2. Visitors are also welcome on Thursday from 7:30 pm to 9:30 pm to listen to the choir rehearse Sunday hymns and from 9:30 am to 10 am as the choir performs for the world's longest-running continuous network broadcast, *Music and the Spoken Word.* ⊠ *50 N. West Temple, Temple Square* ☎ *801/240–4872* ⊕ *www.lds.org* ☒ *Free.*

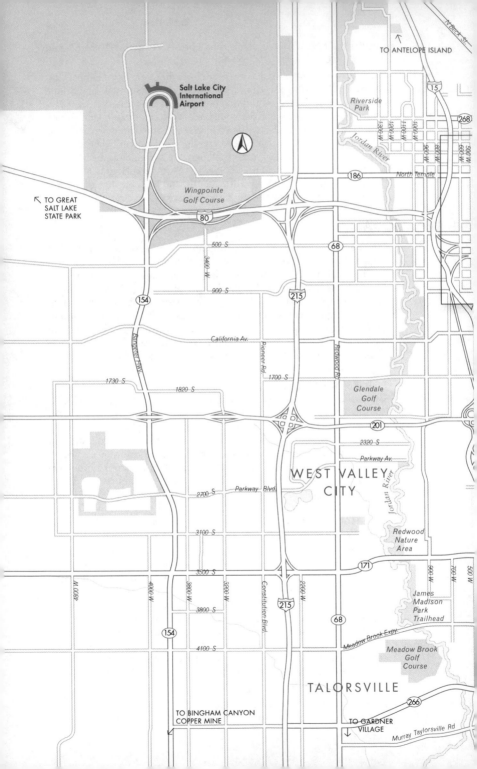

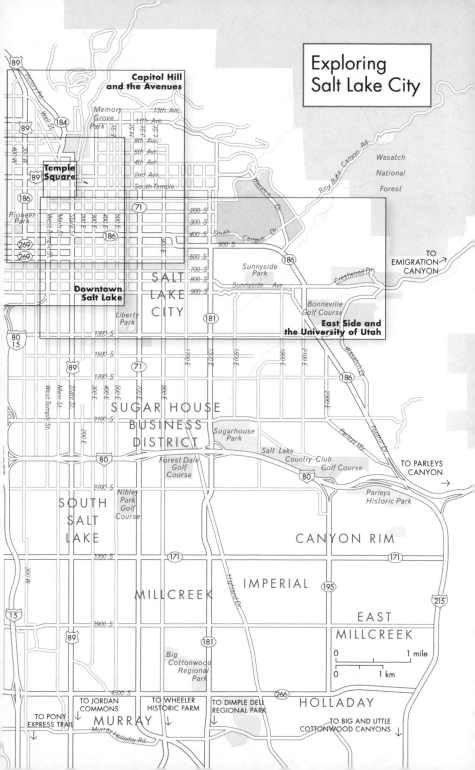

Exploring
Salt Lake City

**Capitol Hill
and the Avenues**

Memory
Grove
Park

13th. Ave.
11th. Ave.
8th. Ave.
6th. Ave.
4th. Ave.
2nd. Ave.
South Temple

**Temple
Square**

Wasatch

National

Forest

Red Butte Canyon Rd.

Wasatch Dr.

200 S
300 S
400 S
500 S
600 S
700 S
800 S
900 S

South Campus Dr.

Pioneer
Park

Liberty
Park

**Downtown
Salt Lake**

**SALT
LAKE
CITY**

Sunnyside Park
Sunnyside Ave.

Crestwood Dr.

TO
EMIGRATION
CANYON

Bonneville
Golf Course

**East Side and
the University of Utah**

1300 S

1500 S

1700 S

**SUGAR HOUSE
BUSINESS
DISTRICT**

Sugarhouse
Park

Salt Lake
Country Club
Golf Course

Parleys Wy.

Foothill Dr.

TO PARLEYS
CANYON
→

2100 S

Forest Dale
Golf Course

2700 S

Nibley
Park
Golf
Course

Parleys
Historic Park

**SOUTH
SALT
LAKE**

CANYON RIM

3300 S

MILLCREEK

IMPERIAL

Highland Dr.

**EAST
MILLCREEK**

3900 S

0   1 mile

0   1 km

Big
Cottonwood
Regional
Park

4500 S

TO JORDAN
COMMONS
↓

TO WHEELER
HISTORIC FARM
↓

TO DIMPLE DELL
REGIONAL PARK
↓

HOLLADAY

TO PONY
EXPRESS TRAIL
↓

MURRAY

Murray Holladay Rd.

TO BIG AND LITTLE
COTTONWOOD CANYONS ↓

West Capitol St.
West St.
300 W
State St.
Main St.
West Temple St.
200 E
300 E
400 E
500 E
600 E

1100 E
1300 E
1500 E
1900 E
2100 E
2300 E

300 W
West Temple St.
Main St.
State St.
200 E
300 E
400 E
500 E
700 E
900 E

300 W

Beehive House ..**1**

Church of Jesus
Christ of
Latter-day
Saints Conference
Center **3**

Family History
Library **6**

Joseph Smith
Memorial
Building **2**

Museum of
Church History
and Art **7**

Salt Lake
Temple **4**

Tabernacle **5**

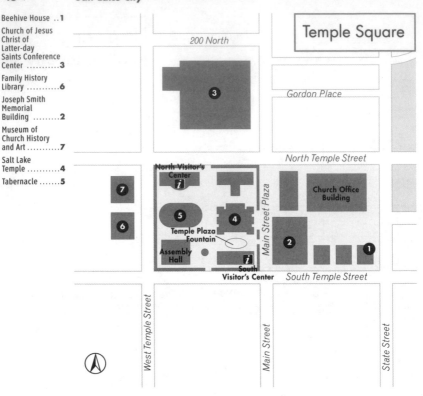

WORTH NOTING

Beehive House. Brigham Young's home, a national historic landmark, was constructed in 1854 and is topped with a replica of a beehive, symbolizing industry. Inside are many original furnishings; a tour of the interior will give you a fascinating glimpse of upper-class 19th-century polygamous life. ⊠ *67 E. South Temple, Temple Square* ☎ *801/240–2681* ⊕ *www.lds.org* ☞ *Free* ☉ *Daily 9:30–8:30.*

Church of Jesus Christ of Latter-day Saints Conference Center. Completed in 2000, this massive center features a 21,000-seat auditorium and an 850-seat theater. Equally impressive are the rooftop gardens landscaped with native plants and streams to mirror the surrounding mountains. Visitors must be accompanied by a guide. Tours are flexible but usually last 45 minutes. The Mormon Tabernacle Choir performs here regularly. ⊠ *60 W. North Temple, Temple Square* ☎ *801/240–0075* ⊕ *www.lds. org* ☞ *Free* ☉ *Daily 9–9.*

**QUICK
BITE**

Hatch Family Chocolates. For a sweet treat, stop at Hatch Family Chocolates, a superfriendly and immaculate candy and ice-cream shop. Jerry Hatch uses his mother's secret recipe for creamy caramel, and each piece of chocolate is hand-dipped and sold by weight. Chocolate turtles here can weigh a full quarter pound. They also serve espresso, Italian soda, ice

CLOSE UP

Genealogy in the Mormon Faith

According to the *Encyclopedia of Mormonism*, "searching for and compiling genealogical information are sacred responsibilities to Latter-day Saints." It is not considered a hobby or even optional; it is a "commandment of God," dating to 1894. LDS church members believe that the family is of eternal significance, and the purpose of compiling detailed genealogical records is to "identify one's roots, to perform saving ordinances in a temple for persons who did not receive them in mortal life, and to seal individuals together for eternity as families." Mormons believe that all people should have the opportunity to hear the gospel in mortal life or the "spirit world," so they actively baptize their ancestors (and others) by proxy. Although church doctrine acknowledges that posthumous baptism may not be accepted by its target, the practice is controversial, with instances of overzealous LDS "Baptists" going well beyond their families to baptize non-church members, including Holocaust victims and U.S. presidents.

2

---

cream, and the best hot chocolate in the city. ⊠ *376 8th Ave., The Avenues* ☎ *801/532–4912* ⊕ *www.hatchfamilychocolates.com* ⊙ *Closed Sun.*

Family History Library. Genealogy is important to Mormons. This four-story library houses the world's largest collection of genealogical data, including books, maps, and census information. Mormons and non-Mormons alike come here to do research. ⊠ *35 N. West Temple, Temple Square* ☎ *801/240–6996* ⊕ *www.lds.org* ▱ *Free* ⊙ *Mon. 8–5, Tues.–Fri. 8 am–9 pm, Sat. 9–5.*

Joseph Smith Memorial Building. Once the Hotel Utah, this building on the National Register of Historic Places is owned and operated by the Mormon Church. You can use a computer program to learn how to do genealogical research at the FamilySearch Center here (no charge; volunteers will assist you) or watch an hour-long film about the church's teaching of how Jesus Christ appeared in the Western Hemisphere after his resurrection. The center has two restaurants and an elegantly restored lobby. Upstairs is the 1920 census and 70,000 volumes of personal histories of the faithful. ⊠ *15 E. South Temple, Temple Square* ☎ *801/240–4085* ⊕ *www.lds.org* ▱ *Free* ⊙ *Weekdays 9–9, Sat. 9–5.*

Museum of Church History and Art. The museum houses a variety of artifacts and works of art relating to the history and doctrine of the Mormon faith, including personal belongings of church leaders Joseph Smith, Brigham Young, and others. There are also samples of Mormon coins and scrip used as standard currency in Utah during the 1800s, and beautiful examples of quilting, embroidery, and other handicrafts. Upstairs galleries exhibit religious and secular works by Mormon artists from all over the world. ⊠ *45 N. West Temple, Temple Square* ☎ *801/240–4615* ⊕ *www. lds.org* ▱ *Free* ⊙ *Weekdays 9–9, weekends 10–5.*

Visitor Centers. The history of the Mormon Church and the Mormon pioneers' trek to Utah is outlined in a North and South Visitor's Center.

City and County
Building **9**

Clark
Planetarium **4**

Discovery
Gateway **5**

Gallivan
Center **1**

Gateway
Mall **3**

The Leonardo **7**

Rio Grande
Depot **6**

Salt Lake City
Main Library **8**

Union
Pacific Building ..**2**

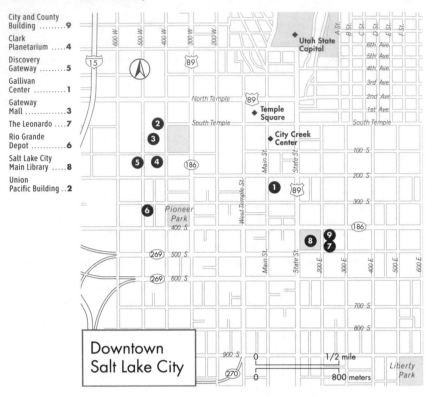

Diligent missionaries stand by to offer tours and answer questions.
⊠ *Temple Sq.* ☎ *801/240–4872* ⊕ *www.lds.org* ⊠ *Free* ☉ *Daily 9–9.*

DOWNTOWN SALT LAKE CITY

Although businesses and homes stretch in all directions, downtown's
core is a compact, six-block area that includes multiple hotels, restaurants, historic buildings, and entertainment venues.

TOP ATTRACTIONS

FAMILY **Discovery Gateway.** The region's premier children's museum has three
floors of lively hands-on experiences. Kids can participate in a television
newscast, tell stories through pictures or radio, climb into a Life Flight
helicopter, or revel in a kid-size town with grocery store, vehicles, a
house, and a construction site. Plan on spending about two hours here
if you have children ages 2 through 10. ⊠ *444 W. 100 S, Downtown*
☎ *801/456–5437* ⊕ *www.childmuseum.org* ⊠ *$9.50* ☉ *Mon.–Thurs.*
10–6, Fri. and Sat. 10–8, Sun. noon–6.

FAMILY **Gateway Mall.** Just west of downtown Salt Lake, Gateway is an all-in-
one family destination with shopping, dining, movie theaters, museums,
and a music venue. In summer, cool off in the Olympic Legacy Plaza,
a choreographed fountain that sprays pillars of water in sync with

the 2002 Olympic theme and other inspiring music. Two parking lots make access easy. The Clark Planetarium, Discovery Gateway children's museum, the Depot (a live-music venue), and a 12-screen movie complex are four of the draws to this mall, across from EnergySolutions Arena. ⊠ *18 N. Rio Grande St., Downtown* ☎ *801/456–0000* ⊕ *www. shopthegateway.com* ☯ *Mon.–Sat. 10–9, Sun. noon–6.*

FAMILY

Fodor'sChoice

★

The Leonardo. Salt Lake's first museum devoted to the convergence of science, art, and technology opened in late 2011 and has become a bucket-list item for any family visit to Salt Lake. Although it hosts large-scale national touring exhibits like the Dead Sea Scrolls, this is quintessentially a hands-on museum dedicated to inspiring children to explore. You'll be greeted by a main-floor lab space where revolving artists in residence offer a menagerie of free programs daily where kids can sculpt with clay, draw, design, or write. Head upstairs to the Tinkering Garage, where volunteers help you build with repurposed household objects, deconstruct electronics, create electric circuits (including a radio), and much more. Throughout this converted library building, exhibits highlight Da Vinci's influence on arts and science, great inventions from Utah (including Philo Farnsworth and the television), and climate change. Technology is integrated everywhere. This place is well worth its modest admission price; allow two to three hours. ⊠ *209 E. 500 S, Downtown* ☎ *801/531–9800* ⊕ *www.theleonardo.org* ☎ *$7–$9* ☯ *Daily 10–5 (to 10 pm Thurs. and Fri.).*

FAMILY

Salt Lake City Main Library. Few libraries in America can match the soaring architectural excitement of the main library in Salt Lake City's system. Designed by Moshe Safdie and built in 2003, this modern building has become a cultural center for the city. Inspired by the Roman Coliseum, it features a six-story walkable wall that serves as both sculpture and function, allowing for great views and a path up the building. Activities are scheduled here all year, in the 300-seat auditorium, the plaza, or the spacious atrium. From the rooftop garden you get a 360-degree view of the valley and mountains. The on-site coffee shop, deli, shops, writing center, and public radio station mean you can stay here all day. Kids can fall in love with reading in the Crystal Cave and Treehouse Room in the huge children's section. Plus, there are five other libraries in the system, including the Tudor-style Sprague Library that opened in 1928 in the city's popular Sugar House neighborhood. ⊠ *210 E. 400 S, Downtown* ☎ *801/524–8200* ⊕ *www.slcpl.lib.ut.us* ☎ *Free* ☯ *Mon.– Thurs. 9–9, Fri. and Sat. 9–6, Sun. 1–5.*

WORTH NOTING

City and County Building. Listed on the National Register of Historic Places, the Romanesque red-sandstone, castle-like seat of city government was the city's tallest building from its 1894 opening to 1973. On Washington Square, at the spot where the original Mormon settlers circled their wagons on their first night in the Salt Lake Valley, this building served as the state capitol for 19 years. Hundreds of trees, including species from around the world, and many winding paths and seating areas make the grounds a calm downtown oasis. In summer the grounds host major Salt Lake arts and music festivals. Free tours are given on Monday during the summer through the Utah Heritage Foundation.

✉ *451 S. State St., Downtown* ☎ *801/533–0858 Heritage Foundation* ⊕ *www.slcgov.com/facilities* ◫ *Free* ⊘ *Weekdays 8–5.*

FAMILY **Clark Planetarium.** With an array of free hands-on exhibits and state-of-the-art 3-D and IMAX theaters, Clark Planetarium is an appealing, affordable family attraction. Traipse across a moonscape and learn about Utah's contributions to spaceflight, but save a few minutes for the Planet Fun store. ✉ *110 S. 400 W, Downtown* ☎ *385/468–7827* ⊕ *www.clarkplanetarium.org* ◫ *Exhibits free; movies $9* ⊘ *Open daily 10:30 am–end of last show* ⌨ *The planetarium will validate 3 hrs of parking at the Gateway; pay for parking as you leave the parking lot.*

Gallivan Center. This outdoor plaza calls itself Salt Lake City's living room, and it's a great spot for a lunch—especially on the weekly Food Truck Thursdays—or evening snack, concert, festival, or other special event. Many events are free. Rent skates and enjoy the festive ice rink in the winter. ✉ *239 S. Main St., Downtown* ☎ *801/535–6110* ⊕ *www. thegallivancenter.com.*

Rio Grande Depot. This 1910 depot was built to compete with the showy Union Pacific Railroad Depot three blocks north. It houses the Rio Grande Café and **Utah History Research Center** (⊘ *Weekdays 9–4* ⊕ *www.historyresearch.utah.gov*), which has rotating exhibits on the history of Utah and the West. The winter counterpart to Salt Lake's thriving farmers' market takes place on selected weekends from November to April. ✉ *300 S. Rio Grande St., Downtown* ☎ *801/533–3535* ◫ *Free.*

Union Pacific Building. This depot, built in 1909 at a cost of $300,000, is a striking monument to the importance of railroads in the settling of the West. The slate-shingle mansard roof sets a distinctive French Second Empire tone for the exterior. Inside, Western-theme murals and stained-glass windows create a setting rich with color and texture. The station has been restored and now functions as the entrance to the Gateway Mall and as a special-events venue. ✉ *400 W. South Temple, Downtown* ☎ *801/456–0000* ⊕ *www.shopthegateway.com* ◫ *Free* ⊘ *Mon.– Sat. 10–9, Sun. noon–6.*

CAPITOL HILL AND THE AVENUES

These neighborhoods overlook the city from the foothills north of downtown. Two days after entering the future Salt Lake City, Brigham Young brought his fellow religious leaders to the summit of the most prominent hill here, which he named Ensign Peak, to plan out their new home. New arrivals built sod homes into the hillside of what is now the Avenues. Two-room log cabins and adobe houses dotted the area. Meanwhile, on the western slope of the hill, fruit and nut trees were planted. Some still remain, as does a neighborhood known as Marmalade, with streets named Apricot, Quince, and Almond.

With the coming of the railroad came Victorian homes. The city's rich and prominent families built mansions along South Temple. As the city has grown over the years, wealthy citizens have continued to live close to the city but farther up the hill where the views of the valley are better. Since the early 1970s the lower Avenues have seen an influx of residents

CAPITOL HILL WALK

A tour of Capitol Hill and the Avenues is a logical extension of a tour of downtown Salt Lake City. To begin the tour of this area, head north along State Street from South Temple to North Temple and turn right. Turn left on Canyon Road to the beginning of **Memory Grove**. The monuments, creek, and trees here have been restored after a freak tornado roared through in 1999. It's a beautiful city sanctuary, and if you head north it turns into City Creek Canyon, which has more than a dozen miles of paved and dirt trails (most free of any motorized traffic). After exploring the Grove and the Canyon, head up the steep hill to the **Utah State Capitol**. The 30- to 45-minute tour of the capitol shows you a grandiose building with surprisingly little activity 10 months

out of the year (the legislature meets for only eight weeks). Exit from the west side of the capitol and cross the street to the free **Pioneer Memorial Museum**, which antiques and history buffs enjoy. Circle back toward downtown and head down the hill, then east on South Temple to see the stately **Cathedral of the Madeleine** and **Kearns Mansion**, home of the governor of Utah.

TIMING

You can spend a half day or more touring the capitol, Kearns Mansion, and the Pioneer Memorial Museum. If you include a picnic in the canyon, your tour could take all day. The views from Capitol Hill are impressive whenever skies are clear. The Kearns Mansion, as the official residence of Utah's governor, is most festive during the Christmas season.

interested in restoring the older homes, making this area a diverse and evolving community.

The state capitol, for which Capitol Hill is named, was completed in 1915. State offices flank the capitol on three sides. City Creek Canyon forms its eastern boundary. The Avenues denotes the larger neighborhood along the foothills, north of South Temple, extending from Capitol Hill east to the University of Utah. Getting around the Avenues is different from following the logic of the grid system of downtown. The Avenues increase in number as you head uphill, 1st Avenue being the beginning. From west to east, the streets are labeled alphabetically.

TOP ATTRACTIONS

Cathedral of the Madeleine. Although the Mormon Temple just to the west is Salt Lake's most prominent religious landmark, this red Romanesque cathedral stands high above the city's north side and is a stunning house of worship in its own right. The exterior bristles with gargoyles, and its Gothic interior showcases bright frescoes, intricate wood carvings, and a 4,066-pipe organ. The highly regarded Madeleine children's choir gives concerts regularly (especially during the Christmas season), and tours of the cathedral are offered every Sunday at 12:30. The building is listed on the National Register of Historic Places. ⊠ *331 E. South Temple, The Avenues* ☎ *801/328–8941* ⊕ *www.saltlakecathedral.org* ⊠ *Free* ☉ *Mon.–Sat. 7 am–9 pm, Sun. 7–7.*

Cathedral of the
Madeleine **4**

Kearns
Mansion **5**

Memory Grove ...**1**

Pioneer
Memorial
Museum **3**

Utah State
Capitol **2**

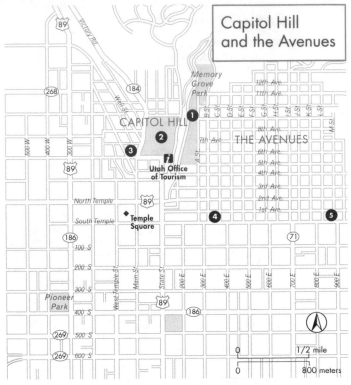

Capitol Hill
and the Avenues

Kearns Mansion. Built by silver-mining tycoon Thomas Kearns in 1902, this limestone structure—reminiscent of a French château with all its turrets and balconies—is now the official residence of Utah's governor. In its early days the mansion was visited by President Theodore Roosevelt and other dignitaries from around the world. The mansion was faithfully restored after Christmas lights caused a fire in 1993 that destroyed much of the interior. ⊠ *603 E. South Temple, The Avenues* ☎ *801/538–1005* ⊕ *www.utah.gov/governor/mansion/index.html* ⊠ *Free* ⊙ *Check website for updates.*

Utah State Capitol. Utah's legislature meets just once a year, for 45 days from January to March. Otherwise the state's grandiose capitol can feel a little like a granite-and-marble ghost town. In 1912, after the state reaped $800,000 in inheritance taxes from the estate of Union Pacific Railroad president Edward Harriman, work began on the Renaissance Revival structure that tops Capitol Hill. From the exterior steps you get a marvelous view of the entire Salt Lake Valley. In the rotunda beneath the 165-foot-high dome, a series of murals, commissioned as part of a Works Progress Administration project during the Depression, depicts the state's history. Don't miss the gold-leafed State Reception Room, the original state supreme court, and the Senate gallery. Free guided tours are offered weekdays 9–5 on the hour. ⊠ *350 N. State St., Capitol*

Hill ☎ 801/538–1800 ⊕ www.utahstatecapitol.utah.gov ⊙ Weekdays 7 am–8 pm, weekends and holidays 8–6.

| QUICK BITE | **Cucina Deli.** Take a break from your tours with a picnic from this Italian deli specializing in gourmet lunches to eat in or take out. Choose a sandwich, like the Sicilian combo with capicola ham, mortadella, salami, provolone, and tomatoes, and a side dish of one of many pasta salads. Bring your freshly packed lunch to Memory Grove or City Creek Canyon to relax and refuel amid beautiful surroundings. ⊠ *1026 E. 2nd Ave., The Avenues* ☎ *801/322–3055* ⊕ *www.cucinadeli.com.* |

2

WORTH NOTING

Memory Grove. Severely damaged by a freak tornado in 1999, Memory Grove was carefully restored as a city park with veterans' monuments, beautiful landscaping, and the waters of City Creek. You can hike, jog, or bike on the paved road or dirt trails along **City Creek Canyon**. More trails take off from the road, including the 100-mile Bonneville Shoreline Trail. ⊠ *300 N. Canyon Rd., Capitol Hill.*

Pioneer Memorial Museum. Covering the pioneer era from the departure of the Mormons from Nauvoo, Illinois, to the hammering of the Golden Spike, this massive collection traces the history of Mormon settlers in 38 rooms—plus a carriage house—on four floors. Administered by the Daughters of Utah Pioneers, its displays include clothing, furniture, tools, wagons, and carriages. Be careful with kids—this museum is as cluttered as a westbound covered wagon loaded with all of a family's possessions. ⊠ *300 N. Main St., Capitol Hill* ☎ *801/532–6479* ⊕ *www. dupinternational.org* 🖾 *Free, donations accepted* ⊙ *Mon.–Sat. 9–5 (until 8 Wed.).*

EAST SIDE AND THE UNIVERSITY OF UTAH

On one of the shorelines of ancient Lake Bonneville, the University of Utah is the state's largest higher-education institution and the oldest university west of the Mississippi. It is home to museums, the football stadium that was the site of the opening and closing ceremonies during the 2002 Winter Olympics, and a 15,000-seat indoor arena that played host to the 1979 NCAA basketball championship game, in which Larry Bird faced off against Magic Johnson. The University Medical Center and its neighbor, the Primary Children's Medical Center, east of the campus, are active in medical training and research. Research Park, south of the campus, houses scores of private companies and portions of 30 academic departments in a cooperative enterprise to combine research and technology to produce marketable products.

As you leave the downtown and university area, there are opportunities to enjoy the outdoors. Hiking trails lead across the foothills above the university. Red Butte Garden and Arboretum is a treat for the eye and a great place to learn about plants that thrive in dry climates such as Utah's. Since relocating to these foothills in 2011, the gleaming copper-colored Natural History Museum of Utah has become a must-visit

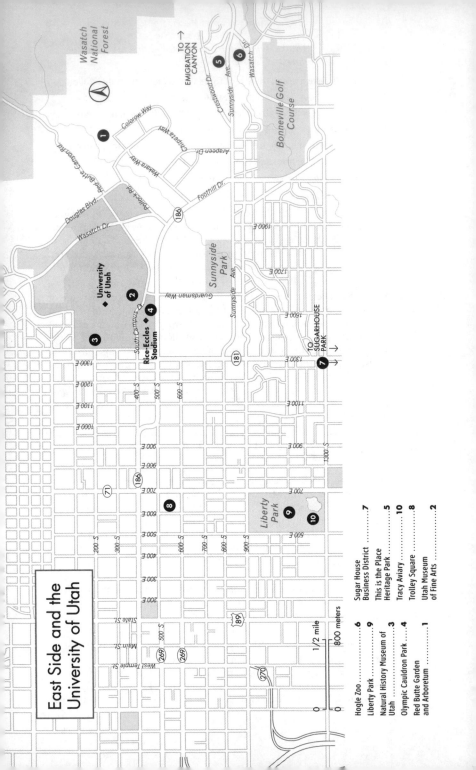

East Side and the University of Utah

Wasatch National Forest

Wasatch Dr.
Douglas Blvd.
Red Butte Canyon Rd.
Pollock Rd.
Colorow Way
Chipeta Way
Wakara Way

University of Utah

South Campus Dr.
Rice-Eccles Stadium

Foothill Dr.
Guardsman Way
Sunnyside Ave.
Crestwood Dr.
Arapeen Dr.
Wasatch Dr.

TO EMIGRATION CANYON →

Sunnyside Park

Bonneville Golf Course

186
181
71
89
269
269
270

TO SUGARHOUSE PARK →

Liberty Park

1900 E
1700 E
1600 E
1300 E
1300 E
1200 E
1100 E
1000 E
900 E
800 E
700 E
600 E
500 E

400 S
500 S
600 S
700 S
800 S
900 S
1300 S

State St.
Main St.
West Temple St.

1/2 mile
800 meters

Hogle Zoo 6
Liberty Park 9
Natural History Museum of Utah 3
Olympic Cauldron Park 4
Red Butte Garden and Arboretum 1

Sugar House Business District 7
This is the Place Heritage Park 5
Tracy Aviary 10
Trolley Square 8
Utah Museum of Fine Arts 2

destination. For living history, wander the boardwalks in This Is the Place Heritage Park, where volunteers dress in 19th-century costume.

TOP ATTRACTIONS

FAMILY **Hogle Zoo.** You'll never confuse this with the San Diego Zoo, but this 42-acre zoo nestled at the base of Emigration Canyon has been a delightful half-day destination for families since 1931. Asian Highlands showcases big cats in natural surroundings; Rocky Shores includes underwater viewing of its polar bears, sea lions, seals, and otters; and Elephant Encounter has elephants and white rhinos in a simulated African plain. In between you'll find many exhibits with species native to the West, including wolves and bison. A children's zoo, interactive exhibits, and special presentations make visits informative and engaging for both adults and children. Just for fun is the Lighthouse Point Splash Zone, with a tube slide and lots of wet play opportunities, the Zoo Train, and a carousel. ⊠ *2600 E. Sunnyside Ave., East Side* ☎ *801/582–1631* ⊕ *www.hoglezoo.org* ⊠ *$14.95 summer; $11.95 winter* ☉ *Mar.–Oct., daily 9–5; Nov.–Feb., daily 9–4, grounds remain open until 5:30.*

FAMILY **Natural History Museum of Utah.** One of the most spectacular natural history museums you will find, this building grabs you from the moment Fodor'sChoice you see its copper-and-granite form sparkling above the eastern foot-★ hills of Salt Lake City. Its dazzling exterior is just a prelude to a gold mine of engaging exhibits about land, sky, water, and life in the West. Learn about the formation of the region's incredible landscape of parks, mountain ranges, lakes, and basins. Study 10,000 years of people and cultures. Immerse yourself in prehistoric Utah, home to prolific research on dinosaurs and some of the most famous fossil recoveries in history. Since its opening in 2011, children and adults alike have counted this as an unforgettable highlight of any Salt Lake City visit. ⊠ *301 Wakara Way, University of Utah* ☎ *801/581–6927* ⊕ *www.nhmu.utah. edu* ⊠ *$11* ☉ *Daily 10–5 (until 9 Wed.).*

Olympic Cauldron Park. Relive the 2002 Olympics through photographs, memorabilia, and a 10-minute film. Step outside to stand beneath the Olympic Torch, which is lit for special events; and Hoberman Arch, the backdrop for medal ceremonies that year. ⊠ *451 S. 1400 E, University of Utah* ☎ *801/581–8849* ⊕ *www.stadium.utah.edu* ⊠ *Free* ☉ *Mon.– Sat. 10–6.*

FAMILY **Red Butte Garden and Arboretum.** With more than 100 acres of gardens Fodor'sChoice and undeveloped acres, the grounds here provide many pleasurable ★ hours of strolling. Of special interest are the Perennial, Fragrance, and Medicinal gardens, the Daylily Collection, the Water Pavilion, and the Children's Garden. Lectures on everything from bugs to gardening in arid climates, workshops, and concerts are presented regularly. The popular Summer Concert Series attracts well-known musicians from Tony Bennett to Vampire Weekend. The pristine amphitheater seats approximately 3,000 people on its expansive lawn. The Botanic Gift Shop offers books, soaps, sculptures, and fine gifts. ⊠ *300 Wakara Way, University of Utah* ☎ *801/581–0556* ⊕ *www.redbuttegarden.org* ⊠ *$10* ☉ *Aug., Mon.–Sat. 9–9, Sun. 9–5; Sept. and Apr., Mon.–Sat. 9–7:30, Sun. 9–5; Oct.–Mar., daily 9–5.*

WORTH NOTING

FAMILY **Liberty Park.** Salt Lake City is blessed with numerous large city parks, and Liberty Park is one of the favorites. Salt Lake's oldest park features the Tracy Aviary, the Chase Home Museum, several playgrounds, a large pond, a swimming pool and tennis complex, and carnival rides in the summer on its eight square city blocks. The city's biggest Pioneer Day celebration (July 24), and running races dot a busy summer schedule annually. Kids will love clambering on the fountain that represents the seven major canyons of the Wasatch Front. ⊠ *600 E. 900 S, East Side* ⊕ *www.slcgov.com/cityparks/parks-liberty-park.*

Sugar House Business District. Utah pioneers tried to produce sugar out of beets at a mill here. Although sugar never made it to their tables, this is a sweet place to find funky little shops and restaurants of all kinds. The **Sprague Library** (⊠ *2131 S. 1100 East*), chosen America's most beautiful library in 1935, is a historic Tudor-style building. Pick up picnic food and head fo tiny Hidden Hollow Park, or cross 1300 East to the expansive Sugar House Park. Catch the city's most spectacular fireworks and arts festival every July 4. ⊠ *2100 S. from 700 E to 1300 E, East Side.*

NEED A BREAK?

Sugar House Park. Rolling grassy hills, athletic fields, multiple playgrounds, a creek, and a pond provide plenty of room to fly a kite or have a picnic at Sugar House Park. Its north-facing hill on the south end of the park is also the "go-to" destination for sledding in winter. The park was once a federal prison famous for incarcerating Utah polygamists. ⊠ *1300 E. 2100 S, East Side* ⊕ *www.sugarhousepark.org.*

FAMILY **This Is the Place Heritage Park.** Brigham Young and his band of Mormon followers descended into the Salt Lake Valley here. On July 24, 1847 (now a statewide holiday that is bigger than July 4 in many communities), he famously declared that this was the place for the Latter-day Saints to end their cross-country trek. A 60-foot-tall statue of Young, Heber Kimball, and Wilbur Woodruff stands prominently in the park, which includes Heritage Village, a re-created 19th-century communityand-visitor center. In summer volunteers dressed in period clothing demonstrate what Mormon pioneer life was like. You can watch artisans at work in historic buildings and take wagon or train rides around the compound. Watch a 20-minute movie depicting the pioneers' trek across America at the visitor center, or browse through the gift and book shop. ⊠ *2601 E. Sunnyside Ave., East Side* ☎ *801/582–1847* ⊕ *www. thisistheplace.org* 🎫 *Village $11 Mon.–Sat., $5 Sun.; monument free* ☉ *Daily 9–5; hours and attractions vary seasonally.*

FAMILY **Tracy Aviary.** Salt Lake City's scale is family-friendly, and the aviary is a prime example. Easily walkable for even the smallest kids, this facility features more than 100 species of birds found on the Western Hemispheric Flyway, a migratory pattern that includes Great Salt Lake. You will see emus, bald eagles, flamingos, parrots, and several types of waterfowl. Don't be startled by the wandering peacocks! One of the aviary's missions is to educate the public about birds native to Utah and their corresponding ecosystems. There are bird shows and educational activities daily. ✉ *600 E. 900 S, East Side* ☎ *801/596–8500* ⊕ *www.tracyaviary.org* ✉ *$7* ☉ *Daily 9–5 (until 8 on Mon., June–Aug.).*

Trolley Square. From 1908 to 1945 this sprawling redbrick structure held nearly 150 trolleys and electric trains for the Utah Light and Railway Company. As trolleys fell out of use, the facility was closed. In the early 1970s the mission-style edifice was completely overhauled. Today it's listed on the National Register of Historic Places and houses a Whole Foods Market in addition to dozens of boutiques and restaurants. ✉ *600 S. 700 E, East Side* ☎ *801/521–9877* ⊕ *www.trolleysquare.com* ☉ *Mon.–Sat. 10–9, Sun. noon–5.*

Utah Museum of Fine Arts. Because it encompasses 74,000 square feet and more than 20 galleries, you'll be glad this modern facility has a café and a sculpture court—perfect places to rest. Special exhibits are mounted regularly, and the vast permanent collection includes Egyptian, Greek, and Roman relics; Italian Renaissance and other European paintings; Chinese ceramics and scrolls; Japanese screens; Thai and Cambodian sculptures; African and Latin American artworks; Navajo rugs; and American art from the 17th century to the present. ✉ *410 S. Campus Dr., University of Utah* ☎ *801/581–7332* ⊕ *www.umfa.utah.edu* ✉ *$9* ☉ *Tues.–Fri. 10–5, Wed. 10–8, weekends 11–5.*

GREAT SALT LAKE

No visit to Utah is quite complete without a trip to the Great Salt Lake. This wonder of the world is actually more popular with tourists than locals. This was not always the case, but drastic changes in lake levels keep the state and private developers from cashing in on this unique site so close to a major city. Because the lake is so shallow, an inch or two of change in the lake's depth translates into yards of sticky mud between the sandy beach and water deep enough to float in. This shouldn't keep anyone from taking a cruise on the lake or visiting Antelope Island, where the shore dynamics are much different.

EXPLORING

Great Salt Lake State Park. The Great Salt Lake is eight times saltier than the ocean and second only to the Dead Sea in salinity. What makes it so briny? There's no outlet to the ocean, so salts and other minerals carried by rivers and streams become concentrated in this enormous evaporation pond. Ready access to this wonder is possible at Great Salt Lake State Park, 16 miles west of Salt Lake City, on the lake's south shore.

The fickle nature of the Great Salt Lake is evident here. From the marina you will see a large, Moorish-style pavilion to the north. This pavilion was built to re-create the glory days of the lake from the 1890s to the 1950s, when first the train, then automobiles, brought thousands of people here for entertainment. Floating in the lake was the biggest draw, but ballroom dancing and an amusement park made for a day's recreation. In addition, three resorts made this a popular place, despite varying lake levels. It was the decline of ballroom dancing together with a severe drop in the lake level that spelled the end of the pavilion's run in the 1960s. In 1981 the present pavilion, souvenir shop, and a dance

The Legendary Great Salt Lake

Legends of an enormous body of water with an outlet to the Pacific Ocean drew explorers north from Mexico as early as the 1500s. By the 1700s, other legends—about piles of gold and mines full of jewels—had been proven false by Spanish explorers, but the lake legend endured. Following a source of water through the West's harsh desert, and traveling along a flat riverbank instead of struggling over mountains, would make trade easier between New Mexico and the settlements springing up along California's coast. Perhaps goods could be shipped to the coast rather than hauled by mules, a trip the Spanish guessed (and they were right) would take months.

Franciscan fathers Francisco Atanasio Dominguez and Francisco Silvestre Velez de Escalante came close to finding Great Salt Lake in 1776, but they cut through the Wasatch Mountains too far to the south. They did blaze a major trade route through Utah, but there is no record of any travelers wandering far enough off the route to see the lake of legend. In 1804–05 Lewis and Clark searched for a water route to the West Coast, but their focus on the Columbia River gave them no reason to travel south of Idaho. They, too, missed the lake.

Mountain men had heard of the lake. Legend has it that an argument about the lake broke out at the alcohol-soaked 1824 rendezvous in northern Utah—the trappers couldn't agree whether the nearby Bear River flowed into the lake. Jim Bridger was chosen to settle the argument, some say because he was the youngest. For whatever reason, he was set adrift on the Bear River in a rickety bull boat and told to report his findings at a future rendezvous—if he survived.

Jim Bridger did survive, and he was able to report that the Bear River did flow into the Great Salt Lake. However, his travels and those of fellow mountain man Jedediah Smith indicated that the lake was landlocked. Plus it was no good for drinking. Even worse, the explorers found that travel around the lake was hampered by vast expanses of marshland, a muddy shoreline, and hundreds of square miles of salt flats that looked solid but were often little more than a thin crust over layers of muck.

With dreams of a freshwater oasis and an easy route to the coast crushed, the legends of the lake changed. The lake became a place where monsters lurked in the water, giants rode elephant-like creatures on the islands, and the bottom periodically opened, swallowing everything nearby. The area became a place to avoid, or to pass by quickly, until 1847, when Brigham Young and the Mormon pioneers crossed the plains to settle on its shore.

floor were built. Two years later record flooding made an island of the pavilion. It sits on dry land today, but its current owners have been unable to re-create its former stature.

The state park used to manage the beaches north of the pavilion, but the lake is too shallow here for convenient floating. The picnic beaches on Antelope Island State Park are the best places to float. If you can't take the time to get to Antelope Island, which is 25 miles north of Salt

CLOSE UP

This Lake Is for the Birds

Although it's too salty for fish, the Great Salt Lake teems with algae and bacteria. These provide food for brine shrimp and brine flies, which must seem like caviar to the millions of shorebirds that stop here during their migrations. The following is a list of some of the more than 250 species that you can spot at natural saltwater marshes, man-made freshwater marshes, and wetland refuges around the lake: avocet, bald eagle, black-necked stilt, California gull, common snipe, cormorant, egret (great and snowy varieties), grebe (eared and western), heron (great blue and black-crowned night), killdeer, long-billed curlew, long-billed dowitcher, marbled godwit, merganser, northern phalarope, plover (black-bellied, lesser, golden, snowy, semipalmated), red knot, sanderling, sandpiper (Baird's, least, pectoral, semipalmated, solitary, spotted, stilt, western), tern (Caspian and Forster's), white-faced ibis, willet, and the yellowlegs (greater and lesser).

It's a bird-watchers' paradise, so bring your binoculars!

Lake City, however, you can walk down the boat ramp at the Great Salt Lake State Marina and stick your legs in the water to experience the unique sensation of floating on water that won't let you sink. Your feet will bob to the surface, and you will see tiny orange brine shrimp floating with you. You can also rent boats and stand-up paddleboards here. Shower off at the marina. ⊠ *Frontage Rd., Magna ✛ 2 miles east of I–80 Exit 104* ☎ *801/250–1898* ⊕ *www.stateparks.utah.gov* ⊠ *$3* ☉ *Daily dawn to dusk.*

SPORTS AND THE OUTDOORS

Salt Lake City's magic lies not in its skyline, but its backdrops. The Great Salt Lake and Wasatch Mountains are more than pretty pictures, however. Rich outdoors experiences await you within minutes of downtown, from a quiet stroll up City Creek Canyon to a peaceful cruise on the Great Salt Lake. The weather usually cooperates with these pursuits—although the city's average 60 inches of snow may often dictate how you spend your winter days. Even on the hottest summer day, you can find a shady canyon with a stream passing through.

Salt Lake City is a gateway to the excellent ski resorts strung along the Wasatch Range. There are also a handful of top-shelf golf courses. In town you can readily bicycle or jog along the wide streets and through the many parks.

TICKETS

Smiths Tix. Tickets to sporting events and concerts are available here. ☎ *801/467–8499, 800/888–8499* ⊕ *www.smithstix.com.*

Ticketmaster. Tickets here are primarily for music and sporting events at the Maverik Center in nearby West Valley City. ⊠ *West Valley City* ☎ *800/745–3000* ⊕ *www.ticketmaster.com.*

BASEBALL

FAMILY **Salt Lake Bees.** Home to minor-league baseball since the 1950s, Salt Lake now loves the Bees, a AAA team just one notch below its parent club, the Los Angeles Angels of Anaheim. Games are played in Smith's Ballpark, where the backdrop of the Wasatch Mountains makes for one of the most picturesque baseball stadiums in America. Games run April through August and are fan-friendly, affordable family fun. ⊠ 77 W. 1300 S, Downtown ☎ 801/325–2273 ⊕ www.slbees.com.

BASKETBALL

Utah Jazz. Salt Lake's NBA team plays at the EnergySolutions Arena. Basketball buffs will want to see the statues of Hall of Famers John Stockton and Karl Malone outside. ⊠ EnergySolutions Arena, 301 W. South Temple, Downtown ☎ 801/355–3865 ⊕ utahjazz.com.

BICYCLING

Bingham Cyclery. Bingham Cyclery operates four popular shops around the state, including one in downtown Salt Lake City across the street from Pioneer Park. The friendly staff sells and rents bikes or will tune up the one you already have. Other branches are in Ogden, Sunset, and Sandy. ⊠ 336 W. Broadway, Downtown ☎ 801/583–1940 ⊕ www. binghamcyclery.com.

Fodor's Choice **City Creek Canyon.** Salt Lake City has fully integrated bicycles into its
★ urban planning, and cyclists will love the GREENBike sharing program, as well as 4-foot-wide bike lanes painted green on several downtown thoroughfares. Within minutes, road and mountain bikers can find all levels of challenge. A favorite is City Creek Canyon, east of the capitol, particularly on odd-number days from Memorial Day through Labor Day and daily between Labor Day and Memorial Day, when the road is closed to vehicles. Liberty Park and Sugar House Park also have good cycling and running paths. ☎ 801/535–6630 ⊕ www.bikeslc.com.

Fodor's Choice **Contender Bicycles.** With a brand-new building in 2013, Contender Bicycles
★ has grown up like the trendy 9th & 9th neighborhood it anchors. From service to sales, this is a must-visit for cyclists. You might catch Tour de France veterans Levi Leipheimer or Dave Zabriskie stopping by to chat or ride with this shop's competitive team. ⊠ 989 E. 900 S, Downtown ☎ 801/364–0344 ⊕ www.contenderbicycles.com ⊗ Closed Sun.

GOLF

Bonneville Golf Course. The city's oldest 18-hole public course, only ten minutes from downtown, was designed by William Bell and opened in 1929. Bonneville presents a satisfying test of skill with its wooded, hilly landscape and tight fairways, but is not a huge challenge and offers a pleasant walk with stunning mountain views. The greens are well kept, with putts breaking toward the valley. ⊠ 954 Connor St., East Side ☎ 801/583–9513 ⊕ www.slc-golf.com/bonneville.html ⊠ $37 ⅃ 18 holes, 6872 yards, par 72.

South Mountain Golf Club. A championship public course and spectacular scenery await you 30 minutes from downtown Salt Lake City at the South Mountain Golf Club. It's a mountainside course, so there are elevation changes, twists and turns that call for every kind of shot—but above all accuracy—and undulating greens that present a good challenge. Choose from five tee boxes that allow for players at all levels. The course hosted the 1999 Utah Open. ⊠ *1247 E. Mike Weir Rd., Draper* ☎ *385/468–1480* ⊕ *www.slco.org/slcountygolf/ cSouthMountain/* ⊠ *$22 for 9 holes Mon.–Thurs., $24 Fri.–Sun., $30 twilight; $42 for 18 holes Mon.–Thurs., $47 Fri.–Sun., $35 twilight* ⅃ *18 holes, 7080 yards, par 72.*

Stonebridge Golf Club. Stonebridge Golf Club is a five-minute drive from Salt Lake International Airport. The links-style course, designed by Gene Bates and Johnny Miller, offers 27 holes amid beautiful scenery. Water hazards come in the form of lakes and streams, and there are plenty of bunkers, but fairways are wide and four sets of tees cater to a range of abilities. ⊠ *4415 Links Dr., West Valley City* ☎ *801/957–9000* ⊕ *www.golfstonebridgeutah.com* ⊠ *$21.50 for 9 holes walking, $28.50 riding; $43 for 18 holes walking, $57 riding (reduced rates for Utah residents and members of the military)* ⅃ *27 holes, 7200 yards, par 36.*

Wingpointe. This Scottish links–style course, adjacent to Salt Lake International Airport, is loved by the golf magazines that hand out awards, regularly figuring within the top five of the state's courses. Golfers seem to like it, too, in spite of the inevitable noise from above as planes fly in and out. It is set out on a rolling landscape of native grass and wildflowers and has a good sprinkling of bunkers and water hazards that call for a good degree of accuracy. The challenging course is often still green when there's snow in the surrounding mountains. ⊠ *3602 W. 100 N, Airport* ☎ *801/575–2345* ⊕ *www.slc-golf.com/wingpoint.html* ⊠ *$18 for 9 holes; $35 for 18 holes* ⅃ *18 holes, 7185 yards, par 72.*

ICE SKATING

One legacy of the Salt Lake Olympics is the ZAP tax (that has since been renewed) to fund zoos, arts, and parks. As a result, some of the finest public facilities in the country are here.

Acord Ice Center. Built as a practice venue for the 2002 Winter Olympics, the rink shares out ice time between hockey, figure skating, and public skating. Call for public ice-skating times. ⊠ *5353 W. 3100 S, West Valley City* ☎ *385/468–1965* ⊕ *www.acordice.slco.org.*

FAMILY **Cottonwood Heights Recreation Center.** Choose to swim, jog, lift weights, play tennis, ice-skate, or much more at the Cottonwood Heights Recreation Center. ⊠ *7500 S. 2700 E, Cottonwood Heights* ☎ *801/943–3190* ⊕ *www.cottonwoodheights.com.*

Fodor'sChoice **Salt Lake City Sports Complex.** With two ice sheets and two Olympic-★ size pools, this recreational complex is a year-round magnet for active families and individuals. ⊠ *645 S. Guardsman Way, University of Utah* ☎ *385/468–1925* ⊕ *www.slco.org/recreation/slcsports/.*

Fodor'sChoice **Utah Olympic Oval.** The stunning venue was built for the 2002 Winter ★ Olympics and is the home of the U.S. Speedskating team. Watch the world's best skaters in major competitions every winter. It's open to the public year-round for myriad activities, including skating, curling, or running on the 442-meter indoor track. ⊠ *5662 S. Cougar Lane, Kearns* ☎ *801/968–6825* ⊕ *www.utaholympiclegacy.com.*

PARKS

Most neighborhoods have a small park, usually with a children's playground.

FAMILY **Fairmont Park.** Perfect for the kids, this is a smallish park with a children's play area, duck pond, and large indoor swimming pool. ⊠ *1040 E. Sugarmont Dr., East Side*.

FAMILY **Liberty Park.** This is one of the local favorite places to run (it's about 1½ miles per lap on the jogging path), and also features tennis courts, an aviary, a swimming pool, picnic areas, a restaurant, and children's playgrounds. ⊠ *600 E. 900 S, East Side* ⊕ *www.slcgov.com/node/725*.

Pioneer Park. In the heart of downtown, this park is home to a substantial farmers' market and a wildly popular twilight concert series in the summer. Parts of the surrounding neighborhoods are a little rough, so be cautious after dark and/or with children. ⊠ *300 W. 350 S, Downtown*.

FAMILY **Sugar House Park.** This is a favorite meeting spot for residents and visitors. Enjoy the open space where you can jog, bicycle, fly a kite, picnic, or soak up some rays. Feed the ducks in the large pond or skip rocks in the creek in the summer, or join dozens of sledders on its hills in winter. ⊠ *2100 S. 1300 E, East Side* ⊕ *www.sugarhousepark.org*.

SKIING

Sports Den. A four-season store, Sports Den can handle any ski, snowboard, and snowshoeing need—as well as bicycles, golf, swimming, and summer gear. ⊠ *1350 Foothill Dr., East Side* ☎ *801/582–5611* ⊕ *www. sportsden.com*.

Utah Ski & Golf. Discounted lift tickets, advance equipment, and clothing rental reservations are available at Utah Ski & Golf's multiple downtown locations and in Park City, with free shuttle service from downtown hotels to their stores. ⊠ *134 W. 600 S, Downtown* ☎ *801/355–9088, 800/858–5221* ⊕ *www.utahskigolf.com*.

SOCCER

Real Salt Lake. Since 2005, Real Salt Lake has competed in Major League Soccer. The gleaming $100 million Rio Tinto Stadium also hosts concerts and other events. ⊠ *9256 S. State St., Sandy* ☎ *801/727–2700* ⊕ *www.realsaltlake.com*.

WHERE TO EAT

The 2002 Winter Olympics cast Salt Lake City in a new, contemporary, more diverse light. Visitors discovered a panoply of cultural influences, brewpubs, ethnic flavors, and progressive chefs. Salt Lake City may not have the depth of restaurants seen in other big cities, but there are a couple of outstanding choices for nearly every budget and cuisine. Restaurants like Lamb's Grill Café, Hire's Big H, and Ruth's Diner trace their roots back five-plus decades, and their colorful proprietors are more than willing to share the history they've witnessed from their kitchens. Returning LDS missionaries have brought back their favorite flavors from Asia, Europe, and Latin America, with impressive results. You may not find the five-star San Francisco dining experience, but you'll find almost as many influences as in the city by the bay. Seafood, Japanese, Tibetan, Indian, Spanish, and Italian are all suitably showcased in Salt Lake eateries, and when all else fails, there are great burgers and Rocky Mountain cuisine, a fusion inspired by frontier big game, seafood fresh from the great Pacific ports, and organic produce grown in Utah's fertile valleys. You'll also find creative wine lists and knowledgeable service. Bakers and pastry chefs defy the 4,400-foot altitude with rustic sourdoughs and luscious berry-filled treats. Multiple weekly summer farmers' markets are thriving, and chefs are building more and more of a food community. All in all, Salt Lake's culinary scene has finally grown up and offers something for every taste, from simple to sophisticated.

Use the coordinates (✛ A1) at the end of each listing to locate a site on the corresponding map.

WHAT IT COSTS

	$	$$	$$$	$$$$
Restaurants	under $12	$12–$20	$21–$30	over $30

Restaurant prices are the average cost of a main course at dinner or, if dinner is not served, at lunch.

DOWNTOWN SALT LAKE

$$$$
AMERICAN
✕ **Bambara.** Seasonal menus reflect regional American and international influences at this artfully designed destination restaurant. A tasty example is the roasted sea bass with mushroom and Sonoma dry jack polenta. The setting, formerly an ornate bank lobby adjacent to the swank Hotel Monaco, is as much of a draw as the food. An open marble-fronted kitchen, big windows framed in fanciful hammered metal swirls, and a definite "buzz" make Bambara a popular gathering spot. You can also dine in the adjoining club, or simply enjoy a cocktail while snuggled in a velvet-lined booth. $ *Average main: $36* ✉ *202 S. Main St., Downtown* ☎ *801/363–5454* ⊕ *www.bambara-slc.com* ☉ *No lunch Sat.* ✛ *C5.*

$$
SOUTHERN
✕ **The Bayou.** You'll find more than 200 microbrews, both bottled and on tap, at chef-owner Mark Alston's lively, often crowded bar and restaurant. There's also a full bar and wine list. The menu offers everything from Cajun specialties such as jambalaya and étouffée to blackened seafood and a terrific garlicky hamburger with sweet-potato fries. Live music, pool tables, and a clean design create a casual, high-energy atmosphere. Because it's considered a bar, no one under the age of 21 is admitted. $ *Average main: $13* ✉ *645 S. State St., Downtown* ☎ *801/961–8400* ⊕ *www.utahbayou.com* ☉ *No lunch weekends* ✛ *E3.*

$$$
MODERN
AMERICAN
Fodor's Choice
★
✕ **Copper Onion.** Adjacent to Salt Lake's arthouse cinema is the best new restaurant in the city in the past decade. Chef Ryan Lowder dazzles with the basics—artful salads, small plates, and charcuterie—and then overwhelms with mouthwatering locally sourced dishes, from Cast Iron Mary's Chicken to rainbow trout. The youthful Lowder studied at the Culinary Institute of America and apprenticed at Jean-Georges and with Mario Batali before bringing his own brand of sophisticated American cuisine to his hometown. Stop in before or after a film, gallery tour,

BEST BETS FOR SALT LAKE CITY DINING

Fodor's Choice ★	$$	Best by Experience
Hire's Big H, $, p. 71	Bombay House, p. 70	
Layla Grill and Mezze, $$, p. 72	Layla Grill and Mezze, p. 72	**BEST BREWPUB**
Log Haven, $$$, p. 72	Mazza Middle Eastern Cuisine, p. 71	Squatters Pub Brewery, $$, p. 69
Lucky 13 Bar and Grill, $, p. 71	Red Iguana, p. 68	**BEST BURGER**
Copper Onion, $$$, p. 63	Ruth's Diner, p. 72	Lucky 13 Bar and Grill, $, p. 71
Red Iguana, $$, p. 68	Settebello Pizzeria Napoletana, p. 68	
Tony Caputo's Market and Deli, $, p. 69		**MOST ROMANTIC**
	$$$	Log Haven, $$$, p. 72
Best by Price	Copper Onion, p. 63	
	Log Haven, p. 72	**CHILD-FRIENDLY**
$	Market Street Grill, p. 65	Hire's Big H, $, p. 71
Hire's Big H, p. 71	Pago, p. 71	Ruth's Diner, $$, p. 72
Lone Star Taqueria, p. 72	$$$$	
Lucky 13 Bar and Grill, p. 71	Bambara, p. 63	**MOST POPULAR**
Tony Caputo's Market and Deli, p. 69		Red Iguana, $$, p. 68
		Mazza Middle Eastern Cuisine, $$, p. 71

or live theater on Salt Lake's Broadway. $ *Average main: $23* ⊠ *111 E. Broadway, Downtown* ☎ *801/355–3282* ⊕ *www.thecopperonion. com* ✛ *F2.*

$$ ✕ **Este Pizzeria SLC.** You may recognize the lettered circles resembling the
PIZZA   New York City subway before you inhale the scent of fresh-baked pies:
FAMILY either will take you back to your favorite borough's pizza joint. Este has
two locations (downtown and 2148 E. 900 South in Sugar House) that
can't be beat for New York–style eats. Grandma Phi Phi's pie has mari-
nara, mozzarella, and basil, and the Italian Flag aligns pizza, pesto, and
ricotta sauces. Vegans and gluten-free diners will do well here, too—and
anyone with a sweet tooth will fall for *zeppole* (Italian doughnuts) and
cream-filled cannoli. $ *Average main: $14* ⊠ *156 E. 200 S, Downtown*
☎ *801/363–2366* ⊕ *www.estepizzaco.com* ✛ *F2.*

$$ ✕ **Hong Kong Tea House.** Lacquered wood-and-marble tables, comfort-
CHINESE able chairs, and warm colors give the three small dining rooms a wel-
coming feel. At lunch, ask for a dim sum menu and mark your choices,
or wait until servers walk by with small dishes or bamboo baskets of
Cantonese-style classics, from steamed pork buns to crunchy chicken
feet. Dinner menus are more formal, with traditional Peking duck, spicy

Szechuan-style chicken with green beans, and other authentic regional Chinese favorites. Don't miss the steamed sea bass with ginger. $ *Average main: $12* ✉ *565 W. 200 S, Downtown* ☎ *801/531–7010* ⊕ *www. hongkongteahouse.com* ⊘ *Closed Mon.* ✛ *A5.*

$$$ **✕Ichiban.** This is one of the most interesting dining destinations in
JAPANESE town. It's set in a former church, complete with exquisite stained-glass windows, vaulted ceilings, and a modernized interior. The specialties include both classic sushi as well as multilayered Americanized interpretations, some with hot chilis, or with esoteric, locally inspired combinations. You can order some fine cold sakes, and there's a full bar. $ *Average main: $28* ✉ *336 S. 400 E, Downtown* ☎ *801/532–7522* ⊕ *watkinsrg.com/Ichiban_Sushi_Utah.html* ⊘ *No lunch* ✛ *F2.*

$ **✕La-Cai Noodle House.** Named for a historic restaurant district in Ho Chi
VIETNAMESE Minh City, this place re-creates the cuisine of southern Vietnam. Despite its unassuming location amid a car dealership strip just south of downtown, a recent complete interior renovation ensures an extraordinary meal and experience once you step through the doors. The menu ranges from traditional basics such as *pho* (beef noodle soup) to unique entrées like walnut shrimp in a creamy white sauce, salt-baked calamari, and fondues. Portions are huge and service is impeccable, so it's no surprise that this seemingly off-the-radar venue is consistently considered one of Salt Lake's best options for authentic Vietnamese and Chinese fare. $ *Average main: $10* ✉ *961 S. State St., Downtown* ☎ *801/322–3590* ⊕ *www.lacainoodlehouse.com* ⊘ *Closed Sun.* ✛ *F3.*

$$ **✕Lamb's Grill Café.** Founded by Greek immigrant George Lamb in 1919,
MEDITERRANEAN this downtown power broker's favorite has demonstrated unusual staying power. With its long marble counter, deco-style trim, and cozy mahogany booths, one of the city's oldest dining establishments has aged well. It's a white-tablecloth kind of place, where you can still indulge in an old-fashioned barbecued lamb shank or blackened salmon at a reasonable price. The longtime Greek owners have added a few Mediterranean touches to the big menu. $ *Average main: $20* ✉ *169 S. Main St., Downtown* ☎ *801/364–7166* ⊕ *www.lambsgrill.com* ⊘ *Closed Sun.* ✛ *C5.*

$$$ **✕Market Street Grill.** See Salt Lake's power brokers sharing stories
SEAFOOD at one of the city's premier choices for seafood, housed in a beautifully restored 1906 building. Popular for breakfast, lunch, and dinner, selections range from daily fresh fish and seafood entrées to certified Angus beef. Portions are large, and include all the side dishes. $ *Average main: $28* ✉ *48 Market St., Downtown* ☎ *801/322–4668* ⊕ *www. marketstreetgrill.com* ⌇ *Reservations not accepted* ✛ *C5.*

$$$ **✕Market Street Oyster Bar.** Some would call this popular bar–restaurant
SEAFOOD more of a "meet market," but it's a fun and upbeat place. Popular items include oysters prepared a half-dozen ways, clam chowder, crab and shrimp cocktails, and more expensive seafood entrées. The decor features original hand-painted pillars, rounded booths that face the action, and televisions on at all hours. $ *Average main: $26* ✉ *54 Market St., Downtown* ☎ *801/531–6044* ⊕ *marketstreetgrill.com* ⌇ *Reservations not accepted* ⊘ *No lunch Sat.* ✛ *C5.*

$$$$ **✕The New Yorker and the Café at the New Yorker.** This subterranean,
STEAKHOUSE clubby bar, café, and restaurant with its modern Continental menu,

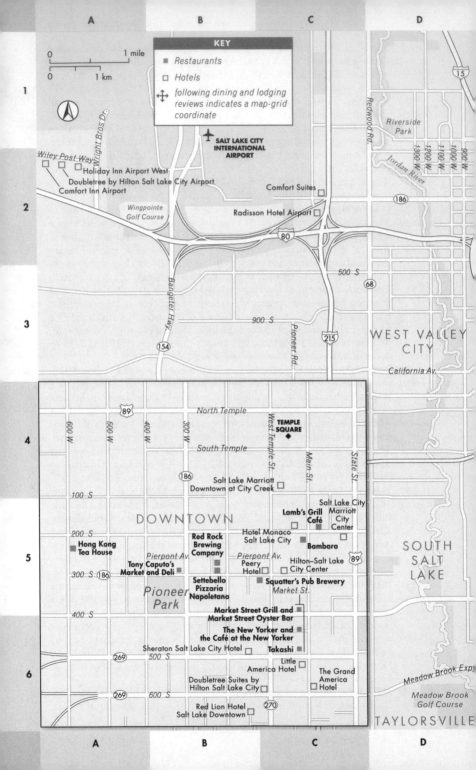

KEY

■ Restaurants
□ Hotels
✛ following dining and lodging reviews indicates a map-grid coordinate

SALT LAKE CITY INTERNATIONAL AIRPORT

Wiley Post Way
Holiday Inn Airport West
Doubletree by Hilton Salt Lake City Airport
Comfort Inn Airport

Comfort Suites
Radisson Hotel Airport

Wingpointe Golf Course

Riverside Park

Jordan River

500 S

WEST VALLEY CITY

900 S

California Av.

North Temple

TEMPLE SQUARE

South Temple

Salt Lake Marriott Downtown at City Creek

DOWNTOWN

Lamb's Grill Café

Salt Lake City Marriott City Center

Hong Kong Tea House

Red Rock Brewing Company

Hotel Monaco Salt Lake City

Bambara

Tony Caputo's Market and Deli

Pierpont Av.
Peery Hotel

Hilton–Salt Lake City Center

SOUTH SALT LAKE

Pioneer Park

Settebello Pizzaria Napoletana

Squatter's Pub Brewery

Market St.

Market Street Grill and Market Street Oyster Bar

The New Yorker and the Café at the New Yorker

Takashi

Sheraton Salt Lake City Hotel

Little America Hotel

The Grand America Hotel

Meadow Brook Expy

Doubletree Suites by Hilton Salt Lake City

Meadow Brook Golf Course

Red Lion Hotel Salt Lake Downtown

TAYLORSVILLE

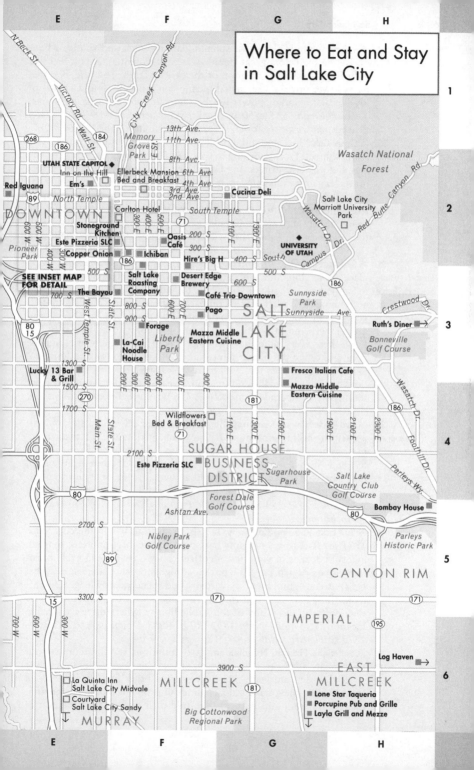

Where to Eat and Stay in Salt Lake City

E   **F**   **G**   **H**

N. Beck St.

Victory Rd.

City Creek Canyon Rd.

268   186   184

Wall St.

13th Ave.
11th Ave.

Memory Grove Park

8th Ave.

Wasatch National Forest

UTAH STATE CAPITOL ◆

Inn on the Hill

Ellerbeck Mansion   6th Ave.
Bed and Breakfast   4th Ave.
3rd Ave.
2nd Ave.

Cucina Deli

Salt Lake City Marriott University Park

89

Red Iguana ■

Em's ■

North Temple

North Temple

South Temple

DOWNTOWN

Carlton Hotel

300 E   400 E   500 E

71

200 S

UNIVERSITY OF UTAH ◆

Campus

Wasatch Dr.

Red Butte Canyon Rd.

Pioneer Park

Stoneground Kitchen

Este Pizzeria SLC ■

Copper Onion ■

186

Ichiban ■

Oasis Café

300 S

400 S

500 S

South

186

SEE INSET MAP FOR DETAIL

500 E

Salt Lake Roasting Company

Desert Edge Brewery

600 S

Sunnyside Park

Crestwood Dr.

The Bayou ■

700 S

Café Trio Downtown ■

Pago ■

SALT LAKE CITY

Sunnyside Ave.

Ruth's Diner ■→

State St.

West Temple St.

800 S

900 S

600 E   700 E

Bonneville Golf Course

80
15

■ Forage

La-Cai Noodle House ■

1300 S

1500 S

Liberty Park

Mazza Middle Eastern Cuisine ■

186

Lucky 13 Bar & Grill ■

270

200 E   300 E   400 E   500 E   700 E   900 E

Fresco Italian Cafe ■

Mazza Middle Eastern Cuisine ■

1700 S

Main St.

State St.

181

1100 E   1300 E   1500 E   1900 E   2100 E   2300 E

Wildflowers Bed & Breakfast ☐

71

SUGAR HOUSE BUSINESS DISTRICT

Parleys Wy.

Wasatch Dr.

Foothill Dr.

Este Pizzeria SLC ■

2100 S

Sugarhouse Park

Salt Lake Country Club Golf Course

80

Ashtan Ave.

Forest Dale Golf Course

80

Bombay House ■

2700 S

2700 S

Nibley Park Golf Course

Parleys Historic Park

89

CANYON RIM

15

3300 S

171

171

195

IMPERIAL

3900 S

EAST MILLCREEK

Log Haven ■→

☐ La Quinta Inn Salt Lake City Midvale

☐ Courtyard Salt Lake City Sandy

↓

MILLCREEK

181

Big Cottonwood Regional Park

■ Lone Star Taqueria
■ Porcupine Pub and Grille
■ Layla Grill and Mezze

↓

MURRAY

E   **F**   **G**   **H**

1   2   3   4   5   6

starched white tablecloths, stained-glass ceilings, and rounded banquette seating offers great people-watching potential. If you feel like indulging, try the filet mignon or the rack of lamb. The café–bar area has a lower-price, more casual menu. You'll usually find a crowd of loyal locals, including power-lunchers mingling and having a good time. [$] *Average main: $35* ☒ *60 W. Market St., Downtown* ☎ *801/363–0166* ⊕ *www.newyorkerslc.com* ☺ *Closed Sun. No lunch Sat.* ⊹ *C6.*

$$ ✕**Oasis Café.** Joel and Jill LaSalle own this comfortable, progressive
ECLECTIC   establishment. From morning to well into the evening, a selection of fine teas and espresso drinks, big breakfasts, and fresh, innovative entrées draws regulars to this café and its serene patio courtyard. The menu leans toward vegetarian and seafood selections, and there are plenty of gluten-free options in addition to rich house-made pastries. Don't overlook the nice wine list. The café is a popular gathering spot, and shares space with the Golden Braid, a shop that sells books and gifts. [$] *Average main: $18* ☒ *151 S. 500 E, Downtown* ☎ *801/322–0404* ⊕ *oasiscafeslc.com* ⊹ *F2.*

$$ ✕**Red Iguana.** One of America's best Mexican restaurants, this lively
MEXICAN FUSION   place doesn't look like much, and it's off the beaten track. But everyone
Fodor's Choice   in Salt Lake City can tell you where to find it, and about its warm and
★   accommodating staff and incomparable house-made moles and chili verde. They pour premium margaritas and good Mexican beers, and always keep the salsa and chips coming. Expect to find rockers Los Lobos here every time they play Salt Lake City. If the wait is out the door and down the block (almost always!), try the new Red Iguana 2 (☒ *866 W. South Temple*) with more tables two blocks away. Both locations have the same vibe and food; make either a stop on your way from the airport. [$] *Average main: $16* ☒ *736 W. North Temple, Downtown* ☎ *801/322–1489* ⊕ *www.rediguana.com* ⊹ *E2.*

$$ ✕**Red Rock Brewing Company.** Enjoy one of their celebrated ales, or grab
AMERICAN   a tasty bite at this contemporary brewpub. Stick to the creative whole-meal salads, thin-crust wood-fired pizzas, and perfectly beer-battered fish-and-chips. An on-site brewery (try the crowd-favorite Amber Ale), house-brewed sodas, a full bar, and an overall sense of style add up to a lively lunch and dinner spot near the EnergySolutions Arena. [$] *Average main: $14* ☒ *254 S. 200 W, Downtown* ☎ *801/521–7446* ⊕ *www.redrockbrewing.com* ⊹ *B5.*

$ ✕**Salt Lake Roasting Company.** Here's a reason to live in the city. Since
CAFÉ   1981 the Roasting Company has sourced, bought, imported, roasted, and sold dozens of varieties of coffees. They open at 6:45 each morning and stay open until 11 pm most nights. Great pastries, desserts, light entrées, complimentary wireless, and friendly, knowledgeable staff make this a Salt Lake institution. You'll detect the distinctive aroma of their coffee in the lobby of the public library, where there's a satellite location. [$] *Average main: $8* ☒ *320 E. 400 S, Downtown* ☎ *801/363–7572* ⊕ *www.roasting.com* ☺ *Closed Sun.* ⊹ *F3.*

$$ ✕**Settebello Pizzeria Napoletana.** Two ambitious restaurateurs set out
PIZZA   to re-create authentic ultra-thin pizza from Naples, and did they ever succeed. Using an oven, flour, cheese, and other ingredients shipped from Naples, they make a dozen kinds of pizza (including margherita, quattro stagioni, and Bianca) that hold their own against the best of

the Old Country. Don't look for pasta or poultry, just pizza and salad. Move over, New York City: Settebello might be the best thin-crust pizza anywhere outside of Italy. $ *Average main: $15* ⊠ *260 S. 200 W, Downtown* ☎ *801/322–3556* ⊕ *www.settebello.net* ⊘ *Closed Sun.* ✛ *B5.*

$$
AMERICAN
✕ **Squatters Pub Brewery.** Check out the gleaming fermentation tanks from the bar at this casual, high-energy brewpub in the 1906 Boston Hotel building. It's a happening spot on summer days and nights when the patio with its cooling mist system is in full swing and the chef fires up the outdoor grill. Featuring plenty of organic and locally sourced ingredients, the menu veers from locally made bratwurst to curry specials, fish tacos, and big, juicy buffalo burgers. If you don't sample one of their array of celebrated beers, you've missed the best part of the Squatters experience. $ *Average main: $14* ⊠ *147 W. Broadway, Downtown* ☎ *801/363–2739* ⊕ *www.squatters.com* ⌕ *Reservations not accepted* ✛ *B5.*

$$
ITALIAN
✕ **Stoneground Kitchen.** On the top floor of a glass-fronted building across the street from the city's architecturally spectacular main public library, this is a casual hangout with New York–style pizza and "Grandma's" pasta dishes. The menu offers better-than-average pub food and pizzas at reasonable prices. Sit on the outdoor deck on glorious summer evenings. $ *Average main: $15* ⊠ *249 E. 400 S, Downtown* ☎ *801/364–1368* ⊕ *www.stonegroundslc.com* ⊘ *No lunch Sun.* ✛ *F2.*

$$$
JAPANESE
✕ **Takashi.** One of Salt Lake's most popular Japanese restaurants is hip and lively, and has the city's finest sushi, including *uni nigiri* (sea-urchin sushi) that defines melt-in-your-mouth. The calamari is a must-try, too, and on many days owner-chef Takashi Gibo can be seen behind the sushi bar. The full-service bar serves up crisp sake and fine martinis. $ *Average main: $24* ⊠ *18 W. Market St., Downtown* ☎ *801/519–9595* ⊘ *Closed Sun. No lunch Sat.* ✛ *C6.*

$
ITALIAN
FAMILY
Fodor's Choice
★
✕ **Tony Caputo's Market and Deli.** The people who line up out the door at lunch hour are usually salivating in anticipation of a generous, authentic deli sandwich at this stocked-to-the-rafters Italian deli and market. Whether you fancy a juicy, sauce-drenched meatball concoction, buffalo mozzarella with basil and fresh tomatoes, salami with roasted red peppers, or a hot daily special such as lasagna, it's a great value and a convivial, casual place. On summer Saturday mornings Caputo's is packed with shoppers leaving the fresh farmers' market in Pioneer Park across the street. Lunch and early dinner are available to eat in or take away. Check out the butcher shop, gourmet chocolate, adjacent fish market, and Italian bakery as well. ■ **TIP→** If wandering around Sugar House, check out their second smaller deli at 1516 S. 1500 E. $ *Average main: $8* ⊠ *314 W. 300 S, Downtown* ☎ *801/531–8669* ⊕ *www.caputosdeli.com* ✛ *B5.*

CAPITOL HILL AND THE AVENUES

$
ITALIAN
✕ **Cucina Deli.** Locals flock to this neighborhood café and take-away food market for the creative salads and colorful entrées displayed like jewels in glass cases. Many people order a sampler of three or four salads, such as orzo with mint, feta, chicken, and artichoke hearts; or wild rice–based concoctions. Also on the menu are house-made soups, generous deli sandwiches, and hot entrées such as meat loaf and mashed potatoes. Big windows and warm mustard and terra-cotta tones are

reminiscent of a Tuscan-style café, with seating indoors and out. $ *Average main: $10* ✉ *1026 E. 2nd Ave., The Avenues* ☎ *801/322–3055* ⊕ *www.cucinadeli.com* ✛ *G2.*

$$
ECLECTIC

✕ **Em's.** Fresh, flavorful, creative, and artsy—chef Emily Gassmann's small café combines it all in a renovated brick storefront in the Marmalade District, west of the capitol. The café has an urban feel with its modern art and polished wood floors. Sit at the counter, at wooden tables, or on the patio and enjoy the varied menu of salads, soups, savory crepes, meats, and vegetarian entrées. Brunch is served on Sunday. $ *Average main: $19* ✉ *271 N. Center St., Capitol Hill* ☎ *801/596–0566* ⊕ *www.emsrestaurant.com* ⊗ *Closed Mon. No dinner Tues. No lunch weekends* ✛ *E2.*

EAST SIDE AND THE UNIVERSITY OF UTAH

$$
INDIAN

✕ **Bombay House.** You're enveloped in exotic aromas the minute you step into this dark, intimate restaurant that shares a massive parking lot with a Wal-Mart. Enjoy good Indian standards, including the softest naan and the spiciest of curries, tandoori dishes, and lots of vegetarian options. There's a selection of domestic and imported beers as well as traditional teas and tea-based drinks. Although the service is extremely attentive, prepare for a longer meal—or call ahead for takeout. $ *Average main: $13* ✉ *2731 E. Parleys Way, East Side* ☎ *801/581–0222* ⊕ *www.bombayhouse.com* ⊗ *Closed Sun. No lunch* ✛ *H5.*

$$
ITALIAN

✕ **Café Trio Downtown.** Start with a selection of cheeses and flatbreads to tempt your appetite, but save room for balsamic-drizzled pizzas, hearty baked pastas, and wood-roasted salmon, all of which vie for attention at this constantly busy Italian eatery. Owner Mikel Trapp has created a comfortable modern dining room with clean lines and sharp staff. You'll want to linger for the crème brulée, flavored martinis, and espresso. $ *Average main: $16* ✉ *680 S. 900 E, East Side* ☎ *801/533–8746* ⊕ *www.triodining.com* ✛ *F3.*

$
AMERICAN

✕ **Desert Edge Brewery.** For more than 40 years, this lively microbrewery inside Trolley Square has offered delicious pub food, house-made beer, loft seating, a sheltered patio, and lots of music and noise. It also offers a great view of the sunset through floor-to-ceiling windows. The menu gets creative with sandwiches such as salmon with pickled ginger-cucumber slaw, whole-meal salads, and Southwestern fare like citrus chicken tacos. $ *Average main: $10* ✉ *273 Trolley Sq., East Side* ☎ *801/521–8917* ⊕ *www.desertedgebrewery.com* ✛ *F3.*

$$$$
MODERN
AMERICAN

✕ **Forage.** With 15 courses on the nightly set menu and a dinner tab that approaches $100/person, this is not your ordinary dining experience—and about the last place you'd expect to find in the historically sleepy Salt Lake dinng scene. But chef Bowman Brown has taken the reins at this upscale favorite, and if crowds are any indicator, Forage's run as the city's most priceless dinner won't end soon. It takes a sophisticated palate to appreciate Forage, where the constantly evolving menu will span from "arugula & juniper" to "lamb with preserved roots." The dining room is as classy and sophisticated as the presentation on some of the bite-size dishes. Prepare to splurge, and don't expect to cheat the restaurant's recommendation that you allot at least 2½ hours for your dining experience. $ *Average main: $87* ✉ *370 E. 900 S, East Side* ☎ *801/708–7834* ⊕ *www.foragerestaurant.com* ⚔ *Reservations essential* ⊘ *No lunch. Closed Mon.* ✚ *F3.*

$$$
ITALIAN

✗**Fresco Italian Cafe.** This intimate restaurant sits back from the street in a clapboard house that adjoins an independent bookstore. Dishes like the daily risotto and housemade sweet-potato ravioli take center stage as the season dictates. In summer seating is available on the small patio. $ *Average main: $24* ✉ *1513 S. 1500 E, East Side* ☎ *801/486–1300* ⊕ *www.frescoitaliancafe.com* ⊘ *Closed Mon. No lunch* ✚ *G3.*

$
BURGER
FAMILY
Fodor's Choice
★

✗**Hire's Big H.** Roll down the car window and place your order at a burger joint that offers a menu, service, and groove that haven't changed much since its 1959 opening. Inside the renovated dining room, root-beer floats are a staple, as are "H" burgers such as the New York H, Canadian H, and Mountain H, all of which pair fresh patties, tasty buns, and the owner's proprietary fry sauce with a variety of condiments. You still might catch a glimpse of the friendliest man in the business, Don Hale, the original owner. $ *Average main: $8* ✉ *425 S. 700 E, East Side* ☎ *801/364–4582* ⊕ *www.hiresbigh.com* ⊘ *Closed Sun.* ✚ *F3.*

$
BURGER
Fodor's Choice
★

✗**Lucky 13 Bar and Grill.** There is no better place in the valley to order up an elaborate monstrous house-made burger and wash it down with a beer and a shot of whiskey. One of the few places in Salt Lake City that does NOT allow kids under 21, Lucky 13 is across the street from Smith's Ballpark, home to Salt Lake's AAA minor-league baseball team. Bacon lovers will adore the house-made slices on many signature burgers, but it's hard to resist Fungus Amongus, a burger with mushrooms sautéed in red wine and garlic, topped with Swiss cheese. Dozens of beers and whiskeys are served here, including six from Park City's High West distillery alone. $ *Average main: $11* ✉ *135 W. 1300 S, Downtown* ☎ *801/487–4418* ⊕ *www.lucky13slc.com* ✚ *E3.*

$$
MIDDLE EASTERN

✗**Mazza Middle Eastern Cuisine.** Consistently voted the city's best Middle Eastern restaurant, Mazza is all about authentic and affordable fare in a casual setting. You can't go wrong with traditional dishes like falafel, stuffed vine leaves, and kebabs, but explore baked kafta, chicken and cauliflower kabsh, and musakhan to truly indulge your taste buds. Fresh desserts include honey-drenched baklava. Due to its success, a second, larger restaurant was added at 9th and 9th. Menus are similar, but not identical. $ *Average main: $15* ✉ *912 E. 900 S, East Side* ☎ *801/521–4572* ⊕ *www.mazzacafe.com* ⊘ *Closed Sun.* ✚ *G4 and G3.* $ *Average main: $15* ✉ *1515 S. 1500 E, East Side* ☎ *801/484–9259* ⊕ *www.mazzacafe.com* ✚ *G4 and G3.*

$$$
MODERN
AMERICAN

✗**Pago.** Bursting onto the burgeoning dining scene in Salt Lake, Pago more than lives up to its promise of farm-to-table freshness in a microscopic neighborhood bistro, albeit with big-city ambition and tastes. The chef-driven restaurant capitalizes on local artisan farmers, with big and small plates anchored around simple ingredients like radishes, beets, or mountain stream trout. There's plenty to satisfy big appetites, such as rack of lamb and rib eye, or gnocchi for vegetarians. Pago has an excellent wine list and attentive service. $ *Average main: $25* ✉ *878 S. 900 E, East Side* ☎ *801/532–0777* ⊕ *www.pagoslc.com* ✚ *F3.*

$$ ✕**Ruth's Diner.** Families love the gussied-up old railcar that serves as
AMERICAN   Ruth's dining room and the city's best creek-side patio in the city—
FAMILY   although you have to navigate your way up gorgeous Emigration Can-
yon to find it. Breakfast (served until 4) has been the diner's trademark
since 1930, and starts with 3-inch-tall biscuits followed by massive
omelets like the King of Hearts (artichokes, garlic, mushrooms, and
two cheeses). In summer the barbecue fires up every Thursday night
for ribs, fish, chicken, or whatever the chef concocts, with live music on
the patio. Ruth's is about 3 miles up the same canyon Brigham Young
traversed to found the city and less than 10 minutes from downtown
but feels a million miles away. Watch the road for deer, moose, and some
of the top cyclists in America, who train here much of the year. Expect
to wait on weekends and many weekday mornings. Ⓢ *Average main:
$12* ✉ *2100 Emigration Canyon, East Side* ☎ *801/582–5807* ✛ *H3.*

FARTHER AFIELD

$$ ✕**Layla Grill and Mezze.** Venture a few miles from downtown to find
MEDITERRANEAN   the Tadros family's Mediterranean restaurant that has debuted with
Fodor's Choice   savory dishes in a crisp, contemporary dining space. Tangy spices
★   enliven old-world favorites such as shawarma and moussaka, and not-
so-common dishes like *muhamarra* (think hummus but with walnuts)
tempt you to stray from your comfort zone. Bright walls, big windows,
and family-friendly banquettes bring a sun-drenched Mykonos feel to
your meal. Lebanese-influenced wine and cocktail offerings are excellent
as well. Ⓢ *Average main: $15* ✉ *4751 S. Holladay Blvd., Cottonwood*
☎ *801/272–9111* ⊕ *www.laylagrill.com* ✛ *G6.*

$$$ ✕**Log Haven.** This elegant mountain retreat was put on the map with
AMERICAN   inventive takes on American cuisine laced with everything from Asian
Fodor's Choice   ingredients to pure Rocky Mountain style. It excels with fresh fish, game,
★   and seasonal local ingredients, creating such dishes as rabbit with white-
corn polenta or ahi tuna served with lime sticky rice and baby bok choy.
The knowledgeable staff can help you pair wines with the menu's multi-
layered flavors. With its romantic setting in a beautifully renovated log
home amid pine trees, waterfalls, and wildflowers, and its summertime
patio seating, this is definitely a restaurant to remember. Ⓢ *Average main:
$25* ✉ *6451 E. Millcreek Canyon Rd., Millcreek Canyon* ✛ *From I–15,
take I–80 E to I–215 S; exit at 39th South; turn left at end of ramp, and
left onto Wasatch Blvd., then turn right at 3800 South. Continue 4 miles
up canyon* ☎ *801/272–8255* ⊕ *www.log-haven.com* ✛ *H6.*

$ ✕**Lone Star Taqueria.** It seems like sacrilege given that the place is in the
MEXICAN   desert, but a prominent magazine (*Sunset*) named Lone Star's signature
fish tacos as "best in the western USA." Among the ordinary storefronts
on busy Fort Union Boulevard, look for the lime-green building sur-
rounded by a fence topped with old cowboy boots and fronted by an
old sticker-covered car that looks as if it crashed through the fence.
With concrete floors, metal tables, and bright umbrellas, the joint serves
some excellent, cheap Mexican food—including house special fish tacos,
handmade tamales, burritos of all types, and plenty of chilled Mexican
beer. It seats less than 50, so fall back on the drive-through window for
takeout, if necessary. Ⓢ *Average main: $8* ✉ *2265 E. Fort Union Blvd.,*

Cottonwood ☎ *801/944–2300* 🌐 *www.lonestartaqueria.com* ✍ *Reservations not accepted* ⏲ *Closed Sun.* ✥ *G6.*

$$ AMERICAN 🍴 **Porcupine Pub and Grille.** Above a ski- and board-rental shop at the mouth of Big and Little Cottonwood canyons sits one of the Valley's most lively pubs. Inside the large A-frame chaletlike building you'll find bright polished wood floors and trim, and a friendly vibe. The menu offers more than 40 variations on standard pub food, including buffalo wings, rock shrimp pizza, burgers, ribs, burritos, and ahi tuna. The full-service bar features spirits, microbrews on tap, and a wine list. [$] *Average main: $15* ✉ *3698 E. Fort Union Blvd., Cottonwood* ☎ *801/942–5555* 🌐 *www.porcupinepub.com* ✍ *Reservations not accepted* ✥ *G6.*

2

WHERE TO STAY

Luxury grand hotels, intimate bed-and-breakfasts, reliable national "all suites" chains—Salt Lake City has plenty of options when it comes to resting your head at night. Unlike those in most cities, hotels, motels, and even bed-and-breakfasts here are all tuned in to serving visiting skiers in winter months. Many offer ski packages, transportation, and equipment-rental options, as well as knowledgeable staff who are probably on the slopes when they're not at work. Most of the hotels are concentrated in the downtown area and west of the airport, but there are also numerous options to the south of Salt Lake proper and closer to the canyon areas, where there are several high-tech companies and corporate headquarters. *Hotel reviews have been shortened. For full information, visit Fodors.com.*

Use the coordinates (✥ A1) at the end of each listing to locate a site on the corresponding map.

WHAT IT COSTS

	$	$$	$$$	$$$$
Hotels	under $100	$100–$150	$151–$200	over $200

Hotel prices are the lowest cost of a standard double room in high season.

DOWNTOWN SALT LAKE

$ HOTEL 🏨 **Carlton Hotel.** An absolute steal on the quiet side of downtown. **Pros:** family-owned for 50 years, pleasant service; made-to-order breakfast included. **Cons:** rooms vary in size, and some are small. Hemmed in by high-rises and a parking garage, some rooms feel claustrophobic. [$] *Rooms from: $79* ✉ *140 E. South Temple, Downtown* ☎ *801/355–3418* 🌐 *www.carltonhotel-slc.com* 🛏 *28 rooms, 7 suites* 🍽 *Breakfast* ✥ *F2.*

$ HOTEL 🏨 **Doubletree Suites by Hilton Salt Lake City.** The sunlit atrium with its soaring ceiling gives the entire hotel a light, airy feeling, and the cool terra-cotta tile floors are soothing in the summer heat. **Pros:** the suites are nice for families; on-site restaurant. **Cons:** a key property when big conventions are in town, so rates may jump higher, if you can even get

BEST BETS FOR SALT LAKE CITY LODGING

Fodor'sChoice★	$$$	BEST GRAND DAME HOTEL
The Grand America Hotel, $$$$, p. 74	Inn on the Hill, p. 76	**The Grand America Hotel**, $$$$, p. 74
Hotel Monaco Salt Lake City, $$$$, p. 74	$$$$	
	The Grand America Hotel, p. 74	HIPSTER HOTELS
Best by Price	**Hotel Monaco Salt Lake City**, p. 74	**Holiday Inn Airport West**, $$, p. 77
$	**Best by Experience**	**Hotel Monaco Salt Lake City**, $$$$, p. 74
Carlton Hotel, p. 73		
La Quinta Inn Salt Lake City Midvale, p. 77		BUILDING ARCHITECTURE
Peery Hotel, p. 75	GREAT CONCIERGE	**The Grand America Hotel**, $$$$, p. 74
$$	**The Grand America Hotel**, $$$$, p. 74	Peery Hotel, $, p. 75
Salt Lake City Marriott City Center, p. 75		BEST-KEPT SECRET
		Peery Hotel, $, p. 75

a room; breakfast not included. $ *Rooms from: $99* ✉ *110 W. 600 S, Downtown* ☎ *801/359–7800* ➽ *244 suites* ❁ *No meals* ✚ *C6.*

$$$$
HOTEL
Fodor'sChoice
★

🏨 **The Grand America Hotel.** With its white Bethel-granite exterior, this 24-story luxury hotel dominates the landscape a few blocks south of downtown. **Pros:** as stately and grand as its name suggests, with luxuries like concierge, executive floor, ritzy spa. **Cons:** by Manhattan standards, luxury here is a bargain, but by Utah standards, Grand America is one of the most expensive properties in the state. $ *Rooms from: $299* ✉ *555 S. Main St., Downtown* ☎ *801/258–6000, 800/304–8696* ⊕ *www.grandamerica.com* ➽ *379 rooms, 396 suites* ❁ *No meals* ✚ *C6.*

$
HOTEL

🏨 **Hilton–Salt Lake City Center.** This Hilton is one of the city's largest and best-appointed places to stay, and it's within walking distance of all downtown attractions and many great restaurants. **Pros:** walking distance from Temple Square, Convention Center, and other downtown sights; concierge; on-site Starbuck's. **Cons:** first hotel to sell out during conventions; nothing intimate about one of Salt Lake's only 500-room hotels; surcharges for parking and wireless access reduce this hotel's value. $ *Rooms from: $94* ✉ *255 S. West Temple, Downtown* ☎ *801/328–2000, 800/445–8667* ⊕ *www.hilton.com* ➽ *479 rooms, 20 suites* ❁ *No meals* ✚ *C5.*

$$$$
HOTEL
Fodor'sChoice
★

🏨 **Hotel Monaco Salt Lake City.** This swank hotel is ensconced in a 14-story former bank (built in 1924), distinguished by an exterior decorated with classical cornices and cartouches. **Pros:** sparkling after $4 million renovation in 2013; distinctive hotel in the heart of downtown; restaurant has impeccable service and innovative food; attentive concierge. **Cons:** $19/day to park here. $\boxed{\$}$ *Rooms from: $209* ✉ *15 W. 200 S, Downtown* ☎ *801/595–0000, 800/805–1801* ⊕ *www.monaco-saltlakecity. com* ⤸ *191 rooms, 32 suites* ⦿ *No meals* ✛ *C5.*

$ 🖥 **Little America Hotel.** This reliably comfortable hotel stands in the
HOTEL   shadow of its world-renowned sister property, but Little America actu-
FAMILY ally has more rooms and its own loyal following. **Pros:** large rooms; trees make the courtyard an oasis; save $13 a day on parking alone compared with the Grand America. **Cons:** restaurants and sports bar lack pizzazz of some downtown eateries. $\boxed{\$}$ *Rooms from: $99* ✉ *500 S. Main St., Downtown* ☎ *801/363–6781, 800/453–9450* ⊕ *www.saltlake.little america.com* ⤸ *850 rooms* ⦿ *No meals* ✛ *C6.*

$ 🖥 **Peery Hotel.** At more than 100 years young, this historic building
HOTEL   on the west side of downtown Salt Lake City has a unique mulberry exterior, a spacious antiques-filled lobby, and canopied beds in every room. **Pros:** a historic building with character that has been well maintained; many "green" features; great location. **Cons:** occasional noise from local bars at night; $10 for valet parking; no on-site restaurant. $\boxed{\$}$ *Rooms from: $89* ✉ *110 W. Broadway, Downtown* ☎ *801/521–4300* ⊕ *www.peeryhotel.com* ⤸ *64 rooms, 9 suites* ⦿ *Breakfast* ✛ *C5.*

$$ 🖥 **Red Lion Hotel Salt Lake Downtown.** With its '70s-era architecture, this
HOTEL   triangular high-rise is best judged by its interior, not its facade. **Pros:** easy access to I–15; free parking and/or free airport shuttle will benefit most guests; take advantage of the ski-rental shop across the street. **Cons:** a little frayed around the edges and showing its age; there are more modern hotels, with better locations, at the same price. $\boxed{\$}$ *Rooms from: $111* ✉ *161 W. 600 S, Downtown* ☎ *801/521–7373, 800/325–4000* ⊕ *salt-lakedowntown.redlion.com* ⤸ *390 rooms, 4 suites* ⦿ *No meals* ✛ *B6.*

$$ 🖥 **Salt Lake City Marriott City Center.** If you want to be in the heart of the
HOTEL   city, this hotel's location is superb. **Pros:** location is superb for all downtown attractions; newer hotel. **Cons:** special events at Gallivan Center can bring big crowds; on-site parking fees can add up. $\boxed{\$}$ *Rooms from: $109* ✉ *220 S. State St., Downtown* ☎ *801/961–8700* ⊕ *www.marriott. com* ⤸ *342 rooms, 17 suites* ⦿ *No meals* ✛ *C5.*

$$ 🖥 **Salt Lake Marriott Downtown at City Creek.** An extensive renovation in
HOTEL   2013 restored this property's status as one of the leading business and convention hotels in downtown Salt Lake City. **Pros:** location can't be beat. **Cons:** not a lot of character; it's easy to confuse the two downtown Marriott hotels; $15 to park your vehicle here. $\boxed{\$}$ *Rooms from: $119* ✉ *75 S. West Temple, Downtown* ☎ *801/531–0800* ⊕ *www.marriott. com* ⤸ *504 rooms, 6 suites* ⦿ *No meals* ✛ *C4.*

$$ 🖥 **Sheraton Salt Lake City Hotel.** One of the city's major full-service hotels,
HOTEL   this business-friendly place has a huge lobby with its own Starbucks coffee shop, oversize chairs, and fireplace. **Pros:** one of the nicer downtown hotels; balcony rooms have great views; flat-panel televisions in rooms. **Cons:** a little far from the heart of downtown, and on busy stretch of 500 South. $\boxed{\$}$ *Rooms from: $119* ✉ *150 W. 500 S, Downtown* ☎ *801/401–2000, 800/364–3295* ⊕ *www.sheraton.com/saltlakecity* ⤸ *332 rooms, 30 suites* ⦿ *No meals* ✛ *B6.*

CAPITOL HILL AND THE AVENUES

$$
B&B/INN
Ellerbeck Mansion Bed and Breakfast. A stay in this Victorian mansion will give you a real appreciation of why city residents flock to live in the historic Avenues district. **Pros:** it's a pleasant walk to Temple Square from this stately Victorian home; some rooms with fireplace. **Cons:** expect room surcharges (and shortages) when conventions are in town. $ *Rooms from: $149* ⊠ *140 North B St., Capitol Hill* ☎ *801/355–2500, 800/966–8364* ⊕ *www.ellerbeckbedandbreakfast.com* ✑ *6 rooms* ⦿| *Breakfast* ✛ *F2.*

$$$
B&B/INN
Inn on the Hill. Owned and restored by former *Salt Lake Tribune* publisher Philip McCarthey, this turn-of-the-20th-century Renaissance Revival mansion makes a striking impression with its red-rock exterior and bold painted trim. **Pros:** elegant stone mansion on Capitol Hill and ideally situated midway between Temple Square and the state capitol. **Cons:** lots of steps and no elevator, and Salt Lake is nearly 4,500 feet above sea level; no kids allowed, unless you rent the Carriage House, which sleeps six. $ *Rooms from: $189* ⊠ *225 N. State St., Capitol Hill* ☎ *801/328–1466* ⊕ *www.innonthehillslc.com* ✑ *6 rooms, 6 suites* ⦿| *Breakfast* ✛ *E2.*

EAST SIDE AND THE UNIVERSITY OF UTAH

$$
HOTEL
Salt Lake City Marriott University Park. Away from the downtown bustle and steps away from hiking and biking trails, this spacious hotel is airy and inviting and a great choice if you like the outdoors at your doorstep. **Pros:** less claustrophobic than downtown and often priced more reasonably; close to hiking and biking trails. **Cons:** traditional amenities like shopping and restaurants are not within walking distance; less convenient to downtown. $ *Rooms from: $109* ⊠ *480 Wakara Way, University of Utah* ☎ *801/581–1000* ⊕ *www.marriott.com* ✑ *189 rooms, 29 suites* ⦿| *No meals* ✛ *H2.*

$
B&B/INN
Wildflowers Bed & Breakfast. An elegant "painted lady" with a private yard full of larkspur, columbine, and foxglove, this Victorian inn was built as a private home in 1891. **Pros:** friendly proprietors make you feel very welcome; listed on National Register of Historic Places; all the artwork is original, and much of it was painted by innkeeper Jeri Parker. **Cons:** clean and tidy—but may be ready for some updating. $ *Rooms from: $90* ⊠ *936 E. 1700 S, East Side* ☎ *801/466–0600, 800/569–0009 reservations* ⊕ *www.wildflowersbb.com* ✑ *4 rooms, 1 suite* ⦿| *Breakfast* ✛ *F4.*

WEST SIDE AND THE AIRPORT

$
HOTEL
Comfort Inn Airport. Spacious, clean, and decked out with amenities, this is a good value for a stay near the airport, with easy access to downtown. **Pros:** caters to business travelers. **Cons:** in a lifeless corporate park west of the airport. $ *Rooms from: $99* ⊠ *200 N. Admiral Byrd Rd., Airport* ☎ *801/746–5200, 800/535–8742* ⊕ *www.slccomfortinn. com* ✑ *153 rooms, 2 suites* ⦿| *Breakfast* ✛ *A2.*

2

$ HOTEL 🏨 **Comfort Suites.** This newer property is an affordable option if downtown hotels are booked because it's closer than most of the airport hotels to restaurants and other services. **Pros:** extensive renovations in rooms, hallways, lobby in 2013; great value. **Cons:** very little within walking distance. [$] *Rooms from: $90* ✉ *171 N. 2100 W, Airport* ☎ *801/715–8688* 🌐 *www.comfortsuites.com* 🛏 *104 rooms* 🍴 *Breakfast* ✥ *C2.*

$ HOTEL 🏨 **Doubletree by Hilton Salt Lake City Airport.** In its own self-contained world beside a man-made lake, this hotel meets business travelers' needs with plenty of business and personal services. **Pros:** completely renovated in 2013; many on-site services, including restaurant and bar; large weight room; it's ¼ mile around the lake if you're a jogger. **Cons:** nothing within walking distance; there's no downtown shuttle service. [$] *Rooms from: $79* ✉ *5151 Wiley Post Way, Airport* ☎ *801/539–1515, 800/999–3736* 🌐 *www.hilton.com* 🛏 *276 rooms, 12 suites* 🍴 *No meals* ✥ *A2.*

$$ HOTEL 🏨 **Holiday Inn Airport West.** This contemporary property, built in 2007, is a stunning departure from your grandfather's Holiday Inn, with stylish interiors and up-to-date amenities. **Pros:** staff is genuine and works hard to ensure your satisfaction; a great value for families or convention goers, as long as you have a car. **Cons:** the cluster of airport hotels feels like the last outpost before miles and miles of desert, and it is; there is nothing within walking distance; the nearest services are downtown. [$] *Rooms from: $109* ✉ *5001 W. Wiley Post Way, Airport* ☎ *801/741–1800* 🌐 *www.holidayinnslcairport.com* 🛏 *61 rooms, 25 suites* 🍴 *No meals* ✥ *A2.*

$ HOTEL 🏨 **Radisson Hotel Salt Lake City Airport.** This very comfortable hotel is a good bet between downtown and the airport. **Pros:** closer to downtown than other airport hotels. **Cons:** downtown Radisson offers nicer property, location, and amenities—often at nearly identical rate; too far to walk to downtown attractions. [$] *Rooms from: $99* ✉ *2177 W. North Temple, Airport* ☎ *801/364–5800, 800/333–3333* 🌐 *www.radisson.com/hotels/saltair* 🛏 *94 rooms, 30 suites* 🍴 *No meals* ✥ *C2.*

FARTHER AFIELD

$$ HOTEL 🏨 **Courtyard Salt Lake City Sandy.** Excellent for business travelers visiting Salt Lake's many South Valley corporations, this full-service hotel offers large in-room desks with broadband and spacious work areas. **Pros:** convenient if you're shopping, visiting south suburbs, or skiing in Cottonwood canyons. **Cons:** in an urban, asphalt island of parking lots and shopping. [$] *Rooms from: $129* ✉ *10701 S. Holiday Park Dr., Sandy* ☎ *801/571–3600* 🌐 *www.marriott.com* 🛏 *117 rooms, 7 suites* 🍴 *No meals* ✥ *E6.*

$ HOTEL 🏨 **La Quinta Inn Salt Lake City Midvale.** It may be farther afield, but you have easy access to the TRAX line (there's a stop a block from the hotel), which will take you downtown, to the south suburbs, or to the University of Utah. **Pros:** interior hallways; breakfast included. **Cons:** industrial neighborhood is hardly family-friendly. [$] *Rooms from: $79* ✉ *7231 S. Catalpa St., Midvale* ☎ *801/566–3291* 🌐 *www.laquinta.com* 🛏 *122 rooms, 3 suites* 🍴 *Breakfast* ✥ *E6.*

NIGHTLIFE AND PERFORMING ARTS

For information on what's happening around town, pick up a *City Weekly* news and entertainment weekly, available at stands outside restaurants and stores in town.

NIGHTLIFE

An increasingly cosmopolitan atmosphere is spreading through downtown Salt Lake City and this has already vastly improved what was once a pretty staid nightlife scene, with bars and clubs serving cocktails and providing live music to meet diverse tastes. Having said that, remnants of the state's quirky liquor laws make for a few surprises to newcomers, however. First of all, don't expect to spend the night barhopping along a single street—zoning prohibits more than two bars on one block. And you won't party until dawn here—last call is 1 AM, and some bars call it earlier. Cabs are not on hand outside every bar or club, so you will probably have to call for one.

DOWNTOWN SALT LAKE

BARS AND LOUNGES

Lumpy's Downtown. Sports fans gather here, and this bar is hopping seven nights a week until 2 am. You'll find televisions at every booth, a dance floor, and more. Lumpy's is within walking distance of most downtown hotels. ✉ *145 Pierpont Ave., Downtown* ☎ *801/883–8714* ⊕ *www.lumpysdowntownslc.com.*

The Red Door. Try a martini at this trendy bar with a cosmopolitan accent, where an eclectic crowd of T-shirt-and-jeans-meets-suit-and-tie hangs out. It's closed on Sunday. ✉ *57 W. 200 S, Downtown* ☎ *801/363–6030* ⊕ *www.behindthereddoor.com.*

Squatters Pub Brewery. They've won dozens of awards at the Great American Beer Festival and World Beer Cup, and will let you have a small taster before you order a full glass. The pub has friendly staff and a nice casual vibe, and is especially lively when conventions are in town; they serve great food too. ✉ *147 W. Broadway, Downtown* ☎ *801/363–2739* ⊕ *www.squatters.com.*

Tavernacle Social Club. Dueling pianos and sing-alongs (Wednesday through Saturday) make for a festive atmosphere in this fixture of a bar just east of downtown. The musicians only play requests, and if you don't like the current song, you can pay $1 to change it. ✉ *201 E. 300 S, Downtown* ☎ *801/519–8900* ⊕ *www.tavernacle.com.*

NIGHTCLUBS

Circle Lounge. Bands, DJs, hookah, and sushi share the billing at Circle Lounge. It's busiest Thursday through Saturday nights. ✉ *328 S. State St., Downtown* ☎ *801/531–5400.*

Kristauf's Martini Bar. You'll have a hard time choosing which martini to try from among the more than 80 varieties, including the crowd-pleasing Crisp Pear. Service is sometimes slow, but the collegiate crowd doesn't seem to mind. ✉ *16 W. Market St., Downtown* ☎ *801/366–9490* ⊕ *www.martinibarslc.com.*

PERFORMING ARTS

Salt Lake City's arts tradition officially started in 1847 with the Deseret Musical and Dramatic Society, founded by Brigham Young. The city has continued to give strong support for the arts, even voting for a special tax to support cultural organizations such as the opera and symphony. Ballet West, the Utah Symphony, and Utah Opera have kept the state on the nation's cultural map. The Capitol Theatre and Rose Wagner Performing Arts Center host Broadway touring companies. The Pioneer Theatre Company and Plan-B Theatre produce the most successful theater productions. Many film lovers forgo the snow and the crowds of Park City to enjoy the 10-day Sundance Film Festival at a half-dozen Salt Lake City venues every January. Lesser-known and locally written plays are presented in small theaters throughout the valley.

TICKETS

ArtTix. For tickets to cultural events, contact ArtTix. ⊠ *50 W. 200 S, Downtown* ☎ *801/355–2787, 888/451–2787* ⊕ *www.arttix.org.*

Smiths Tix. Tickets to sporting events and concerts are available here. ☎ *801/467–8499, 800/888–8499* ⊕ *www.smithstix.com.*

Ticketmaster. Tickets here are primarily for music and sporting events at the Maverik Center in nearby West Valley City. ⊠ *West Valley City* ☎ *800/745–3000* ⊕ *www.ticketmaster.com.*

MAJOR PERFORMANCE VENUES

There are three main performance spaces in Salt Lake City.

Abravanel Hall. The Utah Symphony plays at Abravanel Hall. ⊠ *123 W. South Temple, Downtown* ☎ *801/355–2787* ⊕ *www.slccfa.org/venues/abravanel-hall/.*

Capitol Theatre. Ballet West and the Utah Opera perform at the Capitol Theatre, which also hosts Broadway touring companies. ⊠ *50 W. 200 S, Downtown* ☎ *801/355–2787.*

Rose Wagner Performing Arts Center. Comprising the Black Box Theatre, the Jeanné Wagner Theatre, and the Studio Theatre, this is home to the Ririe-Woodbury Dance Company and the Repertory Dance Theatre, and provides performance space for many of the city's smaller theater and dance companies. ⊠ *138 W. Broadway, Downtown* ☎ *801/355–2787* ⊕ *www.slccfa.org.*

DANCE

Ballet West. This respected professional ballet company performs both classic and original works at the Capitol Theatre. Its inner workings featured in the multiseason reality show *Breaking Pointe.* ⊠ *50 W. 200 S, Downtown* ☎ *801/869–6900* ⊕ *www.balletwest.org.*

Repertory Dance Theatre. This company presents modern-dance performances. ⊠ *138 W. Broadway, Downtown* ☎ *801/534–1000* ⊕ *www.rdtutah.org.*

Ririe-Woodbury Dance Company. This is Salt Lake City's premier modern-dance troupe, recognized for its innovation and commitment to community education. ⊠ *138 W. Broadway, Downtown* ☎ *801/297–4241* ⊕ *www.ririewoodbury.com.*

FILM

Brewvies. A variety of first-run and independent films are shown here. You can have a beer and dinner with the show. ⊠ *676 S. 200 W, Downtown* ☎ *801/355–5500* ⊕ *www.brewvies.com.*

Broadway Centre Theatre. The Salt Lake Film Society shows independent and foreign films here. ⊠ *111 E. Broadway, Downtown* ☎ *801/321–0310* ⊕ *www.saltlakefilmsociety.org.*

Tower Theatre. See independent and foreign films at this historic art deco theater that's also a Sundance Film Festival venue. ⊠ *876 E. 900 S, East Side* ☎ *801/321–0310* ⊕ *www.saltlakefilmsociety.org.*

MUSIC

Mormon Tabernacle Choir. This famous choir, which includes men and women of all ages, performs sacred music, with some secular (classical and patriotic) works. You can hear them during their weekly broadcast, "Music and the Spoken Word," Sunday morning from 9:30 to 10 in the Tabernacle most of the year. Their weekly rehearsal, also open to the public, is held Thursday evening from 7:30 to 9:30 in the Tabernacle. ⊠ *50 N. West Temple, Temple Square* ☎ *801/240–4150* ⊕ *www.mormontabernaclechoir.org.*

Utah Symphony. The premier orchestra in the state, if not the region, the Utah Symphony performs in the acoustically acclaimed Maurice Abravanel Concert Hall and calls the Deer Valley Music Festival its summer home. ⊠ *Abravanel Hall, 123 W. South Temple, Downtown* ☎ *801/533–6683* ⊕ *www.utahsymphony.org.*

OPERA

Utah Opera. Since 1978, this company has performed new and classical works at Capitol Theatre and throughout the state. ⊠ *123 W. South Temple, Downtown* ☎ *801/533–6683* ⊕ *www.utahopera.org.*

THEATER

Off Broadway Theatre. Musicals and plays here include comedies and parodies, as well as improvisational comedy events. ⊠ *272 S. Main St., Downtown* ☎ *801/355–4628* ⊕ *www.theobt.com.*

Pioneer Theatre Company. This professional company, in residence at the University of Utah, stages classic and contemporary musicals and plays. From *Les Miserables* to *The Producers*, it has proved it can put on large-scale and commercially viable theater. ⊠ *300 S. 1400 E, University of Utah* ☎ *801/581–6961* ⊕ *www.pioneertheatre.org.*

Fodor's Choice ★ **Plan-B Theatre.** The resident company of the Rose Wagner Performing Arts Center tends to stage modest productions built on fine original scripts and timely social and cultural themes. Two shows became hits outside of Utah: *Facing East*, which went to New York off Broadway, and *Exposed*, which drew considerable acclaim for tackling the issue of fallout from nuclear testing in the 1950s. ⊠ *138 W. 300 S, Downtown* ☎ *801/297–4200* ⊕ *www.planbtheatre.org.*

Salt Lake Acting Company. Recognized for its development of new regionally and locally written plays, this company's performances run year-round. ⊠ *168 W. 500 N, Capitol Hill* ☎ *801/363–7522* ⊕ *www.saltlakeactingcompany.org.*

SHOPPING

Salt Lake's shopping is concentrated downtown as well as in several malls. Good bets for souvenirs include books, Mormon crafts, and Western collectibles. The vicinity of 300 South and 300 East streets has several shops that specialize in antique jewelry, furnishings, art, and knickknacks.

DOWNTOWN SALT LAKE

PLAZAS AND MALLS

City Creek Center. The centerpiece of a $1 billion downtown redevelopment across from Temple Square in 2012, City Creek has brought luxury shopping to the city with stores like Nordstrom, Tiffany & Co., Porsche Design, and Pandora. Although the outdoor mall is gorgeous and developers were credited with bringing historic City Creek waterway back aboveground, it's somewhat controversial, because the Mormon Church owns the land and most shops are closed on Sunday. The Cheesecake Factory's only Salt Lake City location is here, and the chain restaurant is one of the only restaurants open on Sunday in the mall. ⊠ *50 S. Main St., Downtown* ☎ *801/521–2012* ⊕ *www.shopcitycreekcenter.com* ☾ *Closed Sun.*

Gateway Mall. The Gateway is a combination shopping mall, restaurant district, and business and residential center, all accessible by TRAX, Salt Lake's mass transit. ⊠ *18 N. Rio Grande St., Downtown* ☎ *801/456–0000* ⊕ *www.shopthegateway.com.*

OUTDOOR MARKETS

Farmers bring produce, flowers, and other goodies to the popular downtown farmers' market at **Pioneer Park**, at 300 West and 300 South streets, each Saturday from June through mid-October. Local bakeries and restaurants also sell tasty treats ranging from fresh salsa to cinnamon rolls, and there is live music, too. Find fresh markets in Park City, Murray, South Jordan, and at the University of Utah in the summer as well.

ANTIQUES

Elementé. This store specializes in unique and unusual home furnishings; look for bargains in the basement. ⊠ *353 W. Pierpont Ave., Downtown* ☎ *801/355–7400.*

ART GALLERIES

Alice Gallery at Glendinning. This gallery is housed in the historic Glendinning Mansion, which is also home to the Utah Arts Council. ⊠ *617 E. South Temple, Downtown* ☎ *801/245–7272* ⊕ *www.heritage.utah.gov* ☾ *Weekdays 8–5.*

Phillips Gallery. Find the best of Utah's artists' work here. ⊠ *444 E. 200 S, Downtown* ☎ *801/364–8284* ⊕ *www.phillips-gallery.com.*

BOOKS

Ken Sanders Rare Books. More than 100,000 titles await in this store that specializes in literature about Utah, Mormons, and Western exploration. ⊠ *268 S. 200 E, Downtown* ☎ *801/521–3819.*

Weller Book Works. The name of this store has been synonymous with independent book sales in Salt Lake City since 1929. Catherine and Tony Weller are the third generation to operate this bookstore, which relocated to the historic former train yard in 2012. Bibliophiles will love the space and the helpful and knowledgeable staff. ⊠ *607 Trolley Sq., East Side* ☎ *801/328–2586* ⊕ *www.wellerbookworks.com.*

EAST SIDE AND UNIVERSITY OF UTAH

Explore the smaller neighborhood clusters of shops such as 9th & 9th (900 South, 900 East), Foothill Village, or Trolley Square to find unique souvenirs of Utah.

PLAZAS AND MALLS

Sugar House Business District. The Sugar House Business District is a funky mix of locally owned shops and restaurants between 1700 South and 2700 South streets, from 700 East to 1300 East streets. ⊠ *East Side.*

Trolley Square. The wares here run the gamut from estate jewelry and designer clothes to bath products, baskets, and saltwater taffy. Stores include Pottery Barn, Weller Books, Tabula Rasa, and an assortment of restaurants, as well as a Whole Foods Market. ⊠ *600 S. 700 E, East Side* ☎ *801/521–9877.*

BOOKS

FAMILY **King's English.** This converted cottage is a great place to browse. Local authors, a wide selection of children's books, a dozen reading groups, and a community writing series call King's English home. ⊠ *1511 S. 1500 E, East Side* ☎ *801/484–9100* ⊕ *www.kingsenglish.com.*

FARTHER AFIELD

SPORTING GOODS

Backcountry.com. This is one of the best-known outdoor-equipment retailers on the Internet. Less publicized is the fact that the 24/7 online store also has a small showroom and massive (200,000-square-foot) back room where you can shop or pick up products you've ordered online. Skiers, boarders, campers, and climbers are all welcome. ⊠ *2607 S. 3200 W, West Side* ☎ *800/409–4502* ⊕ *www.backcountry.com.*

Kirkham's Outdoor Products. Locally owned, this store carries a wide spectrum of outdoor gear. ⊠ *3125 S. State St., The Suburbs* ☎ *801/486–4161, 800/453–7756* ⊕ *www.kirkhams.com.*

SIDE TRIPS FROM SALT LAKE CITY

BIG COTTONWOOD CANYON

31 miles from Downtown Salt Lake City.

The history of mining and skiing in Utah often go hand in hand, and that's certainly true of Big Cottonwood Canyon, with its adjacent ski resorts of **Brighton** and **Solitude.** In the mid-1800s, 2,500 miners lived at the top of this canyon in a rowdy tent city. The old mining roads make great hiking, mountain-biking, and backcountry ski trails. Rock climbers congregate in the lower canyon for excellent sport and traditional climbing.

Opened in 1936, Brighton is the second-oldest ski resort in Utah, and one of the oldest in North America. Just down the canyon, Solitude has undergone several incarnations since it opened in 1957, and has invested heavily in overnight accommodations and new base facilities since the early 1990s. As an area, Big Cottonwood is quieter than Park City or neighboring Little Cottonwood Canyon, home of Alta and Snowbird resorts.

GETTING HERE AND AROUND

From downtown Salt Lake City it's a 40-minute drive to Big Cottonwood via Interstate 80 and Interstate 215, then Highway 190 E. Most downtown hotels offer free shuttles to the ski resorts, and Utah Transit Authority runs bus shuttles for $4.50 each way.

SPORTS AND THE OUTDOORS
BICYCLING

Solitude Mountain Resort. There are great single-track trails within Big Cottonwood Canyon as well as routes that connect neighboring canyons. Solitude Mountain Resort offers lift-served mountain biking with rentals available at Solitude Village. ⊠ *12000 Big Cottonwood Canyon Rd.* ☎ *801/534–1400* ⊕ *www.skisolitude.com.*

HIKING

Brighton Lakes Trail. The upper section of Big Cottonwood Canyon is a glacier-carved valley with many side drainages that lead to picturesque alpine lakes. In the Brighton area you can access beautiful mountain lakes (Mary, Margaret, and Catherine) just a short jaunt from the highway. The elevation at Brighton's parking lot is 8,700 feet, so take it easy, rest often, and drink plenty of water. A beautiful hike is along the Brighton Lakes Trail past four alpine lakes and then ascending to Catherine Pass. From here you can choose to descend into Little Cottonwood's Albion Basin near Alta (but remember, you'll need a car for the 45-minute ride back to Brighton), or back along the Brighton Lakes Trail.

Sunset Peak. At Catherine Pass you have the option of continuing up to Sunset Peak, which, at 10,648 feet, is one of the most accessible summits in the Wasatch Range. It's another short grunt to the top, but well worth the effort for the unsurpassed, nearly 360-degree view. The breathtaking vistas include the Heber Valley, Park City, Mount Timpanogos, Big and Little Cottonwood Canyons, and even a portion of the Salt Lake Valley.

SKIING

CROSS-COUNTRY **Solitude Nordic Center.** Accessible from Solitude Village, the Solitude Nordic Center has 20 km (12 miles) of groomed cross-country trails, 10 km (6 miles) of snowshoe trails, and a small shop offering rentals, lessons, food, and guided tours. For $18 you can use the trails all day; for $54 you receive an all-day trail pass and a one-hour group lesson with rentals. ⊠ *12000 Big Cottonwood Canyon Rd.* ☎ *801/536–5774* ⊕ *www.skisolitude.com.*

DOWNHILL **Brighton Ski Resort.** The smallest of the Cottonwood resorts just outside Salt Lake City, Brighton is nonetheless a favorite among serious

Ride on the Pony Express Trail

Imagine a young man racing over the dusty trail on the back of a foaming mustang. A cloud of dust rises to announce him to the station manager, who waits with a new mount, some beef jerky, and water. The rider has galloped 11 miles since breakfast and will cover another 49 before he sleeps. That was the daily life of a courier with the Pony Express.

A rider had to weigh less than 120 pounds. He was allowed only 25 pounds in gear, which included four leather mail pouches, a light rifle, a pistol, and a Bible. The standard uniform consisted of a bright red shirt and blue pants. Hostile Indians, bandits, and rattlesnakes were handled with the guns. The blazing heat of the desert in the summer and blinding blizzards in the winter were his constant foes.

There are few places in the United States where the original trail and stations of the Pony Express survive in such pristine condition as they do in Utah. One of the best-preserved sections of the original Pony Express Trail, which was in operation for 19 months in the mid-19th century, is the 133-mile section through the desert of west-central Utah. You'll see territory that remains much as it was during the existence of the Pony Express, and many of the sights you'll see along the way haven't changed perceptibly since that time. The desert has preserved them.

If you want to traverse the route, the logical starting point is Camp Floyd–Stagecoach Inn State Park in Fairfield. The end is in Ibapah, 133 miles away on the Utah-Nevada border. Stone pillars with metal plaques mark the route that starts and ends on pavement, then becomes a dirt road for 126 miles that is passable when dry. The Bureau of Land Management maintains a campground at Simpson Springs, one of the area's most dependable water sources. Some interesting ruins are still visible at the Faust, Boyd, and Canyon stations. A brochure describing the major stops along the trail is available from the U.S. Bureau of Land Management's Salt Lake Field Office.

It takes a certain breed of romantic to appreciate the beauty of the land and life lived by those who kept the mail moving during the short time that the Pony Express existed. For those with a similar sense of adventure as the wiry young riders, who included "Buffalo Bill" Cody, traveling this trail is a chance to relive history. Historians say that the enterprise enabled communications between Washington, D.C., and California, keeping the state in the Union and helping to secure the North's eventual success in the Civil War. Stagecoaches, freight wagons, the Transcontinental Railroad, and the Lincoln Highway all followed the route pioneered by the Pony Express. The labor-intensive system of communicating cross-country ended with the invention of the telegraph. But before the Pony Express, it took mail six to eight weeks to travel from Missouri to California. By Pony Express, the mail took 10 days to arrive. By the time the telegraph was invented and put into wide use, messages went across the continent in a mere four hours.

snowboarders, parents (who flock to the resort's ski school), and some extreme skiers and riders. There are no megaresort amenities here, just a nice mix of terrain for all abilities, and a basic lodge, ski shop, and ski school. The snow is as powdery and deep as nearby Alta and Snowbird, and advanced (and prepared) skiers can access extensive backcountry areas. There's something for everyone here—at a fraction of the cost of the bigger resorts. Brighton has popular children's programs. ⊠ *8302 S. Brighton Loop Rd., Brighton* ☎ *801/532–4731, 855/201–7669* ⊕ *www. brightonresort.com* ⊨ *Lift tickets $72* ⌒ *1,745-ft vertical drop; 1,050 skiable acres; 21% beginner, 40% intermediate, 39% advanced/expert; 5 high-speed quad chairs, 1 triple chair.*

Solitude Mountain Resort. Offering (since 1957) Big Cottonwood Canyon's most intense ski experience, Solitude Mountain Resort has grown into a European-style village with lodges, condominiums, a luxury hotel, and good restaurants. Downhill skiing and snowboarding are still the main attractions, with steep, pristine terrain in Honeycomb Canyon attracting the experts, and a mix of intermediate cruising runs and beginner slopes beckoning the less accomplished. Day guests will enjoy relaxing after a hard day on the slopes at the comfortable Solitude Mountain Spa. ⊠ *12000 Big Cottonwood Canyon Rd., Solitude* ☎ *801/534–1400, 800/748–4754, 801/536–5774 Nordic Center, 801/536–5777 snow report* ⊕ *www.skisolitude.com* ⊨ *Lift tickets $77* ⌒ *2,047-ft vertical drop; 1,200 skiable acres; 20% beginner, 50% intermediate, 30% advanced; 3 high-speed quad chairs, 2 quad chairs, 1 triple chair, 2 double chairs.*

WHERE TO STAY

$$
HOTEL
Brighton Lodge. There are no frills at Brighton, and if you blink you might miss this 20-bed inn at the base of the ski hill, but, in an area when skiing is increasingly expensive, you can save money and enjoy fantastic family skiing here. **Pros:** unpretentious in every way; a good deal for families. **Cons:** if you don't have kids, the family atmosphere may not appeal. $ *Rooms from: $129* ⊠ *8302 S. Brighton Loop Rd.* ☎ *801/532–4731, 855/201–7669* ⊕ *www.brightonresort.com* ⤷ *16 rooms* ❖ *No meals.*

$$$$
RESORT
The Inn at Solitude. You get ski-in ski-out luxury and VIP treatment at this well-appointed hotel with comfortable and spacious rooms. **Pros:** attentive service; no big-city hustle and bustle. **Cons:** "Solitude" equals "quiet." $ *Rooms from: $369* ⊠ *12000 Big Cottonwood Canyon Rd., Solitude* ☎ *877/517–7717, 801/534–1400* ⊕ *www.innatsolitude.com* ⤷ *42 rooms, 4 suites* ⊗ *Closed May–Nov.* ❖ *No meals.*

$$$$
RENTAL
Powderhorn Lodge. The spacious condo-style units and convenient location allow for the perfect family ski trip. **Pros:** handsome furnishings and full kitchens; convenient to slopes and Solitude's village. **Cons:** this is an early-to-bed spot, so if you want to yodel, do so before dark. $ *Rooms from: $280* ⊠ *12000 Big Cottonwood Canyon Rd.* ☎ *800/748–4754, 801/534–1400* ⊕ *www.skisolitude.com* ⤷ *60 units* ❖ *No meals.*

$$$
B&B/INN
Silver Fork Lodge. Log furniture, wood paneling, and country style make the rooms here warm and inviting, the views are unbeatable, and the food is a major attraction. **Pros:** renowned dining; no in-room phones or TVs to disrupt the peace and quiet. **Cons:** nightlife is lacking;

some may find it a little too quiet. $ *Rooms from: $165* ✉ *11332 Big Cottonwood Canyon Rd.* ☎ *801/533–9977, 888/649–9551* ⊕ *www. silverforklodge.com* ⇄ *6 rooms, 1 suite* ✺ *Breakfast.*

NIGHTLIFE
Molly Green's. Old-time ski bums and younger snowboarders come together to tip back a few at Molly Green's, a 60-year-old watering hole in the A-frame at the base of Brighton Ski Resort. ✉ *Brighton Ski Resort, 8302 S. Brighton Loop Rd.* ☎ *801/532–4731* ⊕ *www. brightonresort.com* ☺ *Call for hrs, May–Nov.*

Thirsty Squirrel. This is a good place to unwind after skiing, but it's quiet once the après-ski crowd leaves. ✉ *Powderhorn Bldg., Solitude Village, 12000 Big Cottonwood Canyon Rd.* ☎ *801/536–5797* ☺ *Closed May–Oct.*

LITTLE COTTONWOOD CANYON

25 miles from Brighton and Solitude; 20 miles from Salt Lake City.

Skiers have been singing the praises of Little Cottonwood Canyon since 1938, when the Alta Lifts Company pieced together a ski lift using parts from an old mine tram to become the **Alta Ski Resort,** the second ski resort in North America. With its 500 inches per year of dry, light snow and unparalleled terrain, this canyon is legendary among diehard snow enthusiasts. A mile down the canyon from Alta, **Snowbird Ski and Summer Resort,** which opened in 1971, shares the same mythical snow and terrain quality. Since 2001 Alta and Snowbird have been connected via the Mineral Basin area. You can purchase an Alta Snowbird One Pass that allows you on the lifts at both areas, making this a huge skiing complex.

But skiing isn't all there is to do here. Many mountain-biking and hiking trails access the higher reaches of the Wasatch-Cache National Forest, and the trails over Catherine Pass will put you at the head of Big Cottonwood Canyon at the Brighton Ski Area. The hike to Catherine Pass is relatively easy and quite scenic. Formed by the tireless path of an ancient glacier, Little Cottonwood Canyon cuts a swath through the Wasatch-Cache National Forest. Canyon walls are composed mostly of striated granite, and traditional climbing routes of varied difficulty abound. Down the canyon from Alta and Snowbird is the trailhead for the Red Pine Lake and White Pine Lake trails. Some 3½ miles and 5 miles in, respectively, these mountain lakes make for great day hikes.

"If it ain't broke, don't fix it," could be the motto at Alta Ski Resort. There's an old-world charm here that many regulars call magic. Most of the lodges have been here since the '40s or '50s, and the emphasis is on efficiency and quality rather than the latest fads.

At Snowbird's base area, modern structures house guest rooms, restaurants, and nightclubs. The largest of these buildings, the Cliff Lodge, is an entire ski village under one roof. The resort mounts a variety of entertainment throughout the year, including live jazz shows, rock, blues, folk, and bluegrass concerts, and an Oktoberfest in fall. You can enjoy a drink at any of several base-area lounges.

All year long, Snowbird's tram takes sightseers to the top, and in summer hikers can ride up to hike atop Hidden Peak. Mountain bikers are discovering that the slopes make for some excellent, if strenuous, riding. The resort also has a competition-class outdoor climbing wall.

GETTING HERE AND AROUND

Travelers to Little Cottonwood Canyon take I–80 E to I–215 S, then hop off the highway at Exit 6 and venture into Little Cottonwood Canyon, following signs for Alta and Snowbird. The canyon's dramatic topography invites very occasional avalanches that block the road, the only entrance and egress.

ESSENTIALS

Visitor Information **Alta Visitors Bureau** ☎ *435/633–1394* ⊕ *www. discoveralta.com.*

EXPLORING

Snowbird Ski and Summer Resort. In summer, the resort is transformed into a summer playground with rides and games for children of all ages, plus concerts, outdoor sports, dining, and more. The thrill seekers in the family will love the mountain coaster, the alpine slide, the zip line, and the mountain flyer, which resembles a roller coaster. You'll also find a climbing wall, trampoline, ropes course, inflatables, and more manmade fun. There are ample options to access stunning hiking terrain and views, including the tram to 11,000-foot Hidden Peak. ⊠ *Hwy. 210* ☎ *801/933–2222* ⊕ *www.snowbird.com* ✉ *All-day activity pass $46 (individual ride tickets are also available);$17 tram ride only.*

SPORTS AND THE OUTDOORS

BICYCLING

Snowbird Ski and Summer Resort. Other than a mile-long beginner-to-intermediate single-track trail, the steep, rocky terrain here is not recommended for novices. Advanced mountain bikers can ride the tram at Snowbird Ski and Summer Resort to the top of the mountain and access a network of trails. Adventure addicts should check out the brand new Big Mountain Trail, which is downhill riding only with a 2,900-foot descent over 7½ miles from the top of Hidden Peak down to Snowbird Center. Road cyclists should note that Little Cottonwood Canyon has been part of the most grueling stage of the Tour of Utah bike race several times. Bike rentals are available. Summer tram tickets are $17/day, with family passes and season passes available. ⊠ *Hwy. 210, Snowbird* ☎ *801/933–2222* ⊕ *www.snowbird.com* ⊙ *Open mid-June–Oct.*

HIKING

The upper canyons provide a cool haven during the hot summer months. Wildflowers and wildlife are plentiful, and most trails provide a good balance of shade and sun. Due to high altitude, even fit hikers often become fatigued and dehydrated faster than they would otherwise, so remember to take it easy, rest often, and drink plenty of water.

Sunset Peak. The trailhead for the 4-mile out-and-back hike to Sunset Peak starts high in Little Cottonwood Canyon, above Alta Ski Resort, in Albion Basin. This is a popular area for finding wildflowers in July and August. After an initial steep incline, the trail wanders through flat meadows before it climbs again to Catherine Pass at 10,240 feet. From here intermediate hikes continue along the ridge in both directions. Continue up the trail to the summit of Sunset Peak for breathtaking views of the Heber Valley, Park City, Mount Timpanogos, Big and Little Cottonwood Canyons, and even a part of the Salt Lake Valley. You can alter your route by starting in Little Cottonwood Canyon and ending your hike in neighboring Big Cottonwood Canyon: from Catherine Pass descend into Big Cottonwood Canyon, passing four lakes and finally ending up at Brighton Ski Resort. If you choose to end your hike in Big Cottonwood, make sure you aren't left stranded without a car.

White Pine Trailhead. White Pine Trailhead, ¾ mile below Snowbird on the south side of the road, accesses some excellent easy hikes to overlooks. If you want to keep going on more intermediate trails, continue up the trail to the lakes in White Pine Canyon, Red Pine Canyon, and Maybird Gulch. All of these hikes share a common path for the first mile.

SKIING

FodorśChoice
★
Alta Ski Area. When it comes to skiing, Alta Ski Area is widely acclaimed for both what it has and what it doesn't have. What it has is perhaps the best snow anywhere in the world—up to 500 inches a year, and terrain to match it. What it doesn't have is glitz and pomp. Neither does it have snowboarders. Alta is one of the few resorts left in the country that doesn't allow snowboarding. Sprawling across two large basins, Albion and Wildcat, Alta has a good mixture of expert, intermediate, and beginner terrain. Much of the best skiing (for advanced or expert skiers) requires either finding obscure traverses or doing some hiking: it takes some time to get to know this mountain so if you can find a local to show you around you'll be ahead of the game. Albion Basin's lower slopes have a terrific expanse of novice and lower-intermediate terrain. Rolling meadows, wide trails, and light dry snow create one of the best places in the country for less-skilled skiers to learn to ski powder. Two-hour lessons start at $60. Half-day group lessons for adults and children are available. In addition to downhill skiing, Alta also has 3 km of groomed track for skating and classic skiing (on a separate ticket), plus a good selection of rental equipment at Alta Ski Shop. ☎ 801/359–1078, 801/572–3939 *snow report* ⊕ *www.alta.com* ✉ *Lift tickets $84; Alta Snowbird One Pass $108* ⟋ *2,020-ft vertical drop; 2,200 skiable acres; 25% novice, 40% intermediate, 35% advanced; 2 high-speed quads, 2 triple chairs, 3 double chairs.*

Fodorś Choice
★
Snowbird Ski and Summer Resort. For many skiers, this is as close to heaven as you can get. Soar aboard Snowbird's signature 125-passenger tram straight from the base to the resort's highest point, 11,000 feet above sea level, and then descend into a playground of powder-filled chutes, bowls, and meadows—a leg-burning top-to-bottom run of more than 3,000 vertical feet if you choose. The terrain here is weighted more toward experts—35% of Snowbird is rated black diamond—and if there is a drawback to this resort, it's a lack of beginner terrain. The open bowls, such as Little Cloud and Regulator Johnson, are challenging; the Upper Cirque and the Gad Chutes are hair-raising. On deep-powder days—not uncommon at the Bird—these chutes are exhilarating for skiers who like that sense of a cushioned free fall with every turn.

With a nod to intermediate skiers, Snowbird opened North America's first skier tunnel in 2006. Skiers and boarders now ride a 600-foot magic carpet through the Peruvian Tunnel, reducing the trek to Mineral Basin. If you're looking for intermediate cruising runs, there's the long, meandering Chip's Run. After a day of powder turns, you can lounge on the 3,000-square-foot deck of Creekside Lodge at the base of Gad Valley. Beginner's lessons start at $110 and include lift ticket, tuition, and rentals. ✉ *Hwy. 210, Snowbird* ☎ *801/933–2222, 800/232–9542 lodging reservations, 801/933–2110 special events, 801/933–2100 snow report* 🌐 *www.snowbird.com* 🎟 *Lift tickets $95; Alta Snowbird One Pass $108* ☞ *3,240-ft vertical drop; 2,500 skiable acres; 27% novice, 38% intermediate, 35% advanced; 125-passenger tram, 4 quad lifts, 6 double chairs, 1 gondola, and a skier tunnel with surface lift.*

SKI TOURS

Ski Utah Interconnect Adventure Tour. Strong intermediate and advanced skiers can hook up with the Ski Utah Interconnect Adventure Tour for a guided alpine ski tour that takes you to as many as six resorts (including Brighton, Solitude, Alta, and Snowbird) in a single day, all connected by backcountry ski routes with unparalleled views of the Wasatch Mountains. Guides test your ski ability before departure. The tour includes guide service, lift tickets, lunch, and transportation back to the point of origin. You'll even walk away with a finisher's pin. The Deer Valley Departure Tour operates Sunday, Monday, Tuesday, Wednesday, and Friday; the Snowbird Departure Tour operates Thursday and Saturday. Reservations are required. ☎ *801/534–1907* 🌐 *www.skiutah.com* 🎟 *$325.*

Wasatch Powderbird Guides. If you don't mind paying for it, the best way to find untracked Utah powder is with Wasatch Powderbird Guides. A helicopter drops you on the top of the mountain, and a guide leads you back down. Itineraries are always weather dependent. Call to inquire about departures from Snowbird (Little Cottonwood Canyon) or Canyons (Park City). ☎ *801/742–2800* 🌐 *www.powderbird.com* 🎟 *$1,190 low season, $1,400 high season for full day.*

WHERE TO EAT

$$$ AMERICAN 🍴 **The Aerie Restaurant, Lounge and Sushi Bar.** Spectacular panoramic views through 15-foot windows, white-linen tablecloths, and dark Oriental rugs set a romantic mood at Little Cottonwood's most elegant dining option on the 10th floor of the Cliff Lodge. For a twist, start with the baby kale Caesar salad, or miso if you're coming in from the slopes. With entrées like lobster mac-and-cheese, pleasant surprises dot the menu. The menu and mood are more casual at the sushi bar and lounge. Be prepared to spend some time paging through the wine list, which has over 1,000 bottles. [$] *Average main: $27* ✉ *Snowbird Ski and Summer Resort, Cliff Lodge, Hwy. 210, 10th fl., Snowbird* ☎ *801/933–2160* 🌐 *www.snowbird.com* 🕒 *No lunch.*

$$$$ AMERICAN 🍴 **Shallow Shaft.** For fine American Kobe beef, seafood, poultry, and pasta dishes, Alta's only sit-down restaurant not in a hotel is the place to go. The small interior is cozy, with a sandy color scheme and walls adorned with 19th-century mining tools found on the mountain. The cuisine has a regional focus, with dishes like Willis lamb T-bone and

boneless beef short rib. Though smaller than wine lists at other gourmet mountain eateries, Shallow Shaft's list has been named best in Utah in years past. The restaurant makes its own ice cream daily. It's across the road from Alta Lodge. [$] *Average main: $31* ✉ *10199 E. Hwy. 210, Alta* ☎ *801/742–2177* 🌐 *www.shallowshaft.com* ✍ *Reservations essential* ⏲ *Closed Apr.–Nov. No lunch.*

$$$$ STEAKHOUSE 🍴 **Steak Pit.** Views and food take precedence over interior design at Snowbird's oldest restaurant. The dining room is warm and unpretentious, with some wood paneling and an expanse of glass. The menu is full of well-prepared steak and seafood choices. Whether you opt for the oven-baked scallops or filet mignon, you can't go wrong. A robust wine list offers bottles up to $950 if you feel like splurging. Be sure to save room for their famous mud pie. [$] *Average main: $35* ✉ *Snowbird Plaza Center, Hwy. 210, Snowbird* ☎ *801/933–2181* 🌐 *www.snowbird.com* ⏲ *No lunch.*

WHERE TO STAY

$$$$ B&B/INN 🏨 **Alta Lodge.** This is a homey place, where many families have been booking the same week each year for several generations. **Pros:** close to Alta's steep-and-deep slopes; views of the Wasatch Mountains; pleasant staff. **Cons:** for the price you pay, few amenities and no sense of luxury; no TVs in guest rooms. [$] *Rooms from: $436* ✉ *10230 Little Cottonwood Canyon Rd., Alta* ☎ *801/742–3500, 800/707–2582* 🌐 *www.altalodge.com* 🛏 *53 rooms, 4 dorms* ⏲ *Closed mid-Apr.–May and early Oct.–mid-Nov.* 🍽 *Some meals.*

$$$$ RESORT 🏨 **Cliff Lodge.** The stark concrete walls of this 10-story structure, designed to complement the surrounding granite cliffs, enclose a self-contained village with restaurants, bars, shops, and a high-end, two-story spa. **Pros:** windows facing the Wasatch Range; nice rooftop spa; several eateries and bars on-site. **Cons:** looking down from the top floor may induce some vertigo. [$] *Rooms from: $349* ✉ *Snowbird Ski and Summer Resort, Little Cottonwood Canyon Rd., Snowbird* ☎ *801/933–2222, 800/232–9542* 🌐 *www.snowbird.com* 🛏 *511 rooms* 🍽 *No meals.*

$$$$ RESORT 🏨 **Iron Blosam Lodge.** A utilitarian lobby with a lot of exposed concrete belies attractive condo-style lodging with accommodations and amenities to suit most any traveler's needs, including studios, bedrooms with lofts, and one-bedroom suites. **Pros:** comfortable accommodations; close to the slopes. **Cons:** there's not much happening in the evening; guests booking through Saturday will be required to change rooms due to property's fixed-week ownership. [$] *Rooms from: $304* ✉ *Hwy. 210, Resort Entry 2, Snowbird* ☎ *801/933–2222, 800/232–9542* 🌐 *www.snowbird.com* 🛏 *159 rooms* ⏲ *Closed 1 wk fall and 1 wk late spring* 🍽 *No meals.*

$$$$ HOTEL 🏨 **Rustler Lodge.** Alta's fanciest lodge resembles a traditional full-service hotel and the interior is decidedly upscale. **Pros:** mountain views; on the slopes of Alta Ski Resort; unpretentious service. **Cons:** though avalanches are rare, you might just end up staying an extra night if Mother Nature says so. [$] *Rooms from: $450* ✉ *10380 E. Hwy. 210, Alta* ☎ *801/742–2200, 888/532–2582* 🌐 *www.rustlerlodge.com* 🛏 *85 rooms, 4 dorms* ⏲ *Closed May–mid-Nov.* 🍽 *Some meals.*

NIGHTLIFE AND PERFORMING ARTS
NIGHTLIFE

Almost all the lodges in Little Cottonwood have their own bar or lounge, and tend to be on the quiet side, centering on the après-ski scene.

Aerie Lounge. Lots of couches and a fireplace give the Aerie Lounge a relaxed feel. You can listen to live music every Wednesday, Saturday, and Sunday night during the winter. ⊠ *Snowbird Ski and Summer Resort, Cliff Lodge, Hwy. 210, 10th fl., Snowbird* ☎ *801/933–2222* ⊕ *www.snowbird.com.*

The Sitzmark Club. Upstairs at the Alta Lodge, the Sitzmark Club is a small, comfortable bar that is a favorite with many of the freeskiers who call Little Cottonwood home. ⊠ *Alta Lodge, Hwy. 210, Alta* ☎ *801/742–3500* ⊕ *www.altalodge.com.*

Tram Club. Windows looking into the gears of the Snowbird tram give the Tram Club its name. Swank leather couches, live music, pool tables, big screens, and video games draw a younger crowd. ⊠ *Snowbird Center, Hwy. 210, Snowbird* ☎ *801/933–2222* ⊕ *www.snowbird.com.*

PERFORMING ARTS

Snowbird Ski and Summer Resort. Even after the snow melts, this is one of the top spots to go in the mountains for special events, including the Friday night films, free outdoor music, and two months of Oktoberfest. ⊠ *Hwy. 210, Snowbird* ☎ *801/933–2222* ⊕ *www.snowbird.com.*

ANTELOPE ISLAND STATE PARK

25 miles north of Salt Lake City.

The best way to experience Great Salt Lake is a half-day excursion to Antelope Island, or longer if you like to hike. There's no place in the country like this state park, home to millions of waterfowl and hundreds of bison and antelope, and surrounded by some of the saltiest water on earth. Driving the 7-mile narrow causeway that links the shoreline provides an appropriate sense of isolation. Once you arrive, you can explore the historic ranch house and miles of hiking trails, and even sample a buffalo burger at the small café.

GETTING HERE AND AROUND

Take Exit 332 off Interstate 15, then drive west on Antelope Drive for 7 miles to the park entrance.

EXPLORING

Antelope Island State Park. In the 19th century, settlers grazed sheep and horses on Antelope Island, ferrying them back and forth from the mainland across the waters of the Great Salt Lake. Today, the park is the most developed and scenic spot in which to experience the Great Salt Lake. Hiking and biking trails crisscross the island, and the lack of cover—cottonwood trees provide some of the only shade—gives the place a wide-open feeling and makes for some blistering hot days. You can go saltwater bathing at several beach areas. Since the salinity level of the lake is always greater than that of the ocean, the water is extremely buoyant (and briny smelling)—simply sit down in the water and bob to the surface like a rubber duck. Hot showers at the marina remove the chill and the salt afterward.

The island has historic sites, as well as desert wildlife and birds in their natural habitat. The island's most popular inhabitants are the members of a herd of more than 500 bison descended from 12 brought here in 1893. Each October at the **Buffalo Roundup** more than 250 volunteers on horseback round up the free-roaming animals and herd them to the island's north end to be counted. The island's **Fielding-Garr House**, built in 1848 and now owned by the state, was the oldest continuously inhabited home in Utah until the last resident moved out in 1981. The house displays assorted ranching artifacts, and guided horseback riding is available from the stables next to the house. Be sure to check out the modern visitor center, and sample a bison burger at the stand that overlooks the lake to the north. If you're lucky, you'll hear coyotes howling in the distance. Access to the island is via a 7½-mile causeway. ⊠ *4528 W. 1700 S, Syracuse* ☎ *801/773–2941* ⊕ *www.stateparks.utah. gov* ⊠ *$10 per vehicle, $3 per person* ☉ *Daily 6 am–10 pm.*

SPORTS AND THE OUTDOORS

HIKING

Antelope Island State Park offers plenty of space for the avid hiker to explore, but keep a few things in mind. All trails are also shared by mountain bikers and horseback riders, so keep an eye out for your fellow recreationists—not to mention the occasional bison. Trees are few and far between on the island, making for high exposure to the elements, so bring (and drink) plenty of water and dress appropriately. In the spring, biting insects make bug repellent a must-have. Pick up a trail map at the visitor center.

Once you're prepared, hiking Antelope Island can be a very enjoyable experience. Trails are fairly level except for a few places, where the hot summer sun makes the climb even more strenuous. Mountain ranges, including the Wasatch Front to the east and the Stansbury Mountains directly to the west, provide beautiful background in every direction, though haze sometimes obscures the view. Aromatic sage plants offer shelter for a variety of wildlife, so don't be startled if your next step flushes a chukar partridge, horned lark, or jackrabbit. A bobcat is a rarely seen island resident that will likely keep its distance.

MOUNTAIN AND ROAD BIKING

Bountiful Bicycle Center. Road bikers race along Legacy Highway, then the causeway to Antelope Island and through the park, which also offers superb mountain-bike trails. Bountiful Bicycle Center rents mountain and road bikes and offers great advice on trails. ⊠ *2482 S. U.S. 89, Woods Cross* ☎ *801/295–6711* ⊕ *www.bountifulbicycle.com.*

WHERE TO EAT

You'll pass a smorgasbord of fast-food outlets in Davis County north of Salt Lake City, including most of the national chain restaurants and a few that are found mainly in Utah. Unless you go as far north as Ogden, there aren't too many choices.

$ ✕ **Island Buffalo Grill.** Some people may have an issue with eating buffalo
BURGER   burgers on a bison sanctuary, but, well, they don't know what they're

missing. No frills here, but there is an unparalleled view. Ⓢ *Average main: $8* ⊠ *Antelope Island Rd., Syracuse* ☎ *801/897–3452* ☺ *Closed Nov.–Feb. No dinner.*

$$ **✗ Roosters Brewing Company.** Even in conservative Davis County north
BURGER   of Salt Lake City, you can find one couple with a passion for beer and
quality brewpub fare. The original Roosters is farther north in Ogden,
but for nearly a decade, the Layton location has served the array of
Roosters beers (from stouts to pale ales), accompanied by individual-
size pizzas, full-meal salads, burgers, and pasta. This is a great stopping
point on the way to or from Antelope Island. Ⓢ *Average main: $15*
⊠ *748 W. Heritage Park Blvd., The suburbs, Layton* ☎ *801/774–9330*
⊕ *www.roostersbrewingco.com.*

THANKSGIVING POINT

28 miles south of Salt Lake City.

Heading south toward ultraconservative Utah County (home of Brigham
Young University), make Thanksgiving Point your first stop. Founded
by WordPerfect computing giant Alan Ashton, Thanksgiving Point is
home to museums, gardens, championship golf, restaurants, and a movie
theater.

GETTING HERE AND AROUND

Thanksgiving Point is centrally located about halfway between Salt
Lake City and Provo just off Interstate 15 at the Point of the Mountain.
Look for the water tower, which can be seen from the freeway. From
Salt Lake City, take Interstate 15 south to Exit 284 (Alpine/Highland).
Turn right and proceed west to the light. Turn left onto Thanksgiving
Way and proceed ½ mile to Water Tower Plaza.

EXPLORING

Thanksgiving Point. Founded by the Ashton family (Alan Ashton founded
computer-software giant WordPerfect), Thanksgiving Point is now an
ever-evolving destination for all visitors to enjoy. Wander among 60
dinosaur skeletons in the Museum of Ancient Life; play golf on an
18-hole Johnny Miller–designed course; or meditate in 55 acres of
carefully landscaped gardens. There are also farm animals, shops, res-
taurants, and a movie theater. The museum is open year-round, but gar-
dens and other attractions are seasonal. ⊠ *3003 N. Thanksgiving Way,
Lehi* ☎ *801/768–2300, 888/672–6040* ⊕ *www.thanksgivingpoint.com*
🖺 *$12 museum, $15 gardens, $7 Farm Country* ☺ *Mon.–Sat. 10–8.*

SHOPPING
PLAZAS AND MALLS

Outlets at Traverse Mountain. Utah's newest outlet mall has some of the
top names in retail, including Nike, Gap, J. Crew, Polo Ralph Lauren,
Coach, and Michael Kors. ⊠ *3700 N. Cabelas Ave., Lehi* ☎ *801/901–
1200* ⊕ *www.outletsattraversemountain.com.*

TIMPANOGOS CAVE NATIONAL MONUMENT

36 miles from Salt Lake City.

Although visitors of all ages and abilities can find easy exploring in the canyons surrounding the Wasatch Front, Timpanogos Cave is suitable only for robust and prepared hikers. The journey is well worth it.

GETTING HERE AND AROUND

From Salt Lake City, take Interstate 15 to Exit 284 (Alpine/Highland exit), then turn east on State Highway 92 for 10 miles to the monument. The highway runs east—west through the monument.

EXPLORING

Timpanogos Cave National Monument. Soaring to 11,750 feet, Mount Timpanogos is the centerpiece of a wilderness area of the same name and towers over Timpanogos Cave National Monument along Highway 92 within American Fork Canyon. After a strenuous hike up the paved 1½-mile trail to the entrance, you can explore three caves connected by two man-made tunnels. Stalactites, stalagmites, and other formations make the three-hour round-trip hike and tour worth the effort. No refreshments are available on the trail or at the cave, and the cave temperature is 45°F throughout the year, so bring water and warm clothes. Although there's some lighting inside the caves, a flashlight will make your explorations more interesting; it will also come in handy should you have to head back down the trail at dusk. These popular tours are often sold out; to guarantee your place on Saturday and holidays, purchase tickets in advance. ✉ *Hwy. 92, 3 miles from American Fork, American Fork* ☎ *801/756–5239 cave info, 801/756–5238 advance tickets* ⊕ *www.nps.gov/tica* 💲 *$7* ⊙ *Early May–Oct., daily 7–5:30.*

OFF THE BEATEN PATH

Alpine Loop Scenic Byway. Beyond Timpanogos Cave, Highway 92 climbs up American Fork Canyon then branches off to loop behind Mount Timpanogos. This twisting road presents stunning scenery before dropping into Provo Canyon to the south. The 9-mile Timpooneke Trail and the 8-mile Aspen Trail, leave the byway for the summit. Closed in winter, the Alpine Loop isn't suitable for motor homes and trucks pulling trailers. A more direct route to Provo Canyon is U.S. 189 east from Orem.

PARK CITY AND THE SOUTHERN WASATCH

Updated by
Caitlin Martz

The Wasatch Range shares the same desert climate as the Great Basin, which it rims, but these craggy peaks rising to more than 11,000 feet stall storms moving in from the Pacific causing massive precipitations. The result is a 160-mile stretch of verdure that is home to 2 million people, or three-fourths of all Utahns. Although its landscape is crisscrossed by freeways and dappled by towns large and small, the Wasatch still beckons adventurers with its alpine forests and windswept canyons. Those who visit follow in the footsteps of Native Americans and in the wagon-wheel ruts of Mormon pioneers and miners.

Where three geologically distinct regions—the Rocky Mountain, the Colorado Plateau, and the Basin and Range provinces—converge, the Wasatch Range combines characteristics of each. You'll find broad glacial canyons with towering granite walls, stream-cut gorges through purple, tan, and green shale, and red-rock bluffs and valleys.

Uppermost in many people's minds is the legendary skiing, but this is truly a year-round destination. Bright-blue lakes afford fantastic boating and water sports, and some of the West's best trout streams flow from the high country. Add picturesque mountain communities, miles of hiking and biking trails, and spectacular alpine scenery, and you have a vacation that's hard to beat.

You can also find cultural activities and entertainment at every turn. The Sundance Film Festival, hosted by actor-director Robert Redford, attracts movie stars and independent filmmakers from all over. Major recording artists of all types play indoor and outdoor venues, and nightlife abounds in the city and resorts, with an increasing number of nightclubs and music venues.

ORIENTATION AND PLANNING

GETTING ORIENTED

Each canyon of the Wasatch is different in topography and scenery. The back (eastern) side of the range is rural, with high-mountain pastures, farms, and small towns, whereas the front side is a long stretch of metropolis. This is not an area that lends itself to checking off points along a straight line. You'll enjoy it more if you let it unfold in a series of loops and meanders, using the larger canyons to move back and forth between the two sides of the range.

TOP REASONS TO GO

Outdoor fun: Regardless of the season, Park City is the epicenter of mountain adventure. You come here to play, not to watch, whether your speed is a hot-air balloon float or an 80 mph bobsled run.

Three top-tier resorts: No place in North America has three resorts so close to one another, not to mention as dynamic, luxurious, and unique as Deer Valley, Park City Mountain, and Canyons Resort, and it's not only skiing on offer—the resorts provide year-round adventures and hospitality.

Olympic spirit: If you think you can feel the legacy of the 2002 Olympic Winter Games on Park City, it's because this town probably contains more Olympians per capita than any town in the country, if not the world, and nearly every U.S. winter

Olympian trains in Park City at some point every four years.

Old Town Park City: First laid out by silver miners in the late 1800s, Park City's historic Main Street has dozens of fine restaurants, bars, galleries, and boutiques. Though always vibrant, its hub is really hopping during big events like the Sundance Film Festival and Kimball Arts Festival.

Sundance Resort: At the base of Mount Timpanogos, Robert Redford's intimate resort pays homage to art and nature, with artists in residence creating works before your eyes and the chance to bond with Mother Nature. You can ski here, too, but mostly it's the calendar of performances and speakers that's the big attraction.

Park City and the Wasatch Back. This is the hospitality heart of the mountains, and you'll be spending a good deal of your time in Park City whatever your budget. There's everything from fine dining on Main Street to athlete training and shows at Utah Olympic Park to nonstop year-round activity at the resorts, with Park City Mountain and Canyons set to combine into one giant resort in 2015. Mountain valleys north and south of Park City are home to stunning wildlife.

South of Salt Lake City. It's worth venturing south to the glorious Sundance Resort for a slice of rural Utah. Even farther south, Provo, home to Brigham Young University, counters Park City's "Sin City" reputation with an overwhelming Mormon temperance.

PLANNING

WHEN TO GO

One of the best reasons to vacation in the Wasatch is that a short drive from the valleys to the mountains will make you feel that you're getting two seasons in a single day. Winter is long in the mountains (ski resorts buzz from November to as late as April) but much more manageable in the valleys. The snow stops falling in April or May, and a month later the temperatures are in the 80s. (Locals joke that if you don't like the weather in spring, wait a minute and it will change.) If you don't mind sometimes-capricious weather, spring and fall are opportune seasons to visit. Rates drop and crowds lessen. Spring may be the shortest season,

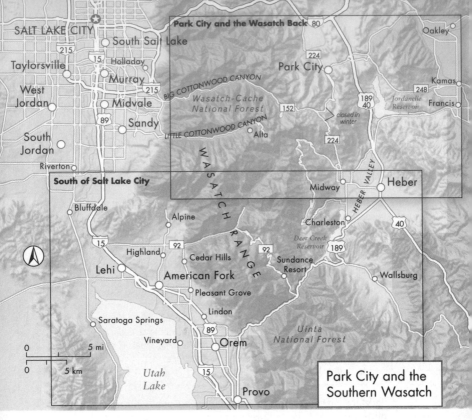

Park City and the Wasatch Back

Park City and the
Southern Wasatch

but it's one of the most interesting. You can ski in the morning with snow still piling up at the ski resorts, and then play 18 holes of golf or hike through fields of wildflowers in the afternoon in any of the Wasatch Valleys or foothills. Spring is also a good time for fishing, rafting on rivers swollen with snowmelt, birding, and wildlife viewing.

In summer, water-sports enthusiasts of all stripes flock to the region's reservoirs, alpine lakes, rivers, and streams to fish, water-ski, windsurf, sail, stand-up paddleboard, kayak, and canoe. The Wasatch Mountains also draw people on foot, bike, and horseback seeking respite from the heat of the valley from June through Labor Day.

Fall's colors rival those of New England. On a walk through a forest or drive along a scenic route, you'll see the yellows, reds, pinks, oranges, and golds of aspens, maples, and oaks against the deep evergreen of fir and spruce. A fall tradition here is to drive along the Alpine Loop east of Provo or up Pine Canyon out of the Heber Valley.

PLANNING YOUR TIME

At your home base in Park City you can ski, snowboard, hike, mountain bike, or simply take in the scenery at the trio of local resorts. Head east to Heber City or Midway for a round of golf at Wasatch State Park, cross-country skiing at Soldier Hollow, or fly-fishing on the Provo River. Plan at least a half-day trip to Sundance Resort. For a glimpse of Utah's

Mormon culture, spend a day in the college town of Provo, particularly if home team Brigham Young University is playing rival University of Utah. Warm-weather drives along the Alpine Loop or Mirror Lake scenic byways are great opportunities for snapping photos of mountain vistas and wildlife.

GETTING HERE AND AROUND

AIR TRAVEL

Commercial air traffic flies in and out of Salt Lake International Airport, which is less than an hour from all destinations in the Wasatch and 7 miles northwest of downtown Salt Lake City. The airport is served by Alaska, American, Delta, SkyWest, Southwest, jetBlue, Frontier, US Airways, and United. Provo Airport has commercial flights from Los Angeles, Oakland, and Mesa, Arizona, on Allegiant Airlines. Heber's airport is open to private planes only.

Contacts Salt Lake City International Airport ⊠ *776 N. Terminal Dr., Salt Lake City* ☎ *801/575–2400* ⊕ *www.slcairport.com.*

CAR TRAVEL

Highway travel around the region is quick and easy. The major routes in the area include the transcontinental I–80, which connects Salt Lake City and Park City; and U.S. 40/189, which connects southwest Wyoming, Utah, and northwest Colorado via Park City, Heber City, and Provo. Along larger highways, roadside stops with restrooms, fast-food restaurants, and sundries stores are well spaced. Scenic routes and lookout points are clearly marked, enabling you to slow down and pull over to take in the views. Off the main highways, roads range from well-paved multilane blacktop routes to barely graveled backcountry trails. Watch out for wildlife on the roads just about anywhere in Utah.

Road Conditions Utah Highway Patrol, Mirror Lake area ☎ *435/655–3445.* **Utah Road Condition Information** ☎ *511 Salt Lake City area, 866/511–8824 within Utah* ⊕ *www.udot.utah.gov.*

SHUTTLE TRAVEL

Shuttles such as All Resort Express, Canyon Transportation, and Park City Transportation are the best way to travel between the airport and Park City, and fares are around $39–$45. A free, efficient Park City transit system operates a reliable network of bus routes, connecting Old Town, the local ski resorts, Kimball Junction, and most neighborhoods.

Shuttle Contacts All Resort Express ☎ *435/649–3999, 877/658–3999* ⊕ *www.allresort.com.* **Canyon Transportation** ☎ *801/255–1841* ⊕ *www. canyontransport.com.* **Park City Direct Shuttle** ☎ *435/649–6648, 866/655–3010* ⊕ *www.parkcitydirectshuttle.com.* **Park City Transportation** ☎ *435/649–8567, 800/637–3803* ⊕ *www.parkcitytransportation.com.* **Premier Transportation** ☎ *435/640–3144* ⊕ *www.premier-transportation.com.*

RESTAURANTS

American cuisine dominates the Wasatch dining scene, with great steaks, barbecue, and traditional Western fare. There's also an abundance of good seafood, which the busier eateries fly in daily from the West Coast. Park City caters to a discriminating clientele with upscale restaurants ranging from Swiss to Japanese, French, and Mexican. Restaurant hours vary seasonally, so it's a good idea to call ahead. Reservations are always a good idea, but are essential during winter holiday weekends and the Sundance Film Festival. ■TIP➜ **Ask about two-for-ones.** Park City restaurants offer great deals, such as two-for-one entrées from spring to fall, so check the local newspaper for coupons or ask your concierge which eateries are offering discounts.

HOTELS

Chain hotels and motels dot I–15 all along the Wasatch Front and nearly always have availability. Every small town on the back side of the range has at least one good bed-and-breakfast, and most towns have both independent and chain motels. Condominiums dominate Park City lodging, but you also find high-end hotels, luxurious lodges, and well-run bed-and-breakfast inns. All this luxury means prices here tend to be higher than in other areas in the state during the winter. Prices drop significantly in the warmer months, when package deals or special rates are offered. Lodging in Provo tends to be most expensive during the week. Make reservations well in advance for busy ski holidays like Christmas, Presidents' Day, and Martin Luther King Jr. Day, and during January's Sundance Film Festival. As the mountain country is often on the cool side, lodgings at higher elevations generally don't have air-conditioning. *Hotel reviews have been shortened. For full information, visit Fodors.com.*

WHAT IT COSTS			
$	$$	$$$	$$$$
Restaurants	under $12	$12–$20	$21–$30	over $30
Hotels	under $100	$100–$150	$151–$200	over $200

Restaurant prices are the average cost of a main course at dinner or, if dinner is not served, at lunch. Hotel prices are the lowest cost of a standard double room in high season.

VISITOR INFORMATION

Ski Utah ✉ *150 W. 500 S, Salt Lake City* ☎ *801/534–1779, 800/754–8824* ⊕ *www.skiutah.com.*

Utah County Convention and Visitors Bureau ✉ *220 W. Center St., Suite 100, Provo* ☎ *801/851–2100, 800/222–8824* ⊕ *www.utahvalley.org.*

PARK CITY AND THE WASATCH BACK

The best-known areas of the Wasatch Mountains lie east of Salt Lake City. Up and over Parley's Canyon via I–80 you'll find the sophisticated mountain town of Park City, with its three ski resorts and myriad summer attractions.

After silver was discovered in Park City in 1868, it quickly became a rip-roaring mining town with more than two-dozen saloons and a thriving red-light district. In the process, it earned the nickname "Sin City." A fire destroyed many of the town's buildings in 1898; this, combined with declining mining fortunes in the early 1900s, caused most of the residents to pack up and leave. It wasn't until 1946 that its current livelihood began to take shape in the form of the small Snow Park ski hill, which opened where Deer Valley Resort now sits.

Park City once again profited from the generosity of the mountains as skiing became popular. In 1963 Treasure Mountain Resort began operations with its skier's subway—an underground train and hoist system that ferried skiers to the mountain's summit via old mining tunnels. Facilities were upgraded over time, and Treasure Mountain became the Park City Mountain Resort. Although it has a mind-numbing collection of condominiums, at Park City's heart is a historic downtown that rings with the authenticity of a real town with real roots.

3

GETTING HERE AND AROUND

If you're arriving at Salt Lake City, a rental car or shuttle bus will get you to Park City in about 35 minutes. Park City has a free transit system running between neighborhoods and to the ski resorts. It operates from roughly 6 am to midnight in summer and winter. The schedule is more limited in fall and spring, so be sure to check schedules at the Transit Center on Swede Alley or on the buses.

Old Town is walkable, but the rest of greater Park City is best explored by bicycle in the spring, summer, and fall. More than 400 miles of bike trails help Park City earn accolades as one of the top cycling communities in the world. Automobile traffic is relatively minimal and limited to slowdowns during morning and evening commutes and the post-ski exodus from the resorts. There are several local taxi businesses.

ESSENTIALS

Visitor Information **Park City Visitor Information Center** ⊠ *1794 Olympic Pkwy., Kimball Junction* ☎ *435/658–9616, 435/649–6100* ⊕ *www.visitparkcity. com* ⊠ *Park City Museum, 528 Main St.* ☎ *435/649–7457* ⊕ *www.visitparkcity. com.*

FESTIVALS

Robert Redford's Sundance Film Festival comes to Park City every January, but the city hosts a number of other festivals and events that might sway your decision about when to visit.

FAMILY **Canyons Summer Concert Series.** Rock, reggae, funk, and country bands draw fans of all ages to the grass-slope amphitheater at the base of Canyons Resort in July and August. Food vendors and family activities surround the Resort Village, and picnics are welcome. ⊠ *4000 Canyons Resort Dr.* ☎ *435/649–5400* ⊕ *www.canyonsresort.com.*

Deer Valley Music Festival. Everything from Utah Symphony performances to country music features in this concert series. Big names like Willie Nelson, Bonnie Raitt, Chris Isaak, and Judy Collins have graced the outdoor amphitheater, which sits on the resort's beginner ski area. ☎ *801/533–5626, 801/533–6683 tickets* ⊕ *www.deervalleymusicfestival.org.*

FAMILY **Independence Day Celebration.** A traditional celebration, complete with a pancake breakfast, parade down Main Street, fireworks, and all-day activities in City Park, is a sure sign that summer has arrived. It culminates in fireworks that illuminate the sky over Old Town. ☎ *435/649–6100* ⊕ *www.visitparkcity.com.*

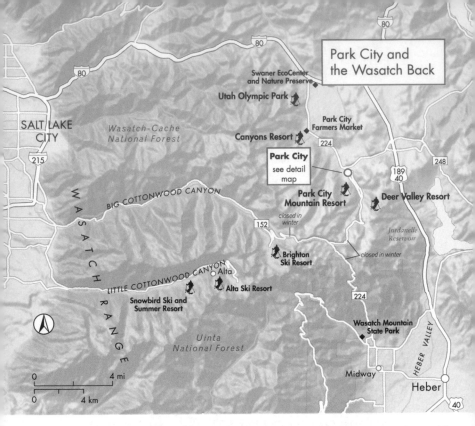

Park City and
the Wasatch Back

FAMILY **Miner's Day.** The end of the summer season is heralded with an old-fashioned parade down Main Street and the Rotary Club's "Running of the Balls"—with golf balls in place of Pamplona-style bulls—followed by miners' competitions of mucking and drilling at Library Park. This Labor Day tradition is a Park City favorite. ☎ 435/649–6100 ⊕ www.visitparkcity.com.

Fodor'sChoice **Park City Food & Wine Classic.** Held in July, this festival offers tastings
★ of hundreds of wines from seemingly every continent, paired with great food, educational seminars, and gourmet dinners around town. It culminates in a grand tasting at Canyons Resort. ■TIP➔ It's increasingly popular, and many events now sell out in advance, so plan ahead. ☎ 877/328–2783 ⊕ www.parkcityfoodandwineclassic.com.

Park City Kimball Arts Festival. Celebrating visual and culinary art, this festival, held the first weekend in August, is the biggest summer event in town. More than 200 artists from all over North America exhibit and offer their work to 40,000 festival attendees. Culinary vendors and beer and wine gardens offer plenty of refreshment to art lovers, and live music is around every corner. ⊠ Main St. ☎ 435/649–8882 ⊕ www.parkcitykimballartsfestival.org.

Fodor'sChoice **Savor the Summit.** When more than 30 of Park City's restaurants—
★ from gourmet to on-the-go—take over Main Street for the Saturday

nearest the Summer Solstice in June, it's a spectacle of food, drink, and music that is unmatched in the country. Restaurateurs line the length of Main Street with a mile-long "Grande Table," creating the largest dinner party you'll witness in Utah. Pick one restaurant (many sell out) and be treated to a special menu, often with a theme related to Park City's colorful history. Visit the website for participating restaurants and reservation information. ☒ *Main St.* ☎ *435/640–7921* ⊕ *www. savorthesummit.com.*

Fodor's Choice
★
Sundance Film Festival. For 10 days each January, Park City morphs into a mountain version of Hollywood as movie stars and film executives gather for the internationally recognized Sundance Film Festival, hosted by Robert Redford's Sundance Institute. In addition to panels, tributes, premieres, and screenings of independent films at various venues in Park City, Sundance, Ogden, and Salt Lake City, there are music and culinary events as well.

■ TIP➜ Book your hotel months in advance. Skip the rental car and use the free shuttle. Park City's legendary ski slopes empty out while the filmgoers pack the screenings, so build in a day of crowd-free skiing. ☎ *435/658– 3456* ⊕ *www.sundance.org/festival.*

EXPLORING

Park City and the surrounding area hosted the lion's share of skiing and sliding events during the 2002 Winter Olympic Games, and the excited spirit of the Games is still evident around town. Visitors often enjoy activities at the Utah Olympic Park or simply taking candid photos at various memorable sports venues.

The city also serves as an excellent base camp for summer activities. Hiking trails are plentiful. A scenic drive over Guardsman Pass is now mostly paved and passable for most vehicles, providing incredible mountain vistas. There are top-rated golf courses, hot-air ballooning is popular, and mountain bikers find the ski slopes and old mining roads truly exceptional pedaling. With so much to offer both summer and winter visitors, dozens of hotels of all levels have sprung up to complement the three resorts, each with its own scene.

All three Park City ski resorts consistently earn high skier-snowboarder rankings. Whereas Park City Mountain Resort is known for its central location, superb family amenities, and gnarly parks and pipes for snowboarders and free skiers, Deer Valley is in a peaceful spot at the edge of town and is renowned for its creature comforts—and its prohibition on snowboarding. Canyons Resort has grown rapidly and is now Utah's largest resort. A city-run free shuttle-bus system serves the three resorts.

TOP ATTRACTIONS

FAMILY **Park City Mountain Resort.** In the warmer months, the resort transforms itself into a mountain amusement park, with attractions such as the Alpine Slide, zip lines, Alpine Coaster, and a climbing wall. The Alpine Slide begins with a chairlift ride up the mountain, and then special sleds carry sliders down 3,000 feet of winding concrete and fiberglass track at speeds controlled by each rider. Two zip lines offer high-flying

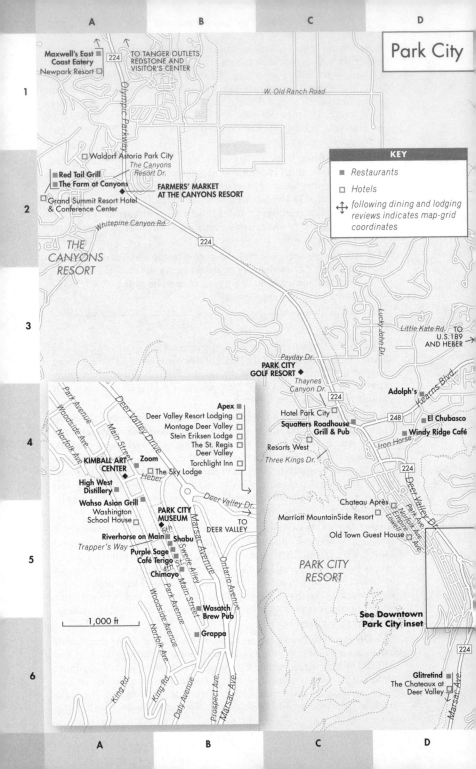

Park City

KEY

- ■ Restaurants
- □ Hotels
- ✛ following dining and lodging reviews indicates map-grid coordinates

Maxwell's East Coast Eatery
Newpark Resort
224
TO TANGER OUTLETS, REDSTONE AND VISITOR'S CENTER

W. Old Ranch Road

Olympic Parkway

□ Waldorf Astoria Park City
The Canyons Resort Dr.

■ Red Tail Grill
■ The Farm at Canyons
FARMERS' MARKET AT THE CANYONS RESORT

□ Grand Summit Resort Hotel & Conference Center

Whitepine Canyon Rd.

THE CANYONS RESORT

224

Little Kate Rd.
TO U.S.189 AND HEBER

Lucky John Dr.

Payday Dr.
PARK CITY GOLF RESORT ◆
Thaynes Canyon Dr.

Kearns Blvd.

Adolph's

224

Hotel Park City □
Squatters Roadhouse Grill & Pub

248
El Chubasco

Windy Ridge Café

Resorts West
Three Kings Dr.

Iron Horse

224

Deer Valley Dr.

Chateau Après □
Marriott MountainSide Resort □
Old Town Guest House □

Park Ave.
Norfolk Ave.
Empire Ave.
Lowell Ave.

PARK CITY RESORT

See Downtown Park City inset

224

Glitretind ■
The Chateaux at Deer Valley

Marsac Ave.

Downtown Park City inset

Park Avenue
Woodside Ave.
Norfolk Ave.

Deer Valley Drive
Main Street

Apex ■
Deer Valley Resort Lodging □
Montage Deer Valley □
Stein Eriksen Lodge □
The St. Regis Deer Valley □
Torchlight Inn □

KIMBALL ART CENTER ◆
Zoom ■
□ The Sky Lodge
Heber

High West Distillery ◆

Wahso Asian Grill ■
Washington School House □

PARK CITY MUSEUM ◆

Deer Valley Dr.
TO DEER VALLEY

Riverhorse on Main ■
6th
Shabu ■

Trapper's Way
Purple Sage ■
Café Terigo ■
4th St.
Chimayo ■

Swede's Alley
Main Street
Marsac Avenue
Ontario Avenue

■ Wasatch Brew Pub

1,000 ft

■ Grappa

Woodside Avenue
Park Avenue
Norfolk Ave.
King Rd.
King Rd.
Daly Avenue
Prospect Avenue
Marsac Ave.

adrenaline rushes as riders strap into a harness suspended from a cable. The gravity-propelled Alpine Coaster (which operates year-round) zooms through aspen-lined twists and turns at speeds up to 35 mph. The climbing wall features five different routes from which to choose. There's also a miniature golf course, trampolines, an adventure zone for younger children, and some of the West's best lift-served mountain biking and hiking. ✉ *1345 Lowell Ave.* ☎ *435/649–8111, 800/222–7275* ⊕ *www.parkcitymountain.com.*

Park City Museum. A must-see for history buffs, this museum is housed in the former library, city hall, and the Bell Tower. With a two-story scale model of the 19th-century Ontario Mine, a 20th-century gondola hanging overhead, and the old jail below, this is an authentic tribute to Park City's mining and skiing past. Climb aboard a re-created Union Pacific train car, hold on to a quivering and noisy jack drill for a feel of the mining experience, and, if you dare, step inside a jail cell. Tours of historic Main Street also depart from here. ✉ *528 Main St.* ☎ *435/649–7457* ⊕ *www.parkcityhistory.org* ⊠ *$10* ⊘ *June–Oct. and early Dec.–Mar., Mon.–Sat. 10–7, Sun. noon–6; Apr., May, and Nov.–early Dec., Mon.–Sat. 11–6, Sun. noon–6 (call to check off-season hrs).*

FAMILY
Fodor's Choice
★

Utah Olympic Park. An exciting legacy of the 2002 Winter Olympics, this is a mecca of bobsled, skeleton, luge, and ski jumping. As it is one of the only places in America where you can try these sports, you might have to wait your turn behind U.S. Olympians and aspirants who train here year-round. In summer or winter, screaming down the track in a bobsled at nearly 80 mph with a professional driver is a ride you will never forget. In summer, check out the freestyle ski jumpers doing flips and spins into a splash pool and Nordic jumpers soaring to soft landings on a synthetic outrun. Ride the zip lines or Alpine Slide, or explore the adventure course. There's also an interactive ski museum and an exhibit on the Olympics; guided tours are offered year-round, or you can take a self-guided tour. ✉ *3419 Olympic Pkwy.* ☎ *435/658–4200* ⊕ *www.utaholympiclegacy.com* ⊠ *Museum and self-guided tours free, guided tours $10* ⊘ *Hrs vary; call for details. Zip line and slide closed in winter.*

WORTH NOTING

Kimball Art Center. A thriving nonprofit community art center, this venue hosts national and regional exhibitions, sells art supplies, and hosts special events. ✉ *638 Park Ave.* ☎ *435/649–8882* ⊕ *www.kimballartcenter.org* ⊠ *Free* ⊘ *Mon.–Thurs. 10–5, Fri. 10–7, Sat. noon–7, Sun. noon–5.*

Park Silly Sunday Market. A funky and constantly changing assortment of artisans, entertainers, and culinary vendors transform Old Town into a street festival complete with beer garden and Bloody Mary bar on Sunday, June through September. The Silly Market strives to be a no-waste event with everything recycled or composted. Look for the free bike valet to park your ride while you walk through the crowds. ✉ *Lower Main St.* ☎ *435/901–9722* ⊕ *www.parksillysundaymarket.com.*

Swaner Preserve and EcoCenter. Home to an array of birds (most notably sandhill cranes) and small critters (like the spotted frog), as well as more elusive larger inhabitants such as foxes, deer, elk, moose, and coyotes, this 1,200-acre preserve is both a bird-watchers' paradise and

CLOSE UP

Alf Engen's Ski Dream

Skiers racing down the runs at one of Utah's many resorts or enjoying a tram or chairlift ride to the top of the Wasatch Mountains might want to consider how much they take for granted. In 1930, when Norwegian Alf Engen came to Utah to compete for the world ski-jumping title, skiers hiked to the top.

The eight-time ski-jumping champion liked Utah's mountains so much that he made his home here. He went on to scope out possible runs at what became the Alta Ski Resort. The Collins lift, the nation's second (the first was in Sun Valley, Idaho), was constructed at Alta in 1939, and lift tickets cost 25¢ a ride or $1.50 a day. Alf also had a hand in designing Brighton and Snowbasin. His legacy lives on at Snowbasin, site of the 2002 Winter Olympics alpine downhill events.

Although Alf left competition at age 55, sharing his love for winter sports was a lifelong passion. He trained soldiers for service in the Alps during World War II, coached the U.S. Olympic ski team in 1948, and spent five decades as an instructor at Alta's ski school. His enthusiasm for life and skiing infected everyone. One look at the smiling senior citizen inspired many skiers to keep in shape. By the time Alf died in 2001 at age 90, skiing had become a major industry in Utah, with 14 resorts. Alta remains the most historic and the closest to his vision. Because of this vision, there's a ski museum named in his honor at the Utah Olympic Park in Park City.

an example of land restoration in action. Naturalist-led walks, snowshoe tours in winter, and other environmentally friendly events are hosted by this nonprofit throughout the year. The EcoCenter is filled with interactive exhibits, such as a climbing wall with microphones emitting the sounds of the wetlands as climbers move through habitats. The facility serves as an exhibit in itself, given its eco-friendly construction, incorporating everything from recycled denim insulation to solar panels. More than 10 miles of hiking and biking trails encompass both sides of I–80. ⊠ *1258 Center Dr., Newpark* ☎ *435/649–1767* ⊕ *www. swanerecocenter.org* ✉ *Free (donation appreciated)* ⊙ *Memorial Day–Labor Day, Mon.–Sat. 10–4; day after Labor Day–day before Memorial Day, Wed.–Sat. 10–4.*

SPORTS AND THE OUTDOORS

BICYCLING

In 2012, Park City was the first community ever designated a Gold Level Ride Center by the International Mountain Bicycling Association, thanks in large part to the relentless work of the Mountain Trails Foundation, which oversees and maintains more than 400 miles of area trails. The accolade is based upon bike shops, trail access, variety, and more. Pick up a map at any local bike shop or get details from the Mountain Trails Foundation (☎ *435/649–6839* ⊕ *www.mountaintrails.org*). With so many miles of public trails and smooth blacktop roads stretching in every direction, it's no wonder Park City is home to a number of the international elite of mountain and road biking. You can join local road or mountain bikers most nights in the summer for free group rides sponsored by Park City bike shops.

Canyons Bike Park. With the opening of the only lift-served bike park in Utah in 2012, Canyons Resort has unique mountain-biking terrain that riders of all levels will want to try. Choose from a half-dozen downhill flow and jump trails of varying difficulty. The natural flow of the trails will carry you and your mountain bike through trees, over bridges and obstacles, and through grassy meadows. Canyons Bike Academy offers lessons with certified instructors for those looking for an introduction to the sport, and those merely looking to refine their skills and explore the trails. Bikes and protective padding are all available in the rental shop. ⊠ *4000 Canyons Resort Dr.* ☎ *435/649–5400* ⊕ *www.canyonsresort.com.*

Canyons Resort. Utah's largest ski resort transforms into a summer adventure land for cyclists, with a lift-served bike park and miles of cross-country and downhill trails. Bike rentals are available. ⊠ *4000 Canyons Resort Dr.* ☎ *435/615–3442* ⊕ *www.canyonsresort.com.*

Cole Sport. Road bikers of all abilities can ride with a pack each Monday evening from June to mid-September from this shop. You can rent mountain and road bikes here, too; be ready to ride at 6 pm. ⊠ *1615 Park Ave.* ☎ *435/649–4806, 800/345–2938* ⊕ *www.colesport.com.*

Deer Valley Resort. For a little help getting uphill, Deer Valley Resort offers lift-assisted mountain biking or hiking daily mid-June to September. Bike rentals are available at Snow Park Lodge, Silver Lake Lodge, and Yurt at Empire Canyon. Deer Valley Mountain Bike School offers tuition and guided tours in a variety of public and private packages from mid-June to Labor Day. ⊠ *Deer Valley Dr. S* ☎ *435/649–1000, 800/424–3337* ⊕ *www.deervalley.com.*

Jans Mountain Outfitters. When the snow melts, Jans has everything you need to hit the road on two wheels. Whether you're into mountain bikes, road bikes, or cruisers, stop by to rent or demo something new, or to tune your own wheels. ⊠ *1600 Park Ave.* ☎ *435/649–4949, 800/745–1020* ⊕ *www.jans.com.*

Park City Mountain Resort. Mountain bikers and hikers can ride several chairs here to access the on-mountain trail complex. An all-day lift pass is about $23. Equipment rentals are available. ⊠ *1310 Lowell Ave.* ☎ *435/649–8111, 800/222–7275* ⊕ *www.parkcitymountain.com.*

Silver Star Ski & Sport. Look for Vidalia and Tallulah, the English and French bulldogs at Silver Star Ski & Sport. While the dogs watch the shop, friendly staff help find the best bike to suit your needs. In addition to the retail area of the store offering top-of-the-line gear and clothing, Silver Star offers cruiser, road, and mountain-bike rentals. ⊠ *1825 Three Kings Dr.* ☎ *435/645–7827* ⊕ *www.silverstarskiandsport.com.*

White Pine Touring. Every Thursday in summer, mountain bikers of all levels gather at 6 pm for a free, guided mountain-bike ride. On the last Thursday of June, July, and August, the White Pine guides prepare a barbecue, too. There's also a women-only ride on Tuesday. For both rides, meet at the shop at 6 pm—earlier if you need to rent a bike. Guided road-biking, mountain-biking, climbing, and hiking tours are also available throughout the summer. ⊠ *1790 Bonanza Dr.* ☎ *435/649–8710* ⊕ *www.whitepinetouring.com.*

FLY-FISHING

The mountain-fed waters of the Provo and Weber rivers and several smaller streams near Park City are prime trout habitat.

Jans Mountain Outfitters. The entire upstairs of this store is dedicated solely to fly-fishing, and knowledgeable staff will help you find the best equipment and gear for your time on the river. Specializing in trout fishing, guides lead fly-fishing excursions year-round in nearby rivers, rent equipment, and provide insight and advice to the local area. Jans is the only outfitter in town with access to private waters. Guides also give free casting lessons at the Deer Valley ponds on Monday at 5 pm from Memorial Day to Labor Day. ⊠ *1600 Park Ave.* ☎ *435/649–4949* ⊕ *www.jans.com.*

Park City Fly Shop. See Chris Kunkel, the owner of this shop, for good advice, guide service, and a modest selection of fly-fishing necessities. ⊠ *2065 Sidewinder Dr.* ☎ *435/645–8382, 800/324–6778* ⊕ *www. parkcityflyshop.com.*

Trout Bum 2. This full-service fly shop can outfit you with everything you need, then guide you to where the fish are. Check the website for fishing reports of the areas rivers and streams. ⊠ *4343 N. Hwy. 224, Suite 101* ☎ *435/658–1166, 877/878–2862* ⊕ *www.troutbum2.com.*

FRISBEE GOLF

Alpine Disc Golf. Frisbee fans can try 18 holes of high-altitude disc golf here. You'll need a gondola pass, but there's no charge to play the course. Rent discs at Canyon Mountain Sports in the resort village. ⊠ *4000 Canyons Resort Dr.* ☎ *435/615–3442* ⊕ *www.canyonsresort. com* ⊠ *$18 for gondola ride* ⊙ *Mid-June–early Oct., daily 10–4.*

GOLF

Within 20 minutes of Park City are 11 golf courses: 5 public and 6 private. The first new public course in more than a decade, Canyons Resort Golf Course, will open for public play spring 2015.

Canyons Resort Golf Course. Spring 2015 marks the opening of this highly anticipated course, which adds to the plethora of summer activities at Canyons Resort. The 97-acre course uses the mountainous terrain at the base of the ski resort for a challenging game. Six holes interact with ski runs, with more than 550 feet of elevation change throughout the course. With seven par-3s, the course is not for the faint of heart, but the views alone make it worth checking out no matter what your level. ⊠ *4000 Canyons Resort Dr., Canyons Resort* ☎ *888/226–9667* ⊕ *www. canyonsresortgolfcourse.com* ⊠ *Call for price information* ⚐ *18 holes, 6256 yards, par 70.*

Park City Municipal Golf Course. On this gorgeous and challenging 6,800-yard, par-72 public course, you'll love the views of ski runs, rising peaks, historic Main Street, and an occasional moose. Popular among locals, it's considered one of the best public courses in the area. Everything you need is in the pro shop, in the Hotel Park City right along the course. ✉ *1541 Thaynes Canyon Dr.* ☎ *435/615–5800* ⊕ *www.parkcity. org/index.aspx?page=171* ✉ *$25 for 9 holes, $32.50 with cart; $50 for 18 holes, $65 with cart* ⚑ *18 holes, 6800 yards, par 72.*

Promontory Club. The only private club in the area to make selected tee times available to the general public, Promontory Club welcomes nonmembers on its challenging and sometimes windy Pete Dye-designed course. The club is renowned for extraordinary views and exemplary service. Six sets of tees on this course make for what some call the most level playing field on any course in Utah. ✉ *8758 Promontory Ranch Rd.* ☎ *435/333–4600* ⊕ *www.promontoryclub.com* ✉ *$175 nonmember, $105 if accompanied by a member* ⚑ *18 holes, 7700 yards, par 72.*

HIKING

The Wasatch Mountains surrounding Park City offer more than 400 miles of hiking trails, ranging from easy, meandering meadow strolls to strenuous climbs up wind-blown peaks. Getting away from civilization and into the aspens is easy, and lucky hikers might spy foxes, coyotes, moose, elk, deer, and red-tailed hawks. Many of the trails take off from the resort areas, but some of the trailheads are right near Main Street. For beginners, or for those acclimating to the elevation, the Rail Trail is a good place to start. Another alternative is to take the McLeod Creek Trail from behind Park City Market all the way to the Redstone Center. The Round Valley and Lost Prospector trails are still mellow but slightly more challenging. To really get the blood pumping, head up Spiro or do a lengthy stretch of Mid-Mountain.

For interactive trail maps, up-to-date information about trail conditions and events, and for answers to your trail questions, contact the nonprofit Mountain Trails Foundation, whose mission is to promote, preserve, advocate for, and maintain Park City's local trail system. Maps detailing trail locations are available at most local gear shops.

Mountain Trails Foundation ☎ *435/649–6839* ⊕ *www.mountaintrails.org.*

HORSEBACK RIDING

Red Pine Adventures. This outfitter leads trail rides through thousands of acres of private land. ✉ *2050 W. White Pine Canyon Rd.* ☎ *435/649– 9445, 800/417–7669* ⊕ *www.redpinetours.com* ✉ *From $75.*

Rocky Mountain Recreation. Saddle up for a taste and feel of the Old West with guided mountain trail rides, from one hour to all-day or overnight excursions, departing from several locations in the Park City area, complete with fantastic scenery and good cowboy grub. ✉ *Stillman Ranch, Oakley* ☎ *435/645–7256* ⊕ *www.rockymtnrec.com* ✉ *From $61.*

Wind In Your Hair Riding. Only experienced riders who are looking for a get-up-and-go kind of mountain riding adventure are allowed on these trail rides, so there will be no inexperienced riders to slow you down, and the Paso Fino horses are noted for their smooth ride. Expect to tip the trail leader extra to the fee. Lessons are available for beginners. ✉ *Cherry Canyon Ranch, 46 E. Cherry Canyon Dr., Wanship*

☎ *435/336–4795, 435/901–4644* ⊕ *www.windinyourhair.com* ✉ *From $150.*

HOT-AIR BALLOONING

Park City Balloon Adventures. Hour-long scenic sunrise flights are offered daily, weather permitting. Fliers meet at Starbucks in Kimball Junction and are shuttled to the take-off site, which varies from day to day. A champagne or nonalcoholic toast is offered on touchdown. Reservations are required. ☎ *435/645–8787, 800/396–8787* ⊕ *www. pcballoonadventures.com* ✉ *$225 per person.*

ICE-SKATING

Park City Ice Arena. The Olympic-size rink here provides plenty of space for testing out that triple-toe loop or slap shot. The hill outside the building is popular sledding terrain. ✉ *600 Gillmor Way* ☎ *435/615–5700* ⊕ *www.parkcityice.org* ✉ *$10.50* ☉ *Call for public skate times.*

RAFTING

Park City Rafting. Two-hour, mostly Class 2 rafting adventures are offered, as well as full-day trips that end with a Class 3 splash. Given the Weber River's mostly benign water, there are plenty of breaks between plunges to look for moose, deer, beavers, badgers, and feathered friends along the shore. ✉ *1245 Taggart La., Morgan* ☎ *435/655–3800, 866/467–2384* ⊕ *www.parkcityrafting.com.*

ROCK CLIMBING

White Pine Touring. If you're looking for some hang time on the local rocks but don't know the area, White Pine Touring offers guided climbing tours, equipment rental, and private and group lessons. Reservations are required. ✉ *1790 Bonanza Dr.* ☎ *435/649–8710* ⊕ *www. whitepinetouring.com* ✉ *$300 for up to 2 climbers, $100 per additional climber.*

SKIING AND SNOWBOARDING

Fodor'sChoice **Canyons Resort.** One of the largest ski resorts in the country, and the
★ largest resort in Utah, Canyons has North America's only chairlift with heated seats (named the Orange Bubble Express). Skiers of all abilities will enjoy this mountain, which has 185 runs and emphasizes service (food, lodging, ski school) in the mold of nearby Deer Valley. Advanced skiers love Ninety-Nine 90, a black-diamond peak named for its altitude. Don't be deceived when you pull into the parking lot—most of the terrain is not visible from the base. Three terrain parks appeal to snowboarders and freeskiers. Vail Resorts, parent company of both Park City Mountain Resort and neighboring Canyons Resort, has plans in place to combine both resorts under the name Park City Mountain Resort by November of 2015. This ski resort will be the largest in the United States, with 7,300 acres of terrain and more than 300 runs. ✉ *4000 Canyons Resort Dr.* ☎ *435/649–5400, 888/226–9667 reservations, 435/615–3456 snow reports* ⊕ *www.canyonsresort.com* ✉ *Lift tickets $107; save by buying online* ☞ *3,190-ft vertical drop; 4,000 skiable acres; 10% beginner, 44% intermediate, 46% advanced; 1 8-passenger gondola, 1 6-passenger high-speed chair, 6 high-speed quad chairs, 5 quad chairs, 2 triple chairs, 2 double chairs, 2 surface lifts.*

FAMILY
Fodor'sChoice
★

Deer Valley Resort. Just to the south of downtown Park City, this resort set new standards in the ski industry by providing such amenities as ski valets and slope-side dining of the highest caliber. For such pampering, the resort has drawn rave reviews from virtually every ski and travel magazine. The careful layout of runs and the quality of the grooming make this an intermediate skier's heaven. With the Empire Canyon and Lady Morgan areas, the resort also offers bona fide expert terrain. For many, part of the ski experience includes a two- to three-hour midday interlude of feasting at the Silver Lake Lodge buffet and catching major rays on the snow-covered meadow in front of the lodge. The ski experience, in other words, fits right in with the resort's overall image. With lessons for kids from preschool through teens, Deer Valley's acclaimed children's ski school is sure to please both children and parents. Note: This is one of the only ski resorts in the United States that prohibits snowboards. ✉ *2250 Deer Valley Dr.* ☎ *435/649–1000, 800/424–3337 reservations* ⊕ *www.deervalley.com* 🎿 *Lift tickets $114* 🏔 *3,000-ft vertical drop; 2,026 skiable acres; 27% beginner, 41% intermediate, 32% advanced; 1 high-speed gondola, 12 high-speed quad chairs, 1 quad chair, 5 triple chairs, 2 double chairs, 4 surface lifts.*

FAMILY
Fodor'sChoice
★

Park City Mountain Resort. This has been one of North America's most popular ski and snowboard destinations for quite some time. With 116 trails and 9 bowls, there is ample terrain to keep skiers of all abilities happy for days. Roughly half the terrain is rated as intermediate, but the slopes that line Jupiter Peak are revered by experts. The east face of Jupiter has some particularly hairy rock-lined chutes. Motherlode Meadows and Mid-Mountain Meadows provide a gentler approach to tree skiing. Known as PCMR to distinguish it from the adjacent town, the resort is widely acclaimed for its family friendliness, for its location (one lift rises out of Park City's Town Lift Square), and for being a freeskiing and snowboarding mecca, especially since hosting 2002 Winter Olympics competitions. The Eagle Superpipe, with 22-foot walls, is one of the largest in North America, and combined with three terrain parks with state-of-the-art rails, jumps, and features, makes this resort an important destination for that crowd. PCMR is the only resort in Park City that offers night skiing. Park City's main drawback is lack of length. Despite a vertical drop of 3,100 feet, it's hard putting together a run of more than about 1,400 vertical feet. The area is made up of a series of ridges and peaks rather than a single mountain face. They have an excellent ski school and also host skiers with disabilities. Vail Resorts, parent company of both Park City Mountain Resort and neighboring Canyons Resort, has plans in place to combine both resorts under the name Park City Mountain Resort by November of 2015. This ski resort will be the largest in the United States, with 7,300 acres of terrain and more than 300 runs. ✉ *1345 Lowell Ave.* ☎ *435/649–8111 reservations and snow reports, 800/222–7275 reservations* ⊕ *www. parkcitymountain.com* 🎿 *Lift tickets $107* 🏔 *3,100-ft vertical drop; 3,300 skiable acres; 17% beginner, 52% intermediate, 31% advanced; 4 high-speed 6-passenger chairs, 3 high-speed quad chairs, 7 triple chairs, 2 double chairs, 3 surface lifts.*

White Pine Nordic Center. Just outside Old Town, White Pine Nordic Center offers around 20 km (12 miles) of set track, in 3-km (2-mile), 5-km (3-mile), and 10-km (6-mile) loops, plus cross-country ski instruction, equipment rentals, and a well-stocked cross-country ski shop. The fee to use the track is $18, or $10 after 3 pm. Reservations are required for their guided backcountry ski and snowshoe tours in the surrounding mountains. ⊠ *On Park City Golf Course, Hwy. 224 and Thaynes Canyon Dr.* ☎ *435/649–6249* ⊕ *www.whitepinetouring.com.*

Wasatch Powderbird Guides. If you don't mind paying for it, the best way to find untracked Utah powder is with Wasatch Powderbird Guides. A helicopter drops you on the top of the mountain, and a guide leads you back down. Itineraries are always weather dependent. Call to inquire about departures from Snowbird (Little Cottonwood Canyon) or Canyons (Park City). ☎ *801/742–2800* ⊕ *www.powderbird.com* ⊠ *$1,190 low season, $1,400 high season for full day.*

SKI RENTALS AND EQUIPMENT

Many shops in Park City rent equipment for skiing and other sports. From old-fashioned rental shops that also offer discount lift tickets to luxurious ski-delivery services that will fit you in your room, you have dozens of choices. Prices tend to be slightly lower if you rent in Salt Lake City. ■TIP→ **If you happen to be visiting during holidays, reserve skiing and snowboarding gear in advance.**

Breeze Winter Sports Rentals. You can reserve your equipment in advance with this company, which has a half-dozen locations in Utah alone. You'll find them near Canyons Resort, Park City Mountain Resort, and in town at Newpark. They're owned by Vail Resorts, and you can expect good quality and service at a value price. ⊠ *4343 N. Hwy. 224* ☎ *435/655–7066, 888/427–3393* ⊕ *www.skirentals.com.*

Cole Sport. With four locations from Main Street to Deer Valley, Cole Sport carries all your winter ski, snowboard, and snowshoe rental needs. Come back in summer for bikes, stand-up paddleboards, hiking gear, and more. No matter the season, Cole Sport offers expert fitting and advice with a broad range of equipment. ⊠ *1615 Park Ave.* ☎ *435/649–4806, 800/345–2938* ⊕ *www.colesport.com.*

Jans Mountain Outfitters. For more than 30 years, this has been the locals' choice for gear rentals, with ski and snowboard equipment packages and clothing in winter, and bikes and fly-fishing gear in summer. With the most knowledgeable staff around, they'll assist you with any outdoor adventure. There are multiple locations, including the flagship Park Avenue store, Deer Valley, and Park City Mountain Resort. ⊠ *1600 Park Ave.* ☎ *435/649–4949* ⊕ *www.jans.com.*

Park City Sport. At the base of Park City Mountain Resort, this is a convenient place to rent ski and snowboard equipment, goggles, and clothing. You can drop off your personal gear at the end of a ski day, and they'll have it tuned and ready for you the next morning. A second location on Main Street is across from Town Lift. ⊠ *1335 Lowell Ave.* ☎ *435/645–7777, 800/523–3922* ⊕ *www.parkcitysport.com.*

Silver Star Ski & Sport. This company rents, tunes, and repairs ski equipment, snowshoes, bike gear, and stand-up paddleboards. Near the municipal golf course, it will also re-grip clubs. ✉ *1825 Three Kings Dr.* ☎ *435/645–7827* ⊕ *www.silverstarskiandsport.com.*

Ski Butlers. The most prominent of a number of companies offering ski and snowboard delivery, Ski Butlers carries top-of-the-line Rossignol equipment. Their experts will fit you in your hotel room or condo and meet you at any of the resorts should something go wrong. You'll pay a little more, but you'll avoid the hassle of rentals when the snow is falling on your first morning in the mountains. ✉ *1821 Sidewinder Dr.* ☎ *877/754–7754* ⊕ *www.skibutlers.com.*

Utah Ski & Golf. Downhill equipment, snowshoes, clothing, and golf-club rental are available here, at the base of Park City Mountain Resort, and in downtown Salt Lake City. ✉ *698 Park Ave.* ☎ *435/649–3020* ⊕ *www.utahskigolf.com.*

SKI TOURS **Ski Utah Interconnect Adventure Tour.** Strong intermediate and advanced skiers can hook up with the Ski Utah Interconnect Tour for a guided alpine ski tour that takes you to as many as six resorts, including Deer Valley and Park City, in a single day, all connected by backcountry ski routes with unparalleled views of the Wasatch Mountains. Guides test your ski ability before departure. The tour includes guide service, lift tickets, lunch, and transportation back to the point of origin. You'll even walk away with a finisher's pin. Reservations are required. ☎ *801/534–1907* ⊕ *www.skiutah.com* 🔖 *$325.*

White Pine Touring. Specializing in telemark, cross-country, and alpine touring gear, White Pine Touring also has top of the line clothing, as well as mountain bikes, snowshoes, and climbing shoes. ✉ *1790 Bonanza Dr.* ☎ *435/649–8710* ⊕ *www.whitepinetouring.com.*

SNOWMOBILING

Red Pine Adventures. For a winter speed thrill of the machine-powered variety, hop on a snowmobile and follow your guide along private groomed trails adjacent to Canyons Resort. You'll need snow clothing, gloves and goggles, but boots and helmets are provided, as is pickup in Park City. ✉ *2050 W. White Pine Canyon Rd.* ☎ *435/649–9445, 800/417–7669 snow* ⊕ *www.redpinetours.com* 🔖 *$165 per machine (up to 2 people)* ⊙ *Daily at 9, 11, 1, and 3 in season.*

Thousand Peaks Snowmobile Adventures. Backcountry snowmobile tours are on one of Utah's largest private mountain ranches, just outside of Park City, where you can catch a free shuttle. Clothing is available to rent. ✉ *100 W. Weber Canyon Rd.* ☎ *888/304–7669* ⊕ *www.thousand peaks.com* 🔖 *From $159 single rider, $198 double.*

SNOW TUBING

FAMILY **Gorgoza Park.** Lift-served snow tubing, mini-snowmobile rentals and skiing lessons for kids ages 5–12 bring families here. ✉ *3863 W. Kilby Rd.* ☎ *435/658–2648* ⊕ *www.gorgoza.com* 🔖 *$8 single ride; $23 2-hrs; $33 4-hrs.*

WHERE TO EAT

Use the coordinates (✣ A1) at the end of each listing to locate a site on the corresponding map.

> **NOT SO DRY**
>
> It's a desert climate, but there's nothing dry about Park City when it comes to tipping back a drink or two. A cocktail contest each fall gets the creative bartending juices flowing, and the momentum keeps up until summer, when a slew of festivals feature beer gardens and wine tastings. Breweries, wine bars, and martini joints pick up where the restaurant wine lists end. Keep in mind that altitude and dehydration go hand in hand so don't forget to drink water along with that blueberry mojito!

$$$$ SWISS 🍴 **Adolph's.** The Swiss Alps meet Park City at this beloved stomping ground of longtime locals and athletes from around the globe. Chef Adolph Imboden's food is European, with strong ties to his Alpine roots. Start off with raclette or escargots, move to the chateaubriand or rack of lamb, then finish with a flambé. Signed photos and posters of skiing greats line the walls. [$] *Average main: $40* ✉ *1500 Kearns Blvd.* ☎ *435/649–7177* 🌐 *www.adolphsrestaurant.com* ✣ *D4.*

$$$$ CONTEMPORARY 🍴 **Apex.** Suitably named, as this restaurant is the highest year-round restaurant in Park City, Apex is also at the top of the class for dining and service. The restaurant is within Montage Deer Valley, and the chefs conjure up seasonal menus with an emphasis on local: think trout from Utah mountain streams, lamb from nearby Morgan Valley, produce from Park City's Copper Moose Farm, and cheeses from purveyors like Gold Creek. The 25-page wine list is creatively formatted and ranges from "sommelier's selections" to "interesting reds" and includes an array of wines by the glass and half bottle. [$] *Average main: $36* ✉ *9100 Marsac Ave.* ☎ *435/604–1300* 🌐 *www.montagedeervalley.com* ✣ *B4.*

$$$ ITALIAN 🍴 **Café Terigo.** Chef-owner Ed Axtell has delighted guests for more than 25 years in this airy café with the best patio in town. He serves well-prepared pasta and seafood dishes using only fresh ingredients. Good picks include the veal Bolognese with pappardelle pasta or herb-breaded Utah trout with citrus butter. An order of bread pudding or chocolate crème brûlée perfectly tops off a meal. [$] *Average main: $29* ✉ *424 Main St.* ☎ *435/645–9555* 🌐 *www.cafeterigo.com* 🕓 *No dinner Sun. Apr.–Nov.* ✣ *B5.*

$$$ SOUTHWESTERN 🍴 **Chimayo.** Star-shape lanterns illuminate the mission-style wrought-iron and terra-cotta tiles of this upscale Southwestern restaurant. Chef Arturo Flores will delight and surprise you with tantalizing flavors in his menu, with items such as duck breast enchiladas, tortilla soup (his grandmother's recipe), trout fajitas, or the melt-off-the-bone spareribs you won't soon forget. Order a house-made margarita (try the serrano margarita for an extra kick) and enjoy the cozy and intimate feel of this popular restaurant. With excellent service and an inspired menu, this is sure to become one of your Main Street favorites. [$] *Average main: $27* ✉ *368 Main St.* ☎ *435/649–6222* 🌐 *www.chimayorestaurant.com* 🕓 *Closed 2 wks in May and 2 wks in Nov. No lunch* ✣ *B5.*

3

$ MEXICAN Fodor's Choice ★ 🍴 **El Chubasco.** For quick and hearty traditional Mexican food, this popular place is perfect. Favorites are *camarones a la diabla* (spicy shrimp), *chiles rellenos* (stuffed chilis), and fish tacos. The smothered burritos are large enough to feed two, and there's plenty of Corona and Dos Equis to cool off even the spiciest items. The low-key atmosphere is part of the charm, and the salsa bar provides some of the best flavor in town. [$] *Average main: $10* ✉ *1890 Bonanza Dr.* ☎ *435/645–9114* 🌐 *www.elchubascomexicangrill.com* ✥ *D4.*

$$$$ MODERN AMERICAN Fodor's Choice ★ 🍴 **The Farm at Canyons.** Chef Steve Musolf and his team relentlessly seek new, fresh, local, and unique ingredients to infuse into memorable meals from the Farm's open kitchen to its dining room with less than a dozen tables. Seasonal menus always spotlights items from regional sustainable farmers, including root vegetables, truffles, berries, and beef. Built as part of a massive reinvention of Canyons Resort in 2010, the Farm is just feet from the slopes on the back side of the Grand Summit Hotel. The darker and cozier lounge features a wine cellar that displays many of its 450-plus varieties of domestic and imported wines. [$] *Average main: $35* ✉ *4000 Canyons Resort Dr.* ☎ *435/615–8080* 🌐 *www.canyonsresort.com* 🕒 *No lunch. Hrs vary seasonally* ✥ *A2.*

$$$$ MODERN AMERICAN Fodor's Choice ★ 🍴 **Glitretind.** Wood trim, white tablecloths, crystal glasses, and fresh-cut flowers set the scene for executive chef Zane Holmquist's creative dishes. Sample specialties like duck and waffles, or Rocky Mountain elk tenderloin. Sommelier Cara Schwindt oversees a wine cellar with more than 10,000 bottles that incorporates every major wine-growing region in the world. Artistic chocolates and desserts provide a perfect finish. You'll be tempted to make an all-day affair out of the Sunday brunch. [$] *Average main: $40* ✉ *7700 Stein Way, Deer Valley* ☎ *435/645–6455* 🌐 *www.steinlodge.com/dining* ✥ *D6.*

$$$$ NORTHERN ITALIAN 🍴 **Grappa.** This restaurant specializes in Italian cuisine with impeccable presentation. Heavy floor tiles, rustic bricks, and exposed timbers lend a warm, rustic farmhouse feel. Tables on the wraparound balcony overlook those on the first floor. The menus, which change seasonally, offer appetizers such as a grapes-and-Gorgonzola salad with roasted walnuts and hearty entrées like Roman-style chicken, osso bucco, or horseradish-encrusted salmon. [$] *Average main: $41* ✉ *151 Main St.* ☎ *435/645–0636* 🌐 *www.grapparestaurant.com* 🕒 *No lunch* ✥ *B6.*

$$$ AMERICAN Fodor's Choice ★ 🍴 **High West Distillery.** Touted as the only ski-in, ski-out distillery in the world, High West sits at the base of the Park City Mountain Resort. The restaurant and bar, housed in a historical home and livery, is a favorite among locals and visitors alike. High West produces whiskey and vodka, and both can be sampled in tasting flights or in one of their specialty handcrafted cocktails, which can be argued as the best cocktails in town. Family-friendly, it serves an eclectically Western, local-focus menu that changes seasonally. [$] *Average main: $21* ✉ *703 Park Ave., Old Town/Main Street* ☎ *435/649–8300* 🌐 *www.highwest.com* ✍ *Reservations not accepted* ✥ *A4.*

$$$ PIZZA FAMILY 🍴 **Maxwell's East Coast Eatery.** Nearly 2 feet across, the Fat Kid "pie" will remind you of Brooklyn or the Bronx—grab a slice of the "Goodfella" veggie pizza or the "Italian Stallion" meat lovers' version. The house-made pastas, such as chicken Parmesan, rival the pizzas as fan favorites.

Top off any meal with the "cookiza," a personal-pan cookie with vanilla ice cream. Located between the Swaner Preserve and a swath of shops, this unpretentious eatery is popular with locals and welcomes the late-night crowd. Live music spices up the scene Thursday through Saturday nights. Sports fans will enjoy the many TVs that always show the game. $ *Average main: $21* ⊠ *1456 Newpark Blvd., Suite 55, Newpark* ☎ *435/647–0304* ⊕ *www.maxwellsparkcity.com* ✛ *A1.*

$$$$ ✕ **Purple Sage.** Plenty of purple-hue touches—velvet upholstered booths,
AMERICAN hand-painted scrims, and Western murals—brighten the 1898 brick building that was once the local telegraph office. "Fancy cowboy" cuisine includes such dishes as grilled veal meat loaf with poblano peppers and pine nuts or the lime-grilled black tiger shrimp. Try a Purple Sage martini (akin to a cosmopolitan, but purple). In summer, eat on the back deck. $ *Average main: $33* ⊠ *434 Main St.* ☎ *435/655–9505* ⊕ *www.purplesageparkcity.com* ☾ *Closed 1 wk in spring and fall* ✛ *B5.*

$$ ✕ **Red Tail Grill.** After a day on the ski slopes or hiking trails at Canyons
SOUTHWESTERN Resort, kick back on the large deck here for lunch, après, or dinner, and
FAMILY people-watch with Park City's best margarita in hand. Red Tail Grill has a full menu of margaritas—try the prickly pear—made from one of the dozens of tequilas in the bar. A Southwestern menu will please all with items such as carnitas nachos and hand-pressed guacamole. Breakfast is offered in summer and fall only, where you can find some of the best *huevos rancheros* in town. $ *Average main: $18* ⊠ *4000 Canyons Resort Dr.* ☎ *435/615–8068* ⊕ *www.canyonsresort.com* ✛ *A2.*

$$$$ ✕ **Riverhorse on Main.** With two warehouse loft rooms, exposed wood
AMERICAN beams, sleek furnishings, and original art, this award-winning restaurant feels like a big-city supper club. Owner-chef Seth Adams pairs imaginative fresh food with an elegant—but ski-town relaxed—atmosphere. On summer nights, request the balcony overlooking Main Street. The menu changes seasonally, but look out for rack of lamb, venison, or buffalo in a port-wine reduction, and original options like the overnight-roasted pork volcano, Chardonnay-poached scallops and lobster tail, filet of beef, or signature macadamia-nut-crusted Alaskan halibut. The mashed potatoes are famous. $ *Average main: $42* ⊠ *540 Main St.* ☎ *435/649–3536* ⊕ *www.riverhorseparkcity.com* ☾ *No lunch; no brunch Mon.–Wed.* ✛ *B5.*

$$$$ ✕ **Shabu.** Hip Asian cuisine matches the chic interior of a restaurant
ASIAN FUSION that draws visiting Hollywood types and in-the-know locals. The red-hued dining room epitomizes "cool," which makes sucking down a Ginger Snap sake martini perfectly acceptable. The firecracker shrimp, volcano sushi roll (tuna, wasabi, pineapple, jalapeno, and cilantro) and shabu shabu, a Japanese hot pot, are all favorites. Dress is casual but smart. $ *Average main: $32* ⊠ *442 Main St.* ☎ *435/645–7253* ⊕ *www. shabuparkcity.com* ☾ *Closed mid-Apr.–Memorial Day; no lunch fall–spring (call to check open dates)* ✛ *B5.*

$$ ✕ **Squatters Roadhouse Grill & Pub.** Raise an organic amber ale (Squat-
AMERICAN ters is one of the largest craft breweries in the state) while savoring a
FAMILY barbecued buffalo burger on the deck, or sidle up to the counter for morning pancakes. Note the eco-friendly leanings, but the vibe is more sporty than hippie at this family-friendly eatery, where skiers, real-estate

agents, prospectors, and lift operators all come for a menu that ranges from pastas to salads to fish sandwiches to an array of burgers. Little ones love the mac-and-cheese almost as much as the bicycles hanging from the ceiling in this bright, cheerful spot at a busy Park City intersection. $ *Average main: $14* ✉ *1900 Park Ave.* ☎ *435/649–9868* ⊕ *www. squatters.com* ⌕ *Reservations not accepted* ✛ *C4.*

$$$$

ASIAN

Fodor's Choice

★

✕ **Wahso Asian Grill.** Warm finger towels, curtained booths, and attentive service in an elegant dining room recall the Jazz-era Orient. Start your evening with a sake martini shaken tableside, then ask your server about starters that span the continent, from steamed Chinese buns to *tom kha gai*, a delicious chicken-and-lemongrass soup from Thailand. Delve into the subcontinent with sweet-and-savory Madras chicken, or stay closer to your comfort zone with a porcini filet mignon. As with many Park City restaurants, summer is a great time to savor Wahso, as prices drop and getting a table is easier. $ *Average main: $41* ✉ *577 Main St.* ☎ *435/615–0300* ⊕ *www.wahso.com* ☾ *No lunch; closed 2 wks in fall (call for dates)* ✛ *A5.*

$$

AMERICAN

FAMILY

✕ **Wasatch Brew Pub.** It's hard to believe it's been nearly 30 years since Wasatch became Park City's first brewery in the post-Prohibition era. At the top of Main Street, this pub stays on top of its game with celebrated beers and down-to-earth pub food. Sidle up to the bar for a mug of Polygamy Porter and a burger, or cozy up with the entire family in a booth. A recent menu overhaul transformed this pub food for the better, with items such as house-made coconut shrimp, a buffalo burger with a Cajun remoulade, and a side of tater tots (both sweet potato and regular) instead of your typical fries. Top it all off with a Brigham's root-beer float. In summer, grab an outside table for people-watching. $ *Average main: $15* ✉ *250 Main St.* ☎ *435/645–0900* ⊕ *www.wasatchbeers.com* ⌕ *Reservations not accepted* ☾ *No brunch weekdays* ✛ *B5.*

$$

AMERICAN

FAMILY

✕ **Windy Ridge Café.** You'll rave about this off-the-beaten-path informal eatery that prepares American favorites with scrumptious results. Don't overlook Windy Ridge because of its industrial park neighborhood, as the dining room is warm and inviting. Lighter diners might fancy the homemade chicken noodle soup and an open-face hot turkey sandwich, or if you've spent the day skiing or biking, tackle the meat loaf or a rack of smoked ribs. It's well worth a short trip away from Main Street for this affordable menu. Just be sure to save room for a pastry or two from the neighboring Bakery at Windy Ridge. $ *Average main: $18* ✉ *1250 Iron Horse Dr.* ☎ *435/647–0880* ⊕ *www.windyridgefoods.com* ✛ *D4.*

$$$$

AMERICAN

✕ **Zoom.** Owned by Robert Redford, and one of five restaurants in the Sundance family, this "Western chic" eatery is housed in an old train depot at the base of historic Main Street, and still has worn woodplank floors. When the weather is warm, the sunken patio is a perfect place to enjoy seared Utah trout or braised short ribs. The wine list leans heavily on California's Napa and Sonoma valleys. Check out the photos of film legends adorning the walls. Leave room for a seasonal dessert. $ *Average main: $32* ✉ *660 Main St.* ☎ *435/649–9108* ⊕ *www. zoomparkcity.com* ✛ *A4.*

WHERE TO STAY

Use the coordinates (✣ A1) at the end of each listing to locate a site on the corresponding map.

$$ B&B/INN **Chateau Après.** In one of the most expensive ski towns around, this reasonably priced classic skiers' lodge is a throwback to ski days gone by. **Pros:** comfortable rooms; inexpensive slope-side place for outdoor enthusiasts to crash; longtime local owners. **Cons:** if you're looking for cushy pampering or fancy hot breakfasts, look elsewhere. [$] *Rooms from: $130* ✉ *1299 Norfolk Ave.* ☎ *435/649–9372, 800/357–3556* 🌐 *www.chateauapres.com* 🛏 *32 rooms* 🕑 *Closed mid-Apr.–Nov.* 🍴 *Breakfast* ✣ *D5.*

$$$$ HOTEL **The Chateaux at Deer Valley.** Just steps away from the Deer Valley lifts at Silver Lake Village, this modern interpretation of a luxury European château incorporates designer furnishings, heated towel racks, full kitchens in suites, gas fireplaces, and numerous windows to take advantage of the spectacular mountain views. **Pros:** luxury digs without stuffy atmosphere; close to the Deer Valley slopes. **Cons:** studios with Murphy beds are not for everyone; too far from Old Town to walk; evenings tend to be quiet; meals expensive in Silver Lake area. [$] *Rooms from: $575* ✉ *7815 Royal St. E* ☎ *435/658–9500, 877/288–2978* 🌐 *www.the-chateaux.com* 🛏 *114 rooms, 46 suites* 🍴 *No meals* ✣ *D6.*

$$$$ RESORT **Grand Summit Resort Hotel & Conference Center.** This slope-side resort is the signature hotel of Utah's largest ski area, steps from a heated chairlift. **Pros:** luxurious; countless activities. **Cons:** rooms need a refresh. [$] *Rooms from: $300* ✉ *4000 Canyons Resort Dr.* ☎ *435/615–8040 front desk, 888/226–9667 reservations* 🌐 *www.canyonsresort.com* 🛏 *375 units* 🍴 *No meals* ✣ *A2.*

$$$$ HOTEL **Hotel Park City.** On the Park City golf course, this all-suites hotel is built in the tradition of the grand old stone-and-timber lodges of the West. **Pros:** close to town and the ski hills; grand lodge-style rooms with views. **Cons:** all this pampering doesn't come cheap. [$] *Rooms from: $549* ✉ *2001 Park Ave.* ☎ *435/200–2000* 🌐 *www.hotelparkcity.com* 🛏 *100 suites* 🍴 *No meals* ✣ *C4.*

$$$$ HOTEL **Marriott MountainSide Resort.** Gabled roofs, rough-hewn stonework, and heavy wood beams re-create the look of Park City's mining-era buildings at this resort with residential condos. **Pros:** ski-in ski-out convenience; heated outdoor pool and hot tubs; helpful, pleasant staff. **Cons:** busy and somewhat congested area. [$] *Rooms from: $300* ✉ *1305 Lowell Ave.* ☎ *435/940–2000, 800/845–5279* 🌐 *www.marriott.com* 🛏 *365 rooms* 🍴 *No meals* ✣ *D5.*

$$$$ RESORT Fodor's Choice ★ **Montage Deer Valley.** The jewel on the top of the crown of Park City, Montage is breathtakingly nestled in Empire Pass at 9,000 feet above sea level like a grand Alpine luxury chalet. **Pros:** exquisite location; everything about Montage is memorable. **Cons:** with its mountaintop location, there's nothing within walking distance in winter; you'll need a car or the resort shuttle even to get to Main Street; not for the faint of wallet. [$] *Rooms from: $899* ✉ *9100 Marsac Ave.* ☎ *435/604–1300* 🌐 *www.montagedeervalley.com* 🛏 *88 rooms, 66 suites* 🍴 *No meals* ✣ *B4.*

$$$$
HOTEL

⊞ Newpark Resort. With Newpark's busy shopping and dining scene on one side and a gorgeous nature preserve on the other, this hotel has a nature-meets-city feel. **Pros:** comfortable suites; affordable rates; within walking distance of shops and restaurants. **Cons:** you may feel you need a car to get around; not all rooms have views. $ *Rooms from: $229* ✉ *1476 Newpark Blvd.* ☎ *435/649–3600, 877/649–3600* ⊕ *www.newparkresort.com* ↻ *62 rooms, 64 suites, 24 townhomes* ❙❀❙ *No meals* ✢ *A1.*

$$$
B&B/INN
Fodor's Choice
★

⊞ Old Town Guest House. Listed on the National Register of Historic Places, this four-room inn offers country style and lodgepole-pine furniture that make it warm and cozy, and the location—steps from the slopes and trails—makes it a magnet for outdoors enthusiasts. **Pros:** if the location doesn't motivate you to get outdoors, the energetic innkeeper will; hearty mountain breakfast and afternoon snacks are included. **Cons:** rooms are cozy but petite. $ *Rooms from: $179* ✉ *1011 Empire Ave.* ☎ *435/649–2642, 800/290–6423* ⊕ *www.oldtownguesthouse.com* ↻ *4 rooms* ❙❀❙ *Breakfast* ✢ *D5.*

$$$$
RESORT
Fodor's Choice
★

⊞ The St. Regis Deer Valley. Take a 90-second ride up the funicular to one of the most luxurious hotels at any alpine resort. **Pros:** glitz, glam, and butlers; ski-in ski-out convenience; champagne in the library, darling. **Cons:** all this luxury comes with a price tag. $ *Rooms from: $1,100* ✉ *2300 Deer Valley Dr. E* ☎ *435/940–5700, 866/932–7059* ⊕ *www.stregisdeervalley.com* ↻ *115 rooms, 66 suites* ❙❀❙ *No meals* ✢ *B4.*

$$$$
HOTEL

⊞ The Sky Lodge. Smack in the middle of Old Town, this contemporary condo-hotel blends historic and modern architecture. **Pros:** superb location; interior design that surprises; great views. **Cons:** you are in the middle of the action in high season (which could also be a pro). $ *Rooms from: $700* ✉ *201 Heber Ave.* ☎ *435/658–2500, 888/876–2525* ⊕ *www.theskylodge.com* ↻ *33 suites* ❙❀❙ *No meals* ✢ *A4.*

$$$$
RESORT
Fodor's Choice
★

⊞ Stein Eriksen Lodge. As enchanting as it gets for a slope-side retreat, this lodge is as perfectly groomed, timelessly gracious, and uniquely charming as its namesake founder, the winner of an Olympic Gold Medal in 1952. **Pros:** it's where the rich and famous stay without fear of being mobbed by fans. **Cons:** expect to spend a lot. $ *Rooms from: $895* ✉ *7700 Stein Way* ☎ *435/649–3700, 800/453–1302* ⊕ *www.steinlodge.com* ↻ *112 rooms, 68 suites* ❙❀❙ *No meals* ✢ *B4.*

$$
B&B/INN

⊞ Torchlight Inn. New in December 2013, this bed-and-breakfast inn offers a nice mix of contemporary and traditional style and incredible views from its rooftop deck and hot tub. **Pros:** rooms are spacious. **Cons:** it's only a matter of time until this property is booked solid year-round. $ *Rooms from: $129* ✉ *255 Deer Valley Dr.* ☎ *508/989–0459* ⊕ *www.torchlightinn.com* ↻ *6 rooms* ❙❀❙ *Breakfast* ✢ *B4.*

$$$$
RESORT

⊞ Waldorf Astoria Park City. A sweeping staircase, Baccarat crystal chandelier, and 300-year-old marble fireplace lend grandeur to the first Waldorf Astoria hotel in an alpine location. **Pros:** refined and renowned service, including concierge and optional majordomo; steps from the gondola; decadent spa; comfortable and chic furnishings. **Cons:** the sense of elegance might make parents with kids nervous; very little within walking distance (but a free shuttle will take you). $ *Rooms from: $239* ✉ *2100 Frostwood Dr.* ☎ *435/647–5500, 866/279–0843*

🌐 *www.parkcitywaldorfastoria.com* 🛏 *178 rooms, 37 suites* 🍴 *No meals* ✣ *A2.*

$$$$ B&B/INN Fodor's Choice ★ 🏛 **Washington School House.** Since 2011, this spectacular boutique hotel has been the hottest "must-stay" destination in Old Town Park City, providing breathtaking rooms and suites within a National Historic Registry landmark. **Pros:** central Park City location; stellar service (they'll even pack and unpack for you). **Cons:** not family-friendly; rooms fill up quickly, so book far in advance; no restaurant on-site (though private dining is available). [$] *Rooms from: $375* ✉ *543 Park Ave., Box 536* ☎ *435/649–3800, 800/824–1672* 🌐 *www.washingtonschoolhouse.com* 🛏 *9 rooms, 3 suites* 🍴 *Breakfast* ✣ *A5.*

CONDOS

Deer Valley Resort Lodging. The reservationists at Deer Valley Resort Lodging are knowledgeable and the service efficient at this high-end property-management company. They can book distinctive hotel rooms, condominiums, or private homes throughout Deer Valley and Park City. Complimentary shuttle service to/from resorts and around town in Cadillac Escalades are a perk. ✉ *2250 Deer Valley Dr. S* ☎ *435/649–4040, 800/424–3337* 🌐 *www.deervalley.com* ✣ *B4.*

Resorts West. One of Park City's largest and best property management companies—and the only one to provide private concierge service for every guest—Resorts West manages roughly 140 properties around the city, ranging from two-bedroom condos to eight-bedroom ski homes. Your concierge will take care of everything from grocery delivery and private chefs to ski rental delivery, and each reservation includes daily housekeeping and shuttle service around town. ✉ *1795 Sidewinder Dr., Suite 100* ☎ *435/655–7006* 🌐 *www.resortswest.com* ✣ *C4.*

NIGHTLIFE AND PERFORMING ARTS

NIGHTLIFE

In a state where nearly every town was founded by Mormons who eschewed alcohol and anything associated with it, Park City has always been an exception. Founded by miners with healthy appetites for whiskey, gambling, and ladies of the night, Park City has been known since its mining heyday as Utah's "Sin City." The miners are gone, but their legacy lives on in this town that has far more bars per capita than any other place in Utah.

Boneyard Saloon and Kitchen. Park City's newest hot spot is in a somewhat unlikely location—in fact, you might think you're lost as you pull into the industrial-looking area in Prospector. But its off-Main location means it's popular with the locals, and ample parking is a huge plus. TVs lining the wall and a special weekend breakfast menu have made Boneyard the new go-to for Sunday football, and the roof-top deck has stunning views of the mountains. A sister restaurant of No Name on Main Street, Boneyard shares the same love for beer with an incredible beer menu featuring draft and an extensive bottle list. ✉ *1251 Kearns Blvd., Prospector* ☎ *435/649–0911.*

Cisero's. This place serves up live music, karaoke, and DJs in the downstairs bar, along with classic Italian food upstairs in the family-friendly restaurant. ✉ *306 Main St.* ☎ *435/649–5044* ⊕ *www.ciseros.com.*

No Name Saloon. A Park City favorite, anchoring Main Street's nightlife, this is a classic wood-backed bar with lots of memorabilia, a shuffleboard table, and a regular local clientele. The upstairs outdoor deck is great for enjoying cool summer nights, but heaters in the winter make this deck comfortable year-round. If you are looking for some late night grub, No Name has the best buffalo burgers in town. ✉ *447 Main St.* ☎ *435/649–6667* ⊕ *www.nonamesaloon.net.*

O'Shucks. If you're looking for a tasty burger and a local beer, this place is a favorite of local ski bums. No frills, no attitude, just the saltiest peanuts—throw the shells on the floor—and the coldest beer around. ✉ *427 Main St.* ☎ *435/645–3999.*

Spur Bar and Grill. Though hard to find (you walk through an alley next to 350 Main Restaurant), the Spur is worth the effort. It's an upscale club with good cowboy-style food and live music. Belly up to the bar on one of the leather bar stools and choose from signature cocktails, many featuring local High West vodka or whiskey. Be prepared to pay a cover charge on busier nights. It's closed Monday and Tuesday. ✉ *352 Main St.* ☎ *435/615–1618* ⊕ *www.thespurbarandgrill.com.*

Troll Hallen Lounge. If quiet conversation and a good single-malt scotch or Swiss raclette in front of a fire is your idea of nightlife, this is your place. ✉ *Stein Eriksen Lodge, 7700 Stein Way* ☎ *435/645–6455.*

PERFORMING ARTS
MUSIC

FAMILY
Fodor'sChoice
★

Mountain Town Music. This is a gem of a nonprofit organization that books dozens of local, regional, and national musical acts in the Park City area, using many different venues around town, including the ski resorts and Main Street. No matter what show you go to, you're likely to see every age group represented and enjoying the music, and most shows are free. ☎ *435/901–7664* ⊕ *www.mountaintownmusic.org.*

THEATER AND DANCE

Eccles Center for Performing Arts. Dance, theater, wide-ranging concerts, family shows, and other performances are on the bill in a state-of-the-art auditorium that also holds the biggest premieres during the Sundance Film Festival. They also program an outdoor summer music series at Deer Valley Resort. ✉ *1750 Kearns Blvd.* ☎ *435/655–3114* ⊕ *www.ecclescenter.org.*

Egyptian Theatre. This historical building has been a Park City theater since its mining days in the 1880s. In 1922 the Egyptian Theatre was constructed on the site of the original Dewey Theatre that collapsed under record-breaking snow. Patrons enjoy an eclectic array of local and regional music, theater, and comedy in the 266-seat space. ✉ *328 Main St.* ☎ *435/649–9371* ⊕ *www.egyptiantheatrecompany.org.*

SHOPPING

Within the colorful structures that line Park City's Main Street are a number of clothing boutiques, sporting-goods stores, and gift shops. The farmers' market (June through October, Wednesday noon–6) at Canyons Resort is a popular stop for local produce, crafts, food, and music.

ART GALLERIES

Park City Gallery Stroll. Main Street is packed with great art galleries, and the best way to see them all is the Park City Gallery Stroll, a free event hosted by the Park City Gallery Association on the last Friday of the month, 6–9 pm—sun or snow! ☎ *435/649–8882* ⊕ *www. parkcitygalleryassociation.com.*

BOOKS AND TOYS

FAMILY **Dolly's Bookstore.** For many returning visitors the first stop in town is Dolly's Bookstore, to check on the three cats, Dolly, Curious George, and Pippi Longstocking, and to browse a great selection of regional books as well as national best sellers. Dolly's also has a uniquely complete selection of children's books and toys. ✉ *510 Main St.* ☎ *435/649–8062.*

FAMILY **J.W. Allen & Sons.** Jam-packed with classic toys and modern fun, J.W. Allen & Sons rescues parents who forgot toys for kids on the family vacation. Scary dinosaurs, giant stuffed bears, dolls, sleds, scooters, and kites are as irresistible as the candy. ✉ *1675 W. Redstone Center, No. 105* ☎ *435/575–8697* ⊕ *www.theparkcitytoystore.com.*

CLOTHING

Mary Jane's. This independently owned boutique has an eclectic selection of trendy clothing and designer jeans, lingerie, and handbags for women. If you like shoes and statement jewelry, this shop is a must. ✉ *613 Main St.* ☎ *435/645–7463* ⊕ *www.maryjanesshoes.com.*

Olive and Tweed. Self-described as an artists-driven boutique, Olive and Tweed features handmade jewelry, many by local artists, and a stylish display of trendy women's clothing, accessories, home style, and even a few baby items. ✉ *608 Main St.* ☎ *435/649–9392* ⊕ *www. oliveandtweed.storenvy.com.*

FOOD AND CANDY

Rocky Mountain Chocolate Factory. You'll find a quick fix for your sweet tooth here, and you can watch them make fudge, caramel apples, and other scrumptious treats. There's another location at 1385 Lowell Avenue. ✉ *510 Main St.* ☎ *435/649–0997, 435/649–2235.*

HOUSEHOLD ITEMS

La Niche. Classical music and the aroma of fresh-roasted coffee greet you at La Niche. While away an hour in this cozy collection of linens, home decorations, quilts, cooking and decorating books, and an intimate espresso and gelato bar in the back. ✉ *401 Main St.* ☎ *435/649–2372.*

Rocky Mountain Christmas. Ornaments, decorations, and a selection of toys crowd the tightly spaced shelves and make every visit feel festive. ✉ *523 Main St.* ☎ *435/649–9169* ⊕ *www.rockymountainchristmas.com.*

OUTLET AND DISCOUNT STORES

Tanger Outlets. Just west of Highway 224 when you exit I–80 toward the ski resorts, this is a bargain shopper's paradise, with dozens of outlets. Foreign tourists spend lavishly here, and locals find deals year-round, too. Represented in this collection of 60 outlets are active brands like Columbia and Nike, plus fashion labels Banana Republic, Gap, Polo Ralph Lauren, Eddie Bauer, and J Crew. ⊠ *6699 N. Landmark Dr.* ☎ *435/645–7078* ⊕ *www.tangeroutlet.com.*

SOUTH OF SALT LAKE CITY

The Utah Valley was a busy place long before the Mormons settled here in 1851. With Utah Lake teeming with fish and game plentiful in the surrounding mountains, several bands of Native Americans lived in the area, and Spanish explorers passed through in 1775. Traders from several countries used the explorers' trail to bring goods here and to capture slaves to sell in Mexico, and fur trappers spent winter seasons in the surrounding mountains. With so many groups competing for the area's resources, conflicts were inevitable. The conflicts became more intense when Mormons settled Provo in 1851 and then began claiming land in other parts of the valley, land that had always been used by Native Americans. Several battles were fought here between Mormon settlers and Native American groups during the Walker and Black Hawk wars.

PROVO

45 miles southeast of Park City; 45 miles south of Salt Lake City; 14 miles south of Lehi.

With Mount Timpanogos to the east and Utah Lake to the west, Provo and the adjacent city of Orem make up one of the prettiest communities in the West. This two-city community is also one of the fastest growing. Provo's historic downtown includes many small shops and family restaurants; in the newer sections you'll find malls, factory outlet stores, a variety of eateries, and the headquarters for several large corporations. The presence of Brigham Young University and the LDS Missionary Training Center imbue the community with a wholesome quality.

GETTING HERE AND AROUND

Highway 189 from Park City or Interstate 15 from Salt Lake City both deposit you into Provo's tidy grid of easy-to-navigate streets. The sprawling Brigham Young University campus and historic downtown are at its center, with shopping malls scattered in all directions. Giant Utah Lake is to the west.

FESTIVALS

America's Freedom Festival. Each June and July, the America's Freedom Festival combines a series of patriotic activities and contests. The event peaks with a hot-air balloon festival, the state's biggest Independence Day parade, and fireworks at BYU's 65,000-seat LaVell Edwards Stadium. ☎ *801/818–1776* ⊕ *www.freedomfestival.org.*

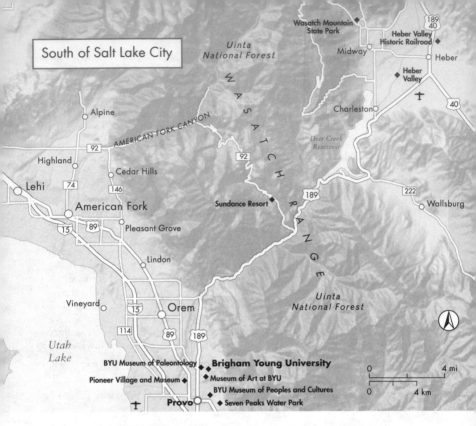

South of Salt Lake City

Wasatch Mountain State Park

Heber Valley Historic Railroad

Midway

Heber

Uinta National Forest

Heber Valley

Charleston

Deer Creek Reservoir

Alpine

AMERICAN FORK CANYON

Highland

Cedar Hills

Lehi

American Fork

Pleasant Grove

Sundance Resort

Wallsburg

Lindon

Uinta National Forest

Vineyard

Orem

Utah Lake

BYU Museum of Paleontology ◆ **Brigham Young University**

Pioneer Village and Museum ◆ ◆ Museum of Art at BYU

◆ BYU Museum of Peoples and Cultures

Provo ◆ Seven Peaks Water Park

0   4 mi

0   4 km

ESSENTIALS

Visitor Information Utah County Convention and Visitors Bureau ✉ 220 W. Center St., Suite 100 ☎ 801/851–2100, 800/222–8824 ⊕ www.utahvalley.com.

EXPLORING

TOP ATTRACTIONS

Brigham Young University. Provo and the entire region are probably best known as the home of BYU. The university was established as the Brigham Young Academy in 1875, with a mandate to combine teaching about the sacred and the secular. It has grown into one of the world's largest church-affiliated universities, and still reflects the conservative nature of the Mormon Church. Students must adhere to a strict dress and honor code, and refrain from alcohol, tobacco, coffee, and tea. BYU is known for its large variety of quality undergraduate and graduate programs and is a considerable force in regional athletics. Heading up BYU attractions is a quartet of museums. A free, guided university tour is offered weekdays on the hour, and reservations are recommended. ✉ *BYU visitor center, Campus Dr.* ☎ *801/422–4678* ⊕ *www.byu.edu.*

FAMILY **BYU Museum of Paleontology.** This museum, across from LaVell Edwards Stadium, features dinosaur bones, fossils, and tours for adults and children. Kids love the hands-on activities, which include several small tables of touchable artifacts. ✉ *1683 N. Canyon Rd.* ☎ *801/422–3680*

⊕ *cpms.byu.edu/ESM/information.html* 🖾 *Free* ⊙ *Weekdays 9–5 (except university holidays).*

FAMILY **Monte L. Bean Life Science Museum.** This museum at BYU, north of the bell tower, has extensive collections of birds, mammals, fish, reptiles, insects, plants, shells, and eggs from around the world, as well as revolving nature-art exhibits. You'll also see current NASA satellite images, wildlife art, and various interactive ecology exhibits. If you bring a toddler, head for the play area themed around animal habitats. ⊠ *645 E. 1430 N* 🕾 *801/422–5051* ⊕ *mlbean.byu.edu* 🖾 *Free* ⊙ *Weekdays 10–9, Sat. 10–5.*

Museum of Art at Brigham Young University. The permanent collection of more than 17,000 works here includes primarily American artists such as Maynard Dixon, Dorothea Lange, Albert Bierstadt, Minerva Teichert, and Robert Henri, and emphasizes the Hudson River School and the American impressionists. Rembrandt, Monet, and Rubens also turn up, along with some fine Far Eastern pieces. The museum's café overlooks the sculpture garden. ⊠ *N. Campus Dr., southeast of LaVell Edwards Stadium* 🕾 *801/422–8287* ⊕ *moa.byu.edu* 🖾 *Free* ⊙ *Weekdays 10–6, Sat. noon–5.*

WORTH NOTING

BYU Museum of Peoples and Cultures. An interesting student-curated collection of artifacts relating to cultures from all over the world is housed here. Clothing, pottery, rugs, weapons, and agricultural tools of Utah's Native American cultures are often on display. A permanent display includes artifacts from the first Provo Tabernacle that BYU students dug up a couple of years ago. ⊠ *700 N. 100 E* 🕾 *801/422–0020* ⊕ *mpc.byu.edu* 🖾 *Free* ⊙ *Weekdays 9–5 (until 7 Tues. and Thurs.).*

Pioneer Village and Museum. This museum re-creates what life was like for the first settlers in the mid-19th century. Original cabins and shops furnished with period antiques are staffed by volunteer history buffs. ⊠ *500 W. 600 N* 🕾 *801/852–6609* ⊕ *www.provopioneervillage.org* 🖾 *Free* ⊙ *Memorial Day weekend–Labor Day, Mon. 5–8, Tues.–Fri. 4–7, Sat. 1–4; museum hrs vary.*

FAMILY **Seven Peaks Water Park.** There are 26 acres of waterborne fun here, with plenty of play areas and a wave pool. When you splash down from a waterslide or rope swing, there won't be a temperature shock, because the water is heated. ⊠ *1330 E. 300 N* 🕾 *801/373–8777* ⊕ *www.sevenpeaks.com* 🖾 *$24.99* ⊙ *Memorial Day–Labor Day, Mon.–Sat. 11–8.*

SPORTS AND THE OUTDOORS

BICYCLING

In the Provo area, road cyclists may make a 100-mile circumnavigation of Utah Lake or tackle U.S. 189 through Provo Canyon or the Alpine Loop Scenic Byway. Mountain bikers can choose from a large selection of trails varying in degrees of difficulty.

Racer's Cycle Service. For information about biking in the area, bicycle sales, and world-class service, go to Racer's Cycle Service and talk to owner "Racer" Jared Gibson. ⊠ *159 W. 500 N* ☎ *801/375–5873* ⊕ *www.racerscycleservice.com.*

FISHING

Utah Lake State Park. Fishing is popular at Utah Lake, which at 96,600 acres is the state's largest freshwater lake. In spring and fall it gets some of the best wind in Utah for windsurfing and sailing. You can also come here for boating—powerboats to canoes. ⊠ *4400 W. Center St.* ☎ *801/375–0731, 801/375–0733* ⊕ *www.stateparks.utah.gov* ⊠ *$10* ⊙ *Daily dawn–dusk.*

GOLF

You'll find 10 public courses within Utah Valley, ranging from canyon or mountain settings to relatively flat and easy-to-walk terrain. Tee times are usually easy to get, and greens fees are reasonable.

Hobble Creek Golf Course. The canyon setting at this affordable course, east of Springville, makes for a beautiful day no matter how you play, particularly in fall, when the hills explode with color. Golfers rave about the views, and warn of tricky greens. This course is consistently rated a favorite among the public courses in Utah. The snack shop and full service pro shop are added conveniences. ⊠ *5984 E. Hobble Creek Canyon Rd.* ☎ *801/489–6297* ⊠ *$14 for 9 holes, $28 for 18 holes* ⚑ *18 holes, 6400 yards, par 71.*

Reserve at East Bay. The 18-hole championship course wends around the beautiful shoreline of Utah Lake and wetlands, with excellent views of the Wasatch Mountains and the chance to spot birds along the way. The 7-hold Executive Course is great for beginners and juniors, and is walk-on only. The individual and group lessons, as well as clinics, provide personalized instruction with PGA professionals. ⊠ *1860 S. East Bay Blvd.* ☎ *801/852–7529* ⊕ *www.eastbaygolf.com* ⊠ *$28 Mon.–Thurs.; $30 Fri., Sat., and holidays; $26 Sun.* ⚑ *18 holes, 6900 yards, par 73.*

Thanksgiving Point. The popular 18-hole Johnny Miller–designed golf course at Thanksgiving Point is a championship course geared toward intermediate and advanced players. Covering more than 200 acres, it is also the largest course in the state. The Jordan River winds around the perimeter and through the course, artistically used throughout the design of the holes. Wind is a factor when playing Thanksgiving point, but many feel adds to the personality of the course. ⊠ *3300 W. Clubhouse Dr., Lehi* ☎ *801/768–7400* ⊕ *thanksgivingpointgolfcourse.com* ⊠ *May 16–Sept. 30, $38 Sun.–Thurs., $48 Fri. and Sat. for 9 holes; $67 Mon.–Wed., $77 Thurs., $87 Fri., Sat., and holidays, $47 Sun. for 18 holes. May 1–15 and Oct. 1–15, $38 for 9 holes; $57 Mon.–Thurs., $67 Fri. and Sat., $42 Sun. for 18 holes. Oct. 16–Apr. 30 prices based on temperature* ⚑ *18 holes, 7714 yards, par 72.*

HIKING

Visitors to the southern part of the Wasatch find many trails from which to choose.

Bonneville Shoreline Trail. The 100-mile Bonneville Shoreline Trail from Brigham City to Nephi spans the foothills of the Wasatch Front following the eastern shoreline of ancient Lake Bonneville. The section near

Provo begins at the Rock Creek trailhead and continues south along the foothills, past the Y trailhead, to the Hobble Creek Parkway trailhead.

Bridal Veil Falls. The trailhead to Bridal Veil Falls is 2½ miles up Provo Canyon; after the moderate climb, hikers are rewarded with a cold mountain-waterfall shower.

Provo Parkway. The easy, paved Provo Parkway meanders along the Provo River from the mouth of Provo Canyon and provides a good mix of shade and sun.

ICE-SKATING

Peaks Ice Arena. A 2002 Olympic Hockey venue, this arena includes two ice sheets, and is open throughout the year for figure skating, hockey, and parties. ✉ *100 N. Seven Peaks Blvd.* ☎ *801/852–7465* 🌐 *www.provo.org/community/peaks-ice-arena/* 🎫 *$5* 🕒 *Mon.–Sat. 7 am–midnight; call to check public skate times.*

ROCK CLIMBING

American Fork Canyon. In the Uinta National Forest, 10 miles north of Provo, American Fork Canyon has northern Utah's best sport climbing, with dozens of fixed routes. The steep walls also offer face, slab, and crack climbs.

WHERE TO EAT

$$$$ FRENCH

🍴 **Chef's Table.** This romantic spot serves freshly made pastas, meat dishes, and seafood. The macadamia nut-crusted halibut and duck in tart cherry reduction sauce are popular choices, and the large wine list is impressive. A pianist, a single red rose decorating each table, and views of the Utah Valley and Wasatch Mountains through wide windows make this *the* place for a romantic meal in Orem. [$] *Average main: $32* ✉ *2005 S. State St., Orem* ☎ *801/235–9111* 🌐 *www.chefstable.net* 🕒 *Closed Sun. No lunch Sat.*

$$$ AMERICAN

🍴 **Communal.** This small but comfortable restaurant will feel a lot like a Sunday dinner family style—a large communal table anchors the space, and you feel as if you are part of the family when dining here. With an ingredient-driven menu (locally sourced, seasonal focus) Communal is more than just food, but about conversation, sharing, and comfort. The open kitchen plates up entrées that are meant to be shared between at least two people, including buttermilk fried chicken or local trout. Don't miss the Saturday brunch with blueberry buttermilk pancakes, better than your childhood favorite. [$] *Average main: $27* ✉ *102 University Ave., Historic Downtown* ☎ *801/373–8000* 🌐 *www.communalrestaurant.com* 🕒 *Closed Sun. and Mon., no brunch weekdays.*

$ ECLECTIC

🍴 **Guru's Café.** An art deco portrait of Gandhi decorates one wall of this downtown hippie refuge. Elsewhere you'll find metal sculptures and blue skyscapes. The vegetarian-friendly fare includes cilantro-lime quesadillas and rice bowls, and options for nonvegetarians include Southwestern chipotle chicken wrap with a side of sweet-potato fries. [$] *Average main: $10* ✉ *45 E. Center St.* ☎ *801/375–4878* 🌐 *www.guruscafe.com.*

$$ MEXICAN

🍴 **Los Hermanos.** In an old downtown building, this long-standing favorite serves great Mexican food in a colorful mazelike space with private rooms and booth tables. Favorites are the halibut Vera Cruz, grilled with a secret blend of spices and extra-virgin olive oil, and the spicy fajitas. Everything can be washed down with a fruity, nonalcoholic *brisa de mora negra* (blackberries, strawberries, and ice cream blended together). $ *Average main: $14* ✉ *16 E. Center St.* ☎ *801/375–5732* 🌐 *www.loshermanosutah.com* 🕒 *Closed Sun.*

$$ PIZZA 🍴 **Pizzeria Seven Twelve.** With a name that comes from the ideal temperature for cooking pizza, the centerpiece of this bright, minimalist establishment is a wood-burning brick oven. Pizzas come topped with delectable items like *speck* (prosciutto) and *soppressata* (salami). The rest of the menu, which largely depends on produce and meats from nearby farmers and artisans, changes with the seasons. Try the braised beef short rib, and top off your meal with buttermilk panna cotta. Local art and quiet conversation make this intimate establishment a pleasant respite. $ *Average main: $15* ✉ *320 S. State St., Orem* ☎ *801/623–6712* 🌐 *www.pizzeria712.com* 🕒 *Closed Sun. No lunch Sat.*

WHERE TO STAY

$$ B&B/INN 🏨 **Hines Mansion Bed & Breakfast.** The welcoming bottle of sparkling cider in your room sets the scene for a stay in this 1895 mansion, where much of the original woodwork, brick, and stained glass has been left intact. **Pros:** close to BYU; antique furnishings. **Cons:** for some, the style in a few rooms may feel a bit outdated. $ *Rooms from: $139* ✉ *383 W. 100 S* ☎ *801/374–8400, 800/428–5636* 🌐 *www.hinesmansion.com* 🛏 *9 rooms* 🍽 *Breakfast.*

NIGHTLIFE AND PERFORMING ARTS

NIGHTLIFE

Although Provo isn't completely "dry," the standards of BYU are evident in the city's dearth of nightlife options. The Madison is the venue everyone talks about.

The Madison. This is the only nightclub and late-night spot you'll find in the area and the crowd is more diverse and welcoming than you might expect in conservative Provo. Three floors make it massive, and DJs and a weekly karaoke night provide entertainment late into the night. It's labeled as a "gastro-pub," and you'll find a varied menu for lunch and dinner. ✉ *295 W. Center St., Downtown* ☎ *801/375–9000* 🌐 *www.facebook.com/themadisonbar* 🕒 *Closed Sun.*

PERFORMING ARTS

Because the university has a considerable interest in the arts, Provo is a great place to catch a play, dance performance, or musical production. BYU has a dozen performing groups in all. The BYU International Folk Dancers and Ballroom Dancers travel extensively, but also perform at home.

BYU Franklin S. Harris Fine Arts Center. Most performances at BYU are held in this center, which houses a concert hall, recital hall, and three theaters. The ticket office is on the third floor, near the south entrance, and is open weekdays 10–3 (until 5 in fall and winter); there's another ticket office on the north side of the Marriott Center, ground level, open weekdays 9–5. ✉ *N. Campus Dr.* ☎ *801/422–4322, 801/422–2981 tickets* 🌐 *arts.byu.edu.*

SHOPPING

Shopping in the Provo–Orem area centers around four primary areas. In addition to the malls, visitors find shopping opportunities at boutiques and galleries in downtown Provo, especially along Center Street.

Provo Towne Centre Mall. On the south end of Provo, this mall has mainstream retailers like Dillard's, JCPenney, and Sears, and specialty shops like Hallmark and Fanzz. It's open 10–9 Monday–Saturday and noon–6 on Sunday. ✉ *1200 S. University Ave.* ☎ *801/852–2400* ⊕ *www.provotownecentre.com.*

Shops at Riverwoods. This mall is home to upscale retailers like Jos. A. Banks, Victoria's Secret, and Williams-Sonoma. It's closed on Sunday. ✉ *4801 N. University Ave.* ☎ *801/802–8430* ⊕ *www.shopsatriverwoods.com.*

University Mall. Catering to the needs of BYU students with stores like Deseret Book and Simply Mac, this mall also has standard retailers like Macy's and H&M—more than 180 shops and restaurants in all. It's closed on Sunday. ✉ *575 E. University Pkwy., Orem* ☎ *801/224–0694* ⊕ *www.shopuniversitymall.com.*

SUNDANCE RESORT

35 miles south of Park City; 12 miles northeast of Provo.

As Thoreau had Walden Pond, so does Redford have Sundance. Lucky for the rest of us, the "Sundance Kid" shares his 5,000-acre bounty. Several miles up a winding mountain lane, Sundance Resort is part retreat and part resort. In winter, it's a full-service ski resort with bustling slopes except during the Sundance Film Festival. In summer, it's a destination for filmmakers, writers, craftsmen, and artists of all sensibilities. Whether you want to write or ski, participate in a film workshop or mountain bike, Sundance has something for you. Or just pamper yourself with the spa, dining, and shopping.

GETTING HERE AND AROUND

From Park City, take Highway 40 and 189 south. From Provo, head northeast on Highway 92.

EXPLORING

Fodor's Choice ★ **Sundance Resort.** Set on the eastern slopes of the breathtaking 11,750-foot Mount Timpanogos, the resort came into being when Robert Redford purchased the land in 1969. In concept and practice, the 5,000-acre mountain community reflects Redford's commitment to the natural environment, outdoor exploration, and artistic expression. All resort facilities—constructed from materials such as indigenous cedar, fir, and pine, and locally quarried stone—blend well with the natural landscape. No matter the season, you'll find plenty of recreational opportunities, including hiking, biking, fly-fishing, horseback riding, alpine and cross-country skiing, snowboarding, and snowshoeing. If you're looking for a more indulgent experience, relax with a body treatment in the Spa at Sundance or take one of many creative classes in the Art Studios. The Sundance Film Festival, based in nearby Park City each January, is an internationally recognized showcase for independent films. Festival screenings and summer workshops are held at the resort. ✉ *8841 N. Alpine Loop Rd.* ☏ *801/225–4107, 800/892–1600* ⊕ *www. sundanceresort.com* 🖫 *Lift tickets $65* ☞ *2,150-ft vertical drop; 450 skiable acres; 20% novice, 40% intermediate, 40% advanced; 2 quad lifts, 2 triple chairs, 1 surface lift.*

SPORTS AND THE OUTDOORS

FLY-FISHING

The Provo River, minutes from Sundance Resort, is a fly-fishing catch-and-release waterway. Access to the rainbow, cutthroat, and German brown trout found in the river is year-round. Tours are provided by Wasatch Guide Service, and include all necessary gear, guides, and some may include drinks and snacks.

Wasatch Guide Service. The preferred outfitter of Sundance Resort, Wasatch Guide Service provides access to some of the best fly-fishing in the state. Guides will take you to the world-class Provo River, right near Sundance Resort, or up to the Weber River, and can even provide access to private waters and lesser-known streams in the area. One guide to every two guests ensures personalized experiences, and they provide all necessary equipment. Half-day and full-day tours are available year-round, with lunch provided in the full-day tour. ☏ *801/830–3316* ⊕ *www.wasatchguideservice.com* 🖫 *From $250 half day; from $350 full day.*

HIKING

Hiking trails in the Sundance area vary from the easy 1.25-mile Nature Trail and the popular lift-accessed Stewart Falls Trail (3 miles) to the 7½-mile Big Baldy Trail, which leads past a series of waterfalls up steep, rugged terrain. You can access moderate- to expert-level trails from the resort base or chairlift. Select from three routes to summit the 11,000-foot Mount Timpanogos. Guided naturalist hikes are available.

MOUNTAIN BIKING

You'll find more than 25 miles of ski lift–accessed mountain-biking trails at Sundance Resort, extending from the base of Mount Timpanogos to Ray's Summit at 7,250 feet. High-tech gear rentals are available for full or half days, as is individual or group instruction.

Sundance Mountain Outfitters. Here, you can rent all the gear you need for mountain biking (or skiing or snowboarding). ✉ *8841 N. Alpine Loop Rd.* ☏ *801/223–4121* ⊕ *www.sundanceresort.com.*

SKIING

CROSS-COUNTRY   Enjoy terrain suitable for all skill levels on nearly 10 miles of groomed trails. Six miles of dedicated snowshoeing trails wind through mature aspen groves and pines. Lessons and equipment rentals, including telemark gear, are available for all techniques of cross-country skiing and snowshoeing.

DOWNHILL   Skiers and snowboarders at Sundance Resort will find 42 trails on 450 acres of varied terrain. The mountain isn't big, but it does offer something for everyone, and you'll almost never find a lift line here. The focus on a total experience, rather than just on skiing or snowboarding, makes this a delightful destination. Services include specialized ski workshops (including ladies' day clinics and personal coaching), a PSIA-certified ski school, and a ski school just for children, with programs that include all-day supervision, lunch, and ski instruction. Children as young as four are eligible for group lessons. Rentals are available for all skill levels. Night skiing is also available four nights a week.

WHERE TO EAT AND STAY

$$$ AMERICAN Fodor's Choice ★

🍴 **Foundry Grill.** Wood-oven pizzas, sizzling steaks, and spit-roasted chicken are among the hearty staples on the menu at this restaurant. Like the rest of Sundance, everything here, from the food presentation to the interior design to the staff, is natural, beautiful, and pleasant. They're open for breakfast, lunch, and dinner, and if you're here on the weekend, the Sunday brunch is an incredible meal. [$] *Average main: $28* ✉ *Sundance Resort, 8841 N. Alpine Loop Rd.* ☎ *866/932–2295* 🌐 *www.sundanceresort.com.*

$$$$ RESORT Fodor's Choice ★

🏨 **Sundance Resort.** With 11,750-foot Mount Timpanogos serving as a backdrop, Robert Redford's 5,000-acre retreat is a genuine tribute to arts and nature. **Pros:** a genuine retreat from urban hubbub; fresh mountain air, glorious scenery, and outdoors adventure; culinary magic plus nourishment for creative souls. **Cons:** cell reception is iffy (which may also be a pro); nightlife doesn't get much more happening than stargazing or lifting a pint at a lone on-site watering hole. [$] *Rooms from: $289* ✉ *8841 N. Alpine Loop Rd.* ☎ *866/259–7468, 800/892–1600* 🌐 *www.sundanceresort.com* 🛏 *95 rooms* 🍽 *No meals.*

NIGHTLIFE AND PERFORMING ARTS

NIGHTLIFE

Owl Bar. Whether you feel like a quiet midday chess game or a livelier atmosphere at night, the Owl Bar is a good gathering space. Here you'll find live music on weekends and a healthy selection of beers and spirits to accompany a limited but satisfying menu. Classic photographs of Paul Newman and Robert Redford as Butch Cassidy and the Sundance Kid hang on the walls, and with the worn plank floors, stone fireplace, and original 1890s rosewood bar (said to have been favored by Cassidy's Hole-in-the-Wall Gang) transported from Thermopolis, Wyoming, you might just feel like cutting loose. ✉ *Sundance Resort, 8841 N. Alpine Loop Rd.* ☎ *801/223–4222* 🌐 *www.sundanceresort.com.*

PERFORMING ARTS

Sundance Art Studios. The studios offer workshops in photography, jewelry making, wheel-thrown pottery, watercolor painting, and charcoal or pencil drawing. Mirroring the Sundance ethic, these classes blend the natural world with artistic process. All workshops and classes are open to resort guests as well as day visitors. ✉ *Sundance Resort, 8841 N. Alpine Loop Rd.* ☎ *801/225–4107* 🌐 *www.sundanceresort.com.*

Sundance Author Series. For more than a decade, the Sundance Author Series has brought literary and political icons like Sue Monk Kidd and Jimmy Carter to the Tree Room for an intimate brunch and lecture. As an added bonus, you'll walk away with a signed copy of the author's book. ✉ *Sundance Resort, 8841 N. Alpine Loop Rd.* ☎ *801/223–4567* 🌐 *www.sundanceresort.com* 🎟 *$75.*

Sundance Bluebird Café. Each summer, Sundance brings a little Nashville to Utah with the Bluebird Café series. Singer-songwriters take the outdoor stage on select summer Fridays to share stories and music in the serene Utah mountains. ⊠ *8841 N. Alpine Loop* ☎ *866/734–4428* ⊕ *www.sundanceresort.com.*

Fodor's Choice ★ **Sundance Film Festival.** Add this to your bucket list. Every January the Sundance Institute, a nonprofit organization supporting independent filmmaking, screenwriters, playwrights, composers, and other film and theater artists, presents the Sundance Film Festival. A world-renowned showcase for independent film, the 10-day festival is based in Park City, but has screenings and workshops at Sundance Resort, Salt Lake City, and Ogden. ☎ *435/658–3456* ⊕ *www.sundance.org/festival.*

Utah Symphony. Performances each summer in Sundance's spectacular outdoor amphitheater start at 8 pm, and you should arrive 30 minutes in advance. The temperature will drop quickly after sundown, so dress in layers. ☎ *801/533–6683* ⊕ *www.utahsymphonyopera.org.*

SHOPPING

Deli. Selling foods from American cottage farmers and artisans as well as homemade oils, soaps, and bath salts, the Deli also has a juice bar and is a good place to get tea, coffee, shakes, pastries, deli meats, organic produce, and other tasty snacks. Stop here before your hike to pick up a fresh sandwich. ⊠ *Sundance Resort, 8841 N. Alpine Loop Rd.* ☎ *801/223–4211* ⊕ *www.sundanceresort.com.*

General Store. Step inside the Sundance catalog, which features distinctive home furnishings, clothing, and jewelry reflecting the rustically elegant Sundance style. Ask about many items that are organic or made of recycled materials. ⊠ *Sundance Resort, 8841 N. Alpine Loop Rd.* ☎ *801/223–4250* ⊕ *www.sundanceresort.com.*

HEBER VALLEY

20 miles south of Park City; 22 miles northeast of Sundance.

Bounded by the Wasatch Mountains on the west and the rolling foothills of the Uinta Mountains on the east, the Heber Valley, including the towns of Heber, Midway, and Charleston, is well supplied with snow in winter for cross-country skiing, snowmobiling, and other snow sports. Summers are mostly cool and green. Events throughout the year entertain locals as well as visitors.

GETTING HERE AND AROUND

From Park City, head east on Highway 40 to enter the Heber Valley. The highway turns into Main Street, which leads straight through Heber City. Turn right on 100 South to reach the Swiss-influenced town of Midway. If you're coming from Sundance, you'd take Highway 92 south then Highway 189 east.

ESSENTIALS

Visitor Information Heber Valley County Chamber of Commerce ⊠ *475 N. Main St., Heber Valley* ☎ *435/654–3666* ⊕ *www.gohebervalley.com.*

CLOSE UP

The Geology of the Wasatch Mountains

The geology of the Wasatch Mountains gives the Salt Lake Valley its character. Few places in the world can show off such distinct geologic features in an area as small as the 50 to 70 miles along the Wasatch Front. One section, from City Creek Canyon in the north to Bells Canyon in the south, has 10 distinct geologic zones. Each canyon has a different look, with rocks of varying ages and colors. Glaciers formed some; flowing water created others.

The reddish rocks visible on a drive up Parley's Canyon come from the Jurassic period. Suicide Rock, at the canyon's mouth, dates from the earlier Triassic age. Lower portions of Big Cottonwood Canyon have billion-year-old Precambrian rock. To the south, Little Cottonwood Canyon has comparatively new formations: a molten igneous mass pushed its

way almost to the surface a mere 32 million years ago. Granite formed here was used to build the Mormon Temple in Salt Lake City.

Tongues of the Wasatch Fault run along the front of the Wasatch Mountains. This fault is where the earth cracks as the Great Basin stretches by a couple of centimeters annually. For this to happen, the valleys from California through the Wasatch Range must fall slightly. Portions of Salt Lake Valley's Wasatch Boulevard and 1300 East Street are on fault lines. You can tell that you're near a fault when the east–west streets suddenly get steeper. Although geologists say that a quake could happen any time, the valley hasn't experienced a major one in recorded history. Where to grab some dinner should be a bigger concern than being shaken by an earthquake.

3

EXPLORING

FAMILY **Heber Valley Railroad.** Following a line that first ran in 1899, this train ride takes you on a nostalgic trip along the Deer Creek Reservoir and through beautiful Provo Canyon. Lunch is available for an extra cost. Each car has been restored, and two of the engines are fully operational, steam-powered locomotives. The railroad offers special events, including cheese-tasting rides, the local favorite North Pole Christmas Train, Raft 'n Rails (pairing rafting with a train excursion), Reins 'n Trains (with horseback riding), and Wilderness Zip Line. ■TIP➜ **There's no climate control in the rail cars, so dress for the weather.** ✉ *450 S. 600 W* ☎ *435/654–5601* ⊕ *www.hebervalleyrr.org* ✑ *Provo Canyon $30; Deer Creek $20; call for special event and activity trip prices* ☺ *Tues.–Sat. 9–5, Sun. 9–3; call for trip departure times.*

FAMILY **Wasatch Mountain State Park.** This 22,000-acre preserve, 3 miles from Heber City, provides for a number of activities, ranging from serene hikes along winding mountain trails to golfing at one of the four 18-hole courses. Children have their own fishing pond near the visitor center. In winter, hiking turns to snowshoeing, cross-country, or backcountry skiing along the Dutch Hollow, Snake Creek, or Pine Creek trails winding up through stands of Gambel oak, aspen, and maple. ✉ *1281 Warm Springs Rd., Midway* ☎ *435/654–1791, 800/322–3770* ⊕ *www.state parks.utah.gov* ✑ *$5 per car.*

Soldier Hollow. On the southern end of the park, this activity center was one site for the 2002 Winter Olympics and still hosts national championship events and other events, including powwows and sheep-dog championships. It's open to the public year-round for hiking, horse-back riding, cross-country skiing, tubing, snowshoeing, biathlon, and other events. A beautiful lodge has food concessions, equipment rentals, and a souvenir shop. ⊠ *2002 Olympic Dr., Midway* ☎ *435/654–2002* ⊕ *www.soldierhollow.com.*

SPORTS AND THE OUTDOORS

GOLF

Crater Springs Golf Course. This incredible course, in the heart of the Heber Valley on the Homestead Resort, offers incredible views of the Wasatch Mountains and plenty of fresh mountain air. A renovation means smoother cart paths, realigned trees, and new water features. GPS enabled-cart paths mean you won't get lost while looking at the scenery. ⊠ *700 N. Homestead Dr., Midway* ☎ *435/654–1102, 800/327–7220* ⊕ *www.cratersspringsgolf.com/Course* 🏌 *$59 for 18 holes Fri.–Sun., $49 Mon.–Wed.; $35 for 9 holes Fri.–Sun., $30 Mon.–Wed* 🏌*. 18 holes, 7040 yards, par 72* ☉ *Closed Nov.–Mar.*

Soldier Hollow Golf Course. Reflecting the Olympic Heritage, the names of the two 18-hole courses are Gold and Silver. While on these greens, golfers enjoy the beauty of both the Heber Valley to the east and the stunning Mount Timpanogos to the west. The Gold course is considered a mountain course, with dramatic elevation changes within each hole. The Silver course is slightly shorter than Gold, but with longer and trickier greens. ⊠ *1371 W. Soldier Hollow La., Midway* ☎ *435/654–7442* 🏌 *$33* 🏌*. Gold: 18 holes, 7598 yards, par 72; Silver: 18 holes, 7335yards, par 72.*

Wasatch Mountain State Park. The setting within the Wasatch Mountain State Park is spectacular, particularly at fall foliage time: and with the challenging Mountain Course as well as the gentler Lake Course, this is one of the most popular public courses in the state. The Mountain Course is designed around the natural contours of the surrounding Wasatch Mountains, and motorized carts are mandatory. The easier Lake Course surrounds eight lakes and ponds, and is a favorite with high, low, and no handicappers. ⊠ *975 W. Golf Course Rd., Midway* ☎ *435/654–0532* ⊕ *www.wasatchgolfcourse.com* 🏌 *$33 weekdays; $35 weekends; $14 for cart rental* 🏌*. Mountain course: 18 holes, 6459 yards, par 71; Lake course: 18 holes, 6942 yards, par 72.*

HIKING

The path connecting the towns of Heber and Midway is an easy walk with spectacular views of the Wasatch Range at a distance and, up close, the Provo River.

Jordanelle State Park. For a quiet experience, start your hike from the Rock Cliff Nature Center, under tall cottonwoods at the east end of Jordanelle State Park, which lies 10 miles east of Heber City. Hikers often report excellent wildlife viewing along this section of the upper Provo River. No dogs are allowed. ⊠ *Hwy. 32* ☎ *435/782–3030* ⊕ *www.state parks.utah.gov.*

Soldier Hollow. Although the trail system here is more exposed than that in the northern end of Wasatch Mountain State Park, hikers will enjoy the stunning view of the east side of Mount Timpanogos as well as the vista of the Uinta Mountains to the east across the Heber Valley. ✉ *2002 Olympic Dr., Midway* ☎ *435/654–2002* 🌐 *www.soldierhollow.com.*

Wasatch Mountain State Park. Hikers will find lots of foliage and wildlife here, on any number of trails in Dutch Hollow, Pine Canyon, and along Snake Creek. ✉ *1281 Warm Springs Rd., Midway* ☎ *435/654–1791* 🌐 *www.stateparks.utah.gov.*

HORSEBACK RIDING

Rocky Mountain Outfitters. Visitors can enjoy the spectacular setting of Wasatch Mountain State Park and surrounding areas on horseback year-round with Rocky Mountain Outfitters. Choose from a variety of ride durations and destinations with the nicest guides in the area. ☎ *435/654–1655* 🌐 *www.rockymountainoutfitters.com.*

WATER SPORTS

Deer Creek State Park. Consistently good fishing, mild canyon winds, and water warmer than you'd expect are responsible for Deer Creek State Park's popularity with windsurfers, sailboaters, swimmers, and those just kicking back in the mountain sunshine. The park is 5 miles south of Heber City. ✉ *U.S. 189* ☎ *435/654–0171* 🌐 *www.stateparks.utah.gov* 🎟 *$10 day-use fee* 🕒 *Daily 6 am–10 pm.*

Jordanelle State Park. This park has two recreation areas on a large mountain reservoir. The Hailstone area, 10 miles north of Heber City via U.S. 40, offers day-use areas, boat ramps, playgrounds, and a marina store where water toys (wave runners and the like) can be rented. To the east, across the reservoir on Highway 32, the Rock Cliff area and facilities are near the Provo River. This is a quiet part of the park known for excellent wildlife-watching, particularly along a series of elevated boardwalks winding through the aspen forest. The Rock Cliff Nature Center provides interpretation of the area's rich natural history. ✉ *Hwy. 32* ☎ *435/649–9540 Hailstone, 435/782–3030 Rock Cliff* 🌐 *www.stateparks.utah.gov* 🎟 *Hailstone $10 per vehicle, Rock Cliff $7 per vehicle.*

WHERE TO EAT

$ PIZZA FAMILY

🍴 **Café Galleria.** This family-friendly restaurant claims to have the best pizza and bagels in the state, and they may not be far off. The wood-fired pizza oven cooks to perfection, and bagel sandwiches, available throughout the day, hit the spot. Plentiful outdoor seating is a great way to enjoy the summer sun. The interior has many rooms, and brown paper tablecloths, with crayons provided, will entertain the kids. [$] *Average main: $11* ✉ *101 W. Main St., Midway* ☎ *435/657–2002* 🌐 *www.cafegalleriapizza.com.*

$ FAST FOOD FAMILY Fodor's Choice ★

🍴 **Dairy Keen.** A welcome respite from chain fast food, this family-owned drive-in serves the best shakes and burgers for miles around. Railroad artifacts line the walls, and an electric train entertains children as it passes over the booths. [$] *Average main: $10* ✉ *199 S. Main St., Heber Valley* ☎ *435/654–5336* 🌐 *www.dairykeen.com* 🕒 *Closed Sun.*

$$ AMERICAN **Snake Creek Grill.** In a refurbished train depot at the end of the Heber Valley Railroad, chef Dean Hottle serves comfort food with a twist. Almond and chive-crusted red trout, cedar plank–roasted salmon with organic couscous, grilled pork tenderloin, and maple-mustard-barbecued baby back ribs are local favorites. Flowers fresh from the garden add to the elegant country ambience. Whatever you do, leave room for dessert; the black-bottom banana-cream pie is to die for. *Average main: $20 650 W. 100 S 435/654–2133 www.snakecreekgrill.com Closed Mon. and Tues. No lunch.*

$ MEXICAN **Tarahumara.** Note the lack of sombreros. Authentic art from the owner's Chihuahua hometown sets the genuine tone in this lively self-serve restaurant, where locals lap up the *carne asada*, seared sea scallops with passion fruit, and other Mexican specialties. Take in a televised soccer game, sip a margarita, and try to sample all 23 of the fresh salsas. *Average main: $11 380 E. Main St., Midway 435/654–3465 www.tarahumara.biz Closed Sun.*

WHERE TO STAY

$$$ B&B/INN **Blue Boar Inn.** Elegant turrets, wrought-iron balconies, an antique alpenhorn, and the boar above the hearth give this 12-room château-style inn a warm, romantic feel. **Pros:** hospitable staff; romantic ambience; full breakfast. **Cons:** not the ideal place for boisterous little ones. *Rooms from: $175 1235 Warm Springs Rd., Midway 435/654–1400, 888/650–1400 www.theblueboarinn.com 12 rooms Breakfast.*

$$ HOTEL **Homestead Resort.** Park City silver miners once soaked in the hot springs of this resort, which has been in operation since 1886. **Pros:** a Bruce Summerhays–designed golf course; natural hot springs. **Cons:** no on-site ski hill. *Rooms from: $150 700 N. Homestead Dr., Midway 435/654–1102, 800/327–7220 www.homesteadresort.com 147 rooms No meals.*

$$$$ RESORT FAMILY **Zermatt Resort & Spa.** Slightly Disney-esque in its re-creation of a Swiss-style estate, this sprawling hotel has everything from a wildlife-theme carousel to a full-service spa. **Pros:** immaculate rooms; stellar views; plenty to do. **Cons:** far from town. *Rooms from: $215 784 W. Resort Dr., Midway 435/657–0180, 866/840–5087 www.zermattresort.com 427 rooms No meals.*

NORTH OF SALT LAKE CITY

Updated
by Amanda
Knoles

When most people think of Utah, they picture the red-rock crags and canyons of the south, but the north, with its cattail marshes and pasturelands framed by the gray cliffs of the Wellsville Mountains and the Bear River Range, has its own kind of beauty—without the throngs of tourists you'll encounter in the south.

Here the Shoshones (Sacagawea's tribe) made their summer camps, living on roots, berries, and the plentiful game of the lowlands. In the 1820s and '30s mountain men came to trap beavers, foxes, and muskrats, taking time out for their annual rendezvous on the shores of Bear Lake. Some, like the famous Jim Bridger, took Native American wives and settled here; to this day, Cache, Rich, and Box Elder counties are collectively known as "Bridgerland." In the 1850s Mormon pioneers were sent by Brigham Young to settle here, and their descendants still populate this rugged land. In 1869 an event occurred here that would change the face of the West, and indeed the nation, forever: the completion of the Transcontinental Railroad was celebrated officially at Promontory Summit.

The region is characterized by alternating mountain ranges and valleys, typical of the Basin and Range geologic province that extends westward into Nevada and California. Much of the landscape has remained unspoiled, preserved for 100 years as part of the Uinta-Wasatch-Cache National Forest. The four counties in this region—Weber, Cache, Rich, and Box Elder—offer a range of outdoor activities for all seasons: hiking, mountain biking, kayaking, skiing, snowmobiling, and birding are popular activities among the locals. The miles of trails here are relatively undiscovered by tourists, who usually head to southern Utah or the Wasatch Mountains east of Salt Lake for such activities.

In the north of Utah as in the south, it's the landscape that steals the show. If you love a stroll through the backcountry, having breakfast with the locals at a small-town café, or exploring the legacy of the Old West, northern Utah may have a particularly strong appeal for you.

ORIENTATION AND PLANNING

GETTING ORIENTED

With two mountain ranges, Mother Nature has neatly divided northern Utah into three major sightseeing areas, each with its own attractions. Ogden and Logan are the main towns that anchor the region. Thirty minutes north of the state capital in Salt Lake City, Ogden served as a major railroad hub in the 19th and 20th centuries, and goods, services, wealth, brothels, and religion all found their way on the rails to this once-rough town. Northwest of Ogden is the Golden Spike Empire, home to the union of transcontinental railroads in 1869 and a thriving agricultural community. Logan, northeast of Ogden, is a fun,

TOP REASONS TO GO

Ski Ogden: Park City gets the accolades, but locals know that the snow is just as good, the slopes less crowded, and the prices much more reasonable at Snowbasin, Powder Mountain, and Nordic Valley. The most memorable moments on skis in the 2002 Winter Olympics happened here, not in Park City.

Hill Air Force Base: One of Utah's largest employers, the base provides worldwide logistics support for America's F-16s and A-10s. Look for Hill's fighters crisscrossing the skies, or get up close with more than 90 air- and spacecraft at the Hill Aerospace Museum.

Logan Canyon National Scenic Byway: A favorite with locals and visitors, the winding Highway 89 from Logan to Bear Lake is best

enjoyed in the fall when changing leaves create stunning panoramas of red, gold, and green. The route offers scenic picnic spots and fun hiking trails, with plenty of historic sites to explore along the way.

Historic 25th Street, Ogden: Once home to brothels and unsavory railside establishments, the community of Ogden has banded together to revitalize 25th Street with art galleries, museums, restaurants, and several unique shops. Downtown Ogden also has one of minor-league baseball's most beautiful ballparks.

Bear Lake: A favorite retreat on the Utah-Idaho border during the hot summer months, this modestly developed lake has a reputation for azure-blue water and the best raspberry shakes in America.

4

thriving college town (Utah State University has 15,000-plus students) that has emerged from the land-grant school. Turquoise-colored Bear Lake straddles the Idaho border farther north.

Ogden City and Valley. The largest city north of Salt Lake City is Ogden, with more than 84,000 residents. Its growth was spurred by the coming of the railroads and Hill Air Force Base, but its 21st-century renaissance is oriented around the easygoing outdoorsy lifestyle here. Hiking, skiing, golf, kayaking, boating, and more are all available either within city limits or in the beautiful valley that lies 8 miles up the canyon.

The Golden Spike Empire. Heading north up I–15 from Ogden (or, if you're in no hurry, up Highway 89, where you'll find plenty of farm stands), you'll come upon the Golden Spike Empire. Pleasant farmlands in the shadow of the Wellsvilles give way to rolling sagebrush-covered hills and eventually the desolate salt flats of the Great Salt Lake. After a visit to the Bear River Migratory Bird Refuge and the Golden Spike National Historic Site, cut east through the Wellsvilles to Logan and the Cache Valley, soaking up the rural scenery along the way.

Cache Valley. North of and roughly half the size of Ogden is the beautiful town of Logan, home to Utah State University and the Utah Festival Opera. You'll want to devote a day or two to the thriving college town, including the university's anthropology museum, which will give you a feel for the area's earliest inhabitants, and a stop at the Nora Eccles Harrison Museum of Art.

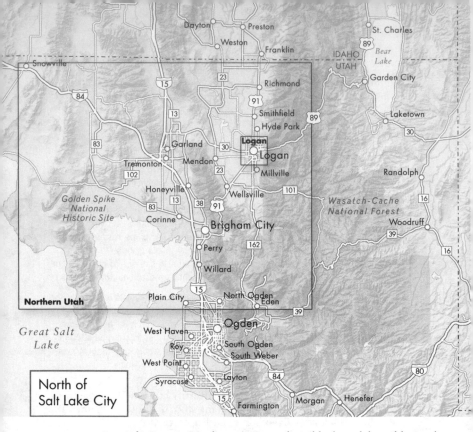

North of
Salt City

Bear Lake Country. It's almost incomprehensible that a lake as blue as the Mediterranean exists in the Intermountain West—but it's true. For sheer beauty, Bear Lake, half of which lies in Idaho, holds its own with Lake Tahoe or Yellowstone Lake. It's not nearly as developed as either, with only a few small motels and campgrounds. But at 109 square miles, it will give you plenty to explore for a few days in the hot summer.

PLANNING

WHEN TO GO

Northern Utah offers four seasons of outdoor fun, just be prepared for hot summer days and extremely cold winter nights. Spring brings vistas of verdant pastures under the still snowcapped mountains. Hot summer afternoons prepare you for a dip in Bear Lake followed by an evening at the Festival Opera. On crisp fall days, breathtaking hues of red scrub oak, orange maple, and bright yellow aspen rub shoulders with blue-green firs. Winter is the domain of skiers, snowshoers, and snowmobilers. This region drops dozens of inches of snow annually in the valleys and hundreds of inches in the mountains. You'll never battle hordes of tourists in this less-discovered part of the state, but you might have to wait in a line of locals for a raspberry shake at Bear Lake on a hot summer weekend.

PLANNING YOUR TIME

Either **Ogden** or **Logan** serves as a great base to begin your exploration of this corner of Utah. Both offer plenty of family-friendly and outdoor activities. Plan on a day in Ogden to check out the Salomon Center, Treehouse Museum, and Historic 25th Street. Head west on Highway 83 to **Golden Spike National Historic Site.** If you've had your fill of railroad history, make your way to Honeyville for a cleanse at **Crystal Hot Springs.** Heading north to **Logan,** enjoy one of the region's more scenic drives, before settling into this college town with plenty to see both in town and on the Utah State University campus. Stock up on cheese, ice cream, and local produce before the leisurely drive up Logan Canyon to **Bear Lake State Park,** where boating, swimming, or lounging await you at Rendezvous Beach.

If it's wintertime, a few days is enough time to get a good sense of skiing in northern Utah. Pick from Nordic Valley, Powder Mountain, and Snowbasin ski resorts. For a taste of what skiing was like before it became a rich person's sport, drive up to Beaver Mountain Ski Resort, or make a trip to Crystal Hot Springs to soak those tired muscles.

GETTING HERE AND AROUND

AIR TRAVEL

Salt Lake International is the primary airport for northern Utah, but Ogden-Hinckley Airport (38 miles north) is Utah's busiest general aviation airport. The Logan-Cache airport is capable of handling small charter jets, and Brigham City has an airport for propeller planes.

Airport Information Brigham City Municipal Airport ⊠ *1800 N. 2000 W, Brigham City* ☎ *435/734–6615* ⊕ *brighamcity.utah.gov/airport.htm.* **Logan-Cache Airport** ⊠ *2500 N. 900 W, Logan* ☎ *435/752–8111* ⊕ *logan-cacheairport.org.* **Ogden-Hinckley Airport** ⊠ *3909 Airport Rd., Ogden* ☎ *801/629–8251* ⊕ *www.flyogden.com.* **Salt Lake International Airport** ⊠ *776 N. Terminal Dr., Salt Lake City* ☎ *801/575–2400* ⊕ *www.slcairport.com.*

AIRPORT TRANSFERS Express Shuttle offers round-trip shuttles to Ogden, and Salt Lake Express makes several stops in Logan including the Transit Center, where you can transfer to local buses. Prices vary by day and time.

Shuttle Information Express Shuttle ☎ *800/397–0773* ⊕ *www.expressshuttleutah.com.* **Salt Lake Express** ☎ *800/356–9796* ⊕ *www.saltlakeexpress.com.*

BUS TRAVEL

The Utah Transit Authority (UTA) is a good option for getting to and from the Wasatch Front. It runs buses more or less hourly between Brigham City and Ogden, with stops in Willard and Perry. From Ogden there are many connections to Salt Lake City. The price is a steal: $2.50 for a two-hour ride (that should get you all the way to Salt Lake). A day pass for $6.25 will allow you to ride TRAX, Salt Lake City's light rail, plus buses and streetcars once you get there. Passes may be purchased from vending machines at TRAX stations or from bus drivers. Within Cache Valley, catch the free blue-and-white Logan Transit District shuttles, which operate within Logan (with an express to Utah State University) or the Cache Valley Transit District between Richmond to the north and Hyrum to the south. The main station is within walking distance of most hotels at 500 North and 100 East streets.

Bus Information Logan Transit District ☎ *435/752-2877* ⊕ *www.cvtdbus.org.* **Utah Transit Authority** ☎ *801/743-3882, 888/743-3882* ⊕ *www.rideuta.com.*

CAR TRAVEL

Northern Utah has two main highways: I–15 running north–south and Highway 89 running northeast–southwest. The latter is a national scenic byway, and the hour's drive between Logan and Bear Lake will reward you with breathtaking vistas and plenty of places to pull off for a picnic. Off the main highways, roads range from well-paved multilane blacktop routes to barely graveled backcountry trails. If you're going to venture off the beaten track at all, it's a good idea to have a four-wheel-drive vehicle or at least a truck with high clearance. Deer, elk, and even bobcats may try to cross a road just as you come along, so watch for wildlife on the highways. In rural and resort towns, expect gas prices to be considerably higher than in large cities. The following Highway Patrol offices are open weekdays from 8:30 to 5.

Information Utah Highway Patrol Logan Office ✉ *1225 W. Valley View, Suite 350, Logan* ☎ *435/752-1110* ⊕ *www.publicsafety.utah.gov.* **Utah Highway Patrol Ogden Office** ✉ *461 Stewart St., Ogden* ☎ *801/393-1136* ⊕ *www. publicsafety.utah.gov.*

Road Conditions Utah Road Condition Information ☎ *511 within Utah, 866/511-8824 outside Utah* ⊕ *udot.utah.gov/traffic.*

TRAIN TRAVEL

The FrontRunner high-speed commuter train operates every half-hour on weekdays and every hour on Saturday between the downtowns of Ogden and Salt Lake City, with a half-dozen stops in between. Fares are based on the distance traveled, starting at $2 one-way.

Train Information Utah Transit Authority ☎ *801/743-3882, 888/743-3882* ⊕ *www.rideuta.com.*

RESTAURANTS

Both Ogden and Logan have fine restaurants, but in general the fare in northern Utah is your basic Western-style grub. If your idea of a nice meal out is a big slab of meat that was on the hoof a few days ago and a giant Idaho potato, then you're in luck. If you can't look at another steak, there's at least one decent Mexican or Italian place in every sizeable town. Be sure to sample the Aggie ice cream made at Utah State University, Cache Valley Swiss cheese, and fresh fruit and vegetables from this rich agricultural area.

HOTELS

Some reputable chains have made their way here, along with interesting family-owned inns and B&Bs in a full range of prices. At Bear Lake you can rent a condo with a kitchen if you feel like putting down roots for a while. Make reservations, especially on summer weekends and holidays; during fall and winter many hotels get booked far in advance when conventions are in town. *Hotel reviews have been shortened. For full information, visit Fodors.com.*

WHAT IT COSTS				
	$	$$	$$$	$$$$
Restaurants	under $12	$12–$20	$21–$30	over $30
Hotels	under $100	$100–$150	$151–$200	over $200

Restaurant prices are the average cost of a main course at dinner or, if dinner is not served, at lunch. Hotel prices are the lowest cost of a standard double room in high season.

VISITOR INFORMATION

Bear Lake–Rendezvous Chamber of Commerce ☎ *435/946–2197* ⊕ *www. bearlakechamber.com.*

Bear River Valley Chamber of Commerce ☎ *435/282–0155* ⊕ *www.brvcc. com.*

Cache Valley Visitors Bureau ✉ *199 N. Main St., Logan* ☎ *435/755–1890, 800/882–4433* ⊕ *www.visitloganutah.com* ☽ *Closed Sun.*

OGDEN CITY AND VALLEY

Settled several years prior to Salt Lake City's historic Mormon influx (in 1847), Ogden has nonetheless been trumped by the capital city to the south for most of its history. Recently, however, a thriving outdoor recreation industry, Hill Air Force Base, three ski areas, and the renovation of Historic 25th Street have brought jobs, recreation, and redevelopment to a community once known as a seedy railroad junction. The city is a small, affordable alternative to Salt Lake City—or head "up the hill" to the Ogden Valley to enjoy a marvelously pastoral community surrounding the Pine View Reservoir and bordered by mountains with some of America's best skiing.

OGDEN

35 miles from Salt Lake City.

As the Wasatch Front population continues to swell, it's harder to tell where Salt Lake City ends and the next major city, Ogden, begins. In between are a string of towns that serve primarily as bedroom communities. The drive north, through and beyond these communities, bordered by the shores of the Great Salt Lake on the west and the Wasatch Mountains on the east, takes you through a world of recreational options. With a population of more than 84,000, Ogden combines a small-town feel with the infrastructure of a larger city. The oldest town in Utah, Ogden was founded by mountain man Miles Goodyear, who settled here with his family in the early 1840s. The Mormons arrived in the area in 1847, and in 1869 Ogden became a hub for the Transcontinental Railroad. The city quickly became a major Western crossroads. During World War II there was a considerable military presence here. This continues today at Hill Air Force Base. Ogden is also a college town; Weber State University is within the city limits.

These days, Ogden has become a multisport mecca, where outdoor adventure blends with emerging urban chic. You can head east into the Upper Ogden Valley—only 20 minutes from downtown—for climbing, biking, hiking, and world-class skiing, or paddle the kayak park on the Ogden River. After your adrenaline binge, recharge in Historic 25th Street, the metropolitan complement to this recreation-heavy stronghold. During the railroad heyday, 25th Street, directly east of the railroad depot, was infamous for its bars and bordellos. The buildings that once housed them have been preserved and now house restaurants, clubs, crafts and antiques shops, and home-style stores.

GETTING HERE AND AROUND

Ogden is about 30 minutes north of Salt Lake City on I–15, with several suburbs and Hill Air Force base in between. Most commuters and visitors take the highway and enter Ogden via Exits 341, 343, or 344. Highway 89 straddles the Wasatch Mountains and offers an alternative route and a shortcut for drivers headed to Ogden Valley from Salt Lake City. FrontRunner trains, taxis, or UTA buses are public options if you don't have a car.

ESSENTIALS

Ogden Convention and Visitors Bureau ⊠ *2438 Washington Blvd.* ☎ *801/778–6254, 866/867–8824* ⊕ *www.visitogden.com.*

Ogden Valley Business Association ⊠ *5460 E. 2200 N, Eden* ☎ *801/745–2550* ⊕ *www.ovba.org.*

Ogden Weber Chamber of Commerce ⊠ *2484 Washington Blvd., Suite 400* ☎ *801/621–8300* ⊕ *www.ogdenweberchamber.com.*

EXPLORING
TOP ATTRACTIONS

FAMILY **George S. Eccles Dinosaur Park.** The 5-acre dinosaur park near the mouth of Ogden Canyon is the stomping ground for about 100 life-size dinosaur models and the delighted children who come to see them. A playground with dinosaurs to crawl on is a lure for the younger set. An on-site café offers quick bites and drinks, and the gift shop is brimming with dinosaur toys, T-shirts, games, and souvenirs. Technicians working with excavated dinosaur bones are on view in the museum area and educational activities for kids put a lot of fun into learning. ⊠ *1544 E. Park Blvd.* ☎ *801/393–3466* ⊕ *www.dinosaurpark.org* 🎟 *$7* ⊗ *Daily 10–5 (until 7 Memorial Day–Labor Day).*

FAMILY **Hill Aerospace Museum.** If you like airplanes old or new, you'll love this museum 5 miles south of downtown Ogden at Hill Air Force Base in Roy, off I–15 at Exit 338. There are more than 90 aircraft on display along with missiles, military vehicles, munitions, uniforms, and thousands of artifacts. ⊠ *Hill Air Force Base, 7961 Wardleigh Rd., Roy* ☎ *801/777–6868* ⊕ *www.hill.af.mil/library/museum* 🎟 *Free* ⊗ *Tues.–Sat. 9–4:30.*

Fodor'sChoice **Historic 25th Street.** Named one of the "10 Best Streets" in the United ★ States by the American Planning Association, this quaint section of downtown Ogden has been the centerpiece of a 30-year urban-renewal initiative. A fun place to hang out for a couple of hours, 25th Street retains the color, flavor, and vitality of its 19th-century roots without the grime and crime that once made it infamous. From Union Station to Washington Boulevard, this three-block stretch includes more than a dozen restaurants, plus galleries, boutiques, and more. Historical markers tell the story of the rough pubs, brothels, and gambling houses that were the anomaly in heavily Mormon Utah a century ago. Relax, though, it's both safe and family-friendly today. The Historic 25th Street Business Association frequently sponsors special events that create a festival atmosphere. ⊕ *www.historic25.com.*

FAMILY **Salomon Center at the Junction.** In a former downtown mall, this massive center is a high-adventure recreational playground, complete with a climbing wall, Flowrider, I Fly wind tunnel, bowling alley, miniature golf, and 13-theater movie complex. ⊠ *2261 Keisel Ave.* ☎ *801/528–5348* ⊕ *www.ogdenjunction.com* ⊠ *Admission varies* ⊙ *Call for hrs.*

FAMILY **Union Station.** Incorporating elements of Ogden's original 1870s train
Fodor'sChoice depot, which was destroyed by fire in 1923, the impressive Spanish
★ Revival replacement houses four museums, three art galleries, a restaurant, and gift shop. ⊠ *2501 Wall Ave.* ☎ *801/393–9890* ⊕ *theunionstation.org* ⊠ *Combined ticket to all 4 museums $5* ⊙ *Mon.–Sat. 10–5.*

John M. Browning Firearms Museum. Celebrating the many achievements of inventor John M. Browing, this museum showcases sporting and military firearms, many of which were built by Winchester, Colt, Remington, and others to become the weapons of choice in the Old West before Browning formed his own company. Original models and working prototypes of many of the guns are displayed.

Browning-Kimball Classic Car Museum. Paying tribute to the golden age of automobiles, this extensive exhibit features almost 60 unique restored cars on display, including a single-cylinder 1901 Oldsmobile and a 16-cylinder Cadillac built in 1930. The 1911 Knox is a highlight. Antique gas pumps, fire engines, and a huge collection of license plates are also on display.

Utah State Railroad Museum. Train enthusiasts will have a ball at this museum featuring exhibits that detail all phases of Utah's railroad history through displays and interpretive signs. You can also watch model trains run through depictions of the Transcontinental Railroad route. The high point of the museum is the Eccles Rail Center, an outdoor exhibit containing several dozen restored train cars, locomotives, and cabooses that date from the late 1800s right up to the 2002 Olympic Games' cauldron car.

Utah Cowboy & Western Heritage Museum. Union Station's newest museum includes the Utah Cowboy Hall of Fame and features a variety of exhibits honoring artists, rodeo champions, entertainers, musicians, ranchers and writers who have promoted the Western lifestyle. As the museum expands it will add books, a research center and memorabilia received from donors. ⊕ *www.utahcowboymuseum.org.*

WORTH NOTING
Eccles Community Art Center. Housed in an impressive Victorian mansion, the museum has a permanent collection of works by such contemporary artists as LeConte Stewart, Henri Mosher, Pilar Pobil, David Jackson,

and Richard Van Wagoner. There is also a sculpture garden. Special exhibits change periodically, and there are monthly displays of works by emerging Utah artists. ⊠ *2580 Jefferson Ave.* ☎ *801/392–6935* ⊕ *www. ogden4arts.org* ✉ *Free* ☉ *Weekdays 9–5, Sat. 9–3.*

FAMILY **Fort Buenaventura Park.** Highlighting a chapter in history that unfolded decades prior to the railroad era, this 84-acre tract has replicas of the stockade and cabins that Miles Goodyear built in 1846. Guides in period costume interpret the ways of the early trappers. Picnicking facilities are available and canoes may be rented ($3 for a half-hour, $5 for an hour) in warmer months. ⊠ *2450 A Ave.* ☎ *801/399–8099* ⊕ *www.co.weber.ut.us/parks/fortb* ✉ *$2* ☉ *Apr.–Nov., daily 9–9.*

FAMILY **Ogden Nature Center.** As one of very few wildlife sanctuaries set within a city, the 152-acre center is home to thousands of trees, marshlands, and ponds, with nature trails used for cross-country skiing in winter. You can see Canada geese, great blue herons, red-tailed hawks, and snowy egrets, as well as red foxes, mule deer, porcupines, and more. The nature center museum has activities for children, and the Nest gift shop sells nature-oriented goods. ⊠ *966 W. 12th St.* ☎ *801/621–7595* ⊕ *www. ogdennaturecenter.org* ✉ *$4* ☉ *Weekdays 9–5, Sat. 9–4.*

FAMILY **Treehouse Museum.** Offering a hands-on learning experience where children literally can step into a story, the downtown museum features interactive exhibits for kids ages 2–12. Visit Jack's Fairy Tale Diner, a Japanese House, the Jupiter Train Locomotive, or the German House Puppet Theater. Other fun activities include songs, theater, and art workshops. ⊠ *347 22nd Ave.* ☎ *801/394–9663* ⊕ *www. treehousemuseum.org* ✉ *$5* ☉ *Mon–Sat. 10–5 (until 8 Fri.).*

SPORTS AND THE OUTDOORS

More than 250 miles of trails for hiking, mountain biking, and horseback riding surround the Ogden area, and the scenic roads are perfect for biking enthusiasts. The Weber and Ogden rivers and a downtown water park provide high-adventure rafting and kayaking. Olympic-caliber skiing is just up the canyon.

BASEBALL

Lindquist Field. Considered one of the best minor-league ballparks in America, this baseball park in downtown Ogden should be on every fan's itinerary. You'll quickly see why it's also considered the best view in baseball. The Raptors are a Dodgers' farm club, and play "rookie ball" from June to August. ⊠ *2330 Lincoln Ave.* ☎ *801/393–2400* ⊕ *www.ogden-raptors.com* ✉ *$12–$25.*

BICYCLING

The Bike Shoppe. Specializing in bikes and bike service for more than 35 years, this shop favored by bike enthusiasts sells and repairs top-of-the-line brands and offers bike rentals by the day ($100). You can also rent snowshoes and wetsuits here. ⊠ *4390 S. Washington Blvd.* ☎ *801/476–1600* ⊕ *www.thebikeshoppe.com* ☉ *Closed Sun.*

GOLF

For a complete list of Ogden area golf courses, contact the Ogden Convention and Visitors Bureau (☎ *801/778–6254* ⊕ *www.visitogden.com*).

Mount Ogden Golf Course. This city-owned course is celebrated for its well-maintained greens and variety of elevation changes. Open since 1984, it was designed by Billy Casper and William H. Neff. Best suited for more experienced players, it's been reviewed by golf enthusiasts as a fun place to play, and has received accolades from golf publications for its stunning views of the Ogden Valley and the creative challenges presented by many of the holes. ✉ *1787 Constitution Way* ☎ *801/629–0699* ⊕ *www.ogdencity.com/en/recreation/classic_rec/golf/ mt_ogden_golf_course.aspx* 🖼 *$33 weekdays, $40 weekends (includes cart)* ⚑ *18 holes, 6342 yards, par 71.*

Schneiter's Riverside Golf Course. Minutes from downtown Ogden and 25 miles from Salt Lake City, this 18-hole course has views of Antelope Island and the Wasatch Mountains. In a scenic valley, it winds along the Weber River and is notable for its tall trees and tight fairways. Appealing to scratch golfers seeking a new challenge and beginners wanting an affordable course to learn on, it's an easy walk and perfect for visitors planning a golf outing. ✉ *5460 S. Weber Dr., Riverdale* ☎ *801/399–4636* ⊕ *www.schneitersgolf.com* 🖼 *$28 for 18 holes, $14 for 9 holes weekends; $26 for 18 holes, $13 for 9 holes weekdays. Carts: $12 for 18 holes, $7 for 9 holes* ⚑ *18 holes, 6177 yards, par 71.*

HIKING

From an urban stroll along the Ogden River Parkway to a challenging hike on the Beus Canyon Trail to the summit of Mount Ogden, hikes in the Ogden area provide something for everyone. Most of the trail system is connected in some way to the North–South Bonneville Shoreline Trail, a pathway following the high mark of prehistoric Lake Bonneville along the Wasatch Front. An excellent resource for detailed trail information is Weber Pathways, a local nonprofit organization dedicated to preserving and maintaining trails in Weber County.

Weber Pathways ☎ *801/393–2304* ⊕ *www.weberpathways.org.*

KAYAKING AND RAFTING

Ogden Kayak Park. On the Weber River, this specially designed kayak park offers great rides for kayakers and thrilling action for spectators. Try to negotiate the Olympic-style slalom gates if you think it looks easy. ✉ *Exchange Rd. and 24th St.* ⊕ *www.ogden.city.com/en/ community/parks/kayak_park_aspx* 🖼 *Free.*

WSU Outdoor Program. Weber State University offers an affordably priced outdoor program designed for students, residents, and visitors seeking custom guided tours. Activities include white-water rafting, kayaking, rock climbing, snowshoeing, and cross-country skiing. All guides are experienced with insider's knowledge of the area. Equipment rentals are available. ✉ *Weber State University, 4022 Stadium Way* ☎ *801/626– 6373* ⊕ *www.weber.edu/outdoor* 🖼 *$70–$125* ⊙ *Mon.–Sat. 8–6.*

WHERE TO EAT

$$$

MODERN
AMERICAN

✕**Bistro 258.** Owners Devin and Nick Cash design and prepare upscale fare such as coconut macadamia halibut, blackberry broiled pork chops, and orange-chili chicken at this popular downtown Ogden eatery. Its chic interiors wouldn't be out of place in Manhattan, but the attitude and vibe is much more laid-back. For lunch, try the Asian chicken wrap or a rice bowl filled with stir-fried vegetables and your choice of meats and sauces. The outdoor patio and glassed-in back dining area are more casual than the front section. Servers are friendly and offer smart suggestions from the menu and wine list. [$] *Average main: $22* ✉ *258 25th St.* ☎ *801/394–1595* 🌐 *bistro258.net* 🕒 *Closed Sun.*

$ AMERICAN FAMILY 🍴 **The Greenery.** Diners enjoy verdant surroundings and views of the Wasatch Mountains at this kitschy eatery that serves up specialties like Mormon muffins and homemade caramel apple pie. The black- and-white tile floors and wrought-iron chairs create a mix of '50s diner and garden-party style. After your meal you can browse the thousands of square feet of trinkets, souvenirs, and books at the gift shops next door for just the right piece of Utah to take home with you. [$] *Average main: $10* ✉ *Rainbow Gardens, 1875 Valley Dr.* ☎ *801/392–1777* 🌐 *www.rainbowgardens.com.*

$$$ CONTEMPORARY Fodor's Choice ★ 🍴 **Hearth on 25th.** Named Best Restaurant in Northern Utah by *Salt Lake Magazine* for two years in a row, this fine-dining gem offers a menu that will please even the most discerning foodie. The *Salt Lake Tribune* named it one of the best places in the state to enjoy wild game, and you'll even find grass-fed yak on the menu. Formerly known as Jasoh!, the owners changed the name to highlight the focus on wood-fired cooking. With an emphasis on farm-to-table freshness, the menu also includes fish presented in creative ways and house-made pastas, breads, and dressings. Diners enjoy a patio overlooking the Historic District and the Wasatch Mountains, an impressive wine and beer list, and a seasonally changing array of fresh desserts. ■ **TIP→ Bags of the slow-dried artisan pasta made on-site are available to take home. Check the pantry at the front of the restaurant.** [$] *Average main: $30* ✉ *195 25th St.* ☎ *801/399–0088* 🌐 *www.hearth25.com* 🕒 *Closed Sun.*

$ AMERICAN 🍴 **Karen's 25th St. Café.** In the heart of the Historic District, this locals' favorite is highly regarded for its tempting breakfasts, homemade soups, and stick-to-your-ribs comfort food. Chicken-fried steak and bacon bleu cheeseburgers are perennial crowd pleasers, but you'll want to save room for a slice of fresh-baked cake (included with the lunch combination plates). Odds are you'll find owners Karen and Troy Waters in the restaurant in the morning whipping up a batch of muffins and making sure your breakfast sizzles. [$] *Average main: $10* ✉ *195 25th St.* ☎ *801/392–0345* 🕒 *No dinner Sun.*

$$ ITALIAN 🍴 **La Ferrovia Ristorante.** You can't go wrong with the pasta specials at this tiny Italian eatery in the heart of Ogden's Historic 25th Street. Owner Giuseppina Ashbridge brought her recipes with her when she left Naples, and she and her husband Jeff serve authentic dishes with genuine hospitality. Specialties include lasagna, ravioli, and tortellini. Pizza and calzones round out the menu, and there's a well-chosen list of mostly Italian wines. A variety of lunch specials is offered, and take-out orders are accepted. [$] *Average main: $17* ✉ *234 25th St.* ☎ *801/394–8628* 🌐 *www.laferrovia.com* 🕒 *Closed Sun. and Mon.*

$$ AMERICAN 🍴 **Rooster's Brewing Company and Restaurant.** On Historic 25th Street, this brewpub offers excellent food and libations brewed on-site. Set in a 104-year-old building that was once a Chinese laundry, the pub offers pizzas created with locally made cheeses, steak, sandwiches, salads, and

daily seafood specials, including the popular grilled Atlantic salmon. Try a Polygamy Pale Ale or any of the two-dozen brewmaster's specials, which vary by season. On a sunny day sit on the patio, which is partly glass-enclosed for year-round use. $ *Average main: $16* ⌧ *253 25th St.* ☏ *801/627–6171* ⊕ *www.roostersbrewingco.com* ☾ *No brunch weekdays.*

WHERE TO STAY

$ | ⊞ **Ben Lomond Suites.** Listed on both the Utah and national historic
HOTEL | registers, this landmark hotel, within walking distance of restaurants, shops, attractions, and a park, offers spacious two-room suites ideal for business trips or family vacations. **Pros:** two on-site restaurants; covered parking; some rooms have mountain views. **Cons:** some bathrooms need updating; elevators are showing their age and can be slow. $ *Rooms from: $90* ⌧ *2510 Washington Blvd.* ☏ *801/627–1900* ⊕ *www.benlomondsuites.com* ↵ *97 suites* |⚬| *Breakfast.*

$$ | ⊞ **Courtyard Ogden.** Renovated in 2014, the former Ogden Marriott
HOTEL | has a convenient downtown location close to government offices and businesses and in walking distance of Historic 25th Street. **Pros:** completely smoke-free; close to businesses, restaurants and nightlife; free Wi-Fi throughout. **Cons:** no complimentary breakfast unless part of a more expensive package; no pets. $ *Rooms from: $125* ⌧ *247 24th St.* ☏ *801/627–1190, 800/321–2211* ⊕ *www.marriott.com* ↵ *182 rooms, 11 suites* |⚬| *No meals.*

$$ | ⊞ **Hampton Inn and Suites.** Gray marble floors, deep-purple chairs, and
HOTEL | ceilings with ornate crown molding greet you in the lobby of this art
Fodor's Choice | deco beauty. **Pros:** free Wi-Fi; complimentary hot breakfast; walking
★ | distance to Historic 25th Street and restaurants. **Cons:** no fridges in many rooms; frequently booked with business travelers; higher rates during special events. $ *Rooms from: $150* ⌧ *2401 Washington Blvd.* ☏ *801/394–9400* ⊕ *www.ogdensuites.hamptoninn.com* ↵ *124 rooms, 21 suites* |⚬| *Breakfast.*

$$ | ⊞ **Hilton Garden Inn.** Near the Ogden Eccles Conference Center and
HOTEL | Union Station, this modern hotel is an ideal choice for both business and leisure travelers. **Pros:** convenient to businesses, attractions and Historic 25th Street; on-site restaurant serves breakfast and dinner and offers room service; scenic view suites have fireplaces. **Cons:** frequently booked up for conventions and conferences; outdoor parking. $ *Rooms from: $129* ⌧ *2271 S. Washington Bd.* ☏ *801/399–2000* ⊕ *www.hilton. com* ↵ *114 rooms, 6 suites* |⚬| *Breakfast.*

NIGHTLIFE AND PERFORMING ARTS
NIGHTLIFE

At the height of the railroad era Ogden's 25th Street was lined with saloons and gambling halls, opium dens, and a thriving red-light district. It's gentrified since then, but is still the center of one of Utah's most vibrant nightlife scenes. The American Planning Association named it one of the "10 Best Streets in the U.S." Beyond 25th Street you'll find good live music and dance clubs throughout the city.

Brewskis. Big-screen TVs, pool tables, and live music are the big draw at this popular bar. The menu features pub fare, including burgers, sandwiches, and pizzas. Anyone (age 21 or older) who enjoys good music will love it here on weekends, when acts ranging from country to hard rock and Indie folk take the stage. ✉ *244 25th St.* ☎ *801/394–1713* ⊕ *www.brewskisonline.net.*

City Club. Decorated with an impressive collection of Beatles memorabilia, this unique bar caters to an upscale crowd, generally in their 30s. Patrons enjoy two floors, a patio, and a menu offering appetizers, specialty drinks, sandwiches, and salads. ✉ *264 25th St.* ☎ *801/392–4447* ⊕ *www.thecityclubonline.net.*

Kamikazes. At this lively nightspot, in a former church, you can dance to live music on one floor and to DJ spins on another, or play pool. ✉ *2404 Adams Ave.* ☎ *801/621–9138.*

Lighthouse Lounge. Once a landmark strip club and then a beer bar, this upscale lounge and music venue is a great spot for sipping a cocktail, sharing some appetizers, and listening to live performers in the Listening Room, some of which are free of a cover charge. ✉ *130 25th St.* ☎ *801/392–3901* ⊕ *lighthouseloungeogden.com.*

Wiseguys Comedy Café. Stand-up comedians perform Friday and Saturday and occasional other nights at this popular venue. You can expect to see recognizable names as well as up-and-coming talent. Openmike night is Wednesday. ✉ *269 25th St.* ☎ *801/622–5588* ⊕ *www.wiseguyscomedy.com.*

PERFORMING ARTS

Ogden Amphitheater. From June through August at this venue with gorgeous views, local and regional artists give free outdoor concerts Tuesday at noon and Wednesday night, and there are free movies on Monday. ✉ *Municipal Gardens, 25th St. and Washington Blvd.* ☎ *801/629–8000* ⊕ *www.ocae.org.*

Peery Egyptian Theater. Built in the 1920s then abandoned for years, the Peery Egyptian Theater is a restored art deco jewel that hosts concerts ranging from world music to national blues, jazz, and country acts, as well as an ongoing film series. The theater also presents screenings and premieres during the Sundance Film Festival in January. ✉ *2415 Washington Blvd.* ☎ *801/689–8600* ⊕ *www.peerysegyptiantheater.com.*

Val A. Browning Center for the Performing Arts. Theater, music, and dance performances by students and visiting artists are offered frequently at Weber State University's performing arts center, home stage for the Ogden Symphony Ballet Association. ✉ *Weber State University, 1901 University Circle, off 3848 Harrison Blvd.* ☎ *801/626–6000* ⊕ *www.browningcenter.org/events.*

SHOPPING

As with nightlife and dining, you'll find the most interesting concentration of shops on Historic 25th Street, with a few don't-miss shopping stops scattered around the rest of town.

ANTIQUES

Sock Monkey N Around Antiques. If the fun name isn't enough to draw you inside, the retro toys and collectibles on display in the window are guaranteed to make you smile. Filled with two stories full of vintage fashions and furniture, dolls, games, vinyl records, jewelry, housewares, and sock monkeys handmade by the owner, this well-organized antiques shop is worth exploring. ⊠ *236 E. 25th St.* ☎ *801/644–3886* ⊙ *Closed Sun.*

ART GALLERIES

25th Street Farmers' & Art Market. Find the work of local artists here on Saturday, July through October from 8 am to 1 pm. There's live music and food stalls, too. ⊠ *25th St. and Municipal Park* ☎ *801/393–3866* ⊕ *www.ogdenfarmersmarket.com.*

Art Stroll. The first Friday of each month more than 20 downtown galleries and artists show off their wares during a street stroll that begins at the Gallery at the Station, Union Station, and ends at the Eccles Community Art Center on the corner of 26th and Jefferson streets. ⊠ *2501 Wall Ave.* ☎ *801/393–3866* ⊕ *www.ogdencityarts.org.*

GIFTS AND SOUVENIRS

Olive & Dahlia. In a redbrick building in the heart of Historic 25th St., this intriguing shop invites exploration. Best known for award-winning flower arrangements, it's also a great place to find unique gift items including glass art, metal sculptures, coasters, birdhouses, and unique home and garden accessories. ⊠ *215 25th St.* ☎ *801/627–0340.*

Rainbow Gardens. If you're looking for a gift or memento that says Utah, this unique store at the mouth of Ogden Canyon is a fun place to browse. More than 20 departments offer souvenirs, cowboy nostalgia, books, baskets, gadgets, seasonal decorations, and regionally made food items. ⊠ *1851 Valley Dr.* ☎ *801/621–1606* ⊕ *www.rainbowgardens.com.*

PERFUME AND COSMETICS

Making Scents Emporium. Create your own signature fragrance at this aromatherapy gift shop in downtown Ogden. Owners Ru Pudlewski and Larry Baird specialize in personalized bath and body products with a wide variety of essential oils, soaps, lotions, and bath salts in stock and more than 500 scents to choose from. ⊠ *290 25th St.* ☎ *801/866–0303* ⊕ *www.mkngscnts.com* ⊙ *Closed Sun.*

UPPER OGDEN VALLEY

8 miles east of Ogden City.

Locals call it "the valley," as if it were the only valley in the world. It's sleepy and slow, and if it had sidewalks they'd roll them up early, but once you see the valley, anchored by Pineview Reservoir, surrounded by the spectacular Wasatch Mountains, and home to the quaint pioneer towns of Eden and Huntsville, you'll see why residents feel this way. With its world-class skiing, accessible water sports, great fishing, golf, climbing, hiking, biking, and camping, the Upper Ogden Valley is a recreation mecca still largely waiting to be discovered. East of the reservoir lies the village of Huntsville, which counts about 600 residents, one monastery, a couple of clay beaches, and the oldest saloons in the state. The 19th-century home of former LDS Church president David MacKay is the primary historical attraction.

GETTING HERE AND AROUND

Most visitors approach the valley from Ogden via 12th Street, which becomes Highway 39. Pineview Reservoir lies at the center of the valley, and resembles an airplane with the nose pointing west, and wings (arms of the lake) extending north and south. You can circle the reservoir in about 30 minutes by car, although it's tempting to stop for the beaches, boat access, milk shakes, and more.

Trapper's Loop (Highway 167) is the scenic shortcut expanded for the 2002 Olympics from I–84 to the south end of the reservoir. It's beautiful in spring and fall, and well maintained for access to Snowbasin ski resort in the winter.

EXPLORING

Pineview Reservoir. In summer this 2,800-acre lake is festooned with colorful sailboats and the graceful arcs of water-skiers and wakeboarders. In winter it's a popular spot for ice-fishing. The fishing is good, and beaches, campgrounds, and marinas dot the shore. Middle Inlet, Cemetery Point, and Anderson Cove are the three developed beaches (fee), but Anderson Cove is the only one that allows overnight camping. The Cove has a boat launch. ⊠ *Ogden, Utah, United States* ☎ *801/625–5112* ⊕ *www.fs.us.usda.gov* ☜ *$13 day use* ☉ *Daily 8 am–10 pm.*

SPORTS AND THE OUTDOORS

GOLF

Wolf Creek Golf Course. With mountains on both sides, this course is known as one of the most scenic in the state. It is the only Audubon-certified course in Utah, with ample chances to see wild birds and local wildlife. Appealing to all skill levels, it was built in 1965 and designed by Mark Dixon Ballif. Winding over foothills, through oak groves and past water features, the challenging course offers stunning views of Pineview Reservoir and the Ogden Valley. ⊠ *3900 N. Wolf Creek Dr., Eden* ☎ *801/745–3365* ⊕ *www.wolfcreekgolfutah.com* ☜ *$20 for 9 holes, $30 for 18 holes; carts: $15 for 18 holes, $10 for 9 holes* ⛳ *18 holes, 6779 yards, par 72.*

HIKING

Many of the beautiful hikes in the Ogden Valley enable you to discover ski terrain in the off-season. For detailed trail maps and information, contact the Ogden Ranger District at ☎ *801/625–5112*; if you're at Snowbasin you can get maps in the Grizzly Center.

Snowbasin. Starting at 6,500 feet and ending at 9,600 feet, the moderate 2½-mile trail (one-way) from the upper parking lot at Snowbasin leads to the saddle south of Mount Ogden. Hikers pass through bowls filled with colorful summer wildflowers. U.S. Forest Service trails branch off at the resort. ⊠ *Ogden* ⊕ *www.snowbasin.com.*

HORSEBACK RIDING

Red Cliff Ranch and Outfitters. Visitors in summer enjoy scenic mountain views on horseback. Guided trail rides are offered in the warmer months along with horse-drawn hayrides that lead to a campfire dinner. Sleigh rides are available in winter. ⊠ *1355 E. Hwy. 39, Huntsville* ☎ *801/745–6900* ⊕ *www.redcliffranch.com.*

SKIING

CROSS-
COUNTRY

North Fork Park. The well-maintained 7½ miles of cross-country and snowshoe trails at this park are perfect for beginners, intermediates, and families looking for a day of fun in the snow. It's also popular for hiking and biking in warmer months. ✉ *1984 North Fork Park Rd., Eden* ☎ *801/648–9020* ⊕ *www.ogdennordic.com.*

DOWNHILL

If you're staying in Ogden and want to head for the mountains for a day of skiing or snowboarding, you can catch the Ski Bus, which runs between several downtown Ogden hotels and the ski resorts in the Upper Ogden Valley. For details of schedules and routes, call ☎ *888/743–3882* or ask at the front desk of your local hotel. Black Diamond Shuttle also offers taxi service from hotels and the airport. Call ☎ *801/920–1774.*

Powder Mountain. Rising north out of Ogden Canyon is one of northern Utah's most popular ski areas. As the name suggests, it receives a generous helping of the white stuff for which Utah is famous. This classic ski resort offers huge terrain (more skiable acres than any other resort in the country) even though it doesn't have as many lifts as some of the destination resorts. Two terrain parks and a half-pipe are popular with snowboarders. You won't find fancy lodges or haute cuisine here, but crowds are nonexistent and the laid-back slope-side eateries serve everything from scones and hot soup to sandwiches or a flame-broiled Powder Burger at the Powder Keg. ✉ *8000 N. 5100 E (Hwy. 158), Eden* ☎ *801/745–3772* ⊕ *www.powdermountain.com* 🎟 *Lift tickets $24–$69* ⛷ *2,205-ft vertical drop; 7,000 skiable acres; 25% beginner, 40% intermediate, 35% advanced; 2 quad chairs, 1 triple chair, 1 double chair, 3 surface lifts.*

Snowbasin. A vertical drop of 2,959 feet and a dramatic start at the pinnacle of Mount Ogden made this ski resort, 17 miles from Ogden, the perfect site for the downhill ski races during the 2002 Olympic Winter Games. With nine lifts accessing more than 2,800 acres of skiable terrain, this is one of Utah's largest resorts. It also offers miles of Nordic trails for cross-country skiing with easy and more challenging routes. Lodging packages are available at area hotels, including downtown locations with shuttles, and nearby condo rentals. The Grizzly Center offers ski and snowshoe rentals, and there are five restaurants on-site. ✉ *3925 E. Snowbasin Rd. (Hwy. 226), Huntsville* ☎ *801/620–1000, 888/437–5488* ⊕ *www.snowbasin.com* 🎟 *Lift tickets $30–$65* ⛷ *2,959-ft vertical drop; 2,820 skiable acres; 7% beginner, 30% intermediate, 67% advanced; 2 high-speed gondolas, 1 tram, 1 high-speed quad chair, 4 triple chairs, 1 double chair, 3 surface lifts.*

Nordic Valley. Utah's smallest ski resort, formerly Wolf Creek Utah, is a good place to go if you're not ready for high-powered mountains. A great place to learn, this family-oriented resort is also the most affordable in the state, and the whole mountain is lighted for night skiing. ✉ *3567 E. Nordic Valley Way, Eden* ☎ *801/745–3511* ⊕ *www.nordicvalley.com* 🎟 *Lift tickets $23–$39* ⊙ *Daily Dec.–Apr.* ⛷ *1,000-ft vertical drop; 100 skiable acres; 30% beginner, 50% intermediate, 20% advanced; 2 double chairs, 1 triple chair.*

4

SNOWMOBILING

Club Rec. Just 30 minutes from three major ski resorts and 45 minutes from Ogden, this outdoor recreation shop offers snowmobile rentals, tours, and clinics. Their location at the Monte Cristo trailhead offers some of the best snow adventures in the West. ✉ *2429 N. Hwy. 158, Eden* ☎ *801/614–0500* 🌐 *www.clubrecnorth.com.*

WHERE TO EAT AND STAY

$$ MODERN MEXICAN 🍴 **Carlos & Harley's.** In a 120-year-old building that was once a dance hall and later a post office and general store, this fun Mexican restaurant specializes in "fresh-Mex" cuisine, a contemporary spin on Tex-Mex, using all made-from-scratch ingredients. While the exterior looks like a building from the Old West, the atmosphere inside is a mix of ski, beach, and Mexican themes, with a sports bar vibe. Four types of salsa come with specialties that include sizzling chicken fajitas, *carne asada* (steak), shrimp tacos, and margaritas. There are daily specials and several make-your-own-combination options. [$] *Average main: $17* ✉ *5510 E. 2200 N, Eden* ☎ *801/745–8226* 🌐 *www.carlosandharleys.com.*

$ AMERICAN Fodor's Choice ★ 🍴 **Shooting Star Saloon.** The only Utah bar listed in *Esquire* magazine's ranking of top bars in the United States is also the oldest remaining saloon in the state. In operation since the 1880s, it's a favorite hangout of skiers in winter and a beloved destination for bikers in summer. On the outside it could have come straight out of a Western movie; on the inside rustic accoutrements draw the eye in every corner—dollar bills pinned to the ceiling, comical signs, scruffy old boots, rifles, teapots, and the mounted head of a Saint Bernard dog on the wall. The menu doesn't stray far from beer and burgers, but many consider the burgers among the best in the country. If you're really hungry, the Star Burger is a hefty double cheeseburger topped with a Polish hot dog. [$] *Average main: $10* ✉ *7350 E. 200 S, Huntsville* ☎ *801/745–2002.*

$$ B&B/INN 🏨 **Jackson Fork Inn.** For those willing to stay a bit off the beaten path, this quaint country inn offers attentive service and lots of charm. **Pros:** a gorgeous setting near ski resorts and summer recreation areas; complimentary Continental breakfast. **Cons:** no in-room phones; stairs can be awkward with luggage; by reservation only on Monday and Tuesday. [$] *Rooms from: $150* ✉ *7345 E. 900 S, Huntsville* ☎ *801/745–0051, 800/609–9466* 🌐 *www.jacksonforkinn.com* 🛏 *7 rooms* 🕒 *Restaurant closed Mon. and Tues* 🍽 *Breakfast.*

THE GOLDEN SPIKE EMPIRE

Deserts, marshes, farmlands, mountains: there's enough landscape in the vast reaches of eastern Box Elder County to please any palate. The star attraction here, though, is history, specifically one day in history that changed the world: May 10, 1869. That's the date the Union Pacific and Central Pacific railroad officials met to drive their symbolic golden spike in celebration of the completion of the First Transcontinental Rail route. It happened at Promontory Summit, an ironically desolate spot about 15 miles north of the Great Salt Lake. The Wild West was about to be tamed.

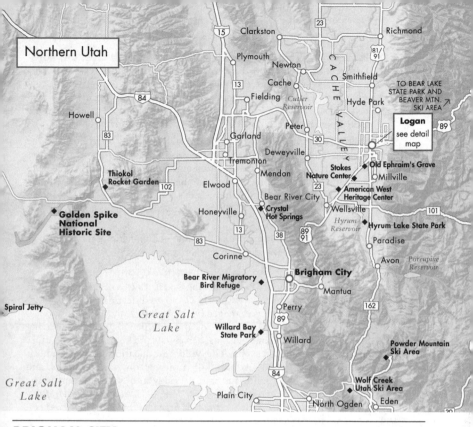

BRIGHAM CITY

21 miles north of Ogden.

People passing through Brigham City are charmed by its sycamore-lined Main Street and old-fashioned downtown, but may not realize they are in one of Utah's most progressive towns. ATK, which manufactures rocket motors about 45 minutes west of here, has brought in a lot of highly paid, well-educated professionals who have settled here and molded the city to their liking. The local museum outclasses those in many of the state's larger cities, and the Box Elder Stake Tabernacle at 251 Main Street is listed on the National Register of Historic Places. Free guided tours are offered each summer.

GETTING HERE AND AROUND

Brigham City lies just to the east of I–15 on Highway 89/91. Like many cities settled by LDS pioneers, it's laid out on a grid system with Main Street running north/south and each street numbered by 100s as you head in all four directions. Head north on Main to get to the quaint center of the town. Highway 89/91 to Logan bypasses the town.

FESTIVALS

Peach Days Celebration. In honor of the famous local crop, this popular event has been held the Wednesday to Saturday after Labor Day since 1904—the longest continually celebrated harvest festival in Utah. There's a Peach Queen pageant, a parade, a carnival, theater and concerts, classic car events, art and craft booths, and, of course, freshly baked peach cobbler. ☎ *435/723–3931* ⊕ *www.peachdays.org.*

Railroader's Festival. Held on the second Saturday in August at the Golden Spike National Historic Site, this free annual festival celebrates the completion of the Transcontinental Railroad. Visitors of all ages enjoy reenactments, talks by railroad historians, and games including a spike-driving contest and handcar rides. ✉ *Golden Spike Rd., Promontory Summit* ☎ *435/471–2209* ⊕ *www.nps.gov/gosp.*

ESSENTIALS

Visitor Information Brigham City Chamber of Commerce ✉ *6 N. Main St.* ☎ *435/723–3931* ⊕ *www.brighamchamber.com.*

EXPLORING

FAMILY
Fodor's Choice
★
Bear River Migratory Bird Refuge. Established in 1928 to conserve the Bear River habitat for migratory waterfowl and wildlife, this refuge, 13 miles west of Brigham City, is managed by the U.S. Fish and Wildlife Service. You'll get a chance to observe birds and wildlife along a 4-mile driving route, with ducks, geese, pelicans, herons, swans, shore birds, and more arriving in various seasons. The Wildlife Education Center contains interactive displays, an exhibit hall, a theater, observation decks, and teaching labs, with guided tours on Friday and Saturday during the summer. ✉ *2155 W. Forest St.* ☎ *435/734–6425* ⊕ *www.fws.gov/refuge/ bear_river_migratory_bird_refuge* 🖼 *Free* ☉ *Park daily dawn–dusk; visitor center weekdays 8–5, Sat. 10–4.*

Brigham City Museum-Gallery. Documents and artifacts from the city's early settlement and Mormon cooperative periods are the focus of this 3,300-square-foot museum and gallery, which also contains displays on the railroad and agricultural history of the Bear River valley. The northern gallery includes treasures brought across the plains by the pioneers and furniture made in Brigham City around 1860. The south end of the gallery holds regional art collections and hosts monthly regional and national touring shows. ✉ *24 N. 300 W* ☎ *435/723–6769* ⊕ *www. brighamcity.utah.gov/museum* 🖼 *Free* ☉ *Tues.–Fri. 11–6, Sat. 1–5.*

FAMILY
Crystal Hot Springs. Originally used as a winter camp by the Shoshones, this popular recreation area has one of the world's largest natural hot and cold springs. Mixing water from the two springs allows for a variety of pools with temperatures ranging from 80°F to 105°F. The complex is in Honeyville, about 8 miles north of Brigham City, has its own campground, hot tubs, a large soaker pool, a cold freshwater swimming pool, two water slides, and a lap pool. ✉ *8215 N. Hwy. 38, Honeyville* ☎ *435/279–8104, 801/547–0777* ⊕ *www.crystalhotsprings. net* 🖼 *$6 pool; $10 pool and slide* ☉ *Pool: Memorial Day–Labor Day, Mon.–Sat. 10–10, Sun. 10–8; day after Labor Day–day before Memorial Day, Mon.–Thurs. noon–10, Fri. noon–11, Sat. 10 am–11 pm, Sun. 10–8. Hrs vary for other attractions; call to check.*

Willard Bay State Park. Measuring 10,000 acres in size, this freshwater arm of the Great Salt Lake is a popular spot for water sports, fishing, boating, and observing more than 200 species of birds. Fed by canals in spring, it's effectively protected from the saltwater of the Great Salt Lake by a series of dikes. Facilities include a marina, campground, concession stands, and shady picnic spots. Bald and golden eagles are spotted frequently in tall trees along the park's Eagle Beach. Access if via Exit 357 off I–15, 6 miles south of Brigham City. ⊠ *900 W. 650 N, Willard* ☎ *435/734–9494* ⊕ *www.stateparks.utah.gov/parks/willard-bay* ⊒ *$10 per vehicle* ⊗ *Daily 6 am–10 pm.*

SPORTS AND THE OUTDOORS

BICYCLING

Box Elder County's long rural roads are excellent for road biking, but the dirt roads in the Wellsvilles are generally much too steep for good mountain biking.

GOLF

Eagle Mountain Golf Course. Featuring mountain views and a scenic overlook of the Great Salt Lake, this golf course in Brigham City has a PGA pro, a complete pro shop, and snack bar. It's a nice mix of challenging holes, water hazards, and straightforward greens, but rent a cart, because the switchbacks up the front nine will leave you puffing, although the back nine levels off. ⊠ *960 E. 700 S* ☎ *435/723–3212* ⊕ *www.eaglemountaingc.com* ⊒ *$13 for 9 holes, $26 for 18 holes* ⅄ *18 holes, 6781 yards, par 71.*

HIKING

The pink-and-gray crags of the Wellsvilles beckon the adventurous, and you can practically hike out your back door in Brigham City because the mountains rise straight up from town. But the range is one of the steepest in the world, so you must pace yourself. Although the peaks are all federal wilderness, gaining access isn't always a straightforward proposition. North of Brigham City the foothills encompass a string of private ranches. If you knock on a farmhouse door, however, the landowner will usually oblige and tell you the best place to cross his land.

Brigham City's 700 North Street dead-ends in the east at the head of a nice hiking trail. East of Honeyville the only good public access to the Wellsvilles is from 7200 North Street, 9 miles north of Brigham City on Highway 38; the road dead-ends at a gate, which you can open (don't forget to close it behind you) or just climb over. Beyond it are miles of hiking trails to explore.

In spite of all that irrigated farmland you see, you're still in the desert, so bring water on any trip, even if you only plan to be gone an hour.

WHERE TO EAT

$$
AMERICAN ✗**Idle Isle Café.** You'll feel like you're in Mayberry at this quaint café built in 1921. Visitors and locals cozy into original wooden booths to savor old-fashioned comfort foods like pot roast and au gratin potatoes, chicken-fried steak, and homemade soups. The authentic soda fountain from the 1920s is a great spot to enjoy ice cream or a shake, but you'll also want to save room for the signature idleberry pie—a two-crust beauty brimming with several types of berries. ■TIP➔ Grab

a box of chocolates for the road at the Idle Isle candy factory across the street. $ *Average main: $13* ✉ *24 S. Main St.* ☎ *435/734-2468* ⊕ *www. idleislecafe.com* ⊘ *Closed Sun.*

$$
AMERICAN
Fodor's Choice
★

✕ **Maddox Ranch House.** Despite an off-the-beaten path location 2 miles south of Brigham City, this family-owned eatery is one of the most visited restaurants in Utah. The Maddox family has been serving down-home Western food—fried chicken, prime rib, and bison steak—since 1949. Portions are big enough to satisfy a ranch hand, and the fresh-baked dinner rolls served with raspberry butter are as popular as any entrée. Every dish is made from scratch, and side vegetables and salads are prepared with locally grown produce. People drive here from surrounding states just for a slice of the fresh peach pie in season. Reservations are recommended even on weeknights, and kids eat free on Tuesday night. ■ TIP➔ **Everything on the regular menu can be ordered at the drive-thru if you're in a hurry or want to take food back to your hotel.** $ *Average main: $20* ✉ *1900 S. Hwy. 89, Perry* ☎ *435/723-8545, 800/544-5474* ⊕ *www.maddoxfinefood.com* ⚖ *Reservations essential* ⊘ *Closed Sun. and Mon.*

WHERE TO STAY

$
HOTEL

⌗ **Crystal Inn Brigham City.** Conveniently off I–15, this two-story hotel with views of the mountains is popular with families stopping off on their way to Yellowstone as well as business travelers and weekend visitors on a road trip to nearby Logan and Bear Lake. **Pros:** value price; convenient to the freeway; child- and pet-friendly; free high-speed Wi-Fi. **Cons:** books up quickly in summer; a bit isolated. $ *Rooms from: $80* ✉ *480 Westland Dr.* ☎ *435/723-0440, 800/408-0440* ⊕ *www.crystalinnbrigham.com* ⇝ *52 rooms* ⎮◎⎮ *Breakfast.*

PERFORMING ARTS

Heritage Theatre. Since 1970 this dedicated community theater group has produced plays in an old church, 4 miles south of Brigham City, on Friday, Saturday, and Monday nights; there are also some matinees. Performances span a variety of genres from comedies and dramas to mysteries and musicals. ✉ *2509 S. Hwy. 89, Perry* ☎ *435/723-8392* ⊕ *www.heritagetheatreutah.com.*

GOLDEN SPIKE NATIONAL HISTORIC SITE

32 miles west of Brigham City.

Golden Spike National Historic Site offers a variety of activities in addition to the annual reenactment that celebrates the anniversary of the completion ceremony for the nation's first transcontinental railroad. Replicas of the 1869 steam locomotives operate May to October and visitors can take engine house tours, hike on Big Fill Loop Trail, or take two auto tours that detail how the railroad was constructed.

GETTING HERE AND AROUND

One of the more remote outposts in the National Park System, Golden Spike is almost two hours north and west of Salt Lake City and not on the way to anywhere. Be aware that once you leave I–15, there are virtually no services. Make sure you have enough gas to make the round-trip.

EXPLORING

Golden Spike National Historic Site. The Union Pacific and Central Pacific railroads met here at Promontory Summit on May 10, 1869, to celebrate the completion of the First Transcontinental Rail route. Under the auspices of the National Park Service, the site has a visitor center and two beautifully maintained locomotives that are replicas of the originals that met here for the "wedding of the rails." Every May 10 (and on Saturday and holidays in summer), a reenactment of the driving of the "Golden Spike" is held. In August, boiler stoking, rail walking, and handcar racing test participants' skills at the Railroader's Festival. The Winter Steam Festival around Christmas time gives steam buffs opportunities to photograph the locomotives in the cold, when the steam from the smokestacks forms billowing clouds. ⊠ *Golden Spike Rd., off Hwy. 83, Promontory* ☎ *435/471–2209* ⊕ *www.nps.gov/gosp* ☑ *$7 per vehicle; $4 per person on foot or bike* ☉ *Visitor center daily 9–5.*

CACHE VALLEY

East of Brigham City Highway 89/91 tops Sardine Summit in Wellsville Canyon before dropping into the highly scenic Cache Valley. Walled in on the west by the imposing Wellsville Mountains (often touted as having the steepest incline of any range in the country) and on the east by the Bear River Range (a subrange of the Wasatch), Cache Valley is 15 miles wide and 60 miles long.

The valley was originally home to bands of Northwestern Shoshone. During the 1820s it became a favorite haunt for Jim Bridger and other mountain men, who often stashed (or "cached") their furs and held rendezvous here. Mormon pioneers, led by Peter Maughan, arrived in 1856 and created permanent settlements. Today Cache Valley is one of Utah's most important agricultural regions. Topping the list of foods produced here is cheese. Cache Valley Cheese, one of the valley's three cheese factories, is one of the nation's largest producers of Swiss cheese.

LOGAN

25 miles northeast of Brigham City.

Mormon pioneers created the permanent settlement of Logan in 1859, but the town didn't become prominent until 1888, when it was chosen as the site for Utah's land-grant agricultural college, now called Utah State University (USU). Logan is now the hub of the Cache Valley. The historic Main Street is best explored on a walking tour; an illustrated brochure is available from the visitor information center. Interesting buildings include St. John's Episcopal Church, representing Cache Valley's first non-Mormon denomination; the Ellen Eccles and Lyric theaters; and the Cache County Courthouse.

GETTING HERE AND AROUND

Head up Highway 89 from Brigham City through Logan Canyon and you'll arrive at the beautiful Cache Valley. As it cuts north through the central historic district, Highway 89 becomes Main Street. Turn right (east) at 400 North to skirt the south end of Utah State University and head northeast to Bear Lake. Take 700 North, which bisects the campus, or 1000 North to reach the north end of the campus and the football stadium.

FESTIVALS

Summerfest Arts Faire. Held on the Logan Tabernacle grounds for three days (Thursday–Saturday) over Father's Day weekend, this annual festival features more than 100 artists, live music, and a variety of food vendors. Admission is free. ⊠ *50 N. Main St.* ☎ *435/213–3858* ⊕ *www. logansummerfest.com.*

EXPLORING

TOP ATTRACTIONS

FAMILY **American West Heritage Center.** To learn about Cache Valley's history from 1820 to 1920, drive 6 miles south of Logan to visit this living-history complex that spans 160 acres. At the farm, antique implements are on display, draft horses still pull their weight, docents dressed in period clothing demonstrate sheep shearing and quilting, and special events take place throughout the year. The Pioneer Festival, held at the center in late July, features additional displays and reenactments, along with food booths, cowboy poetry readings, and concerts. Visitors can also shop for authentic Western jewelry and clothing. ⊠ *4025 S. Hwy. 89/91, Wellsville* ☎ *435/245–6050* ⊕ *www.awhc.org* ⊠ *$5–$9* ☉ *Early June– late Aug., Tues.–Sat. 11–4; Sept. 1–early June, welcome center, exhibit area and special events only (call for hrs).*

Utah State University. Established in 1888, USU has an enrollment of 27,800 and is a leader in such diverse fields as agriculture, sustainability, and technology. It ranks fourth in the nation for total research dollars received by a college and was named a Tree Campus USA by the Arbor Day Foundation. The scenic campus is best toured by starting at the historic Old Main administration building east of downtown Logan—look for the bell tower. ⊠ *500 Old Main Hill* ☎ *435/797–1351* ⊕ *www.usu.edu* ⊠ *Free.*

Museum of Anthropology. More than 13,000 visitors each year view the collection of prehistoric and contemporary Native American artifacts and cultural works from around the world on display here. Exhibits are designed by students with faculty guidance as part of the anthropology program at USU. ⊠ *USU Old Main Bldg., 730 Old Main Hill, Room 252* ☎ *435/797–7545* ⊕ *anthromuseum.usu.edu* ⊠ *Free* ☉ *Weekdays 10–5, 1st Sat. 10–2.*

Nora Eccles Harrison Museum of Art. USU's Chase Fine Arts Center includes this impressive art museum. Revolving exhibits of works by locally, nationally, and internationally recognized artists are featured in the galleries with an emphasis on artists living and/or working in the western United States. ⊠ *650 N. 1100 E* ☎ *435/797–0163* ⊕ *www. artmuseum.usu.edu* ⊠ *Free* ☉ *Tues.–Sat. 10–5.*

QUICK BITES

Aggie Ice Cream. There are plenty of ice-cream shops in Utah but this one is the pride and joy of Utah State University dairy students. On the USU campus, the historic shop even occasionally offers a tour ($4, includes a scoop to taste). Watch a video about ice-cream and cheese production, then choose from more than a dozen flavors. With scoops starting at $1.79 and sandwiches priced under $9, your money will go a lot farther than in national chain ice-cream shops. ⊠ *Nutrition & Food Science Bldg., USU, 750 N. 1200 E* ☎ *435/797-2109, 888/586-2735* ⊕ *www.aggieicecream.usu.edu* ⊗ *May–Sept., weekdays 9 am–10 pm, Sat. 10–10.*

WORTH NOTING

Cache Valley Center for the Arts. Housed in a beautifully restored historic mansion, this very active community arts organization presents a variety of traveling art exhibits and showcases regional artists with gallery walks and other events throughout the year. The organization hosts an impressive selection of shows and concerts at the historic Ellen Eccles Theater. ⊠ *35 W. 100 S* ☎ *435/753-2970* ⊕ *www.cachearts.org* ⊠ *Fees vary* ⊗ *Artists' Gallery Wed.–Fri. 10:30–5:30, Sat. 10–2.*

Daughters of Utah Pioneers Cache Museum. A branch of Salt Lake City's organization, this museum has mountain-man displays as well as musical instruments, furniture, clothing, and a collection of personal journals from the 1850s to the early 1900s. ⊠ *160 N. Main St.* ☎ *435/752-5139, 435/753-1635* ⊕ *www.dupinternational.org* ⊠ *Free* ⊗ *June–Aug., Tues.–Fri. 10–4; Sept.–May by appointment.*

Logan Mormon Temple. The majestic towers remind all that this college town is also a conservative community with Mormon roots. Built on a terrace of the ancient Lake Bonneville, this impressive limestone edifice took settlers seven years to complete. The site was chosen by Brigham Young himself in 1877, and the work was directed by architect Truman O. Angell, designer of the Salt Lake temple. Like all Mormon temples, it's open only to followers of the faith but visitors may walk around the grounds. ⊠ *175 N. 300 E* ☎ *435/752-3611.*

FAMILY **Stokes Nature Center.** About a mile up Logan Canyon, the nature center is a great way to get acquainted with the natural wonders of this area. The center has animal and bird exhibits and demonstrations. There are special programs for adults and children on some Saturdays; visit the website for listings. ⊠ *2696 E. Hwy. 89* ☎ *435/755-3239* ⊕ *www.logannature.org* ⊠ *Free* ⊗ *Wed.–Fri. 10–4, 2nd Sat. 10–4.*

CACHE VALLEY FOOD TOUR

Fodor'sChoice★ Cache Valley Food Tour. Cache Valley is famous for ice cream, coffee, honey, cheese, chocolates, and artisanal bread, among other gourmet delights. This self-guided tour takes you behind the scenes to see how goat's milk soap is made and what goes into making organic bread; visit a coffee-roasting plant, view honeybees in action, and sample artisanal candy and ice cream. Tours are more frequent in summer but some run year-round. ⊠ *199 N. Main St.* ☎ *435/755-1890* ⊕ *www.explorelogan.com* ⊠ *Free.*

Logan

KEY

- ■ Restaurants
- □ Hotels
- ⊕ following dining and lodging reviews indicates map-grid coordinates

Map labels:
600 N · 500 N · 400 N · 300 N · University Boulevard · Valley View Highway · 300 N · 200 N · 100 N · Center St. · 100 S · 200 S · 300 S · 400 S · 500 S · 600 S · 700 S · 200 S · 500 W · 600 W · 500 W · 400 W · 300 W · 200 W · 100 W · Main St. · 100 E · 200 E · 300 E · 400 E · 600 E · 950 W · 850 W · 750 W · 500 W · 300 W · S West St. · Park Av. · Center Av.

Angie's · El Toro Viejo · STOKES NATURE CENTER ◆ · UTAH STATE UNIVERSITY ◆ · Tandoori Oven · Best Western Plus Weston Inn · DAUGHTERS OF UTAH PIONEERS CACHE MUSEUM · LOGAN MORMON TEMPLE · Canyon Blvd. · Herm's Inn ■ → · Caffé Ibis · Le Nonne · Seasons at the Riter Mansion · Canyon Rd. · Bluebird ■ · ◆ LOGAN TABERNACLE · CACHE VALLEY CENTER FOR THE ARTS · Best Western Baugh Motel · LOGAN/CACHE COUNTY FAIRGROUNDS · ◆ ZOO · Willow Park · Willow West Park · Logan River · Summerhill Suites by Marriott · Crystal Inn · AMERICAN WEST HERITAGE CENTER · OLD EPHRAIM'S GRAVE · Country Road

0   1/4 mi
0   1/4 km

SPORTS AND THE OUTDOORS

It is hard to ignore the outdoors in beautiful Cache Valley, which is dominated by mountains east and west and by the lazy Bear River snaking through the bottomlands. Fly-fishers enjoy the Logan River and Black Smith Fork, and birders love to canoe the marshes. Hikers, skiers, picnickers, and mountain bikers head for the hills. Trails for all abilities are just minutes away from downtown Logan.

BICYCLING AND HIKING

Road cyclists pedal out to the long, flat country roads of scenic Cache Valley or venture up Logan and Blacksmith Fork canyons. Mountain bikers can spend an afternoon on the 9-mile round-trip from Wood Camp, in Logan Canyon, to the 1,500-year-old Jardine juniper tree that grows on a high ridge offering views of Wyoming and Idaho.

Naomi Peak. Mountain bikers and hikers alike can access a prime wilderness area via the 3-mile route from Tony Grove Lake to the summit of Naomi Peak. In the Wellsville Mountains a 2-mile trail climbs steeply from Maple Bench to Stewart Pass, a lofty ridge along the migration route of eagles and hawks; on a clear day the view from here extends for more than 80 miles. ⊠ *Tony Grove Rd.* ⊕ *From Logan take Hwy. 89 northeast to Tony Grove Rd. (19¼ miles) and follow that for 7 miles to Tony Grove Lake* ⊕ *www.utah.com/hike/naomi_peak.htm.*

Red Bridge–River Trail. Just a few miles up Logan Canyon, the wide passageway of the Red Bridge–River Trail continues 4¼ miles on the south side of the canyon along the Logan River.

Uinta-Wasatch-Cache National Forest. You can get maps and brochures for hiking trails from the Logan Ranger District office (✉ *1500 E. Highway 89*) or at the Cache Valley Visitors Bureau at 199 N. Main St. ✉ *Hwy. 101* ☎ *435/755–3620* ⊕ *www.fs.usda.gov/uwcnf.*

BOATING AND FISHING

Anglers cast dry flies into the Logan River or angle for rare albino trout in the depths of Tony Grove Lake. Although you can paddle a canoe on virtually any body of water in

the region, the best places include Tony Grove Lake in Logan Canyon and Bear River, northwest of Logan. Snaking through Cache Valley, Bear River has several nice stretches, including a particularly satisfying 11 miles between Amalga and Tremonton, passing a blue heron rookery along the way.

Bridgerland Audubon Society. Boat trips on the Bear River are often sponsored by the society. ⊕ *www.bridgerlandaudubon.org.*

Hyrum Lake State Park. A 450-acre reservoir within the park draws boaters in summer and fall. A campground, shady picnic areas, peaceful rural setting, and great views of the Wellsville Mountains and the Bear River Range make this a popular spot for family gatherings. In winter ice fishing is the activity of choice. Day use is $6 per vehicle. ✉ *405 W. 300 S, Hyrum* ☎ *435/245–6866* ⊕ *www.stateparks.utah.gov.*

Muddy Road Outfitters. Canoe rentals start at $20 per day, including life vests, paddles, and the car accessories for transporting them. ✉ *4705 W. 3800 N, Benson* ☎ *435/753–3693* ⊕ *www.muddyroad.net.*

GOLF

Birch Creek Golf Course. Considered by many to be one of the best golf courses in the state, this scenic course, with great mountain views, is long and exceptionally well maintained. Generally wide open and of moderate difficulty, it has a few easy holes and some that are quite challenging, with an uphill finish on the 18th. The clubhouse has one of the best views in Cache Valley. ✉ *550 E. 100 N (Summit Dr.), Smithfield* ☎ *435/563–6825* ⊕ *www.birchcreekgolf.com* ✐ *$26 weekdays, $28 weekends* ⚑ *18 holes, 6768 yards, par 72.*

Logan River Golf Course. This course is also a wetlands preserve, as you'll discover when your ball plops irretrievably into one of the many cattail marshes. All that water can make for high humidity in summer, too, but the lush greenery and great mountain views compensate. It's a very challenging course; the front nine has a tighter width, while the back nine has a tighter length. ✉ *550 W. 1000 S* ☎ *435/750–0123* ⊕ *www.loganutah.org* ⚲ *$14 for 9 holes walking; $28 for 18 holes. Riding, it's an extra $7 and $14 per rider* 🏌 *18 holes, 6502 yards, par 71.*

WHERE TO EAT

Use the coordinates (✚ A1) at the end of each listing to locate a site on the corresponding map.

$$
AMERICAN

✘ **Angie's.** An institution in Logan since 1938, this family-owned restaurant lives up to its slogan: "Where The Locals Eat." One glance at the line of friendly folks waiting to be seated and you'll know you're in for a good time and a hearty meal. Whether you choose to rub shoulders with regulars at the long counter or snuggle into a cozy booth, you'll be in comfort-food heaven with a long menu featuring malt waffles piled high with fruit, chicken-fried steak and eggs, homemade soups and desserts, and much more. Ⓢ *Average main: $14* ✉ *690 N. Main St.* ☎ *435/752–9252* ⊕ *www.angiesrest.com* ✚ *C1.*

$$
AMERICAN

✘ **Bluebird.** Utah's oldest continuously operated restaurant attracts a loyal clientele for its classic meat-and-potatoes fare and homemade dinner rolls, but the real draw is the soda counter that dates back to the 1920s. Sip an Ironport cherry soda or savor an ice-cream sundae while enjoying the photos, murals, and furnishings that depict Cache Valley history. The old-fashioned chocolates display will halt your progress on the way out. Ⓢ *Average main: $12* ✉ *19 N. Main St.* ☎ *435/752–3155* ⊙ *Closed Sun.* ✚ *C2.*

$
CAFÉ

✘ **Caffé Ibis.** Hang out with Logan's hip and earthy crowd while sipping some of the state's best—and most eco-friendly—coffee. Shiny brass canisters are filled with triple-certified (shade-grown, organic, and fair-trade) coffee beans ground daily at the off-site local plant. You can also enjoy homemade soups, savory sandwiches, and hearty breakfasts. Brunch is served 8–1 on Sunday. Local musicians perform for tips on Friday and Sunday nights. Both indoor and outdoor seating are available. ■ TIP➜ **Ask about roasting demonstrations at the roasting house.** Ⓢ *Average main: $10* ✉ *52 Federal Ave.* ☎ *435/753–9515* ⊕ *www.caffeibis.com* ⊙ *No dinner* ✚ *C2.*

$$
MEXICAN

✘ **El Toro Viejo.** Decorated in festive colors with metalwork, paintings, and carvings adorning the walls, Logan's most popular Mexican eatery offers a spacious dining room and authentic south-of-the-border cuisine. Tortillas, guacamole, and savory sauces are all made fresh on-site daily and most of the entrées are large enough for sharing. Since 1995 locals have insisted that this is some of the best Mexican food in the region, with unique entrées like *burrito en el huerto* (tortillas stuffed with veggies, including cactus) and steak, chicken, or chorizo and cheese served steaming hot in a *molcajete* (traditional stoneware mortar). ■ TIP➜ **Lunch combination plates are a bargain at less than $10.** Ⓢ *Average main: $15* ✉ *1111 N. Main St.* ☎ *435/753–4084* ⊕ *www.eltoroutah.com* ✚ *C1.*

$$
AMERICAN
Fodor's Choice
★

✘ **Herm's Inn.** Famous for its pizza-size cinnamon swirl pancakes and French toast topped with seasonal fresh fruits, this popular breakfast and lunch spot is often jam-packed with students from nearby Utah State University, but it's worth the wait. Diners enjoy savory omelets, homemade soups, hearty sandwiches, and huge salads created from locally grown produce. Housed in what once was a historic gas station and inn, the restored building is easy to spot—just look for the bright red vintage gas pump out front. $ *Average main: $12* ⊠ *1435 Canyon Rd.* ☎ *435/792–4321* ⊕ *www.hermsinn.com* ☾ *No dinner* ⊹ *D1.*

$$$
NORTHERN
ITALIAN

✕ **Le Nonne.** Housed in a lovely Victorian home converted into a restaurant, this upscale Italian eatery features Northern Italian cuisine and live jazz on Wednesday and Friday evenings. Offering a romantic dining room and outdoor patio seating in the warmer months, the specialty here is attentive service and a variety of pasta, steak, chicken, and seafood dishes with Tuscan flair. Regulars rave about the sweet potato ravioli and the homemade gnocchi with Gorgonzola sauce. The tiramisu is made fresh daily and worth savoring. ■ **TIP**➔ **Combine dinner with an opera at the nearby Eccles Theatre and you might forget you're in rural Utah.** $ *Average main: $24* ⊠ *129 N. 100 E* ☎ *435/752–9577* ⊕ *lenonne.com* ☾ *Closed Sun. No lunch Sat.–Wed.* ⊹ *C2.*

$$
INDIAN

✕ **Tandoori Oven.** Near the USU football stadium and usually mobbed with students for the lunch buffet, this family-owned eatery serves up some of the best Indian food in the Cache Valley. Sharing a building with a gas station and minimart, the low-key restaurant has been delighting fans of the subcontinent's cuisine since 2004. Due to its small size and popularity, seating can be a bit cramped, but the dishes that emerge from the tandoor ovens more than make up for it. Chicken tikka is a crowd favorite but you can't go wrong with tandoori chicken or lamb coconut kurma. Vegetarian dishes include *biryani* (spicy rice with vegetables). $ *Average main: $15* ⊠ *720 E. 1000 N* ☎ *435/750–6836* ☾ *Closed Sun.* ⊹ *D1*

WHERE TO STAY

Use the coordinates (⊹ A1) at the end of each listing to locate a site on the corresponding map.

$
HOTEL

🏨 **Best Western Baugh Motel.** Operated by the Baugh family since 1957, this place still looks like a 1950s-era drive-in motel, but ongoing renovations have kept rooms updated and comfortable. **Pros:** rooms are larger than most cookie-cutter chains; walk to Ellen Eccles Theatre and Main Street; on-site pool is family-friendly. **Cons:** in some rooms you may hear the Main Street traffic. $ *Rooms from: $79* ⊠ *153 S. Main St.* ☎ *435/752–5220* ⊕ *www.bestwestern.com* ⇴ *76 rooms* ❙❂❙ *Breakfast* ⊹ *C2.*

$$
HOTEL

🏨 **Best Western Plus Weston Inn.** In a central location and only five minutes from Utah State University, this popular inn is close to many shops and restaurants. **Pros:** close to everything; easy access to parks and hiking trails. **Cons:** motel feel, with exterior corridors and noisy air-conditioners. $ *Rooms from: $109* ⊠ *250 N. Main St.* ☎ *435/752–5700* ⊕ *www. westoninn.com* ⇴ *89 rooms* ❙❂❙ *Breakfast* ⊹ *C1.*

$$
HOTEL
FAMILY

🏨 **Crystal Inn Logan.** With a sleek and welcoming lobby and spacious, modern rooms, this popular Utah-based chain is known for its attention to detail and above-average standards of cleanliness and customer service. **Pros:** good value for the price; shuttle van provides local transportation. **Cons:** fills up fast for conferences and special events. $ *Rooms from: $125* ⊠ *853 S. Hwy. 89/91* ☎ *435/752–0707* ⊕ *www.crystalinnlogan.com* ⇴ *82 rooms, 4 suites* ❙❂❙ *Multiple meal plans* ⊹ *C3.*

$$ B&B/INN **Seasons at the Riter Mansion.** Centrally located in a quiet residential area just a short walk from Main Street, this beautifully restored historic mansion is perfect for a romantic bed-and-breakfast getaway or as a cozy retreat. **Pros:** peaceful area, but walking distance to downtown. **Cons:** popular for weddings and other special events, which can impact on the serenity. [$] *Rooms from: $149* ✉ *168 N. 100 E* ☎ *435/752–7727* 🌐 *www.theritermansion.com* 🛏 *6 rooms* 🍴 *Breakfast* ✣ *C2.*

$$ HOTEL Fodor's Choice ★ **Summerhill Suites by Marriott.** Logan's most upscale hotel offers all-suite accommodations and from the contemporary elegance of the lobby to the luxurious touches in the rooms, it's clear the goal is to make you feel pampered. **Pros:** spacious rooms; complimentary breakfast buffet; good location; fine dining on-site at Elements restaurant. **Cons:** frequently sells out when business conferences are in town. [$] *Rooms from: $139* ✉ *635 S. Riverwoods Pkwy.* ☎ *435/750–5180* 🌐 *www.marriott.com* 🛏 *115 suites* 🍴 *Breakfast* ✣ *C3.*

NIGHTLIFE AND PERFORMING ARTS

NIGHTLIFE

White Owl. There are several chain sports bars in town but the White Owl offers a chance to rub shoulders with both townies and university types in a tavern with more local flavor. If it's nice out, toast the sunset view of the Wellsvilles from the rooftop beer garden. The popular watering hole features pub grub including burgers, hot dogs, beer, and wine. ✉ *36 W. Center St.* ☎ *435/753–9165* ⏲ *Closed Sun.*

PERFORMING ARTS

Thanks to both the presence of Utah State University and the community's keen interest in the arts, Logan offers many fine theater productions. USU's theater and music departments present a variety of exciting performances.

Caine Lyric Theatre. Built in 1913 by a prominent local family, this historic venue is home to the Old Lyric Repertory Company. The theater group entertains audiences with a musical, drama, mystery, and farce each summer, from about mid-June through early August. ✉ *28 W. Center St.* ☎ *435/797–8022* 🌐 *arts.usu.edu/lyric/.*

Fodor's Choice ★ **Ellen Eccles Theatre.** National and international touring productions perform here along with a diverse mix of high-quality performances from local arts organizations. Known as the "crown jewel" of Cache Valley, the theater was built in 1923 and restored to its original grandeur in 1993. ✉ *43 S. Main St.* ☎ *435/752–0026* 🌐 *www.centerforthearts.org.*

Utah Festival Opera Company. Each summer this highly respected opera company presents a five-week season at the Ellen Eccles Theatre. Featuring performers from Broadway, the Metropolitan Opera, and San Francisco Opera, the productions dazzle. ✉ *43 S. Main St.* ☎ *435/750–0300, 800/262–0074* 🌐 *www.utahfestival.org.*

SHOPPING

ANTIQUES AND HOME STYLE

Country Village Antique Mall. The wide range of antiques here ranges from vintage gas station signs and posters to dolls and retro jewelry. Stocked floor to ceiling with glassware, books, collectibles, quilts, coins, and other fabulous finds, it's a fascinating place to explore whether you have 10 minutes or an hour. ✉ *730 S. Main St.* ☎ *435/752–1678* ⊕ *countryvillagemall.net.*

The Valley Outlet. A few miles south of Logan in the small town of Nibley, this beautifully decorated shop features handcrafted picture frames, wall art, sculptures, pillows, and seasonal items, along with whimsical gifts, wind chimes, souvenirs and more. ✉ *2707 S. Hwy. 89/91, Nibley* ☎ *435/232–4444* ⊕ *www.thevalleyoutlet.com.*

GIFTS AND SOUVENIRS

Cox Honeyland and Gifts. Specializing in honey products, this Logan landmark, operated by the Cox family for four generations, offers a wide variety of flavored, creamed honeys, berry juices, fudge, and raspberry jam. You can also shop for a variety of home design items and souvenirs, or have gift baskets shipped. ✉ *1780 S. Hwy. 89* ☎ *435/752–3234* ⊕ *www.coxhoney.com.*

Fodor's Choice
★

The Spirit Goat. On a side street just steps from Main, this family-owned shop specializes in skin care products made from goat's milk. Filled with aromatic fragrances like cranberry orange, citrus and ginger, the quaint shop has shelves brimming with more than 80 varieties of soaps, plus body lotions, and gift items. A behind-the-scenes tour of the soap-making process is offered on Friday at 10 am. ✉ *28 Federal Ave.* ☎ *435/512–9040* ⊕ *www.spiritgoat.com.*

MARKETS

Cache Valley Gardeners' Market. From early-May through mid-October, Utah's oldest local farmers' market is held every Saturday from 9 to 1 at Horseshoe Willow Park. The market features regional produce vendors, locally made products, and live music. ✉ *500 W. 700 S* ⊕ *www.gardenersmarket.org.*

BEAR LAKE COUNTRY

Bear Lake is one of the most beautiful alpine lakes in America, nearly 6,000 feet above sea level and extremely remote. A few hardy ranchers live here year-round, but raspberries are the only crop besides hay that can stand the short growing season, and you'll see them everywhere in the form of syrup, jam, and the famous Bear Lake raspberry shakes. The deep Bear Lake Valley is generally 5 to 10 degrees cooler than the Cache Valley, so when the mercury hits 90°F in Logan there's a mass migration over the Bear River Range. The handful of lodgings fill quickly (and in the winter some close up entirely), so call to check availability.

BEAR LAKE STATE PARK

41 miles from Logan (to Garden City).

Known for its vibrant blue water rivaling the Caribbean and Lake Tahoe in beauty, Bear Lake is a perfect summer destination offering swimming, boating, fishing, jet skiing, and a chance to sample the region's famous raspberry shakes. In winter it's one of Utah's best-kept secrets, with miles of snowy terrain for cross-country skiing and snow-mobiling and easy access to affordable and family-friendly ski resorts.

GETTING HERE AND AROUND

Perhaps the remote nature of Bear Lake explains why it's such a well-kept secret in the West. About the only way to get here is by driving 41 miles on Highway 89 from Logan. Once you're here, it can take an hour and a half or longer to circle the lake by car, especially if it's a busy summer weekend; and it may be impossible in the winter due to weather. Services are limited, and clustered on the lake's western shore. Garden City (population 562) is the largest town and the best place to stock up on gas, basic groceries, and other supplies. Otherwise, it's mostly no-stoplight communities on the lakefront.

EXPLORING

FAMILY **Bear Lake State Park.** Eight miles wide and 20 miles long, Bear Lake is an unusual shade of blue, thanks to limestone particles suspended in the water. It is home to five species of fish found nowhere else, including the Bonneville cisco, which draws anglers during its spawning season in January. Among the lake's more discreet inhabitants is the Bear Lake Monster, which according to local lore lurks somewhere in the depths like its Loch Ness counterpart. The abundance of Bear Lake's raspberries is celebrated each year in early August at **Raspberry Days.** A parade, a craft fair, and entertainment are almost eclipsed by the main event: sampling myriad raspberry concoctions.

Along the south shore of Bear Lake, Route 30 traces an old route used by Native Americans, mountain men, and settlers following the Oregon Trail. The lake was a popular gathering place for mountain men, who held two rendezvous here in the 1820s. Harsh winters persuaded most travelers to move on before the first snow flew, but hardy Mormon pioneers settled in the area and founded Garden City. You'll find several hotel and restaurant options in town, which sits at the junction of U.S. 89 and Route 30, and you can follow the quarter-mile board-walk through a small wetlands preserve to the lakeshore. ⊠ *Hwy. 89* ☎ *435/946–3343, 800/322–3770* ⊕ *www.stateparks.utah.gov* ⊠ *$8 per vehicle* ⊗ *Daily 8 am–10 pm.*

SPORTS AND THE OUTDOORS

BICYCLING

Cyclists of all abilities can enjoy all or any portion of the level 48-mile ride on the road circling Bear Lake. The paved Lakeside Bicycle Path curves from Bear Lake Marina south and east along the shore, with several rest stops. Interpretive signs relate stories about Bear Lake's history and local lore.

Bear Lake KOA. Right on the trail, this campground rents bikes, including a four-wheel, surrey-top bicycle-built-for-four that can actually carry a family of six. ⊠ *485 N. Bear Lake Blvd., Garden City* ☎ *435/946–3454.*

BOATING

Fodor's Choice Bear Lake's turquoise waters are a bit chilly for swimming on all but the
★ hottest summer days, but boating is a popular way to enjoy the lake. Personal watercraft, kayaks, pontoons, and motorboats are available at the Bear Lake Marina, at Rendezvous Beach, and in the surrounding towns.

Prices vary from about $70 per hour for a PWC to $150 an hour and up for large motorboats capable of towing water-skiers and wakeboarders. Be advised that the winds at this mountain lake can change 180 degrees within minutes (or go from 30 knots to completely calm), so it's wise to be cautious and make sure everyone on board has life jackets.

Bear Lake Fun. In addition to sailboats and motorized craft this water-sports equipment specialty shop rents paddleboats, canoes, and kayaks that are great for poking around the lake's vast shoreline and marshes. You can also rent water skis, wet suits, tubes, and wakeboards here. ⊠ *Rendezvous Beach, Hwy. 30, Laketown* ☎ *435/946–2900* ⊕ *www.bearlakefun.com.*

Cisco's Landing. At the Bear Lake Marina this go-to shop for gear offers everything from personal watercraft to full-size ski boats. You can also grab a quick bite at the grill. ■**TIP→ Don't neglect to pick owner Bryce Nielson's brain—he's a wildlife biologist and a former Garden City mayor, and he can tell you everything you need to know about the lake and its denizens, both above and below the water.** ⊠ *Bear Lake Marina, Hwy. 89, Garden City* ☎ *435/946–2717* ⊕ *www.ciscoslanding.com.*

FISHING

The Logan River and Blacksmith Fork are blue-ribbon trout streams. You can pull indigenous Bear Lake cutthroat, which are found nowhere else in the world, out of Bear Lake, or join the locals in dip-netting Bear Lake cisco when they come to shore to spawn in January. Warm-water species are found in abundance in Mantua Reservoir, 4 miles east of Brigham City on Highway 89. In the Bear River, it's mostly carp these days. For a novelty fishing experience, boat out to the middle of Tony Grove Lake and use a long line with plenty of sinkers to land one of the rare albino trout that frequent the depths of the lake.

Utah Division of Wildlife Resources. You can get a fishing license at most local sporting goods stores, but if you want to obtain your license online, go to the Utah Division of Wildlife Resources website. ⊠ *Bear Lake State Park, Utah, United States* ☎ *801/476–2740* ⊕ *www.wildlife.utah.gov.*

GOLF

Bear Lake Golf Course. Golfers looking for a quick game can play nine holes in this beautiful lakeside setting when the weather permits (generally May–October). It's suitable for all levels of play, good for beginners, but also with some challenging greens and water hazards, generally calling for accurate shots—not easy, given the distraction of the stunning views and activity on the lake. There's a good restaurant at the clubhouse, with occasional live entertainment. ⊠ *2180 S. Country Club Dr., Garden City* ☎ *435/946–8742* ⊕ *www.bearlake.com/golf* ☑ *$15 weekdays, $17 weekends; with cart: $23 weekdays, $25 weekends* ⌃ *9 holes, 3376 yards, par 36.*

HIKING

FAMILY At 9,980 feet, Naomi Peak is the highest point of the Bear River Range in Cache National Forest. The 3.2-mile **Naomi Peak Trail** starts in the parking lot of the Tony Grove Campground and gains almost 2,000 feet in elevation. You hike through conifer forests and open meadows and along sub-alpine basins and rocky ledges. A shorter hike to **White**

Pine Lake, which begins on the same trail and splits after a quarter of a mile, is also lovely. To reach the trailhead, take Highway 89 southwest from Garden City for approximately 15 miles to the Tony Grove turnoff, then follow the signs. Closer to Garden City is the **Limber Pine Nature Trail,** a popular and easy hike (1 mile round-trip) at the summit between Logan Canyon and Bear Lake that features interpretive information especially designed for children.

SKIING

Beaver Mountain Ski Area. Owned and operated by the same family since 1939, this locals' favorite offers skiing as it was before it became a rich man's sport. A terrain park invites aerial tricks. There aren't any trendy nightspots at the foot of this mountain, just an old-fashioned A-frame lodge with burgers and chili. ✉ *40000 E. Hwy. 89* ☎ *435/946–3610, 435/753–0921* 🌐 *www.skithebeav.com* 🎫 *Lift tickets $48* ☞ *1,600-ft vertical drop; 664 skiable acres; 45 runs; 35% beginner, 40% intermediate, 25% advanced; 2 double chairs, 2 triple chairs, 1 surface lift.*

WHERE TO EAT AND STAY

$ MEXICAN

🍴 **Café Sabor.** Offering a welcome respite for hungry tourists, fishermen, and water-sports enthusiasts returning from a day on Bear Lake, this family-owned Mexican restaurant treats diners to a fiesta-like atmosphere with comfortable indoor seating or outdoor dining on the spacious patio. Featuring a full lunch and dinner menu filled with traditional favorites like quesadillas, tacos, and burritos, the options also include sizzling fajita platters for two, chicken mole, shrimp enchiladas, and homemade tortilla soup. Chips, tortillas, and guacamole are made fresh daily on-site, and the bar features a variety of tasty margaritas and other south of the border–inspired cocktails. For dessert you can't go wrong with fried ice cream. [$] *Average main: $11* ✉ *100 N. Bear Lake Bd., Garden City* ☎ *435/946–3297* 🌐 *www.cafesabor.com* 🕒 *Closed Sun. year-round and Mon.–Wed. Nov.–Apr.*

$ FAST FOOD

🍴 **LaBeau's Drive-in.** The Bear Lake region is well known for its locally grown raspberries and this is the most popular spot in town to enjoy a thick and creamy raspberry shake. Choose from 45 other shake flavors along with a menu of old-fashioned hamburgers, hot dogs, and chicken sandwiches topped with homemade sauce. Picnic tables outside provide a great spot to enjoy the food and the view. [$] *Average main: $9* ✉ *69 N. Bear Lake Blvd., Garden City* ☎ *435/946–8821* 🕒 *Closed Sun. and mid-Oct.–late Apr.*

$$$ RESORT FAMILY

🏨 **Ideal Beach Resort.** A private beach awaits at this family-style resort open year-round, and there's a wide range of accommodations options, from rooms for two to condos sleeping up to 20. **Pros:** a wonderful place for families; lots of activities; within walking distance of the lake. **Cons:** with so many kids around, it's not a spot for peace and quiet; limited amenities in winter. [$] *Rooms from: $159* ✉ *2176 S. Bear Lake Blvd., Garden City* ☎ *435/946–3364, 800/634–1018* 🌐 *www.idealbeachresort.com* 🛏 *8 rooms, 200 condos* 🍽 *No meals.*

5

DINOSAURLAND AND EASTERN UTAH

Updated by
Kellee Katagi

The rugged beauty of Utah's northeastern corner, wedged neatly between Wyoming to the north and Colorado to the east, is the reward for those willing to take the road less traveled. Neither I–80 nor I–70 enters this part of the state, so most visitors who pass through the western United States never even see it. That, of course, is part of its appeal. Small towns, rural attitudes, and a more casual and friendly approach to life are all part of the eastern Utah experience.

Northeastern Utah is most spectacular when viewed out-of-doors and out of your vehicle. It's home to superb boating and fishing at Flaming Gorge, Red Fleet, and the Steinaker reservoirs. Hundreds of miles of hiking and mountain-biking trails (often available to cross-country skiers, snowmobilers, or snowshoers in winter) crisscross the region. The Green and Yampa rivers entice white-water rafters as well as less ambitious float-trippers. The pine- and aspen-covered Uinta (pronounced *You-in-tah*) Mountains offer campers and hikers hidden, pristine lakes and streams. Even if you don't get out of your car, exploring this region takes you through vast red-rock basins, over high mountain passes, and between geologic folds in the earth.

Dinosaurs once dominated this region, and in many ways, they still do. Paleontology labs and fossil displays abound, as do corny dino statues and impressive life-size skeleton casts. Excavation sites such as Dinosaur National Monument make northeastern Utah one of the most important paleontological research areas in the world.

Ancient Native American cultures also left their marks throughout the region. Cliff walls and boulders are dotted with thousands of examples of rock art of the Fremont people (AD 600 to 1300), so called because they inhabited the region near the Fremont River. Today the Uintah and Ouray Reservation is the second largest in the United States, and covers a significant portion of eastern Utah, though much of the reservation's original land grant was reclaimed by the U.S. government for its mineral and timber resources. The Ute Tribe, whose 3,000-some members inhabit the land, hold powwows and other cultural ceremonies, which help visitors understand their way of life.

Museums throughout the region are full of fascinating pioneer relics, and there are a number of restored homesteads in and around Vernal. The rich mining and railroad history of the Price–Helper area fuels the tall tales you're certain to hear of outlaws, robberies, mine disasters, and heroic deeds.

TOP REASONS TO GO

One great gorge: The most jaw-dropping spot in northeastern Utah is the Flaming Gorge National Recreation Area. The deep-blue water under the gorge's reddish, steep walls is a serene place for fishing and boating, and the surrounding open space makes for good camping and hiking.

Dino-mite: Come to Dinosaur National Monument to see the famous dinosaur fossils or just to explore some truly remote country. For the most exciting introduction to the monument, take a guided river-rafting trip through it.

Ancient art: The cliffs near Vernal and Price are striking not only for their interesting rock formations,

but also for voluminous displays of ancient petroglyphs and picto-graphs, drawn once upon a time by members of the Fremont tribe.

Bike Vernal: In the last decade almost 200 miles of former cow trails around Vernal have been converted for use by mountain bikes. The sport is still getting a foothold in the area, so that means the paths are often blissfully empty—for now.

Alone in the swell: The San Rafael Swell is one of the least crowded spots in a region that's already known for its sparse population. If you're looking for solitude while hiking, biking, and boating, these miles of domed rock might be exactly what you need.

5

ORIENTATION AND PLANNING

GETTING ORIENTED

This section of Utah is large, but traffic is light and the towns are few, so it's easy to get around. The main highways are U.S. 191 and U.S. 40, which run north–south. The biggest towns are Vernal and Price, both of which make comfortable bases for the backcountry.

Northeast–Central Utah (Castle Country). Nicknamed for the impressive castle-like rock formations that dot the landscape, Castle Country is one of those secret spots that many vacationers miss. Most of the attractions are near the town of Price, such as the huge crop of petroglyphs at Nine Mile Canyon. The San Rafael Swell, one of the largest natural wonders you may never have heard about, lies 25 miles south of Price.

The Uinta Basin (Dinosaurland). Dubbing the Uinta Basin "Dinosaurland" is no overstatement. Named in honor of the large quantity of dinosaur fossils in the area (and especially the 1909 discovery of a huge cache of dino fossils in what is now Dinosaur National Monument), this slice of Utah boasts about its paleontological history whenever possible. Here you can see the ancient bones at the monument and get a crash course in dinosaur history at Vernal's Utah Field House of Natural History State Park. If dinosaurs don't hold your interest (blasphemy around here), you can still have a grand time taking river trips, hiking, and mountain biking. The breathtaking Flaming Gorge National Recreation Area is an excellent place to fish, boat, swim, and catch up-close glimpses of wildlife such as bighorn sheep and wild turkeys.

PLANNING

WHEN TO GO

In northeastern Utah most museums, parks, and other sights extend their hours from Memorial Day to Labor Day—sometimes through the end of September. (Some museums and parks are open only in summer.) Summer also brings art festivals, pioneer reenactments, rodeos, and other celebrations. This hottest period of the year, when temperatures can reach 100°F, is an ideal time for rafting trips down the Green River or boating on the region's reservoirs. Spring and autumn are cooler and less crowded, and nicer for hiking or biking, but you'll miss out on some of the festivities. Some campgrounds are open year-round, but the drinking water is usually turned off after Labor Day. In winter you can cross-country ski or snowshoe on many of the hiking trails; maps are available at local visitor centers.

> ### CAMPING
>
> Wilderness makes up the majority of this beautifully undeveloped region. Consequently, many visitors choose to immerse themselves in the outdoors by camping for at least part of their stay. For campground information contact **Dinosaur National Monument Quarry Visitor Center** (☎ 435/781–7700 ⊕ www.nps.gov/dino), the state government's recreation department (☎ 877/444–6777 ⊕ www.recreation.gov), or **Utah State Parks** (☎ 800/322–3770 ⊕ www.stateparks.utah.gov/reservations).

PLANNING YOUR TIME

Vernal is a good base for your eastern Utah wanderings. From there it's not far to the two biggest draws in this area: **Flaming Gorge National Recreation Area** and **Dinosaur National Monument.** While it's reasonable to see the fossils on display at Dinosaur in just a day, you'll get a better sense of park's untouched natural beauty if you stay overnight. Likewise, you can spend a day or several hiking the trails and playing in the water at Flaming Gorge. Besides Vernal, many of the towns in the area can be driven through or stopped in without spending the night. The one exception is **Price,** a pleasant town that's close to the tiny, historic town of **Helper** and less than two hours from the stunning **San Rafael Swell,** a huge, oval-shape, geologic dome that's far from everything but worth the trek. You could easily spend a few days exploring these unique areas. If you can make the time, a one or multiday excursion on the **Green, White,** or **Yampa rivers** would be an unforgettable—and occasionally heart-pounding—addition to your stay.

GETTING HERE AND AROUND

AIR TRAVEL

The closest major airport is Salt Lake City International Airport—two hours from Price and three hours from Vernal; it's served by most major airlines.

CAR TRAVEL

Both U.S. 40 and U.S. 191 are well maintained but have some curvy, mountainous stretches, and away from major towns, be prepared for dirt roads. Keep your vehicle fueled up, because gas stations can be far apart, and some are closed on Sunday. Watch for wildlife on the road, especially at night. Price is the largest city on U.S. 6, the major route between the Wasatch Front and the southeastern part of the state. Vernal and Dinosaur National Monument (which spans the Utah–Colorado border) are three hours east of Salt Lake City on U.S. 40, or three hours northeast of Price via U.S. 191 and U.S. 40. Flaming Gorge is 40 miles north of Vernal via U.S. 191. The Uinta Mountains and the High Uintas Wilderness Area are about 1½ hours east of Salt Lake City, first via I–80, U.S. 40, and Highway 248 to Kamas and then via Highway 150.

Information Road Conditions ☎ 866/511–8824 ⊕ www.udottraffic.utah.gov.

RESTAURANTS

Because the towns in eastern Utah are small, dining options are generally more casual and less innovative than in urban areas. The area has only two brewpubs: the refreshingly trendy Vernal Brewing Company, which opened just off Vernal's Main Street in 2013, and Grogg's Pinnacle Brewing Co., between Helper and Price; happily, both turn out good food and beer. Price has a mix of ethnic restaurants (with surprisingly low prices) that represents its immigrant railroad and mining history. Vernal, a farming and ranching town, has good steak houses and tasty diner eats. The best dining in this part of the state can be found in upscale lodges—Falcon's Ledge Lodge, between Duchesne and Roosevelt, and Red Canyon Lodge and Flaming Gorge Resort, both near Flaming Gorge—which pride themselves on having gourmet menus. Bear in mind that most locally owned restaurants are closed on Sunday, so plan ahead or you'll likely be stuck eating in motel restaurants or fast-food joints.

HOTELS

Most hotels and motels in eastern Utah are chains, and you can expect clean, comfortable rooms and standard amenities. The area's lodges make for a nice change of pace, surrounding you with natural beauty and more individualized rooms and services. Though it goes against logic, many hotels here offer cheaper rates on weekends than weekdays, due to the high number of workers who stay during the week. On weekends, hotels and motels do their best to attract tourists. *Hotel reviews have been shortened. For full information, visit Fodors.com.*

WHAT IT COSTS				
	$	$$	$$$	$$$$
Restaurants	under $12	$12–$20	$21–$30	over $30
Hotels	under $100	$100–$150	$151–$200	over $200

Restaurant prices are the average cost of a main course at dinner or, if dinner is not served, at lunch. Hotel prices are the lowest cost of a standard double room in high season.

VISITOR INFORMATION
Visitor Information Bureau of Land Management ⊠ *125 S. 600 W, Price*
☎ *435/636–3600* ⊕ *www.blm.gov/ut* ⊠ *170 S. 500 E, Vernal* ☎ *435/781–4400*
⊕ *www.blm.gov/ut.* **Visit Dinosaurland** ⊠ *149 E. Main St., Vernal* ☎ *435/781–
6765, 800/477–5558* ⊕ *www.dinoland.com.*

NORTHEAST–CENTRAL UTAH (CASTLE COUNTRY)

While Castle Country feels desolate, people have been in the area for centuries. Spanish explorers and traders crossed northeast–central Utah as early as 1598, on a trail now followed by Highway 10. In the 19th century fur trappers passed through the mountains in their search for beaver and other animals, and in the 1870s some of them decided to return to do some ranching. However, the area didn't thrive until a new kind of wealth was discovered in the mountains—coal. Railroad tracks were laid in the valley in 1883 to bring miners from around the world to dig the black mineral and to carry the coal out to markets across the country. Coal continues to provide the economic base for many towns in Castle Country, but so does tourism, which is growing every year.

PRICE

120 miles southeast of Salt Lake City.

Thousands of visitors annually come to Price to look at Utah's prehistoric past in the Prehistoric Museum, USU Eastern. Like many Utah towns, Price began as a Mormon farming settlement in the late 1800s. In 1883 the railroad arrived, bringing immigrants from around the world to mine coal reserves. Mining became the town's primary industry, which it remains to this day.

GETTING HERE AND AROUND

To get to Price from Salt Lake City: go 50 miles south via I–15, then 70 miles southeast on U.S. 6. To get here from Green River: head 65 miles north via U.S. 191. The town is easy to navigate, with most of the main attractions on, or close to, Main Street.

FESTIVALS

Greek Festival Days. A sizable number of Greeks came to the Price area to work in the mines in the early 1900s, and this festival in mid-July celebrates that heritage with two days of traditional Greek food, dance, and music. ⊠ *Assumption Greek Orthodox Church, 61 S. 200 E* ☎ *435/636–3701* ⊕ *www.castlecountry.com/GREEK-FESTIVAL-DAYS.*

Price City International Days. At the end of July, this festival uses music, dance, and food to celebrate the many nationalities that make up the Price community. ⊠ *Pioneer Park, 100 E. 550 N* ☎ *435/636–3701* ⊕ *www.castlecountry.com/Price-City-International-Days.*

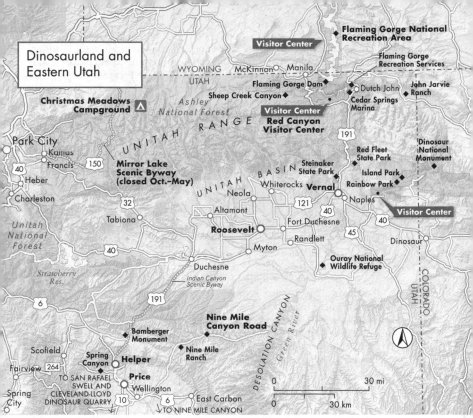

Dinosaurland and Eastern Utah

ESSENTIALS

Visitor Information Carbon County Office of Tourism and Visitors Center. Relocating during 2015; call to check before visiting. ⌧ *81 N. 200 E* ☎ *435/637–3701* ⊕ *www.castlecountry.com.*

EXPLORING

FAMILY **Cleveland-Lloyd Dinosaur Quarry.** Paleontologists and geologists have excavated more than 15,000 dinosaur bones from the Cleveland-Lloyd Dinosaur Quarry, making this "predator trap" the densest concentration of Jurassic fossils ever found. Since the quarry's discovery by herders in the 1920s, scores of dinosaur remains have been discovered here, including the oldest fossilized egg. Although many of the bones found in the quarry now reside in museums around the world, a trip to the remote landscape surrounding the quarry pit is worth the journey. The visitor center, which generates its own electricity from rooftop solar panels, has a reconstructed dinosaur skeleton and exhibits about the quarry, and the area has some short hiking trails. The center is 15 miles on a gravel road from the nearest services, so bring food and water and dress for desert conditions. It's 32 miles south of Price: take Highway 10 south to the Cleveland/Elmo turnoff and follow the signs. ■**TIP→ Bonus for families: free admission for ages 15 and younger.** ⌧ *Off Hwy. 10* ☎ *435/636–3600* ⊕ *www.blm.gov/ut* ⌧ *$5* ⊙ *Call for hrs.*

Fodor's Choice   **Nine Mile Canyon.** The hundreds of petroglyphs etched into the boulders
★   and cliffs of Nine Mile Canyon may be one of the world's largest outdoor art galleries. They're the handiwork of the Fremont people, who
lived in much of what is now Utah from AD 600 to 1300. The canyon
also shelters the remnants of many early homesteads, stage stops, and
ranches. However, the petroglyphs and pictographs are the main draws.
It's important not to touch the fragile rock art because oils from your
fingers can damage them. The drive spans about 100 miles round-trip,
so plan a day to complete it. Bring water and a picnic, because there
are no services. A brochure detailing significant sites is available at the
Carbon County Visitors Center in Price. Without it, many panels will
go unnoticed. ✉ *Nine Mile Canyon Rd.* ✚ *To reach canyon, go 7½ miles
southeast of Price on U.S. 6 and then turn north on Soldier Creek Rd.,
which eventually connects with Nine Mile Canyon Rd.* ☎ *435/637–
3701* ⊕ *www.castlecountry.com/Nine-Mile-Canyon.*

FAMILY   **The Prehistoric Museum, USU Eastern.** Miners working in the coal fields
around Price in the late 1800s often saw and excavated rare treasures
that most scientists could only dream of finding—dinosaur bones, eggs,
skeletons, and fossilized tracks. These are all on view here, along with a
small, but excellent kids discovery area. A second hall is devoted to early
humans, with displays of beadwork, clay figurines, a walk-in teepee,
and other area artifacts, as well as a gigantic wooly mammoth and a
saber-toothed cat. ✉ *155 E. Main St.* ☎ *435/613–5060, 800/817–9949*
⊕ *www.usueastern.edu/museum* ✆ *$6* ☉ *Mon.–Sat. 9–5.*

Price Mural. The 200-foot-long mural inside the Price Municipal Building
is a visual narration of the history of the town and of Carbon County,
beginning with the first trappers and white settlers. The painting took
artist Lynn Fausett almost four years to complete back in the late 1930s.
✉ *200 E. Main St.* ☎ *435/637–5010* ✆ *Free* ☉ *Weekdays 8–5.*

Fodor's Choice   **San Rafael Swell.** Tremendous geological upheavals pushed through the
★   earth's surface eons ago, forming a giant oval-shape dome of rock about
80 miles long and 30 miles wide, giving rise to the name "swell." Over
the years, the harsh climate beat down the dome, eroding it into a wild
array of multicolor sandstone and creating buttes, pinnacles, mesas, and
canyons that spread across more than 600,000 acres—an area slightly
smaller than the state of Rhode Island.

Managed by the Bureau of Land Management, the Swell offers visitors
spectacular sights similar to those in Utah's national parks but without
the crowds. In the northern Swell, the Wedge Overlook peers into the
Little Grand Canyon and the San Rafael River below, for one of the
most scenic vistas in the state. The strata at the edges of the southern
Swell are angled near vertical, creating the San Rafael Reef. Both are
known for fantastic hiking, canyoneering, and mountain biking.

I–70 bisects the San Rafael Swell, and is the only paved road in the
region. Although there are many off-road opportunities, the main gravel
road and many of the graded dirt roads through the Swell are accessible
to two-wheel-drive vehicles. The Swell is about 25 miles south of Price,
and the closest towns—Green River, Castle Dale, and Cleveland—are

not that close, so bring whatever supplies you might need, including plenty of water, food, and a spare tire.

Proposals have been made to designate the Swell a national monument. Until then, the San Rafael Swell remains one of the little-known natural wonders of the American West. ✉ *125 S. 600 W* ☎ *435/636–3600* 🌐 *www.blm.gov/ut.*

SPORTS AND THE OUTDOORS

Carbon County covers a wide range of geography, from mountains to gorges to plateaus. Hundreds of miles of hiking and biking trails crisscross the region.

GOLF

Carbon Country Club. The 18-hole championship course at the Carbon Country Club is open to the public and offers an enjoyable game to golfers at all levels of expertise, and has a pleasant relaxed feel. Keep in mind that it may be hard to concentrate on your game when you're surrounded by sandstone cliffs, a waterfall, hidden Native American petroglyphs, and a pioneer burial ground. ✉ *3055 N. U.S. 6* ☎ *435/637–2388* 🌐 *www.carboncountryclub.com* 🎫 *$27* ⛳ *18 holes, 6209 yards, par 70.*

5

HIKING AND MOUNTAIN BIKING

The canyons and expanses around Price include trails that rival the slickrock of Moab, but without the crowds. The visitor center in Price has a mountain-biking guide that shows several trails you can tackle, including Nine Mile Canyon. Adventurous hikers can use many of these trails as well. Bicyclewerks is also a source of information.

Bicyclewerks. The co-owners here—Fuzzy "the Bike Guy" Nance and Mark Jespersen—are Price's go-to guys for trail details, fix-its, or area information. ✉ *82 N. 10 W* ☎ *435/637–7676* 🌐 *www.facebook.com/Bicyclewerks.*

WHERE TO EAT

$ AMERICAN 🍴 **Farlaino's Café.** In a historic building on Main Street, this casual restaurant attracts locals with its large portions of American fare for breakfast, lunch, and early dinners (it closes at 7). It's known for its hand-cut curly fries, homemade soups (on weekdays), and pancakes so big they could be mistaken at first glance for a pizza. [$] *Average main: $9* ✉ *87 W. Main St.* ☎ *435/637–9217* 🕒 *Closed Sun.*

$ GREEK 🍴 **Greek Streak.** On the site of a Greek coffeehouse from the early 1900s, this low-key café is a reminder of Price's strong Greek heritage. The menu includes traditional recipes from Crete: gyros, dolmades, lemon-rice soup, and such. The baklava and other desserts made here are among the best Greek pastries in the state. [$] *Average main: $9* ✉ *84 S. Carbon Ave.* ☎ *435/637–1930* 🕒 *Closed Sun.*

$ ITALIAN 🍴 **Nicki Spaghetti.** In a welcome departure from the region's typical bar-and-grill fare, this restaurant serves traditional Italian dishes at very reasonable prices. The atmosphere evokes the Rat Pack era with a Sinatra soundtrack, black-and-white photographs of Bogart and gang, and a low-light ambience. The food is the real deal, using the chef's old family recipes; as the story goes, when the chef was four years old, his mother whisked him, and the recipes, away from his East Coast mobster father (named Nicki Spaghetti) and headed west. [$] *Average* *main: $8* ✉ *40 W. Main St.* ☎ *435/637–4393* 🌐 *www.nickispaghetti.com* 🕒 *Closed Sun. No lunch.*

$ FAST FOOD FAMILY Fodor's Choice ★ 🍴 **Sherald's.** If you hanker for the nostalgia, and the prices, of an old-fashioned hamburger stand, you're in luck. You can either order at the window and eat on outside picnic tables or use the carhop service. Stop at Sherald's and see why locals stand in line here for their burgers, fries, and incredibly thick milk shakes, ignoring the McDonald's across the street. [$] *Average main: $5* ✉ *434 E. Main St.* ☎ *435/637–1447* 🕒 *Closed Sun.*

WHERE TO STAY

$ HOTEL 🏨 **Greenwell Inn & Convention Center.** With more amenities than most local hotels but still reasonably priced, the Greenwell is a good choice. **Pros:** convenient downtown location; nice pool. **Cons:** motel-style room entrances are a downside in inclement weather; fitness center is large but is in lobby/pool area. [$] *Rooms from: $90* ✉ *655 E. Main St.* ☎ *435/637–3520, 800/666–3520* 🌐 *www.greenwellinn.com* 🛏 *130 rooms, 6 suites* 🍽 *No meals.*

$ B&B/INN 🏨 **Nine Mile Ranch.** Ben Mead grew up in beautiful Nine Mile Canyon, and now runs this "bunk and breakfast" establishment on his working cattle ranch. **Pros:** a place to get a true cowboy experience; unrivaled silence. **Cons:** this spot is very far from everything, which can be an acquired taste for some; breakfast is not included with cabin rental (but available). [$] *Rooms from: $90* ✉ *Nine Mile Canyon Rd., Post 24, Wellington* ✣ *To reach the ranch, travel 7 miles southeast of Price to Wellington via Highway 6, then make a left onto Soldier Creek Canyon Road, which will become Nine Mile Canyon Road, and drive north for 25 miles* ☎ *435/637–2572* 🌐 *www.ninemilecanyon.com* 🛏 *2 rooms, 3 cabins* 🍽 *Multiple meal plans.*

$$ HOTEL 🏨 **Ramada.** This tastefully decorated hotel has a large atrium containing the pool, and the rooms are clean and comfortable. **Pros:** a lot of amenities; pleasant and well-lit interiors. **Cons:** no meals included; though worth it, the price feels high for Price. [$] *Rooms from: $124* ✉ *838 Westwood Blvd.* ☎ *435/637–8880, 877/492–4803* 🌐 *www.ramada.com/hotel/48661* 🛏 *137 rooms, 14 suites* 🍽 *No meals.*

NIGHTLIFE

The Club at the Tuscan. This club's classy atmosphere renders it a pleasant place to park for the evening. Come early for dinner; it's attached to a tasty fine-dining restaurant with ridiculously low prices. Then step across the hall for drink and a mellow game of pool. The atmosphere livens up on the weekends, when the doors stay open till 2 am and a live DJ inspires dancing. ✉ *23 E. 100 N* ☎ *435/613–2582* 🕒 *Open 4–midnight Wed. and Thurs., 4–2 am Fri. and Sat. Closed Sun.–Tues.*

Sports Page Bar. Inside the Ramada, this bar has a pool table and big-screen TV to keep patrons amused when there isn't a comedy act performing, karaoke being sung, or a DJ spinning tunes. ✉ *Ramada Hotel, 838 Westwood Blvd.* ☎ *435/637–8880, 877/492–4803* 🌐 *www.ramada.com/hotel/48661.*

THE UINTA BASIN (DINOSAURLAND)

The Uinta Basin, originally home to the ancient Fremont people, is a vast area of gently rolling land bordered by the Uinta Mountains to the north, the Wasatch Mountains to the west, and a series of high plateaus and cliffs to the south. In the 1860s the Mormons thought about settling here, but decided the land was not fit for agriculture. At their suggestion, President Abraham Lincoln set aside several million acres of the basin as a Native American reservation, and moved members of Ute and other tribes here from their traditional lands in the Salt Lake and Utah Lake valleys. In the 1900s the U.S. government took back much of the Uinta Basin land that had been set aside as a reservation and opened it to settlers from the East. Following the Indian Reorganization Act of 1934, the Northern Ute Tribe repurchased the majority of this land, which now constitutes the second-largest reservation in the United States.

> **BY ANY OTHER NAME . . .**
>
> Before Roosevelt took its modern-day moniker, it had the utilitarian name of Dry Gulch City (due to a nearby gulch that spent most of the year without water). According to legend, the name was changed in honor of Teddy Roosevelt at the request of the wife of the man who laid out the town. Roosevelt became the adopted name in 1906, when the city was officially founded.

In the early 1900s an unbelievably rich trove of dinosaur fossils was discovered in the sandstone layers near the eastern Utah border. Since then, archaeologists have unearthed hundreds of tons of fossils, and the region encompassing Daggett, Duchesne, and Uintah counties has become known as Dinosaurland. An area particularly rich in fossils, straddling the Utah and Colorado borders, has been preserved as Dinosaur National Monument.

ROOSEVELT

80 miles northeast of Price.

Roosevelt, a small town named for President Theodore Roosevelt, lies between blocks of the sovereign land of the Uintah and Ouray Indian Reservation. Its tiny main street is pure Americana, and resembles any number of the other little towns in the area. It's a good place to stop for a cup of coffee or a meal, or to spend the night on the way to somewhere else.

GETTING HERE AND AROUND

Roosevelt is more of a place you end up than a planned destination. Its location, between Price and Vernal on U.S. 40, makes it an ideal place to get out and stretch your legs. If you're headed here from Price, go north on U.S. 191, then east on U.S. 40.

EXPLORING

Ouray National Wildlife Refuge. Established in 1960, this refuge consists of 11,987 acres of land along the Green River, where you can see more than 200 species of migratory birds in spring and fall, mule deer and golden eagles year-round, and bald eagles in early winter. An information kiosk at the refuge has a bird checklist and other leaflets. Best times to visit are in the early morning and early evening. ✉ *Wildlife Refuge Rd., off Hwy. 88, Ouray ✣ To reach refuge, go 15 miles east of Roosevelt on U.S. 40, then 13 miles south on Rte. 88* ☎ *435/545–2522* 🌐 *www.fws.gov/ouray* 🎟 *Free* 🕒 *Daily.*

Uintah and Ouray Reservation. The 1.3 million acres of the reservation spread out in patchwork fashion across the Uinta Basin and northeastern Utah to the eastern edge of the state. Fort Duchesne is the tribal headquarters for the Uintah and Ouray branch of the Ute Tribe. Because it's sometimes difficult to tell whether you're on reservation land, public land, or private land, you should stay on main roads unless you have permission to be on the reservation lands. ✉ *Fort Duchesne* 🌐 *www.utetribe.com.*

Northern Ute Pow Wow. Each July 4 weekend the Northern Ute Pow Wow has drumming, dancing, and singing competitions, featuring top performers from throughout North America. The powwow is one of the largest in the West and is free to the public, who are welcome to attend and camp on the powwow grounds. Other attractions include a rodeo, golf and softball tournaments, and an arts-and-crafts fair. The tribe also celebrates two Ute Bear Dances in May and a smaller powwow, held over Thanksgiving weekend at the tribal gymnasium in Fort Duchesne. ✉ *U.S. 40, 8 miles east of Roosevelt, Fort Duchesne* ☎ *435/722–5141* 🌐 *www.utetribe.com.*

SPORTS AND THE OUTDOORS

FISHING

Ute Tribe Fish & Wildlife Department. Information about camping, sporting, and photo safaris on the Uintah and Ouray Reservation is available from the Ute Tribe Fish & Wildlife Department. ☎ *435/722–5511* 🌐 *www.uitfwd.com.*

WHERE TO STAY

$$ HOTEL 🏨 **Best Western Plus Landmark Hotel.** Ample amenities, including one of the few indoor pools in the region and a hot breakfast, make this chain hotel a reliable choice. **Pros:** hot breakfast; free Wi-Fi; indoor pool open year-round. **Cons:** rates seem high for the area; not much to do in Roosevelt except move on to somewhere else. [$] *Rooms from: $143* ✉ *2477 E. U.S. 40, Ballard* ☎ *435/725–1800, 800/780–7234* 🌐 *www.bestwestern.com* 🛏 *49 rooms, 7 suites* 🍴 *Breakfast.*

$$$ B&B/INN Fodor's Choice ★ 🏨 **Falcon's Ledge Lodge.** With an emphasis on escaping the workaday world, this small lodge on a 600-acre private ranch caters to fly-fishers, hunters, or anyone wanting to immerse himself or herself in the outdoors without sacrificing comfort. **Pros:** far from crowds; exquisite food. **Cons:** location is quite remote; the inn has few technological distractions (a bonus for some); no children under 12 allowed. [$] *Rooms from: $195* ✉ *Hwy. 87, 15 miles north of Duchesne or 25 miles west of Roosevelt, Altamont* ☎ *435/454–3737, 877/879–3737* 🌐 *www.falconsledge.com* 🛏 *9 rooms* 🍴 *Breakfast.*

$$ RENTAL 🏨 **J/L Ranch.** This is a place for the family to come explore, where you can sleep in cowboy-theme comfort, hike, bird-watch, and fish in the numerous lakes, rivers, and mountain streams. **Pros:** perfect for a fly-fishing getaway. **Cons:** if you're not into outdoor activities, you may not

be happy in this remote setting. $ *Rooms from: $138* ✉ *White Rocks Canyon Rd., Whiterocks* ☎ *435/353–4049* ⊕ *www.jlranch.com* ⌖ *2 cabins* ⦿ *No meals.*

PERFORMING ARTS
CINEMA
Echo Drive-In. For a taste of Americana, catch a show at the Echo Drive-In on summer weekends. ✉ *250 W. Hwy. 40* ☎ *435/722–2095* ⊕ *www. rooseveltmovies.com* ☉ *June–Aug. weekends.*

VERNAL

22 miles east of Fort Duchesne.

Vernal is the hub of Dinosaurland, mixing the region's ancient heritage with a certain kitschy charm—think down-home diners and giant dino statues. Dinosaurs aren't the only things they're proud of in Vernal, however. The town claims a connection to the ancient Fremont people, a rowdy ranching past, and more than a passing acquaintance with outlaws like Butch Cassidy, who frequented the area whenever he felt it was safe to be seen around town. Legend has it that the saloon-keepers of Vernal gave Butch's gang the name "Wild Bunch," muttering "There goes that wild bunch" whenever the outlaws rolled in. Now the largest town (population 10,000) in the northeast corner of the state, the cattle-ranching community of Vernal is one of the few Utah towns founded by non-Mormons. However, it was the town's remote location—at the eastern edge of Utah, far from government authorities—not a lack of religion that led to its early reputation as a wild and lawless place. These days it's more of a tame, friendly spot to cool your heels between trips to outlying areas as well as biking and river adventures.

> ### MEET DINAH
>
> Vernal is packed to the gills with dinosaur replicas, but none are as famous as the tall, pink one towering over U.S. 40 on the east side of town. Dinah, as she's known around town, has long eyelashes and a girlish smile, and has become Vernal's unofficial mascot over the years. She was originally built in the early 1970s to hold the sign for the now-defunct Dine-A-Ville motel. After that venture went belly-up, the city took over her care and eventually moved her to the current location.

GETTING HERE AND AROUND
Though far from pretty much everything, it's simple to reach Vernal. From Salt Lake City, first go 25 miles via I–80, then 145 miles east via U.S. 40/U.S. 191; from Price go east on U.S. 40. Most of Vernal's attractions are right on Main Street. From Vernal, take U.S. 40 east to reach Dinosaur National Monument, or head north on U.S. 191 to explore Flaming Gorge National Recreation Area.

FESTIVALS
Dinosaur Roundup Rodeo. For three days in early or mid-July each year, Vernal celebrates the town's Western heritage when it hosts the Dinosaur Roundup Rodeo. Three days of rodeo events, dances, and parades

CLOSE UP

Butch Cassidy, the Robin Hood of Utah

One of the West's most notorious outlaws was born and raised in southern Utah by Mormon parents, and his footprints and legends are scattered over southern and eastern Utah like buckshot. Butch Cassidy (born Robert LeRoy Parker in 1866) started out as a migrant cowboy dabbling in rustling. A brief career as a butcher in Wyoming earned him the nickname "Butch," and "Cassidy" was likely the name of his old rustling mentor.

By 1896 he'd formed a gang of accomplices and had turned from rustling to the more lucrative pursuits of bank and train robberies. His Wild Bunch of loosely knit companions fancied themselves the "Robin Hoods" of the West. Outraged by the way wealthy cattle barons were squeezing out the smaller ranchers, the outlaws justified their lifestyle choice by sharing their bounty with the local people, who often struggled in the harsh environment of the Utah desert. Of course, the fact that this generosity helped buy allies and protectors in the area didn't hurt. Butch Cassidy was well known for being shrewd, quick-witted, and charming.

The only major heist he pulled in Utah was in Price Canyon, near Helper, with his friend Elza Lay. Butch and Elza stole $8,800 in gold coins from the Pleasant Valley Coal Mine office by shoving a gun in the paymaster's belly while 200 men stood nearby waiting for their pay. The steps from the Castle Gate store, where the robbery occurred, are still on display at the Western Mining & Railroad Museum in Helper. The Wild Bunch often wintered near Vernal in Browns Park—a major hideout along the so-called Outlaw Trail, which stretched from Mexico to Montana. Many of the buildings are still visible and on display to visitors today. After masterminding one of the longest strings of successful bank and train robberies in America, Cassidy eventually escaped to Argentina with Harry Longabaugh (the Sundance Kid) and Longabaugh's girlfriend, Etta Place. What happened then is a source of continuing mystery. Some believe Cassidy and Longabaugh were killed there; others swear the two returned to the American West, living out their days in peaceful anonymity.

on Main Street celebrate the real-life cowboys who wear cowboy boots because they're practical, not because they're fashionable. ⊠ *Western Park Convention Center, 302 E. 200 S* ☎ *435/781–6765* ⊕ *vernalrodeo. com* ⊡ *$14–$17.*

ESSENTIALS

Visitor Information Vernal Area Chamber of Commerce ⊠ *134 W. Main St.* ☎ *435/789–1352* ⊕ *www.vernalchamber.com* .**Visit Dinosaurland** ⊠ *149 E. Main St.* ☎ *435/781–6765, 800/477–5558* ⊕ *www.dinoland.com.*

EXPLORING

FAMILY **Dry Fork Canyon.** An impressive array of easily accessible Native American petroglyphs and pictographs adorn the 200-foot-high cliffs in Dry Fork Canyon, making the 22-mile round-trip drive from Vernal well worth your time. Two trails leading to the rock art are on **McConkie Ranch,** a privately owned property that asks only for a $4 per vehicle donation and respect for the art and trails. ✉ *3500 West St. (Dry Fork Canyon Rd.)* ☎ *435/789–6733* ✉ *Free, $4 per vehicle donation requested* ⊙ *Daily.*

Uintah County Heritage Museum. Inside the Uintah County Heritage Museum are collections of Fremont and Ute Indian artifacts, including baskets, water jugs, and beadwork pieces, as well as pioneer items like carriages, guns, saddles, and old-fashioned toys. Kids can try out an old-school typewriter, while their parents check out the most off-beat installation: a collection of handmade porcelain dolls modeled after the nation's First Ladies, from Martha Washington to Nancy Reagan; they are a kitschy delight. ✉ *155 E. Main St.* ☎ *435/789–7399* ⊕ *www. uintahmuseum.org* ✉ *Free* ⊙ *Weekdays 9–6 (until 7:30 Mon.–Thurs., Memorial Day–Labor Day), Sat 10–4.*

FAMILY
Fodor'sChoice
★

Utah Field House of Natural History State Park. Around 150 million years ago, this was the stomping ground of dinosaurs, and you can see rock samples, fossils, Fremont and Ute nation artifacts, and a viewing lab where you can watch paleontologists restore actual fossils. The biggest attraction for kids is undoubtedly the outdoor Dinosaur Garden with its 18 life-size models of prehistoric creatures, including a *T. rex* and a woolly mammoth. The Field House also doubles as a visitor center for all of Dinosaurland, so stop here for maps and guides for the entire area. ✉ *496 E. Main St.* ☎ *435/789–3799* ⊕ *stateparks.utah.gov/parks/ field-house* ✉ *$6* ⊙ *Apr.–Sept., daily 9–5; Oct.–Mar., Mon.–Sat. 9–5.*

OFF THE
BEATEN
PATH

Browns Park. If you hanker for a glimpse of the Wild West, head to Browns Park. Lying along a quieter stretch of the Green River and extending into Colorado, this area features plenty of high-desert scenery, a national waterfowl refuge, and a history complete with notorious outlaws of the late 1800s. Inside the park you can explore several buildings on the **John Jarvie Ranch.** Buildings date from 1880 to the early 1900s, and there's also a cemetery containing the graves of a few men who met violent ends nearby. In addition to his ranch, Jarvie ran a post office, store, and river ferry, and his spread was a major hideout on the so-called Outlaw Trail. In late May, the **Jarvie Festival** celebrates this past with mountain men, wagon rides, pioneer demonstrations, rope- and leather-making, and live music. A similar festival takes place the last Saturday of October. Reach the park and ranch by driving 65 miles north of Vernal on U.S. 191, then 22 miles east on a gravel road, following signs to the ranch. ✉ *Browns Park Rd., Browns Park* ☎ *435/885–3307 John Jarvie Ranch* ⊕ *www.blm.gov/utah/vernal* ✉ *Free* ⊙ *Memorial Day–Labor Day, daily 10–4:30; day after Labor Day–day before Memorial Day, Wed.–Sat. 10–4:30.*

SPORTS AND THE OUTDOORS
BICYCLING
Because Dinosaurland is less well known than other parts of the state, bikers can often escape the crowds and enjoy some scenic solitude. The Uinta Basin has some 100 miles of trails. Bring plenty of water and sunblock.

Altitude Cycle. To talk to knowledgeable cyclists about local trails off the beaten path, stop in here; they can set you up with trail guides, repairs, and accessories. Ask for a map of biking hot spot **McCoy Flats,**

just 6½ miles west of the shop, off Highway 40. There you'll find 45 miles of trails to explore. ✉ *580 E. Main St.* ☎ *435/781–2595* ⊕ *www. altitudecycle.com.*

Dinosaur River Expeditions. Explore the best local mountain biking trails with guides from Dinosaur River Expeditions. Most of the biking tours take you just west of Vernal to McCoy Flats. There your guide will lead you on the best trails for your abilities. Novices might start on the 1½-mile Milk and Cookies loop, while advanced riders may head for the 5½-mile technical single track of Slippery when Wet. For a discounted rate, tack on a full-day rafting excursion on the Green River the day before or after. ✉ *550 E. Main St.* ☎ *800/345–7238* ⊕ *www.dinosaurriver expeditions.com* ✉ *$65 for half-day tour; does not include bike rental.*

BOATING

Red Fleet State Park. Like the other reservoirs in the region, this one, 10 miles north of Vernal, is great for boating and fishing. What really attracts visitors are the colorful sandstone formations surrounding the lake. In addition, a section of 200-million-year-old dinosaur tracks can be reached by a short hike or by boat, and camping is available. ✉ *Off U.S. 191* ☎ *435/789–4432* ⊕ *www.stateparks.utah.gov* ✉ *$7 day use.*

Steinaker State Park. Boating and waterskiing enthusiasts love Steinaker State Park, 7 miles north of Vernal. With 829 surface acres, Steinaker Reservoir relinquishes a fair number of largemouth bass and rainbow trout. There's a sandy swimming beach, hiking trails begin at the park, and wildlife-viewing areas are nearby. A campground and covered group pavilions make this a popular park. ✉ *U.S. 191* ☎ *435/789–4432* ⊕ *www.stateparks.utah.gov* ✉ *$7 day use.*

HIKING

Jones Hole Creek. One of the most beautiful hikes in the area begins at the Jones Hole National Fish Hatchery, 40 miles northeast of Vernal on the Utah-Colorado border, and follows Jones Hole Creek through riparian woods and canyons, past petroglyphs and wildlife. The full trail is an 8-mile round-trip to the Green River and back, but you can stop halfway at Ely Creek and return for an easier, but still lovely, 4-mile hike. There are numerous trails in this area that are unmarked and not maintained, but easy to follow if you use reasonable caution. ✉ *24495 E. Jones Hole Hatchery Rd.*

Dinosaur National Monument Quarry Visitor Center. Or check with the rangers at this visitor center, 20 miles east of Vernal, for more information about the numerous hiking trails in the area. ✉ *Hwy. 149, Dinosaur National Monument* ☎ *435/781–7700* ⊕ *www.nps.gov/dino.*

RAFTING

⇨ *For information on rafting, see Dinosaur National Monument.*

SCENIC FLIGHTS

Dinaland Aviation. For a bird's-eye view of Dinoland's deep canyons, wide-open deserts, and blue reservoirs, take to the air with Dinaland Aviation. They offer flight-seeing tours from 30 minutes to more than an hour. ✉ *830 E. 500 S* ☎ *435/789–4612* ✉ *From $39 per person.*

WHERE TO EAT

$ AMERICAN
🍴 **Betty's Café.** The atmosphere says "dive" (think plumbing and bail-bond ads on the tables) and the food may inch you a notch closer to a heart attack, but your taste buds will loudly sing the praises of Betty's Café. Locals swear by the breakfasts, especially the biscuits, jams, and scalloped-cut home fries—all homemade. Lunches are standard American fare. [$] *Average main: $9* ✉ *416 W. Main St.* ☎ *435/781–2728* 🕒 *Closes at 2 on weekdays and noon on weekends.*

$$$ STEAKHOUSE
🍴 **Club XS.** The atmosphere is odd at this combo nightclub and family steakhouse, but the steaks are the best in town, as locals will attest. Seafood, sandwiches, and salads are also available. Come for dinner and stay until 1 am for dancing. [$] *Average main: $24* ✉ *1080 E. Hwy. 40* ☎ *435/781–0122* 🌐 *www.clubxsrocks.com* 🕒 *Closed Sun. No lunch Sat.*

$$ AMERICAN FAMILY
🍴 **Dinosaur Brew Haus.** This friendly spot serves higher-quality food than your average sports pub, including hand-cut fries (try them Cajun-style), house-smoked meats, and grilled salmon. Snack on peanuts and watch a game on one of the TVs while you wait for your food, or drop a coin in the jukebox and shoot some pool. There's a kids' menu, too. [$] *Average main: $12* ✉ *550 E. Main St.* ☎ *435/781–0717.*

$$ MEXICAN
🍴 **Plaza Mexicana.** Festive, colorful interiors and authentic Mexican specialties make Plaza Mexicana a sure bet if you need a break from Vernal's ubiquitous American eateries. There are 22 varieties of burritos to choose from, as well as a large selection of seafood options. The homemade salsas are fantastic—enjoy them with your complimentary chips while you peruse the enormous menu. [$] *Average main: $14* ✉ *55 E. Main St.* ☎ *435/781–2931.*

$$ MODERN AMERICAN Fodor's Choice ★
🍴 **Vernal Brewing Company.** Breweries are rare in this corner of the state, as are eateries with modern style and trendy menu items such as tempura-fried portobellos or honey-glazed Cornish game hen with watermelon salsa. The VBC fits both bills, with a half-dozen home brews on tap and a creative array of menu items ranging from thin-crust pizzas to delectable dishes served in mini cast-iron skillets. Finish your meal with an order of Oreo nachos. [$] *Average main: $15* ✉ *55 S. 500 E* ☎ *435/781–2337* 🌐 *www.vernalbrewingcompany.com.*

WHERE TO STAY

$$$ HOTEL FAMILY
🏨 **Best Western Dinosaur Inn.** Remodeled rooms and a new pizza place spruce up this comfortable chain motel located within blocks of all downtown attractions. **Pros:** family-friendly; central location. **Cons:** Main Street location leads to traffic noise in some rooms; feels pricey considering that it's a basic chain offering. [$] *Rooms from: $160* ✉ *251 E. Main St.* ☎ *435/789–2660, 800/780–7234* 🌐 *www.bestwestern.com* 🛏 *55 rooms, 5 suites* 🍽 *Breakfast.*

$$ HOTEL
🏨 **Landmark Inn and Suites.** Just one block off Main Street, this inn offers rooms that are classy for the area and come with kitchenettes. **Pros:** central location; well-appointed rooms. **Cons:** the area isn't very pretty; in-room fans are loud. [$] *Rooms from: $119* ✉ *301 E. 100 S* ☎ *435/781–1800, 888/738–1800* 🛏 *36 rooms, 3 suites* 🍽 *Breakfast.*

5

PERFORMING ARTS

Outlaw Trail Theater. In late June and early July, enjoy musicals, melo-dramas, or comedies under the stars. Shows typically run Monday through Saturday. ✉ *Western Park Outdoor Amphitheater, 302 E. 200 S* ☎ *888/240–2080* ⊕ *www.outlawtrailtheater.com.*

SHOPPING

Ashley Trading Post. Dinosaur memorabilia, rocks, fossils, and Native American jewelry and baskets are available here. ✉ *236 E. Main St.* ☎ *435/789–8447.*

R. Fullbright Studios and Rock Shop. Stop here to enjoy artist Randy Full-bright's collection of gorgeous Dinosaur National Monument photographs. His paper castings of petroglyphs make nice mementos, too. ✉ *216 E. Main St.* ☎ *435/789–2451* ⊕ *www.randyfullbright.com.*

EN ROUTE

Flaming Gorge-Uintas National Scenic Byway. Past Red Fleet Reservoir north of Vernal, U.S. 191 begins to ascend the eastern flank of the Uinta uplift as you head toward Flaming Gorge. The section of U.S. 191 and Highway 44 between Vernal and Manila, Utah, is known as the Flaming Gorge-Uintas National Scenic Byway. Within a distance of 30 miles the road passes through 18 uptilted geologic formations, including the billion-year-old exposed core of the Uinta Mountains, with explanatory signs. The route also provides plenty of opportunity for wildlife-watching and fossil hunting. Before setting out, pick up a guide at the Utah Field House of Natural History. ✉ *U.S. 191.*

DINOSAUR NATIONAL MONUMENT

20 miles east of Vernal.

Dinomania rules at this 330-square-mile park that straddles the Utah–Colorado border. Although the main draws are obviously the ancient dinosaur fossils, the park's setting is something to savor as well, from craggy rock formations to waving grasslands to the Green and Yampa rivers. The best part is that complete solitude is easy to find, as desolate wilderness surrounds even the busiest spots within the park.

GETTING HERE AND AROUND

Coming from Vernal, go east about 10 miles to the town of Jensen, via U.S. 40. Once there, be on the lookout for Utah Highway 149 on your left and then follow the signs to the park.

EXPLORING

FAMILY

Fodor's Choice

★

Quarry Exhibit Hall. The monument's astoundingly large collection of fossils was discovered by Earl Douglass in 1909, when he stumbled upon eight enormous dinosaur tailbones exposed on a sandstone ridge. Although most of the park's acreage is in Colorado, the Utah side features its prime attraction: the Quarry Exhibit Hall. Here you can view some 1,500 genuine fossils, displayed in their original burial positions in an excavated river bed, several stories high, 150-feet long, and now enclosed by a large, airy museum. A "touch wall" allows you to run your hands over some of the ancient bones, and various displays and dinosaur replicas help you put the jumble of bones in their prehistorical context. ■TIP➔ **Use one of the interactive kiosks to identify the**

massive bones imbedded in the wall, or, better yet, flag down a ranger, who can add interesting tidbits about the bones and their excavation. To reach the Exhibit Hall, first stop by the **Quarry Visitor Center,** near the monument's west entrance. There you can view a 12-minute video and see displays that give an overview of the site and its paleontological significance. Then hop a shuttle (in summer) or drive (in winter) up to the Exhibit Hall. ⊠ *Hwy. 149, 20 miles east of Vernal* ☎ *435/781–7700* ⊕ *www.nps.gov/dino* ⊠ *$10 per vehicle to enter the monument* ⊗ *Daily, late May–Sept., 8–5:30; Oct.–mid-May 9–5.*

SCENIC DRIVES

Island Park Road. A scenic drive on the unpaved Island Park Road, along the northern edge of the park, not only passes some impressive Fremont petroglyph panels but also reaches a put-in point for rafters.

Tour of the Tilted Rocks. This especially scenic 20-mile round-trip drive runs from the Quarry Visitor Center east to the Josie Morris Cabin. Josie's sister, Ann Bassett, was reputedly the "Etta Place" of Butch Cassidy legends. Ms. Morris lived alone for 50 years at her isolated home. Along the drive, watch for ancient rock art, geological formations, views of Split Mountain, the Green River, and hiking trails.

SPORTS AND THE OUTDOORS

HIKING

Desert Voices Nature Trail. Four miles past the Quarry Visitor Center, the moderate 1½-mile trail has interpretive signs (including some designed by children for children) that describe the arid environment you're hiking through. You can make a longer hike by using the Connector Trail to link up with the Sound of Silence Trail (⇨ *below*).

Sound of Silence Trail. More challenging than the Desert Voices trail, this 3-mile trail, which begins 2 miles past the Dinosaur Quarry, delivers excellent views of Split Mountain. To hike both trails without returning to your car, use the easy ¼-mile **Connector Trail**, which links the two.

RAFTING

Fodor'sChoice
★

The best way to experience the geologic depths of Dinosaur National Monument is to take a white-water rafting trip on the Green or Yampa rivers. Joining forces near Echo Park in Colorado, the two waterways have each carved spectacular canyons through several eons' worth of rock, and contain thrilling white-water rapids. River-running season is May through September. ⚠ **Permits are required for all boaters.**

Adrift Adventures. The closest guide service to the Dinosaur National Monument, this outfitter offers one-day or multiday rafting trips on the Green and Yampa rivers. ⊠ *9500 E. 6000 S, Jensen* ☎ *435/789–3600, 800/824–0150* ⊕ *www.adrift.com* ⊠ *From $96 (day trip, including lunch and pass to Dinosaur National Monument).*

Dinosaur River Expeditions. Single-day trips on the Green River and multiday trips on both the Green and Yampa rivers are available. Ask about custom trips as well. ⊠ *550 E. Main St., Vernal* ☎ *800/345–7238* ⊕ *www. dinosaurriverexpeditions.com* ⊠ *From $87 (day trip including lunch).*

Don Hatch River Expeditions. The region's original river-running company has been at it since 1929. Their one-day and multiday rafting trips take

CLOSE UP

Environmental Controversy at Echo Park

Few public land controversies tell the tale of the modern environmental movement like the debate over the Echo Park Dam.

To achieve economic expansion after World War II and encourage settlement in the arid American West, the federal Bureau of Reclamation created the Colorado River Compact, a proposal to build a series of hydroelectric dams on the West's greatest river. One of these proposed dams was at Echo Park, in the heart of the remote Dinosaur National Monument, where two Colorado River tributaries, the Green and the Yampa, meet.

Although the relatively unknown Dinosaur National Monument wasn't the public icon that parks such as Yosemite, Yellowstone, or the Grand Canyon were, the dam proposal galvanized a number of environmental organizations. The National Parks Association, Sierra Club, Izaak Walton League, and the Wilderness Society began an unprecedented national campaign to raise awareness of the potentially submerged national monument. They raised the question: if national parks and monuments—supposedly under government protection—could not escape development, how could they be safeguarded?

Through photographs, these organizations showcased the area's astounding geologic history, wild white-water rivers, spectacular canyons, and role as a wildlife haven. Historians view the Echo Park Dam controversy as the start of an era—the first time conservation organizations used their voices to oppose government actions on public lands. When Secretary of the Interior Douglas McKay announced in 1955 that the Echo Park Dam project would not go forward, it was the first of several major conservationist victories that led to legislation including the Wilderness Act (1964) and the Wild and Scenic Rivers Act (1968).

Through this controversy, the U.S. public began to realize the value of national parks and monuments, even those in remote locations. "Environmental" entered the vocabulary.

you through both calm and white waters on the Green and Yampa rivers. ✉ *221 N. 400 E, Vernal* ☎ *800/342–8243* 🌐 *www.hatchriver.com* 🎟 *From $99 (day trip, including lunch).*

WHERE TO STAY

$ B&B/INN **Fodor's Choice** ★ 🏨 **The Jensen Inn.** Tucked just off the road to Dinosaur National Monument, this is a bright, cheery bed-and-breakfast with friendly owners and tasteful modern interiors, including a Japanese-style room. **Pros:** close to Dinosaur National Monument; excellent breakfasts. **Cons:** far from stores or restaurants; closed December through February. [$] *Rooms from: $95* ✉ *5056 S. 9500 E, Jensen* ☎ *435/789–5905* 🌐 *www.thejenseninn.com* 🛏 *4 rooms* 🕒 *Closed Dec.–Feb.* 🍴 *Breakfast.*

FLAMING GORGE NATIONAL RECREATION AREA

40 miles north of Vernal (to Flaming Gorge Dam).

If you are standing in front of the Flaming Gorge or its reservoir with a crowd of people, you'll likely hear gasps and exclamations of surprise. The sheer size of these bodies of water is astounding, as are the red, narrow walls on either side of the gorge. Though not far from the suburban town of Vernal, the Flaming Gorge area feels like its own world—the kind of place where you notice the aspen trees quiver and hear the birds chirp. The lake and 91-mile gorge also has some of the best boating and fishing in the state. The Flaming Gorge Reservoir stretches north into Wyoming, but most facilities lie south of the state line in Utah.

A BRIEF HISTORY OF FLAMING GORGE

In May 1869, during his mapping expedition on the Green and Colorado rivers, explorer John Wesley Powell named this canyon Flaming Gorge for its "flaming, brilliant red" color. Flaming Gorge remained one of Utah's most remote and least-developed inhabited areas well into the 1950s. In 1964 Flaming Gorge Canyon and the Green River running through it were plugged with a 500-foot-high wall of concrete, creating the gorge of today.

GETTING HERE AND AROUND

From Vernal, getting to the gorge is a straight shot north via U.S. 191. Follow the highway for about 38 miles, which will take you into some magnificent country at high elevations. Then simply follow the signs to the gorge. The road will veer downward for a few miles before you reach it. From Salt Lake City, go 30 miles east via I–80 past Evanston, Wyoming. Take the Fort Bridge exit, and drive to Manila via Highway 414, which becomes Highway 43. Once in Manila, turn right on Highway 44 for 38 miles until you reach U.S. 191, then follow signs.

ESSENTIALS

Flaming Gorge Dam Visitor Center. The main information center for the Utah side of the gorge, 2 miles north of Greendale Junction, includes displays and an explanatory movie, and, depending on national terrorism alert levels and the weather, this engineering marvel may be open for free guided tours. ✉ *U.S. 191* ☎ *435/885–3135* ⊕ *www. flaminggorgecountry.com* ⊗ *Mid-Apr.–mid-Oct., daily 9–5, longer hrs Memorial Day–Labor Day; mid-Oct.–mid-Mar., call for hrs.*

Red Canyon Visitor Center. Displays here explain the geology, flora and fauna, and human history of the Flaming Gorge area, but the best thing is the cliff-top location 1,300 feet above the lake. The views are outstanding, and you can enjoy them while having a picnic. To get here, head west from the Greendale Junction of U.S. 191 and Highway 44, and follow the signs. ✉ *Hwy. 44* ☎ *435/889–3713* ⊕ *www.flaminggorge country.com* ⊗ *Memorial Day–Labor Day, daily 8–6.*

EXPLORING

Sheep Creek Canyon Geological Area. A scenic 13-mile drive, on paved and gravel roads, crosses the Sheep Creek Canyon Geological Area, which is full of upturned layers of rock, craggy pinnacles, and hoodoos. Watch for a herd of bighorn sheep, as well as a popular cave alongside the road. In the fall, salmon return to Sheep Creek to spawn; a kiosk and several bridges provide unobtrusive viewing. The area, 28 miles west of Greendale Junction off U.S. 191 and Highway 44, is open from May to October. ⊠ *Forest Service Rd. 218* ☎ *435/784–3445.*

Spirit Lake Scenic Backway. This 17-mile round-trip add-on to the Sheep Creek Canyon Loop road leads past the **Ute Lookout Fire Tower,** which was in use from the 1930s through the 1960s.

Swett Ranch. This isolated homestead that belonged to Oscar and Emma Swett and their nine children through most of the 1900s. The U.S. Forest Service has turned the ranch into a working historic site, complete with restored and decorated houses and buildings. ⊠ *Off U.S. 191* ✛ *At Greendale Junction of U.S. 191 and Hwy. 44, stay on U.S. 191; about ½ mile north of junction there's a sign for 1½-mile dirt road to ranch* ☎ *435/784–3445* ⊕ *www.flaminggorgecountry.com/swett-ranch* ⊠ *Free* ☉ *Memorial Day–Labor Day, Sat. 10–5.*

SPORTS AND THE OUTDOORS

BICYCLING

Because it mixes high-desert vegetation—blooming sage, rabbit brush, cactus, and wildflowers—and red-rock terrain with a cool climate, Flaming Gorge is ideal for road and trail biking. The 3-mile round-trip **Bear Canyon–Bootleg** ride begins south of the dam off U.S. 191 at the Firefighters' Memorial Campground, and runs west to an overview of the reservoir. For the intermediate rider, **Dowd Mountain Hideout** is a 10-mile ride with spectacular views through forested single-track trail, leaving from Dowd Springs Picnic Area off Highway 44. Fliers describing cycling routes are at area visitor centers or online at ⊕ *www.dinoland. com.* Several local lodges rent bikes.

BOATING AND FISHING

Fodor's Choice ★ Flaming Gorge Reservoir provides ample opportunities for boating and water sports of all kinds, whether you prefer lounging on the deck of a rented houseboat or skiing behind a high-performance speedboat. Old-timers maintain that Flaming Gorge provides the best lake fishing in the state, yielding rainbow and lake trout, smallmouth bass, and Kokanee salmon. The Green River below Flaming Gorge Dam has been identified as one of the best trout fisheries in the world. Rainbow and brown trout are plentiful and big, but only artificial lures and fly-fishing are permitted; bait fishing isn't allowed. Fed by cold water from the bottom of the lake, this stretch is a calm, scenic stretch of water, ideal for risk-averse folk or for families who want to take smaller children on rafting trips, but who don't want to worry about them falling into white water. Most boating facilities close from October through mid-March.

Cedar Springs Marina. If you have your own boat, you can launch it, gas it up, or rent a slip here. You can also rent a boat or hire a fishing guide. The marina is approximately 2 miles southwest of Flaming Gorge Dam. ✉ *U.S. 191* ☎ *435/889–3795* 🌐 *www.cedarspringsmarina.com.*

Flaming Gorge Recreation Services. Boat rentals, guided fishing trips, and daily float trips on the Green River are available here. ✉ *U.S. 191 at Dutch John Blvd.* ☎ *435/885–3191* 🌐 *www.fishthegreen.com.*

Lucerne Valley Marina. Seven miles east of Manila you'll find this marina, with a boat launch, slips, mooring buoys, boat rentals, fishing licenses, mechanical services, gas, RV camping with electricity, and houseboat and floating-cabin rentals. ✉ *5570 E. Lucerne Valley Rd.* ☎ *435/784–3483, 888/820–9225* 🌐 *www.flaminggorge.com.*

HIKING

There's plenty of hiking in the Flaming Gorge area and any of the local visitor centers or lodges can recommend hikes. From the Red Canyon Visitor Center, three different hikes traverse the **Canyon Rim Trail** through the pine forest: an easy ½-mile round-trip trek leads to the Red Canyon Rim Overlook (above 1,300-foot cliffs), a moderate 3½-mile round-trip hike finds you at the Swett Ranch Overlook, and a 7-mile round-trip hike winds through brilliant layered colors to the Green River at the canyon's bottom below the dam. In the Sheep Creek Canyon Geological Area, the 4-mile **Ute Mountain Trail** leads from the Ute Lookout Fire Tower down through pine forest to Brownie Lake, and back the same way. The **Tamarack Lake Trail** begins at the west end of Spirit Lake (on Highway 44, go past the Ute Lookout Fire Tower turnoff and take F.S. Road 221 to Spirit Lake) and goes to Tamarack Lake and back for a moderate 3-mile trek, round-trip.

5

RAFTING

⇨ *For information on rafting, see Dinosaur National Monument.*

WHERE TO STAY

$$ HOTEL 🏨 **Flaming Gorge Resort.** With motel rooms and condo-style suites, a good American-cuisine restaurant, and a store just a short drive from the water, this is a practical base for activities. **Pros:** plenty of amenities and recreational options; good restaurant. **Cons:** aging rooms and suites; motel rooms don't have air-conditioning; can be very busy in summer, and too quiet in winter. [$] *Rooms from: $125* ✉ *1100 E. Flaming Gorge Resort Rd., off U.S. 191, Dutch John* ☎ *435/889–3773* 🌐 *www.flaminggorgeresort.com* 🛏 *21 rooms, 24 suites* 🍴 *No meals.*

$$ RESORT FAMILY Fodor's Choice ★ 🏨 **Red Canyon Lodge.** A pleasant surprise in the woods, this lodge is surrounded by well-built, handcrafted log cabins with kitchenettes (some with wood-burning stoves) that face a private trout-stocked lake. **Pros:** beautiful setting; cabins are comfortable for families or groups. **Cons:** for summer lodging, you need to book 3–6 months in advance; Wi-Fi only in restaurant; no air-conditioning; some beds are small. [$] *Rooms from: $119* ✉ *2450 W. Red Canyon Lodge Rd., Dutch John* ☎ *435/889–3759* 🌐 *www.redcanyonlodge.com* 🛏 *18 cabins* 🍴 *No meals.*

MIRROR LAKE SCENIC BYWAY

Kamas is 42 miles from Salt Lake City.

Although the Wasatch may be Utah's best-known mountain range, the Uinta Mountains, the only major east–west mountain range in the United States, are its tallest, topped by 13,528-foot Kings Peak. This area, particularly in the High Uintas Wilderness, where no vehicles are allowed, is great for pack trips, horseback day rides, hiking, and overnight backpacking in summer. The Uintas are ribboned with streams and dotted with small lakes set in rolling meadows.

GETTING HERE AND AROUND

From Salt Lake City, take I–80 and Highway 32 south to Kamas. You can access the Uinta Mountains either from Kamas or Evanston, Wyoming. From Kamas, go 65 miles east via Highway 150. From Evanston, travel 30 miles south on the same highway.

EXPLORING

Mirror Lake. A mile north of the crest of Bald Mountain Pass on Highway 150, this is arguably the best-known lake in the High Uintas Wilderness. At an altitude of 10,000 feet, it offers a cool respite from summer heat. It's easy to reach by car, and families enjoy fishing, hiking, and camping along its rocky shores. Its campgrounds provide a base for hikes into the surrounding mountains, and Highline Trail accesses the 460,000-acre High Uintas Wilderness Area to the east. There's a $6 day-use fee for Mirror Lake, but it's good for three days. ⊠ *Hwy. 150, mile marker 32.*

Fodor's Choice ★ **Mirror Lake Scenic Byway.** This scenic road begins in Kamas and winds its way up to the High Uinta country. The 65-mile drive follows Highway 150 through heavily wooded canyons past mountain lakes and peaks, cresting at 10,687-foot Bald Mountain Pass. Because of heavy winter snows, much of the road is closed from October to May. A three-day pass is required to use facilities in the area. You can buy a guide to the byway from the Wasatch-Cache National Forest's Kamas Ranger District office in Kamas (⊠ *50 E. Center St.* ☎ *435/783–4338* ⊕ *www.utah.com/byways*). ⊠ *Kamas* 🌐 *$6 for 3-day pass.*

Upper Provo Falls. This is a good place to stop en route, near mile marker 24, where you can stroll the boardwalk to the terraced falls cascading with clear mountain water.

SPORTS AND THE OUTDOORS

Bear River Lodge. This is an ideal jumping-off spot to explore the Uinta Mountains. Well-informed employees can steer you to the right hiking trails for you, and the lodge rents fishing gear, ATVs, snowmobiles, kayaks, cross-country skis, and snowshoes. ⊠ *Mirror Lake, Hwy. 150, mile marker 49* ☎ *435/642–6289* ⊕ *www.bearriverlodge.com.*

WHERE TO STAY

$$$$ **RENTAL** 🏠 **Bear River Lodge.** Log cabins in the forest let you reconnect with nature via a range of on-site activities without giving up creature comforts. **Pros:** comfortable cabins; plenty of outdoor activities. **Cons:** prices seem high for level of amenities; no other restaurants within 30 miles. 💲 *Rooms from: $289* ⊠ *Mirror Lake Hwy., mile marker 49* ☎ *435/642–6289* ⊕ *www.bearriverlodge.com* 🛏 *16 cabins* 🍽 *No meals.*

6

CAPITOL REEF
NATIONAL PARK

Visit Fodors.com for advice, updates, and bookings

WELCOME TO CAPITOL REEF NATIONAL PARK

TOP REASONS TO GO

★ **The Waterpocket Fold:** See an excellent example of a monocline, a fold in Earth's crust with one very steep side in an area that is otherwise horizontal. This one's almost 100 miles long.

★ **No crowds:** Experience the best of southern Utah weather, rock formations, and wide-open spaces without the crowds of nearby parks such as Zion and Bryce Canyon.

★ **Fresh fruit:** Pick apples, pears, apricots, and peaches in season at the pioneer-planted orchards at historic Fruita. These trees still produce plenty of fruit.

★ **Rock art:** View ancient pictographs and petroglyphs left by the Fremont people, who lived in this area from AD 300 to 1300.

★ **Pioneer artifacts:** Buy faithfully reproduced tools and utensils, like those used by Mormon pioneers, at the Gifford House Museum and Store.

1 Fruita. This historic pioneer village is at the heart of what most people see of Capitol Reef. The one and only park visitor center nearby is the place to get travel and weather information and maps. The scenic drive through Capitol Gorge provides a view of the Golden Throne.

2 Cathedral Valley. The views are stunning and the silence deafening in the park's remote northern section. High-clearance vehicles are required, as is a crossing of the Fremont River. Driving in this valley is next to impossible when the Cathedral Valley Road is wet, so ask at the visitor center about current weather and road conditions.

3 Muley Twist Canyon. At the southern reaches of the park, this canyon is accessed via Notom-Bullfrog Road from the north, and Burr Trail Road from the west and southeast. High-clearance vehicles are required for much of it.

Above: Gifford Farmhouse in Fruita; Left: Chimney Rock; Below: Springtime blossoms

GETTING ORIENTED

At the heart of this 381-square-mile park is the massive natural feature known as the Waterpocket Fold, which runs roughly northwest to southeast along the park's spine. Capitol Reef itself is named for a formation along the fold near the Fremont River. A historic pioneer settlement, the green oasis of Fruita, is easily accessed by car, and an 8-mile scenic drive provides a good overview of the canyons and rock formations that populate the park. Colors here range from deep, rich reds to sage greens to crumbling gray sediments. The absence of large towns nearby ensures that night skies are brilliant starscapes.

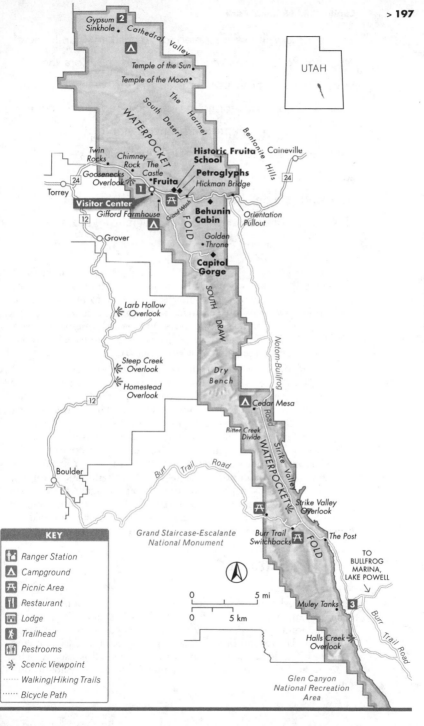

UTAH

Gypsum Sinkhole 2

Cathedral Valley

Temple of the Sun

Temple of the Moon

The Hartnet

South Desert

WATERPOCKET

Bentonite Hills

Caineville

24

Twin Rocks

Chimney Rock

The Castle

Historic Fruita School

Petroglyphs

Hickman Bridge

Goosenecks Overlook

•Fruita

1

24

Torrey

Visitor Center

12

Gifford Farmhouse

Behunin Cabin

Grand Wash

FOLD

Golden Throne

Orientation Pullout

Grover

Capitol Gorge

SOUTH DRAW

6

Larb Hollow Overlook

Steep Creek Overlook

Dry Bench

Homestead Overlook

Notom-Bullfrog

12

Cedar Mesa

Bitter Creek Divide

WATERPOCKET

Strike Valley

Boulder

Burr Trail Road

Road

Strike Valley Overlook

Grand Staircase-Escalante National Monument

Burr Trail Switchbacks

The Post

FOLD

TO BULLFROG MARINA, LAKE POWELL

0   5 mi

0   5 km

Muley Tanks

3

Burr Trail Road

Halls Creek Overlook

Glen Canyon National Recreation Area

KEY

🏕️ *Ranger Station*

🔺 *Campground*

🎪 *Picnic Area*

🍴 *Restaurant*

🏨 *Lodge*

🥾 *Trailhead*

🚻 *Restrooms*

🔆 *Scenic Viewpoint*

.... *Walking/Hiking Trails*

.... *Bicycle Path*

Updated by
John Blodgett

Your senses will be delighted by a visit to Capitol Reef National Park. Here, you are saturated in colors that are more dramatic than anywhere else in the West. The dominant Moenkopi rock formation is a rich, red-chocolate hue. Deep blue-green juniper and pinyon stand out against it. Other sandstone layers are gold, ivory, and lavender. Sunset brings out the colors in an explosion of copper, platinum, and orange, then dusk turns the cliffs purple and blue. The texture of rock deposited in ancient inland seas and worn by subsequent erosion is pure art.

The park preserves the Waterpocket Fold, a giant wrinkle in the earth that extends 100 miles between Thousand Lake Mountain and Lake Powell. When you climb high onto the rocks or into the mountains, you can see this remarkable geologic wonder and the jumble of colorful cliffs, massive domes, soaring spires, and twisting canyons that surround it. It's no wonder Native Americans are said to have called this part of the country the "land of sleeping rainbow."

But your eyes will not be alone in their joy. The fragrance of pine and sage rises from the earth, and canyon wrens sing to you as you sit by the water. Flowing across the heart of Capitol Reef is the Fremont River, a narrow little creek that can turn into a swollen, raging torrent during desert flash floods. The river sustains cottonwoods, wildlife, and verdant valleys rich with fruit. During the harvest, your sensory experience is complete when you bite into a perfect ripe peach or apple from the park's orchards. Your soul, too, will be gratified here. You can walk the trails in relative solitude and enjoy the beauty without confronting crowds on the roads or paths. All around you are signs of those who came before: ancient peoples of the Fremont culture, Mormon pioneers who settled the land, and other courageous explorers who traveled the canyons. It is a rare thrill to feel the past overtake the present.

CAPITOL REEF PLANNER

WHEN TO GO

Spring and early summer are most bustling. Folks clear out in the midsummer heat, and then return for the apple harvest and crisp temperatures of autumn. Still, the park is seldom crowded—though the Fruita campground can fill quickly. Annual rainfall is scant, but when it does rain, flash floods can wipe out park roads. Snowfall is usually light. Sudden, short-lived snowstorms—and thunderstorms—are not uncommon in the spring.

AVG. HIGH/LOW TEMPS.

Jan.	Feb.	Mar.	Apr.	May	June
41/20	46/26	57/33	66/40	76/49	86/58

July	Aug.	Sept.	Oct.	Nov.	Dec.
92/65	88/63	80/54	66/43	51/30	41/21

FESTIVALS

AUGUST **Wayne County Fair.** The great American county-fair tradition is at its finest in Loa. Horse shows, demolition derby, rodeo, and a parade are part of the fun. There are also crafts such as handmade quilts, agricultural exhibits, children's games, and plenty of good food. It takes place over six days in mid-August. ☎ *435/836–2765* ⊕ *waynecountyutah.org.*

Women's Redrock Music Festival. Held at the Robber's Roost Bookstore, this two-day event has been attracting independent female musicians from all corners of the globe, as well as hundreds of fans, since 2007. Run by the nonprofit Entrada Institute, a regional arts and education organization, the festival benefits Utah women through donations and scholarships. ⊠ *185 W. Main St., Torrey* ☎ *435/425–3265* ⊕ *womensredrockmusicfest.com.*

OCTOBER **Harvest Time Scarecrow Festival.** Events for this monthlong celebration of the end of another busy season are held throughout Wayne County. In addition to a scarecrow contest, there are plenty of family-friendly events, including music, arts and crafts, pumpkin carving, and a Halloween party at Torrey's Rim Rock restaurant. ⊠ *Torrey* ☎ *435/425–3265* ⊕ *www.entradainstitute.org.*

PLANNING YOUR TIME
CAPITOL REEF IN ONE DAY

Pack a picnic lunch, snacks, and cold drinks to take with you, because there are no restaurants in the park. As you enter the park, look to your left for Chimney Rock; in a landscape of spires, cliffs, and knobs, this deep-red landmark is unmistakable. Start your journey at the **visitor center,** where you can study a three-dimensional map of the area, watch the 18-minute park movie, and browse the many books and maps related to the park. Then head for the scenic drive, stopping at the **Fruita Historic District** to see some of the sites associated with the park's Mormon history. Stop at the **Gifford House Museum and Store** for a tour and a visit to the gift shop. That lunch you packed can be enjoyed at picnic tables on rolling green lawns lining both sides of the road between here and the orchard.

As you continue on with your tour, check out the **Fremont Indian Petroglyphs,** and if you feel like some exertion, take a hike on the Hickman Bridge Trail. From the trail (or if you skip the hike, from Highway 24 about 2 miles east of the visitor center), you'll see **Capitol Dome.** Along this stretch of Highway 24 stop to see the old one-room **Fruita Schoolhouse,** the **petroglyphs,** and the **Behunin Cabin.** Next you'll have to backtrack a few miles on Highway 24 to find the **Goosenecks Trail.** At the same parking lot, you'll find the trailhead for **Sunset Point Trail;** time

6

this short hike toward the end of the day and linger to watch the setting sun hit the colorful cliffs.

GETTING HERE AND AROUND

BUS TRAVEL

Once inside the park, there is no shuttle service as at nearby Zion and Bryce Canyon national parks.

CAR TRAVEL

Though far from big cities, Capitol Reef country can be reached by a variety of approaches. The main high-speed arteries through the region are Interstates 70 and 15, but any route will require travel of some secondary roads such as U.S. 50, U.S. 89, Highway 24, or Highway 72. All are well-maintained, safe roads that bisect rich agricultural communities steeped in Mormon history (such as the nearby towns of Bicknell and Loa). Interstate 15 is the fastest way through central Utah, but U.S. 89 and the local roads that feed onto it will give you a more direct path into Utah's past and present-day character. Highway 24 runs across the middle of Capitol Reef National Park, so even those traveling between points west and east of the park with no intention of touring it get a scenic treat on their way.

PARK ESSENTIALS

PARK FEES AND PERMITS

There is no fee to enter the park, but it's $5 per vehicle (or $3 per bicycle) to travel on Scenic Drive beyond Fruita Campground; this fee is good for one week, paid via the "honor system" at a drop box versus a staffed entry gate. Backcountry camping permits are required and free; pick them up at the visitor center.

PARK HOURS

The park is open 24/7 year-round. It is in the mountain time zone.

CELL-PHONE RECEPTION

Cell-phone reception is virtually nonexistent within the park (though available in nearby Torrey). Pay phones are at the visitor center and at Fruita Campground.

RESTAURANTS

There are no restaurants inside the Capitol Reef National Park, but dining options do exist close by in Torrey, where there are all kinds of eateries. These range from one of Utah's most memorable restaurants serving high-end Southwestern cuisine to basic hamburger joints with consistently good food.

HOTELS

There are no lodging options within Capitol Reef, but you'll have no problem finding clean and comfortable accommodations nearby, no matter what your budget. Torrey is the closest place, and Bicknell and Loa are not far beyond. Drive farther into the region's towns, and you are more likely to find locally owned low- to moderate-priced motels and a few nice bed-and-breakfasts. Reservations are recommended in summer. *Hotel reviews have been shortened. For full information, visit Fodors.com.*

Plants and Wildlife in Capitol Reef

The golden rock and rainbow cliffs are at their finest at sunset, when it seems as if they are lighted from within. That's also when mule deer wander through the orchards near the campground. The deer have become habituated to human presence, but do not feed them; their digestive systems are harmed by food for humans. Many of the park's animals move about only at night to escape the heat of the day, but pinyon jays and black-billed magpies flit around the park all day. The best place to see wildlife is near the Fremont River, where animals are drawn to quench their thirst. Mammals such as the yellow-bellied marmot and white-tailed antelope ground squirrel are frequently seen in Fruita. Desert bighorn sheep also live in Capitol Reef, but they are elusive. Your best chance for spotting the sheep is during a long hike deep within the park. If you should encounter a sheep, do not approach it, as they've been known to charge human beings. In fact, all wildlife is protected; rangers ask that you give animals space and don't disrupt their natural behavior.

6

WHAT IT COSTS				
	$	$$	$$$	$$$$
Restaurants	under $12	$12–$20	$21–$30	over $30
Hotels	under $100	$100–$150	$151–$200	over $200

Restaurant prices are the average cost of a main course at dinner or, if dinner is not served, at lunch. Hotel prices are the lowest cost of a standard double room in high season.

VISITOR INFORMATION
PARK CONTACT INFORMATION
Capitol Reef National Park ⊠ *Off Hwy. 24* ☎ *435/425–3791* ⊕ *nps.gov/care.*

VISITOR CENTER
Capitol Reef Visitor Center. Watch a park movie, talk with rangers, or peruse the many books, maps, and materials offered for sale in the bookstore. Towering over the center, which is 11 miles east of Torrey, is the Castle, one of the park's most prominent rock formations. ⊠ *Hwy. 24 and Scenic Dr.* ☎ *435/425–3791* ☉ *Late May–Sept., daily 8–6; Oct. and mid-Apr.–late May, daily 8–5; Nov.–mid-Apr., daily 8–4:30.*

EXPLORING

SCENIC DRIVES

Capitol Reef Scenic Drive. This 8-mile road, called simply Scenic Drive by locals, starts at the visitor center and winds its way through the Fruita Historic District and colorful sandstone cliffs into Capitol Gorge; a side road, Grand Wash Road, provides access into the canyon. At Capitol

Gorge, the canyon walls become steep and impressive but the route becomes unpaved for about the last 2 miles, and road conditions may vary due to weather and usage. Check with the visitor center before setting out. ⊠ *Off Hwy. 24, 11 miles east of Torrey.*

SCENIC STOPS

Behunin Cabin. Elijah Cutlar Behunin used blocks of sandstone to build this cabin in 1882. Floods in the lowlands made life too difficult, and he moved before the turn of that century. The house, 5.9 miles east of the visitor center, is empty, but you can peep through a window. ⊠ *Hwy. 24.*

Capitol Dome. One of the rock formations that gave the park its name, this giant, sandstone dome is visible in the vicinity of the Hickman Bridge trailhead, 1.9 miles east of the visitor center. ⊠ *Hwy. 24.*

Fodor's Choice
★
Capitol Gorge. At the entrance to this gorge, 9 miles south of visitor center, Scenic Drive becomes unpaved. The narrow, twisting road on the floor of the gorge was a route for pioneer wagons traversing this part of Utah starting in the 1860s. After every flash flood, pioneers would laboriously clear the route so wagons could continue to go through. The gorge became the main automobile route in the area until 1962, when Highway 24 was built. The short drive to the end of the road has striking views of the surrounding cliffs and leads to one of the park's most popular walks, the hiking trail to the water-holding "tanks" eroded into the sandstone. ⊠ *Scenic Dr.*

Chimney Rock. Even in a landscape of spires, cliffs, and knobs, this deep-red landform, 3.9 miles west of the visitor center, is unmistakable. ⊠ *Hwy. 24.*

FAMILY
Fremont Petroglyphs. Nearly 1,000 years ago the Capitol Reef area was occupied by people of the Fremont culture. A nice stroll along a boardwalk bridge, 1.1 mile east of visitor center, allows close-up views of the Fremont rock art, which can be identified by the large trapezoidal figures often depicted wearing headdresses and ear baubles. ⊠ *Hwy. 24.*

FAMILY
Fruita Historic District. In the 1880s Nels Johnson became the first homesteader in the Fremont River Valley, building his home near the confluence of Sulphur Creek and the Fremont River. Other Mormon settlers followed and established small farms and orchards, creating the village of Junction. The orchards thrived, and by 1900 the name was changed to Fruita. The orchards, less than a mile from the visitor center, are preserved and protected as a Rural Historic Landscape. ⊠ *Scenic Dr.*

Pioneer Register. Travelers passing through Capitol Gorge in the 19th and early 20th centuries etched the canyon wall with their names and the date they passed. Directly across the canyon from the Pioneer Register and about 50 feet up are signatures etched into the canyon wall by an early United States Geologic Survey crew. Though it's illegal to write or scratch on the canyon walls today, plenty of damage has been done by vandals over the years. You can reach the register via an easy hike from the sheltered trailhead at the end of Capitol Gorge Road, 10.3 miles south of the visitor center; the register is about 10 minutes along the hike to the sandstone "tanks." ⊠ *Off Scenic Dr.*

The Waterpocket Fold. A giant wrinkle in the earth extends almost 100 miles between Thousand Lake Mountain and Lake Powell. You can glimpse the fold by driving south on Scenic Drive, after it branches off Highway 24, past the Fruita Historic District, but for complete immersion enter the park via the 36-mile Burr Trail from Boulder. Travel through the southernmost reaches of the park is largely on unpaved roads. It's accessible to most vehicles during dry weather, but check with the visitor center for current road conditions.

EDUCATIONAL OFFERINGS

RANGER PROGRAMS

From May to October, ranger programs are offered at no charge as budget and staffing allow. You can obtain current information at the visitor center or campground bulletin boards.

Evening Program. Learn about Capitol Reef's geology, Native American cultures, wildlife, and more at the campground amphitheater about a mile from the visitor center. Programs begin typically around sunset. A schedule of topics and times is posted at the visitor center. ⊠ *Amphitheater, Loop C, Fruita Campground, Scenic Dr.* ☎ *435/425–3791.*

Junior Ranger Program. Each child who participates in this self-guided, year-round program completes a combination of activities in the Junior Ranger booklet, attends a ranger program, watches the park movie, interviews a park ranger, and/or picks up litter. ⊠ *National Park Visitor Center, 16 Scenic Dr.* ☎ *435/425–3791* ⊠ *Free.*

Ranger Talks. Typically, the park offers a daily morning geology talk at the visitor center and a daily afternoon Fremont Culture talk at the petroglyph panel. Occasional geology hikes and history tours are also sometimes offered. Times can vary. ⊠ *National Park Visitor Center, 16 Scenic Rd.* ☎ *435/425–3791* ⊠ *Free* ☉ *May–Sept., daily.*

> ### GEOLOGY BEHIND THE PARK'S NAME
>
> When water wears away layers of sandstone, basins can appear in the rock. These are called waterpockets. The nearly 100-mile-long Waterpocket Fold—a massive wrinkle in Earth's crust, where an ancient fault pushed one side 7,000 feet higher than the other (today it's settled to 2,600 feet)—is full of these waterpockets. Early explorers with seafaring backgrounds called the fold a reef, because it was a barrier to travel. Some of the rocks, due to erosion, also have dome-like formations resembling capitol rotundas.

6

SPORTS AND THE OUTDOORS

The main outdoor activity at Capitol Reef is hiking. There are trails for all levels. Remember: Whenever you venture into the desert—that is, wherever you go in Capitol Reef—take, and drink, plenty of water.

BICYCLING

Bicycles are allowed only on established roads in the park. Highway 24 is a state highway and receives a substantial amount of through traffic, so it's not the best place to pedal. Scenic Drive is better, but the road is narrow, and you have to contend with drivers dazed by the beautiful surroundings. Four-wheel-drive roads are certainly less traveled, but they are often sandy, rocky, and steep. You cannot ride in washes or on hiking trails.

Cathedral Valley Scenic Backway. In the remote north of the park you can enjoy solitude (but for the occasional off-roader) and a true backcountry ride on this trail. Surfaces include dirt, sand, bentonite clay, and rock, and you will also ford the Fremont River; be prepared to

> **WHAT TO READ**
>
> ■ *Capitol Reef: Canyon Country Eden*, by Rose Houk, is an award-winning collection of photographs and lyrical essays on the park.
>
> ■ *Dwellers of the Rainbow, Fremont Culture in Capitol Reef National Park*, by Rose Houk, offers a brief background to the Fremont culture in Capitol Reef.
>
> ■ *Geology of Capitol Reef National Park*, by Michael Collier, teaches the basic geology of the park.
>
> ■ *Red Rock Eden*, by George Davidson, tells the story of historic Fruita and its orchards.

encounter steep hills and switchbacks, wash crossings, and stretches of deep sand. Summer is not a good time to try this ride, as water is very difficult to find and temperatures may exceed 100°F. The entire route is about 58 miles long, and can be accessed at Caineville, off Highway 24, or at River Ford Road, 5 miles west of Caineville; for a multiday trip, there's a primitive campground about midway through the loop. ⊠ *Off Hwy. 24.*

South Draw Road. This is a very strenuous ride that traverses dirt, sand, and rocky surfaces, and crosses several creeks that may be muddy. It's not recommended in winter or spring because of deep snow at higher elevations. The route starts at an elevation of 8,600 feet on Boulder Mountain, 13 miles south of Torrey, and ends 15.7 miles later at 5,500 feet in the Pleasant Creek parking area at the end of Scenic Drive. ⊠ *Bowns Reservoir Rd. and Hwy. 12.*

FOUR-WHEELING

You can explore Capitol Reef in a 4x4 on a number of exciting backcountry routes. Road conditions can vary greatly depending on recent weather patterns. Spring and summer rains can leave the roads impassable even to four-wheel-drive vehicles. Always check at the park visitor center for current conditions before you set out, and take water, supplies, and a cell phone with you—though it's highly unlikely reception will be available.

Cathedral Valley Scenic Backway. The north end of Capitol Reef, along this backcountry road, is filled with towering monoliths, panoramic vistas, two water crossings, and a stark desert landscape. The area is remote and the road through it unpaved, so do not enter without a high-clearance vehicle, some planning, and a cell phone (although reception is virtually nonexistent). The drive through the valley is a 58-mile loop that you can begin at River Ford Road, 11¾ miles east of the visitor center off Highway 24; allow half a day. ■TIP→ If your time is limited, you can tour only the Caineville Wash Road, which takes about two hours. Pick up a self-guided-auto-tour brochure for $2 at the visitor center. ⊠ *River Ford Rd., off Hwy. 24.*

> ### NOTABLE QUOTE
>
> "The colors (at Capitol Reef) are such as no pigments can portray. So luminous are they that the light seems to flow or shine out of the rock rather than to be reflected from it."
>
> —Clarence Dutton

HIKING

Many park trails in Capitol Reef include steep climbs, but there are a few easy-to-moderate hikes. A short drive from the visitor center takes you to a dozen trails, and a park ranger can advise you on combining trails or locating additional routes.

EASY

Goosenecks Trail. This nice little walk gives you a good introduction to the land surrounding Capitol Reef. Enjoy the dizzying views from the overlook. It's only a 0.3 mile round-trip. *Easy.* ⊠ *Trailhead at Hwy. 24, about 3 miles west of visitor center.*

Grand Wash Trail. At the end of unpaved Grand Wash Road you can continue on foot through the canyon to its end at Highway 24. You're bound to love the trip. This flat hike takes you through a wide wash between canyon walls. It's an excellent place to study the geology up close. The round-trip hike is 4½ miles; allow two to three hours for your walk. Check at the ranger station for flash-flood warnings before entering the wash. *Easy.* ⊠ *Trailhead at Hwy. 24, east of Hickman Bridge parking lot, or at end of Grand Wash Rd., off Scenic Dr. about 5 miles from visitor center.*

Sunset Point Trail. The trail starts from the same parking lot as the Goosenecks Trail. Benches along this easy, 0.8-mile round-trip invite you to sit and meditate surrounded by the colorful desert. At the trail's end, you will be rewarded with broad vistas into the park; it's even better at sunset. *Easy.* ⊠ *Trailhead at Hwy. 24, about 3 miles west of visitor center.*

MODERATE

Capitol Gorge Trail and the Tanks. Starting at the Pioneer Register, about a mile from the Capitol Gorge parking lot, is a trail that climbs to the Tanks, holes in the sandstone, formed by erosion, that hold water after it rains. After a scramble up about a quarter-mile of steep trail with cliff drop-offs, you can look down into the Tanks and can also see a natural bridge below the lower tank. Including the walk to the Pioneer Register, allow an hour or two for this interesting hike, one of the park's most popular. *Moderate.* ⊠ *Trailhead at end of Scenic Dr., 10 miles south of visitor center.*

FAMILY **Cohab Canyon Trail.** Children particularly love this trail for the geological features and native creatures, such as rock wrens and Western pipistrelles (canyon bats), that you see along the way. One end of the trail is directly across from the Fruita Campground on Scenic Drive,

6

and the other is across from the Hickman Bridge parking lot. The first ¼ mile from Fruita is pretty strenuous, but then the walk becomes easy except for turnoffs to the overlooks, which are strenuous but short. Along the way you'll find miniature arches, skinny side canyons, and honeycombed patterns on canyon walls where the wrens make nests. The trail is 3.2 miles round-trip to the Hickman Bridge parking lot. The Overlook Trail adds 1 mile to the journey. Allow one to two hours to overlooks and back; allow two to three hours to Hickman Bridge parking lot and back. *Moderate.* ⊠ *Scenic Dr., about 1 mile south of visitor center, or Hwy. 24, about 2 miles east of visitor center.*

Fremont River Trail. What starts as a quiet little stroll beside the river turns into an adventure. The first ½ mile of the trail is wheelchair accessible as you wander past the orchards next to the Fremont River. After you pass through a narrow gate, the trail changes personality and you're in for a steep climb on an exposed ledge with drop-offs. The views at the top of the 480-foot ascent are worth it. It's 2 miles round-trip; allow two hours. *Moderate.* ⊠ *Trailhead near amphitheater off Loop C of Fruita Campground, about 1 mile from visitor center.*

Golden Throne Trail. As you hike to the base of the Golden Throne, you may be lucky enough to see one of the park's elusive desert bighorn sheep, but you're more likely to spot their split-hoof tracks. The trail is about 2 miles of gradual rise with some steps and drop-offs. The Golden Throne is hidden until you near the end of the trail, then suddenly you see the huge sandstone monolith. If you hike near sundown the throne burns gold. The round-trip hike is about 3.8 miles and will take two to three hours. *Moderate.* ⊠ *Trailhead at end of Capitol Gorge Rd., 10 miles south of visitor center.*

Hickman Bridge Trail. This trail is a perfect introduction to the park. It leads to a natural bridge of Kayenta sandstone, which has a 133-foot opening carved by intermittent flash floods. Early on, the route climbs a set of steps along the Fremont River, and as the trail tops out onto a bench, you'll find a slight depression in the earth. This is what remains of an ancient Fremont pit house, a kind of home that was dug into the ground and covered with brush. The trail splits, leading along the right-hand branch to a strenuous uphill climb to the Rim Overlook and Navajo Knobs. Stay to your left to see the bridge, and you'll encounter a moderate up-and-down trail. As you continue up the wash on your way to the bridge, you'll notice a Fremont granary on the right side of the small canyon. Allow about 2 hours to walk the 2-mile round-trip. The walk is one of the most popular trails in the park, so expect lots of company. *Moderate.* ⊠ *Hwy. 24, 2 miles east of visitor center.*

DIFFICULT

Chimney Rock Trail. You're almost sure to see ravens drifting on thermal winds around the deep red Mummy Cliff that rings the base of this trail. This loop trail begins with a steep climb to a rim above Chimney Rock. The trail is 3.6 miles round-trip, with a 590-foot elevation change. No shade. Use caution during monsoon storms due to lightning hazards. Allow three to four hours. *Difficult.* ⊠ *Hwy. 24, about 3 miles west of visitor center.*

HORSEBACK RIDING

Many areas in the park are closed to horses and pack animals, so it's a good idea to check with the visitor center before you set out with your animals. Day use does not require a permit, but you need to get one (it's free) for overnight camping with horses and pack animals.

South Draw. This 15.7-mile route gives you access to Tantalus Flats and Boulder Mountain or a return via Pleasant Creek. ⊠ *At end of Scenic Dr., 9 miles south of visitor center.*

WHERE TO EAT

IN THE PARK

PICNIC AREAS

Museum and Store. In a grassy meadow with the Fremont River flowing by, this is an idyllic shady spot in the Fruita Historic District for a sack lunch. Picnic tables, drinking water, grills, and a convenient restroom make it perfect. It's 1 mile south of the visitor center. ⊠ *Scenic Dr.*

OUTSIDE THE PARK

$ ✕ **Little L's Bakery.** If you are traveling by way of Panguitch, stop by this
AMERICAN charming bakery for the homemade cheddar-and-bacon muffins, pot pies, or a raspberry donut and your favorite coffee drink priced at half the big-city version. The surroundings alone are worth a peek at this roomy bakery/coffeehouse, with tabletops made from antique doors and a counter area reminiscent of an old-time grocery. $ *Average main: $5* ⊠ *37 N. Main St., Panguitch* ☎ *435/676–8750* ⊗ *Closed Sun.*

$ ✕ **Stan's Burger Shak.** This is the traditional pit stop between Lake
FAST FOOD Powell and Capitol Reef, featuring great burgers, fries, and shakes—and the only homemade onion rings you'll find for miles and miles. Keep in mind it generally closes for the winter in early December and reopens in February. $ *Average main: $8* ⊠ *140 S. Hwy. 95, Hanksville* ☎ *435/542–3330* ⊕ *www.stansburgershak.com* ⊗ *Closed Dec.–early to mid-Feb.*

WHERE TO STAY

OUTSIDE THE PARK

$ 🛏 **Aquarius Inn.** Large, comfortable rooms and recreational facilities
HOTEL such as an indoor pool, playground, and basketball and volleyball
FAMILY courts make this an attractive place for families. **Pros:** not too far from Torrey and Capitol Reef; Laundromat on-site; hot tub and workout room. **Cons:** Bicknell might be too tiny and quiet for some; can fill quickly on summer weekends. $ *Rooms from: $77* ⊠ *292 W. Main St., Bicknell* ☎ *435/425–3835, 800/833–5379* ⊕ *aquariusinn.com* ↩ *28 rooms, 1 suite* ⦿ *No meals.*

Best Campgrounds in Capitol Reef

Campgrounds in Capitol Reef fill up fast in the spring and fall, though that goes mainly for the superconvenient, first-come, first-served Fruita Campground and not the more remote backcountry sites. Most of the area's state parks have camping facilities, and the region's two national forests offer many wonderful sites.

Cathedral Valley Campground. You'll find this primitive (no water, pit toilet) campground, about 30 miles from Highway 24, in the park's remote northern district. ✉ *Hartnet Junction, on Caineville Wash Rd.* ☎ *435/425–3791.*

Cedar Mesa Campground. Wonderful views of the Waterpocket Fold and Henry Mountains surround this primitive campground in the park's southern district. ✉ *Notom-Bullfrog Rd., 21 miles south of Hwy. 24* ☎ *435/425–3791.*

Fruita Campground. Near the orchards, the Gifford House Museum and Store, and the Fremont River, the park's developed (flush toilets, running water, dump station), shady campground is a great place to call home for a few days. The sites nearest the river or the orchards are the very best. ✉ *Scenic Dr., about 1 mile south of visitor center* ☎ *435/425–3791.*

$ **Fish Lake Resorts.** Here you can find everything from rustic cabins that
RESORT sleep two to deluxe rental cabins with six bedrooms, all of which focus on function rather than cute amenities. **Pros:** great place for families and groups to congregate. **Cons:** some cabins are a little close together—so not the best for solitude. $ *Rooms from: $65* ✉ *2 N. Hwy. 25, Fish Lake* ☎ *435/638–1000* ⊕ *fishlake.com* ⌁ *41 cabins* ⎮◎⎮ *No meals.*

$$$ **Lodge at Red River Ranch.** You'll swear you've walked into one of the
HOTEL great lodges of Western legend when you walk through the doors at
Fodor'sChoice Red River Ranch. **Pros:** furnishings and artifacts so distinctive they
★ could grace the pages of a design magazine; plenty of outdoor activities, including private fly-fishing. **Cons:** rooms are on the small side. $ *Rooms from: $175* ✉ *2900 W. Hwy. 24, Teasdale* ☎ *435/425–3322, 800/205–6343* ⊕ *redriverranch.com* ⌁ *15 rooms* ⎮◎⎮ *No meals.*

$$ **Muley Twist Inn.** This gorgeous inn sits on 15 acres of land, with
B&B/INN expansive views of the colorful landscape in just about every direction. **Pros:** dramatic setting against a beautiful rock cliff; a place you can slow down and unwind; all rooms have private baths. **Cons:** might be too far away from it all for some. $ *Rooms from: $135* ✉ *249 W. 125 S, Teasdale* ☎ *435/425–3640, 800/530–1038* ⊕ *www.muleytwistinn. com* ⌁ *5 rooms* ☉ *Closed Nov.–Mar.* ⎮◎⎮ *Breakfast.*

ZION NATIONAL PARK

WELCOME TO ZION NATIONAL PARK

TOP REASONS TO GO

★ **Eye candy:** Pick just about any trail in the park and it's all but guaranteed to culminate in an astounding viewpoint full of pink, orange, and crimson rock formations.

★ **Auto immunity:** From mid-March through October, and during weekends in November, cars are generally not allowed in Zion Canyon, allowing for a quiet and peaceful park.

★ **Botanical wonderland:** Zion Canyon is home to approximately 900 species of plants, more than anywhere else in Utah.

★ **Animal tracks:** Zion has expansive hinterlands where furry, scaly, and feathered residents are common. Hike long enough and you'll encounter deer, elk, rare lizards, birds of prey, and other zoological treats.

★ **Unforgettable canyoneering:** Zion's array of rugged slot canyons is the richest place on earth for scrambling, rappelling, climbing, and descending.

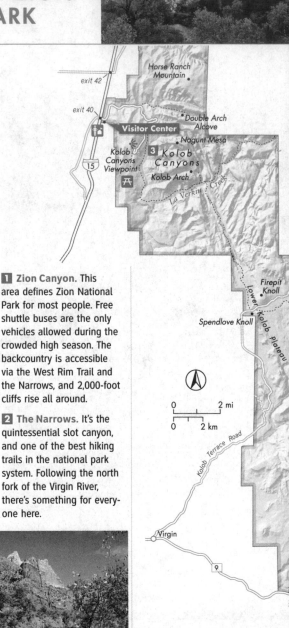

1 Zion Canyon. This area defines Zion National Park for most people. Free shuttle buses are the only vehicles allowed during the crowded high season. The backcountry is accessible via the West Rim Trail and the Narrows, and 2,000-foot cliffs rise all around.

2 The Narrows. It's the quintessential slot canyon, and one of the best hiking trails in the national park system. Following the north fork of the Virgin River, there's something for everyone here.

3 Kolob Canyons. Zion's northwestern corner is a secluded wonderland with only one entrance. Don't miss the Kolob Arch, and keep looking up to spot Horse Ranch Mountain, the park's highest point.

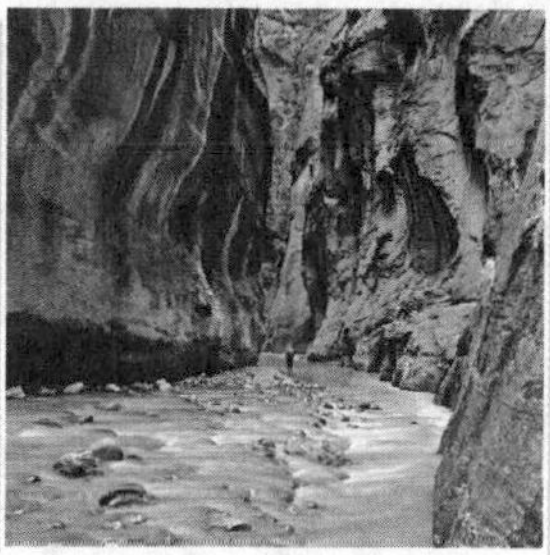

Hiking through the river in Zion Narrows

4 Lava Point. Infrequently visited, this area has two nearby reservoirs that offer the only significant fishing in the park. From Lava Point Overlook view Zion Canyon from the north.

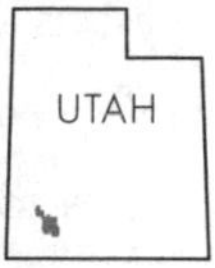
UTAH

GETTING ORIENTED

The heart of Zion National Park is Zion Canyon, which follows the North Fork of the Virgin River for 6½ miles beneath cliffs that rise 2,000 feet from the river bottom. The Kolob area is considered by some to be superior in beauty, and because it's isolated from the rest of the park, you aren't likely to run into any crowds here. Both sections hint at the extensive backcountry beyond, open for those with the stamina, time, and the courage to go off the beaten paths of the park.

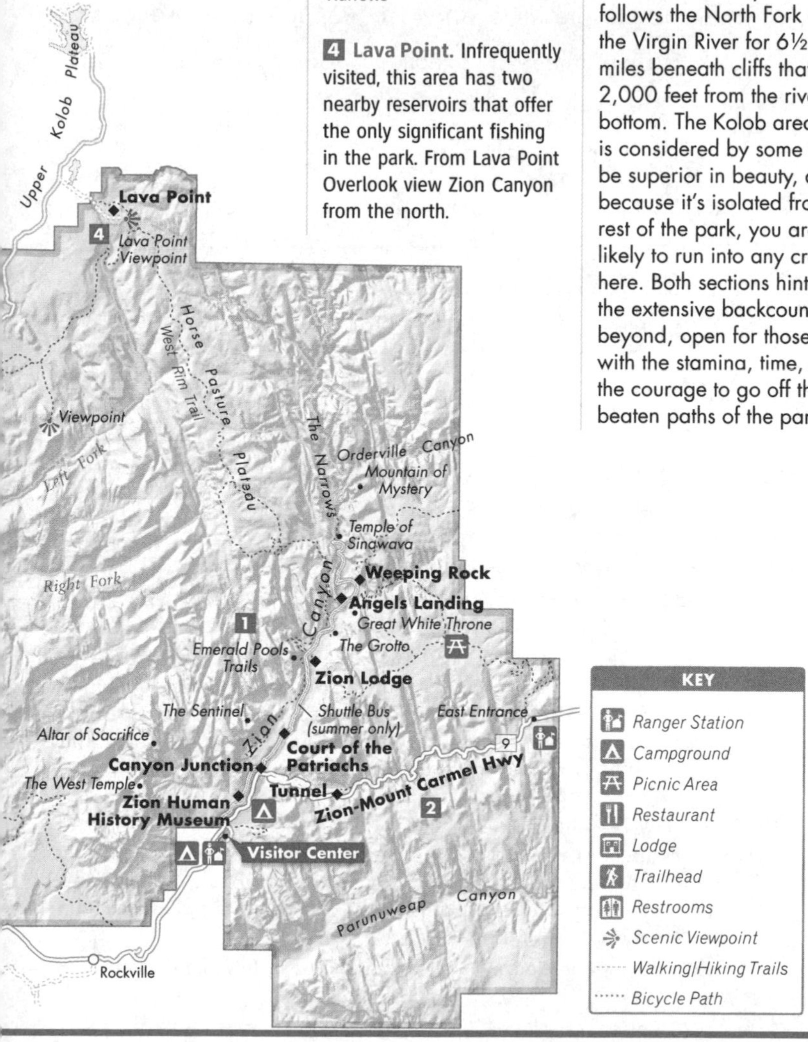
Upper Kolob Plateau
Lava Point
4
Lava Point Viewpoint
Horse Pasture Plateau
West Rim Trail
Viewpoint
Left Fork
The Narrows
Orderville Canyon
Mountain of Mystery
Temple of Sinawava
Right Fork
Weeping Rock
Angels Landing
Great White Throne
1
Zion Canyon
Emerald Pools Trails
The Grotto
Zion Lodge
The Sentinel
Shuttle Bus (summer only)
East Entrance
Altar of Sacrifice
Court of the Patriachs
9
Canyon Junction
Zion-Mount Carmel Hwy
The West Temple
Tunnel
Zion Human History Museum
2
Visitor Center
Parunuweap Canyon
Rockville
KEY
Ranger Station
Campground
Picnic Area
Restaurant
Lodge
Trailhead
Restrooms
Scenic Viewpoint
Walking/Hiking Trails
Bicycle Path

Updated by
John Blodgett

The walls of Zion Canyon soar more than 2,000 feet above the valley below, but it's the character, not the size, of the sandstone forms that defines the park's splendor. Throughout the park, stratigraphic evidence points to the distant past, with fantastically colored bands of limestone, sandstone, and lava. Stripes and spots of greenery high in the cliff walls create a "hanging garden" effect, and invariably indicate the presence of water seepage or a spring. Erosion has left behind a collection of domes, fins, and blocky massifs bearing the names and likenesses of cathedrals and temples, prophets and angels.

Trails lead deep into side canyons and up narrow ledges to waterfalls, serene spring-fed pools, and shaded spots of solitude. So diverse is this place that 85% of Utah's flora and fauna species are found here. Some, like the tiny Zion snail, appear nowhere else in the world.

The Colorado River helped create the Grand Canyon, while the Virgin River—the Colorado's muddy progeny—carved Zion's features. Because of the park's unique topography, distant storms and spring runoff can transform a tranquil slot canyon into a sluice.

ZION PLANNER

WHEN TO GO

Zion is the most heavily visited national park in Utah, receiving nearly 3 million visitors each year. Locals used to call the spring and fall the shoulder seasons because traffic would drop off from the highly visited summer months. Not so much anymore. Warmer temperatures mean the park is packed April to October.

Summer in the park is hot and dry, punctuated with sudden cloudbursts that can create flash flooding and spectacular waterfalls. Expect afternoon thunderstorms between July and September. Whether the day starts out sunny or not, wear sunscreen and drink lots of water, even if you aren't exerting yourself or spending much time outside. The sun is very powerful at this elevation.

Winters are mild at lower desert elevations. You can expect to encounter winter driving conditions November through March, and although most park programs are suspended, winter is a wonderful and solitary time to see the canyons.

⚠ **Extreme highs in Zion can often exceed 100°F in July and August.**

CLOSE UP

Plants and Wildlife in Zion

Zion Canyon's unique geography—the park is on the Colorado Plateau and bordered by the Great Basin and Mojave Desert provinces—supports more than 900 species of plants in environments that range from desert to hanging garden to high plateau. (Those so inclined can pick up a plant identification guide at the Zion Canyon Visitor Center.) And yes, poison ivy is among the plant species. If you're not sure how to recognize it, take a quick lesson from a ranger prior to your first hike or you'll wind up with an itchy souvenir.

With car traffic having been almost completely replaced by a shuttle bus system from mid-March through October, wildlife has returned in force to the park. Even in high season you can spot mule deer wandering in shady glens as you ride through the park, especially in early morning and near dusk. You'll also see scores of lizards and wild turkeys everywhere you go.

If you're looking for more exotic fauna, hit the hiking trails. Nearly 300 species of birds occupy (either part-time or full-time) the park, from tiny hummingbirds and chickadees to surprisingly large wild turkeys, eagles, and even pelicans. Ringtail cats (which are not cats but are similar to raccoons) prowl the park. Evening hikes may reveal foxes, but you're more likely to spot their tracks than the elusive animals themselves. All animals, from the smallest chipmunk to the biggest elk, should be given plenty of space, but only the extremely rare mountain lion or black bear pose any kind of threat to humans.

7

AVG. HIGH/LOW TEMPS.

Jan.	Feb.	Mar.	Apr.	May	June
52/29	57/31	63/36	73/43	83/52	93/60
July	Aug.	Sept.	Oct.	Nov.	Dec.
100/68	97/66	91/60	78/49	63/37	53/30

PLANNING YOUR TIME
ZION IN ONE DAY

Begin your visit at the **Zion Canyon Visitor Center,** with outdoor exhibits about the park's geology, wildlife, history, and trails. Get a taste of what's in store by viewing the far off Towers of the Virgin, then head to the **Court of the Patriarchs** viewpoint to take photos. Then take the shuttle (or your car, if it's off-season) to **Zion Canyon Lodge,** where you can take a trail to one of the most beautiful spots in the park, the **Emerald Pools.** The Lower Pool Trail is the second most popular walk at Zion (after the Riverside Walk); other trails branch off if you're fit and have time. Ride the next shuttle to the end of the road and walk the paved, accessible **Riverside Walk.**

Reboard the shuttle to return to the Zion Canyon Visitor Center to pick up your car (or continue driving off-season). Head out onto the beautiful **Zion–Mount Carmel Highway,** with its long, curving tunnels, your camera at the ready for stops at viewpoints. Once you reach the park's east entrance, turn around, and on your return trip stop for the short hike up to **Canyon Overlook**. Now you're ready to rest your feet and watch *Zion Canyon: Treasure of the Gods* at the **Zion Canyon Giant Screen Theatre**. In the evening you can attend a ranger program at one of the campground amphitheaters or at Zion Lodge. Or have dinner and a stroll in **Springdale**.

GETTING HERE AND AROUND
AIR TRAVEL
The nearest commercial airport is 46 miles away in St. George, Utah, with daily flights from Los Angeles and Salt Lake City.

CAR TRAVEL
In southwestern Utah, not far from the Nevada border, Zion National Park is closer to Las Vegas (158 miles) than to Salt Lake City (310 miles). The 46 miles from the interstate to the main entrance has become busier over the years, with more roadside development along the way. From I–15, head east on Highway 9. After 21 miles you'll reach Springdale, which abuts the main entrance to the park.

If you're arriving mid-March through October, or weekends in November, you can drive your vehicle into Zion Canyon only if you have reservations at the Zion Lodge. Otherwise, you'll have to park it in Springdale or at the Zion Canyon Visitor Center and take the shuttle.

The visitor center parking lot fills up quickly. You can avoid parking heartburn by leaving your car in Springdale and riding the shuttle to the park entrance. Shuttles are accessible for people with disabilities and have plenty of room for gear. Town shuttle stops are at Majestic View, Driftwood Lodge, Bit & Spur Restaurant, Best Western Zion Park Inn, Bumbleberry Inn, Zion Pizza & Noodle Co., Watchman Café, Flanigan's Inn, and Zion Canyon Giant Screen Theatre. Times for the shuttle service vary according to season, but you can generally count on the first bus arriving at 5:45 am and the last bus leaving at 10:30 pm. You won't likely wait more than 15 minutes at any stop before you see one.

PARK ESSENTIALS
PARK FEES AND PERMITS
Entrance to Zion National Park is $25 per vehicle for a seven-day pass. People entering on foot or by bicycle or motorcycle pay $12 per person (not to exceed $25 per family) for a seven-day pass. Entrance to the Kolob Canyons section of the park also costs $25, and allows you access to the entire park.

Permits are required for backcountry camping and overnight hikes. Depending on which parts of the trails you're going to explore, you'll need a special permit for the Narrows and Kolob Creek or the Subway slot canyon. Climbing and canyoneering parties will also need a permit before using technical equipment.

Zion National Park limits the total number of overnight and canyoneering permits issued per day and has a reservation system with most of the permits now issued in an online lottery to apportion them fairly. Permits to the Subway, Mystery Canyon, the Narrows through-hikes, and West Rim are in short supply during high season. The maximum size of a group hiking into the backcountry is 12 people. The cost for a permit for 1 to 2 people is $10; 3 to 7 people, $15; and 8 to 12 people, $20. Permits and hiking information are available at either visitor center. For more information, visit ⊕ *www.nps.gov/zion* prior to your trip.

PARK HOURS
The park, open daily year-round, 24 hours a day, is in the mountain time zone.

CELL-PHONE RECEPTION
Cell-phone reception is good in Springdale but spotty in Zion Canyon. Public telephones may be found at South Campground, Watchman Campground, Zion Canyon Visitor Center, Zion Lodge, and Zion Human History Museum.

RESTAURANTS
There is only one full-service restaurant in Zion National Park, but there are numerous places around the park. Springdale is the obvious choice for family-friendly restaurants.

HOTELS
Zion Canyon Lodge is rustic but clean and comfortable. Springdale has dozens of options, from quaint bed-and-breakfasts to modest motels to chain hotels with riverside rooms. Panguitch and Hurricane have some good budget and last-minute choices. *Hotel reviews have been shortened. For full information, visit Fodors.com.*

WHAT IT COSTS				
	$	$$	$$$	$$$$
Restaurants	under $12	$12–$20	$21–$30	over $30
Hotels	under $100	$100–$150	$151–$200	over $200

Restaurant prices are the average cost of a main course at dinner or, if dinner is not served, at lunch. Hotel prices are the lowest cost of a standard double room in high season.

VISITOR INFORMATION
PARK CONTACT INFORMATION
Zion National Park ✉ *Hwy. 9, Springdale* ☎ *435/772–3256* ⊕ *nps.gov/zion*.

VISITOR CENTERS
The visitor center should be the first stop on your itinerary regardless of how deep into the bush you plan to go. Because access to Kolob Canyons is separate from the rest of the park, Zion has a dedicated visitor center in that section of the park in addition to the main facility at the south entrance of the park.

Kolob Canyons Visitor Center. Make this your first stop as you enter this remote section of the park. There are books and maps, a small gift shop, and helpful rangers to answer questions about Kolob Canyons exploration. Clean public restrooms can also be found here. Take exit 40 off I–15, 17 miles south of Cedar City. ✉ *3752 E. Kolob Canyons Rd.* ☎ *435/586–9548* ⊕ *www.nps.gov/zion* ☾ *Late May–early Sept.,* *daily 8–6; late Apr.–late May and early Sept.–mid-Oct., daily 8–5; mid-Oct.–Apr., daily 8–4:30.*

Zion Canyon Visitor Center. Most of the information here is presented in an appealing outdoor exhibit next to a gurgling runnel shaded by cottonwood trees. These displays introduce the area's geology, flora, and fauna. Inside, a large shop sells everything from field guides to souvenirs. Zion Canyon shuttle buses leave regularly from the center and make several stops along the canyon's beautiful scenic drive; ranger-guided shuttle tours depart twice a day. ✉ *Zion Park Blvd. at south entrance, Springdale* ☎ *435/772–3256* ⊕ *www.nps.gov/zion* ⊗ *June–early Sept., daily 8–7:30; late Apr.–late May and Sept.–mid Oct., daily 8–6; mid Oct.– late Apr., daily 8–5.*

EXPLORING

SCENIC DRIVES

Zion Canyon's grandeur is best experienced on foot whenever possible, but there is something to be said for covering a lot of ground on wheels. Driving is the only way to easily access Kolob Canyons, for example, and from November through mid-March, driving your own vehicle is the only way to access the Zion Canyon scenic drive.

Kolob Canyons Road. The beauty starts modestly at the junction with Interstate 15, but as you move along this 5-mile road the red walls of the Kolob finger canyons rise suddenly and spectacularly out of the earth. With the crowds left behind at Zion Canyon, this drive offers the chance to take in incredible vistas at your leisure. Trails include the short but rugged Middle Fork of Taylor Creek Trail, which passes two 1930s homestead cabins then, after 2¾ miles, culminates in the Double Arch Alcove. During heavy snowfall Kolob Canyons Road may be closed.

Zion–Mount Carmel Highway and Tunnels. Two narrow tunnels as old as the park itself lie between the east entrance and Zion Canyon on this breathtaking 24-mile (round-trip) stretch of Highway 9. One was once the longest man-made tunnel in the world. As you travel the (1.1 mile) passage through solid rock, five arched portals along one side provide fleeting glimpses of cliffs and canyons. When you emerge you'll find that the landscape has changed dramatically. Large vehicles require traffic control and a $15 permit, available at the park entrance, and have restricted hours of travel. This includes nearly all RVs, trailers, dual-wheel trucks, and campers. The Canyon Overlook Trail starts from a parking area between the tunnels. The road is open April through October. ✉ *Hwy. 9, 5 miles east of Canyon Junction.*

HISTORIC SITES

Zion Human History Museum. Enrich your visit with a stop at this quaint museum, ½ mile north of south entrance, which tells the story of the park from the perspective of humans who have lived here throughout history, including Ancestral Puebloans and early Mormon settlers.

Permanent exhibits show how inhabitants dealt with wildlife, plants, and other natural forces. Temporary exhibits include finds from recent archaeological excavations. A 22-minute film screens throughout the day. ■ TIP➜ There's an incredible view of the Towers of the Virgin from back patio area. ⊠ *Zion Canyon Scenic Dr.* ☎ *435/772–3256* ⊕ *www. nps.gov/zion/historyculture/zion-human-history-museum.htm* 🔁 *Free* ⊙ *Mar.–Nov., daily 10–5.*

Zion Lodge. Built by Union Pacific Railroad in 1925, the original lodge was destroyed by fire in 1966. Today's scenic structure recaptures the look and feel of the first building. Some of the original cabins are still in use today. Set on a sprawling lawn shaded by giant cottonwoods, the lodge has a restaurant, snack bar, gift shop, and a spacious patio with rocking chairs with views of the canyon. It's 3 miles north of Canyon Junction. ⊠ *Zion Canyon Scenic Dr.* ☎ *435/772–7700.*

SCENIC STOPS

The park comprises two distinct sections—Zion Canyon and the Kolob Plateau and Canyons. Most people restrict their visit to the better-known Zion Canyon, especially if they have only one day to explore, but the Kolob area has much to offer. Though there's little evidence of Kolob's beauty from the entrance point off Interstate 15, once you negotiate the first switchback on the park road, you are hit with a vision of red-rock cliffs shooting out of the earth. As the road climbs, you are treated first to a journey through these canyons, then with a view into the chasm. ■ TIP➜ You have to exit the park to get between Zion Canyon and Kolob Canyons, so it is not easy to explore both sections in one day.

Checkerboard Mesa. The distinctive waffle patterns on this huge, white mound of sandstone were created by eons of freeze/thaw cycles creating vertical fractures, along with the exposure of horizontal bedding planes by erosion. The crosshatch effect is stunning and well worth stopping at the pull-out, 1 mile west of the east entrance, for a long gaze. ⊠ *Zion–Mount Carmel Hwy.*

Court of the Patriarchs. This trio of peaks bears the names of, from left to right, Abraham, Isaac, and Jacob. Mount Moroni is the reddish peak on the far right, which partially blocks your view of Jacob. Hike the trail that leaves from the Court of the Patriarchs Viewpoint, 1½ miles north of Canyon Junction, to get a much better view of the sandstone prophets; you may catch a glimpse of rock climbers camming their way up Isaac's sheer face. ⊠ *Zion Canyon Scenic Dr.*

Great White Throne. Dominating the Grotto picnic area near Zion Lodge is this massive Navajo sandstone peak, which juts 2,000 feet above the valley floor. The Throne was for decades the most popular formation in the park. You'll find it about 3 miles north of Canyon Junction. ⊠ *Zion Canyon Scenic Dr.*

Fodor's Choice
★

The Narrows. This sinuous 16-mile crack in the earth where the Virgin River flows over gravel and boulders is one of the most stunning gorges in the world. If you hike through it, you'll find yourself surrounded—sometimes nearly closed in by—smooth walls stretching high into the heavens. Plan to get wet. ⊠ *Begins at Riverside Walk.*

Weeping Rock. Surface water from the rim of Echo Canyon spends several thousand years seeping down through the porous sandstone before exiting at this picturesque alcove 4½ miles north of Canyon Junction. A paved walkway climbs a quarter mile to this flowing rock face where wildflowers and delicate ferns grow. In fall, the maples and cottonwoods riot with color, and an abundance of lizards point the way down the path. It's not suitable for wheelchairs. ⊠ *Canyon Scenic Dr.*

EDUCATIONAL OFFERINGS

CLASSES AND SEMINARS

Zion Canyon Field Institute. The educational arm of the Zion Natural History Association offers one-, two-, and three-day workshops on the park's natural and cultural history with an expert instructor. Many classes include a hike into the field to apply what you've learned. Take a deep dive into subjects like edible plants, bat biology, river geology, photography, or bird-watching. Classes are limited to small groups; reserve ahead to ensure placement. Visitors can also volunteer to help out with ongoing park projects, gaining a behind-the-scenes glimpse at Zion's inner workings. ☎ *435/772–3264, 800/635–3959* ⊕ *www. zionpark.org* ⊠ *$25–$80 per day.*

RANGER PROGRAMS

Evening Programs. Held each evening in campground amphitheaters and at Zion Lodge, these entertaining ranger-led talks cover geology, biology, and history. You might learn about wildfires, migratory birds, or observing nature with all your senses. Slide shows and audience participation are often part of the talk. Check the park guide for times and locations. ☎ *435/772–3256* ⊕ *www.nps.gov/zion.*

Fodor's Choice **Expert Talks.** These free, informal lectures take place on the Zion Human
★ History Museum patio and Kolob Canyons area of the park. Recent sessions have included "Animals of Zion," "Water, Rocks, and Time," and "Snapshots of History," highlighting stories of the early settlers. There are no reservations, and you can come and go as you please. Talks are usually 20 to 30 minutes, but some run longer. Park bulletin boards and publications have schedules. ☎ *435/772–3256.*

FAMILY **Junior Ranger Program.** The park offers an array of worthy educational activities aimed at younger visitors. This includes the chance to earn their Junior Ranger badge by attending at least one nature program and completing the free Junior Ranger Handbook, available at visitor centers, the Zion Human History Museum, and Zion Nature Center. The ranger-led programs cover topics such as plants, animals, geology, and archaeology through hands-on activities, games, and hikes. Check the park guide for scheduled talks. ⊠ *Zion Nature Center, near South Campground entrance, ½ mile north of south entrance* ☎ *435/772– 3256* ⊕ *www.nps.gov/zion* ⊠ *Free.*

Ranger-Led Hikes. These guided hikes are perfect if you crave to know more about the sites and sounds of the trail but don't have the time to get a degree in botany or zoology prior to the trip. Itineraries vary between easy 1-mile to moderate 2.5-mile walks and have recently included a Riverside Ramble, a geologic tour called Rock and Stroll, and a natural-history walk taking in the incredible vistas of Kolob Canyons. Inquire at the Zion Canyon and Kolob Canyons visitor centers, or check park bulletin boards for locations and times. Wear sturdy footgear and bring a hat, sunglasses, sunscreen, and water. ⊕ *www.nps.gov/zion.*

FAMILY **Ride with a Ranger Shuttle Tours.** Listening to the audiotape narration that Fodor's Choice accompanies every shuttle ride is one thing, but having your very own ★ expert along for the trip is quite another. Twice a day the park provides ranger-led shuttle tours that stop at various points of interest along Zion Canyon Scenic Drive, offering details on the canyon's geology, ecology, and history, as well as great photo ops. The two-hour tours take place in the morning and evening and depart from the Zion Canyon Visitor Center. Make reservations, in person, at the visitor center up to three days in advance; seating is limited. ⊠ *Zion Canyon Visitor Center* ☎ *435/772–3256* ⊕ *www.nps.gov/zion* ⊠ *Free* ☉ *May–Sept., daily at 9 and 6:30.*

SPORTS AND THE OUTDOORS

Hiking is by far the most popular activity at Zion, with a panoply of trails leading to rewarding destinations in the hinterlands: extreme slot canyons, gorgeous overlooks, verdant meadows, and dripping springs. Some sections of the Virgin River are ideal for canoeing (inner tubes are not allowed). In winter, hiking boots can be exchanged for snowshoes and cross-country skis, but check with a ranger to determine backcountry snow conditions.

BICYCLING

Zion National Park has something for every kind of biker. Mountain bikers can cake themselves with mud on the park's trails, and racers will find enough up and down to make their pulse race.

The park has become much more bicycle-friendly, including having bike racks at some of the facilities and on the shuttle buses themselves. If you are renting bikes by the hour from a Springdale outfitter, you can load your bike on the bus, have the shuttle take you to the last stop (Temple of Sinawava), and take an easy one-way pedal back to Springdale. ■TIP➜ **When you're on the park road, shuttle buses and cars have the right of way and you're expected to pull off to the side and let them pass.**

Within the park proper, bicycles are allowed only on established park roads and on the 3½-mile Pa'rus Trail, which winds along the Virgin River in Zion Canyon. You cannot walk or ride your bicycle through the Zion–Mount Carmel Tunnels; the only way to get your bike past this stretch of the highway is to transport it by motor vehicle.

OUTFITTERS

Bicycles Unlimited. A trusted resource on mountain biking in southern Utah, this bike shop rents bikes and sells parts, accessories, and guidebooks. ✉ *90 S. 100 E, St. George* ☎ *888/673–4492* ⊕ *bicyclesunlimited. com* ⊙ *Mon.–Sat. 9–6.*

Zion Cycles. This is a full-service shop offering bike rentals for novices to seasoned pros. Rentals can be for a few hours or multiple days; tag-a-longs and trailers are also available. The shop includes repair services and a large selection of parts. ✉ *868 Zion Park Blvd., Springdale* ☎ *435/772–0400* ⊕ *zioncycles.com.*

BIRD-WATCHING

More than 270 bird species call Zion Canyon home, and scores more pass through the park on their annual migrations. Some species, such as the white-throated swift and ospreys, make their home in the towering cliff walls. Red-tailed and Cooper's hawks are abundant. Closer to the ground you'll doubtless see the bold Steller's jay and scrub jay rustling around the pinyon thickets. The wild turkey population has been booming in recent years, and some of the flock just might come your way looking for a handout. Five species of hummingbirds are residents of the park, with the black-chinned variety being the most common. The park service says four other species of hummers may zip by you on their way to some nectar-filled destination, but these birds are just tourists here like you. Climb to the top of Angels Landing and you may catch a glimpse of a bald eagle. The luckiest bird-watchers might even see two of the park's rarest species: the Mexican spotted owl and the enormous California condor. ■TIP➜ Ask for a bird checklist at the visitor center.

HIKING

The best way to experience Zion Canyon is to walk beneath, between, and, if you can bear it (and have good balance!), along its towering cliffs. Trails vary, from paved and flat river strolls to precarious cliff-side scrambles. Whether you're heading out for a day of rock hopping or an hour of meandering, pack and consume plenty of drinking water to counteract the effects of a high-altitude workout in the arid climate.

Keeping the sun at bay is a real challenge at Zion National Park (though by midafternoon the canyon is shaded by its walls). Put on sunscreen before you set out, and reapply at regular intervals. Hikes usually include uneven surfaces and elevation changes, so wear sturdy footwear. Many veteran hikers carry good walking sticks—invaluable on trails that ford or follow the Virgin River or its tributaries.

Zion is one of the most popular parks in the country, so it can be hard to envision just how alone you'll be on some of the less traveled trails. If you want to do a backcountry hike, make a reservation and let park rangers know where you're going and when you plan to be back.

■TIP➜ Park rangers warn hikers to remain on alert for flash floods; walls of water can appear out of nowhere, even when the sky above is clear.

EASY

FAMILY **Emerald Pools Trail.** Multiple waterfalls cascade (or drip, in dry weather) into algae-filled pools along this trail, about 3 miles north of Canyon Junction. The path leading to the lower pool is paved and appropriate for strollers and wheelchairs. If you've got any energy left, keep going past the lower pool. The mile from there to the middle pool gets rocky and steep but offers increasingly scenic views. A less crowded and exceptionally enjoyable return route follows the Kayenta Trail connecting on to the Grotto Trail. Allow 50 minutes for the 1¼-mile round-trip hike to the lower pool, and 2½ hours round-trip to the middle (2 miles) and upper pools (3 miles). *Easy.* ✉ *Trailhead at Zion Canyon Scenic Dr.*

> ### GOOD READS
>
> *Zion Adventure Guide,* by Greer Chesher, the complete guide to exploring Zion National Park.
>
> *An Introduction to the Geology of Zion,* by Al Warneke, is a good pick for information on Zion's geology.
>
> *The Zion Tunnel, from Slickrock to Switchback,* by Donald T. Garate, tells the fascinating story of the construction of the mile-long Zion Tunnel in the 1920s.
>
> *Zion National Park: Sanctuary in the Desert,* by Nicky Leach, gives you a photographic overview and a narrative journey through the park.

FAMILY **Grotto Trail.** This flat trail takes you from Zion Lodge, about 3 miles north of Canyon Junction, to the Grotto picnic area, traveling for the most part along the park road. Allow 20 minutes or less for the walk along the half-mile trail. If you are up for a longer hike, and have two to three hours, connect with the Kayenta Trail after you cross the footbridge, and head for the Emerald Pools. You will begin gaining elevation, and it's a steady, steep climb to the pools, which you will begin to see after about 1 mile. *Easy.* ✉ *Trailhead at Zion Canyon Scenic Dr.*

Pa'rus Trail. This 2-mile, relatively flat walking and biking path parallels and occasionally crosses the Virgin River, starting at South Campground, ½ mile north of south entrance, and proceeding north along the river to the beginning of Zion Canyon Scenic Drive. It's paved and gives you great views of the Watchman, the Sentinel, the East and West temples, and Towers of the Virgin. Dogs are allowed on this trail as long as they are leashed. *Easy.* ✉ *Trailhead at Canyon Junction.*

FAMILY **Riverside Walk.** Beginning at the Temple of Sinawava shuttle stop at the end of Zion Canyon Scenic Drive, 6½ miles north of Canyon Junction, this 1-mile round-trip shadows the Virgin River, and in spring wildflowers bloom on the opposite canyon wall in lovely hanging gardens. This is the park's most trekked trail, so be prepared for crowds at high season; it is paved and suitable for strollers and wheelchairs. A round-trip walk takes one to two hours. At the end of the trail, the Narrows Trail begins. *Easy.* ✉ *Trailhead at Zion Canyon Scenic Dr.*

7

MODERATE

FAMILY
Fodor's Choice
★

Canyon Overlook Trail. The parking area just east of Zion–Mount Carmel tunnel leads to this popular 1-mile, one-hour trail. The overlook at the trail's end gives views of the West and East temples, Towers of the Virgin, the Streaked Wall, and other Zion Canyon cliffs and peaks. The elevation change is 160 feet. *Moderate.* ⊠ *Trailhead at Hwy. 9.*

Taylor Creek Trail. In the Kolob Canyons area of the park, about 1½ miles east of visitor center, this trail immediately descends parallel to Taylor Creek, sometimes crossing it, sometimes shortcutting benches beside it. The historic Larsen Cabin precedes the entrance to the canyon of the Middle Fork, where the trail becomes rougher. After the old Fife Cabin, the canyon bends to the right and delivers you into Double Arch Alcove, a large, colorful grotto with a high blind arch (or arch "embryo") towering above. To Double Arch it's 2¾ miles one way— about a four-hour round-trip. The elevation change on this trail is 440 feet. *Moderate.* ⊠ *Trailhead at Kolob Canyons Rd.*

Watchman Trail. For a view of Springdale and a look at lower Zion Creek Canyon and the Towers of the Virgin, this strenuous hike begins on a service road east of Watchman Campground. Some springs seep out of the sandstone to nourish hanging gardens and attract wildlife here. There are a few sheer cliff edges, so supervise children carefully. Plan on two hours for the 3-mile hike with a 380-foot elevation change. *Moderate.* ⊠ *Trailhead at main visitor center.*

DIFFICULT

Fodor's Choice
★

Angels Landing Trail. As much a trial as a trail, this hike beneath the Great White Throne is one of the most challenging in the park. Leave your acrophobia at home as you work your way through Walter's Wiggles, a series of 21 switchbacks built out of sandstone blocks. From here you traverse sheer cliffs with chains bolted into the rock face to serve as handrails in some (but not all!) places. In spite of its hair-raising nature, this trail is popular. Allow 2½ hours round-trip if you stop at Scout's Lookout (2 miles), and four hours if you keep going to where the angels (and birds of prey) play. The trail is 5 miles round-trip and is not appropriate for children. *Difficult.* ⊠ *Trailhead at Zion Canyon Scenic Dr., about 4½ miles north of Canyon Junction.*

Narrows Trail. After leaving the paved ease of the Gateway to the Narrows trail behind, the real fun begins. Rather than following a trail or path, you walk on the riverbed itself. In places you'll find a pebbly shingle or dry sandbar path, but when the walls of the canyon close in you'll be forced into the chilly waters of the Virgin River, walking against the current (tack back and forth, don't fight it head-on). The hike is a stunning and unique nature experience, but it's no picnic. A walking stick and shoes with good tread and ankle support are highly recommended and will make hiking the riverbed much more enjoyable. Be prepared to swim, as chest-deep holes may occur even when water levels are low. Like any narrow desert canyon, this one is famous for sudden flash flooding, even when skies are clear. ■TIP➔ **Before hiking into the Narrows, check with park rangers about the likelihood of flash floods.** A day trip up the lower section of the Narrows is 6 miles one-way to the turnaround point. Allow at least five hours round-trip. *Difficult.* ✉ *Trailhead at end of Riverside Walk.*

HORSEBACK RIDING

TOURS AND OUTFITTERS

FAMILY **Canyon Trail Rides.** Grab your hat and boots and see Zion Canyon the way the pioneers did—on a horse or mule. Easygoing, one-hour and half-day guided rides are available (minimum age 7 and 10 years, respectively). Maximum weight is 220 pounds. These friendly folks have been around for years, and are the only outfitter for trail rides inside the park. Reservations are recommended and can be made online. ✉ *Across from Zion Lodge* ☎ *435/679–8665* 🌐 *canyonrides.com* 🎟 *$40–$80 per person* 🕒 *Late Mar.–Oct.*

SWIMMING

Swimming is allowed in the Virgin River, but be careful of cold water, slippery rock bottoms, and the occasional flash floods whenever it rains. Swimming is not allowed in the Emerald Pools. The use of inner tubes is prohibited within park boundaries, but some companies offer trips on a tributary of the Virgin River just outside the park.

WINTER SPORTS

Cross-country skiing and snowshoeing are best experienced in the park's higher elevations in winter, where snow stays on the ground longer. Inquire at the Zion Canyon Visitor Center for backcountry conditions. Snowmobiling is allowed only for residential access.

WHERE TO EAT

$ CAFÉ 🍴 **Castle Dome Café & Snack Bar.** Next to the Zion Lodge shuttle stop, 3¼ miles north of Canyon Junction, this small fast-food restaurant is all about convenience. Hikers on the go can grab a banana, burger, smoothie, or salad, or you can while away an hour with ice cream on the shaded patio. Gets quite busy during high-season months. [$] *Average main: $6* ✉ *Zion Canyon Scenic Dr.* ☎ *435/772–7700* 🌐 *zionlodge.com.*

$$ AMERICAN 🍴 **Red Rock Grill at Zion Lodge.** This restaurant's monopoly on in-park fine dining has not made it complacent. The menu is solid American fare, with steaks, seafood, and surprises like house-made Western bison meat loaf. The spacious dining room has photos of the area landscape, but a large patio has views of the real thing. Lunch includes a generous selection of salads, sandwiches, and specialties such as the Wrangler cheeseburger with onion straws and chipotle mayo. Breakfast is also served. You'll need to make a reservation for dinner. [$] *Average main: $18* ✉ *Zion Canyon Scenic Dr.* ☎ *435/772–7760* 🌐 *zionlodge.com.*

7

CLOSE UP

Best Campgrounds in Zion

The three campgrounds within Zion National Park—Watchman, South, and Lava Point—are family-friendly, convenient, and quite pleasant, but in the high season they do fill up fast. Outside the park you'll find a number of private campgrounds.

Lava Point Campground. The six primitive sites here are available at no charge on a first-come, first-served basis. Located in the Kolob Canyons section of the park, the campground is typically open June to October, though if weather permits it can open earlier. ✉ *Off Kolob Terrace Rd., 25 miles north of Virgin.* ☎ *435/772–3256.*

South Campground. All the sites here are under big cottonwood trees, providing some relief from the summer sun. The campground operates on a first-come, first-served basis, and sites are usually filled before noon each day during high season. ✉ *Rte. 9, ½ mile north of south entrance* ☎ *435/772–3256.*

Watchman Campground. This large campground on the Virgin River operates on a reservation system between April and October, but you do not get to choose your own site. ✉ *Access road off Zion Canyon Visitor Center parking lot* ☎ *435/772–3256, 800/365–2267* 🌐 *www.recreation.gov.*

PICNIC AREAS

FAMILY **The Grotto.** Get your food to go at the Zion Lodge, take a short walk to this lunch retreat, and dine beneath a shady oak. There are lots of amenities—drinking water, picnic tables, and restrooms—but no fire grates. A trail leads to the Emerald Pools if you want to walk off your lunchtime calories. ✉ *Zion Canyon Scenic Dr.*

Kolob Canyons Viewpoint. Take in a shaded meal with a view at this charming picnic site 100 yards down the Timber Creek Trail, 5 miles from Kolob Canyons Visitor Center. ✉ *End of Kolob Canyons Rd.*

FAMILY **Zion Nature Center.** On your way to or from the Junior Ranger Program feed your kids at the nature center picnic area, near the entrance to South Campground, ½ mile north of the south entrance. When the nature center is closed, you can use the restrooms in South Campground. ✉ *Zion Canyon Scenic Dr.* ☎ *435/772–3256.*

WHERE TO STAY

$$$ HOTEL 🏨 **Zion Lodge.** Pine and log furnishings re-create the look and feel of this 1920s lodge, but rooms are modern (not fancy), and each has its own balcony or patio. **Pros:** guests can drive their cars here all year; incredible views; gets quiet and dark at night. **Cons:** pathways dimly lit so bring a flashlight; staff seems overwhelmed at busiest times. [$] *Rooms from: $185* ✉ *Zion Canyon Scenic Dr.* ☎ *888/297–2757* 🌐 *zionlodge.com* 🛏 *76 rooms, 6 suites, 40 cabins* 🍴 *No meals.*

BRYCE CANYON NATIONAL PARK

WELCOME TO BRYCE CANYON NATIONAL PARK

TOP REASONS TO GO

★ **Hoodoo heaven:** The brashly colored, gravity-defying limestone tentacles reaching skyward—known as "hoodoos"—are the main attraction of Bryce Canyon.

★ **Famous fresh air:** With some of the clearest skies anywhere, the park offers views that, on a clear day, extend more than 100 miles and into three states.

★ **Spectacular sunrises and sunsets:** The deep orange and crimson hues of the park's hoodoos are intensified by the sun's light at either end of the day.

★ **Dramatically different zones:** From the highest point of the rim to the canyon base, the park drops 2,000 feet, so you can explore three distinct climatic zones: spruce-fir forest, ponderosa-pine forest, and pinyon pine–juniper forest.

★ **Snowy fun:** Bryce gets almost 100 inches of snowfall a year, and is a popular destination for skiers and snowshoe enthusiasts.

Spire in Bryce Canyon

1 Bryce Amphitheater. It's the heart of the park. From here you can access the historic Bryce Canyon Lodge as well as Sunrise, Sunset, and Inspiration points. Walk to Bryce Point at sunrise to view the mesmerizing collection of massive hoodoos known as Silent City.

2 Under-the-Rim Trail. This 23-mile trail is the best way to reach Bryce Canyon backcountry. It can be a challenging three-day adventure or a half day of fun via one of the four access points from the main road. A handful of primitive campgrounds lines the route.

Hoodoo Towers

Inspiration Point at Bryce Canyon

3 Rainbow and Yovimpa Points. The end of the scenic road, but not of the scenery, here you can hike a trail to see some ancient bristlecone pines and look south into Grand Staircase–Escalante National Monument.

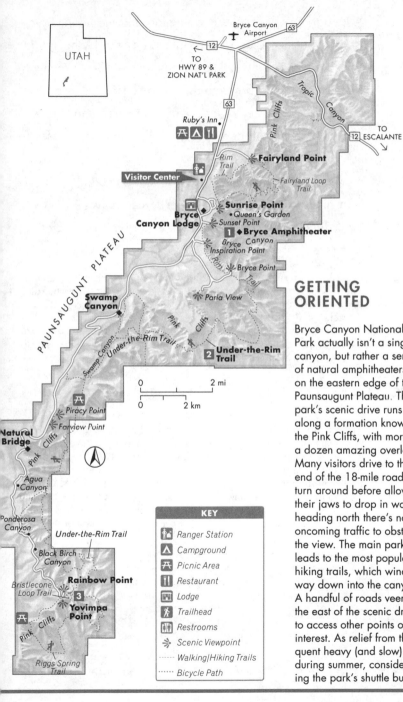

GETTING ORIENTED

Bryce Canyon National Park actually isn't a single canyon, but rather a series of natural amphitheaters on the eastern edge of the Paunsaugunt Plateau. The park's scenic drive runs along a formation known as the Pink Cliffs, with more than a dozen amazing overlooks. Many visitors drive to the end of the 18-mile road and turn around before allowing their jaws to drop in wonder; heading north there's no oncoming traffic to obstruct the view. The main park road leads to the most popular hiking trails, which wind their way down into the canyons. A handful of roads veer to the east of the scenic drive to access other points of interest. As relief from the frequent heavy (and slow) traffic during summer, consider riding the park's shuttle buses.

KEY

- 🚹 *Ranger Station*
- 🔺 *Campground*
- 🌲 *Picnic Area*
- 🍴 *Restaurant*
- 🏨 *Lodge*
- 🚶 *Trailhead*
- 🚻 *Restrooms*
- ⚜ *Scenic Viewpoint*
- ····· *Walking/Hiking Trails*
- ······ *Bicycle Path*

Updated by
John Blodgett

A land that captures the imagination and the heart, Bryce is a favorite among Utah's national parks. Although its splendor had been well known for decades, Bryce Canyon wasn't designated a national park until 1928. The park is named for Ebenezer Bryce, a pioneer cattleman and the first permanent European settler in the area. His description of the landscape—he reportedly said it was "a hell of a place to lose a cow"—has oft been repeated. Even more than his famous quote, however, Bryce Canyon is known for its fanciful "hoodoos," best viewed at sunrise or sunset, when the light plays off the red rock.

In geological terms, Bryce is actually an amphitheater, not a canyon. The hoodoos in the amphitheater took on their unusual shapes because the top layer of rock—"cap rock"—is harder than the layers below it. If erosion undercuts the soft rock beneath the cap too much, the hoodoo will tumble. Bryce continues to evolve today, but the hoodoos are a permanent feature; old ones may die, but new ones are constantly forming as the amphitheater rim recedes.

BRYCE CANYON PLANNER

WHEN TO GO

Around Bryce Canyon National Park and the nearby Cedar Breaks National Monument area, elevations approach and surpass 9,000 feet, making for temperamental weather, intermittent and seasonal road closures due to snow, and downright cold nights well into June. The air is cooler on the rim of the canyon than it is at lower altitudes. ■TIP➜ If **you choose to see Bryce Canyon in summer, you'll be visiting with the rest of the world. During these months, traffic on the main road can be crowded with cars following slow-moving RVs, so consider taking one of the park shuttle buses.**

If it's solitude you're looking for, come to Bryce any time between November and February. The park is open all year long, so if you come during the cooler months you might just have a trail all to yourself.

AVG. HIGH/LOW TEMPS.

Jan.	Feb.	Mar.	Apr.	May	June
39/8	41/13	48/17	56/25	68/31	75/38
July	Aug.	Sept.	Oct.	Nov.	Dec.
83/47	80/45	74/37	63/29	51/19	42/11

FESTIVALS AND EVENTS

FEBRUARY **Bryce Canyon Winter Festival.** This event at the Best Western Ruby's Inn features cross-country ski races, snow-sculpting contests, ski archery, and ice-skating. Clinics to hone skills such as snowshoeing and photography also take place, and there's entertainment, too. ☎ *435/834–5341* ⊕ *www.rubysinn.com.*

PLANNING YOUR TIME
BRYCE CANYON IN ONE DAY

Begin your day at the **visitor center** to get an overview of the park and to purchase books and maps. Watch the video and peruse exhibits about the natural and cultural history of Bryce Canyon. Then, drive to the historic **Bryce Canyon Lodge** (closed November–March). From here, stroll along the relaxing **Rim Trail.** If you have the time and stamina to walk into the amphitheater, the portion of the Rim Trail near the lodge gets you to the starting point for either of the park's two essential hikes, the **Navajo Loop Trail** from **Sunset Point** or the **Queens Garden Trail** that connects Sunset to **Sunrise Point.**

Afterward (or if you skip the hike), drive the 18-mile **main park road,** stopping at the overlooks along the way. Allowing for traffic and stops at all 14 overlooks, this drive will take you two to three hours.

If you have time for more walking, a short, rolling hike along the **Bristlecone Loop Trail** at **Rainbow Point** rewards you with spectacular views and a cool walk through a forest of bristlecone pines. If you don't have time to drive the 18 miles to the end of the park, skip Bryce Canyon Lodge and drive 2 miles from the visitor center to **Inspiration Point** and then to the next overlook, **Bryce Point.**

8

End your day with sunset at Inspiration Point or dinner at Bryce Canyon Lodge. As you leave the park, stop at **Ruby's Inn** for Native American jewelry, souvenirs for the kids, and groceries or snacks for the road.

GETTING HERE AND AROUND
AIR TRAVEL

The nearest commercial airport to Bryce Canyon is 80 miles west in Cedar City, Utah.

BUS TRAVEL

A shuttle bus system operates in Bryce Canyon from early-May through early-October. Buses run every 12 to 15 minutes, and are free with your admission fee. The route stops at all the major hotels and campgrounds, as well as the visitor center and the main trailheads.

CAR TRAVEL

The closest major cities to Bryce Canyon are Salt Lake City and Las Vegas, each about 270 miles away. The park is reached via Highway 63, just 3 miles south of the junction with Highway 12. You can see the park's highlights by driving along the well-maintained road running the length of the main scenic area. Bryce has no restrictions on automobiles on the main road, but in the summer you may encounter heavy traffic and full parking lots.

PARK ESSENTIALS
PARK FEES
The entrance fee is $25 per vehicle for a seven-day pass and $12 for pedestrians or bicyclists. The entrance fee includes unlimited use of the park shuttle. An annual Bryce Canyon park pass, good for one year from the date of purchase, costs $30. If you leave your private vehicle outside the park—at the shuttle staging area or Ruby's Inn—the 7-day entrance fee, including transportation on the shuttle, is $25 per party. ■ TIP→ **At the time of writing, the National Park Service was considering increasing some of its fees. If approved, the increases will take effect some-time during 2015; call to check.**

A $5 backcountry permit, available from the visitor center, is required for camping in the park's wilderness, allowed only on Under-the-Rim Trail and Rigg's Spring Loop, both south of Bryce Point. Campfires are not permitted.

PARK HOURS
The park is open 24/7, year-round. It's in the mountain time zone.

CELL-PHONE RECEPTION
Cell-phone reception is hit-and-miss in the park. If you're getting reception, take advantage of it and make your calls; you may not have another chance. Bryce Canyon Lodge, General Store, Ruby's Inn, Sunset Campground, and the visitor center all have public telephones.

RESTAURANTS
Dining options in the park proper are limited to Bryce Canyon Lodge; the nearby Ruby's Inn complex is your best eating bet before you pay to enter the park. The restaurants in nearby locales tend to be of the meat-and-potatoes variety. Utah's drinking laws can be confusing, so ask your server what is available: beer is more common than wine and spirits.

HOTELS
Lodging options in and around Bryce Canyon include both rustic and modern amenities, but all fill up fast in summer. Bryce Canyon Lodge is the only hotel inside the park, but there are a number of options in Bryce Canyon City, just north of the park entrance. Panguitch and Tropic are small towns nearby with good options for budget and last-minute travelers. *Hotel reviews have been shortened. For full information, visit Fodors.com.*

WHAT IT COSTS			
$	**$$**	**$$$**	**$$$$**
Restaurants	under $12	$12–$20	$21–$30	over $30
Hotels	under $100	$100–$150	$151–$200	over $200

Restaurant prices are the average cost of a main course at dinner or, if dinner is not served, at lunch. Hotel prices are the lowest cost of a standard double room in high season.

VISITOR INFORMATION
PARK CONTACT INFORMATION
Bryce Canyon National Park ☎ *435/834–5322* ⊕ *www.nps.gov/brca.*

Plants and Wildlife in Bryce Canyon

Due to elevations approaching 9,000 feet, many of Bryce Canyon's 400 plant species are unlike those you'll see at less lofty places. Look at exposed slopes and you might catch a glimpse of the pygmy pinyon, or the gnarled, 1,000-year-old bristle-cone pine. At lower altitudes are the Douglas fir, ponderosa pine, and the quaking aspen, sitting in groves of twinkling leaves. No fewer than three kinds of sagebrush—big, black, and fringed—grow here, as well as the blue columbine.

Mule deer and chipmunks are common companions on the trails and are used to human presence. You might also catch a glimpse of the endangered Utah prairie dog. Give them a wide berth; they may be cute, but they bite. Other animals include elk, black-tailed jackrabbits, and the desert cottontail. More than 170 species of bird live in the park or pass through as a migratory stop. Eagles, peregrine falcons, and even the rare California condor have all been spotted in the park.

VISITOR CENTER

Bryce Canyon Visitor Center. Even if you're anxious to hit the hoodoos, the visitor center, 1 mile south of park entrance, is the best place to start if you want to know what you're looking at and how it got there. You can't miss the visitor center—the spacious building looks like a cross between a barn and a fire station. There are also multimedia exhibits, books, maps, and backcountry camping permits for sale. First aid, emergency, and lost-and-found services are offered here, along with free Wi-Fi. If you want coffee, head to nearby Ruby's Inn. ⊠ *Hwy. 63* ☎ *435/834–5322* ⊕ *www.nps.gov/brca* ⊗ *May–Sept. 8–8; Apr. and Oct. 8–6; Nov.–Mar. daily 8–4:30.*

8

EXPLORING

SCENIC DRIVES

Fodor'sChoice
★
Main Park Road. Following miles of canyon rim, this thoroughfare gives access to more than a dozen scenic overlooks between the park entrance and Rainbow Point. Major overlooks are rarely more than a few minutes' walk from the parking areas, and many let you see more than 100 miles on clear days. ■ TIP→ **Remember that all overlooks lie east of the road—to keep things simple, proceed to the southern end of the park and stop at the overlooks on your northbound return.** Allow two to three hours to travel the entire 36-mile round-trip. The road is open year-round, but may close temporarily after heavy snowfalls. Keep your eyes open for wildlife as you drive. Trailers are not allowed at Bryce Point and Paria View, but you can park them at the parking lot across the road from the visitor center. RVs can drive throughout the park, but vehicles longer than 25 feet are not allowed at Paria View.

HISTORIC SITES

Bryce Canyon Lodge. The lodge's architect, Gilbert Stanley Underwood, was a national park specialist, having designed lodges at Zion and Grand Canyon before turning his T-square to Bryce in 1923. The results are worth a visit, even if you plan to sleep elsewhere, as this National Historic Landmark has been faithfully restored, right down to the lobby's huge limestone fireplace and log and wrought-iron chandelier. The bark-covered hickory furniture isn't original, but renovators ordered it from the same company that created the originals. Inside the historic building are a restaurant and a gift shop, as well as plenty of information on park activities. Guests of the lodge, which is 2 miles south of park entrance, can stay in the numerous log cabins on the wooded grounds. ⊠ *Hwy. 63* ☎ *435/834–8700.*

SCENIC STOPS

Agua Canyon. This overlook in the southern section of the park, 12 miles south of park entrance, has a nice view of several standout hoodoos. Look for the top-heavy formation called the Hunter, which actually has a few small hardy trees growing on its cap. As the rock erodes, the park evolves; snap a picture because the Hunter may look different the next time you visit.

Fairyland Point. Best seen as you exit the park, this scenic overlook adjacent to Boat Mesa, ½-mile north of the visitor center and a mile off the main park road, has splendid views of Fairyland Amphitheater and its delicate, fanciful forms. The Sinking Ship and other formations stand before the grand backdrop of the Aquarius Plateau and distant Navajo Mountain. Nearby is the Fairyland Loop trailhead; it's a stunning five-hour hike in summer and a favorite of snowshoers in winter. ⊠ *Off Hwy. 63.*

Inspiration Point. Not far (1.5 miles) east along the Rim Trail from Bryce Point is Inspiration Point, site of a wonderful vista on the main amphitheater and one of the best places in the park to see the sunset. ⊠ *Inspiration Point Rd.*

Natural Bridge. Formed over millions of years by wind, water, and chemical erosion, this 85-foot rusty-orange arch formation—one of several rock arches in the park—is an essential photo op. Beyond the parking lot lies a rare stand of aspen trees, their leaves twinkling in the wind. ⚠ **Watch out for distracted drivers at this stunning viewpoint.** ⊠ *Off Hwy. 63, 11 miles south of park entrance.*

Rainbow and Yovimpa Points. Separated by less than half a mile, Rainbow and Yovimpa points offer two fine panoramas facing opposite directions. Rainbow Point's best view is to the north overlooking the southern rim of the amphitheater and giving a glimpse of Grand Staircase–Escalante National Monument. Yovimpa Point's vista spreads out to the south. On a clear day you can see all the way to Arizona, 100 miles away. Yovimpa Point also has a shady and quiet picnic area with tables and restrooms. You can hike between them on the Bristlecone Loop Trail or tackle the more strenuous 8¾-mile Riggs Spring Loop Trail, which passes the tallest point in the park. ✉ *Off Hwy. 63, 18 miles south of park entrance.*

Fodor's Choice ★ **Sunrise Point.** Named for its stunning views at dawn, this overlook is a short walk from Bryce Canyon Lodge, 2 miles south of park entrance, and so one of the park's most popular stops. It's also the trailhead for the Queens Garden Trail and the Fairyland Loop Trail. You have to descend the Queens Garden Trail to get a regal glimpse of **Queen Victoria,** a hoodoo that appears to sport a crown and glorious full skirt. The trail is popular and marked clearly, but moderately strenuous with 350 feet of elevation change. ✉ *Off Hwy. 63.*

> ### GOOD READS
>
> *Bryce Canyon Auto and Hiking Guide,* by Tully Stroud, includes information on the geology and history of the area.
>
> Supplement the free park map with *Bryce Canyon Hiking Guide,* which includes an amphitheater hiking map and aerial photo.
>
> To prepare kids ages 5–10 for a trip to the park, consider ordering the 32-page *Kid's Guide to Bryce Canyon.*

Sunset Point. Watch the late-day sun paint the hoodoos here. You can see **Thor's Hammer,** a delicate formation similar to a balanced rock, from the rim, but when you hike 550 feet down into the amphitheater on the Navajo Loop Trail, you can walk through the famous and very popular Wall Street—a deep, shady "slot" canyon. The point is 2 miles south of park entrance near Bryce Canyon Lodge.

EDUCATIONAL OFFERINGS

RANGER PROGRAMS

Campfire and Auditorium Programs. Bryce Canyon's natural diversity comes alive in the park's North Campground amphitheater, the Visitor Center Theater, or in the Bryce Canyon Lodge Auditorium. Lectures, multimedia programs, and ranger walks introduce you to geology, astronomy, wildlife, history, and many other topics related to Bryce Canyon and the West. ☎ *435/834–5322.*

Canyon Hike. June to August, a ranger-led tour of the Queens Garden or Navajo Loop Trail, stopping at multiple points along the way, explains the amphitheater's features and formations. The hike is 2–3 miles long and takes two to three hours to complete.

Full Moon Hike. Rangers lead guided hikes on the nights around each full moon (two per month May–October). Wear heavy-traction shoes, and reserve a spot at the visitor center on the day of the hike. ■ TIP→ **These free tours are a popular activity, so sign up early.**

Geology Talk. Rangers regularly host discussions about the long geological history of Bryce Canyon; they are nearly always held at Sunset Point. Talks are free and last 30 minutes.

FAMILY **Junior Ranger Program.** Children ages three and above can sign up to be Junior Rangers at the Bryce Canyon Visitor Center. The park takes that title seriously, so kids have to complete several activities in their free Junior Ranger booklet, as well as collect some litter, and attend a ranger program. Allow three to six hours for all this. Schedules of events and topics are posted at the visitor center, Bryce Canyon Lodge, and on North and Sunset campgrounds' bulletin boards.

Fodor's Choice ★ **Night Sky Program.** City folk are lucky to see 2,500 stars in their artificially illuminated skies, but out here among the hoodoos you see three times as many. The Night Sky Program includes low-key astronomy lectures and multimedia presentations, followed by telescope viewing (weather permitting). The program is typically offered on Tuesday, Thursday, and Saturday, May–September; the monthly full-moon hike is offered in October as well. Reservations are necessary only for the latter event; check at the visitor center for locations, times, and other details. ☎ 435/834–4747 ⊠ Free.

Rim Walk. Join a park ranger for a 1-mile, 90-minute stroll along the gorgeous rim of Bryce Canyon starting at the Sunset Point overlook. Reservations are not required for the walk, which is usually offered daily from May to September. Start time is usually 5 pm, but it sometimes begins at 4 earlier or later in the season. Check at the visitor center for details. ⊠ Free.

SPORTS AND THE OUTDOORS

Because Bryce Canyon is easily visited by car—the park road itself can seem a main feature of the park—it can be tempting to spend too much time viewing rock formations from within the confines of safety glass or from behind a scenic turnout's fence. Fortunately, there is plenty more to do here once you do get outside. You can get tours by air and horseback, birds and other wildlife can be seen with a little diligence and quietude, and don't forget all those wonderful hiking trails. In fact, most trailheads are readily accessed from your parking space.

AIR TOURS

OUTFITTERS

Bryce Canyon Airlines & Helicopters. For a bird's-eye view of Bryce Canyon National Park, take a dramatic helicopter ride or airplane tour over the fantastic sandstone formations. Longer full-canyon tours and added excursions to sites such as the Grand Canyon, Monument Valley, or Zion are also offered. Flight time can last anywhere from 35 minutes to 4 hours; family and group rates are available. ☎ 435/834–8060, 435/691–8813, 435/619–0017 ⊕ rubysinn.com/bryce-canyon-airlines.html ⊠ From: $110.

BIRD-WATCHING

More than 170 bird species have been identified in Bryce. Violet green swallows and white-throated swifts are common, as are Steller's jays, rufous hummingbirds, and mountain bluebirds. Lucky bird-watchers will see golden eagles floating across the skies above the pink rocks of the amphitheater, and experienced birders might spot a peregrine falcon nest high in the canyon wall. The best time in the park for avian variety is from May through July.

HIKING

To get up close and personal with the park's hoodoos, set aside a half day to hike into the amphitheater. There are no elevators, so remember that after you descend below the rim you'll have to get back up. The air gets warmer the lower you go, and the altitude will have you huffing and puffing unless you're a mountain native. The uneven terrain calls for lace-up shoes on even the well-trodden, high-traffic trails and sturdy hiking boots for the more challenging ones. No below-rim trails are paved. Hiking farther into the depths of the park is not difficult so long as you don't pick a hike that is beyond your abilities. At these elevations, you'll have to stop to catch your breath more often than you're used to, but although it gets warm in summer, it's rarely uncomfortably hot. For trail maps, information, and ranger recommendations, stop at the visitor center. Bathrooms are at most trailheads but not down in the amphitheater.

OUTFITTERS **Escalante Outfitters.** Natural history tours of Grand Staircase–Escalante National Monument are offered here, as well as more adventurous day and overnight hikes and guided fly-fishing excursions. The business also has an outdoor store with camping gear, café, and a few homey sleeping berths out back, including some rustic private cabins and campsites. ⊠ *310 W. Main St., Escalante* ☎ *435/826–4266* ⊕ *www.escalante outfitters.com* ⊠ *From: $250.*

EASY

Bristlecone Loop Trail. This 1-mile trail with a modest 200 feet of elevation gain alternates between spruce and fir forest and wide-open vistas across the Grand Staircase-Escalante National Monument and beyond. You might see yellow-bellied marmots and dusky grouse, critters not found at lower elevations in the park. The most challenging part of the hike is ungluing your eyes from the scenery long enough to read the signage at the many trail forks. Plan on 45 minutes to an hour. *Easy.* ⊠ *Trailhead at Rainbow Point parking area, 18 miles south of park entrance.*

FAMILY **Queens Garden Trail.** This hike is the easiest way down into the amphitheater, with 350 feet of elevation change leading to a short tunnel, quirky hoodoos, and lots of like-minded hikers. Allow two hours total to hike the 1½-mile trail plus the ½-mile rim-side path and back. *Easy.* ⊠ *Trailhead at Sunrise Point, 2 miles south of park entrance.*

MODERATE

Navajo Loop Trail. One of Bryce's most popular and dramatic attractions is this steep descent via a series of switchbacks leading to Wall Street, a claustrophobic hallway of rock only 20-feet wide in places with walls 100-feet high. After a walk through the Silent City, the northern end of the trail brings Thor's Hammer into view. A well-marked intersection offers a shorter way back or continuing on the Queens Garden Trail to Sunrise Point. For the short version allow at least an hour on this

8

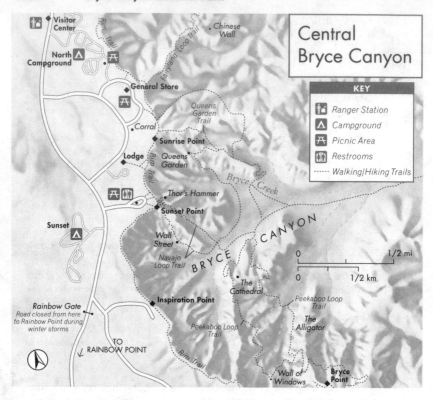

Central Bryce Canyon

KEY

👫	*Ranger Station*
🅰	*Campground*
⛱	*Picnic Area*
🚻	*Restrooms*
-----	*Walking/Hiking Trails*

Visitor Center

North Campground

General Store

Queens Garden Trail

Corral

Sunrise Point

Lodge

Queens Garden

Chinese Wall

Thor's Hammer

Bryce Creek

Sunset Point

Sunset

Wall Street

Navajo Loop Trail

BRYCE CANYON

0 _____ 1/2 mi

0 _____ 1/2 km

Inspiration Point

The Cathedral

Peekaboo Loop Trail

The Alligator

Rainbow Gate
Road closed from here to Rainbow Point during winter storms

Peekaboo Loop Trail

TO RAINBOW POINT

Rim Trail

Wall of Windows

Bryce Point

1½-mile trail with 550 feet of elevation change. *Moderate.* ⊠ *Trailhead at Sunset Point, 2 miles south of park entrance.*

Fodor's Choice ★ **Navajo/Queens Garden Combination Loop.** By walking this extended 3-mile loop, you can see some of the best of Bryce; it takes a little more than two hours. The route passes fantastic formations and an open forest of pine and juniper on the amphitheater floor. Descend into the amphitheater from Sunrise Point on the Queens Garden Trail and ascend via the Navajo Loop Trail; return to your starting point via the Rim Trail. *Moderate.* ⊠ *Trailheads at Sunset and Sunrise points, 2 miles south of park entrance.*

DIFFICULT

Fairyland Loop Trail. Hike into whimsical Fairyland Canyon on this trail that gets more strenuous and less crowded as you progress along its 8 miles. It winds around hoodoos, across trickles of water, and finally to a natural window in the rock at Tower Bridge, 1½ miles from Sunrise Point and 4 miles from Fairyland Point. The pink-and-white badlands and hoodoos surround you the whole way. Don't feel that you have to go the whole distance to make it worthwhile. But if you do, allow at least five hours for the round-trip with 1,700 feet of elevation change. You can pick up the loop at Fairyland Point or Sunrise Point. *Difficult.*

✉ *Trailhead at Fairyland Point, 1 mile off main park rd., 1 mile south of park entrance; Sunrise Point, 2 miles south of park entrance.*

Peekaboo Loop. The reward of this steep trail is the Wall of Windows and the Three Wise Men. ■**TIP→ Horses use this trail in spring, summer, and fall and have the right-of-way.** Start at Bryce, Sunrise, or Sunset Point and allow four to five hours to hike the 5-mile trail or 7-mile double-loop. *Difficult.* ✉ *Trailheads at Bryce Point, 2 miles off main park road, 5½ miles south of park entrance; Sunrise and Sunset points, 2 miles south of park entrance.*

Trail to the Hat Shop. The sedimentary haberdashery sits 2 miles from the trailhead. Hard gray caps balance precariously atop narrow pedestals of softer, rust-color rock. Allow three to four hours to travel this strenuous but rewarding 4-mile round-trip trail, the first part of the longer Under-the-Rim Trail. *Difficult.* ✉ *Trailhead at Bryce Point, 2 miles off main park road, 5½ miles south of park entrance.*

Under-the-Rim Trail. Starting at Bryce Point, the trail travels 23 miles to Rainbow Point, passing through the Pink Cliffs, traversing Agua Canyon and Ponderosa Canyon, and taking you by several springs. Most of the hike is on the amphitheater floor, characterized by up-and-down terrain among stands of ponderosa pine; the elevation change totals about 1,500 feet. Four trailheads along the main park road allow you to connect to the Under-the-Rim Trail and cover its length as a series of day hikes. Allow at least two days to hike the route in its entirety, and although it's not a hoodoo-heavy hike there's plenty to see to make it a more leisurely three-day affair. *Difficult.* ✉ *Trailheads at Bryce Point, Swamp Canyon, Ponderosa Canyon, and Rainbow Point.*

HORSEBACK RIDING

Many of the park's hiking trails were first formed beneath the hooves of cattle wranglers. Today, hikers and riders share the trails. A concession outfitter can set you up with a gentle mount and lead you to the park's best sights. Not only can you cover more ground than you would walking, but equine traffic has the right-of-way at all times. Call ahead to the stables to reserve a two-hour or half-day ride. People under the age of 7 or who weigh more than 220 pounds are prohibited from riding.

TOURS AND OUTFITTERS

Canyon Trail Rides. Descend to the floor of the Bryce Canyon amphitheater via horse or mule—and most visitors have no riding experience, so don't hesitate to join in. A two-hour ride ambles along the amphitheater floor to the Fairy Castle before returning to Sunrise Point. The half-day expedition follows Peekaboo Loop Trail, winds past the Fairy Castle and the Alligator, and passes the Wall of Windows before returning to Sunrise Point. Two rides a day of each type leave in the morning and early afternoon. Trips can now be booked online; there are no rides in winter. ✉ *Bryce Canyon Lodge, off Hwy. 63* ☎ *435/679–8665* ⊕ *canyonrides.com* ✉ *$60 for 2 hrs; $80 for half-day excursion.*

FAMILY **Ruby's Horseback Adventures.** Mount up and retrace trails taken by outlaw Butch Cassidy in Red Canyon National Forest, Bryce Canyon, or

Grand Staircase–Escalante National Monument on Ruby's Horseback Adventures rides, which last from one hour to all day. Riders must be seven or older. Wagon rides to the rim of Bryce Canyon are available for all ages, as are sleigh rides in winter. ☎ *866/782–0002* 🌐 *horserides.net* 🎟 *From: $55.*

WINTER SPORTS

Unlike Utah's other national parks, Bryce Canyon receives plenty of snow, making it a popular cross-country ski and snowshoe area. The unplowed roads to Fairyland Point and Paria View, along with the Paria Ski Loop are popular destinations. Be advised that only snowshoes are permitted below the rim of Bryce Canyon; using skis, snowboards, sleds, snow tubes, toboggans, and other snow-sliding devices is prohibited. The visitor center sells shoe-traction devices, and ranger-guided snowshoe activities include snowshoes and poles.

OUTFITTERS

Ruby's Winter Activities Center. This facility grooms miles of private, no-cost trails that connect to the ungroomed trails inside the park. Rental snowshoes, ice skates, and cross-country ski equipment are available. ✉ *Hwy. 63, 1 mile north of park entrance, Bryce* ☎ *435/834–5341* 🌐 *www.rubysinn.com/winter.html.*

WHERE TO EAT

IN THE PARK

$$$ AMERICAN

🍴 **Bryce Canyon Lodge.** Set among towering pines, this rustic old lodge, 2 miles south of park entrance, is the featured place to dine within the park. The menu changes each year, but always uses organic, regional foods. The menu emphasizes local choices such as Utah trout and ranges from prime rib to vegetarian-friendly quinoa primavera. A beer and wine selection includes Utah microbrews. No reservations are accepted, so you may encounter a wait. [$] *Average main: $24* ✉ *Hwy. 63* ☎ *435/834–8700* 🌐 *brycecanyonforever.com* ✍ *Reservations not accepted* 🕑 *Closed Nov.–Mar.*

$ ITALIAN FAMILY

🍴 **Valhalla Pizzeria & Coffee Shop.** Addressing the need for a family-friendly, fast-casual alternative to Bryce Canyon Lodge's formal dining, a former recreation room across the parking lot from the lodge was converted into this 40-seat pizzeria and coffee shop. The patio is a nice place to have a beer or glass of wine in balmy weather (as long as you buy at least a banana to go with it, thanks to Utah liquor laws). In addition to pizza, the menu includes calzones, lasagna, salads, appetizers, and desserts. Hours are odd: daily 6–11:30 and 3–10. [$] *Average main: $10* ✉ *Off Hwy. 63, 2 miles south of park entrance* ☎ *435/834–8709* 🌐 *brycecanyonforever.com/lodge-pizza* ✍ *Reservations not accepted* 🕑 *Closed mid-Oct.–mid-May. No lunch.*

PICNIC AREAS

North Campground. On the south end of the campground, about ¼ mile south of the visitor center, this picnic area in the shade of the ponderosa pines has tables and grills along with freshwater taps.

Yovimpa Point. At the southern end of the park, 18 miles south of the park entrance, this shady, quiet spot has tables and restrooms nearby. A short walk leads to the edge of the Paunsaugunt Plateau and offers long-distance, panoramic views.

OUTSIDE THE PARK

$$ ✕ **Bryce Canyon Restaurant.** Part of the Bryce Canyon Pines motel, about
AMERICAN   15 miles west from Tropic, this cozy eatery offers homemade soups like cream of broccoli and corn chowder, or settle down for a steak and mashed potatoes. They are known for their delicious homemade pies. $ *Average main: $12* ✉ *Hwy. 12, mile marker 10, Bryce* ☎ 800/892–7923 ⊕ *brycecanyonmotel.com.*

$$ ✕ **Foster's Family Steakhouse.** This steak house is known for its prime rib
STEAKHOUSE   and sautéed mushrooms, but you'll also find seafood on the menu, and some choices include the soup and salad bar. Whatever you choose, be sure to leave room for dessert—try the namesake mixed-berry pie that includes raspberries, rhubarb, and strawberries. Beverages include beer and wine, and you can take out homemade breads and pastries. The restaurant is open early for breakfast, too, and you'll find it 2 miles west of the Highway 63 intersection. $ *Average main: $15* ✉ *1150 Hwy. 12, Bryce* ☎ 435/834–5227 ⊕ *www.fostersmotel.com* ☾ *Closed Mon.–Thurs. in Jan.*

WHERE TO STAY

IN THE PARK

$$$ ⊡ **Bryce Canyon Lodge.** A few feet from the amphitheater's rim and trail-
HOTEL   heads is this rugged stone-and-wood lodge with suites on the lodge's
Fodor's Choice   second level, motel-style rooms with balconies or porches in separate
★   buildings, and cozy lodgepole-pine cabins, some with cathedral ceilings and gas fireplaces. **Pros:** only lodging inside the park; friendly and attentive staff; cabins have fireplaces. **Cons:** closed in winter; books up fast; no TV; grounds can be dark at night, so bring a flashlight to dinner. $ *Rooms from: $183* ✉ *Off Hwy. 63* ☎ 435/834–8700, 877/386–4383 ⊕ *brycecanyonforever.com/lodging/* ⇗ *70 rooms, 3 suites, 40 cabins* ☾ *Closed Nov.–Mar.* ⊠ *No meals.*

OUTSIDE THE PARK

$$$ ⊡ **Best Western Bryce Canyon Grand Hotel.** If you're into creature comforts
HOTEL   but can do without charm, this four-story hotel is the place—rooms are relatively posh, with comfortable mattresses, pillows, and bedding, spacious bathrooms, and modern appliances. **Pros:** clean and squared away; lots of indoor amenities. **Cons:** no pets allowed. $ *Rooms from:*

8

CLOSE UP

Best Campgrounds in Bryce Canyon

The two campgrounds in Bryce Canyon National Park fill up fast, especially in summer, and are family-friendly. All sites are drive-in, except for the handful of backcountry sites that only backpackers and gung-ho day hikers ever see. Both campgrounds completed a welcome renovation of their restrooms and shared facilities in 2012.

North Campground. A cool, shady retreat in a forest of ponderosa pines, this is a great home base for your

exploration of Bryce Canyon. You're near the general store (with laundry facilities and showers), trailheads, and the visitor center. Open year-round. ⊠ *Main park rd. ½ mile south of visitor center* ☎ *435/834–5322.*

Sunset Campground. This serene campground is within walking distance of Bryce Canyon Lodge and many trailheads. Open mid-April through mid-Oct. ⊠ *Main park rd., 2 miles south of visitor center* ☎ *435/834–5322.*

$169 ⊠ 30 N. 100 E, Bryce ☎ *866/866–6636, 435/834–5700* ⊕ *brycecanyongrand.com* ⊅ *164 rooms* ⏐◎⏐ *Breakfast.*

$$
HOTEL
⏺ **Best Western Plus Ruby's Inn.** As the park has grown more popular, so has Ruby's Inn, expanding over the years to include various wings with rooms that vary widely in terms of size and appeal but are consistently comfortable. **Pros:** a good place to mingle with other park visitors and swap canyon adventure stories. **Cons:** the lobby can get very busy, especially when the big tour buses roll in. ⓢ *Rooms from: $135 ⊠ 26 S. Main St., Bryce* ☎ *435/834–5341, 866/866–6616* ⊕ *www.rubysinn.com* ⊅ *370 rooms, 11 suites* ⏐◎⏐ *No meals.*

$
HOTEL
⏺ **Bryce View Lodge.** Right next to the park entrance, on Route 63, this motel is a good, reasonably priced option, with comfortable rooms and access to the pool and other amenities across the way at the Best Western Plus Ruby's Inn, its sister property. **Pros:** ideal location for park access; well-stocked general store. **Cons:** a bit dated inside and out. ⓢ *Rooms from: $88 ⊠ 105 E. Center St., Canyon City* ☎ *435/834–5180, 888/279–2304* ⊕ *www.bryceviewlodge.com* ⊅ *160 rooms* ⏐◎⏐ *No meals.*

SOUTHWESTERN
UTAH

Updated
by Amanda
Knoles

Towering cliffs, dramatic canyons, and awe-inspiring rock formations define much of this region's appeal, but as the seasons change stunning displays of wildflowers and breathtaking fall foliage add an artist's palate of colors to soften the landscape. Blanketed in snow in winter, it's perfect for cross-country skiing, snowmobiling, and holiday sleigh rides. The state's lowest point, Beaver Dam Wash is here, and the Pine Valley Mountains, north of the growing city of St. George are among the highest in Utah.

Such contrasts have always attracted the curious. Famed explorer John Wesley Powell charted the uncharted; the young idealist and dreamer Everett Reuss left his well-to-do family and lost himself without a trace in the canyons (though his bones are thought to have been found and identified in 2008); the author and curmudgeon Ed Abbey found himself, and has since been thought of, depending on who you ask, as either a voice crying in the wilderness or a pariah in Pahreah. But that's the beauty of this place, the joy of choice in a land that confronts and challenges. We come, ostensibly, to escape; yet we really come to discover.

Southwestern Utah is a land of adventure and contemplation, of adrenaline and retreat. It's not an either-or proposition; you rejuvenate whether soaking at a luxury spa or careening on a mountain bike down an alpine single-track headed straight for an aspen tree. The land settlers tamed for planting cotton and fruit is now a playground for golfers, bikers, and hikers. Arts festivals and concerts under canyon walls have smoothed the rough edges hewn by miners and the boomtowns that evaporated as quickly as they materialized. Ruins, petroglyphs, pioneer graffiti, and ghost towns—monuments to what once was—beckon new explorers. The region's secrets reveal themselves to seekers, yet some mysteries remain elusive—the paradox of the bustling world that lies hidden under the impression of spare, silent, and open space.

ORIENTATION AND PLANNING

GETTING ORIENTED

Southwestern Utah is remarkable in the range of activities and terrain it has to offer. On one summer day you can explore an arid desert canyon at Snow Canyon State Park, the next you can camp in a high-alpine aspen grove in Dixie National Forest and bundle up for warmth. In winter you can sample mountain biking (at Gooseberry Mesa near Hurricane) and skiing (at Brian Head Resort) on the same trip.

TOP REASONS TO GO

Go with the (lava) flow: As you hike along the lower trails of Snow Canyon State Park, look up to see ridges capped in lava from eruptions that may have happened as recently as 20,000 years ago.

Sit in a stagecoach: Imagine travel in pioneer days in the one restored stagecoach that visitors can hop aboard at Iron Mission State Park Museum.

Drive the Scenic Byway: The stretch of Highway 12 that begins at Escalante and passes through Grand Staircase-Escalante National

Monument and on to Capitol Reef National Park offers spectacular views along with some hair-raising twists and turns.

Pay your respects to the Bard: Watch productions such as *Othello* on a stage that replicates the old Globe Theatre during the Utah Shakespeare Festival.

Walk where dinosaurs stepped: The St. George Dinosaur Discovery Site at Johnson Farm would be developed real estate today if a backhoe hadn't unearthed ancient footprints in 2000.

Utah's Dixie. Many of southwestern Utah's Mormon settlers hailed from the American South and brought the name Dixie with them. St. George, the main population center in this area, is often the hottest place in the state.

Along U.S. 89—Utah's Heritage Highway. U.S. 89 is known as the Heritage Highway for its role in shaping Utah history. Many of the towns along this road provide quiet, uncrowded, and inexpensive places to stay near Zion and Bryce Canyon national parks.

Grand Staircase—Escalante National Monument. Three distinct sections define the 1.7 million acres of this region—the Grand Staircase, the Kaiparowits Plateau, and the Canyons of the Escalante. Here, among the waterfalls, Native American ruins and petroglyphs, and slot canyons, improbable colors abound.

9

PLANNING

WHEN TO GO

Year-round, far southwestern Utah is the warmest region in the state; St. George is usually the first city to break 100°F every year, and even the winters remain mild at lower desert elevations. Despite the heat, most people visit from June to September, making the off-season a pleasantly uncrowded experience for those willing and able to travel from fall to spring. Incidentally, Utahns from the north tend to stay away from the southern parts of the state during peak months for the very reasons—intense, dry heat and unyielding sun—that attract so many travelers from out of state. If you decide to brave the heat, wear sunscreen and drink lots of water, regardless of your activity level.

Farther east, around the Brian Head–Cedar Breaks National Monument area, elevations approach and surpass 9,000 feet, making for more temperamental weather, intermittent and seasonal road closures due

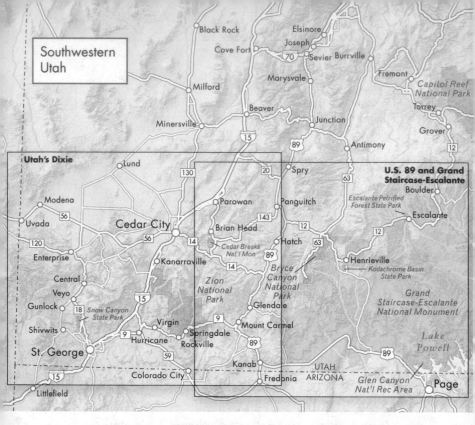

to snow, and downright cold nights well into June. At this altitude the warm summer sun is perfectly balanced by the coolness of the alpine forests during the day. Although the peak season at most locations is summer, it's a different story at Brian Head, where snow sports dominate; still, the resort has been pushing its summer recreation lineup of mountain biking and hiking, and the trails here are some of the finest in all of Utah.

PLANNING YOUR TIME

What brings you to Utah's southwest will determine how best to plan your time. If you're here for Zion National Park and only have a few days, for example, you might choose to forego visiting Cedar City or St. George. No matter which part you visit, however, driving time will take up a fair number of your hours. Zion National Park and Grand Staircase–Escalante experiences are more outdoorsy and potentially exerting than ambling about on St. George's downtown walking tour or attending a Shakespeare play in Cedar City. No one town is a convenient base for exploring the entire region. For Zion National Park, choose Springdale or Hurricane; for St. George or Cedar City, the cities themselves are the best bases of exploration.

GETTING HERE AND AROUND
AIR TRAVEL
SkyWest flies to St. George Municipal Airport, and operates as a carrier for both United Express and Delta Connection flights. Las Vegas's McCarran International Airport is 116 miles from St. George, and the St. George Shuttle makes nine trips a day between the two. Aztec Shuttle provides round-trip service from Salt Lake City, with stops in St. George and Cedar City. Reservations are required.

Airport Contacts McCarran International Airport ⊠ *5757 Wayne Newton Blvd., Las Vegas, Nevada* ☎ *702/261–5211* ⊕ *www.mccarran.com.* **St. George Municipal Airport** ⊠ *4550 S. Airport Way, St. George* ☎ *435/627–4080* ⊕ *www. flysgu.com.*

Airport Shuttle Aztec Shuttle. ⊠ *St. George* ☎ *435/656–9040* ⊕ *www. aztecshuttle.com.* **St. George Shuttle** ⊠ *1275 E. Redhills Pkwy., St. George* ☎ *435/628–8320, 800/933–8320* ⊕ *www.stgshuttle.com.*

CAR TRAVEL
I–15 is the main route into southwestern Utah from Las Vegas to the southwest and Salt Lake City to the northeast. Farther east, U.S. 89 is a more scenic north–south route with access to Bryce Canyon National Park, the east side of Zion National Park, and the Kanab area. Highways 143 and 14 are the main east–west connecting routes.

Highway 9 is the primary access to Springdale and Zion National Park. ■ TIP➔ **If you need to travel between I-15 and U.S. 89 via Route 9 during the day, you must pay the $25 admission fee to Zion National Park even if you do not plan to stop and visit.** Access to the massive and remote Grand Staircase–Escalante National Monument is via Highway 12 to the north and U.S. 89 to the south.

In winter the primary access roads to Brian Head and Cedar Breaks National Monument may be closed for snow removal (Highway 143 from the north and east) or for the season (Highway 148 from the south). Call the Cedar City office of the Utah Department of Transportation at ☎ *866/511–8824* for current road conditions.

RESTAURANTS
In the southwestern corner of the state, reflecting the pioneer heritage of the region, traditional and contemporary American cuisines are most common, followed closely by those with Mexican and Southwestern influences. St. George and Springdale have the greatest number and diversity of dining options. Around St. George there are a number of restaurants that serve seafood; keep in mind that at nicer restaurants the fish is flown in daily from the West Coast; at the less expensive locales the fish is usually frozen. Because this is conservative Utah, don't presume a restaurant serves beer, much less wine or cocktails, especially in the smaller towns, and don't be surprised if you are carded no matter what your age. Most restaurants are family-friendly, and dress tends to be casual.

9

HOTELS

Southwestern Utah is steeped in pioneer heritage, and you'll find many older homes that have been refurbished as bed-and-breakfasts. Green Gate Village in St. George, a collection of pioneer homes gathered from around the state, is an excellent example. The area also has its share of older independent motels in some of the smaller towns. Most major hotel and motel chains have at least one facility in the region. With the exception of Brian Head, high season is summer, and logic dictates that the closer you want to be to a major attraction, the earlier you have to make reservations. If you are willing to stay upward of an hour from your destination, perhaps with fewer amenities, you may get same-day reservations and much lower room rates. Panguitch has a number of no-frills motels for budget and last-minute travelers. The Utah Office of Tourism website has information on lodging and amenities in the southwestern part of the state. *Hotel reviews have been shortened. For full information, visit Fodors.com.*

WHAT IT COSTS			
	$	$$	$$$	$$$$
Restaurants	under $12	$12–$20	$21–$30	over $30
Hotels	under $100	$100–$150	$151–$200	over $200

Restaurant prices are the average cost of a main course at dinner or, if dinner is not served, at lunch. Hotel prices are the lowest cost of a standard double room in high season.

VISITOR INFORMATION

Contacts Utah Office of Tourism ⊠ *300 N. State St., Salt Lake City* ☎ *800/200–1160* ⊕ *www.visitutah.com.*

UTAH'S DIXIE

Mormon pioneers from the American South settled this part of Utah to grow cotton, and they brought the name Dixie with them. Some thought the move was a gamble, but the success of the settlement may be measured in the region's modern-day definition of risk: hopping the border to nearby Mesquite, Nevada, to roll the dice. St. George is often the hottest place in the state, but the Pine Valley Mountains and Brian Head offer alpine relief and summer recreation.

CEDAR CITY

250 miles southwest of Salt Lake City.

Rich iron-ore deposits here grabbed Mormon leader Brigham Young's attention, and he ordered a Church of Jesus Christ of Latter-day Saints (LDS) mission established. The first ironworks and foundry opened in 1851 and operated for only eight years; problems with the furnace, flooding, and hostility between settlers and Native Americans eventually put out the flame. Residents then turned to ranching and agriculture for their livelihood, and Cedar City thrived thereafter.

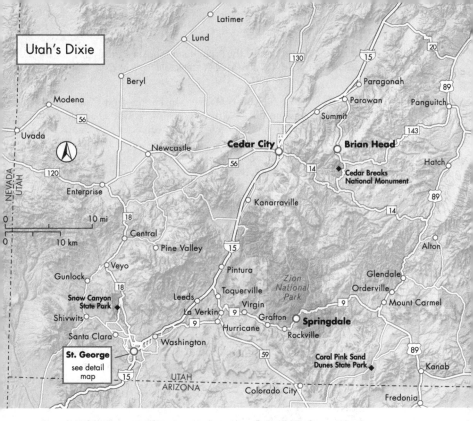

The Southern Utah University campus hosts the city's major event, the Utah Shakespeare Festival, with a season that gets longer as its reputation grows. Though better known for festivals than recreation, the city is well placed for exploring the Brian Head area.

GETTING HERE AND AROUND

Cedar City is off I–15, Utah's major north-south interstate. Travelers coming from the Brian Head area use the scenic Highway 14, winding down from Cedar Canyon into downtown. Though downtown is walkable, you might want your car for getting around.

FESTIVALS

Fodor's Choice **Utah Shakespeare Festival.** For more than 50 years Cedar City has gone
★ Bard-crazy, staging productions of Shakespeare's plays June through October in theaters both indoors and outdoors at Southern Utah University. The Tony award–winning regional theater offers literary seminars, backstage tours, cabaret featuring festival actors, and an outdoor preshow with Elizabethan performers. The outdoor theater is a replica of the original Globe Theatre from Shakespeare's time and showcases Shakespearian plays during the festival. Reserve well in advance as tickets sell out quickly. ☎ 435/586–7878 ⊕ www.bard.org.

ESSENTIALS

Visitor Information Cedar City/Brian Head Tourism Bureau ✉ 581 N. Main St. ☏ 800/354–4849, 435/586–5124 ⊕ scenicsouthernutah.com.

EXPLORING

Daughters of the Utah Pioneers Museum. Inside the Iron County Visitor Center, this museum displays pioneer artifacts such as an old treadle sewing machine, an antique four-poster bed, and photographs of old Cedar City and its inhabitants. ✉ 581 N. Main St. ☏ 435/586–8269 ▣ Free ⊙ Weekdays 9–5.

Frontier Homestead State Park Museum. Created as a memorial to the county's iron-industry heritage, this local attraction allows visitors to explore the bullet-scarred stagecoach that ran in the days of Butch Cassidy, plus tools and other mining artifacts. A log cabin built in 1851—the oldest standing home in southern Utah—and a collection of wagon wheels and farm equipment are displayed outside. Local artisans demonstrate pioneer crafts. ✉ 585 N. Main St. ☏ 435/586–9290 ⊕ www.frontier homestead.org ▣ $3 ⊙ Mon.–Sat. 9–5.

SPORTS AND THE OUTDOORS

Dixie National Forest. The forest's expansive natural area is divided into four noncontiguous swaths covering a total of two million acres. Adjacent to three national parks, two national monuments, and several state parks, the forest has 26 campgrounds in a variety of backdrops: lakeside, mountainside, in the depths of pine and spruce forests. Recreational opportunities abound, including hiking, picnicking, horseback riding, and fishing. ✉ Dixie National Forest Headquarters, 1789 N. Wedgewood La. ☏ 435/865–3700 ⊕ www.fs.usda.gov/dixie ▣ Free.

HIKING

Southern Utah Scenic Tours. Experienced tour guides accompany visitors on all-day tours to some of southern Utah's most popular destinations. Day trips include the ATV Slot Canyons Tour, a fun journey that combines riding ATVs and hiking through scenic terrain. Multi-day trips like the Mighty Five take visitors to Utah's five national parks, with transportation, lodging, and some meals included. For shorter tours you can create your own custom itinerary or join a tour group. Day trips include hotel pickup and drop-off in St. George or Cedar City, park entrance fees, bottled water, and snacks. ☏ 435/656–1504, 888/404–8687 ⊕ www.utahscenictours.com ▣ ATV Slot Canyons Tour $310; Mighty Five $1,595; call for prices of other tours.

WHERE TO EAT

$$
ITALIAN
Fodor'sChoice
★

✕ **Centro Woodfired Pizzeria.** You can watch your handmade thin-crust pizza being pulled from the fires of the brick oven, then sit back and enjoy a seasonal pie layered with locally grown figs, prosciutto, and Asiago cheese, or try year-round selections featuring roasted cremini mushrooms or Italian soppressata salami. The creamy vanilla gelato layered with a balsamic reduction and sea salt can actually be addictive. Wine and beer selections are offered as well. $ Average main: $12 ✉ 50 W. University Blvd. ☏ 435/867–8123 ⚘ Reservations not accepted ⊙ Closed Sun.

$$$
ITALIAN
✗**Chef Alfredo Italiano Ristorante.** With linen tablecloths, a decent wine list and soft music playing in the background, this Sicilian-style restaurant, tucked away in a strip mall, may be the closest you'll get to fine dining in Cedar City. The menu features traditional antipasto appetizers and specials like butternut ravioli or eggplant Parmesan. You can choose from favorites including linguini and clam sauce, or signature dishes like chicken parmigiana and fettuccini primavera. Fresh-baked bread is served with olive oil. Dessert options include made-on-the-premises tiramisu, cannoli, and several varieties of cheesecake. $ *Average main: $25* ✉ *2313 W. Hwy. 56* ☎ *435/586–2693* ⊕ *www.chefalfredos.com* ◷ *No lunch Sun.*

$$$
STEAKHOUSE
Fodor'sChoice
★
✗**Milt's Stage Stop.** Locals and an increasing number of tourists have discovered the lodge-like surroundings, friendly service, and spectacular canyon views at this dinner spot a 10-minute drive from Cedar City. It's known for hearty steak-house cuisine: rib-eye steaks, prime rib, seafood dishes, and a bountiful salad bar, accompanied by loaded baked potatoes or other sides. Hunting trophies decorate the log cabin–style interior, and in winter deer feed outside while logs blaze away in the big stone fireplace inside. ■**TIP➔ Don't miss the raspberry or cherry cheesecake.** $ *Average main: $25* ✉ *3560 E. Hwy. 14* ☎ *435/586–9344* ⊕ *miltsstagestop.com* ⌑ *Reservations essential* ◷ *No lunch.*

$
CAFÉ
FAMILY
✗**The Pastry Pub.** Don't be fooled by the name—coffee and tea are the only brews here, and pastries aren't the only things on the menu. Build a sandwich of meat, egg, cheese, and more on a freshly baked bagel, croissant, artisanal bread, or one of four flavors of wraps. For dinner, chicken, steak, quesadilla, and tostada are added to the menu. Enjoy your meal in the spacious dining room or have fun people-watching on the outdoor patio. ■**TIP➔ Festival goers, take note: This is the best bet for a late-night bite after the show.** $ *Average main: $8* ✉ *86 W. Center St.* ☎ *435/867–1400* ⊕ *www.cedarcitypastrypub.com* ◷ *Closed Sun.*

WHERE TO STAY

$$$
B&B/INN
Fodor'sChoice
★
🛏**Amid Summer's Inn Bed & Breakfast.** The individually styled rooms at this cozy B&B feature historical themes—think designer, not Disney—with rich color-coordinated fabrics and fine paintings and other works of art. **Pros:** innkeepers bend over backwards to make your stay memorable; many repeat customers attest to quality; minutes from downtown. **Cons:** some rooms are accessible only by a narrow stairway; may be too intimate for some. $ *Rooms from: $165* ✉ *140 S. 100 W* ☎ *435/586–2600, 888/586–2601* ⊕ *www.amidsummersinn.com* ⮌ *9 rooms, 1 suite* ⦿ *Breakfast.*

$$
B&B/INN
🛏**Bard's Inn Bed and Breakfast.** Rooms in this restored turn-of-the-20th-century house are named after famous females from Shakespeare's plays, and handcrafted quilts grace the beds. **Pros:** immaculate rooms; good restaurant next door; enforced quiet at night. **Cons:** thin walls and creaky floors; books up fast for festival season. $ *Rooms from: $109* ✉ *150 S. 100 W* ☎ *435/586–6612* ⊕ *thebardsinn.com* ⮌ *8 rooms* ◷ *Closed Sept.–May* ⦿ *Breakfast.*

$$
HOTEL
🛏**Best Western Town & Country Inn.** In downtown Cedar City, this renovated motel offers spacious rooms, complimentary breakfast, a fitness center, and two on-site eateries. **Pros:** convenient to shops and restaurants; nice

9

pool. **Cons:** breakfast gets mixed reviews; Wi-Fi reception can be spotty. $ *Rooms from: $119* ⊠ *189 N. Main St.* ☎ *435/586–9900* ⊕ *www. bwtowncountry.com* ⊅ *128 rooms, 17 suites* ⦿ *Breakfast.*

$$
HOTEL

🏨 **Springhill Suites by Marriott Cedar City.** Close to Brian Head ski resort, Bryce Canyon, and Zion, and convenient for downtown shops and eateries, this upscale hotel features spacious suites with contemporary style. **Pros:** close to parks; breakfast included. **Cons:** not within walking distance of downtown. $ *Rooms from: $150* ⊠ *1477 S. Old Hwy. 91* ☎ *435/586–1685* ⊕ *www.marriott.com/hotels/travel/cdcsh-springhill-suites-cedarcity* ⊅ *72 suites* ⦿ *Breakfast.*

BRIAN HEAD

29 miles northeast of Cedar City.

Brian Head Resort is Utah's southernmost and highest ski area, at well over 9,000 feet, but the area's summer recreation, especially mountain biking, has been developed energetically. There are now more than 200 miles of trails for bikers, many of which are served by chairlift or shuttle services. The bright red-orange rock formations of Cedar Breaks Monument are several miles south of town.

The snow season is still the high season here, so book winter lodging in advance and expect high room rates. Food prices are high year-round. The fall "mud season" (October to November) and spring "slush season" (April to May) shut down some area businesses.

GETTING HERE AND AROUND

From Cedar City, take Highway 14 east then highways 143 and 148 north, but whichever way you arrive, the drive into Brian Head is scenic. The town isn't large, but the layout doesn't encourage walking. Come winter, snow closes highways 143 and 148 from the south.

EXPLORING

Cedar Breaks National Monument. From the rim of Cedar Breaks, 23 miles east of Cedar City, a natural amphitheater plunges 2,000 feet into the Markagunt Plateau. Short hiking trails along the rim make this a wonderful summer stop. ⊠ *Hwy. 14* ☎ *435/586–0787* ⊕ *nps.gov/cebr* ☒ *$4* ⊙ *Visitor center open late May–mid-Oct., daily 9–6.*

SPORTS AND THE OUTDOORS
BICYCLING

Brian Head is a good place to base mountain-biking excursions. The area's most popular ride is the 12-mile **Bunker Creek Trail,** which winds through forests and meadows to Panguitch Lake. Brian Head Resort runs one of its ski lifts in summer, giving access to several mountain-bike trails, and Brianhead Sports, among others, shuttles riders to other trails at the resort. Five miles south of Brian Head, road cyclists can explore Cedar Breaks National Monument and vicinity.

SKIING AND SNOWBOARDING

Brian Head Ski Resort. Eight lifts, including a new high-speed, detachable quad chairlift, transport skiers to trails covering more than 650 acres of terrain, starting at a base elevation of 9,600 feet. Expert skiers head for the 11,300-foot summit of Brian Head Peak for access to more-challenging runs. A half-pipe, trails, and terrain park attract hordes of snowboarders. From the top you can see the red-rock cliffs of Cedar Breaks National Monument to the southwest. During summer and fall the resort is a favorite with mountain biking enthusiasts. ✉ *329 S. Hwy. 143* ☎ *866/930–1010* ⊕ *www.brianhead.com* 🎫 *Lift tickets $49* ⊙ *Mid Nov.–mid Apr., daily 9:30–4:30.*

Brian Head Sports. The largest outfitter in town caters to cyclists, skiers, and snowboarders with equipment and accessories for rent or purchase. The store runs a mountain-bike shuttle that's handy for riding area trails that end far from where they start. ✉ *269 S. Village Way* ☎ *435/677–2014* ⊕ *www.brianheadsports.com.*

Georg's Ski Shop and Bikes. Just down the road from Brian Head Resort, this popular ski shop has new and rental skis, snowboards, and bikes. The friendly staff is experienced at helping both beginning and advanced skiers find the perfect gear. ✉ *612 S. Hwy. 143* ☎ *435/677–2013* ⊕ *www.georgsskishop.com.*

WHERE TO EAT AND STAY

$$$
STEAKHOUSE

✕ **Double Black Diamond Steak House.** Pecan-crusted trout and rib-eye steaks are favorites at this elegant yet relaxed steak and seafood restaurant in Cedar Breaks Lodge, but you'll also find fish-and-chips and a variety of tempting appetizers on the menu. Desserts range from cheesecake and crème brûlée to decadent chocolate cake. Low lights, a crackling fire, and the clink of wineglasses set an upscale mood, but there's no need to dress up. Reservations are not essential but recommended. 💲 *Average main: $28* ✉ *223 Hunter Ridge Rd.* ☎ *435/677–4242* ⊕ *www.cedarbreakslodge.com* ⊙ *Closed Mon.–Wed. No lunch.*

$$
AMERICAN

✕ **The Lift Bar and Grill.** Within the Grand Lodge Resort, this upscale bar and grill features expansive views of the mountains and an eclectic menu of contemporary entrées. With a rustic lodge feel, it features stone fireplaces and floor-to-ceiling windows to maximize the views, and the bar attracts a steady local clientele as well as resort guests. You can't go wrong with the smoked cheddar bacon burger, but try the rosemary lemon chicken wings to stimulate your taste buds. The outdoor patio with gas-powered fire pits is a great spot to enjoy one of the creative cocktails. 💲 *Average main: $16* ✉ *314 Hunter Ridge Rd.* ☎ *435/677–9000* ⊕ *www.grandlodgeatbrianhead.com.*

$$
RESORT

🛏 **Cedar Breaks Lodge & Spa.** At the north end of town at an altitude of 9,600 feet, this lodge-style resort offers scenic views. **Pros:** scenic location with easy access to skiing, hiking, and mountain biking. **Cons:** early checkout; noisy parking lot; food gets mixed reviews. 💲 *Rooms from: $150* ✉ *223 Hunter Ridge Rd.* ☎ *435/677–3000, 888/282–3327* ⊕ *www.cedarbreakslodge.com* ⬎ *118* 🍴 *No meals.*

$$$
RESORT

🛏 **Grand Lodge at Brian Head.** This modern resort amid stunning mountain scenery is in a great location for skiing and snowmobiling in winter or mountain biking, hiking, and fishing in summer. **Pros:** modern comforts in a mountain setting; spa; every room has a view. **Cons:** a bit pricey; breakfast included only with certain packages; on-site restaurant has mixed reviews. 💲 *Rooms from: $200* ✉ *314 Hunter Ridge Rd.* ☎ *435/677–9000* ⊕ *www.grandlodgebrianhead.com* ⬎ *88 rooms, 12 suites* 🍴 *Multiple meal plans.*

9

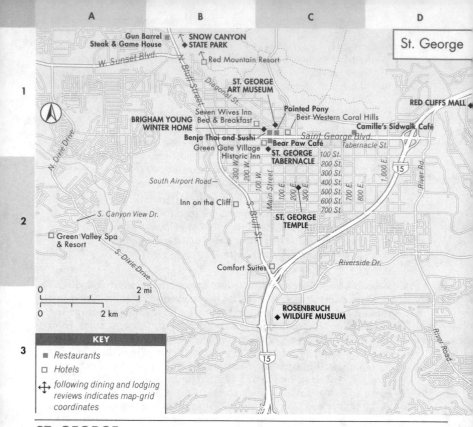

St. George

Gun Barrel Steak & Game House
SNOW CANYON STATE PARK
W. Sunset Blvd.
Red Mountain Resort
ST. GEORGE ART MUSEUM
RED CLIFFS MALL
Seven Wives Inn Bed & Breakfast
Painted Pony
Best Western Coral Hills
BRIGHAM YOUNG WINTER HOME
Camille's Sidewalk Café
Benja Thai and Sushi
Saint George Blvd.
Green Gate Village Historic Inn
Bear Paw Café
Tabernacle St.
ST. GEORGE TABERNACLE
100 St.
200 St.
South Airport Road
300 St.
400 St.
500 St.
Inn on the Cliff
600 St.
700 St.
S. Canyon View Dr.
ST. GEORGE TEMPLE
Green Valley Spa & Resort
Comfort Suites
Riverside Dr.
ROSENBRUCH WILDLIFE MUSEUM

0   2 mi
0   2 km

KEY
■ Restaurants
□ Hotels
⬥ following dining and lodging reviews indicates map-grid coordinates

ST. GEORGE

50 miles southwest of Cedar City.

Believing the mild year-round climate ideal for growing cotton, Brigham Young dispatched 309 LDS families in 1861 to found St. George. They were to raise cotton and silkworms and to establish a textile industry, to make up for textile shortages resulting from the Civil War. The area was subsequently dubbed "Utah's Dixie," a name that stuck even after the war ended and the "other" South could once again provide cotton to Utah. The settlers—many of them originally from southern states—found the desert climate preferable to northern Utah's snow, and they remained as farmers and ranchers. Crops included fruit, molasses, and grapes for wine that the pioneers sold to nearby mining communities. St. Georgians now number approximately 75,000, many of whom are retirees attracted by the hot, dry climate and the numerous golf courses. But historic Ancestor Square, the city's many well-preserved, original pioneer and Mormon structures, and a growing shopping district make St. George a popular destination for families, as well. Walking tours are set up by the St. George Area Convention and Visitors Bureau.

GETTING HERE AND AROUND

This burgeoning city is easily reached via I–15 from north and south. Unless your hotel is downtown, it's best to get around by car.

FESTIVALS

St. George Arts Festival. Artisan booths, food, children's activities, and entertainment, including cowboy poets, are all part of this annual festival held at Town Square on the Friday and Saturday of Easter weekend. ☎ 435/627–4500 ⊕ *www.sgcity.org.*

St. George Winter Bird Festival. Bird-watchers gather in St. George every January to peep at the nearly 400 feathered species. After a Thursday-night kickoff event, join in two full days of field trips, exhibits, lectures, and activities. ✉ *1851 S. Dixie Dr.* ☎ *435/627–4560* ⊕ *www.sgcity.org/ departments/recreation/birdfestival/* ✉ *$10.*

ESSENTIALS

St. George Area Convention & Visitors Bureau ✉ *1835 Convention Center Dr.* ☎ *800/869–6635* ⊕ *www.visitstgeorge.com.*

EXPLORING

TOP ATTRACTIONS

Brigham Young Winter Home. Mormon leader Brigham Young spent the last five winters of his life in the warm, sunny climate of St. George. Built of adobe on a sandstone-and-basalt foundation, Young's winter home has been restored to its original condition. A portrait of Young hangs over one fireplace, and authentic furnishings from the late-19th-century time period have been donated by supporters. Guided tours are available. ✉ *67 W. 200 N* ☎ *435/673–2517* ⊕ *www.lds.church.org/ locations/brigham-young-winter-home* ✉ *Free* ☉ *Daily 9–dusk.*

FAMILY **Rosenbruch Wildlife Museum.** This modern 35,000-square-foot facility displays more than 300 species of wildlife created using fiberglass or foam forms and real skin and fur. The animals are displayed in representations of their native habitat—including Africa, the Arctic, Asia, Australia, Europe, and North America. Two waterfalls cascade from a two-story mountain, and hidden speakers provide ambient wildlife and nature sounds. Before your tour, check out the children's interactive area, and don't miss the art gallery and video theater. ✉ *1835 Convention Center Dr.* ☎ *435/656–0033* ⊕ *www.rosenbruch.org* ✉ *$8* ☉ *Mon. 10–8, Tues.–Sat. 10–6.*

St. George Art Museum. Spend a few quiet hours out of the Dixie sun at this museum. The permanent collection celebrates local potters, photographers, painters, and more. Special exhibits highlight local history. ✉ *47 E. 200 N* ☎ *435/627–4525* ⊕ *www.sgartmuseum.org* ✉ *$3* ☉ *Mon.–Sat. 10–5 (to 9 on 3rd Thurs.).*

St. George Temple. The red-sandstone temple, plastered over with white stucco, was completed in 1877 and served as a meeting place for both Mormons and other congregations. Today, only Mormons can enter the temple, but a visitor center next door offers guided tours. ✉ *250 E. 400 S* ☎ *435/673–5181* ⊕ *www.lds.org/locations/st-george-utah-temple-visitors-center* ✉ *Free* ☉ *Visitor center daily 9–9.*

Snow Canyon State Park. Named not for winter weather but after a pair of pioneering Utahns named Snow, this overlooked gem of a state park is filled with natural wonders. Hiking trails lead to lava cones, sand dunes, cactus gardens, and high-contrast vistas. From the campground you can scramble up huge sandstone mounds and overlook the entire valley. Park staff lead occasional guided hikes. The park is about 10 miles northwest of St. George, and about an hour from Zion. ✉ *1002 Snow Canyon Dr., Ivins* ☎ *435/628–2255* ⊕ *www.stateparks.utah.gov* ⌨ *$6 per vehicle* ⊙ *Daily 6 am–10 pm.*

WORTH NOTING

FAMILY **St. George Dinosaur Discovery Site at Johnson Farm.** Unearthed 15 years ago by property developers, this site allows visitors to view the ancient footprints left by dinosaurs from the Jurassic period, millions of years ago. Fossils unearthed at the site are also on display, accurate replicas portray the creatures that left these tantalizing remains, and themed displays cover many aspects of the Jurassic era. There's an interactive area for children and a Dino Park is being developed outside the museum. ✉ *2180 E. Riverside Dr.* ☎ *435/574–3466* ⊕ *www.dinosite.org* ⌨ *$6* ⊙ *Mar.–Sept., Mon.–Sat. 10–6, Sun. 11–5; Oct.–Feb., Mon.–Sat. 10–5.*

St. George Tabernacle. This is one of the best-preserved pioneer buildings in the entire state, and is still used for public meetings and programs for the entire community. Mormon settlers began work on the tabernacle in June 1863, a few months after the city of St. George was established. Upon completion of the sandstone building's 140-foot clock tower 13 years later, Brigham Young formally dedicated the site. ✉ *18 S. Main St.* ☎ *435/628–4072* ⊙ *Daily 9–dusk.*

SPORTS AND THE OUTDOORS
BICYCLING
Bicycles Unlimited. A trusted resource on mountain biking in southern Utah, this bike shop rents bikes and sells parts, accessories, and guidebooks. ✉ *90 S. 100 E* ☎ *888/673–4492* ⊕ *bicyclesunlimited.com* ⊙ *Mon.–Sat. 9–6.*

GOLF
Dixie Red Hills Golf Club. Well known as the first golf club developed by the city, this popular course in the heart of St. George has been a favorite of golfers in southern Utah for more than 40 years. Featuring stunning views of red cliffs, the 9-hole course has gorgeous greens surrounded by cottonwood, pine, and other trees, providing welcome shade in the hotter months. It's an easily walkable course that's perfect for beginners, seniors, and those seeking a short round. ✉ *645 W. 1250 N* ☎ *435/627–4444* ⊕ *www.stgeorgecitygolf.com/dixieredhills.php* ⌨ *$21 for 9 holes, $7 per rider for cart* ⚑ *9 holes, 2775 yards, par 34.*

St. George Golf Club. A favorite of local golfers for more than 30 years, this municipal course has a more traditional feel, with straight fairways offering average golfers a chance to make putts at longer distances. With its open-course layout, it's very walkable. The unique design includes several par-3 water challenges as the course winds past the Fort Pearce wash and a peninsula that hosts the 9th and 18th greens. ✉ *2190 S. 1400 E* ☎ *435/627–4404* ⊕ *www.stgeorgecitygolf.com/stgeorge.php* ⌨ *$33 for 18 holes, $21 for 9 holes; $7 for golf cart per rider per 9 holes* ⚑ *18 holes, 7238 yards, par 73.*

Southgate Golf Club. Featuring greens that wind around the Santa Clara River and gorgeous views of the hillsides surrounding the city, this 18-hole public course is fun for all levels, but also provides plenty of challenges. On the front nine water hazards from the lake and river frequently come into play. It's testing without being too intimidating. ✉ *1975 Tonaquint Dr.* ☎ *435/627–4440* 🌐 *www.stgeorgecitygolf.com/southgate.php* 🎫 *$33 for 18 holes; $7 for golf cart per rider per 9 holes* ⛳ *18 holes, 6321 yards, par 71.*

Sunbrook Golf Club. With three separate courses featuring 27 championship holes, this golf club was rated one of the top-50 municipal courses in the country, and it will test every skill level. The 5th hole at the Pointe looks easy until golfers realize it's a par four right next to a desert cliff. The Woodbridge course is known for its 5th hole offering scenic lake views and ample chances for a bogey. Black Rock Nine has three holes carved from lava rock, with the par four 7th being one to watch out for. ✉ *2366 W. Sunbrook Dr.* ☎ *435/627–4400* 🌐 *www.stgeorgecitygolf.com/sunbrook.php* 🎫 *$56 for 18 holes, $32 for 9 holes* ⛳ *The Pointe: 9 holes, 3397 yards, par 37; Woodbridge: 9 holes, 3691 yards, par 36; Black Rock Nine: 9 holes, 3384 yards, par 36.*

HIKING

Snow Canyon State Park. This park, 8 miles northwest of St. George off Highway 18, has several short trails and lots of small desert canyons to explore. ☎ *435/628–2255* 🌐 *www.stateparks.utah.gov.*

HORSE RACING AND RODEO

Dixie Downs Horse Races. For more than 40 years, two Saturdays in April are reserved for quarter-horse racing at the Washington County Fair Grounds in Hurricane. ☎ *435/632–2136* 🌐 *stgeorgelions.com.*

Dixie Roundup. This annual rodeo has been a tradition for more than 80 years. Held over three days in mid-September, the event includes both young mutton busters and professional bull riders, and is held in the evenings on the green grass of Sun Bowl Stadium. ☎ *435/632–2136* 🌐 *stgeorgelions.com* 🎫 *$10.*

9

WHERE TO EAT

Use the coordinates (✥ A1) at the end of each listing to locate a site on the corresponding map.

$ AMERICAN Fodor's Choice ★

🍴 **Bear Paw Café.** Prepare to wait for a table on busy weekend mornings, but it's worth it at this cozy Western-theme diner where the French toast is nearly two inches thick, flavorful crepes come in choices such as cherries jubilee or spiced apple, and the waffles are legendary. The lunch menu includes the Bear Paw Two-Story Club, panini sandwiches, and a variety of salads. For dessert, try the Forgotten Baked Apple, an apple dumpling stuffed with cranberries and baked to perfection. The long, long list of beverages includes dozens of specialty teas and coffee blends, juices, smoothies, and sodas. Breakfast service starts at 7 am; lunch is served until 3. [$] *Average main: $9* ✉ *75 N. Main St.* ☎ *435/634–0126* 🌐 *bearpawcafe.com* ⏲ *No dinner* ✥ *C1.*

$$ THAI

🍴 **Benja Thai and Sushi.** In St. George's charming Ancestor Square, you can dine on exotic Thai soups, salads, and specialty dishes, and choose from an extensive sushi menu. The room's tapestries, intricate wood carvings, and lilting music give it a warmth and tranquillity, and large windows provide views of the landscaped courtyard dotted with quaint historic buildings. $ *Average main: $12* ⊠ *2 W. St. George Blvd.* ☎ *435/628–9538* ⊕ *benjathai.com* ◷ *No lunch Sun.* ✛ *C1.*

$

CAFÉ

FAMILY

✕ **Camille's Sidewalk Café.** This charming café offers a variety of healthy breakfast and lunch choices that you can enjoy at cozy tables inside or on the covered patio. Decorated in beach-inspired style, the popular eatery offers an extensive menu of fresh fruit smoothies, artisanal flatbread pizzas, breakfast sandwiches, gourmet wraps, paninis, and salads. The prices are quite reasonable and the fresh-tasting fare will make you happy you passed on the fast-food chains down the street. $ *Average main: $8* ⊠ *661 E. St. George Blvd.* ☎ *435/767–9727* ⊕ *www.camillesutah.com* ◷ *Closed Sun.* ✛ *C1.*

$$$

AMERICAN

✕ **Gun Barrel Steak & Game House.** With an interior inspired by the Wyoming Wildlife and Taxidermy Museum and dotted with unique artifacts, you'll feel as if you're dining in the Old West at this family-owned restaurant, known for hearty steaks and wild game. There's an impressive stone fireplace, tabletops made from railroad trestles, and an open grill so you can view your dinner being cooked over mesquite wood. Specialties include buffalo and elk steaks, but there's a variety of chicken and seafood choices. Try the chocolate chip cookie skillet topped with ice cream, chocolate sauce, and whipped cream for dessert. $ *Average main: $25* ⊠ *1091 N. Bluff St.* ☎ *435/652–0550* ⊕ *www.gunbarrelutah.com* ◷ *Closed Sun. No lunch* ✛ *B1.*

$$$

AMERICAN

Fodor'sChoice

★

✕ **Painted Pony.** Shaded patio dining and contemporary Southwestern art on the walls provide a romantic setting in which to savor the creative meals. The focus is on fresh ingredients, many from the owners' organic garden, and the wine list is arguably the best in St. George. Try the duck with apple stuffing or prosciutto-wrapped free-range chicken. Standout sides include sweet cornbread pudding, herb-whipped potatoes, and Parmesan-crusted asparagus. White-chocolate banana-nut bread pudding is among the delicious desserts. $ *Average main: $28* ⊠ *2 W. St. George Blvd.* ☎ *435/634–1700* ⊕ *www.painted-pony.com* ◷ *No lunch Sun.* ✛ *C1.*

WHERE TO STAY

Use the coordinates (✛ A1) at the end of each listing to locate a site on the corresponding map.

$$

HOTEL

Best Western Coral Hills. If you're looking for a downtown location, this attractive two-story hotel gets you close to the Convention Center, Dixie State University, the Tuacahn Amphitheater, and several restaurants. **Pros:** family suites; amid downtown attractions and walking tours; breakfast included; 19 restaurants nearby. **Cons:** rooms near the road and the indoor pool can suffer some noise. $ *Rooms from: $100* ⊠ *125 E. St. George Blvd.* ☎ *435/673–4844, 800/542–7733* ⊕ *www.coralhills.com* ➥ *95 rooms, 3 suites* ⦿ *Breakfast* ✛ *C1.*

$$$

B&B/INN

Green Gate Village Historic Inn. For a truly unique experience, you can book a room or an entire home in this 1860s village, where fully restored pioneer homes are furnished with antiques combined with modern amenities. **Pros:** authentic historic properties; close to downtown; hot breakfast included. **Cons:** village setting may limit privacy; might not suit active young children. $ *Rooms from: $159* ⊠ *76 W. Tabernacle*

St. ☎ *435/628–6999, 800/350–6999* 🌐 *www.greengatevillageinn.com* 🛏 *4 rooms, 10 suites* 🍴 *Breakfast* ✣ *C1.*

$$$ RESORT 🏨 **Green Valley Spa & Resort.** Minutes from downtown but in a world of its own, this serene, luxurious resort and spa has been ranked one of America's best midsize spas. **Pros:** park-like pool and garden area; full gym plus numerous activities. **Cons:** adult-oriented setting wouldn't suit families; resort fees are charged. [$] *Rooms from: $179* ✉ *1871 W. Canyon View Dr.* ☎ *435/628–8060, 800/237–1068* 🌐 *www.greenvalleyspa.com* 🛏 *50 suites* 🍴 *Multiple meal plans* ✣ *A2.*

$$ HOTEL 🏨 **Inn on the Cliff.** This modern boutique hotel features panoramic views of St. George, spacious accommodations, and attentive service. **Pros:** high quality at an affordable price; stunning views. **Cons:** boxed Continental breakfast delivered to your room; can't walk to downtown. [$] *Rooms from: $138* ✉ *511 S. Airport Rd.* ☎ *435/216–5864* 🌐 *www.innonthecliff.com* 🛏 *27 rooms* 🍴 *Breakfast* ✣ *B2.*

$$$$ RESORT Fodor's Choice ★ 🏨 **Red Mountain Resort.** One of Fodor's Top Fitness and Wellness Resorts for 2014, this luxury retreat in stunning surroundings near the mouth of Snow Canyon offers a range of outdoor adventures and fitness packages for the body and mind. **Pros:** down-to-earth spa experience with activities suited to all levels of fitness; packages are among the least expensive among fitness resorts; rate includes meals and spa/fitness facilities; pet-friendly. **Cons:** you might feel guilty if you don't wake up at dawn to hit the gym or the trails. [$] *Rooms from: $215* ✉ *1275 E. Red Mountain Circle, Ivins* ☎ *435/673–4905, 877/246–4453* 🌐 *www.redmountainresort.com* 🛏 *82 rooms, 24 villa suites* ⏲ *7 miles northwest of St. George* 🍴 *All meals* ✣ *B1.*

$$$ B&B/INN 🏨 **Seven Wives Inn Bed & Breakfast.** Named for an ancestor of the owner who indeed had seven wives, this quaint bed-and-breakfast occupies two Victorian homes and is full of historic charm. **Pros:** near Ancestor Square and other downtown attractions; nice pool; children are welcome. **Cons:** rooms fill quickly in summer; setting too quiet for some travelers. [$] *Rooms from: $189* ✉ *217 N. 100 W* ☎ *435/628–3737* 🌐 *www.sevenwivesinn.com* 🛏 *13 rooms* 🍴 *Breakfast* ✣ *C1.*

9

PERFORMING ARTS

Tuacahn. A rotating series of musicals such as *Beauty & The Beast, Sister Act,* and *The Wizard of Oz* entertain at this outdoor amphitheater nestled in a natural sandstone cove. The venue is also used for big-name rock concerts and movies. ✉ *1100 Tuacahn Dr., Ivins* ☎ *800/746–9882, 435/652–3300* 🌐 *www.tuacahn.org.*

SHOPPING

Ancestor Square. The centerpiece shopping area of downtown St. George is a great place to browse stores and art galleries before grabbing lunch or dinner at one of the nearby restaurants. ✉ *St. George Blvd. and Main St.* ☎ *435/656–8238* 🌐 *www.ancestorsquare.com.*

The Outlets at Zion. Southern Utah's popular factory-outlet center, at I–15 Exit 8, has more than 30 stores, including Eddie Bauer, Pendleton, Levis, and Downeast Outfitters. ✉ *250 N. Red Cliffs Dr.* ☎ *435/674–0133* 🌐 *www.theoutletsatzion.com.*

Red Cliffs Mall. Serving the needs of both residents and visitors this popular mall has a variety of specialty shops and sporting goods stores, with anchors like Barnes & Noble, Dillard's, and JCPenney. ✉ *1750 E. Red Cliffs Dr.* ☎ *435/673–0099* ⊕ *www.redcliffsmall.com.*

SPRINGDALE

40 miles east of St. George.

Springdale's growth has followed that of next-door neighbor and main attraction Zion National Park, the most popular park destination in Utah and one of the most popular in the United States. Hotels, restaurants, and shops keep popping up, yet the town still manages to maintain its small-town charm. And oh, that view!

GETTING HERE AND AROUND

You'll need a car to get to Springdale, via Highway 9, but getting around once you're there is easy. The canyon-road shuttle bus—from April through October—makes getting from one end of Springdale to the other easy, with bus stops throughout town. But it's also a pleasant town to walk about, with shops, galleries, and restaurants all within a central district.

EXPLORING

FAMILY **Grafton.** A stone school, dusty cemetery, and a few wooden structures are all that remain of the nearby town of Grafton, a ghost town that has starred in films such as *Butch Cassidy and the Sundance Kid.* Attacks by Native Americans drove the original settlers from the site. ✉ *Bridge La., 2 miles west of Rockville.*

WHERE TO EAT

$$$ ✕ **Bit & Spur Restaurant and Saloon.** Creative Southwestern fare such as
SOUTHWESTERN   sweet-potato tamales and blue crab and roasted corn cannelloni high-
Fodor's Choice   light the menu at this Springdale institution, which has been serving
★   patrons for more than 30 years. Gluten-free and vegetarian options are available and all sauces and salsas are homemade. There is an impressive craft-beer selection, and the standout dessert is German chocolate cake. An outside dining area with fountain, stone pathways, and shade trees is an oasis on warm days. $ *Average main: $22* ✉ *1212 Zion Park Blvd.* ☎ *435/772–3498* ⊕ *www.bitandspur.com* ⊘ *No lunch.*

$$ ✕ **Oscar's Café.** A popular destination for hikers and tourists with hearty
CAFÉ   appetites, this café has a surprisingly extensive menu. You can set your-
FAMILY   self up for an active day from the tempting breakfast menu, which includes omelets, pancakes, French toast, and specialties like the Lean Hiker breakfast burrito, with egg whites, spinach, tomatoes, beans, and cheese. The lunch and dinner menu has steaks and ribs, a dozen burger choices, salads, sandwiches, and Mexican favorites, with plenty of vegetarian options. Eat on the inviting patio for stunning mountain views. $ *Average main: $15* ✉ *948 Zion Park Blvd.* ☎ *435/772–3232* ⊕ *www.cafeoscars.com.*

$$ ✕ **Zion Pizza & Noodle Co.** It may look like a church (and once was),
PIZZA   but the only thing being worshipped here now is beer and incredible
FAMILY   pizza. After a long day on the trails, put up your feet and dig into the

meat-laden Cholesterol Hiker or Good for You pizza with grilled zucchini and Asiago cheese. You can also order pasta dishes like linguine with peanuts and grilled chicken, or chicken Parmesan. A selection of Utah microbrews and wines by the glass is also served. Enjoy dinner indoors or in the beer garden. $ *Average main: $16* ✉ *868 Zion Park Blvd.* ☎ *435/772–3815* 🌐 *zionpizzanoodle.com* 🕒 *No lunch. Closed Dec.–Feb.*

WHERE TO STAY

$$$ HOTEL 🏨 **Cliffrose Lodge and Gardens.** The acres of flowers, lush lawns, and canyon views at this riverside hotel make it more than a place to rest your head, and you could throw a rock and hit the south entrance to the park. **Pros:** expansive, scenic pool area; airport shuttle service available; bedding and linens are absolutely top-notch. **Cons:** some walls are thin. $ *Rooms from: $189* ✉ *281 Zion Park Blvd.* ☎ *435/772–3234, 800/243–8824* 🌐 *cliffroselodge.com* 🛏 *52 rooms, 12 suites, 3 villas* 🍴 *Breakfast.*

$$$ HOTEL Fodor's Choice ★ 🏨 **Desert Pearl Inn.** At this riverside lodge every room has vaulted ceilings, oversize windows, and soaking tubs, and a 1,000-square-foot suite with a full kitchen is also available. **Pros:** cute gift shop; striking views; rooms facing river have balconies or terraces; some rooms sleep six. **Cons:** bedding is plush but minimalist; cooking smells can permeate the walls (the wrong neighbor can spoil your retreat). $ *Rooms from: $178* ✉ *707 Zion Park Blvd.* ☎ *435/772–8888, 888/828–0898* 🌐 *desertpearl.com* 🛏 *72 rooms, 1 suite* 🍴 *No meals.*

SHOPPING

Bumbleberry Gifts. Next to the Bumbleberry Inn, this quaint gift shop is best known for its fresh-baked bumbleberry pies and locally produced bumbleberry jams. You'll also find a wide array of gifts and souvenirs, plus an extensive selection of outdoor apparel and footwear. ✉ *897 Zion Park Blvd.* ☎ *435/772–3224* 🌐 *www.bumbleberrygifts.com.*

9

Fodor's Choice ★ **Worthington Gallery.** Opened in 1980 by a single potter in a pioneer-era home near the mouth of Zion Canyon, this ever-expanding gallery now features more than 30 artists who create with paper, metal, glass, paint, and pottery. Even if you only have time for a quick stop, it is worth the trip to see some of the best craftwork and fine art in the area. ✉ *789 Zion Park Blvd.* ☎ *435/772–3446* 🌐 *worthingtongallery.com* 🕒 *Daily, Mar.–Oct., 9–9; Nov.–Feb., 10–5.*

ALONG U.S. 89—UTAH'S HERITAGE HIGHWAY

Winding north from the Arizona border all the way to Spanish Fork Canyon an hour south of Salt Lake City, U.S. 89 is known as the Heritage Highway for its role in shaping Utah history. At its southern end, Kanab is known as "Little Hollywood," having provided the backdrop for many famous Western movies and television commercials. The town has since grown considerably to accommodate tourists who flock here to see where Ronald Reagan once slept and Clint Eastwood drew his guns. Other towns north along this famous road may not have the same notoriety in these parts, but they do provide quiet, uncrowded,

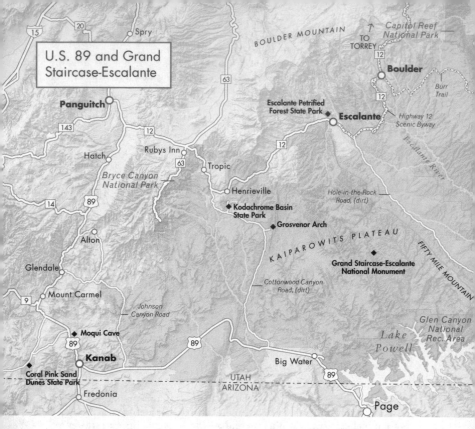

U.S. 89 and Grand
Staircase-Escalante

and inexpensive places to stay near Zion and Bryce Canyon national parks. East of Kanab, U.S. 89 runs along the southern edge of the Grand Staircase–Escalante National Monument.

KANAB

43 miles southeast of Springdale.

Kanab is Hollywood's vision of the American West. Soaring vermilion sandstone cliffs and sagebrush flats with endless vistas have lured filmmakers to this area for more than 75 years. The welcoming sign at city limits reads "Greatest Earth on Show"—Kanab has been used as a setting in more than 100 movies and television shows. Abandoned film sets have become tourist attractions, and old movie posters or still photographs are a decorating staple at local businesses. In addition to a movie-star past, Kanab is ideally positioned as a base for exploration. With major roads radiating in four directions, it offers easy access to three national parks, three national monuments (including Grand Staircase–Escalante), two state parks, and several historic sites.

GETTING HERE AND AROUND

Most of Kanab's lodging facilities are close to downtown, where a handful of restaurants make this a reasonably walkable destination. U.S. 89 from the north and south is the main road in.

FESTIVALS

FAMILY **Western Legends Roundup.** Held every August at various venues in town, this festival is a must for anyone with a love of the cowboy era. For three days in late August, Kanab plays host to cowboy poets, musicians, and character actors from Old West TV series of yesteryear. Native American dancers and weavers, arts-and-crafts vendors, quilt shows, a parade, tours to Western movie sites, a chuck wagon dinner, campfire entertainment, and a film festival draw enthusiasts from all over the country. ☎ *435/644–3444* ⊕ *westernlegendsroundup.com.*

ESSENTIALS

Visitor Information **Kanab Visitor Center.** In addition to information on self-guiding driving tours, hiking and road conditions, this visitor center has exhibits on archaeology and geology. ✉ *745 E. U.S. 89* ☎ *435/644–1300* ⊕ *www.blm. gov/ut/st/en/fo/grand_staircase-escalante/recreation/visitor_centers/Kanab* ⌚ *Daily 8–4:30.* **Kane County Office of Tourism** ✉ *78 S. 100 E* ☎ *800/733–5263* ⊕ *www.visitsouthernutah.com.*

EXPLORING

Coral Pink Sand Dunes State Park. Visitors to this sweeping expanse of pink sand enjoy a slice of nature that is the result of eroding sandstone. Funneled through a notch in the rock, wind picks up speed and carries grains of sand into the area. Once the wind slows down, the sand is deposited, creating this giant playground for dune buggies, ATVs, and dirtbikes. A small area is fenced off for walking, but the sound of wheeled toys is always with you. ⚠ **Children love to play in the sand, but check the surface temperature; it can become very hot.** ✉ *Yellowjacket and Hancock Rds., 12 miles off U.S. 89* ☎ *435/648–2800* ⊕ *www.state parks.utah.gov* ⌚ *$8* ☉ *Daily.*

Little Hollywood Museum. Stop at this replica of a frontier town and see buildings that were actually used on movie sets dating as far back as 1924 (*The Deadwood Coach*). A long list of classic westerns, sci-fi, and other genres requiring barren scenery ensued, including the 2001 *Planet of the Apes* and *Evolution*. TV shows filmed here include *The Lone Ranger, Six Million Dollar Man,* and *How the West Was Won.* An all-you-can eat buffet is served on tin plates and cups. ✉ *297 W. Center St.* ☎ *435/644–5337* ⊕ *www.littlehollywoodmuseum.com* ⌚ *Free* ☉ *Apr.– Oct., daily 8 am–9 pm; Nov., Dec., and Mar., daily 9–5.*

Moqui Cave. In a replica of an ancient Native American cliff dwelling, this cave, 5½ miles north of Kanab, offers a little bit of everything. Native American artifacts are displayed alongside dinosaur footprints, a fluorescent mineral display, and pre-Columbian artifacts from Mexico. The inside temperature of the cave never exceeds 70°F, even on hot summer days. ✉ *518 N. Hwy. 89* ☎ *435/644–8525* ⌚ *$5* ☉ *May–Sept., Mon.–Sat. 9–7; Oct.–Apr., Mon.–Sat. 10–4.*

9

WHERE TO EAT AND STAY

$$$
SOUTHWESTERN

✗**Rocking V Cafe.** Offering specialties like jalapeño lime chicken and fish tacos, this popular eatery focuses on slow-cooked meals made from scratch. Housed in a quirky building that was once a post office, the restaurant gets very busy even on weeknights. Even those with hearty appetites will have a hard time finishing the Kanab-A-Dab-A-Doo burger, a half-pound patty topped with ham, cheese, and avocado. Patio dining is available in the warmer months. The drink menu includes beer, wine, and margaritas. $ *Average main: $22 ⊠ 97 W. Center St. ☎ 435/644–8001 ⊕ www.rockingvcafe.com ☉ Closed Tues. and Wed. in winter (dates vary).*

$
AMERICAN
FAMILY

✗**Three Bears Creamery Cottage.** Designed with a storybook theme that will appeal to children and nostalgic adults, this popular Kanab eatery serves soup, sandwiches, salads, and hot dogs, but the real draw is the homemade ice cream. Choose from more than 20 unique flavors or splurge on a decadent hot fudge sundae. Shakes can also be customized with a mix of seasonal fruits, nuts, and other goodies—you'll need a spoon instead of a straw. $ *Average main: $8 ⊠ 210 S. 100 E ☎ 435/644–3300 ⊕ www.threebearscreamery.com ☉ Closed Sun.*

$$
HOTEL

Best Western Red Hills. One of Kanab's larger motels has a hearty dose of cowboy flavor accenting its city-style amenities. **Pros:** within a half hour of Zion National Park; children under 17 stay free. **Cons:** no on-site restaurant. $ *Rooms from: $139 ⊠ 125 W. Center St. ☎ 435/644–2675, 800/830–2675 ⊕ www.bestwesternredhills.com ☜ 75 rooms ⦿ Breakfast.*

$$
HOTEL

Parry Lodge. Listed on the National Register of Historic Places, this landmark lodge hosted dozens of movie stars during Kanab's movie location heyday. **Pros:** film buffs will enjoy sleeping among the ghosts of Hollywood's past. **Cons:** some rooms could use a new look; no elevator. $ *Rooms from: $108 ⊠ 89 E. Center St. ☎ 435/644–2601 ⊕ www.parrylodge.com ☜ 89 rooms ⦿ No meals.*

PANGUITCH

67 miles north of Kanab.

An elevation of 6,650 feet helps this town of 1,500 residents keep its cool. Main Street is lined with late-19th-century buildings, and its early homes and outbuildings are noted for their distinctive brick architecture. Decent amenities, inexpensive lodging (mainly strip motels), and an excellent location 24 miles northwest of Bryce Canyon National Park make Panguitch a comfortable launching pad for recreation in the area.

GETTING HERE AND AROUND

Panguitch is quickly accessible to those touring Bryce Canyon National Park, and is a bit farther for those exploring the Kanab and Grand Staircase–Escalante areas. U.S. 89 is the well-maintained and scenic route to take.

FESTIVALS

JUNE **Panguitch Valley Balloon Rally.** The population of tiny Panguitch triples with this annual festival, which includes a morning launch of about 35 hot-air balloons, an evening balloon-glow, bands, food, and a Harley-Davidson parade. ☎ *435/676–8585* 🌐 *www.panguitch.org.*

Quilt Walk Festival. During the bitter winter of 1864, Panguitch residents set out over the mountains to fetch provisions from the town of Parowan, 40 miles away. Legend says the men, frustrated and ready to turn back, laid a quilt on the snow and knelt to pray. Soon they realized the quilt had kept them from sinking into the snow. Spreading quilts before them as they walked, leapfrog style, the men traveled to Parowan and back. This three-day event in June commemorates the event with quilting classes, a tour of pioneer homes, a dinner-theater production, and other events. ☎ *435/690–9228* 🌐 *quiltwalk.org.*

JULY **Panguitch Pioneer Day Celebration.** Panguitch celebrates Pioneer Day (officially July 24) with a parade, carnival chuck-wagon breakfast, kids' games, and roast beef barbecue in honor of Brigham Young's arrival in the Salt Lake area. ☎ *435/676–1160* 🌐 *panguitch.com.*

ESSENTIALS

Visitor Information **Garfield County Office of Tourism** ✉ *55 S. Main St.* ☎ *800/444–6689, 435/676–1160* 🌐 *www.brycecanyoncountry.com.*

SPORTS AND THE OUTDOORS

FISHING

Panguitch Lake. Reportedly, the lake takes its name from a Paiute word meaning "big fish." They may not all be big, but several types of trout are plentiful, and ice fishing is popular in winter. With 10 miles of shoreline you're sure to find a quiet spot to wet a line, or you can rent a boat for the day. ✉ *Hwy. 143, 17 miles south of Panguitch, Bryce Canyon National Park* ☎ *435/676–1161* 🌐 *www.panguitchlake.com.*

9

WHERE TO EAT AND STAY

$$ AMERICAN 🍴 **Cowboy's Smokehouse Café.** From the Western-style interior and creaky floors to the smoker out back, this rustic café has an aura of Texan authenticity with cowboy collectibles and game trophies lining the walls. The menu includes mesquite-smoked beef, pork, turkey, and chicken, and a secret sauce with no fewer than 15 ingredients (bottles may be purchased to take home). Lighter fare includes burgers, sandwiches, and salads served with cornbread and cinnamon butter. ■ **TIP→ Payment is cash only but there is an ATM on the premises.** [$] *Average main: $18* ✉ *95 N. Main St.* ☎ *435/676–8030* 🌐 *www.cowboyssmokehousecafe.com* 💳 *No credit cards* ⏰ *Closed Sun.*

$ HOTEL 🏨 **Canyon Lodge.** Within walking distance of restaurants, a gift shop and grocery store, this family-owned no-frills motel offers clean and comfortable guest rooms. **Pros:** just 25 miles from Bryce Canyon; barbecue and picnic area for guests to use; affordably priced. **Cons:** small bathrooms; breakfast not included; a little noisy from highway traffic. [$] *Rooms from: $89* ✉ *210 N. Main St.* ☎ *435/676–8292* 🌐 *www.canyonlodgemotel.com* 🛏 *9 rooms, 1 suite* 🍽 *No meals.*

$$ B&B/INN 🏨 **Red Brick Inn B&B.** A historic Dutch Colonial building offers uniquely decorated rooms for a charming stay. **Pros:** close to downtown shops

and eateries; convenient access to Bryce and Zion parks; gourmet breakfast; nice deck and shady garden. **Cons:** open spring through early fall only; rooms on the small side. $ *Rooms from: $130* ⊠ *161 N. 100 W* ☎ *435/676–2141* ⊕ *www.redbrickinnutah.com* ⌐ *6 rooms* ☉ *Closed mid-Oct.–Mar.* ¶⊙*Breakfast.*

SHOPPING

Cowboy Collectibles. Dusty old boots in need of a cowhand sit ready to walk and ride again at this store, which covers more than 2,000 square feet. The owners travel all over the country to find saddles, chaps, vintage clothing, quilts, and other antiques from the days when men on horseback roamed the ranges. There are also toys and other items that celebrate the Old West, along with memorabilia once owned by the likes of Roy Rogers and Buffalo Bill. ⊠ *57 N. Main St.* ☎ *435/676–8168* ⊕ *cowboycollectiblesutah.com* ☉ *Sun.–Thurs. by appointment.*

GRAND STAIRCASE–ESCALANTE NATIONAL MONUMENT

In September 1996 President Bill Clinton designated 1.9 million acres in south-central Utah as the Grand Staircase–Escalante National Monument. Its three distinct sections—the Grand Staircase, the Kaiparowits Plateau, and the Canyons of the Escalante—offer remote backcountry experiences hard to find elsewhere in the Lower 48. Waterfalls, Native American ruins and petroglyphs, shoulder-width slot canyons, and improbable colors all characterize this wilderness. Straddling the northern border of the monument, the small towns of Escalante and Boulder offer access, information, outfitters, lodging, and dining to adventurers. The highway that connects them, Highway 12, is one of the most scenic stretches of road in the Southwest.

Visitor centers in Big Water, Kanab, Cannonville, and Escalante can provide current information on road conditions and self-guided tours. Each center has a different theme, with exhibits on archaeology, geology, paleontology, and biology. Popular day trips include Lower Calf Creek Falls, Spooky Canyon, Devil's Garden, and Grosvenor Arch. Other worthwhile destinations include Johnson Canyon/Skutumpah Road, Cottonwood Canyon Road, and nearby Kodachrome Basin State Park.

A good way to plan your visit is to hire one of the many experienced outfitters and guides who offer options ranging from narrated tours in air-conditioned vehicles to hiking and backpacking adventures. Most tours feature areas with colorful sandstone rock formations, slot canyons, dramatic cliffs, waterfalls, and scenic back roads.

ESCALANTE

47 miles east of Bryce Canyon National Park entrance.

Though the Dominguez and Escalante expedition of 1776 came nowhere near this area, the town's name does honor the Spanish explorer. It was bestowed nearly a century later by a member of a survey party led by

John Wesley Powell, charged with mapping this remote area. Today, it has modern amenities and is a gateway to the national monument.

GETTING HERE AND AROUND

Escalante is only reachable via Highway 12 from the north and south. Fortunately, it's a drive not to be missed. The tiny downtown is where most amenities are found.

ESSENTIALS

Visitor Information Big Water Visitor Center. Housed in a spiral-designed building this visitor center features exhibits on local paleontology and includes a display of dinosaur bones. ⊠ *100 Upper Revolution Way, Big Water* ☎ *435/675–3200* ⊕ *www.blm.gov/ut/st/en/fo/grand_staircase-escalante/recreation/visitor_centers/Big_Water_Visitor_Center* ⊠ *9–5:30 Apr–Oct; 8–4:30 Nov.–Mar.* **Cannonville Visitor Center.** This small visitor center features outdoor cultural exhibits that you can view year-round but the center itself is open seasonally. ⊠ *10 Center St., Cannonville* ☎ *435/826–5640* ⊕ *www.blm.gov/ut/st/en/fo/grand_staircase-escalante/recreation/visitor_centers/Cannonville_Visitor_Center* ⊗ *Closed mid-Nov.–mid-Mar.* **Escalante Interagency Visitor Center.** A good starting point if you are trying to decide what to explore first, and solo adventurers should check in here before going into the wild, so somebody knows where they are. The museum has ecology and biology exhibits, a short film, and a relief map of the area. ⊠ *755 W. Main St.* ☎ *435/826–5499* ⊗ *Mid-Mar.–mid Nov., daily 8–4:30; mid-Nov.–mid-Mar., weekdays 8–4:30.*

TOURS

Opportunities for getting out and exploring this fascinating area abound, and a good way to start is in the company of an expert tour guide. Activity-based tours include hiking, canyoneering, and horseback riding; special interest tours cover such subjects as photography, geology, and the area's flora and fauna.

Escape Goats. Providing guided tours of the slot canyons and other southwest Utah destinations for more than 10 years, this family-owned operation offers a variety of day and evening hikes, multiday backpacking trips, and photo and artist tours. The company offers shuttle services and personalized attention, and can customize tours for families with children and travelers with limited mobility. ⊠ *Boulder* ☎ *435/826–4652* ⊕ *www.escalantecanyonguides.com* ⊠ *From $90.*

Excursions of Escalante. Hiking and canyoneering tours are custom-fit to your needs by experienced guides whose specialty is taking canyoneers into the slot canyons to move through slot chutes or rappel down walls and other obstacles. All gear is provided, and trips last from one day to a week. ⊠ *125 E. Main St.* ☎ *800/839–7567* ⊕ *excursionsofescalante.com* ⊠ *From $130* ⊗ *Mid-Apr.–mid-Nov.*

Grand Staircase Discovery Tours. Half-day and full-day hikes are offered, with services including hiking/camping gear, shuttle service, photography, and customized trips. Tours take visitors to ghost towns, slot canyons, rock formations, and more. ⊠ *Big Water* ☎ *928/614–4099* ⊕ *www.grandstaircasediscoverytours.com* ⊠ *From $125.*

Hondoo Rivers & Trails. With a reputation for high-quality educational trips into the backcountry of Capitol Reef National Park, Escalante

9

Canyons, and the High Plateaus, this tour company delivers a unique experience. From April to October they'll take you on hiking, horse-back-riding, and Jeep day tours. Trips are designed to explore the geologic landforms in the area, seek out wildflowers in season, and to encounter free-roaming mustangs, bison, and bighorn sheep when possible. Multiday trips can also be arranged. ⊠ *90 E. Main St., Torrey* ☎ *435/425–3519* ⊕ *www.hondoo.com* ☜ *From $90.*

Southwest Adventure Tours. This experienced tour operator partners with Paria Outpost and Outfitters to offer hikes that wind past incredible scenery, including the Wahwaep hoodoos (sandstone rock formations), Sidestep Canyon, the Rimrocks, Deer Range Point, and the Cockscomb area. Hikes range from 1½ to 8 miles round-trip with some moderate climbing. Multiday backpacking and camping trips are offered along with advice about self-guided driving tours and tours of other Utah parks. ⊠ *382 E. 650 S, Cedar City* ☎ *435/590–5864, 800/970–5864* ⊕ *www.southwestadventuretours.com* ☜ *$125 half-day hike, $175 full-day hike.*

EXPLORING

FAMILY **Escalante Petrified Forest State Park.** This state park was created to protect a huge repository of petrified wood, easily spotted along two moderate-to-strenuous hiking trails. There's an attractive swimming beach at the park's Wide Hollow Reservoir, which is also good for boating, fishing, and birding. ⊠ *710 N. Reservoir Rd.* ☎ *435/826–4466* ⊕ *stateparks. utah.gov* ☜ *$8* ☉ *Daily 8 am–10 pm.*

NEED A BREAK? **Kiva Koffeehouse.** A fun place to stop along the way for the spectacular view and a quick bite, this unusual coffeehouse at mile marker 73.86, 13 miles east of Escalante, was constructed by the late artist and inventor Bradshaw Bowman. He began building it when he was in his 80s and spent two years finding and transporting the 13 Douglas fir logs surrounding the structure. Today the eatery serves breakfast and lunch and is run by his daughter and granddaughters. Enjoy homemade soups, sandwiches, and desserts, an espresso bar, and Wi-Fi access. It's open from March to October, and there are two rooms for rent in the nearby cabin. ⊠ *7144 S. Hwy. 12* ☎ *435/826–4550* ⊕ *www.kivakoffeehouse.com.*

Fodor'sChoice ★ **Highway 12 Scenic Byway.** Keep your camera handy and steering wheel steady along this route between Escalante and Loa, near Capitol Reef National Park. Though the highway starts at the intersection of U.S. 89, west of Bryce Canyon National Park, the stretch that begins in Escalante is one of the most spectacular. The road passes through Grand Staircase–Escalante National Monument and on to Capitol Reef along one of the most scenic stretches of highway in the United States. Be sure to stop at the scenic overlooks; almost every one will give you an eye-popping view, and information panels let you know what you're looking at. ⚠ **Don't get distracted while driving, though; the paved road is twisting and steep, and at times climbs over a hogback with sheer drop-offs on both sides.** ⊕ *scenicbyway12.com.*

OFF THE BEATEN PATH

Kodachrome Basin State Park. As soon as you see it, you'll understand why the park earned this colorful photographic name from the National Geographic Society. The sand pipes here cannot be found anywhere else in the world. Hike any of the trails to spot some of the 67 pipes in and around the park. The short Angels Palace Trail takes you quickly into the park's interior, up, over, and around some of the badlands. ✉ *Cottonwood Canyon Rd., Cannonville* ☎ *435/679–8562* 🌐 *stateparks.utah.gov* 🎟 *$8* 🕐 *Daily 6 am–10 pm.*

SPORTS AND THE OUTDOORS

Larger than most national parks at 1.7 million acres, the Grand Staircase–Escalante National Monument is popular with backpackers and hard-core mountain-bike enthusiasts. You can explore the rocky landscape, which represents some of America's last wilderness, via dirt roads with a four-wheel-drive vehicle; most roads depart from Highway 12. Roadside views into the monument are most impressive from Highway 12 between Escalante and Boulder. It costs nothing to enter the park, but fees apply for camping and backcountry permits.

BICYCLING

Hell's Backbone Road. For a scenic and challenging mountain-bike ride, follow the 44-mile Hell's Backbone Road from Panguitch to the Escalante region and beyond. The route, also known as Highway 12, gives riders stunning views and a half-dozen kitschy townships as a reward for the steep grades. The road begins 7 miles south of Panguitch.

HIKING

Lower Escalante River. Some of the best backcountry hiking in the area lies 15 miles east of Escalante on Route 12, where the Lower Escalante River carves through striking sandstone canyons and gulches. You can camp at numerous sites along the river for extended trips, or spend a little time in the small park where the highway crosses the river.

Utah Canyons Guided Tours. This outfitter offers a variety of guided tours into Grand Staircase–Escalante and Glen Canyon, whether you want to traverse slot canyons, discover the area's natural waterfalls, or enjoy breathtaking sunsets. There's a two-person minimum, and discounts for children. Their location includes a store with hiking and camping gear, and some serious, freshly made espresso. ✉ *325 W. Main St.* ☎ *435/826–4967* 🌐 *utahcanyons.com* 🎟 *From: $110.*

9

WHERE TO EAT AND STAY

$$ AMERICAN

🍴 **Cowboy Blues.** Step back into the Old West for basic but bountiful American food in this rustic restaurant adorned with ranching memorabilia. This locals' favorite serves steaks, ribs, blackened salmon, and a variety of burgers and sandwiches. You can enjoy a cocktail or beer on the patio, along with appetizers like jalapeño poppers or spicy cheese fries. Homebaked desserts include pies, bread pudding, and brownie sundaes. [$] *Average main: $15* ✉ *530 W. Main St.* ☎ *435/826–4577* 🌐 *cowboyblues.net* ✍ *Reservations not accepted.*

$$ CAFÉ

🍴 **Esca-Latte Internet Cafe & Pizza Parlor.** When you're spent after a day of exploration, this is a great place to sit back and relax. Try one of the build-your-own pizzas, known for fresh, local ingredients such as applewood-smoked bacon and slow-roasted tomatoes, and pair it with an icy Utah microbrew. There are also sandwiches, salads, homemade desserts, and perhaps the best cup of coffee in town, fresh ground from fair-trade beans. [$] *Average main: $17* ✉ *310 W. Main St.* ☎ *435/826–4266* 🌐 *www.escalanteoutfitters.com/restaurant/.*

$$ B&B/INN 🏨 **Escalante's Grand Staircase Bed & Breakfast Inn.** Rooms are set apart from the main house, giving this property some motel-type privacy along with B&B amenities. **Pros:** spacious rooms; wireless Internet; cute back porch for horizon gazing. **Cons:** the rooms are packed in tight. [$] *Rooms from: $145* ✉ *280 W. Main St.* ☎ *435/826–4890* 🌐 *escalantebnb.com* 🛏 *8 rooms* 🍴 *Breakfast.*

$ HOTEL 🏨 **Escalante Outfitters.** A good option if you want a one-stop place to plan and gear up for your outdoor adventure or if you're on a budget and don't care about amenities. **Pros:** the food is a pleasant surprise; store and bike rentals on-site; pet-friendly. **Cons:** right on the highway; you may have to wait in line for a shower. [$] *Rooms from: $45* ✉ *310 W. Main St.* ☎ *435/826–4266* 🌐 *www.escalanteoutfitters.com* 🛏 *7 cabins* 🍴 *No meals.*

SHOPPING

Serenidad Gallery. Southwestern art lines the walls and shelves of this seven-room gallery, but there's also contemporary or antique pieces of Native American jewelry, pioneer soap, a fossil, or book to take home. ✉ *360 W. Main St.* ☎ *435/826–4720, 435/826–4577* 🌐 *serenidadgallery.com* 🕒 *Mar.–Oct., Mon.–Sat. 8–6, Sun. 1–6.*

BOULDER

29 miles northeast of Escalante.

That mail was delivered to Boulder by horse and mule until 1940 should give an idea of how out-of-the-way it is. (Highway 12 helps make it less so.) Cattle ranchers founded the town, and ranching continues to occupy many residents. The town of Escalante is larger, but Boulder has one of the finest lodges and restaurants in the state.

GETTING HERE AND AROUND

Highway 12 is the only way into town. The attractions are spare; if you're staying at the lodge, you can walk to the state park if you have some time to wander, but most people drive around.

TOURS

Fodor's Choice ★ **Earth Tours.** Led by Dr. Kenneth Watts, a respected geologist and lifelong student of natural history, small group tours explore some of southern Utah's most breathtaking destinations. While exploring Utah's many wonders of nature, participants are entertained with behind-the-scenes stories and anecdotes that make the tour both fun and memorable. ✉ *Burr Trail Outpost, 10 N. Hwy. 12* ☎ *435/691–1241* 🌐 *www.earthtours.com* 🎟 *$110 per person for full-day hikes.*

SPORTS AND THE OUTDOORS

BICYCLING

Burr Trail. Mountain bikers may want to pedal a portion of the Burr Trail, a 66-mile backcountry route (also passable by most vehicles when dry) that crosses east through the monument into the southern portion of Capitol Reef National Park.

HIKING

Calf Creek Falls Trail. Those seeking a moderately difficult 5½-mile round-trip hike will enjoy the excursion that begins from the trailhead at Calf Creek Recreation Area, 8 miles south of Boulder. Along the way hikers will pass sandstone cliffs, beaver ponds, and prehistoric rock-art sites. At the end of the trail, 126-feet-tall Lower Calf Creek Falls explodes over a cliff. Bird-watchers should keep an eye out for many species, including golden eagles, hummingbirds, woodpeckers, and western bluebirds that enjoy the vegetation and water at the bottom of the canyon. ✉ *Hwy. 12* ⊕ *www.blm.gov/ut/st/escalante.*

WHERE TO EAT AND STAY

$$ ✕ **Burr Trail Outpost & Grill.** Local cowboys still ride up to the back porch
SOUTHWESTERN for meals at this restaurant, which serves contemporary fare like spicy Thai burgers, pesto pizza, and grilled trout. With Southwestern style and a laid-back atmosphere, diners enjoy outdoor seating with views of Boulder Mountain and the Aquarius Plateau. Favorite appetizers are the Burr Trail wings and fried green tomatoes. Vegetarians will find creative offerings like the sweet potato burger, while omnivores will appreciate the Red Rock burger with white cheddar, guacamole, chipotle, and salsa. You might want to share an entrée and save room for fresh-baked ginger berry or caramel apple pie topped with homemade ice cream. $ *Average main: $15* ✉ *10 N. Hwy. 12* ☎ *435/335–7503* ⊕ *www.burrtrailgrill.com* ✆ *Closed Nov.–Feb.*

$$$ ✕ **Hell's Backbone Grill.** On the grounds of the Boulder Mountain Lodge
ECLECTIC and voted Best Restaurant in Southern Utah for eight years in a row
Fodor's Choice by *Salt Lake Magazine,* this remote eatery is well worth the drive. The
★ menu, featuring specialties like smoked trout quesadillas and strip steak with lemony mashed potatoes, is inspired by Native American, Western range, Southwestern, and Mormon pioneer recipes (a cookbook is to be published in 2015). The owners, who are also the chefs, have a historical connection to the area, and many of the ingredients they use come directly from their own organic farm. Because they insist on fresh ingredients, the menu changes seasonally. The restaurant closes between lunch and dinner, 2:30–5. $ *Average main: $25* ✉ *20 N. Hwy. 12* ☎ *435/335–7464* ⊕ *www.hellsbackbonegrill.com* ✆ *Closed Dec.–mid-Mar.*

$$$ ◫ **Boulder Mountain Lodge.** If you're traveling scenic Highway 12
HOTEL between Capitol Reef and Bryce Canyon national parks, don't miss
Fodor's Choice this wonderful lodge with a fireplace and library in the two-story
★ great room and award-winning Hell's Backbone restaurant on the premises. **Pros:** a perfect spot for peace and solitude; the service and care given to guests are impeccable. **Cons:** some might find the middle-of-nowhere location too remote. $ *Rooms from: $160* ✉ *20 N. Hwy. 12* ☎ *435/335–7460, 800/556–3446* ⊕ *www.boulder-utah.com* ✆ *20 rooms, 2 suites* ⬦ *No meals.*

9

TORREY

36 miles north of Boulder.

The pretty little town of Torrey, just outside the Capitol Reef National Park, has lots of personality and dates back to the 1880s, when Mormon settlers first arrived. Giant old cottonwood trees alongside a narrow canal make it a shady spot, and its altitude of 6,830 feet makes it a cool place to stay in the height of the summer. The townspeople, numbering fewer than 200, are friendly and accommodating and there are places to eat and stay and some interesting shopping opportunities.

GETTING HERE AND AROUND

Highway 24 passes right through Torrey, but if you're driving up from Boulder you'll be traveling a particularly lovely section of the Highway 12 Scenic Byway.

TOURS

Alpine Adventures. With a stellar reputation for personalized attention during fly-fishing trips into the high backcountry around Capitol Reef and the Fremont River, Alpine Adventures also leads trophy hunting and horseback tours. ⊠ *310 W. Main St.* ☎ *435/425–3660* ⊕ *alpineadventuresutah.com* ⊠ *From: $225.*

PERFORMING ARTS

Robber's Roost. This shop, named after Butch Cassidy's hideout, is home base for the Entrada Institute, an alliance of arts and outdoors enthusiasts that holds musical events and talks, usually on Saturday nights, from May through October. The annual women's music festival, held each August, attracts more than 600 attendees to hear performance art, blues, rock, jazz, and folk. (⇨ *See also Shopping.*) ⊠ *185 W. Main St. (Hwy. 24)* ☎ *435/425–3265* ⊕ *robbersroostbooks.com.*

SHOPPING

ART GALLERIES

Gallery 24. This pleasing space sells contemporary fine art from southern Utah–based artists that includes paintings, photography, and ceramics. ⊠ *135 E. Main St.* ☎ *435/425–2124* ⊕ *www.gallery24.biz* ☾ *Easter–mid-Oct., Fri.–Mon. 11–5.*

Torrey Gallery. At this lovely gallery, the art on display from regional artists includes oil paintings, photographs, Navajo rugs, and sculptures. ⊠ *80 E. Main St. (Hwy. 24)* ☎ *435/425–3909* ⊕ *torreygallery.com* ☾ *Mid-Mar.–late Nov., Mon.–Sat. 10–6.*

BOOKS

Robber's Roost. The inviting and well-stocked Robber's Roost is part bookstore, part coffee and snack bar, and part performance space (⇨ *see also Performing Arts*), all contained in the late Utah writer Ward Roylance's practically teepee-shape house. It has books by regional authors, guidebooks, maps, and T-shirts. Unexpected offerings include authentic Native American jewelry and crafts, vintage guitars, and other stringed instruments. A seasonal Saturday farmers' market offers local produce. It's an excellent place to browse, talk about trails, or find out what's going on around town. ⊠ *185 W. Main St. (Hwy. 24)* ☎ *435/425–3265* ⊕ *robbersroostbooks.com* ☾ *Mar.–Oct., daily 8–8.*

CRAFTS

Flute Shop Trading Post. Unique and unexpected, the nifty Flute Shop is open year-round and sells Native American–style flutes, handcrafted by owner Vance Morrill. You can also find Native American jewelry, rocks, fossils, and other unusual gifts. A quiet and inexpensive four-unit motel has been added to the premises. You'll find it 4 miles south of the junction of Highways 12 and 24. ✉ *1705 S. Scenic Rte. 12* ☎ *435/425–3144* 🌐 *www.fluteshopmotel.com* 🕑 *Mon.–Sat. 8–8.*

FAMILY **Torrey Trading Post.** Come here for Native American jewelry and pottery, T-shirts, wood carvings, stone figures, gifts for children, and more. ✉ *75 W. Main St.* ☎ *435/425–3716* 🌐 *torreytradingpost.com* 🕑 *Daily 8:30 am–9 pm.*

WHERE TO EAT

$$$ AMERICAN Fodor's Choice ★ 🍴 **Cafe Diablo.** This restaurant is one of the state's best. White plaster walls are a perfect setting for the local art on display in the intimate dining room, or you can dine outside on the patio. Innovative Southwestern entrées include marinated Utah lamb, and beef tenderloin medallions topped with roasted-shallot butter. The rattlesnake cakes, made with free-range desert rattler and served with ancho-rosemary aioli, are delicious and a steadfast menu item. House-made pastries, served with ice cream, are made with fruits picked at nearby Fruita, many of the vegetables and herbs come from the restaurant's own organic farm, just down the road, and other ingredients are carefully selected from local producers. The international wine list is well chosen and reasonably priced. [$] *Average main: $26* ✉ *599 W. Main St. (Hwy. 24)* ☎ *435/425–3070* 🌐 *cafediablo.net* 🕑 *Closed late Oct.–early Apr.*

$$ AMERICAN FAMILY 🍴 **Capitol Reef Café.** For a varied selection of solid and healthy fare, visit this unpretentious eatery. Favorites include the vegetable salad and the flaky smoked or grilled fillet of rainbow trout, and the breakfasts are both delicious and hearty. A handful of vegetarian offerings includes mushroom lasagna, and there's a surprisingly expansive beer and wine list. Earth tones and Native American flute music make for a truly laid-back vibe, and the attached gift shop has an eclectic selection of books about the Southwest. [$] *Average main: $13* ✉ *360 W. Main St. (Hwy. 24)* ☎ *435/425–3271* 🌐 *capitolreefinn.com* 🕑 *Closed Nov.–Mar.*

9

WHERE TO STAY

$ HOTEL 🏨 **Austin's Chuckwagon Motel.** Foremost at this pleasant complex are friendly service and immaculate rooms: choose between standard rooms at the motel-style lodge or stand-alone cabins that sleep up to six. **Pros:** shady and cool; perfect for families; oversize pool. **Cons:** family atmosphere might not please solitary travelers. [$] *Rooms from: $91* ✉ *12 W. Main St.* ☎ *435/425–3335, 800/863–3288* 🌐 *austinschuckwagonmotel.com* 🛏 *25 rooms, 1 suite, 3 cabins* 🕑 *Closed Nov.–Mar.* 🍽 *No meals.*

$ HOTEL 🏨 **Rim Rock Inn.** On a bluff with outstanding views into the desert, this motel was the first one to accommodate visitors to Capitol Reef. **Pros:** stunning views in every direction; reasonable price. **Cons:** predictable motel-style rooms; no shade on property; only a Continental breakfast is included in the price. [$] *Rooms from: $74* ✉ *2523 E. Hwy. 24*

☎ 435/425–3398 🌐 therimrock.net 🛏 19 rooms ⏲ Closed Nov.–Mar. 🍴 Breakfast.

$$ B&B/INN 🏨 **SkyRidge Inn Bed and Breakfast.** Each of the inn's windows offers an exceptional year-round view of the desert and mountains surrounding Capitol Reef National Park. **Pros:** supremely comfortable; convenient to gas and other amenities. **Cons:** no pets. [$] *Rooms from: $119 ✉ 950 E. Hwy. 24 ☎ 435/425–3222, 877/824–1508 🌐 skyridgeinn.com 🛏 3 rooms, 3 suites 🍴 Breakfast.*

ARCHES
NATIONAL PARK

10

WELCOME TO ARCHES NATIONAL PARK

Delicate Arch

TOP REASONS TO GO

★ **Arch appeal:** Nowhere in the world has such a large array and quantity of natural arches.

★ **Legendary landscape:** This section of Utah is every photographer's dream. No wonder it's been the backdrop for Hollywood legends from John Wayne to Indiana Jones and *Thelma & Louise.*

★ **Treasures hanging in the balance:** Landscape Arch and Balanced Rock look like they might topple tomorrow, and they could! Come quick as the features in this park erode and evolve constantly.

★ **Fins and needles:** Fins are parallel vertical shafts of eroding rock that slowly disintegrate into towerlike "needles." The spaces around and between them will carve their way into your memories like the wind and water that formed them.

★ **Moab:** Utah's alternative town is a great base from which to explore by foot, bicycle, balloon, watercraft, and four-wheeler.

Balanced Rock

1 Devils Garden. About 18 miles from the visitor center, this is the end of the paved road in Arches. The park's only campground, a picnic area, and access to drinking water give way to several trails, including the incomparable Landscape Arch.

2 Fiery Furnace. This forbiddingly named area about 14 miles from the visitor center is so labeled because its orange spires of rock look much like tongues of flame, especially in the late-afternoon sun. Reservations are required weeks in advance to join the twice-daily ranger-guided treks here from March to October; otherwise, you need a permit and canyoneering savvy.

3 The Windows. Reached on a spur 11¾ miles from the visitor center, this area of the park is where visitors with little time stop. Here you can see many of the park's natural arches from your car or on an easy rolling trail.

4 Balanced Rock. This is the kind of landmark only nature can conjure up—a giant rock teetering atop a pedestal, creating a 128-foot formation of red-rock grandeur right along the roadside, 9¼ miles from the visitor center.

5 Petrified Dunes. Just a tiny pull-out about 5 miles from the visitor center, this scenic stop is where you can take pictures of acres and acres of petrified sand dunes.

6 Courthouse Towers. The Three Gossips, Sheep Rock, and Tower of Babel are the rock formations to see here. Enter this section of the park 3 miles past the visitor center. The Park Avenue Trail winds through the area, which was named for its steep walls and towers that look like buildings.

7 Moab. A river-running, mountain-biking, canyoneering hub, unconventional Moab is the can't-miss base for all your adventures—and comforts—about 5 miles south of the park.

Bighorn Sheep

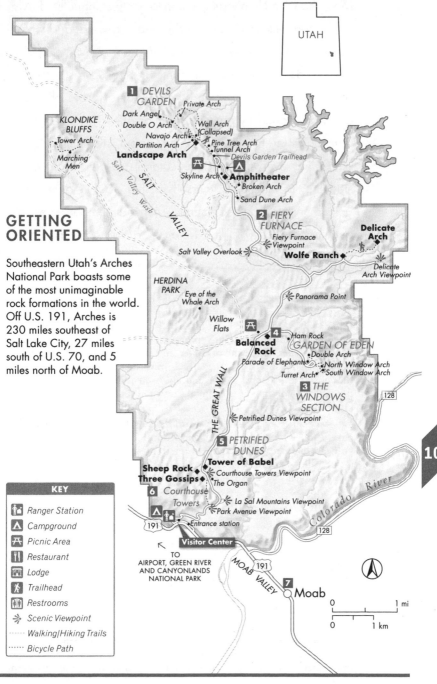

UTAH

1 DEVILS GARDEN

KLONDIKE BLUFFS
Tower Arch
Marching Men

Dark Angel
Double O Arch
Navajo Arch
Partition Arch
Landscape Arch

Private Arch
Wall Arch (Collapsed)
Pine Tree Arch
Tunnel Arch
Devils Garden Trailhead

Skyline Arch
Amphitheater
Broken Arch
Sand Dune Arch

SALT VALLEY
Salt Valley Wash

2 FIERY FURNACE
Fiery Furnace Viewpoint
Salt Valley Overlook
Wolfe Ranch

Delicate Arch
Delicate Arch Viewpoint

HERDINA PARK
Eye of the Whale Arch

Panorama Point

Willow Flats

Balanced Rock
4
Ham Rock
GARDEN OF EDEN
Double Arch
Parade of Elephants
North Window Arch
Turret Arch
South Window Arch

3 THE WINDOWS SECTION

128

10

Petrified Dunes Viewpoint

THE GREAT WALL

5 PETRIFIED DUNES

Tower of Babel
Sheep Rock
Courthouse Towers Viewpoint
Three Gossips
The Organ
6 Courthouse Towers
La Sal Mountains Viewpoint
Park Avenue Viewpoint
191
Entrance station

GETTING ORIENTED

Southeastern Utah's Arches National Park boasts some of the most unimaginable rock formations in the world. Off U.S. 191, Arches is 230 miles southeast of Salt Lake City, 27 miles south of U.S. 70, and 5 miles north of Moab.

KEY

- 🧍 Ranger Station
- ⛺ Campground
- 🍴 Picnic Area
- 🍽 Restaurant
- 🏨 Lodge
- 🚶 Trailhead
- 🚻 Restrooms
- 🌿 Scenic Viewpoint
- ----- Walking/Hiking Trails
- ······ Bicycle Path

Visitor Center

TO AIRPORT, GREEN RIVER AND CANYONLANDS NATIONAL PARK

Colorado River

128

MOAB VALLEY
191
7 Moab

0   1 mi
0   1 km

Updated by
John Blodgett

More than 1 million visitors come to Arches annually, drawn by the red-rock landscape and its teasing wind- and water-carved rock formations. The park is named for the 2,500-plus sandstone arches that frame horizons, cast precious shade, and nobly withstand the withering forces of nature and time. Fancifully named attractions like Three Penguins, Queen Nefertiti, and Tower of Babel stir the curiosity, beckoning even the most delicate of travelers from road-side locales. Immerse yourself in this 76,519-acre park, but don't lose yourself entirely—summer temperatures frequently crack 100°F, and water is hard to come by inside the park boundaries.

ARCHES PLANNER

WHEN TO GO

The busiest times of year are spring and fall. In the spring blooming wildflowers herald the end of winter, and temperatures in the 70s bring the year's largest crowds. The crowds remain steady in summer as the thermostat approaches 100°F and above in July and August. Sudden dramatic cloudbursts create rainfalls over red rock walls in late-summer "monsoon" season.

Fall weather is perfect—clear, warm days and crisp, cool nights. The park is much quieter in winter, and from December through February you can hike any of the trails in relative solitude. Snow seldom falls in the valley beneath La Sal Mountains, and when it does, Arches is a photographer's paradise, as snow drapes slickrock mounds and natural rock windows.

AVG. HIGH/LOW TEMPS.

Jan.	Feb.	Mar.	Apr.	May	June
44/19	53/25	64/33	76/39	84/49	98/58
July	Aug.	Sept.	Oct.	Nov.	Dec.
100/62	99/61	86/50	77/40	58/32	48/21

Note: Extreme highs often exceed 100°F in July and August.

FESTIVALS AND EVENTS

SUMMER **Canyonlands PRCA Rodeo.** Cowboys come to the Old Spanish Trail Arena (just south of Moab) for three days in late May or early June to try their luck on thrashing bulls and broncs at this annual Western tradition. ✉ *3641 S. Hwy. 191, Moab* ☎ *435/259–4852* ⊕ *www. moabcanyonlandsrodeo.com* ✉ *From $10.*

FALL **Green River Melon Days.** The town claims its melon festival, dating to 1906, is the world's oldest. All the watermelon you can eat, an old-fashioned parade, a 5k run, and other small-town-America activities await you on the third Saturday of September. ☎ *435/564–3448* ⊕ *melondays.com.*

PLANNING YOUR TIME

There's no food service within the park, so you'll need to pack snacks, lunch, and plenty of water each day before you head into the park. You'll also need to plan ahead to get tickets to the daily Fiery Furnace walk with a ranger. It's a highlight for those who are adventurous and in good shape, but during most of the year, you must reserve your spot in advance at ⊕ *www.recreation.gov.* If you don't have a reservation, you can check for spots at the visitor center (make that your very first stop). The one-day itinerary *(⇨ below)* is based on what to do if you can't take the walk or what to do on a different day. On the day of your Fiery Furnace walk, you can fill in your spare time with a walk on the Park Avenue trail. And if you have a third day, take a rafting trip on the Colorado River, which runs along the park's boundary.

ARCHES IN ONE DAY

Start as early as sunrise for cool temperatures and some of the best natural light, and head out on the 3-mile round-trip hike on the **Delicate Arch Trail.** The route is strenuous but quite rewarding. Pause for a healthy snack before heading to **Devils Garden,** another great spot for morning photography, where you'll also find the easy, primarily flat trail to **Landscape Arch,** the second of the park's two must-see arches. Along the way, picnic in the shade of a juniper or in a rock alcove. By the time you return, you'll be ready to see the rest of the park by car, with some short strolls on easy paths.

In the mid- to late afternoon, drive to **Balanced Rock** for photos, then on to the **Windows.** Wander around on the easy gravel paths for more great photo ops. Depending on what time the sun is due to set, go into town for dinner before or after you drive out to Delicate Arch or the Fiery Furnace and watch the sun set the rocks on fire.

10

GETTING HERE AND AROUND

AIR TRAVEL

The nearest airport is Canyonlands Field (aka Grand County Airport ☎ *435/259–4849*), 18 miles north of Moab. Delta SkyWest flies daily to and from Salt Lake City. Grand Junction Airport (GJT) is 110 miles away in Colorado.

CAR TRAVEL

Interstate 70 is the highway that gets you across Utah from Denver. To dip southeast toward Moab, exit the interstate onto U.S. 191, a main artery running all the way south to the Arizona border, skirting Arches' western border, Moab, and the Manti–La Sal National Forest along the way. Alternatively, you can take Highway 128, Colorado River Scenic Byway, traveling just east of Arches. On either road, services can be far apart.

Branching off the main, 18-mile park road are two spurs, one 2½ miles to the Windows section and one 2¾ miles to the Delicate Arch trailhead and viewpoint. There are several four-wheel-drive roads in the park; always check at the visitor center for conditions before attempting to drive them. U.S. 191 tends to back up midmorning to early afternoon. There's likely to be less traffic at 8 am or sunset.

TRAIN TRAVEL

The California Zephyr, operated by Amtrak (☎ 800/872–7245), stops daily in Green River, about 50 miles northwest of Moab.

PARK ESSENTIALS

PARK FEES AND PERMITS

Admission to the park is $10 per vehicle and $5 per person on foot, motorcycle, or bicycle, good for seven days. You must pay admission to Canyonlands separately. A $25 local park pass grants you admission for one year to both Arches and Canyonlands parks as well as Natural Bridges and Hovenweep national monuments.

Fees are required for the Fiery Furnace ranger-led hike ($10) and for a permit ($4) to hike without a park ranger in the Fiery Furnace. Reservations must be made months in advance.

PARK HOURS

Arches National Park is open year-round, seven days a week, around the clock. It's in the mountain time zone.

CELL-PHONE RECEPTION

Cell-phone reception is available intermittently in the park. You can find a public telephone at the park's visitor center.

RESTAURANTS

Because most people come to Arches to play outside, casual trekking-wear rules—sandals, shorts, and T-shirts in the very hot summers. Whether you select an award-winning Continental restaurant in Moab, a nearby resort, or the tavern in Green River, you can dress comfortably. But don't let the relaxed attire fool you. There are some wonderful culinary surprises waiting for you, and some come with a side of spectacular views as a bonus.

In the park itself, there are no dining facilities and no snack bars. Supermarkets, bakeries, and delis in downtown Moab will be happy to make you food to go. If you bring a packed lunch, there are several picnic areas from which to choose.

HOTELS

Though there are no hotels or cabins in the park itself, in the surrounding area every type of lodging is available, from economy chain motels to B&Bs and high-end, high-adventure resorts. It's important to know when popular events take place, however, as accommodations can, and do, fill up weeks ahead of time.

VISITOR INFORMATION

PARK CONTACT INFORMATION

Arches National Park ⊠ N. U.S. 191, Moab ☎ 435/719–2299 ⊕ www. nps.gov/arch.

CLOSE UP

Plants and Wildlife in Arches

As in any desert environment, the best time to see wildlife in Arches is early morning or evening. Summer temperatures keep most animals tucked away in cool places, though ravens and lizards are exceptions. If you happen to be in the right place at the right time, you may spot one of the beautiful turquoise-necklace-collared lizards. It's more likely you'll see the western whiptail. Mule deer, jackrabbits, and small rodents are usually active in cool morning hours or near dusk. You may spot a lone

coyote foraging day or night. The park protects a small herd of desert bighorns, and in winter some of them can be seen early in the morning grazing beside U.S. 191 south of the Arches entrance. If you encounter bighorn sheep, do not approach them. They have been known to charge people who attempt to get too close. The park's mule deer and small mammals such as chipmunks are very used to seeing people and may allow you to get close—but don't feed them.

VISITOR CENTER
Arches Visitor Center. ⊠ *N. U.S. 191* ☎ *435/719–2299* ⊕ *nps.gov/arch* ⊗ *Hrs vary but generally daily 9–4, with frequently extended hrs Apr.–Oct.*

EXPLORING

Wolfe Ranch. Built in 1906 out of Fremont cottonwoods, this rustic one-room cabin housed Civil War veteran John Wesley Wolfe and his family after their first cabin was lost to a flash flood. Look for remains of a root cellar and a corral as well. Even older than these structures is the nearby Ute rock-art panel by the Delicate Arch trailhead. About 150 feet past the footbridge and before the trail starts to climb, you can see images of bighorn sheep and figures on horseback, as well as some smaller images believed to be dogs. To reach the panel, follow the narrow dirt trail along the rock escarpment until you see the interpretive sign. The cabin is 12.9 miles from park entrance, 1.2 miles off main road. ⊠ *Off Delicate Arch Rd.*

10

SCENIC DRIVES

Arches Main Park Road. Although they are not formally designated as such, the main park road and its two short spurs are scenic and allow you to enjoy many park sights from your car. The main road leads through Courthouse Towers, where you can see Sheep Rock and the Three Gossips, then alongside the Great Wall, the Petrified Dunes, and Balanced Rock. A drive to the Windows section takes you to attractions like Double Arch, and you can see Skyline Arch along the roadside as you approach the campground. The road to Delicate Arch is not particularly scenic, but it allows hiking access to one of the park's main features. Allow about two hours to drive the 45-mile round-trip, more if you explore the spurs and their features and stop at viewpoints along the way. ⊕ *www.nps.gov/arch*.

Fodor's Choice
★ **Colorado River Scenic Byway—Highway 128.** One of the most scenic drives in the country, Highway 128 intersects U.S. 191 3 miles south of Arches. The 44-mile highway runs along the Colorado River with 2,000-foot red rock cliffs rising on both sides. This gorgeous river corridor is home to a winery, orchards, and a couple of luxury lodging options. It also offers a spectacular view of world-class climbing destination Fisher Towers before winding north to Interstate 70. The drive from Moab to I–70 takes at least an hour. ⊠ *Hwy. 128, Moab.*

> **WHAT'S AN ARCH?**
>
> To be defined as an arch, a rock opening must be in a continuous wall of rock and have a minimum opening of 3 feet in any one direction. A natural bridge differs from an arch in that it is formed by water flowing beneath it.

SCENIC STOPS

It's easy to spot some of the arches from your car, but you should really take the time to step outside and walk beneath the spans and giant walls of orange rock. This gives you a much better idea of their proportion. No doubt you will feel as writer Edward Abbey did when he awoke on his first day as a park ranger in Arches: that you're walking in the most beautiful place on Earth. ■TIP→ **Visit as the sun goes down.** At sunset, the rock formations in Arches glow like fire, and you'll often find photographers waiting for magnificent rays to descend on Delicate Arch or some other site. The Fiery Furnace earns its name as its narrow fins glow red just before the sun dips below the horizon. Full-moon nights are particularly dramatic in Arches as the creamy white Navajo sandstone reflects light, and eerie silhouettes are created by towering fins and formations.

Balanced Rock. One of the park's favorite sights, 9¼ miles from park entrance, this rock is visible for several minutes as you approach—and just gets more impressive and mysterious as you get closer. The formation's total height is 128 feet, with the huge balanced rock rising 55 feet above the pedestal. Be sure to hop out of the car and walk the short (530-yard) loop around the base. ⊠ *Arches Scenic Dr.*

Fodor's Choice
★ **Delicate Arch.** The iconic symbol of the park and the state (it appears on many of Utah's license plates), the Delicate Arch is frankly tall and muscular compared to many of the spans in the park—and it's big enough to shelter a four-story building. The arch is a remnant of an Entrada Sandstone fin; the rest of the rock has eroded and now frames La Sal Mountains in the background. Drive 2¼ miles off the main road to view the arch from a distance, or hike right up to it. The trail, 13 miles from park entrance and 2¼ miles off the main road, is a moderately strenuous 3-mile round-trip hike. ⊠ *Delicate Arch Rd.*

Double Arch. In the Windows section of the park, 11¾ miles from park entrance, Double Arch has appeared in several Hollywood movies, including *Indiana Jones and the Last Crusade*. The northern arch is visible from the parking lot, but walk the short trail to see the southern one, as well as Turret Arch. ⊠ *The Windows Rd.*

Fiery Furnace. Fewer than 10% of the park's visitors ever descend into the chasms and washes of Fiery Furnace (a permit or a ranger-led hike is the only way to go), but you can gain an appreciation for this twisted, unyielding landscape from the overlook, 14 miles from the park entrance. At sunset, the rocks glow a vibrant flamelike red, which gives the formation its daunting moniker. ⊠ *Off Arches Scenic Dr.*

Skyline Arch. A quick walk from the parking lot at Skyline Arch, 16½ miles from park entrance, gives you closer views and better photos. The short trail is less than a half-mile round-trip and only takes a few minutes to travel. ⊠ *Devil's Garden Rd.*

FAMILY **The Windows.** As you head north from the park entrance, turn right at Balanced Rock to find this concentration of natural windows, caves, and needles 11¾ miles from park entrance. Stretch your legs on the easy paths that wind between the arches and soak in a variety of geological formations. ⊠ *The Windows Rd.*

EDUCATIONAL OFFERINGS

RANGER PROGRAMS

As you explore Arches, look for sandwich boards announcing "Ranger on Trail" and stop for a 3- to 10-minute program led by park staff. Topics range from geology and desert plants to mountain lions and the Colorado River. Most nights, spring through fall, more in-depth campfire programs are available at Devils Garden Campground amphitheater. You may also find guided walks (in addition to the beloved Fiery Furnace walk) during your visit. For information on current schedules and locations of park programs, contact the visitor center (☎ *435/719–2299*) or check the bulletin boards throughout the park.

FAMILY **Fiery Furnace Walk.** Join a park ranger on a two- or three-hour walk
Fodor's Choice through a labyrinth of rock fins and narrow sandstone canyons. You'll
★ see arches that can't be viewed from the park road and spend time listening to the desert. You should be relatively fit and not afraid of heights if you plan to take this moderately strenuous walk. Wear sturdy hiking shoes, sunscreen, and a hat, and bring at least a liter of water. Walks into the Fiery Furnace are usually offered twice a day (hours vary) and leave from Fiery Furnace Viewpoint, off the main road, about 15 miles from park visitor center. Tickets must be reserved up to six months in advance (at ⊕ *www.recreation.gov*) of mid-March–October, or purchased at the visitor center from November–February. Children ages 7–12 pay half price; the walk is not recommended for children under 5. ■TIP➜ **Book**

10

GOOD READS

Arches Visitor Center Bookstore. Operated by Canyonlands Natural History Association, this bookstore at the park entrance is the place in the park to buy maps, guidebooks, driving tours on CD, and material about the natural and cultural history of Arches National Park. ✉ *Off Hwy. 191* ☎ *435/259–6003.*

■ *127 Hours: Between a Rock and a Hard Place,* by Aron Ralston. This true story—made into a movie of the same name starring James

Franco—took place southeast of Arches and is a modern-day survivor story of solitary man in nature.

■ *Canyon Country Wildflowers,* by Damian Fagan, can help you name the colorful blossoms you see during wildflower season (spring and early summer).

■ *Desert Solitaire.* Eminent naturalist Edward Abbey's first ranger assignment was Arches; this classic is a must-read.

early as the program usually fills months prior to each walk. ✉ *Trailhead on Arches Scenic Dr.* ☎ *$10* ⏰ *Mid-Mar.–Oct., daily (hrs vary).*

FAMILY **Junior Ranger Program.** Kids 2 through 12 can pick up a Junior Ranger booklet at the visitor center. It's full of activities, word games, drawings, and thought-provoking material about the park and the wildlife. To earn your Junior Ranger badge, you must complete several activities in the booklet, attend a ranger program, or watch the park film and pick up some trash in the park. ■TIP➜ **For ranger program veterans ages 8 and up, ask about the "extra credit" Red Rock Ranger Program.** ☎ *435/719–2299* 🖰 *Free.*

LEARNING RESOURCES

FAMILY **Red Rock Explorer Pack.** Better than borrowing from a library, families can check out a youth backpack filled with tools for learning about both Arches and Canyonlands national parks. Four books, a three-ring binder of activities, hand lens magnifier and binoculars are just some of the loaner items. Backpacks can be returned to either Arches or Island in the Sky visitor centers. Use of the backpack is free with a credit-card imprint in case of loss or damage to the pack or enclosed items. ☎ *435/719–2299* 🖰 *Free.*

SPORTS AND THE OUTDOORS

Arches National Park lies in the middle of one of the adventure capitals of the United States. Deep canyons and towering walls are everywhere you look. Slick sandstone surfaces, known as slickrock, make for some of the world's best mountain biking. Thousand-foot sandstone walls draw rock climbers from across the globe. Hikers can choose from shady canyons or red rock ridges that put you in the company of the West's big sky. The Colorado River forms the southeast boundary of the park and can give you every grade of white-water adventure.

Moab-based outfitters can set you up for any sport you may have a desire to try: mountain biking, ATVs, dirt bikes, four-wheel-drive vehicles, kayaking, climbing, stand-up paddleboarding, and even sky-diving. Within the park, it's best to stick with basics such as hiking, sightseeing, and photography. Climbers and other adventure seekers should always inquire at the visitor center about restrictions. Climbing on any arch inside the park is prohibited.

> **NOTABLE QUOTE**
>
> "You can't see *anything* from a car; you've got to get out and walk, better yet crawl, on hands and knees, over the sandstone and through the thornbush and cactus. When traces of blood begin to mark your trail you'll see something, maybe."—Edward Abbey, *Desert Solitaire*

BICYCLING

There's world-class biking all around Arches National Park, but the park proper is not the best place to explore on two wheels. Bicycles are allowed only on established roads, and because there are no shoulders, cyclists share the roadway with drivers and pedestrians gawking at the scenery. If you do want to take a spin in the park, try the dirt-and-gravel Willow Flats Road, the old entrance to the park. The road is about 6½ miles long one-way and starts directly across from the Balanced Rock parking lot. It's a pretty mountain-bike ride on dirt and sand through slickrock, pinyon, and juniper country. You must stay on the road with your bicycle or you chance steep fines for destroying fragile vegetation and soils.

BIRD-WATCHING

Within the park you'll definitely see plenty of the big, black, beautiful raven. Look for them perched on top of a picturesque juniper branch or balancing on the bald knob of a rock. The noisy black-billed magpie populates the park, as do the more melodic canyon and rock wrens. Lucky visitors will spot a red-tailed hawk and hear its distinctive call.

Serious birders will have more fun visiting the 875-acre **Scott M. Matheson Wetlands Preserve** 5 miles south of the park. The wetlands is home to more than 225 species of birds including the wood duck, western screech owl, indigo bunting, and plumbeous vireo.

BOATING AND RIVER EXPEDITIONS

Although the Colorado River runs along the border of the park, there is no boating within the park proper. You can, however, enjoy a splashy ride nearby on the Fisher Towers stretch of the river north of Moab, and there are plenty of fine outfitters in Moab that can set you up for expeditions.

10

FISHING

There is no fishing in Arches National Park, and the Colorado River is too silty to offer good fishing. The nearby La Sal Mountains are dotted with small lakes that are stocked with small trout, but finding good native trout fishing in the area will take some effort.

FOUR-WHEELING

With thousands of acres of nearby Bureau of Land Management lands to enjoy, it's hardly necessary to use the park's limited trails for four-wheel adventures. You can, however, go backcountry in Arches on the Willow Flats Road and the Salt Valley Road—just don't set out for this expedition without first stopping at the visitor center to learn of current conditions. Salt Valley Road is very sandy and requires special driving skills.

HIKING

Getting out on any one of the park trails will surely cause you to fall in love with this Mars-like landscape. But remember, you are hiking in a desert environment and approximately 1 mile above sea level. Many people succumb to heat and dehydration because they do not drink enough water. Park rangers recommend a gallon of water per day per person.

EASY

FAMILY **Balanced Rock Trail.** You'll want to stop at Balanced Rock for photo opportunities, so you may as well walk the easy, partially paved trail around the famous landmark. This is one of the most accessible trails in the park and is suitable for small children and folks who may have difficulty walking. The trail is only about 530 yards round-trip; you should allow 15 minutes for the walk. *Easy.* ⊠ *Trailhead approximately 9¼ miles from park entrance.*

Broken Arch Trail. An easy walk across open grassland, this loop trail passes Broken Arch, which is also visible from the road. The arch gets its name because it appears to be cracked in the middle, but it's not really broken. The trail is 1¼ miles round-trip, and you should allow about an hour for the walk. *Easy.* ⊠ *Trailhead at end of Sand Dune Arch trail, off Devils Garden Rd., 16½ miles from park entrance.*

Double Arch Trail. If it's not too hot, anyone can walk here from Windows Trail. This relatively flat trail leads you to two massive arches that make for great photo opportunities. The ¾-mile round-trip gives you a good taste of desert flora and fauna. *Easy.* ⊠ *Trailhead 2½ miles from main road, on Windows Section spur road, 9¼ miles from main entrance.*

Landscape Arch. This natural rock opening competes with Kolob Arch at Zion for the title of largest geologic span in the world. Measuring 306 feet from base to base, it appears as a delicate ribbon of rock bending over the horizon. In 1991, a slab of rock about 60 feet long, 11 feet wide, and 4 feet thick fell from the underside, leaving it even thinner. You can reach it by walking a rolling, gravel 1.4-mile-long trail. *Easy.*

✉ *Trailhead at Devils Garden Rd., 18 miles north of park entrance off main road.*

Park Avenue Trail. The first named trail that park visitors encounter, this is an easy, 2-mile round-trip walk (with only one small hill) amid walls and towers that resemble a New York City skyline. You'll walk under the gaze of Queen Nefertiti, a giant rock formation that some observers think has Egyptian-looking features. If you are traveling with companions, make it a one-way, 1-mile downhill trek by having them pick you up at the Courthouse Towers Viewpoint. Allow about 45 minutes for the one-way journey. *Easy.* ✉ *Trailhead on Arches Scenic Drive, 2 miles from park entrance.*

> **PAW PRINTS**
>
> If Fido is along for the Arches adventure, keep in mind that pooches aren't allowed on national park trails and must be on leash in the Devils Garden Campground. However, canines can join you on Bureau of Land Management trails, such as Negro Bill Canyon (named for one of the town's first nonnative settlers, William Granstaff), which match the beauty of in-park hikes. The heat can be stifling, so remember to bring enough water for you and your four-legged friend, hit the trails in the early morning hours, and avoid midsummer scorchers.

FAMILY **Sand Dune Arch Trail.** Your kids will return to the car with shoes full of bright red sand from this giant sandbox in the desert and will love exploring in and around the rock. ⚠ **Do not climb or jump off the arch, as doing so has frequently resulted in injuries.** Set aside five minutes for this shady, 530-yard walk and as much time as your children's imaginations allow for play. The trail intersects with the Broken Arch Trail, so if you visit both arches it's a 1½-mile round-trip. *Easy.* ✉ *Trailhead off Arches Scenic Drive, about 16½ miles from park entrance.*

FAMILY **Windows Trail.** The first stop for many visitors to the park, Windows Trail gives you an opportunity to get out and enjoy the desert air. Here you'll see three giant openings in rock and walk on a trail that leads you right through the holes. Allow about an hour on this gently inclined, 1-mile round-trip hike. As 90% of visitors won't follow the "primitive" trail around the backside of the two windows, take advantage if you want some desert solitude. The primitive trail adds an extra half hour to the trip. *Easy.* ✉ *Trailhead on the Windows Rd., off Arches Scenic Dr., 12 miles from park entrance.*

10

MODERATE

Fodor's Choice **Delicate Arch Trail.** To see the park's most famous freestanding arch up
★ close takes effort and won't offer you much solitude—but it's worth every step. The 3-mile round-trip trail ascends via steep slickrock, sandy paths, and along one narrow ledge (at the very end) that might give pause to anyone afraid of heights. Plus, there's almost no shade. First-timers should start early to avoid the midday heat in summer. Still, at sunrise, sunset, and every hour in between, it's the park's most popular and busy trail. ■ **TIP→ Heat mixed with lack of shade makes this a strenuous hike in the summer. Bring plenty of water, as heat stroke is a very real possibility.** Allow two to three hours for this hike, depending

on your fitness level and how long you plan to linger at the arch. If you go at sunset or sunrise, bring a headlamp or flashlight. Don't miss Wolfe Ranch and some ancient rock art near the trailhead. *Moderate.* ⊠ *Trailhead on Delicate Arch Rd., 13 miles from park entrance, 2¼ miles off main road.*

Fodor's Choice
★
Devils Garden Trail. Landscape Arch is the highlight of this trail but is just one of several arches within reach depending on your ambitions and the heat. It's an easy ¾-mile one-way trip (mostly gravel, relatively flat) to Landscape Arch, one of the longest stone spans in the world at 306 feet and one of the most fragile-looking. In fact, you can see where a 60-foot-long piece fell off the underside in 1991, leading to the closure of the trail that used to go under the span. This serves as a reminder of the impermanence of the features in the park. Beyond Landscape Arch the scenery changes dramatically and the hike becomes more strenuous, as you must climb and straddle slickrock fins and negotiate some short, steep inclines. Finally, the stacked spans that compose Double O Arch come into view around a sharp bend. Allow up to three hours for this round-trip hike of just over 4 miles. For a still longer hike, venture on to see a formation called Dark Angel and then return to the trailhead on the primitive loop. The hike to Dark Angel is a difficult route through fins with a short side trip to Private Arch. If you hike all the way to Dark Angel and return on the primitive loop, the trail is about 6 miles round-trip, not including possible (and worthwhile) detours to Navajo Arch, Partition Arch, Tunnel Arch, and Pine Tree Arch. Allow about five hours for this adventure, take plenty of water, and watch your route carefully. ■TIP→ **Pick up the park's useful guide to Devils Garden, or download it from the website before you go.** *Moderate.* ⊠ *Trailhead on Devils Garden Rd., off main road, 18 miles from park entrance.*

Tower Arch Trail. Check with park rangers before attempting the dirt road to Klondike Bluffs parking area. If rains haven't washed out the road, a trip to this seldom-visited area provides a solitude-filled hike climaxed with a giant rock opening. Allow from two to three hours for this 3½-mile round-trip hike, not including the drive. *Moderate.*

✉ *Trailhead at Klondike Bluffs parking area, 24½ miles from park entrance, 7¾ miles off main road.*

DIFFICULT

Fiery Furnace. This area of the park has taken on a near-mythical lure for park visitors, who are drawn to the forbidden nature of Fiery Furnace. Rangers strongly discourage inexperienced hikers from entering here—in fact, you can't enter without watching a safety video and getting a permit ($4). As a result, up to one month's advance reservations are now required to get a spot on the 2-mile round-trip ranger-led hikes ($10) through this unique formation. *(⇨ Ranger Programs)* A hike here is a challenging but fascinating trip amid rugged rocks and sandy washes into the heart of Arches. The trek may require the use of hands and feet to scramble up and through narrow cracks and along vertigo-inducing ledges above drop-offs and there are no trail markings. If you're not familiar with the Furnace you can easily get lost and cause resource damage, so watch your step and use great caution. ■TIP➜ **Call or visit the website (⊕ recreation.gov) for reservations, which are a must.** The less intrepid should look into Fiery Furnace from the overlook off the main road. *Difficult.* ✉ *Trailhead off main road, about 15 miles from visitor center.*

ROCK CLIMBING AND CANYONEERING

Rock climbers travel from across the country to scale the sheer red rock walls of Arches National Park and surrounding areas. Most climbing routes in the park require advanced techniques. ■TIP➜ **Permits (free) are required, available 24 hours a day outside the visitor center.** Two popular routes ascend Owl Rock in the Garden of Eden (about 10 miles from the visitor center); the well-worn route has a difficulty of 5.8, while a more challenging option is 5.11. Many climbing routes are available in the Park Avenue area, about 2¼ miles from the visitor center. These routes are also extremely difficult climbs. No commercial outfitters are allowed to lead rock-climbing excursions in the park. Before climbing, it's imperative that you stop at the visitor center and check with a ranger about climbing regulations.

WHERE TO EAT

PICNIC AREAS

Balanced Rock. The view is the best part of this picnic spot opposite the Balanced Rock parking area. There are no cooking facilities or water, but there are tables. If you sit just right, you might find some shade under a small juniper; otherwise, this is an exposed site. Pit toilets are nearby. ✉ *Arches Scenic Dr., 9¼ miles from park entrance on main road.*

Devils Garden. There are grills, water, picnic tables, and restrooms here, and depending on the time of day, some shade from junipers and rock walls. It's a good place for lunch before or after a hike. ✉ *On main road, 18 miles from park entrance.*

Best Campgrounds In and Around Arches

Campgrounds in and around Moab range from sprawling RV parks with myriad amenities to quaint, shady retreats near a babbling brook. The Devils Garden Campground in the park is a wonderful spot to call home for a few days, though it is often full and does not provide an RV dump station. More than 350 campsites are operated in the vicinity by the Bureau of Land Management—their sites on the Colorado River and near the Slickrock Trail are some of the nicest (and most affordable) in the area. The most centrally located campgrounds in Moab will generally provide services needed by RV travelers.

IN THE PARK
Devils Garden Campground. This campground is one of the most unusual—and gorgeous— in the West, and in the national park system, for that matter. Reservations often fill six months in advance. ⊠ *Off main road, 18 miles from park entrance* ☎ *435/719–2299, 435/259–4351 for group reservations, 877/444–6777 for NRRS reservations* ⊕ *www.recreation. gov.*

OUTSIDE THE PARK
Bureau of Land Management Campgrounds. Most of the more than 350 sites at 26 different BLM campgrounds are in the Moab area, including some stunning sites along the Colorado River (Route 128 and

Route 279), Sand Flats Recreation Area (near the Slickrock Trail), and Canyon Flats Recreation Area (outside Needles District of Canyonlands). ☎ *435/259–2100* ⊕ *www.blm.gov/ utah/moab.*

Canyonlands Campground. Although this camping park is in downtown Moab, the campground is astride Mill Creek and has many shade trees. ⊠ *555 S. Main St., Moab* ☎ *435/259–6848 or 888/522–6848* ⊕ *moabrvresorts.com/canyonlands/.*

Moab Valley RV Resort. Near the Colorado River, this campground with an expansive view feels more like a mall than a campground with its abundant space, activities, and services. ⊠ *1773 N. U.S. 191, Moab* ☎ *435/259–4469* ⊕ *moabrvresorts. com/moab-valley/.*

Slickrock Campground. At one of Moab's older campgrounds you find lots of mature shade trees and all the basic amenities—plus a heated pool and two hot tubs where adults have priority. ⊠ *1301½ N. U.S. 191, Moab* ☎ *435/259–7660 or 800/448–8873* ⊕ *www.slickrockcampground.com.*

Up the Creek Campground. Perhaps the quietest of the in-town campgrounds, Up the Creek lies under big cottonwoods on the banks of Mill Creek. ⊠ *210 E. 300 S, Moab* ☎ *435/260–1888* ⊕ *www.moabup thecreek.com.*

CANYONLANDS
NATIONAL PARK

WELCOME TO CANYONLANDS NATIONAL PARK

Colorado River

TOP REASONS TO GO

★ **Endless vistas:** The view from the Island in the Sky stretches for miles as you look out over millennia of sculpting by wind and rain.

★ **Seeking solitude:** Needles, the most interesting part of the park to explore on foot, sees very few visitors, so you'll have it all to yourself.

★ **Radical rides:** The Cataract Canyon rapids and the White Rim Trail are world-class adventures by boat or bike.

★ **Native American artifacts:** View rock art and Ancestral Puebloan dwellings in the park.

★ **Wonderful wilderness:** Some of the country's most untouched landscapes are within the park's boundaries, and they're worth the extra effort needed to get there.

★ **The night skies:** Far away from city lights, Canyonlands is ideal for stargazing.

Great Gallery

1 **Island in the Sky.** From any of the overlooks here you can see for miles and look down thousands of feet to canyon floors. Chocolate-brown canyons are capped by white rock, and deep-red monuments rise nearby.

2 **Needles.** Pink, orange, and red rock is layered with white rock and stands in spires and pinnacles around grassy meadows. Extravagantly red mesas and buttes interrupt the horizon, as in a postcard of the Old West.

3 **The Maze.** Only the most intrepid adventurers explore these remote rock formations.

4 **Rivers.** For many, rafting the rivers is the best way to see the park. They are as wild as when John Wesley Powell explored them in the mid-1800s.

5 **Horseshoe Canyon.** Plan on several hours of dirt-road driving to get here, but the famous rock-art panel "Great Gallery" is a grand reward at the end of a long hike.

GETTING ORIENTED

Canyonlands National Park, in southeastern Utah, is divided into three distinct land districts and the river district, so it can be a little daunting to visit. It's exhausting, but not impossible, to explore the Island in the Sky and Needles in the same day.

Chesler Park

KEY
👪 Ranger Station
⛰ Campground
🛏 Picnic Area
🍴 Restaurant
🏨 Lodge
🚶 Trailhead
🚻 Restrooms
⇝ Scenic Viewpoint
······ Walking/Hiking Trails
······ Bicycle Path

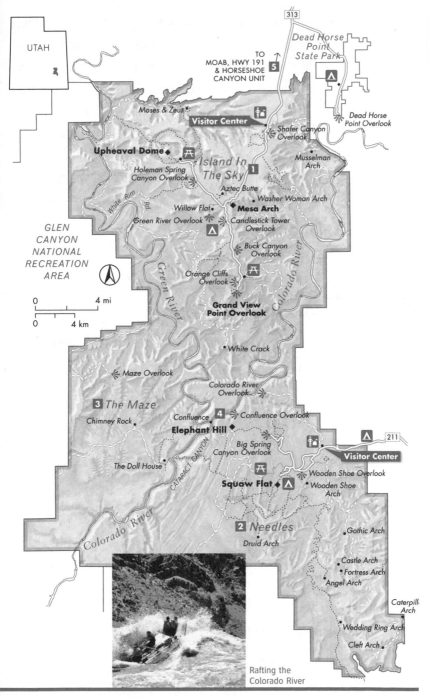

UTAH

TO
MOAB, HWY 191
& HORSESHOE
CANYON UNIT
5
313

Dead Horse
Point
State Park

Dead Horse
Point Overlook

Moses & Zeus

Visitor Center

Shafer Canyon
Overlook

Upheaval Dome

*Island In
The Sky* **1**

Musselman
Arch

Holeman Spring
Canyon Overlook

Aztec Butte

White Rim

Washer Woman Arch

Willow Flat

Mesa Arch

GLEN
CANYON
NATIONAL
RECREATION
AREA

Green River Overlook

Candlestick Tower
Overlook

Green River

Buck Canyon
Overlook

Orange Cliffs
Overlook

0   4 mi

0   4 km

**Grand View
Point Overlook**

Colorado River

White Crack

Maze Overlook

Colorado River
Overlook

3 *The Maze*

Confluence **4** Confluence Overlook

Chimney Rock

Elephant Hill

Big Spring
Canyon Overlook

Visitor Center
211

The Doll House

CATARACT CANYON

Squaw Flat

Wooden Shoe Overlook

Wooden Shoe
Arch

Colorado River

2 *Needles*

Gothic Arch

Druid Arch

Castle Arch
Fortress Arch
Angel Arch

Caterpill
Arch

Wedding Ring Arch

Cleft Arch

Rafting the
Colorado River

Updated by
John Blodgett

Canyonlands is truly four parks in one, but most visitors drive through the panoramic vistas of Island in the Sky and barely venture anywhere else. If you've come this far, plan a half day to hike around the Needles District and see the park from the bottom up. To truly experience Canyonlands, you should also float down the Green and Colorado rivers on a family-friendly rafting trip—and if it's rapids you seek, you can take on the white water in the legendary Cataract Canyon. The Maze is so remote that its riverbeds, slot canyons, and stark rock formations are only for the truly hardy. There's a reason Butch Cassidy hid out here.

CANYONLANDS PLANNER

WHEN TO GO

Gorgeous weather means that spring and fall are most popular for visitors. Canyonlands is seldom crowded, but in the spring backpackers and four-wheelers populate the trails and roads. During Easter week, some of the four-wheel-drive trails in the park are used for Jeep Safari, an annual event drawing thousands of visitors to town.

The crowds thin out by July as the thermostat approaches 100°F and beyond for about four weeks. It's a great time to get out on the Colorado or Green River winding through the park. October can be rainy, but the region receives only 8 inches of rain annually.

The well-kept secret is that winter is the best time in the park. Crowds are gone, roads are good, and snowcapped mountains stand in the background. Winter here is one of nature's most memorable shows, with red rock dusted white and low-floating clouds partially obscuring canyons and towers.

AVG. HIGH/LOW TEMPS.

Jan.	Feb.	Mar.	Apr.	May	June
44/22	52/28	64/35	71/42	82/51	93/60
July	Aug.	Sept.	Oct.	Nov.	Dec.
100/67	97/66	88/55	74/42	56/30	45/23

PLANNING YOUR TIME
CANYONLANDS IN ONE DAY

Your day begins with a choice: Island in the Sky or Needles. If you want expansive vistas looking across southeast Utah's canyons, head for the island, where you stand atop a giant mesa. If you want to walk among Canyonlands' needles and buttes, Needles is your destination. If you have a second or third day in the area, consider contacting an outfitter to take you on a rafting or 4x4 trip. ■**TIP➜ Before venturing into the park, top off your gas tank, pack a picnic lunch, and stock up on plenty of water.**

ISLAND IN THE SKY

Make your first stop along the main park road at **Shafer Canyon Overlook.** A short walk takes you out on a finger of land with views of the canyon over both sides. From here you can see Shafer Trail's treacherous descent as it hugs the canyon wall below.

Stop at the visitor center to learn about ranger talks or special programs, then drive to **Mesa Arch.** Grab your camera and water bottle for the short hike out to the arch perched on the cliff's edge. After your excursion, take the spur road to Upheaval Dome, with its picnic spot in the parking lot. A short walk takes you to the first viewpoint of this crater. If you still have energy, 30 more minutes and a little sense of adventure, continue to the second overlook.

Retrace your drive to the main park road and continue to **Grand View Point.** Stroll along the edge of the rim, and see how many landmarks you can spot in the distance. White Rim Overlook is the best of the scenic spots, particularly if you're not afraid of heights and venture all the way out to the end of the rocky cliffs (no guardrail here). On the way back to dinner in Moab, spend an hour in Dead Horse Point State Park.

NEEDLES

If you can stay overnight as well, then begin by setting up camp at Squaw Flat or one of the other wonderful campgrounds in Needles. Then hit the **Joint Trail,** or any of the trails that begin from Squaw Flat, and spend the day hiking in the backcountry of the park. Save an hour for the brief but terrific little hike to **Cave Springs.** Sleep under more stars than you've seen in a long time.

GETTING HERE AND AROUND

AIR TRAVEL

The nearest airport is Grand County Airport, 18 miles north of Moab. Great Lakes Airlines flies here daily from Denver. Colorado's Grand Junction Airport, 120 miles east, has limited flights.

CAR TRAVEL

Access is west off U.S. 191. The Island in the Sky visitor center is 21 miles from Arches National Park and 32 miles from Moab on Route 313; the Needles District is reached via Route 211.

Before starting a journey to any of Canyonlands' three districts, make sure your gas tank is topped off, as there are no services inside the large park. Island in the Sky is 32 miles from Moab, Needles District is 80 miles from Moab, and the Maze is more than 100 miles from Moab. The Island in the Sky road from the district entrance to Grand View Point is 12 miles, with one 5-mile spur to Upheaval Dome. The Needles scenic drive is 10 miles with two spurs about 3 miles each. Roads in the Maze, suitable only for rugged, high-clearance, four-wheel-drive vehicles, wind for hundreds of miles through the canyons. Within the parks, safety and courtesy mandate that you always park only in designated pull-outs or parking areas.

TRAIN TRAVEL

The nearest train "station" is a solitary Amtrak stop in Green River, about 50 miles northwest of Moab.

PARK ESSENTIALS

PARK FEES AND PERMITS

Admission is $10 per vehicle and $5 per person on foot, motorcycle, or bicycle, good for seven days and for all the park's districts. There's no entrance fee to the Maze District. A $25 local park pass grants you admission for one year to both Arches and Canyonlands as well as Natural Bridges and Hovenweep national monuments.

You need a permit for overnight backpacking, four-wheel-drive camping, mountain-bike camping, four-wheel-drive day use in Horse and Lavender canyons, and river trips. Reservations need to be made at least two weeks in advance.

PARK HOURS

Canyonlands National Park is open 24 hours a day, seven days a week, year-round. It is in the mountain time zone.

CELL-PHONE RECEPTION

You may get reception in some parts of the park, but not reliably so. Public telephones are at the park's visitor centers.

RESTAURANTS

There are no dining facilities in the park itself. Needles Outpost, just outside the entrance to the Needles District, has a small general store for picnicking necessities. Restaurants in Monticello and Blanding offer simple meals, and most do not serve alcohol. Moab has a multitude of options.

HOTELS

There is no lodging inside Canyonlands. Most visitors use Moab as a base to explore the park. The towns of Monticello and Blanding offer basic motels, both family-owned and national chains. Bluff also has motels and B&Bs and offers a quiet place to stay. *Hotel reviews have been shortened. For full information, visit Fodors.com.*

WHAT IT COSTS			
$	**$$**	**$$$**	**$$$$**
Restaurants	under $12	$12–$20	$21–$30	over $30
Hotels	under $12	$100–$150	$151–$200	over $200

Restaurant prices are the average cost of a main course at dinner or, if dinner is not served, at lunch. Hotel prices are the lowest cost of a standard double room in high season.

VISITOR INFORMATION

PARK CONTACT INFORMATION

Canyonlands National Park ☎ *435/719–2313* ⊕ *www.nps.gov/cany.*

VISITOR CENTERS

Hans Flat Ranger Station. This remote outpost—46 miles east of Route 24; 21 miles south and east of the Y junction and Horseshoe Canyon kiosk on dirt road—is a treasure trove of books, maps, and other documents about the unforgiving Maze District of Canyonlands. The slot canyons, pictographs, and myriad rock formations are tempting, but you need to know what you're doing. The rangers will be direct with you—inexperienced off-road drivers and backpackers can get themselves into serious trouble in the Maze. Just to get here you must drive 46 miles on a dirt road that is sometimes impassable even to 4x4 vehicles. There's a pit toilet, but no water, food, or services of any kind. If you're headed for the backcountry, permits cost $30 per group for up to 7 days. ⊠ *Recreation Rds. 777 and 633, Maze* ☎ *435/259–2652* ⌚ *Daily 8–4:30.*

Island in the Sky Visitor Center. The gateway to world-famous White Rim Road, this visitor center, 21 miles from U.S. 191, past the park entrance off the main park road, is often filled with a mix of mountain bikers, hikers, and tourists. Enjoy the orientation film, then browse the bookstore for information about the Canyonlands region. Exhibits help explain animal adaptations as well as some of the history of the park. Rangers give short talks twice a day. ⊠ *Grand View Point Rd., Island in the Sky* ☎ *435/259–4712* ⌚ *Daily 9–4, with some extended hrs Mar.–Oct. and closures possible Nov.–Feb.*

Needles District Visitor Center. This gorgeous building is 34 miles from U.S. 191 and less than 1 mile from the park entrance, off the main park road. Needles is remote, so it's worth stopping to inquire about road, weather, and park conditions. You can also watch the interesting orientation film and get books, trail maps, and other information. ⊠ *Hwy. 211, Needles* ☎ *435/259–4711* ⌚ *Mar.–Oct., daily 9–4, hrs may vary; Nov.–Feb., hrs vary and closures may occur.*

EXPLORING

SCENIC DRIVES

Island in the Sky Park Road. This 12-mile-long main road is bisected by a 5-mile side road to the Upheaval Dome area. To enjoy dramatic views, including the Green and Colorado rivers, stop at the overlooks and take the short walks. Once you get to the park, allow at least two hours to explore. ⊠ *Island in the Sky.*

Needles District Park Road. You'll feel like you've driven into a Hollywood Western as you roll along the park road in the Needles District. Red mesas and buttes rise against the horizon, blue mountain ranges interrupt the rangelands, and the colorful red-and-white needles stand like soldiers on the far side of grassy meadows. You should get out of the car at a few of the marked roadside stops, including both overlooks at Pothole Point. Allow at least 90 minutes in this less-traveled section of the park. ⊠ *Needles.*

Plants and Wildlife in Canyonlands

Wildlife is not the attraction in Canyonlands, as many of the creatures sleep during the heat of the day. On the bright side, there are fewer people and less traffic to scare the animals away. Cool mornings and evenings are the best time to spot them, especially in summer when the heat keeps them in cool, shady areas. Mule deer are nearly always seen along the roadway as you enter the Needles District, and you'll no doubt see jackrabbits and small rodents darting across the roadway. Approximately 250 bighorns populate the park in the Island in the Sky District, and the Maze shelters about 100 more. If you happen upon one of these regal animals, do not approach it even if it is alone, as bighorn sheep are skittish by nature and easily stressed. Also, report your sighting to a ranger.

HISTORIC SITES

ISLAND IN THE SKY

Shafer Trail. This road was probably first established by ancient Native Americans, but in the early 1900s ranchers used it to drive cattle into the canyon. Originally narrow and rugged, it was upgraded during the uranium boom, when miners hauled ore by truck from the canyon floor. Check out the road's winding route down canyon walls from Shafer Canyon Overlook before you drive it to see why it's mostly used by daring four-wheelers and energetic mountain bikers. Off the main road, less than 1 mile from the park entrance, it descends 1,400 feet to the White Rim. ⊠ *Island in the Sky.*

NEEDLES

FAMILY **Cowboy Line Camp.** This fascinating stop on the **Cave Springs Trail** is an authentic example of cowboy life more than a century ago. You do not need to complete the entire trail (which includes two short ladders and some rocky hiking) to see the 19th-century artifacts at the Cowboy Camp. ⊠ *Off Cave Springs Rd., 2.3 miles from visitor center, Needles.*

SCENIC STOPS

ISLAND IN THE SKY

Grand View Point. This 360-degree view is the main event for many visitors to Island in the Sky. Look down on the Colorado and Green rivers and contemplate the power and persistence of water and the vast canyons carved over the millennia. Stretch your legs on the trails along the canyon edge. ⊠ *Off main road, 12 miles from park entrance, Island in the Sky.*

Green River Overlook. From the road it's just 100 yards to this stunning view of the Green River Canyon to the south and west. It's not far from Island in the Sky campground. ⊠ *About 1 mile off Upheaval Dome Rd., 8 miles from park entrance, Island in the Sky.*

Mesa Arch. If you don't have time for the 2,000 arches in nearby Arches National Park, you should take the half-mile walk to Mesa Arch. The arch is above a cliff that drops 800 feet to the canyon bottom. Views through Washerwoman Arch and surrounding buttes, spires, and canyons make this a favorite photo opportunity. ✉ *Off main road, 7 miles from park entrance, Island in the Sky.*

Upheaval Dome. This mysterious crater is one of the wonders of Island in the Sky. Some geologists believe it's an eroded salt dome, but others have theorized that it was made by a meteorite. To see it, you'll have to walk about a mile, round-trip, to the first overlook. Energetic visitors should continue to the second overlook as well for a better perspective. ✉ *Off Upheaval Dome Rd., 12 miles from park entrance, Island in the Sky.*

> **MEET ME AT SUNSET**
>
> Sunset is one of the picture-perfect times in Canyonlands, as the slanting sun shines over the vast network of canyons that stretch out below Island in the Sky. A moonlight drive to Grand View Point can also give you lasting memories as the moonlight drenches the white sandstone. Likewise, late-afternoon color in the spires and towers at the Needles District is a humbling, awe-inspiring scene.

NEEDLES

Pothole Point Trail. Microscopic creatures lie dormant in pools that fill only after rare rainstorms. When the rains do come, some eggs hatch within hours and life becomes visible. If you're lucky, you'll hit Pothole Point after a storm. Otherwise, you'll have to use your imagination. The dramatic views of the Needles and Six Shooter Peak make this easy, 0.6-mile round-trip walk worthwhile in their own right. Plan for about 45 minutes. There's no shade, so wear a hat. ✉ *Off main road, about 10 miles from Needles District park entrance, Needles.*

Wooden Shoe Arch. Kids will enjoy looking for the tiny window in the rock that looks like a wooden shoe with a turned-up toe. If you can't find it on your own; there's a marker to help you. ✉ *Off main road, about 6 miles from Needles entrance to park, Needles.*

EDUCATIONAL OFFERINGS

For more information on current schedules and locations of park programs, contact the visitor centers or check the bulletin boards throughout the park. Last-minute changes sometimes occur.

FAMILY **Red Rock Explorer Pack.** Just like borrowing a book from a library, kids can check out a backpack filled with tools for learning about both Canyonlands and Arches national parks. The sturdy backpack includes binoculars, a magnifying glass, and a three-ring binder full of activities. It can be cumbersome to carry everything on a hike, but the backpack is great for around the campfire or back in your hotel room. ☎ *435/719–4712* ✉ *Free.*

RANGER PROGRAMS

Grand View Point Overlook Talk. Between April and October, rangers lead short geology presentations at Grand View Point. You'll learn something about the geology that created Utah's Canyonlands. ⊠ *Grand View Point, 12 miles from park entrance off main park road, Island in the Sky* 🖾 *Free* ☉ *Apr.–Oct., daily; check at park visitor centers for times and locations.*

FAMILY **Junior Ranger Program.** Kids ages 5 to 12 can pick up a Junior Ranger booklet at the visitor centers. It's full of puzzles, word games, and fun facts about the park and its wildlife. To earn the Junior Ranger badge, they must complete several activities in the booklet, attend a ranger program, watch the park film, and/or gather a bag of litter. ☎ *435/259–4712 Island in the Sky, 435/259–4711 Needles* 🖾 *Free.*

SPORTS AND THE OUTDOORS

Canyonlands is one of the world's best destinations for adrenaline junkies. You can rock climb, mountain bike treacherous terrain, tackle world-class white-water rapids, and make your 4x4 crawl over steep cliffs along precipitous drops. Compared with other national parks, Canyonlands allows you to enjoy an amazing amount of solitude while having the adventure of a lifetime.

BICYCLING

TOURS AND OUTFITTERS

Magpie Cycling. Seasoned bikers Mike Holme and Maggie Wilson lead groups (or lone riders) on daylong and multiday bike trips exploring the Moab region's most memorable terrain, including the White Rim, Needles, and the Maze. If you need to rent a bike, Magpie will meet you at its preferred shop, Poison Spider Bicycles (⊠ *497 N. Main St., Moab* ☎ *435/259–7882 or 800/635–1792* ⊕ *poisonspiderbicycles.com*). ☎ *435/259–4464, 800/546–4245* ⊕ *www.magpieadventures.com.*

TRAILS

White Rim Road. Mountain bikers from all over the world like to brag that they've conquered this 100-mile ride. The trail's fame is well deserved: it traverses steep roads, broken rock, and dramatic ledges, as well as long stretches that wind through the canyons and looks down onto others. If you're biking White Rim without an outfitter, you'll need careful planning, vehicle support, and much sought-after backcountry reservations. ■ TIP→ **Permits are available no more than four months, and no less than two days, prior to permit start date.** There is a 15-person, 3-vehicle limit for groups. Most White Rim Road journeys begin at the end of Shafer Trail. ⊠ *Off main park road about 1 mile from entrance, then about 11 miles on Shafer Trail, Island in the Sky* ☎ *435/259–4351* ⊕ *www.nps.gov/cany.*

BIRD-WATCHING

Without getting on the Colorado River, you can see a variety of wrens, including the rock wren, canyon wren, and Bewick's wren. Blue-gray gnatcatchers are fairly common in the summer, along with the solitary vireo and black-throated gray warbler and Virginia's warbler. You'll have the most fun spotting the American kestrel, peregrine falcon, or prairie falcon and watching golden and bald eagles soar overhead. The common raven is everywhere you look, as are the juniper titmouse, mountain chickadee, and a variety of jays. Once on the Colorado River, you'll stand a chance of glimpsing the elusive white-faced ibis, and you'll almost certainly see a great blue heron swooping along the water or standing regally on a sandbar.

BOATING AND RAFTING

Seeing Canyonlands National Park from the river is a great and rare pleasure. Long stretches of calm water on both the Green and Colorado rivers are perfect for lazy canoe or raft trips. Still, be sure to wear life preservers as drownings happen nearly every summer in the area. In Labyrinth Canyon, north of the park boundary, and in Stillwater Canyon, in the Island in the Sky District, the river is quiet and calm and there's plenty of shoreside camping. The Island in the Sky leg of the Colorado River, from Moab to its confluence with the Green River and downstream a few more miles to Spanish Bottom, is ideal for both canoeing and for jet-boat rides. If you want to take a self-guided flat-water float trip in the park, you must obtain a $30 permit from park headquarters (☎ 435/259–4351 ⊕ canypermits.nps.gov); apply by mail or fax only. Make your upstream travel arrangements with a shuttle company before you request a permit.

Below Spanish Bottom, about 64 miles downstream from Moab, 49 miles from the Potash Road ramp and 4 miles south of the confluence, the Colorado churns into the first rapids of legendary Cataract Canyon. With some of the best white water in the United States, this piece of river between the Maze and the Needles districts rivals the Grand Canyon stretch of the Colorado River for adventure. During spring melt-off these rapids can rise to staggering heights and deliver heart-stopping excitement. The canyon cuts through the very heart of Canyonlands, where you can see this amazing wilderness area in its most pristine form. The water calms down a bit in summer but still offers enough thrills for most people. Outfitters will take you for the ride of your life in this wild canyon, where the river drops more steeply (39 feet in ¾ mile) than anywhere else on the Colorado River. You can join an expedition lasting anywhere from one to six days, or you can purchase a $30 permit for a self-guided trip from park headquarters.

FOUR-WHEELING

Nearly 200 miles of challenging backcountry roads lead to campsites, trailheads, and natural and cultural features in Canyonlands. All of the roads require high-clearance, four-wheel-drive vehicles, and many are inappropriate for inexperienced drivers. The 100-mile White Rim Trail, for example, can be extremely challenging, so make sure that your four-wheel-drive skills are well honed and that you are capable of making basic road and vehicle repairs. Carry at least one full-size spare tire, extra gas, extra water, a shovel, a high-lift jack, and—October through April—chains for all four tires. Double-check to make sure that your vehicle is in top-notch condition, because you definitely don't want to break down in the interior of the park: towing expenses can exceed $1,000.

For overnight four-wheeling trips you must purchase a $30 permit, which you can reserve no more than four months, and no fewer than two days in advance by contacting the Backcountry Reservations Office (☎ 435/259–4351 ⊕ canypermits.nps.gov). Cyclists share all roads, so be aware and cautious of their presence. Vehicular traffic traveling uphill has the right-of-way. It's best to check at the visitor center for current road conditions before taking off into the backcountry. You must carry a washable, reusable toilet with you in the Maze District and carry out all waste.

ISLAND IN THE SKY
White Rim Road. Winding around and below the Island in the Sky mesa top, the dramatic, 100-mile White Rim Road offers a once-in-a-lifetime driving experience. As you tackle Murphy's Hogback, Hardscrabble Hill, and more formidable obstacles, you will get some fantastic views of the park. A trip around the loop can be done in one long day, or you can camp overnight with advance reservations. Campsite reservations open in July for the subsequent year, and popular spring and fall weekends fill up immediately. Bring plenty of water, a spare tire, and a jack, as no services are available on the road. White Rim Road starts at the end of Shafer Trail. ⊠ Off main park road about 1 mile from entrance, then about 11 miles on Shafer Trail, Island in the Sky ☎ 435/259–4351 ⊕ www.nps.gov/cany.

THE MAZE
Flint Trail. This remote, rugged road is the most popular in the Maze District, but it's not an easy ride. It has 2 miles of switchbacks that drop down the side of a cliff face. You reach Flint Trail from the Hans Flat Ranger Station, 46 miles from the closest paved road. From Hans Flat to the end of the road at the Doll House it's 41 miles, a drive that takes at least six hours one-way. The Maze is not generally a destination for a day trip, so you'll have to purchase an overnight backcountry permit for $30. ■ TIP→ Despite its remoteness, the Maze District can fill to capacity during spring and fall, so plan ahead. ⊠ Hans Flat Ranger Station, National Park Rd. 777, 46 miles east of Rte. 24, Maze.

NEEDLES
Elephant Hill. The first 3 miles of this route are designated as passable by all vehicles, but don't venture out without asking about road conditions. For the rest of the trail, only 4x4 vehicles are allowed. The route is so difficult that many people get out and walk—it's faster than you can drive it in some cases. From Elephant Hill Trailhead to Devil's Kitchen it's 3½ miles; from the trailhead to the Confluence Overlook, it's a

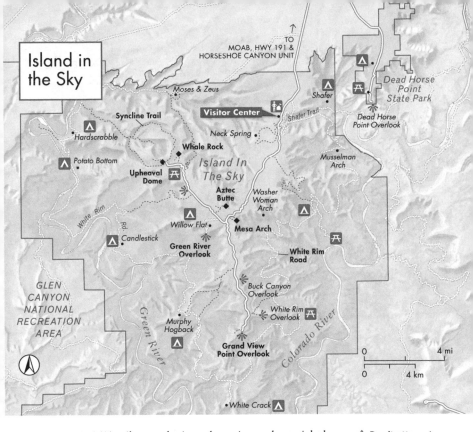

Island in the Sky

TO
MOAB, HWY 191 &
HORSESHOE CANYON UNIT

Moses & Zeus

Syncline Trail

Hardscrabble

Potato Bottom

Upheaval
Dome

Whale Rock

Island In
The Sky

Aztec
Butte

Neck Spring

Visitor Center

Shafer

Shafer Trail

Dead Horse
Point
State Park

Dead Horse
Point Overlook

Musselman
Arch

Washer
Woman
Arch

White Rim Rd.

Candlestick

Willow Flat

Green River
Overlook

Mesa Arch

White Rim
Road

GLEN
CANYON
NATIONAL
RECREATION
AREA

Green River

Murphy
Hogback

Buck Canyon
Overlook

White Rim
Overlook

Colorado River

Grand View
Point Overlook

White Crack

0   4 mi

0   4 km

14½-mile round-trip and requires at least eight hours. ⚠ **Don't attempt this without a well-maintained 4x4 vehicle and spare gas, tires, and off-road knowledge.** ⊠ *Off main park road, 7 miles from park entrance, Needles.*

HIKING

Canyonlands is a good place to saturate yourself in the intoxicating colors, smells, and textures of the desert. Many trails are long, rolling routes over slickrock and sand in land dotted with juniper, pinyon, and sagebrush. Interconnecting trails in the Needles District are excellent for weeklong backpacking excursions. The Maze trails are primarily accessed via four-wheel-drive vehicle. In the separate Horseshoe Canyon area, Horseshoe Canyon Trail takes a considerable amount of effort to reach, as it is more than 100 miles from Moab, 32 miles of which are a bumpy, and often sandy, dirt road.

ISLAND IN THE SKY
EASY
Aztec Butte Trail. The highlight of the 2-mile round-trip hike is the chance to see Ancestral Puebloan granaries. *Easy.* ⊠ *Trailhead on Upheaval Dome Rd., about 6 miles from park entrance, Island in the Sky.*

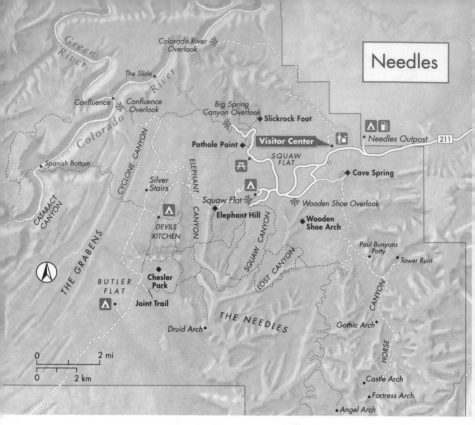

Needles

Grand View Point Trail. If you're looking for a level walk with some of the best scenery in the West, stop at Grand View Point and wander this 2-mile round-trip trail along the cliff edge. Many people just stop at the paved overlook and drive on, but you'll gain breathtaking perspective by strolling along this flat cliff-side trail. On a clear day you can see up to 100 miles to the Maze and Needles districts of the park, the confluence of the Green and Colorado rivers, and each of Utah's major laccolithic mountain ranges: the Henrys, Abajos, and La Sals. *Easy.* ⊠ *Trailhead on main park road, 12 miles from visitor center, Island in the Sky.*

FAMILY
Fodor's Choice
★

Mesa Arch Trail. After the overlooks, this is the most popular trail in the park, a ½-mile loop that acquaints you with desert plants and terrain and offers vistas of the LaSal Mountains. The highlight of this hike is a natural arch window perched over an 800-foot drop, giving a rare downward glimpse through the arch rather than the usual upward view of the sky. Park rangers say this is one of the best spots to enjoy the sunrise. *Easy.* ⊠ *Trailhead 6 miles from visitor center, Island in the Sky.*

FAMILY

Whale Rock Trail. If you've been hankering to walk across some of that pavement-smooth stuff they call slickrock, the hike to Whale Rock will make your feet happy. This 1-mile round-trip adventure, complete with handrails to help you make the tough final 100-foot climb, takes

CLOSE UP

Best Campgrounds in Canyonlands

11

Canyonlands campgrounds are some of the most beautiful in the National Park system. At the Needles District, campers will enjoy fairly private campsites tucked against red rock walls and dotted with pinyon and juniper trees. At Island in the Sky, starry nights and spectacular vistas make the small campground an intimate treasure. Hookups are not available in either of the park's campgrounds; however, the sites are long enough to accommodate units up to 28 feet long.

Squaw Flat Campground. The defining features of the camp sites at Squaw Flat are house-size red rock formations, which provide some shade, offer privacy from adjacent campers, and make this one of the more unique campgrounds in the National Park system. ⊠ *Off main road, about 5 miles from park entrance, Needles* ☎ *435/259–7164.*

Willow Flat Campground. From this little campground on a mesa top, you can walk to spectacular views of the Green River. Most sites have a bit of shade from juniper trees. ⊠ *Off main park road, about 9 miles from park entrance, Island in the Sky* ☎ *435/259–4712.*

---

you to the very top of the whale's back. Once you get there, you are rewarded with great views of Upheaval Dome and Trail Canyon. *Easy.* ⊠ *Trailhead on Upheaval Dome Rd., 11 miles from park entrance, Island in the Sky.*

MODERATE
Upheaval Dome Trail. It's fun to imagine that a giant meteorite crashed to earth here, sending shockwaves around the planet. But some people believe that salt, collecting and expanding upward, formed a dome and then exploded, causing the crater. Either way, it's worth the steep hike to see it and decide for yourself. You reach the main overlook after just 0.8 miles, but you can double your pleasure by going on to a second overlook for a better view. The trail is steeper and rougher after the first overlook. Round-trip to the second overlook is 2 miles. *Moderate.* ⊠ *Trailhead on Upheaval Dome Rd., 12 miles from park entrance, Island in the Sky.*

DIFFICULT
Syncline Loop Trail. If you're up for a strenuous day of hiking, try this 8-mile trail that circles Upheaval Dome. You get limited views of the dome itself as you actually make a complete loop around the outside of the crater. Stretches of the trail are rocky, rugged, and steep. *Difficult.* ⊠ *Trailhead on Upheaval Dome Rd., 12 miles from park entrance, Island in the Sky.*

THE MAZE
DIFFICULT
Horseshoe Canyon Trail. This remote region of Canyonlands National Park is accessible by dirt road, and then only in good weather. Park at the lip of the canyon and hike 6½ miles round-trip to the Great Gallery,

considered by some to be the most significant rock-art panel in North America. Ghostly life-size figures in the Barrier Canyon style populate the amazing panel. The hike is moderately strenuous, with a 750-foot descent. Allow at least six hours for the trip and take a gallon of water per person. There's no camping allowed in the canyon, although you can camp on top near the parking lot. *Difficult.* ⊠ *Trailhead 32 miles east of Rte. 24, Maze.*

NEEDLES
EASY
Slickrock Trail. Wear a hat if you're on this trail in summer, because you won't find any shade along the 2.4-mile round-trip trek. This is the rare frontcountry site where you might spot one of the few remaining native herds of bighorn sheep in the national park system. *Easy.* ⊠ *Trailhead on main park road, about 10 miles from park entrance, Needles.*

MODERATE
FAMILY **Cave Spring Trail.** One of the best, most interesting trails in the park takes you past a historic cowboy camp, prehistoric pictographs, and great views. Two wooden ladders and one short, steep stretch may make this a little daunting for the extremely young or old, but it's also a short hike, features some shade, and has many features packed into half a mile. Allow about 45 minutes. *Moderate.* ⊠ *Trailhead off main park road on Cave Springs Rd., 2.3 miles from visitor center, Needles.*

DIFFICULT
Chesler Park Loop. Chesler Park is a grassy meadow dotted with spires and enclosed by a circular wall of colorful "needles." One of Canyonlands' more popular trails leads through the area to the famous Joint Trail. The trail is 6 miles round-trip to the viewpoint. The entire loop is 11 miles. *Difficult.* ⊠ *Accessed via Elephant Hill Trailhead, off main park road, about 7 miles from park entrance, Needles.*

Joint Trail. Part of the Chesler Park Loop, this well-loved trail follows a series of deep, narrow fractures in the rock. A shady spot in summer, it will give you good views of the Needles formations for which the district is named. The loop travels briefly along a four-wheel-drive road and is 11 miles round-trip; allow at least five hours to complete the hike. *Difficult.* ⊠ *Accessed by Elephant Hill Trailhead, off main park road, 7 miles from park entrance, Needles.*

ROCK CLIMBING

Fodor's Choice ★ Canyonlands and many of the surrounding areas draw climbers from all over the world. Permits are not required, but because of the sensitive archaeological nature of the park, it's imperative that you stop at the visitor center to pick up regulations pertaining to the park's cultural resources. Popular climbing routes include Moses and Zeus towers in Taylor Canyon, and Monster Tower and Washerwoman Tower on the White Rim Road. Like most routes in Canyonlands, these climbs are for experienced climbers only. Just outside the Needles District, in Indian Creek, is one of the country's best traditional climbing areas.

MOAB AND SOUTHEASTERN UTAH

Updated by
Lisa Church

Southeastern Utah—especially Moab—is full of converts, and not so much in a religious sense. These are people formerly of suburbs or cities who cut through this country once on a road trip or came here long ago for a family vacation. They spent a few days surrounded by the vast, unpeopled desert and the clean, welcoming rivers, and the land became a part of them. Years or decades later, they have rejected the urban lifestyle and now work remotely by Internet; own restaurants, breweries, bike shops, or galleries; or do seasonal work—whatever they must to stay here. As much as the red rock, big sky, and nearby mountains, the rich, pioneering energy of these residents makes this part of Utah what it is. For them, this is a place to be reborn.

Although the towns tend to be visually unstimulating in this part of the world, the beauty that surrounds them is off the charts. You can hear about the canyons, arches, natural bridges, and such, but no words come close to their enormous presence. Not even pictures do them justice, and once you're standing in front of the famed Delicate Arch or riding your bike on an endless stretch of red slickrock, that will become crystal clear. It's probably why many people come here, actually—to see this place for themselves. Ostensibly, visitors arrive to run the gorgeous stretch of the Colorado River near Moab or to explore the unique landscape of the area's national parks and monuments. Or perhaps they are history buffs, excited about checking out the ancient ruins and rock art left behind by various Native American tribes. Truly, however, most tourists must come out of curiosity, to find out if this landscape is just as special and disarming as they have heard it is. And although that sort of thing is a personal matter, it's more than likely that after even a little while in this environment, you'll understand how it can be so hard to leave.

ORIENTATION AND PLANNING

GETTING ORIENTED

Interstate 70 is the speedway that gets you across Utah, but to dip into southeastern Utah you'll need to use the main artery, U.S. 191, which runs south toward the Arizona border. The only road that stretches any distance westward across the region is Highway 95, which dead-ends at Lake Powell. No matter which of the state roads you use to explore

12

TOP REASONS TO GO

Beauty from another world: There is simply nothing like the scenery here. Whether you're visiting the national parks or exploring a remote trail on your own, it's almost certain that the terra-cotta expanse of moonlike rock and open desert will affect you at your very core.

Get out and play: About the only outdoor activity not available here is surfing. Mountain and road biking, rafting, rock climbing, hiking, four-wheeling, and cross-country skiing are all wildly popular.

Creature comforts: Remote, southeastern Utah—and Moab, in

particular—has an array of lodging and dining options, including elegant bistros, fancy hotels, and quaint bed-and-breakfasts.

Catch a festival: Especially in the spring and summer months, this area is chock-full of gatherings focused on art, music, and recreation.

Another state of being: Something about the openness of this desert creates a scrappy, friendly culture, in which time and money aren't the main focus. Once that red sand gets in your blood, you might never leave.

the area, you're in for a treat. Here, the earth is red, purple, and orange. The Manti–La Sal Mountains rise out of the desert like ships. Mesas, buttes, and pinnacles interrupt the horizon in a most surprising way. But this is some of the most remote country in the United States, so services are sometimes far apart.

Moab. Small but unbelievably busy in spring, summer, and fall, Moab is on the Colorado River, south of I–70 on U.S. 191. More than 100 miles from any large town, it's close to nothing, and its residents are just fine with that.

Southeastern Utah. From Green River to Mexican Hat, this large swath of desert has a very small population. The most easily reached destinations are the small towns right on U.S. 191 or I–70, but some of the most beautiful stops require substantial but worthwhile detours off these main roads. Lake Powell, about three hours southwest of Moab, remains a favorite among visitors and locals alike.

PLANNING

WHEN TO GO

The most enjoyable times to be in this part of Utah are the beginning and end of high season, right before (March) or directly after (October) the huge summer swells of visitors. April and May have the best weather, but also the most visitors. May to September is the best time to hit the river, but is also when the towns and national parks are swollen with people, and the temperatures can be downright fiery. From the beginning of November through the end of February some restaurants and stores shut down, and things can get eerily quiet. To compensate, almost all hotels offer steep discounts (sometimes as much as 40% off high-season prices), which can make visiting in the off-season a steal.

PLANNING YOUR TIME

With its variety of restaurants and lodgings, Moab is the most obvious and fun place to base your southeastern Utah walkabout. From here, it's an easy drive to both **Arches** and **Canyonlands national parks,** each of which take at least a day to take in. They should be your first priority. At Arches, a great, if sometimes crowded, hike is the trail to the famous **Delicate Arch.** At Canyonlands, the **Island in the Sky District** is a stunning area to visit, with its crow's-nest views of deep canyons, thin spires, and the Colorado River. After a few days surrounded by rock and dust, you can spend one or several days on the **Green, San Juan,** or **Colorado rivers.** Outfitters also offer half-day, one-day, or multiday trips on mountain bikes and jeeps, if either of those are more your speed. Many side trips from Moab can be taken in a day, some worthwhile treks being to the **La Sal Mountains, Goblin Valley State Park,** and the little town of **Bluff.** More southern locales, like **Natural Bridges National Monument, Lake Powell,** and **Monument Valley,** will be much more enjoyable with an overnight stay. Whatever you do, wherever you go, make sure to leave time to just kick back, hang out, and enjoy the outdoors. Moab locals joke that this region has its own sense of time—it would be a shame not to enjoy the slower pace.

GETTING HERE AND AROUND

AIR TRAVEL

The nearest large airport to southeastern Utah is Walker Field Airport in Grand Junction, Colorado, 110 miles from Moab. Rental cars are now available at the Moab Airport, although advance reservations are recommended.

Air Contacts Grand Junction Regional Airport ⊠ *2828 Walker Field Dr., Grand Junction, Colorado* ☎ *970/244–9100* ⊕ *www.gjairport.com.*

CAR TRAVEL

To reach southeastern Utah from Salt Lake City, take I–15 to U.S. 6 and then U.S. 191 south. Take I–70 or U.S. 491 from Colorado and the east. Take U.S. 191 from either Wyoming or Arizona. Most roads are well-maintained two-lane highways, though snow can be a factor during winter travel. Be sure your car is in good working order and keep the gas tank topped off, as there are long stretches of empty road between towns.

Information Utah State Road Conditions ☎ *511 toll-free within Utah, 866/511–8824 toll-free outside Utah* ⊕ *www.udot.utah.gov.*

RESTAURANTS

Including even a few surprising twists, Moab-area restaurants have pretty much anything you might be craving. The other smaller towns in southeastern Utah don't have quite the culinary kaleidoscope and focus mostly on all-American, meat-centered meals. Though not the best destination for vegetarians or those watching their weight, the comfort food can be quite good and satisfying. One thing is for sure: no matter what restaurant you choose, you won't have to worry about a dress code. Shorts or jeans and sandals are always acceptable.

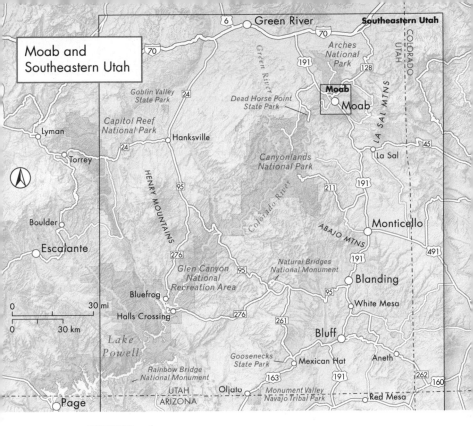

Moab and
Southeastern Utah

HOTELS

Every type of lodging is available in southeastern Utah, from economy chain motels to B&Bs and high-end, high-adventure resorts. Some of the best values in Moab are condominiums. Start with the Moab Travel Council for listings and suggestions of accommodations to suit your group size and budget. *Hotel reviews have been shortened. For full information, visit Fodors.com.*

Contacts Moab Property Management ☎ *435/259–5955, 800/505–5343* 🖷 *435/514–7281* ⊕ *www.moabutahlodging.com.*

Contacts Moab Travel Council ✉ *84 N. 100 E, Moab* ☎ *435/259–8825* ⊕ *www.discovermoab.com.*

WHAT IT COSTS				
	$	$$	$$$	$$$$
Restaurants	under $12	$12–$20	$21–$30	over $30
Hotels	under $100	$100–$150	$151–$200	over $200

Restaurant prices are the average cost of a main course at dinner or, if dinner is not served, at lunch. Hotel prices are the lowest cost of a standard double room in high season.

MOAB

When you first drive down Main Street, Moab's commercial, downtown strip, you might not get the town's appeal right away. The wide thoroughfare is lined with T-shirt shops and touristy restaurants, and is low on charm. But don't let Moab's impersonal exterior fool you. All you have to do is take a few walks, enter some storefronts, and talk to some of the residents to realize that this is a town centered on community. Here local theater, local radio, and local art rule, and Moabites are proud of that. At its core, this is a frontier outpost, where people have had to create their own livelihoods for more than 100 years. In the late 1880s, it was settled as a farming and ranching community. In the 1950s it became a center for uranium mining after Charlie Steen found a huge deposit of the stuff outside town. After about a decade of unbelievable monetary success, there was a massive downturn in the mining industry, and Moab plunged into an economic free fall. Then came tourism, and Moab was able to rebuild itself with the dollars of sightseers, four-wheelers, bikers, and boaters. Today the town is dealing with environmental and development issues while becoming more and more popular with tourists and second-home owners from around the world. No matter how it changes, however, one thing simply doesn't. This town has a different flavor from any other in the state.

GETTING HERE AND AROUND

Although Moab is fairly friendly to bikes and pedestrians, the only practical way to reach it is by car. If you're coming from the south, U.S. 191 runs straight into Moab. If you're arriving from Salt Lake City, travel 50 miles via I–15, then go 150 miles southeast via U.S. 6 and finally 30 miles south via U.S. 191. Signs for Moab will be obvious past Green River. ■ TIP→ If you happen to be approaching from the east on U.S. 70, you can treat yourself to a drive that will knock your socks off. Take Exit 214 into the ghost town of Cisco, and then drive down Colorado River Scenic Byway—Route 128 into Moab. The views of the river, rocks, and mesas are second to none.

FESTIVALS

As much as Moab is a place for the outdoors, it's also a spot to experience extremely popular festivals and events in a small-town setting. For the most part, these are time-honored institutions that draw quite a crowd of both locals and visitors.

Easter Jeep Safari. Each year during the weeklong Easter Jeep Safari thousands of four-wheel-drive vehicles descend on Moab to tackle some of the toughest backcountry roads in America. Although it's great fun for Jeep lovers, non-Jeepers might want to stay away, as this week is notoriously loud and hectic. ☎ 435/259–7625 ⊕ www.rr4w.com.

Moab Arts Festival. Every Memorial Day weekend, artists from across the West gather at Moab's Swanny City Park to show their wares, including pottery, photography, and paintings. This fun festival is small enough to be manageable, charges no admission, and offers an array of affordable artwork. There's live music, cultural entertainment, a kids' tent, and lots of food. Beginning in 2014, the arts festival partnered with local

12

breweries and wineries for the first wine and beer festival at the park. ☎ *435/259–2742 Moab Arts Council* ⊕ *www.moabartsfestival.org.*

Moab Music Festival. Moab's red rocks resonate with world-class music—classical, jazz, and traditional—during this annual festival that takes place in indoor and outdoor venues including the city park, local auditoriums, private homes, and a natural stone grotto along the Colorado River. Musicians from all over the globe perform, and it's one of the West's top music showcases. The festival starts the Thursday before Labor Day and runs about two weeks. ☎ *435/259–7003* ⊕ *www. moabmusicfest.org.*

Pumpkin Chuckin' Festival. A unique event, on the last Saturday in October, pulls together the diverse Moab community in October, when people from all over the region build contraptions—catapults, trebuchets, and slingshots—that toss pumpkins across the sky. Live music, about 25 vendor booths, a weiner dog race, and typically beautiful weather make this a popular event. Proceeds go toward the Youth Garden Project. ✉ *Grand County High School, 400 E. and Red Devil Dr.* ☎ *435/259–2326* ⊕ *www.youthgardenproject.org/pumpkinchuckin* 🎫 *$10.*

TOURS

Canyonlands by Night & Day. For more than 50 years, this outfitter was best known for its two-hour, after-dark boat ride on the Colorado River (March–October). While illuminating the canyon walls with 40,000 watts, the trip includes music and narration highlighting Moab's history, Native American legends, and geologic formations along the river. You can combine the boat trip with a Dutch-oven dinner, too. These days, daytime jetboat tours are offered, too, as well as tours by Hummer, airplane, and helicopter (land and air tours are offered year-round). ✉ *1861 Hwy. 191* ☎ *435/259–5261* ⊕ *www.canyonlandsbynight.com.*

ESSENTIALS

The Moab Information Center, right in the heart of town, is the best place to find information on Arches and Canyonlands national parks as well as other destinations in Utah's southeast, with brochures, maps, and knowledgeable staff on hand. It has a wonderful bookstore operated by Canyonlands Natural History Association. The hours vary, but in the peak tourist season it's open until at least 7 PM, sometimes later; in winter the center is open a few hours each morning and afternoon.

Visitor Information Moab Information Center ✉ *25 E. Center St.* ☎ *435/259–8825, 800/635–6622* ⊕ *www.discovermoab.com/visitorcenter.htm.*

EXPLORING

Fodor's Choice **Colorado River Scenic Byway—Highway 128.** One of the most scenic drives ★ in the country, Highway 128 intersects U.S. 191 3 miles south of Arches. The 44-mile highway runs along the Colorado River with 2,000-foot red rock cliffs rising on both sides. This gorgeous river corridor is home to a winery, orchards, and a couple of luxury lodging options. It also offers a spectacular view of world-class climbing destination Fisher Towers before winding north to Interstate 70. The drive from Moab to I–70 takes at least an hour. ✉ *Hwy. 128.*

Colorado River Scenic Byway—Highway 279. If you're interested in Native American rock art, Highway 279 northwest of Moab is a perfect place to spend a couple of hours. To get there, go north on U.S. 191 about 3.5 miles and turn left onto Highway 279. If you start late in the afternoon, the cliffs will be glowing orange as the sun sets. Along the first part of the route, you'll see signs reading "Indian Writings." Park only in designated areas to view the petroglyphs on the cliff side of the road. At the 18-mile marker, you'll see Jug Handle Arch on the cliff side of the road. A few miles beyond this point the road turns to four-wheel-drive only, and takes you into the Island in the Sky District of Canyonlands. ⚠ **Do not continue onto the Island in the Sky unless you are in a high-clearance four-wheel-drive vehicle with a full gas tank and plenty of water.** Allow about two hours round-trip for the Scenic Byway drive. ■**TIP**➔ **If you happen to be in Moab during a heavy rainstorm, Highway 279 is also a good option for viewing the amazing waterfalls caused by rain pouring off the cliffs on both sides of the Colorado River.** ✉ *Hwy. 279.*

> **DESERT SOUNDTRACK**
>
> **KZMU, Moab Community Radio.** Since 1992, locals have turned to KZMU for solar-powered, off-the-grid community radio. At 106.7 and 90.1 FM, the programming is a crazy quilt of music and community news shows provided entirely by a parade of local volunteers. One block of tunes might be dance themed, the next could be country twang or big band music. Don't be shy about calling in a request. Tune in Friday at noon for the Trading Post—a lively, funny, and always entertaining radio swap shop. ☎ *435/259–5968 request line* ⊕ *www.kzmu.org.*

Fodor's Choice
★   **Dead Horse Point State Park.** One of the gems of Utah's state park system, 34 miles southwest from Moab, this park overlooks a sweeping oxbow of the Colorado River, some 2,000 feet below. Dead Horse Point itself is a small peninsula connected to the main mesa by a narrow neck of land. As the story goes, cowboys used to drive wild mustangs onto the point and pen them there with a brush fence. There's a modern visitor center with a coffee shop (March–October) and museum. The park's Intrepid Trail System has become popular with mountain bikers and hikers alike. Be sure to walk the 4-mile rim trail loop and drive to the park's eponymous point if it's a nice day. ✉ *Hwy. 313* ☎ *435/259–2614, 800/322–3770 camping reservations* ⊕ *www.stateparks.utah.gov* 🖃 *$10 per vehicle* ☉ *Park daily 6 am–10 pm; visitor center Mar.–Oct., daily 8–6; Nov.–Feb., daily 9–5.*

Museum of Moab. Exhibits on the history, geology, and paleontology of the Moab area include settler-era antiques, and ancient and historic Native Americans are remembered in displays of baskets, pottery, sandals, and other artifacts. Displays also chronicle early Spanish expeditions into the area, regional dinosaur finds, and the history of uranium discovery. ✉ *118 E. Center St.* ☎ *435/259–7985* ⊕ *www.moabmuseum. org* 🖃 *$5 suggested donation; free Mon.* ☉ *Mar. 15–Oct. 15, Mon.–Sat. 10–6; Oct 16.–Mar. 14, Mon.–Sat. noon–5.*

Scott M. Matheson Wetlands Preserve. Owned and operated by the Nature Conservancy, this is the best place in the Moab area for bird-watching.

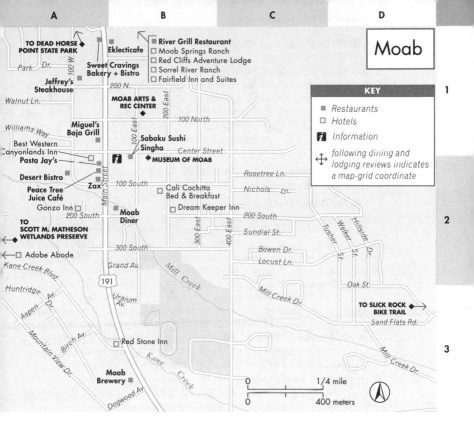

The 894-acre oasis is home to more than 200 species, including such treasures as the pied-billed grebe, the cinnamon teal, and the northern flicker. It's also a great place to spot beavers and muskrats playing in the water. An information kiosk greets visitors just inside the preserve and a boardwalk winds through the property to a viewing shelter. To reach the preserve, turn northwest off U.S. 191 at Kane Creek Boulevard and continue northwest approximately 2 miles. ✉ *934 W. Kane Creek Blvd.* ☎ *435/259–4629* ⊕ *www.nature.org* ✉ *Free* ☽ *Daily dawn–dusk.*

SPORTS AND THE OUTDOORS

Moab's towering cliffs and deep canyons can be intimidating and unreachable without the help of a guide. Fortunately, guide services are abundant in Moab, whether you are interested in a 4x4 expedition into the rugged backcountry, a river-rafting trip, a jet-boat tour on calm water, bicycle tours, rock-art tours, or a scenic flight. It's always best to make reservations, but don't hesitate to call if you make a last-minute decision to join an expedition. Cancellations or unsold spots sometimes make it possible to jump on a tour with short notice. One notable exception is the Fiery Furnace tour in Arches National Park: book at least one month in advance!

SHUTTLES

If you need a ride to or from your trailhead or river trip put-in point, a couple of Moab companies provide the service (and also provide airport shuttle service by reservation), with vehicles large enough to handle groups. Coyote's website is worth checking out for trail and river conditions and other information. Enquiries for Roadrunner are handled by Dual Sport, under the same ownership.

Coyote Shuttle. ⊠ *55 W. 300 S* ☎ *435/260–2097, 435/259–8656* ⊕ *www. coyoteshuttle.com.*

Roadrunner Shuttle. ⊠ *197 W. Center St.* ☎ *435/259–9402* ⊕ *www. roadrunnershuttle.com.*

FOUR-WHEELING

There are thousands of miles of four-wheel-drive roads in and around Moab suitable for all levels of drivers. The rugged terrain, with its hair-raising ledges, steep climbs, and smooth expanses of slickrock, is the perfect place for drivers to test their mettle. Seasoned 4x4 drivers might tackle the daunting Moab Rim, Elephant Hill, or Poison Spider Mesa. Novices will be happier touring Long Canyon, Hurrah Pass, or, if you're not afraid of precipitous cliff edges, the famous Shafer Trail. All routes offer spectacular scenery in the vast desert lands around Moab. Prices vary depending on the outfitter and location, but you can expect to pay around $75 for a half-day tour, $120 for a full day; multiday safaris usually start at around $600. Almost all of Moab's river-running companies also offer four-wheeling excursions.

OUTFITTERS AND EXPEDITIONS

Coyote Land Tours. Imposing Mercedes Benz Unimog trucks (which dwarf Hummers) take you to parts of the backcountry where you could never wander on your own. Technical tours challenge drivers with imposing rock formations, washes, and assorted obstacles, and there are tamer sunset excursions and camp-style ride-and-dine trips. They stand by their money-back "great time" guarantee. ☎ *435/260–6056* ⊕ *www. coyotelandtours.com* ▭ *From $59.*

Dual Sport Utah. If you're into dirt biking, this is the only outfitter in Moab specializing in street-legal, off-road dirt-bike tours and rentals. Follow the Klondike Bluffs trail to Arches, or negotiate the White Rim Trail in Canyonlands in a fraction of the time you would spend on a mountain bike. ⊠ *197 W. Center. St.* ☎ *435/260–2724* ⊕ *www.dual sportutah.com* ▭ *From $225.*

High Point Hummer & ATV. You can rent vehicles, including ATVs, UTVs, Jeeps, and motorcycles, or get a guided tour of the backcountry in open-air Hummer vehicles, ATVs, dirt bikes, or dune buggy–like "side-by-sides" that seat up to six people. The enthusiastic owners love families and small, intimate groups, and offer hiking and canyoneering as well. ⊠ *281 N. Main St.* ☎ *435/259–2972, 877/486–6833* ⊕ *www.highpoint hummer.com* ▭ *Guided tours from $69.*

12

GOLF

Moab Golf Club. A spectacular red-sandstone backdrop, wide fairways, and lush well-kept greens make for a breathtaking combination. Moab's 4,000-foot elevation and dry air make this municipal course fun to hit. It is open year-round and a relative bargain. ⊠ *2705 S. East Bench Rd.* ☎ *435/259–6488* ⊕ *www.moab countryclub.com* ✉ *$47, including cart* ⚓ *18 holes, 6819 yards, par 72.*

HIKING

Ramble through the desert near a year-round stream or get your

LEAVE NO TRACE

While doing any activity out in the desert, make sure to tread lightly. The dry, dusty landscape might look unbreakable, but it actually houses a fragile ecosystem, one that can take years to recover from just a set of footprints in the wrong place. In other words, it's best to stay on the trail or make sure you walk on rock or washes (dry stream beds).

muscles pumping with a hike up the side of a steep slickrock slope. Hiking is a sure way to fall in love with the high-desert country, and there are plenty of hiking trails for all fitness levels. For a great view of the Moab valley and surrounding red-rock country, hike up the steep **Moab Rim Trail.** For something a little less taxing, hike the shady, cool path of **Negro Bill Canyon,** which is off Route Highway 129. At the end of the trail you'll find giant Morning Glory Arch towering over a cool pool created by a natural spring. If you want to take a stroll through the heart of Moab, hop on the **Mill Creek Parkway,** which winds along the creek from one side of town to the other. It's paved and perfect for bicycles, strollers, or joggers. For a taste of slickrock hiking that feels like the backcountry but is easy to access, try the **Corona Arch Trail,** off Highway 279. You'll be rewarded with two large arches hidden from view of the highway. The Moab Information Center carries a free hiking trail guide.

MOUNTAIN BIKING

Fodor's Choice ★ Moab has earned a well-deserved reputation as the mountain-biking capital of the world, drawing riders of all ages onto rugged roads and trails. It's where the whole sport started, and the area attracts bikers from all over the globe. One of the many popular routes is the **Slickrock Trail,** a stunning area of steep Navajo Sandstone dunes a few miles east of Moab. ■TIP→ Beginners should master the 2½-mile practice loop before attempting the longer, and very challenging, 10-mile loop. More moderate rides can be found on the **Gemini Bridges** or **Monitor and Merrimac** trails, both off U.S. 191 north of Moab. **Klondike Bluffs,** north of Moab, is an excellent novice ride, as are sections of the newest trails in the Klonzo trail system. The Moab Information Center carries a free biking trail guide. Mountain-bike rentals range from $40 for a good bike to $75 for a top-of-the-line workhorse. If you want to go on a guided ride, expect to pay between $120 and $135 per person for a half day and $155 to $190 for a full day, including the bike rental. You can save money by joining a larger group to keep the per-person rates down; even a party of two will save drastically over a single rider. Several companies offer shuttles to and from the trailheads.

OUTFITTERS AND EXPEDITIONS

Poison Spider Bicycles. In a town of great bike shops, this fully loaded shop is considered one of the best. Poison Spider serves the thriving road-cycling community as well as mountain bikers. Rent, buy, or service your bike here. You can also arrange for shuttle and guide services and purchase merchandise. Want to ship your bike to Moab for your adventure? Poison Spider will store it until you arrive and the staff will reassemble it for you and make sure everything is in perfect working order. ⊠ *497 N. Main St.* ☎ *435/259–7882, 800/635–1792* ⊕ *www. poisonspiderbicycles.com.*

Rim Tours. Reliable, friendly, and professional, Rim Tours has been taking guests on guided one-day or multiday mountain-bike tours, including Klondike Bluffs (which enters Arches) and the White Rim Trail (inside Canyonlands) since 1985. Road-bike tours as well as bike rentals are also available. Bike skills a little rusty? Rim Tours also offers mountain-bike instructional tours and skill clinics. ⊠ *1233 S. U.S. 191* ☎ *435/259–5223, 800/626–7335* ⊕ *www.rimtours.com* ✉ *Day tours from $140; multiday from $800.*

Western Spirit Cycling Adventures. Head here for fully supported, go-at-your-own-pace, multiday mountain-bike and road-bike tours throughout the Western states, including trips to Canyonlands, Trail of the Ancients, and the 140-mile Kokopelli Trail, which runs from Grand Junction, Colorado, to Moab. Guides versed in the geologic wonders of the area cook up meals worthy of the scenery each night. Ask about family rides, and road-bike trips, too. There's also the option to combine a Green River kayak trip with the three-night White Rim Trail ride. ⊠ *478 Mill Creek Dr.* ☎ *435/259–8732, 800/845–2453* ⊕ *www. westernspirit.com* ✉ *From $925.*

MULTISPORT

Lovers of the outdoors wear many hats in Moab, sometimes being boaters, bikers, and Jeepers too. Here are a few companies that cater to a range of adventure seekers.

OUTFITTERS AND EXPEDITIONS

Adrift Adventures. This outfitter takes pride in well-trained guides who can take you via foot, raft, kayak, 4x4, jet boat, and more, all over the Moab area, including the Colorado and Green rivers. They also offer history, movie, and rock-art tours. They've been in business since 1978 and have a great reputation around town. ⊠ *378 N. Main St.* ☎ *435/259–8594, 800/874–4483* ⊕ *www.adrift.net* ✉ *From $50.*

Moab Adventure Center. At the prominent storefront on Main Street you can schedule most any type of local adventure experience you want, including rafting, 4x4 tours, scenic flights, hikes, balloon rides, and much, much more. You can also purchase clothing and outdoor gear for your visit. ⊠ *225 S. Main St.* ☎ *435/259–7019, 866/904–1163* ⊕ *www. moabadventurecenter.com* ✉ *From $67.*

NAVTEC. Doc Williams was the first doctor in Moab in 1896, and some of his descendants have never left, sharing his love for the area through this rafting, canyoneering, and 4x4 company. Whether you want to explore by boat, boots, or wheels, you'll find a multitude of one-day and multiday options here. ✉ *321 N. Main St.* ☎ *435/259–7983 1278* ⊕ *www.navtec.com.*

Tag-A-Long Expeditions. This outfitter, 50 years in business been taking people into the white water of Cataract Canyon anᴅ yonlands for longer than any other outfitter in Moab. They also run 4x4 expeditions into the backcountry and calm-water excursions on the Colorado and Green rivers. Trips, for 3 to 11 people, run from a half day to six days. ✉ *452 N. Main St.* ☎ *435/259–8946, 800/453–3292* ⊕ *www.tagalong.com* ✉ *From $170.*

RIVER EXPEDITIONS

Fodor'sChoice ★ On the Colorado River northeast of Arches and very near Moab you can take one of America's most scenic—yet unintimidating—river-raft rides. This is the perfect place to take the family or to learn to kayak with the help of an outfitter. The river rolls by the red Fisher Towers as they rise into the sky in front of the La Sal Mountains. A day trip on this stretch of the river will take you about 15 miles. Outfitters offer full-, half-, or multiday adventures here.

White-water adventures await more adventuresome rafters. Upriver, in narrow, winding Westwater Canyon near the Utah–Colorado border, the Colorado River cuts through the oldest exposed geologic layer on Earth, with craggy black granite jutting out of the water and red sandstone walls towering above. This section of the river is considered highly technical for rafters and kayakers, but dishes out a great white-water experience in a short period of time. Most outfitters offer this trip as a one-day getaway, but you may also take as long as three days to complete the journey. A permit is required from the Bureau of Land Management (BLM) in Moab to run Westwater Canyon.

OUTFITTERS AND EXPEDITIONS

FAMILY
Fodor'sChoice ★ **Canyon Voyages Adventure Co.** This is an excellent choice for rafting or kayaking adventures on the Colorado or Green rivers. Don and Denise Oblak run a friendly, professional company with a retail store and rental shop that's open year-round. Most of their customers take one-day trips, but they also offer multiday itineraries, guided tours, and rentals. It's also the only company that operates a kayak school for those who want to learn how to run the rapids on their own. Ask about stand-up paddleboarding, biking, and horseback riding, too. ✉ *211 N. Main St.* ☎ *435/259–6007, 800/733–6007* ⊕ *www.canyonvoyages. com* ✉ *From $59.*

Holiday River Expeditions. Since 1966, this outfitter has offered one- to eight-day adventures on the San Juan, Green and Colorado rivers, including inside Canyonlands National Park. They also offer multisport trips, women's retreats, and bike adventures, including the White Rim Trail. ✉ *2075 E. Main St., Green River* ☎ *435/564–3273, 800/624–6323* ⊕ *www.bikeraft.com* ✉ *From $155.*

Sheri Griffith Expeditions. In addition to trips through the white water of Cataract, Westwater, and Desolation canyons, on the Colorado and Green rivers, this company also offers specialty expeditions for women, writers, and families. One of their more luxurious expeditions features dinners cooked by a professional chef and served at linen-covered tables. Cots and other sleeping amenities also make roughing it a little more comfortable. ✉ *2231 S. U.S. 191* ☎ *435/259–8229, 800/332–2439* ⊕ *www.griffithexp.com* ✉ *From $79.*

ROCK CLIMBING

Rock climbing—or simply climbing, as most who do it call it—is an integral part of Moab culture. The area's rock walls and towers bring climbers from around the world, and a surprising number end up sticking around.

OUTFITTERS AND EXPEDITIONS

Desert Highlights. This guide company takes adventurous types on descents and ascents through canyons (with the help of ropes), including those found in the Fiery Furnace at Arches National Park. Full-day and multiday canyoneering treks are available to destinations both inside and outside the national parks. Desert Highlights does not offer guided rock climbing. ✉ *50 E. Center St.* ☎ *435/259–4433, 800/747–1342* ⊕ *www.deserthighlights.com* ✉ *From $120.*

Moab Cliffs & Canyons. In a town where everyone seems to offer rafting and 4x4 expeditions, Moab Cliffs & Canyons focuses exclusively on canyoneering, climbing, and rappelling—for novice and veteran adventurers. This is the outfitter that provided technical assistance to the crew on the movie *127 Hours.* ✉ *253 N. Main St.* ☎ *435/259–3317, 877/641–5271* ⊕ *www.cliffsandcanyons.com* ✉ *From $84.*

Pagan Mountaineering. Climbers in need of gear and advice on local terrain should chat up the friendly staff here. ✉ *59 S. Main St., No. 2* ☎ *435/259–1117* ⊕ *www.paganmountaineering.com.*

SKYDIVING

Although Moab's beauty will surely hit you from any vantage point, a truly stunning (and completely frightening) one is from above. Because the area gets only a few days of rain, the skydiving season is long, lasting from March 1 to November 15.

OUTFITTERS AND EXPEDITIONS

Skydive Moab. This is certainly a different way to view the local landscape. All flights take off from Moab's Canyonlands Field, 16 miles north of town. Skydive Moab also hosts the annual Mother of All Boogies Skydiving Festival each year in September. ✉ *Canyonlands Field/ Moab Airport, Hwy. 191 N* ☎ *435/259–5867* ⊕ *www.skydivemoab. com* ✉ *From $199 for a tandem skydive.*

WHERE TO EAT

Use the coordinates (✛ A1) at the end of each listing to locate a site on the corresponding map.

$$$$
MODERN
AMERICAN
Fodor's Choice
★

✕**Desert Bistro.** Moab's finest dining experience is in a small adobe house just off Main Street. Whether you dine inside or on either peaceful patio, anticipate thoughtful flavor combinations in artful salads, locally sourced beef, and delicious vegetables. The handmade agnolotti pasta stuffed with mushrooms and Italian cheeses, and the beef fillet crusted with gorgonzola are both impressive. Proprietors Karl and Michelle pour their hearts into this cozy bistro, and diners rave. The menu changes seasonally, but you can count on creative pastas, sweet and savory salad combinations, and surprise ingredients from kiwi to quinoa. $ *Average main: $32* ✉ *36 S. 100 W* ☎ *435/259–0756* ⊕ *www. desertbistro.com* ⌕ *Reservations essential* ⊙ *Closed Dec.–Feb., Mon. in Sept. and Oct., and Mon. and Tues. in Nov. No lunch* ✛ *A2.*

$
ECLECTIC
Fodor'sChoice
★

✕ **Eklecticafe.** The funky font on the sign makes this place easy to miss but worth finding for one of the more creative, healthy menus in Moab. Breakfast and lunch items include a variety of burritos and wraps, scrambled tofu, salmon cakes, Indonesian satay kebabs, and many fresh, organic salads. The *huevos rancheros* have just the right amount of heat and the wakame with either scrambled eggs or tofu is a great way to start the day. Excellent coffee, too. On nice days you can take your meal outside to the large covered patio. In winter you'll want to stay inside by the wood-burning stove. $ *Average main: $9* ✉ *352 N. Main St.* ☎ *435/259–6896* ⊙ *No dinner* ✛ *B1.*

$$$$
STEAKHOUSE

✕ **Jeffrey's Steakhouse.** Melt-in-your-mouth tender Wagyu beef is this restaurant's specialty. Jeffrey's offers plenty of salads and side dishes, but remember—this is a steak house, so there's a separate charge for everything, and that can quickly make for a pricey meal. The menu also features lamb and pork chops, chicken and salmon, and a few other entrée options. But it's really the Wagyu that brings in the crowds. A good selection of wines is also available and the knowledgeable staff is happy to help you choose a good pairing. With no more than a dozen or so tables in this historic adobe home just off Main Street, it's sometimes hard to get a reservation at this popular eatery, so plan ahead if possible. $ *Average main: $32* ✉ *218 N. 100 W* ☎ *435/259–3588* ⊕ *www. jeffreyssteakhouse.com* ⌕ *Reservations essential* ⊙ *No lunch* ✛ *A1.*

$$
MEXICAN

✕ **Miguel's Baja Grill.** This isn't the cheapest Mexican food around, but it's definitely the best. Not your standard south-of-the-border fare, the food comes from the culinary spirit of Baja, California, which means some excellent fish dishes like ceviche, a tangy blend of raw fish, onions, tomatoes, and spices. If you like fish tacos, you won't be disappointed. ■ TIP➔ **Both the tomatillo and the red sauce are fairly spicy so taste them first if you aren't fond of hot foods.** $ *Average main: $15* ✉ *51 N. Main St.* ☎ *435/259–6546* ⊕ *www.miguelsbajagrill.com* ⊙ *Closed Dec.–Feb. No lunch* ✛ *A1.*

$$
AMERICAN
FAMILY

✕ **Moab Brewery.** Southern Utah's award-winning brewery is known for its Scorpion Pale Ale, Dead Horse Amber Ale, and an assortment of other brews from light to dark. Their on-site restaurant is spacious and comfortable and decorated with kayaks, bikes, and other adventure paraphernalia. In the bar, you can always find someone to talk to about canyon-country adventure, because river runners, rock climbers, and locals all hang out here. There's a wide selection of menu choices, including fresh salads (try the gazpacho spinach salad), poultry (honey almond), St. Louis–style ribs, vegetarian pasta, and fish (including fish tacos). The house-made gelato is rich but not as good as their beer. $ *Average main: $12* ✉ *686 S. Main St.* ☎ *435/259–6333* ⊕ *www.the moabbrewery.com* ✛ *B3.*

$
AMERICAN
FAMILY

✕ **Moab Diner.** For breakfast, lunch, and dinner, this is the place where old-time Moabites go. Try the dishes smothered in green chili (burritos, burgers, omelets, and more), which they claim is Utah's best. The menu offers standard diner fare and the service is always friendly. Breakfast is served all day, and the ice-cream counter is as popular as ever—the diner did start out as an ice-cream parlor after all. $ *Average main: $10* ✉ *189 S. Main St.* ☎ *435/259–4006* ⊕ *www.moabdiner.com* ☽ *Closed Sun.* ⊹ *B2.*

$$
ITALIAN
FAMILY

✕ **Pasta Jay's.** Mountain bikers, families, and couples pack this downtown restaurant's patio from noon until well into the evening. This bustling spot's friendly servers rapidly dish up a dozen kinds of pasta in an equal number of preparations, perfect for hungry adventurers. If ravioli and manicotti aren't your thing, there's pizza, sandwiches, and salads, too. Linger over your meal and enjoy the people-watching on Moab's main drag. $ *Average main: $15* ✉ *4 S. Main St.* ☎ *435/259–2900* ⊕ *www.pastajays.com* ⊹ *A2.*

$$
CAFÉ

✕ **Peace Tree Juice Café.** Start with your choice of a dozen smoothies, then select from a menu that ranges from wraps to sandwiches to full entrées prepared primarily from local, natural, and organic ingredients for a healthy, filling meal. Try the quinoa-stuffed red pepper, Mediterranean penne, or sweet-and-salty beet salad for interesting new flavor combinations. The dinner menu includes steaks and salmon. Peace Tree's downtown location is as clean and contemporary as its food. For dinner, you may have to wait for a table on the patio. Take out is also an option. There's another location in Monticello, Utah. $ *Average main: $15* ✉ *20 S. Main St.* ☎ *435/259–0101* ⊕ *www.peacetreejuice cafe.com* ⊹ *A2.*

$$$
AMERICAN

✕ **River Grill Restaurant.** The most scenic dining experience in the area is 17 miles upstream from Moab at the Sorrel River Ranch, beside the Colorado River, with views of La Sal Mountains, and the red-rock spires and towers surrounding the ranch. This fine-dining restaurant follows a farm-to-table ethic and its seasonal menu changes regularly; look for local options like buffalo, pheasant, lamb, and trout as well as vegetarian entrées. Even if you don't splurge on a full wine dinner, know that the wine list is high quality and fairly priced. For lunch (which is served until 5 pm) you can sit out on the River Deck, for uninterrupted views. Reservations are recommended. $ *Average main: $28* ✉ *Sorrel River Ranch, Hwy. 128, mile marker 17.5* ☎ *435/259–4642* ⊕ *www.sorrelriver.com* ⊗ *Reservations essential* ☽ *Lunch for takeout only, Nov.–Mar.* ⊹ *B1.*

$$
MODERN ASIAN
Fodor's Choice
★

✕ **Sabaku Sushi.** Sushi in the desert? It may seem surprising, but the chefs here know what they're doing. The fish is flown in fresh several times a week, the veggies are crisp and the sauces are spicy—locals particularly love the spicy tuna roll with cucumber and avocado served with siracha and eel sauce. The tempura is light and crunchy and the stir-fry noodles with vegetables in a spicy miso are a taste treat. For those who aren't so into fish, the menu has chicken and steak options, along with plenty of dishes for vegetarians. The place has a trendy vibe and is often crowded, so call for reservations if you mind waiting for a table. $ *Average main: $15* ✉ *90 E. Center St.* ☎ *435/259–4455* ⊕ *www. sabakusushi.com* ☽ *Closed Sun.–Tues. No lunch* ⊹ *B1.*

12

$$ ✕ **Singha.** Authentic Thai food may not be what you expect in the middle of the desert, and that's exactly what makes this smallish, central place so liked by locals. Some of the tastiest dishes here are the noodle options, such as the tangy pad thai or the spicy, panfried drunken noodles. The curry dishes are also very popular. ■ TIP→ **The best deals are the lunch specials, which feature many of the dinner items in combination plates for a good deal less than the dinner prices.** If it looks crowded, however, you might want to find other eats; it has famously spotty service and quality when busy. $ *Average main: $15* ✉ *92 E. Center St.* ☎ *435/259–0039* ☽ *Closed Sun.* ✛ *B1.*

THAI

$ ✕ **Sweet Cravings Bakery + Bistro.** Cinda Culton has created a sensation in Moab with some of the largest and most delicious cookies and cinnamon rolls you've ever seen, but the secret here is an amazing roster of breakfast and lunch panini, wraps, and sandwiches, and daily comfort foods like pot pies and soups. Baked goods are all from scratch, gluten-free options abound, produce is local, meats are preservative-free, and coffee is 100% Rainforest Alliance and organic. Everything is available to go (in eco-friendly containers), but the Canyon Ham with spinach and tarragon aioli on marbled rye is so good it might not make it to the trail. Breakfast starts at 7 am and lunch is served until 4 pm. $ *Average main: $10* ✉ *397 N. Main St.* ☎ *435/259–8983* ⊕ *www.cravemoab.com* ☽ *No dinner. Closed weekends Nov.–Feb.* ✛ *A1.*

BAKERY
FAMILY

$$ ✕ **Zax.** Wood-fired pizza ovens are the focal point of this downtown eatery and sports bar, where baseball bats double as door handles. For $14 you can try the pizza-salad-soup buffet (a popular choice, so the pies are constantly coming out of the oven), but while the pizza is a grand slam, the salad bar is dull as a 1–0 game. The best seats in the house are out on the patio for people-watching. Burgers, sandwiches, and salads make up most of the rest of the menu, but there are pasta dishes and steaks, too. The bar has a good selection of local microbrewed beers. $ *Average main: $15* ✉ *96 S. Main St.* ☎ *435/259–6555* ⊕ *www.zaxmoab.com* ✛ *A2.*

AMERICAN
FAMILY

WHERE TO STAY

Use the coordinates (✛ A1) at the end of each listing to locate a site on the corresponding map.

$$ ⌂ **Adobe Abode.** A lovely B&B near the nature preserve, this single-story inn surrounds you with solitude. **Pros:** relaxing in the beautifully decorated common area; the entrée-of-the-day (sometimes ham and eggs or waffles) accompanying the Continental breakfast; peace and quiet. **Cons:** you can bicycle to town, but it's too far to walk; no children under 16. $ *Rooms from: $139* ✉ *778 W. Kane Creek Blvd.* ☎ *435/260–2932 innkeeper's cell, 435/259–7716* ⊕ *www.adobeabodemoab.com* ☜ *4 rooms, 2 suites* ⫽⊙⫽ *Breakfast* ✛ *A2.*

B&B/INN

$$$$ ⌂ **Best Western Canyonlands Inn.** The confluence of Main and Center streets is the epicenter of Moab, and this comfortable, contemporary, impeccably clean hotel anchors the intersection, providing a perfect base camp for families. **Pros:** downtown location; smiling and helpful staff; updated, sparkling rooms; breakfast alfresco on outdoor patio. **Cons:**

HOTEL
FAMILY
Fodor'sChoice
★

pricier than some comparable properties due to its location; for those seeking solitude, family-friendliness means the property bustles with happy children. [$] *Rooms from: $229* ✉ *16 S. Main St.* ☎ *435/259–2300, 800/649–5191* 🌐 *www.canyonlandsinn.com* 🛏 *34 rooms, 46 suites* 🍴 *Breakfast* ✥ *A2.*

$$ B&B/INN 🏨 **Cali Cochitta Bed & Breakfast.** One of the first homes built in Moab, this 19th-century Victorian in the heart of town, two blocks from Main Street shops and restaurants, has been restored to its classic style by owners David and Kim Boger. **Pros:** gracious owners pay attention to the details; easy walk to the hub of town; accomplished chef means scrumptious breakfast in the garden. **Cons:** given its historic construction, some quarters may feel a little tight. [$] *Rooms from: $140* ✉ *110 S. 200 E* ☎ *435/259–4961* 🌐 *www.moabdreaminn.com* 🛏 *3 rooms, 1 suite, 2 cottages* 🍴 *Breakfast* ✥ *B2.*

$$$$ HOTEL 🏨 **Fairfield Inn and Suites.** Views of the Colorado River are sure to wow guests at this new hotel, which opened in November 2014. **Pros:** warm, inviting and very clean; great views of the river and surrounding red-rock scenery; buffet, Continental, or hot breakfasts included. **Cons:** about 4 miles from downtown Moab, so not in walking distance to restaurants and shops; pricey (but most Moab hotels are these days). [$] *Rooms from: $219* ✉ *1863 N. Hwy. 191* ☎ *435/259–5350, 888/236–2427* 🌐 *www.marriott.com* 🛏 *65 rooms, 24 suites* 🍴 *Breakfast* ✥ *B1.*

$$$ HOTEL 🏨 **Gonzo Inn.** Unconventional Moab's most original hotel property, this eclectic inn stands out for its design, color, art, and varnished adobe construction. **Pros:** unique, spotless, and hip; steps to Main Street but still one of downtown's quietest properties; friendly staff. **Cons:** interior hallways can be dark; no elevator; not all rooms have a good view. [$] *Rooms from: $169* ✉ *100 W. 200 S* ☎ *435/259–2515, 800/791–4044* 🌐 *www.gonzoinn.com* 🛏 *21 rooms, 22 suites* 🍴 *Breakfast* ✥ *A2.*

$$$$ RENTAL 🏨 **Moab Springs Ranch.** First developed by William Granstaff in the late 19th century, this 18-acre property about 3 miles from Arches and 2 miles from downtown Moab features comfortable hotel rooms and condos set by a meandering spring and decades-old sycamores, mulberries, and cottonwoods. **Pros:** large, green, shaded space filled with a natural spring and ponds; along recently built bike path to town. **Cons:** little within walking distance; some Highway 191 traffic noise. [$] *Rooms from: $216* ✉ *1266 N. Main St.* ☎ *435/259–7891, 888/259–5759* 🌐 *www.moabspringsranch.com* 🛏 *3 rooms, 14 condos* 🍴 *No meals* ✥ *B1.*

$$$$ RESORT 🏨 **Red Cliffs Adventure Lodge.** Discovered in the late 1940s by director John Ford, this former ranch was the setting for several old Westerns in the 1950s. **Pros:** great riverfront views; private cabins are woodsy but modern; the movie museum, which chronicles filmmaking in the area, is a treat. **Cons:** far from town; spotty cell-phone service. [$] *Rooms from: $239* ✉ *Hwy. 128, mile marker 14* ☎ *435/259–2002, 866/812–2002* 🌐 *www.redcliffslodge.com* 🛏 *79 rooms, 30 cabins, 1 suite* 🍴 *No meals* ✥ *B1.*

$$ HOTEL 🏨 **Red Stone Inn.** One of the best bargains in town, this timber-frame motel offers small, clean rooms at the south end of the Moab strip near restaurants and shops. **Pros:** walking distance to Moab restaurants

and shops; the price is right. **Cons:** pool is at sister property across busy Main Street; no frills. [$] *Rooms from: $110* ✉ *535 S. Main St.* ☎ *435/259–3500, 800/722–1972* 🌐 *www.moabredstone.com* 🛏 *52 rooms* 🍴 *No meals* ✥ *B3.*

$$$$ RESORT Fodor's Choice ★ 🏨 **Sorrel River Ranch.** This lavish ranch resort is the biggest splurge around—and it's worth every penny. **Pros:** the most luxurious hotel in the Moab area by far; very attentive staff. **Cons:** half an hour from Moab; resort fee of 9% is added to your bill. [$] *Rooms from: $479* ✉ *Hwy. 128, mile marker 17* ☎ *435/259–4642, 877/359–2715* 🌐 *www.sorrelriver.com* 🛏 *39 rooms, 16 suites* 🍴 *No meals* ✥ *B1.*

NIGHTLIFE AND PERFORMING ARTS

Moab Happenings is a great resource for visitors to the area; it includes a calendar of events and options for activities, shopping, restaurants, and other necessities for travelers.

NIGHTLIFE

Moab's nightlife can be pretty quiet, especially in winter. In high season, however, live bands play every weekend.

Club Rio. At this local hangout and sports bar, decent bar food and cold beer make a perfect pairing for watching a weekend game on TV. Live music, DJs, karaoke, comedy, and lots of local flair make it worth a visit. There's a cover charge for some events. ✉ *2 S. 100 W* ☎ *435/259–2654* 🌐 *www.theriomoab.com* ⏲ *Daily 11:30 am–1 am.*

World Famous Woody's Tavern. An old-school style tavern that's a favorite hangout for locals, this Main Street standby offers beer, bands, and a little bit of ruckus. The front porch still looks like a perfect place to ride up and secure a horse, and there's a great patio. ✉ *221 S. Main St.* ☎ *435/259–3550* 🌐 *www.worldfamouswoodystavern.com* ⏲ *Mon.–Sat. 2 pm–1 am, Sun. 11 am–1 am.*

FRIENDLY FOLK DANCING

Community Contra Dance. Locals come together for nights of folk dancing with live music from the Moab Community Dance Band, and even if you've never tried this all-American dance form, don't be intimidated. A caller shouts out the moves and other dancers are happy to show you the ropes. You don't need rhythm or a partner, just a $5 donation, which goes to a different charity each month. The dances spring into action the third Saturday of most months at the Moab Arts and Recreation Center. ✉ *111 E. 100 N* ☎ *435/259–6272* 🌐 *www.facebook.com/MoabCommunityDanceBand.*

PERFORMING ARTS

Moab Arts and Recreation Center. For a slice of Moab's arts scene, from "Quick Draw Sales" where artists have three hours to create pieces during the annual Plein Air Festival, to dance, crafts, and fitness classes, this has been the spirited hub of arts activities in Moab since 1997. ✉ *111 E. 100 N* ☎ *435/259–6272* 🌐 *www.moabrecreation.com.*

SHOPPING

Shopping opportunities are plentiful in Moab, with art galleries, jewelry stores, and shops carrying T-shirts and souvenirs all over Main Street.

ART GALLERIES

Lema's Kokopelli Gallery. The Lema family has built a reputation for fair prices on a large selection of Native American and Southwest-themed jewelry, art, pottery, rugs, and more. Everything sold here is authentic. ⊠ *70 N. Main St.* ☎ *435/259–5055* ⊕ *www.kokopellioutlet.com* ⊗ *Mar.–Oct., daily 9 am–10 pm; Dec.–Feb., daily 9–5.*

Moab Art Walk. Moab galleries and shops celebrate the perfect weather of spring and fall with a series of exhibits. Art Walks are held the second Saturday of the month from March through June and September through November. Stroll the streets (6–9 pm) to see and purchase original works by Moab artists. ☎ *435/259–4912* ⊕ *www.moabart walk.com.*

Western Image. This is a fun place to browse for Old West antiques, Western art, cowboy hats, boots, belts, coins, badges, and other classy souvenirs. ⊠ *39 N. Main St.* ☎ *435/259–3006* ⊗ *Mar.–Oct., daily 9 am–10 pm; Nov.–Feb., 10–6.*

BOOKS

FAMILY   **Back of Beyond Books.** A Main Street treasure, this comprehensive bookstore features the American West, environmental studies, Native American cultures, water issues, and Western history, as well as rare antiquarian books on the Southwest. There's also a nice nook for kids. ⊠ *83 N. Main St.* ☎ *435/259–5154, 800/700–2859* ⊕ *www.backof beyondbooks.com* ⊗ *Daily 9–6 (to 9 pm Mar.–Nov.).*

SUPPLIES

Dave's Corner Market. You can get most anything you might need here, including some of the best cappuccino and Colombian coffee in town. The store is also the heartbeat of the local community, where everyone discusses local politics. ⊠ *401 Mill Creek Dr.* ☎ *435/259–6999.*

GearHeads. If you forget anything for your camping, climbing, hiking, or other outdoor adventure, you can get it here. It's packed with not only essentials, but things like booties and packs for your dog. The store's owners invented a high-end LED flashlight that has become very popular with the U.S. military and is available at the store. ⊠ *471 S. Main St.* ☎ *435/259–4327* ⊕ *www.moabgear.com.*

Walker Drug Co. A Moab landmark since the 1950s, this is as close as you'll get to a department store for more than 100 miles. Besides pharmacy and drugstore items, you can buy forgotten camping supplies, swimsuits, hats, sunglasses, souvenirs, and almost anything else. The pharmacy section is closed on weekends. ⊠ *290 S. Main St.* ☎ *435/259– 5959* ⊗ *Mon.–Sat., 7:30 am–9 pm, Sun., 8:30 am–6 pm.*

SIDE TRIP FROM MOAB

LA SAL MOUNTAINS
8 miles south of Moab.

Although Moab is best known for its slickrock desert, it's also the gateway to the second-highest mountain range in the state—the 12,000-foot La Sal Mountains. Long a favorite stomping ground of locals, the often-snowcapped peaks have been discovered by out-of-towners as a welcome retreat from the summer heat.

GETTING HERE AND AROUND
Go south from Moab via U.S. 191.

EXPLORING
La Sal Mountain Loop. With beautiful lakes and welcoming shade, these mountains outside Moab offer cool relief from the desert's hot summers, and striking scenery as the aspen leaves turn gold in the fall. On Old Airport Road (a left turn off U.S. 191) 8 miles south of Moab, the 62-mile loop climbs over the laccolithic mountain range, affording some great vistas of the valley. The road enters La Sal Division of the Manti-La Sal National Forest just as the dominant red-rock cliffs east of Moab begin to alternate with sagebrush and juniper flats. Passing through the cool heights of La Sal Mountains, the loop winds north through red-rock country to Castle Valley and an intersection with Highway 128. The road is paved, except for a couple of gravel sections, but it has steep switchbacks, and it does become snow-packed in winter. Check road closures with the National Forest Service. ⊠ *U.S. 191* ☎ *435/259–7155, 435/637–2817* ⊕ *www.fs.usda.gov/mantilasal* ⊙ *Year-round.*

SOUTHEASTERN UTAH

Don't think of southeastern Utah the way you would any other tourist destination. It's a rough-and-tumble world, not a locale of cutesy towns and built-up attractions. The scenery is dramatic, from the wide span of water at Lake Powell to the huge, sandstone formations (called "mittens") in Monument Valley. This is a place to hit the trail or river and lap up the feeling of desolation that occurs just miles from any town. Up in Green River you'll encounter a world of agriculture and boating, with melon stands popping up in the late summer and fall. From there, the farther south you travel the more you'll see the influence of Native American culture, and by the time you near Mexican Hat you might have eaten more Navajo tacos and bought more hand-made jewelry than you had planned.

GREEN RIVER

70 miles west of the Colorado state line.

Named for the river that runs through town, Green River, Utah, and its namesake are historically important. Early Native Americans used the river for centuries, the Old Spanish Trail crossed it, and the Denver and Rio Grande Railroad bridged it in 1883. Some say the "green" refers to the color of the water; others claim it's the plants along the riverbank.

Another story gives the credit to a mysterious trapper named Green. Whatever the etymology, Green River remains a sleepy little town, and a nice break from some of the more "hip" tourist towns in southern Utah, with a real community under the surface. At any rate, it remains a good place from which to base trips.

GETTING HERE AND AROUND

Reaching Green River is as easy as finding I–70. The town is 180 miles southeast of Salt Lake City, 100 miles west of Grand Junction, Colorado, and 50 miles northwest of Moab.

ESSENTIALS

Green River Information Center ⊠ *John Wesley Powell River History Museum, 1765 E. Main St.* ☎ *435/564–3427* ⊕ *destinationgreenriver.com* ⊗ *Apr.–Oct., daily 8–7; Nov.–Mar., Tues.–Sat. 9–5.*

> ### THE GRANDFATHER OF RIVER RUNNING
>
> A hundred years before there were tourists flocking to river outfitters, there was a one-armed Civil War vet named John Wesley Powell and his famous expedition of 1869. For three months he traveled down the Colorado River, and made the first passage through the Grand Canyon with his ever-dwindling crew. If that weren't enough to cement him into river history, he made the same journey again in 1871, during which time he made sure that pictures, maps, and papers about the trip were produced. His 1875 account of the journey, *The Exploration of the Colorado River and Its Canyons*, is still a great read.

EXPLORING

Green River State Park. A shady respite on the banks of the Green River, the park is best known for its golf course. It's also the starting point for boaters drifting along the river through Labyrinth and Stillwater canyons. Fishing and bird-watching are favorite pastimes here. ⊠ *450 S. Green River Rd.* ☎ *435/564–3633, 800/322–3770 for campground reservations* ⊕ *www.stateparks.utah.gov* ⊠ *$5 per vehicle* ⊗ *Mar.–Nov., daily 6 am–10 pm; Dec.–Feb., daily 8–5.*

John Wesley Powell River History Museum. Learn what it was like to travel down the Green and Colorado rivers in the 1800s in wooden boats. A series of displays tracks the Powell Party's arduous, dangerous 1869 journey, and visitors can watch the award-winning film *Journey Into the Unknown* for a cinematic taste of the white-water adventure. The center also houses the River Runner's Hall of Fame, a tribute to those who have followed in Powell's wake. River-themed art occupies a gallery and there's a dinosaur exhibit in the lower level. ⊠ *1765 E. Main St.* ☎ *435/564–3427* ⊕ *www.johnwesleypowell.com* ⊠ *$6* ⊗ *Apr.–Oct., daily 8–7; Nov.–Mar., Tues.–Sat. 9–5.*

Sego Canyon Rock Art Panels. Large, ghostlike rock-art figures painted and etched by Native Americans approximately 4,000 years ago cover these canyon walls, making Sego one of the most dramatic and mystifying rock-art sites in the area. There's also art left by the Utes from the 19th-century. Distinctive for their large anthropomorphic figures, and for horses, buffalo, and shields painted with red-and-white pigment, these rare drawings are some of the finest in the region. ⊠ *I–70, Exit 187,*

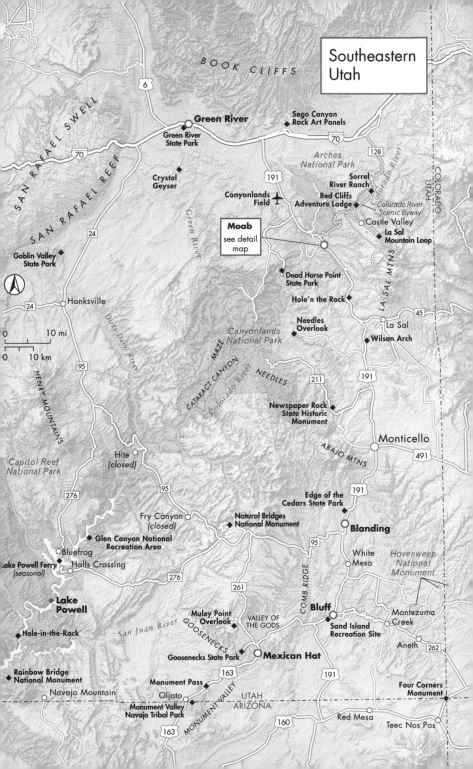

Southeastern Utah

BOOK CLIFFS

SAN RAFAEL SWELL

SAN RAFAEL REEF

6

Green River

Green River
State Park

70

70

Sego Canyon
Rock Art Panels

128

*Arches
National Park*

Colorado
UTAH

Crystal
Geyser

191

Sorrel
River Ranch

Red Cliffs
Adventure Lodge

*Colorado River
Scenic Byway*

Castle Valley

La Sal
Mountain Loop

Canyonlands
Field

24

Goblin Valley
State Park

Moab
see detail
map

Dead Horse Point
State Park

LA SAL MTNS

Hanksville

Hole'n the Rock

Needles
Overlook

La Sal

45

Wilson Arch

0   10 mi

0   10 km

Dirty Devil River

Green River

*Canyonlands
National Park*

MAZE

Colorado River

CATARACT CANYON

NEEDLES

211

Newspaper Rock
State Historic
Monument

95

HENRY MOUNTAINS

*Capitol Reef
National Park*

Hite
(closed)

ABAJO MTNS

Monticello

491

276

95

Fry Canyon
(closed)

Natural Bridges
National Monument

Edge of the
Cedars State Park

191

Blanding

*Hovenweep
National
Monument*

Glen Canyon National
Recreation Area

95

Bluefrog

Lake Powell Ferry
(seasonal)

Halls Crossing

276

White
Mesa

COMB RIDGE

261

**Lake
Powell**

Muley Point
Overlook

VALLEY OF
THE GODS

GOOSENECKS

San Juan River

Bluff

Sand Island
Recreation Site

Montezuma
Creek

Hole-in-the-Rock

Gooosenecks State Park

Mexican Hat

163

191

Aneth

262

Rainbow Bridge
National Monument

Navajo Mountain

Monument Pass

Oljato

MONUMENT VALLEY

UTAH
ARIZONA

Four Corners
Monument

Red Mesa

Teec Nos Pos

Monument Valley
Navajo Tribal Park

163

160

Thompson Springs ✦ *25 miles east of Green River on I–70, at Exit 187 go north onto Hwy. 94 through Thompson Springs* ☎ *435/259–2100 Bureau of Land Management Office in Moab* ⊕ *www.blm.gov.*

OFF THE BEATEN PATH **Goblin Valley State Park.** Strange-looking hoodoos rise up from the desert landscape 12 miles north of Hanksville, making Goblin Valley home to some of the weirdest, goblin-like rock formations in southeast Utah—hundreds of them, with a dramatic orange hue. Short, easy trails wind through the goblins, which delight children. ⊠ *Hwy. 24* ☎ *435/564–3633* ⊕ *stateparks.utah.gov* 🖼 *$8 per vehicle* ☉ *Mar.–Nov., daily 8 am–10 pm; Dec.–Feb., daily 8–5.*

SPORTS AND THE OUTDOORS
RIVER FLOAT TRIPS

Bearing little resemblance to its name, Desolation Canyon acquaints those who venture down the Green River with some of the last true American wilderness, a lush, verdant canyon, where the rapids promise more laughter than fear. It's a favorite destination of canoe paddlers, kayakers, and novice rafters. May through September, raft trips can be arranged by outfitters in Green River or Moab. South of town the river drifts at a lazier pace through Labyrinth and Stillwater canyons, and the stretch south to Mineral Bottom in Canyonlands is best suited to canoes and motor boats.

⇨ *For river-trip outfitters, see the Moab Sports and the Outdoors section.*

WHERE TO EAT AND STAY

$$
MEXICAN
✗ **La Veracruzana.** The Polito family continues the long tradition of good food in this older, unassuming building on Green River's main drag. Couples and families should try the *molcajete*, a two-person entrée with meat, chicken, shrimp, and nopal (cactus) served on a volcanic-rock stone mortar. Savory pork and *chile verde* combinations also impress on a menu that offers enchiladas, tacos, and other standard Mexican fare. 💲 *Average main: $15* ⊠ *125 Main St.* ☎ *435/564–3257.*

$
AMERICAN
✗ **Ray's Tavern.** Ray's is something of a Western legend and a favorite hangout for river runners. The bar that runs the length of the restaurant reminds you this is still a tavern and a serious watering hole—but all the photos and rafting memorabilia make it comfortable for families as well. It's worth stopping in for the great tales about working on the river and the coldest beer and the best hamburger in two counties. For dessert, owner Cathy Gardner makes homemade apple pie daily. 💲 *Average main: $10* ⊠ *25 S. Broadway* ☎ *435/564–3511.*

$
HOTEL
🏨 **Green River Comfort Inn.** This clean, updated motel is convenient if you're staying only one night, as many do on family rafting outings (Holiday River Expeditions is behind the hotel). Rooms have a somewhat contemporary look, but mainly the style is modern motel. Splurge on a suite for a four-poster bed and pine-trimmed jetted tub. **Pros:** clean, and comfortable; close to town's premier rafting outfitter; kids under 18 stay for free. **Cons:** remote, barren town; no elevator to second-floor; Green River's two best restaurants are not in walking distance. 💲 *Rooms from: $99* ⊠ *1975 E. Main St.* ☎ *435/564–3300* ⊕ *www. comfortinn.com* ➥ *54 rooms, 3 suites* 🍽 *Breakfast.*

BLANDING

12

126 miles south of Green River.

For nearly the first 20 years of its life, this small place near the base of the Abajo and Henry mountains, was known as Grayson. This changed when wealthy Thomas Bicknell offered a huge library of books to any town willing to take his name. In the end, another town got the name, and Blanding was so named to honor Bicknell's wife's maiden name, but it did get a share of the book bounty. These days the name seems fitting, as there is famously little to do around here. Many residents love it for its peaceful quality, however, and as the biggest town in San Juan County it remains vital in its own way.

GETTING HERE AND AROUND

The town is about a 30-minute drive from Monticello and about 90 minutes from Moab traveling south on U.S. 191. There are several gas stations, and it's always a good idea to keep your tank filled because in this area there are long stretches of road with few services.

ESSENTIALS

The Blanding Visitor Center has an on-site pioneer museum, and it's staffed by friendly locals who really know the area and are happy to give out goody bags of free samples. You can also connect to the Internet here.

Visitor Information Blanding Visitor Center ⊠ *12 N. Grayson Pkwy.* ☎ *435/678–3662* ⊕ *www.blanding-ut.gov* ⊗ *Closed Sun.*

EXPLORING

FAMILY

Fodor's Choice

★

Edge of the Cedars State Park Museum. Possibly the most interesting state park in Utah, Edge of the Cedars is one of the nation's foremost museums dedicated to the Ancestral Puebloan culture. Behind the museum, an interpretive trail leads to an ancient village that they once inhabited. Portions of the village have been partially excavated and visitors can climb down a ladder into a 1,000-year-old ceremonial room called a kiva. The museum displays a variety of pots, baskets, spear points, and rare artifacts—even a pair of sandals said to date back 1,500 years. ⊠ *660 W. 400 N* ☎ *435/678–2238* ⊕ *stateparks.utah.gov/park/edge-of-the-cedars-state-park-museum* ⊠ *$5* ⊗ *Mon.–Sat. 9–5; also Sun. 10–4, Apr.–Sept.*

OFF THE
BEATEN
PATH

Newspaper Rock State Historic Monument. One of the West's most famous rock-art sites, about 15 miles west of U.S. 191, Newspaper Rock contains Native American designs engraved on the rock over the course of 2,000 years. Apparently, early pioneers and explorers to the region named the site Newspaper Rock because they believed the rock, crowded with drawings, constituted a written language with which early people communicated. Archaeologists now agree that the petroglyphs do not represent language. ⊠ *Hwy. 211.*

WHERE TO EAT

$$

DINER

✕ Homestead Steak House. The folks here specialize in authentic Navajo fry bread and Navajo tacos. At lunch the popular—and big!—sheepherder's sandwich, is made with fry bread, and comes with your choice of beef, turkey, or ham and all the trimmings. A range of steaks and other meat dishes is available for dinner. The salad bar and homemade soup are a nice touch. No alcohol is served. [$] *Average main: $14* ✉ *121 E. Center St.* ☎ *435/678–3456.*

SHOPPING

Thin Bear Indian Arts. The Hosler family has operated this tiny little trading post in the same location since 1973. Authentic jewelry, rugs, baskets, and pottery are for sale at this friendly spot. ✉ *1944 S. Main St.* ☎ *435/678–2940* ⏲ *Weekdays 9–5, Sat. 10–2.*

BLUFF

25 miles south of Blanding via U.S. 191.

Bluff is a tiny but unexpectedly interesting town with a big personality, and it's building a reputation for fun events. Like Moab, it doesn't have a palpable Mormon feel, and it remains a mini–melting pot of Navajos, river rats, hippies, and old-time Utahns. It's a nice place to relax for a while—and to check out what it might be like living in the middle of nowhere; the town is surrounded by red-rock mesas, so there's no cell phone service for several miles around.

Bluff, settled in 1880, is one of southeastern Utah's oldest towns. Mormon pioneers from the original Hole in the Rock journey built a ranching empire that made the town at one time the richest per capita in the state. Although this early period of affluence has passed, several historic Victorian-style homes remain. Pick up the free brochure "Historic Bluff by Bicycle and on Foot" at any business in town. Most of the original homes from the 1880 town-site of Bluff City are part of the Bluff Historic District. In a dozen or so blocks are 42 historic structures, most built between about 1890 and 1905.

TRAIL OF THE ANCIENTS

As you head toward the southeast corner of Utah you are not only entering the Four Corners Region, but approaching what is known as the "Trail of the Ancients." Route 95 is designated as such because it's rich with ancient Indian dwellings. Deep in the canyons of this area are petroglyphs, pictographs, and artifacts of the Ancestral Puebloan peoples. Enjoy looking but never touch, remove, or vandalize these historic sites or their artifacts; it's a federal offense to do so.

GETTING HERE AND AROUND

Bluff is just under two hours from Moab south on U.S. 191.

EXPLORING

Sand Island Recreation Site. Three miles southwest of Bluff you'll find a large panel of Ancestral Puebloan rock art. The panel includes several large images of Kokopelli, the mischief maker from Puebloan lore. ✉ *U.S. 191* ☎ *435/587–1500 Monticello BLM office.*

NEED A BREAK?

Comb Ridge Coffee. A good place to grab a cup of joe, maybe breakfast, and get a feel for the local color, this coffee house is pure Western, with big wooden posts breaking up the barnlike space and works by local artists on the walls. The coffee is rich and delicious and the beans are fair trade, so

you can feel good about enjoying it. Local crafts, including jewelry, pottery, photography, and textiles, is for sale. ⊠ *680 S. U.S. 191* ☎ *435/485-5555* ⊕ *www.combridgecoffee.com* ☉ *Mar.–Oct., Tues.–Sun. 7 am–12:30 pm.*

FESTIVALS

Bear Dance. In September you can see traditional Ute ceremonial dances at the Bear Dance, sponsored by the Ute Mountain Ute Tribe in a four-day celebration held Labor Day weekend on the Ute Reservation. ⊠ *Beaver La., White Mesa* ☎ *435/678–3621.*

Bluff Arts Festival. A growing local artist community shows off its chops during this annual festival in mid-October. Each year has a different theme, and features four days of artist receptions, lectures, and workshops, along with the Bluff Film Festival. ☎ *435/672–2253* ⊕ *bluffarts festival.org.*

SPORTS AND THE OUTDOORS

RIVER EXPEDITIONS

While somewhat calmer than the Colorado, the San Juan River offers some truly exceptional scenery and abundant opportunities to visit archaeological sites. It can be run in two sections: from Bluff to Mexican Hat, and from Mexican Hat to Lake Powell. Near Bluff (3 miles southwest on U.S. 191), the Sand Island Recreation Site is the launch site for most river trips. You'll find a primitive campground there. Permits from the Bureau of Land Management are required for floating on the San Juan River.

Bureau of Land Management, Monticello Field Office. For permits, contact the Bureau of Land Management, Monticello Field Office. ⊠ *365 N. Main St., Monticello* ☎ *435/587–1544* ⊕ *www.blm.gov/ut.*

Wild River Expeditions. The San Juan River is one of the prettiest floats in the region, and this reliable outfitter can take you on one- to eight-day trips. They are known for educational trips, which emphasize the geology, natural history, and archaeological wonders of the area. ⊠ *2625 S. U.S. 191* ☎ *435/672–2244* ⊕ *www.riversandruins.com.*

WHERE TO EAT AND STAY

$$ ✕ **Cottonwood Steakhouse.** These ribs blow your mind, and the Western
STEAKHOUSE theme runs thick here, visible from the moment you drive up to the old-timey fake front. Inside, animal pelts, guns, and other paraphernalia adorn the walls. You can sit outside at picnic tables and watch as plump and tender baby back ribs and T-bone steaks are cooked over the outdoor grill—one reason the place closes in winter. Make sure to take home your napkin, which is a free bandana. Beer and wine are available. $ *Average main: $18* ⊠ *409 W. Main St.* ☎ *435/672–2282* ⊕ *www.cottonwoodsteakhouse.com* ☉ *Closed Nov.–Mar. No lunch.*

$$ 🏨 **Desert Rose Inn and Cabins.** Bluff's largest hotel is an attractive, wood-
HOTEL sided lodge with a huge two-story front porch. **Pros:** clean, comfortable rooms; friendly staff. **Cons:** has no historic charm; town not a culinary hub. $ *Rooms from: $140* ⊠ *701 W. Main St.* ☎ *435/672–2303, 888/475–7673* ⊕ *www.desertroseinn.com* ⮐ *30 rooms, 16 suites, 7 cabins* 🍽 *No meals.*

$ 🖭 **Recapture Lodge.** The knowledgeable owners of this family-owned and
HOTEL   -operated inn have detailed tips for exploring the surrounding canyon
country. **Pros:** set on shady grounds; owner is a wildlife biologist happy
to share his knowledge; horses welcome. **Cons:** older property; small
rooms and basic amenities; no phones or Wi-Fi in rooms. Ⓢ *Rooms
from: $85* ⊠ *220 E. Main St. (U.S. 191)* ☎ *435/672–2281* ⊕ *www.
recapturelodge.com* ⊅ *26 rooms, 2 houses* ⦿ *Breakfast.*

MEXICAN HAT

20 miles southwest of Bluff.

Tiny Mexican Hat lies on the north bank of the San Juan River. Named
for a nearby rock formation, which you can't miss on the way into
town, this is a jumping-off point for two geological wonders: Utah's
Goosenecks and Arizona's Monument Valley. The latter, stretching
south into Arizona, is home to generations of Navajo farmers, and is
very recognizable as the backdrop for many old Westerns.

GETTING HERE AND AROUND
From Bluff, go south on U.S. 191 for about 4½ miles to the intersection
of U.S. 191 and U.S. 163. Take U.S. 163 into Mexican Hat.

EXPLORING
Goosenecks State Park. From the overlook you can peer down on what
geologists claim is the best example of an "entrenched meander" in
the world. The river's serpentine course resembles the necks of geese in
spectacular 1,000-foot-deep chasms. Although the Goosenecks of the
San Juan River is a state park, no facilities other than pit toilets are
provided, and no fee is charged. You'll find it 10 miles northwest of
Mexican Hat, off Highway 261. ⊠ *Hwy. 316.*

Monument Valley Navajo Tribal Park. For the best breathtaking (and recognizable) views of the iconic West, this is the place. The soaring red
buttes, eroded mesas, deep canyons, and naturally sculpted rock formations found here are an easy 21-mile drive south of Mexican Hat on
U.S. 163 across Navajo land. Monument Valley is a small part of the
nearly 16-million acre Navajo Reservation, and is sacred to the Navajo
Nation, or Diné (pronounced din-*eh,* which means "the people"), as
they refer to themselves. For generations, the Navajo have grown crops
and herded sheep in Monument Valley, considered to be one of the most
scenic and mesmerizing destinations in the Navajo Nation. Director
John Ford made this amazing land of buttes, towering rock formations, and mesas popular when he filmed *Stagecoach* here in 1938. The
30,000-acre Monument Valley Navajo Tribal Park lies within Monument Valley. A 17-mile self-guided driving tour on a dirt road (there's
only one road, so you can't get lost) passes the memorable **Mittens** and
Totem Pole formations, among others. Drive slowly, and be sure to
walk (15 minutes round-trip) from North Window around the end of
Cly Butte for the views. Call ahead for road conditions in winter. The
Monument Valley **visitor center** holds a small crafts shop and exhibits
devoted to ancient and modern Native American history. Most of the
independent guided tours here use enclosed vans and you will usually

be approached in the parking lot; you can find about a dozen approved Navajo Native American guides in the center. They will escort you to places you are not allowed to visit on your own. Bring your camera (and extra batteries) to capture this surreal landscape that constantly changes with the rising and setting sun. ✉ *Visitor center, off U.S. 163, 21 miles south of Mexican Hat, Monument Valley* ☎ *435/727–5870 park visitor center, 928/871–6647 Navajo Parks & Recreation Dept.* 🌐 *www.navajonationparks.org* 🎟 *$20 per vehicle up to 4 people; $10 per person above 4* 🕒 *Visitor center May–Sept., daily 6 am–8:30 pm; Oct.–Apr., 8–4:30.*

WHERE TO STAY

$$$ HOTEL 🏨 **Goulding's Lodge.** With spectacular views of Monument Valley from each room's private balcony, this motel often serves as a base for film crews. **Pros:** truly a slice of American history; the views. **Cons:** it's miles from anything in any direction; rooms are dated and feel overpriced. [$] *Rooms from: $168* ✉ *Off U.S. 163, Monument Valley* ☎ *435/727–3231* 🌐 *www.gouldings.com* 🛏 *77 rooms* 🍴 *No meals.*

$ HOTEL 🏨 **San Juan Inn & Trading Post.** This peaceful spot is a well-known take-out point for white-water runners on the San Juan, a river that's famed as the setting of many of Tony Hillerman's Jim Chee mystery novels. **Pros:** the location overlooking the San Juan River. **Cons:** there's not much to do besides watching the river roll by (but that may be just what you're looking for). [$] *Rooms from: $99* ✉ *U.S. 163* ☎ *435/683–2220* 🌐 *www.sanjuaninn.net* 🛏 *39 rooms* 🍴 *No meals.*

$$$$ HOTEL 🏨 **The View Hotel.** Aptly named, the hotel is all about the vista—prices increase the higher the floor, and each room looks out to the Navajo Tribal Park's famous "mittens." **Pros:** wonderful views from private decks; the only hotel actually inside the tribal park. **Cons:** architecture inside and out isn't that interesting; Internet only available in the lobby and restaurant; bad cell-phone reception. [$] *Rooms from: $209* ✉ *Monument Valley Navajo Tribal Park, Off U.S. 163, about 25 miles southwest of town* ☎ *435/727–5555* 🌐 *www.monumentvalleyview.com* 🛏 *93 rooms, 3 suites* 🍴 *No meals.*

NIGHTLIFE AND PERFORMING ARTS

Earth Spirit Show. If you find yourself at Goulding's Lodge in the evening, take in this sound-and-sight show produced by photographer Ric Ergenbright. Admission is free if you're staying at the lodge or have purchased a Goulding's guided trip through Monument Valley; otherwise, tickets are $2. ✉ *1000 Oljato Rd., Monument Valley* 🌐 *www.gouldings.com.*

NATURAL BRIDGES NATIONAL MONUMENT

For so long the hidden gem of southeast Utah's national parks and monuments, the secret is now out. The scenery and rock formations found in this national monument must be seen to be believed.

Natural Bridges National Monument. Stunning natural bridges and ancient Native American ruins, plus magnificent scenery throughout make Natural Bridges National Monument a must see for anyone who has time to make the trip. Sipapu is one of the largest natural bridges in the world, spanning 225 feet and standing more than 140 feet tall. You can take

CLOSE UP

Hoodoos, Bridges, and Arches

After a while, the fantastically eroded landscapes and formations found in southern Utah can all begin to look the same. Don't worry. It happens to everyone. A brief course in the geology of the Colorado Plateau can get your vacation back on track and clear up any confusion while you're busy making memories.

An **arch** is an opening created primarily by the ceaseless erosional powers of wind and weather. Airborne sand constantly scours cliff faces; tiny and huge chunks of stone are pried away by minuscule pockets of water as it freezes, expands, and thaws again and again over the course of thousands or millions of years. Arches are found in all stages, from cavelike openings that don't go all the way through a stone fin to gigantic stone ribbons shaped by an erosional persistence that defies imagination.

Bridges are the product of stream or river erosion. They span what at some time was a water source powerful enough to wear away softer layers of sedimentary stone through constant force and motion. As softer stone is washed away, the harder capstone layers remain in the form of natural bridges.

The most bizarrely shaped formations have the strangest name. **Hoodoos** are chunks of rock chiseled through time into columns or pinnacles. Like all rock formations, hoodoos are constructed of layers and layers of horizontal bands. Each band or stratum has its own composition. When wind or water, particularly in the form of heavy, sporadic rainstorms, goes to work on these pillars, the eventual result is a hoodoo—an eccentric and grotesque formation usually found in the company of other hoodoos.

in the Sipapu, Owachomo, and Kachina bridges via an 8.6-mile round-trip hike that meanders around and under them. A 13-site primitive campground is an optimal spot for stargazing. The national monument is about 120 miles southwest of the Needles District of Canyonlands National Park and approximately 45 miles from Blanding. ⌖ *Hwy. 275, off Hwy. 95* ☎ *435/692–1234* ⊕ *www.nps.gov/nabr* ⌖ *$6 per vehicle* ☼ *May–Sept., daily 8–6; Oct. and Apr., daily 8–5; Nov.–Mar., daily 9–5.*

LAKE POWELL

If you really want to get away from it all, the placid waters of Lake Powell allow you to depart the landed lifestyle and float away on your own houseboat. With 96 major side canyons spread across 186 miles, you can literally spend months exploring more than 2,000 miles of shoreline. Most of us have only a few days or a week, but that's still plenty of time for recreation in the second-largest reservoir in the nation. Be safe (children under 12 must always wear life jackets on motorboats or the exterior of houseboats) and every water sport imaginable awaits you, from waterskiing to fishing. Small communities around marinas in Page (Arizona), Bullfrog, Wahweap, Hite, and Hall's Crossing have hotels, restaurants, and shops where you can restock vital supplies.

GETTING HERE AND AROUND

AIR TRAVEL

Getting here can be your biggest challenge. Great Lakes Airlines serves Page, Arizona, from Phoenix. To get to Bullfrog, Utah, it's a three-and-a-half-hour drive from Canyonlands Airport in Moab (served by Delta) and five hours from Walker Field Airport in Grand Junction, Colorado.

CAR TRAVEL

Many people visit Lake Powell as part of grand drives across the southwestern United States. Bullfrog, Utah, is about 300 miles from Salt Lake City via I–15 to I–70 to U.S. 95 south. Take I–70 from Colorado and the east. Take U.S. 191 from either Wyoming or Arizona. Most roads are well-maintained two-lane highways, though snow can be a factor in winter. Be sure your car is in good working order, as there are long stretches of empty road, and keep the gas tank topped off.

FERRY TRAVEL

Hall's Crossing Marina is the eastern terminus of the ferry. You and your car can float across a 3-mile stretch of the lake to the Bullfrog Basin Marina in 25 minutes, from which it's an hour's drive north to rejoin Highway 95. Ferries run daily, a few or several times a day, depending on the time of year. Call ahead for departures information.

Lake Powell Ferry ⊠ *Hall's Crossing Marina, Hwy. 276* ☎ *435/684–3088* ⊕ *www.lakepowell.com* 🚗 *$25 per car* ⊙ *Mid-Apr.–mid-May, daily 8–3; mid-May–mid-Sept., 8–7; mid-Sept.–Oct., 8–5; Nov.–mid-Apr., Sat. only; call for times.*

Information Utah State Road Conditions ☎ *511 toll-free within Utah, 866/511–8824 toll-free outside Utah* ⊕ *www.udot.utah.gov.*

EXPLORING

Lake Powell. With a shoreline longer than America's Pacific coast, Lake Powell is the heart of the huge 1,255,400-acre **Glen Canyon National Recreation Area**. Created by the Glen Canyon Dam—a 710-foot wall of concrete in the Colorado River—Lake Powell took 17 years to fill. The second-largest man-made lake in the nation, it extends through terrain so rugged it was the last major area of the country to be mapped. Red cliffs ring the lake and twist off into 96 major canyons and countless inlets with huge, red-sandstone buttes randomly jutting from the sapphire waters. You could spend 30 years exploring the lake and still not see everything. Several years ago, the Sierra Club started a movement to drain the lake to restore water-filled Glen Canyon, which some believe was more spectacular than the Grand Canyon, but the lake is likely to be around for years to come.

The most popular thing to do at Lake Powell is renting a houseboat and chugging leisurely across the lake, exploring coves and inlets. You'll have plenty of company, however, since more than 2 million people visit the lake each year. Fast motorboats, jet skis, and sailboats all share the lake. It's a popular spot for bass fishing, but you'll need a Utah fishing license from one of the marinas. Remember also that the lake extends into Arizona, and if your voyage takes you across the state line, you'll need a fishing license that covers the southern end of the lake. Unless you love crowds and parties, it's best to avoid visiting during Memorial

Day or Labor Day weekends. It is important to check with the National Park Service for current water levels, closures, and other weather-related conditions.

Guided day tours are available for those who don't want to rent a boat. A popular full-day or half-day excursion sets out from the Bullfrog and Hall's Crossing marinas to **Rainbow Bridge National Monument**, the largest natural bridge in the world, and this 290-foot-high, 275-foot-wide span is a breathtaking sight. The main National Park Service visitor center is at Bullfrog Marina; there's a gas station, campground, general store, and boat docks there. ✉ *Bullfrog visitor center, Hwy. 276* ☎ *435/684–7420* 🌐 *www.nps.gov/glca* 🎟 *$15 per vehicle* 🕒 *Recreation area year-round; services close seasonally; call for info.*

SPORTS AND THE OUTDOORS

Lake Powell Resorts & Marinas. Boating and fishing are the major sports at Lake Powell. Conveniently, all powerboat rentals and tours are conducted by this company. Daylong tours (departing from Wahweap Marina near Page, Arizona, only) go to Rainbow Bridge or Antelope Canyon, and there's also a tour that goes into some of the more interesting canyons and a dinner cruise. The company also rents houseboats. ✉ *Bullfrog Marina, Rte. 276* ☎ *800/528–6154* 🌐 *www.lakepowell.com* 🎟 *Tours $45–$120.*

WHERE TO STAY

$$$$ RESORT Fodor's Choice ★

🏨 **Amangiri.** One of just two U.S. properties operated by the famously luxurious Aman resort company, this ultraplush 34-suite compound lies just a few miles north of Lake Powell on a 600-acre plot of rugged high desert. **Pros:** stunning accommodations inside and out; exceedingly gracious staff; world-class restaurant and spa. **Cons:** it's many times more expensive than most accommodations in the area; extremely remote. [$] *Rooms from: $1,200* ✉ *1 Kayenta Rd., 15 miles northwest of Page off U.S. 89, Canyon Point* ☎ *435/675–3999, 877/695–3999* 🌐 *www.amanresorts.com* 🛏 *34 suites* 🍴 *All meals.*

$$$ HOTEL

🏨 **Defiance House Lodge.** At the Bullfrog Marina this cliff-top lodge has comfortable and clean rooms, but the real draw is the view. **Pros:** beautiful lakefront setting; adjacent restaurant. **Cons:** very remote; no general store for miles. [$] *Rooms from: $160* ☎ *435/684–2233, 888/896–3829* 🌐 *www.lakepowell.com* 🛏 *48 rooms* 🍴 *No meals.*

$$ B&B/INN

🏨 **Dreamkatchers' B&B.** This sleek, contemporary Southwestern-style home sits on a bluff a few miles northwest of Lake Powell, with dramatic views of the lake, mountains, and sweeping high-desert mesas. **Pros:** peaceful and secluded location that's perfect for stargazing; delicious breakfasts; laid-back, friendly hosts. **Cons:** often booked more than a couple of months in advance; two-night minimum stay. [$] *Rooms from: $135* ✉ *1055 S. American Way, Big Water* ☎ *435/675–5828* 🌐 *www.dreamkatcherslakepowell.com* 🛏 *3 rooms* 🕒 *Closed mid-Nov.–early Apr.* 🍴 *Breakfast.*

TRAVEL SMART UTAH

GETTING HERE AND AROUND

Salt Lake City is Utah's major air gateway, although if southern Utah is your primary destination, Las Vegas is a convenient and often less expensive alternative. Once on the ground, a car or other vehicle is your best bet for getting around. Outside of the urban corridor from Provo to Ogden (including Salt Lake City), much of the state's interest lies in natural attractions, including five national parks and terrain that ranges from sun-baked desert to mountain peaks that soar above 10,000 feet. Be prepared for wide-open vistas, extreme temperature variations and long, long stretches of asphalt.

▮ AIR TRAVEL

Salt Lake City has a reputation for having one of the nation's easiest airports for travelers—with a low rate of delayed or canceled flights. Plus, it's a Western hub for Southwest and Delta, so your Utah explorations should get off to a timely start. Nonstop flights are available from larger U.S. cities as well as one-stop connections to Asia, Europe, and South America.

Salt Lake City is approximately 16 hours from Sydney, 12 hours from London, 3 hours from Dallas, 5 hours from New York, 4 hours from Chicago, 2 hours from Los Angeles, and an hour from Las Vegas.

If you're traveling during snow season, allow extra time for the drive to the airport, as weather conditions can slow you down. If you'll be checking skis, arrive even earlier.

Airlines and Airports Airline and Airport Links.com. This website has links to many of the world's airlines and airports. ⊕ *www. airlineandairportlinks.com.*

Airline Security Issues Transportation Security Administration. You'll find answers here for almost every question that might come up. ⊕ *www.tsa.gov.*

AIRPORTS

The major gateway to Utah is Salt Lake City International Airport. If you're staying in Salt Lake City, you'll appreciate that it's one of the closest airports to downtown of any American city. Be advised that the construction of a new terminal could affect your experience through at least 2019.

Flights to smaller, regional, or resort-town airports generally connect through the state capital. A convenient gateway to southern Utah, particularly Zion and Bryce Canyon national parks, is McCarran International Airport in Las Vegas. More and more visitors to southern Utah (and the north rim of the Grand Canyon) are using St. George Municipal Airport, which has daily Delta and United flights to Salt Lake City and Denver. There are limited services, but you can rent cars here and it's less than an hour's drive to Zion National Park once you're on the road.

▮ **TIP→ Long layovers don't have to be only about sitting around or shopping. These days they can be about burning off vacation calories. Check out www.airportgyms.com for lists of health clubs that are in or near many U.S. and Canadian airports.**

Airport Information McCarran International Airport (LAS) ☎ *702/261–5211* ⊕ *www.mccarran.com.* **Salt Lake City International Airport (SLC)** ☎ *801/575–2400* ⊕ *www.slcairport.com.* **St. George Municipal**

Airport (SGU) ⊠ *4550 S. Airport Pkwy., St. George* ☎ *435/627-4080* ⊕ *www.flysgu.com.*

GROUND TRANSPORTATION

You can get to and from the Salt Lake City Airport by light-rail, taxi, bus, or hotel shuttle. A light-rail line called TRAX now connects you in less than 30 minutes (and for just $2.50) from Terminal 1 to downtown Salt Lake City and the rest of the rapid-transit network. It runs approximately every 15 minutes. Taxis, though, are faster (15 minutes); the trip to downtown costs $20–$25. Shared-ride shuttle services are similarly priced to taxis, but can take longer.

Public transportation information counters are near baggage claim in all terminals, or at the front desk at hotels. If you're in downtown Salt Lake City, your best bet is to call ahead for a taxi rather than hope to flag one down.

Contacts **City Cab Company** ☎ *801/363-8400.* **Utah Transit Authority (UTA)** ☎ *801/743-3882, 888/743-3882* ⊕ *www. rideuta.com.* **Ute Cab Company** ☎ *801/359-7788.* **Yellow Cab** ☎ *801/521-2100.*

FLIGHTS

Salt Lake City has a large international airport, so you'll be able to fly here from anywhere, though you may have to connect somewhere else first. The airport is a major hub for Delta Airlines, with more than five-dozen flights daily from around the country. SkyWest, which serves regional destinations in alliance with both Delta and United, offers more than 100 flights daily. Southwest ranks third in terms of daily flights. American, jetBlue, United, and Frontier have a handful of flights each.

If you're flying in from somewhere other than the United States, you'll likely connect in Los Angeles or San Francisco if you're coming from Asia, or a major airport in the East, such as Detroit, Atlanta, or New York, if you're traveling from Europe. Occasionally in winter you may be delayed by a major snowstorm, but

these generally affect the mountain areas, not the airport.

If you're heading to southern Utah, you may find it more convenient to fly into Las Vegas, which has more flights and is often a cheaper destination. Be advised that the 120-mile drive from Las Vegas to St. George passes through extremely remote country, and the Virgin River Canyon near the Arizona/Utah border can make for treacherous driving, especially at night.

More visitors to southern Utah are flying directly to St. George, which has daily flights from Denver and Salt Lake City. Provo, Cedar City, Logan, Ogden, and Moab are about the only other destinations reachable via commercial airlines; it's often just as easy (and cheaper) to drive.

Airline Contacts **American Airlines** ☎ *800/433-7300* ⊕ *www.aa.com.* **Delta Airlines** ☎ *800/221-1212 for U.S. reservations, 800/241-4141 for international reservations* ⊕ *www.delta.com.* **Frontier** ☎ *800/432-1359* ⊕ *www.frontierairlines.com.* **jetBlue** ☎ *800/538-2583* ⊕ *www.jetblue.com.* **SkyWest** ⊕ *www.skywest.com.* **Southwest Airlines** ☎ *800/435-9792* ⊕ *www.southwest. com.* **United Airlines** ☎ *800/864-8331 for U.S. reservations, 800/538-2929 for international reservations* ⊕ *www.united.com.*

▌CAR TRAVEL

You'll need a car in Utah. Public transportation is available primarily along the Wasatch Front (Ogden to Salt Lake City to Provo), but caters to commuters, not tourists. You'll seldom be bored driving. Scenery ranges from snowcapped mountains to endless stretches of desert with strange rock formations and intense color. There are more national parks here than in any other state except Alaska and California, although their interiors are not always accessible by car.

Outside of the Salt Lake City and Park City areas, much of what draws most people to Utah is in the southern part of the state. I–15 is the main north–south thoroughfare, branching off to U.S. 6 toward Moab and to Arches and Canyonlands National Parks in the southeast, passing west of Capitol Reef National Park in the south–central region, and continuing all the way to the St. George area for Zion and Bryce National Parks in the southwest. Many visitors approach the southern Utah parks by way of I–70, which runs west from Denver through Grand Junction, Colorado, and Moab. Highway 89 parallels I–15 for much of the state, offering a slower, back roads alternative and includes Main Street in many small towns. Highway 12 is a nationally recognized Scenic Byway in the Grand Staircase-Escalante National Monument and is also worth incorporating into your itinerary if you have time.

TRAVEL TIMES FROM SALT LAKE CITY BY CAR	
TO	HOURS
Park City	40 min
Zion National Park	4¾ hours
Bryce National Park	4¼ hours
Arches National Park and Moab	4 hours
Canyonlands National Park	4¼ hours
Capitol Reef National Park	3¾ hours

GASOLINE

In major cities throughout Utah, gas prices are roughly similar to those in the rest of the continental United States; in rural and resort towns prices are considerably higher. In urban areas stations are plentiful, and most stay open late (some are open 24 hours). In rural areas stations are less numerous, and hours are more limited, particularly on Sunday; you can sometimes drive more than 100 miles on back roads without finding a gas station. It's best to always keep your tank at least half full.

PARKING

Parking is generally plentiful and easy to find, even in Salt Lake City. Many parking garages offer free visitor parking, typically for one or two hours. Meters are usually free for two hours at a stretch on Saturday and all day on Sunday.

ROAD CONDITIONS

Utah has some of the most spectacular vistas—and challenging driving—in the world. Roads range from multilane divided blacktop to narrow dirt roads; from twisting switchbacks bordered by guardrails to primitive backcountry paths so narrow that you must back up to the edge of a steep cliff to make a turn. Scenic routes and lookout points are clearly marked, enabling you to slow down and pull over to take in the views. You'll find highways and the national parks crowded in summer, and almost deserted (and occasionally impassable) in winter.

In many locations, particularly in the burgeoning Salt Lake Valley and St. George areas, there always seems to be road construction, which slows traffic. Check road conditions before you set out, and allow a little extra time when traveling in these busier regions.

Unpleasant sights along the highway are road kills—animals struck by vehicles. Deer, elk, and even bears may try to get to the other side of a road just as you come along, so watch out for wildlife on the highways. Exercise caution, not only to save an animal's life, but also to avoid possible extensive damage to your car.

Road Conditions In Utah ☎ *511* ⊕ *commuterlink.utah.gov.*

ROADSIDE EMERGENCIES

Throughout Utah, call 911 for any travel emergency, such as an accident or a serious health concern. For automotive breakdowns, 911 is not appropriate. Instead, find a local directory and dial a towing service. When out on the open highway, call the nonemergency central administration phone number of the Utah Highway Patrol for assistance.

Emergency Services Utah Highway Patrol
☎ 801/965–4518 ⊕ highwaypatrol.utah.gov.

RULES OF THE ROAD

Utah law requires seat belts for drivers and all passengers in vehicles so equipped. Always strap children under age 5 into approved child-safety seats. Helmets are required for motorcyclists and passengers under the age of 18.

You may turn right at a red light after stopping if there is no sign stating otherwise and no oncoming traffic. Right turns on red are prohibited in some areas, but these are signed accordingly. When in doubt, wait for the green.

The speed limit on U.S. interstates is 75–80 mph in rural areas and 65 mph in urban zones. But watch out. "Rural areas" are determined by census boundaries, and sometimes make little sense. Increased speeds are allowed only where clearly posted. Transition zones from one speed limit to the next are indicated with pavement markings and signs. Fines are doubled for speeding in work zones and school zones.

It is illegal in Utah to send text messages while driving, punishable by a fine and a misdemeanor charge and/or more serious penalties if it causes an accident or death.

WINTER AND DESERT DRIVING

It is best to have a complete tune-up before setting out. At the least, you should check the following: lights, including brake lights, backup lights, and emergency lights; tires, including the spare; oil; engine coolant; windshield-washer fluid; windshield-wiper blades; and brakes. For emergencies, take along flares or reflector triangles, jumper cables, an empty gas can, a flashlight, a plastic tarp, blankets, water, and coins or a calling card for phone calls (cell phones don't always work in high mountain areas).

Modern highways make mountain driving safe and generally trouble-free even in cold weather. Although winter driving can occasionally present some real challenges, road maintenance is good and plowing is prompt. However, severe winter storms occasionally close I–80 between Salt Lake City and Park City and I–15 near Cedar City. Tire chains and/or all-wheel drive or four-wheel-drive vehicles are often required in the canyons surrounding the Wasatch Front during storms, including Parley's Canyon between Salt Lake City and Park City and Big and Little Cottonwood canyons. Also, Highway 6 between Provo and Green River is considered the most dangerous road in the state. Its windy stretches and dramatic elevation changes cause slide-offs and mishaps, particularly in winter. If you're planning to drive into high elevations (and even Salt Lake City is at 4,000-plus feet above sea level), be sure to check the weather forecast and call for road conditions beforehand. Even main highways can close. Be prepared for stormy weather: carry an emergency kit containing warm clothes, a flashlight, some food and water, and blankets. It's also good to carry a cell phone, but the mountains can disrupt service, so also bring along coins for a pay phone. If you do get stalled by deep snow, do not leave your car. Wait for help, running the engine only if needed, and remember that assistance is never far away. Winter weather isn't confined to winter in the high country (it's been known to snow on July 4), so be prepared year-round. Keep your tank full of gas and remember water, even in winter. Always tell someone, even if it's the hotel clerk or gas-station attendant, where you're going and when you expect to return.

Desert driving can be dangerous in winter or summer. You may encounter extreme conditions in remote areas with drifting snow, blowing sand, and flash floods, with little chance of anyone driving by to help. Never leave children or pets in a car—summer temperatures climb quickly above 100°F. Before setting out on any driving trip, it's important to make sure your vehicle is in top condition.

CAR RENTAL

You can rent an economy car with air-conditioning, automatic transmission, and unlimited mileage in Salt Lake City for about $30 a day and $150 a week. This does not include tax on car rentals, which is 16.35% in Salt Lake City. If you're planning to do any skiing, biking, four-wheeling, or towing, check into renting an SUV, van, or pickup from a local company like Rugged Rentals, which specializes in outdoor vehicles and provides supplemental insurance as part of the rental charge. For around $60 per day or $300 per week (plus taxes and other fees), you can rent a relatively new SUV or van with bike rack, ski rack, or towing equipment included.

Renting a car in Las Vegas can be less expensive than renting one in Salt Lake City, especially if you're visiting southern Utah. The driving time between Las Vegas and Salt Lake City is seven to nine hours, but it's only a two- to three-hour trip from Las Vegas to Zion National Park.

In Utah you must be 21 or over and have a valid driver's license to rent a car; most companies also require a major credit card. If you're over 65, check the rental company's policy on overage drivers. You may pay extra for child seats (but shop around; some companies don't charge extra for them), which are compulsory for children under five, and for additional drivers. Non-U.S. residents will need a reservation voucher, a passport, a driver's license, and a travel policy that covers each driver to pick up a car.

Local Agencies Advantage ☎ 800/777-5500 ⊕ www.advantage.com. **Rugged Rental** ☎ 800/977-9111 ⊕ www.ruggedrental.com.

Major Rental Agencies Alamo ☎ 800/462-5266 ⊕ www.alamo.com. **Avis** ☎ 800/331-1212 ⊕ www.avis.com. **Budget** ☎ 800/527-0700 ⊕ www.budget.com. **Hertz** ☎ 800/654-3131 ⊕ www.hertz.com. **National Car Rental** ☎ 800/227-7368 ⊕ www.nationalcar.com.

■ TRAIN TRAVEL

Amtrak connects Utah to Chicago and San Francisco Bay Area daily via the *California Zephyr,* which stops in Salt Lake City, Provo, Helper, and Green River. However, trains are notorious for delays.

Information Amtrak ☎ 800/872-7245 ⊕ www.amtrak.com.

SCENIC TRAIN TRIPS

On the Heber Valley Historic Railroad you can catch the *Heber Creeper,* a turn-of-the-20th-century steam-locomotive train that rides the rails from Heber City across Heber Valley, alongside Deer Creek Reservoir, and down Provo Canyon to Vivian Park. Depending on the time of year, you can catch the Comedy Murder Mystery Train, the Polar Express, the Cowboy Poetry Train, or special holiday rides.

Information Heber Valley Historic Railroad ⊠ 450 S. 600 W, Heber City ☎ 435/654-5601 ⊕ www.hebervalleyrr.org.

ESSENTIALS

■ ACCOMMODATIONS

Utah is home to the founders of the Marriott chain of hotels, and its accommodations are plentiful, varied, and reasonably priced throughout the state. Chain motels are everywhere. The ski resorts along the Wasatch Front—especially in Park City—cater to the wealthy jet set, and there are posh resorts such as Deer Valley, the Waldorf Astoria Park City, and Canyons, and pampering spas at Green Valley or Red Mountain. Salt Lake City has hotels in every price range. National chains like Holiday Inn, Marriott, Hilton, Best Western, Super 8, and Motel 6 are dependable in Utah, and are occasionally the best beds in town. The gateway towns to the national parks usually have a large range of accommodations. There are also more bed-and-breakfasts, as international tourists often prefer to meet the locals at such places. Independent motels can also be found all over the state. Look for guest ranches if you're trying to find an authentic Western experience. They often require a one-week stay, and the cost is all-inclusive. During the busy summer season, from Memorial Day to Labor Day, it's a good idea to book hotels and bed-and-breakfasts in advance. Most motels and resorts have off-season rates. Take advantage of these, because hiking is best in the south in cool weather and the mountains are beautiful even without snow.

■ TIP→ Assume that hotels do not include any meals in their room rates, unless we specify otherwise.

General Information Utah Hotel & Lodging Association ☎ 801/593–2213 ⊕ www.uhla. org.

APARTMENT AND HOUSE RENTALS

Increasingly, condos and private homes are available for rent. Rentals range from one night to month-long stays. Enjoy slope-side accommodations with all the amenities of home such as multiple bathrooms and full kitchens at most ski resorts. Condo and home rentals are also available outside Zion, Bryce, Arches, and Canyonlands national parks. There are multiple national services, but Vacation Rentals By Owner is tried and true.

Rental Information Vacation Rentals By Owner ⊕ www.vrbo.com.

BED-AND-BREAKFASTS

Charm is the long suit of these establishments, which generally occupy a restored older building with some historical or architectural significance. Towns with notable B&Bs include Salt Lake City, Park City, Moab, and Springdale (outside Zion National Park). They're generally small, with fewer than 20 rooms. Breakfast is usually included in the rates. Call ahead to determine the extent of ADA compliance; most B&Bs do not have elevators, for instance.

Reservation Services BB Getaways ⊕ www. bbgetaways.com. **Bed & Breakfast.com** ☎ 512/322–2710, 800/462–2632 ⊕ www. bedandbreakfast.com. **Bed and Breakfast Inns of Utah** ⊕ www.bbiu.org. **Bed & Breakfast Inns Online** ☎ 800/215–7365 ⊕ www. bbonline.com. **BnB Finder.com** ☎ 888/469–6663 ⊕ www.bnbfinder.com.

HOSTELS

Hostels are almost too scarce in Utah to serve as a useful way to see the mountains and the desert. Salt Lake City has a couple, but only one, the Avenues, is in a nice neighborhood. In Moab the Lazy Lizard is an old standby. Check with the national hosteling networks for other Utah locations.

Information Hostels.com ⊕ www.hostels. com. **The Avenues Hostel** ☎ 801/539–8888 ⊕ www.saltlakehostel.com. **Lazy Lizard** ✉ 1213 S. Hwy. 191, Moab ☎ 435/259–6057 ⊕ www.lazylizardhostel.com.

HOTELS

Most Salt Lake City hotels cater to business travelers with such facilities as restaurants, cocktail lounges, Internet, swimming pools, exercise equipment, and meeting rooms. Room rates usually reflect the range of amenities available. Most other Utah towns and cities have less expensive hotels that are clean and comfortable but have fewer facilities. A popular accommodations trend is the all-suite hotel, which gives you more room for the money; examples include Courtyard by Marriott and Embassy Suites. In resort towns hotels are decidedly more deluxe, with every imaginable amenity in every imaginable price range; rural areas generally have simple, and sometimes rustic, accommodations.

Many properties have special weekend rates, sometimes up to 50% off regular prices. However, these deals are usually not extended during peak months (summer near the national parks and winter in the ski resorts), when hotels are normally full. Salt Lake City hotels are generally full only during major conventions such as the Outdoor Retailers Show (winter and summer).

All hotels listed have private bath unless otherwise noted.

RESORTS

Ski towns throughout Utah such as Park City, Sundance, and Brian Head, are home to resorts in all price ranges (but primarily high-end); any activities lacking in any individual property are usually available in the town itself—in summer as well as winter. Off the slopes, there are both wonderful rustic and luxurious resorts in the southern part of the state: Zion Ponderosa Ranch Resort near Zion, Sorrel River Ranch and Red Cliffs Adventure Lodge near Arches, and Amangiri near Lake Powell and Four Corners.

∎ COMMUNICATIONS

INTERNET

Most hotels and many smaller motels throughout Utah now offer Wi-Fi or other Internet access at no cost to guests. Many coffee shops provide Wi-Fi free of charge (although it's a little harder to find in southern Utah), as do most libraries, which also provide computers with Internet access. There's also free Wi-Fi along Main Street in downtown Salt Lake City.

Contacts Cybercafes ⊕ www.cybercafes.com.

PHONES

To dial any number in Utah you must dial at least 10 digits, including the three-digit area code. The area code for the Wasatch Front (roughly from Ogden to Provo, including Salt Lake City) has always been 801, but new numbers are being assigned with a new 385 area code. The area code 435 covers all the rest of the state. To confuse matters, the "801" district is divided geographically between Salt Lake County and neighboring counties (Utah to the south and Davis to the north)—you must dial "1" if you're calling *between* counties but not if you're calling *within* one of the counties.

∎ EATING OUT

Dining in Utah is generally casual. Menus are becoming more varied, but you can nearly always order a hamburger or a steak. There are a growing number of fine restaurants in Salt Lake City and Park City, and good places are cropping up in various other areas. Also look for good dining in Springdale, Moab, and Torrey. Seek out colorful diners along the secondary highways like U.S. 89; they usually serve up meat and potatoes along with the local flavor of each community. Authentic ethnic food is easy to find in Salt Lake City, but generally not available elsewhere. The restaurants we list are the cream of the crop in each price category.

MEALS AND MEALTIMES

Although you can find all types of cuisine in the major cities and resort towns of Utah, be sure to try native dishes like trout, elk, and buffalo (the latter two have less fat than beef and are just as tasty); organic fruits and vegetables are also readily available, especially in finer establishments in Salt Lake City and Park City. Southwestern food is popular, and you'll find several restaurants that specialize in it or show Southwestern influences in menu selections. Asian and Latin American cuisines are both gaining in popularity (and quality) in the Salt Lake area.

Unless otherwise noted, the restaurants listed in this guide are open daily for lunch and dinner. Dinner hours are usually from 6 to 9 pm. Outside of the large cities and resort towns in the high seasons, many restaurants close by 10 and are closed on Sunday.

PAYING

Credit cards are widely accepted, though not always at restaurants in rural areas.

⇨ *For guidelines on tipping see Tipping below.*

RESERVATIONS AND DRESS

Reservations are relatively rare outside of the top restaurants in the urban and resort areas. It's a good idea to call ahead if you can. We only mention them specifically when reservations are essential (there's no other way you'll ever get a table) or when they are not accepted. Large parties should always call ahead to check the reservations policy. We mention dress only when men are required to wear a jacket or a jacket and tie—which is almost never in casual Utah. Even at nice resorts dress is usually casual, and in summer you're welcome nearly everywhere in your shorts, T-shirt, and hiking shoes.

Contacts OpenTable ⊕ *www.opentable.com.*

WINES, BEER, AND SPIRITS

Despite what you've heard, it's not hard to get a drink in Utah, though you must be 21 to purchase or consume alcohol.

The state overhauled liquor laws in 2009 to bring it more in line with the rest of the United States. The state abolished the "private club" system, which required each patron have an annual or short-term membership in order to enter the premises. Many restaurants have licenses, which allow them to serve you wine and beer—and occasionally liquor—with a meal. At restaurants, you will have to order food in addition to alcohol. Some restaurants—generally those that cater to families—opt not to carry a liquor license. If you're set on having a drink with your meal, check before you go. Some restaurants will allow you to bring your own wine, but may charge a corkage fee. Call ahead if you want to take your own wine or other liquor to a restaurant—lots of regulations cover brown bagging.

Utah has a thriving microbrewery scene, with local lagers produced in Salt Lake City, Park City, Moab, Springdale, and Ogden. There are several brewpubs with their own beers on tap—try St. Provo Girl and Polygamy Porter to get a taste of the local drinking humor. Some brewpubs also have a liquor license that allows the sale of wine and spirits.

Most hotel restaurants carry a liquor license, and you'll be able to get your own drinks from the minibar in your room.

Beer with 3.2% alcohol is available in grocery stores and some convenience stores. For anything else, you'll have to go to a state liquor store. There are 16 liquor stores throughout Salt Lake City and others throughout the state. They are closed on Sunday, Election Day, and holidays.

▌ HEALTH

Salt Lake City and Logan are surrounded by mountains, which can trap pollution and create some of the worst air quality in the nation, particularly in winter. Red Alert action days happen several times a year (often for more than a week at a time) when strenuous activity, particularly by young and elderly people, is discouraged. Visit the Utah Department of Environmental Quality website to find out about air quality if you have asthma, allergies, or other breathing sensitivities.

Information Utah Department of Environmental Quality ⊕ *www.airquality.utah.gov.*

∎ MONEY

Hotel prices in Salt Lake City run the gamut, but on average the prices are a bit lower than in most major cities. You can pay $100–$350 a night for a room in a major business hotel, though some "value" hotel rooms go for $50–$75, and budget motels are also readily available. Weekend packages at city hotels can cut prices in half (but may not be available in peak winter or summer seasons). As a rule, costs outside cities are lower, except in the deluxe resorts, where costs can be double those anywhere else in the state. Look for senior and kids' discounts at many attractions.

Prices throughout this guide are given for adults. Substantially reduced fees are almost always available for children, students, and senior citizens.

CREDIT CARDS

Some small-town restaurants may not accept credit cards, but otherwise plastic is readily accepted at dining, lodging, shopping, and other facilities throughout the state. Minimum purchase amounts may apply.

Throughout this guide, we only mention credit cards when they are not accepted.

∎ PACKING

Informality reigns here; jeans, sport shirts, and T-shirts fit in almost everywhere, for both men and women. The few restaurants and performing-arts events where dressier outfits are required, usually in resorts and larger cities, are the exception.

If you plan to spend much time outdoors, and certainly if you go in winter, choose clothing appropriate for cold and

wet weather. Cotton clothing, including denim—although fine on warm, dry days—can be uncomfortable and even dangerous when it gets wet and when the weather's cold. A better choice is clothing made of wool or any of a number of new synthetics that provide warmth without bulk and maintain their insulating properties even when wet.

In summer you'll want shorts during the day. But because early morning and night can be cold, and high passes windy, pack a sweater and a light jacket, and perhaps also a wool cap and gloves. Try layering—a T-shirt under another shirt under a jacket—and peel off layers as you go. For walks and hikes, you'll need sturdy footwear. To take you into the wilds, boots should have thick soles and plenty of ankle support; if your shoes are new and you plan to spend much time on the trail, break them in at home. Bring a day pack for short hikes, along with a canteen or water bottle, and don't forget rain gear, a hat, sunscreen, and insect repellent.

In winter, prepare for subfreezing temperatures with good boots, warm socks and liners, thermal underwear, a well-insulated jacket, and a warm hat and mittens. Dress in layers, so you can add or remove clothes as the temperatures fluctuate.

If you attend dances and other events at Native American reservations, dress conservatively—skirts or long pants for women, long pants for men—or you may be asked to leave.

When traveling to mountain areas, remember that sunglasses and a sun hat are essential at high altitudes, even in winter; the thinner atmosphere requires sunscreen with a greater SPF than you might need at lower elevations. Bring moisturizer even if you don't normally use it. Utah's dry climate can be hard on your skin.

▌SAFETY

All those strenuous activities in high altitudes can be fun but dangerous. Utah is full of wide-open, lonely spaces. Though you may enjoy the freedom, openness, and solitude, it's always best to tell someone—the hotel desk clerk, the ski-rental person—where you're going. Cell phones don't always work in the backcountry, and even a general idea of where you are can help rescuers find you quickly. Regardless of the outdoor activity or your level of skill, safety must come first. Remember: Know your limits.

Many trails are at high altitudes, where oxygen is thinner. They're also frequently desolate. Hikers and bikers should carry emergency supplies in their backpacks. Proper equipment includes a flashlight, a compass, waterproof matches, a first-aid kit, a knife, and a light plastic tarp for shelter. Backcountry skiers should add a repair kit, a blanket, an avalanche beacon, and a lightweight shovel to their lists. Always bring extra food and a canteen of water as dehydration is a common occurrence at high altitudes. Never drink from streams or lakes, unless you boil the water first or purify it with tablets. Giardia, an intestinal parasite, may be present.

Always check the condition of roads and trails, and get the latest weather reports before setting out. In summer take precautions against heat stroke or exhaustion by resting frequently in shaded areas; in winter take precautions against hypothermia by layering clothing. Ultimately, proper planning, common sense, and good physical conditioning are the strongest guards against the elements.

You may feel dizzy and weak and find yourself breathing heavily—signs that the thin mountain air isn't giving you your accustomed dose of oxygen. Take it easy and rest often for a few days until you're acclimatized. Throughout your stay, drink plenty of water and watch your alcohol consumption. If you experience severe headaches and nausea, see a doctor. It is easy—especially in Utah, where highways climb to 9,000 feet and higher—to go too high too fast. The remedy for altitude-related discomfort is to go down quickly into heavier air. Other altitude-related problems include dehydration and overexposure to the sun due to the thin air.

Flash floods can strike at any time and any place with little or no warning. The danger in mountainous terrain intensifies when distant rains are channeled into gullies and ravines, turning a quiet streamside campsite or wash into a rampaging torrent in seconds; similarly, desert terrain can become dangerous when heavy rains fall on land that is unable to absorb the water and thus floods quickly. Check weather reports before heading into the backcountry, and be prepared to head for higher ground if the weather turns severe.

One of the most wonderful features of Utah is its abundant wildlife. And although a herd of grazing elk or a bighorn sheep high on a hillside is most certainly a Kodak moment, an encounter with a bear or mountain lion is not. To avoid such an unpleasant situation while hiking, make plenty of noise and keep dogs on a leash and small children between adults. While camping, be sure to store all food, utensils, and clothing with food odors far away from your tent, preferably high in a tree or in a bear box. If you do come across a bear or big cat, do not run. For bears, back away quietly; for lions, make yourself look as big as possible. In either case, be prepared to fend off the animal with loud noises, rocks, sticks, and so on. And, as the saying goes, do not feed the bears—or any wild animals, whether they're dangerous or not.

When in any park, give all animals their space. If you want to take a photograph, use a long lens and keep your distance. This is particularly important for winter visitors. Approaching an animal can cause stress and affect its ability to survive the sometimes-brutal climate. In all cases, remember that the animals have the right-of-way; this is their home, you are the visitor.

▌ TAXES

State sales tax is 4.65% in Utah. Most areas have additional local sales and lodging taxes, which can be quite significant. For example, in Salt Lake City the combined sales tax is 6.85%, plus a 1% tax on all restaurant checks. Utah sales tax is reduced for some items, such as groceries.

▌ TIME

Utah is in the mountain time zone. Mountain time is two hours earlier than eastern time and one hour later than Pacific time. It is one hour earlier than Chicago, seven hours earlier than London, and 17 hours earlier than Sydney. In summer Utah observes Daylight Savings Time. Timeanddate.com can help you figure out the correct time anywhere.

Time Zones Timeanddate.com ⊕ *www. timeanddate.com/worldclock.*

▌ TIPPING

Utahans are notoriously stingy tippers, so don't ask a local what to tip. It is customary to tip 15% at restaurants; 18%–20% in resort towns is increasingly the norm. For coat checks and bellmen, $1 per coat or bag is the minimum. Taxi drivers expect 15% to 20%, depending on where you are. In resort towns, ski technicians, sandwich makers, coffee baristas, and the like also appreciate tips.

TIPPING GUIDELINES FOR UTAH	
Bartender	$1 to $5 per round of drinks, depending on the number of drinks
Bellhop	$1 to $5 per bag, depending on the level of the hotel
Hotel Concierge	$5 or more, if he or she performs a service for you
Hotel Doorman	$1–$2 if he helps you get a cab
Hotel Maid	$1–$3 a day (either daily or at the end of your stay, in cash)
Hotel Room-Service Waiter	$1 to $2 per delivery, even if a service charge has been added
Porter at Airport or Train Station	$1 per bag
Skycap at Airport	$1 to $3 per bag checked
Taxi Driver	15%–20%, but round up the fare to the next dollar amount
Tour Guide	10% of the cost of the tour
Valet Parking Attendant	$1–$2, but only when you get your car
Waiter	15%–20%, with 20% being the norm at high-end restaurants; nothing additional if a service charge is added to the bill

▌ TOURS

SPECIAL INTEREST TOURS
BICYCLING
Utah offers a wide range of topography and scenery to satisfy cyclists of all styles. Moab has been heralded for years as a mecca for mountain bikers, but fat-tire lovers pedal all corners and all elevations of the state; bike shops in St. George, Salt Lake City, and Ogden can also help you find an itinerary. Excellent multiday (and multisport) tours crisscross the desert including the incomparable White Rim Trail in Canyonlands National Park. Hard-core road cyclists, including pros in training, challenge themselves by climbing

the grueling canyons to the east of Salt Lake City. But there are plenty of roads for the less gonzo rider to explore, and biking is an excellent way for a family to bond while getting some exercise.

■ TIP→ Most airlines accommodate bikes as luggage for an extra fee, provided they're dismantled and boxed.

Contacts **Bicycle Adventures.** Several multiday tours in southern Utah including an epic seven-day road ride from St. George to Lake Powell. ☎ 800/443–6060 ⊕ www. bicycleadventures.com ✉ From $1,995. **Escape Adventures.** More than 20 itineraries for road cyclists and mountain bikers alike range from three to seven days. Beginners can enjoy road rides of less than 30 miles per day, single-track daredevils can conquer slickrock trails, and independent travelers will love the "do it yourself" itineraries. ☎ 800/596–2953 ⊕ www.escapeadventures.com ✉ From $100 per day. **Western Spirit.** This outfitter offers a half-dozen fully supported itineraries (such as Bryce to Zion National Parks) that range from family-oriented to expert-only, and from four to seven days. The common denominator is challenging wilderness conditions that are best undertaken with an expert guide unless you're a seasoned, experienced back-road or off-road biker. ☎ 800/845–2453 ⊕ www.westernspirit. com ✉ From around $250 per day. **Rim Tours.** Half-, full- or multiday tours in southern Utah include Moab, Gooseberry Mesa, and the White Rim Trail. ☎ 435/259–5223, 800/626–7335 ⊕ www.rimtours.com ✉ From $95 per person for a half-day tour.

FISHING

Close to Salt Lake City, the Provo and Logan rivers are world-class trout-fishing rivers that attract anglers from around the globe. In some parts of the Provo, it is said that there are upward of 7,500 trout per square mile.

Contacts **Four Seasons Fly Fishers.** These knowledgeable anglers will lead you to trout-filled streams, and set up tents and hot meals for you on multiday trips. ☎ 435/657–2010, 800/498–5440 ⊕ www.utahflyfish.com ✉ From $500 per day.

GOLF

From a dozen public courses in the Salt Lake Valley, to world-class courses in Park City to the sunny southern Utah courses set against red-rock backdrops, Utah offers a proliferation of golf courses. You will find variety in terrain, scenery, and level of difficulty.

HORSEBACK RIDING

You can still throw on some jeans and boots and head out on a multiday horseback trek. Several Utah operators will match you with your steed, give you as much or as little instruction as you need, and get you out on the trail. Excursions range from day trips to weeklong adventures.

RAFTING

For an instant respite from summer heat that ranges from toasty to torrid, book a one-to-five-day river-rafting adventure. Itineraries exist for families with adventurers as young as three years old and range from leisurely multiday floats to days that culminate in unforgettable rapids. Utah's river guides have been at it for decades, and will gladly share river-bottom views of red rock cliffs, petroglyphs, and wildlife. The Utah tourism website (⊕ www. utah.com/raft) is a useful resource.

SKIING

If ever an outdoor activity was synonymous with Utah tourism, skiing is it. The bulk of the state's resorts, known for the fluffy powder that falls on average 400 to 600 inches or more a year, are within a one-hour drive from the Salt Lake City Airport. Ski the same runs that Olympians traversed in 2002: the downhill and slaloms were held at Snowbasin near Ogden, while aerials, slalom, and snowboarding took place at Park City or Deer Valley. Finally, challenge yourself on the same Nordic competition trails at Heber Valley's Soldier Hollow Olympic venue. Every ski resort and many private travel agents can assist you with your ski planning. Ski Utah is the state's official and very useful website for ski information; it should be your starting point for any ski activity in the state.

Information SkiUtah. Whether you have 2 days or 10, Ski Utah can help you make the most of your time on the snow. The Interconnect Tour gives advanced to expert skiers the chance to ski backcountry terrain in and around as many as six resorts in one day. ☎ *800/754–8824* ⊕ *www.skiutah.com* ✉ *From $325 for Interconnect tour.*

▌ TRIP INSURANCE

Comprehensive trip insurance is valuable if you're booking a very expensive or complicated trip (particularly to an isolated region) or if you're booking far in advance. Comprehensive policies typically cover trip-cancellation and interruption, letting you cancel or cut your trip short because of illness, or, in some cases, acts of terrorism in your destination. Such policies might also cover evacuation and medical care. Some also cover you for trip delays because of bad weather or mechanical problems as well as for lost or delayed luggage.

Another type of coverage to consider is financial default—that is, when your trip is disrupted because a tour operator or airline goes out of business. Generally you must buy this when you book your trip or shortly thereafter, and it's available to you only if your operator isn't on a list of excluded companies.

Always read the fine print of your policy to make sure that you're covered for the risks that most concern you. Compare several policies to be sure you're getting the best price and range of coverage available.

Comprehensive Insurers AIG Travel Guard ☎ *800/826–4919* ⊕ *www.travelguard.com.* **Allianz Global Assistance** ☎ *866/884–3556* ⊕ *www.allianztravelinsurance.com.* **CSA Travel Protection** ☎ *800/711–1197* ⊕ *www. csatravelprotection.com.* **Travelex Insurance** ☎ *800/228–9792* ⊕ *www.travelexinsurance.*

INSPIRATION: BOOKS AND MOVIES

The desert environment has been explored by a host of writers: Everett Reuss (*A Vagabond for Beauty*); Terry Tempest Williams (*Refuge: An Unnatural History of Family and Place*); Edward Abbey (*Desert Solitaire*); Wallace Stegner (*Mormon Country*); Jon Krakauer (*Under the Banner of Heaven*). Visitors can brush up on religious customs with *Mormonism for Dummies*; while the *Book of Mormon* has been the church's foundation since its publication in 1830.

Utah's famous desert landscape makes it a top destination for filmmakers as well: *How the West Was Won* (1963); *2001: A Space Odyssey* (1968); *Butch Cassidy and the Sundance Kid* (1969); *Thelma and Louise* (1991); *High School Musical* (2006); *127 Hours* (2011); and many more.

---

com. **Travel Insured International** ☎ *800/243–3174* ⊕ *www.travelinsured.com.*

Insurance Comparison Information Insure My Trip ☎ *800/487–4722* ⊕ *www.insuremytrip. com.* **Square Mouth** ☎ *800/240–0369* ⊕ *www. squaremouth.com.*

▌ VISITOR INFORMATION

Utah Office of Tourism (across the street from the state capitol) is open six days a week.

Contacts Utah Office of Tourism ✉ *Council Hall, Capitol Hill, 300 N. State St., Salt Lake City* ☎ *801/538–1030, 800/200–1160* ⊕ *www. visitutah.com.*

INDEX

A

Accommodations, *343–344*
Agua Canyon, *232*
Air tours, *234*
Air travel, *18, 338–339*
Arches National Park, 277
Bryce Canyon National Park, 229
Canyonlands National Park, 293
Dinosaurland and Eastern Utah, 174
Moab and Southeastern Utah, 308, 335
North of Salt Lake City, 141
Park City and the Southern Wasatch, 99
Salt Lake City, 40
Southwestern Utah, 245
Zion National Park, 214
Alpine Loop Scenic Byway, *94*
Alta Ski Resort, *86, 88*
Amangiri ⊡ **,** *336*
American West Heritage Center, *160*
Amid Summer's Inn Bed & Breakfast ⊡ **,** *249*
Angels Landing Trail, *222*
Antelope Island State Park, *91–93*
Apartment and house rentals, *343*
Arches Main Park Road, *279–280*
Arches National Park, *16, 34, 273–288*
camping, 288
itineraries, 277
lodging, 278
permits, 278
plants and wildlife, 279
restaurants, 278
scenic drives, 279–280
transportation, 277–278
visitor information, 278, 279
Art galleries. ⇨ *See* Museums and art galleries

B

Balanced Rock, *274, 280*
Banks. ⇨ *See* Money matters
Baseball, *60, 146*
Basketball, *60*
Bear Lake Country, *140, 167–170*
Bear Lake State Park, *167–170*

Bear Paw Café ✕ **,** *255*
Bear River Migratory Bird Refuge, *156*
Bed & Breakfasts, *343*
Beehive House, *46*
Behunin Cabin, *202*
Best Western Canyonlands Inn ⊡ **,** *321–322*
Bicycling, *20–21*
Arches National Park, 283
Canyonlands National Park, 298
Capitol Reef National Park, 204
Dinosaurland and Eastern Utah, 179, 185–186, 192
Moab and Southeastern Utah, 315–316
North of Salt Lake City, 146, 157, 162–163, 168
Park City and the Southern Wasatch, 106–108, 125–126, 130
Salt Lake City and environs, 60, 83, 87, 92
Southwestern Utah, 250, 254, 267, 269
tours, 348–349
Zion National Park, 219–220
Big Cottonwood Canyon, *82–83, 85–86*
Bird-watching, *56, 57, 59, 156, 220, 234–235, 283, 299*
Bit & Spur Restaurant and Saloon ✕ **,** *258*
Blanding, *329–330*
Blanding Visitor Center, *329*
Bluff, *330–332*
Boating, *163, 168–169, 186, 192–193, 283, 299, 336*
Books and movies, *221, 233, 282, 350*
Boulder, *268–269*
Boulder Mountain Lodge ⊡ **,** *269*
Brian Head, *250–251*
Brigham City, *155–158*
Brigham City Museum-Gallery, *156*
Brigham Young University, *124*
Brigham Young's Winter Home, *253*
Browning Firearms Museum, *145*
Browning-Kimball Car Museum, *145*

Browns Park, *185*
Bryce Amphitheater, *226*
Bryce Canyon Lodge ⊡ **,** *232, 239*
Bryce Canyon National Park, *16, 34, 225–240*
campgrounds, 240
itineraries, 229
lodging, 230, 239–240
permits, 230
plants and wildlife, 231
restaurants, 230, 238–239
scenic drives, 231
tours, 237–238
transportation, 229
visitor information, 230, 231
Bryce Canyon Visitor Center, *231*
Bus travel, *40–41, 99, 141–142, 200, 229, 314*
BYU Museum of Paleontology, *124–125*
BYU Museum of Peoples and Culture, *125*

C

Cache Valley, *139, 159–167*
Cache Valley Center for the Arts, *161*
Cache Valley Food Tour, *161*
Cafe Diablo ✕ **,** *271*
Camping
Arches National Park, 288
Bryce Canyon National Park, 240
Canyonlands National Park, 303
Capitol Reef National Park, 208
Dinosaurland and Eastern Utah, 174
Canyon Overlook Trail, *222*
Canyon Voyages Adventure Company, *317*
Canyonlands National Park, *16, 34, 289–304*
camping, 303
itineraries, 292–293
lodging, 294
permits, 294
plants and wildlife, 296
restaurants, 294
scenic drives, 295
tours, 298
transportation, 293–294
visitor information, 294, 295

Canyons Resort, 110
Capitol Dome, 202
Capitol Gorge, 202
Capitol Reef National Park, 14,
    34, 195–208
    camping, 208
    itineraries, 199–200
    lodging, 200, 207–208
    permits, 200
    plants and wildlife, 201
    restaurants, 200, 207
    scenic drives, 201–202
    transportation, 200
    visitor information, 201
Capitol Reef Scenic Drive,
    201–202
Car travel and rentals, 18, 19,
    339–342
    Arches National Park,
    277–278, 279–280
    Bryce Canyon National Park,
    229, 231
    Canyonlands National Park,
    293, 295
    Capitol Reef National Park,
    200, 201–202
    Dinosaurland and Eastern
    Utah, 174–175, 189
    Moab and Southeastern Utah,
    308, 335
    North of Salt Lake City, 142
    Park City and the Southern
    Wasatch, 99
    Salt Lake City, 26
    Southwestern Utah, 245
    Zion National Park, 214, 216
Cassidy, Butch, 184
Castle Country, 173, 176–180
Cathedral of the Madeleine, 51
Cathedral Valley, 196
Cedar Breaks National Monu-
    ment, 250
Cedar City, 246–250
Centro Woodfired Pizzeria
    ✕, 248
Checkerboard Mesa, 217
Children, attractions for, 33
    Arches National Park, 281–
    282, 284, 285
    Bryce Canyon National Park,
    233–234, 235, 237–238
    Canyonlands National Park,
    296, 297, 298, 302–303, 304
    Capitol Reef National Park,
    202, 205–206
    Dinosaurland and Eastern
    Utah, 177, 178, 184–185
    Moab and Southeastern Utah,
    324, 329

North of Salt Lake City, 144,
    145, 146, 156, 160, 161,
    168, 169–170
Park City and the Southern
    Wasatch, 101, 102, 103,
    105, 111, 113, 121, 122,
    124–125, 133–134
Salt Lake City and environs, 40,
    48–49, 50, 55, 60, 61, 62, 82
Southwestern Utah, 253, 254,
    258, 261, 266, 271
Zion National Park, 218–219,
    221, 222, 223
Chimney Rock, 202
Church of Jesus Christ of
    Latter-day Saints Conference
    Center, 46
City and County Building,
    49–50
City Creek Canyon, 60
Clark Planetarium, 50
Cleveland-Lloyd Dinosaur
    Quarry, 177
Colorado River Scenic Byway -
    Route 128, 280, 311
Colorado River Scenic Byway -
    Route 279, 312
Communications, 344
Community Contra Dance, 323
Condo rentals, 120
Contender Bicycles, 60
Copper Onion ✕, 63–64
Coral Pink Sand Dunes Park,
    261
Court of the Patriarchs, 217
Courthouse Towers, 274
Cowboy Line Camp, 296
Credit cards, 11, 346
Crystal Hot Springs, 156

D

Dairy Keen ✕, 135
Daughters of the Utah Pioneers
    Museum (Cedar City), 248
Daughters of Utah Pioneers
    Cache Museum (Logan), 161
Dead Horse Point State Park,
    312
Deer Valley Resort, 111
Delicate Arch, 280
Delicate Arch Trail, 285–286
Desert Bistro ✕, 318–319
Desert Pearl Inn 🖵, 259
Devils Garden, 274
Devils Garden Campground
    ⚠, 288
Devils Garden Trail, 286
Dining. ⇨ See Restaurants

Dinosaur National Monument,
    188–190
Dinosaur National Monument
    Quarry and Visitor Center,
    186
Dinosaur Roundup Rodeo,
    183–184
Dinosaur sites, 26
Dinosaurland and Eastern Utah,
    177, 178, 183, 185, 188
    North of Salt Lake City, 144
    Southwestern Utah, 243, 254
Dinosaurland and Eastern
    Utah, 14, 171–194
    campgrounds, 174
    lodging, 175, 180, 182–183,
    187, 190, 193, 194
    nightlife and the arts, 180,
    183, 188
    restaurants, 175, 179–180, 187
    tours, 186, 189–190
    transportation, 174–175
    visitor information, 176, 177,
    184
Discovery Gateway, 48
Double Arch, 280–281
Dry Fork Canyon, 184–185

E

Earth Tours, 268
Eastern Utah. ⇨ See Dinosaur-
    land and Eastern Utah
Eccles Community Art Center,
    145–146
Echo Park Dam, 190
Edge of the Cedars State Park
    Museum, 329
Eklecticafe ✕, 319
El Chubasco ✕, 115
Ellen Eccles Theater, 166
Escalante, 264–268
Escalante Petrified Forest State
    Park, 266

F

Fairyland Point, 232
Falcon's Ledge Lodge 🖵, 182
Family History Library, 47
Farm at the Canyons ✕, 115
Ferry travel, 335
Festivals and seasonal
    events, 19
    Arches National Park, 276–277
    Bryce Canyon National Park,
    229
    Capitol Reef National Park, 199
    Dinosaurland and Eastern
    Utah, 176, 183–184

Moab and Southeastern Utah, 310–311, 331
North of Salt Lake City, 156, 160
Park City and the Southern Wasatch, 101–103, 123, 132
Salt Lake City, 39–40
Southwestern Utah, 247, 253, 261, 263
Fiery Furnace, 274, 281
Fishing, 21, 108, 126, 130, 163, 169, 182, 192–193, 263, 284
tours, 349
Flaming Gorge Dam Visitor Center, 191
Flaming Gorge National Recreation Area, 191–193
Flaming Gorge–Uintas National Scenic Byway, 188
Fly fishing, 108, 126, 163, 169, 182, 192–193
Fort Buenaventura Park, 146
Foundry Grill ✕, 131
Four-wheeling, 204–205, 284, 299–301, 314
Fremont Petroglyphs, 202
Frisbee golf, 108
Frontier Homestead State Park Museum, 248
Fruita Historic District, 196, 202

G
Gateway Mall, 48–49
Geology, 133, 203, 334
George S. Eccles Dinosaur Park, 144
Glen Canyon National Recreation Area, 335
Glitretind ✕, 115
Goblin Valley State Park, 328
Golden Spike Empire, 139, 154–159
Golden Spike National Historic Site, 158–159
Golf, 60–61, 108–109, 126, 134, 146–147, 152, 157, 163–164, 169, 179, 254–255, 315
tours, 349
Goosenecks State Park, 332
Grafton, 258
Grand America Hotel, The 🏨, 74
Grand Staircase-Escalante National Monument, 243, 264–272
Grand View Point, 296

Great Salt Lake, 38–39, 57–59
Great Salt Lake State Park, 57–59
Great White Throne, 217
Green River, 325–326, 328
Green River Overlook, 296
Green River State Park, 326

H
Hampton Inn and Suites 🏨, 149
Hatch Family Chocolates ✕, 46–47
Health concerns, 345–346
Hearth on 25th ✕, 148
Heber Valley, 132–136
Heber Valley Railroad, 133
Hell's Backbone Grill ✕, 269
Herm's Inn ✕, 164–165
High West Distillery ✕, 115
Highway 12 Scenic Byway, 266
Hiking, 22–23
Arches National Park, 284–287
Bryce Canyon National Park, 235–237
Canyonlands National Park, 301–304
Capitol Reef National Park, 205–206
Dinosaurland and Eastern Utah, 179, 186, 189, 193
Moab and Southeastern Utah, 315
North of Salt Lake City, 117, 16=52, 157, 162–163, 169–170
Park City and the Southern Wasatch, 109, 126–127, 130, 134–135
Salt Lake City environs, 83, 87–88, 92
Southwestern Utah, 248, 255, 269
Zion National Park, 220–223
Hill Aerospace Museum, 144
Hire's Big H ✕, 71
Historic 25th Street District, 144–145
Hogle Zoo, 55
Hoodoos, 334
Horse racing, 255
Horseback riding, 23–24, 109–110, 135, 152, 207, 223, 237–238
Tours, 349
Horseshoe Canyon Trail, 290
Hostels, 343
Hot-air ballooning, 110

Hotel Monaco Salt Lake City 🏨, 74–75
Hotels, 11, 344. ⇨ *See also* Lodging

I
Ice-skating, 61, 110, 127
Inspiration Point, 232
Internet, 344
Island in the Sky Park Road (Canyonlands National Park), 290, 295, 296–297
Itineraries, 28–31. ⇨ *See also* under specific cities and areas

J
Jensen Inn 🏨, 190
John Jarvie Ranch, 185
John M. Browning Firearms Museum, 145
John Wesley Powell River History Museum, 326
Joseph Smith Memorial Building, 47

K
Kanab, 260–262
Kayaking, 147
Kearns Mansion, 51, 52
Kimball Art Center, 105
Kodachrome Basin State Park, 267
Kolob Canyon, 211
Kolob Canyon Road, 216

L
La Sal Mountain Loop, 325
La Sal Mountains, 325
Lake Powell, 334–336
Lake Powell Ferry, 335
Lava Point, 211
Layla Grill and Mezze ✕, 72
Leonardo, The, 49
Liberty Park, 56
Little America Hotel 🏨, 86–91
Little Hollywood Museum, 72
Lodging, 11. ⇨ *See also* Hotels
Logan, 159–167
Logan Mormon Tabernacle, 161
Log Haven ✕, 72
Lucky 13 Bar and Grill ✕, 71

M
Maddox Ranch House ✕, 158
Main Park Road (Bryce Canyon National Park), 231
Maze, The 290

Memory Grove, *51, 53*
Mesa Arch, *297*
Mesa Arch Trail, *302*
Mexican Hat, *332–333*
Milt's Stage Stop ✕, *249*
Mirror Lake, *194*
Mirror Lake Scenic Byway, *194*
Moab and Southeastern Utah, *16, 274, 305–336*
itineraries, *308*
lodging, *308, 321–323, 328, 331–332, 333, 336*
nightlife and the arts, *323, 333*
restaurants, *308, 318–321, 328, 329–331*
tours, *316–318*
transportation, *308*
visitor information, *311, 326, 329*
Moab Information Center, *311*
Moab Music Festival, *311*
Money matters, *346*
Montage Deer Valley ☒ , *118*
Monte L. Bean Life Science Museum, *125*
Monument Valley Navajo Tribal Park, *332–333*
Moqui Cave, *261*
Mormon Tabernacle Choir, *43*
Mormons in Utah, *19, 32, 41, 47*
Mountain biking. ⇨ See Bicycling
Mountain Town Music, *121*
Movies, *350*
Muley Twist Canyon, *196*
Museum of Anthropology, *160*
Museum of Art at Brigham Young University, *125*
Museum of Church History and Art, *47*
Museum of Moab, *312*
Museums and art galleries
Capitol Reef National Park, *202*
Dinosaurland and Eastern Utah, *178, 185, 192*
Moab and Southeastern Utah, *312, 324, 326–328, 329*
North of Salt Lake City, *144, 145–146, 151, 156, 160, 161*
Park City and the Southern Wasatch, *105–106, 122, 124–125*
Salt Lake City, *47, 48, 49, 53, 55, 57*
Southwestern Utah, *248, 253, 259, 261, 270*
Zion National Park, *216–217*

N
Narrows, The *210, 217–218*
Natural Bridge, *232*
Natural Bridges National Monument, *333–334*
Natural History Museum of Utah, *55*
Navajo/Queen's Garden Combination Loop, *236*
Needles District Park Road (Canyonlands National Park), *290, 295, 296, 297*
Newspaper Rock State Historic Monument, *329*
Night Sky Program, *234*
Nine Mile Canyon, *178*
Nora Eccles Harrison Museum, *160*
North of Salt Lake City, *14, 137–170*
itineraries, *141*
lodging, *142, 149, 154, 158, 165–166, 170*
nightlife and the arts, *149–150, 158, 166*
restaurants, *142, 147–149, 154, 157–158, 160–161, 164–165, 170*
transportation, *141–142*
visitor information, *143, 144, 156*
Northeast-Central Utah, *173, 176–180*
Northern Ute Pow Wow, *182*

O
Ogden, *143–151*
Ogden City & Valley, *139, 143–154*
Ogden Nature Center, *146*
Olympic Cauldron Park, *55*
Ouray National Wildlife Refuge, *181–182*
Outdoor Retailer Expo, *19*

P
Packing, *346–347*
Painted Pony ✕ , *256*
Panguitch, *262–264*
Park City and the Southern Wasatch, *14, 95–136*
lodging, *100. 118–120, 128, 131, 136*
nightlife and arts, *120–121, 128, 131–132*
restaurants, *99–100, 114–117, 127–128, 131, 135–136*
transportation, *99*

visitor information, *100, 124, 132*
Park City Food & Wine Classic, *102*
Park City Mountain Resort, *103, 105, 111*
Park City Museum, *105*
Park Silly Sunday Market, *105*
Permits, *200, 214–215, 230, 278, 294*
Petrified Dunes, *274*
Pets, *285*
Phones, *345*
Picnic areas, *207, 224, 239, 287*
Pineview Reservoir, *152*
Pioneer Day, *19*
Pioneer Memorial Museum, *51, 53*
Pioneer Register, *202*
Pioneer Village and Museum, *125*
Plan-B Theater, *80*
Poison Spider Bicycles, *316*
Pony Express Trail, *84*
Pothole Point Trail, *297*
Prehistoric Museum USU Eastern, *178*
Price, *176–180*
Price categories, *11*
dining, *63, 100, 143, 175, 201, 215, 230, 246, 294, 308*
lodging, *73, 100, 143, 175, 201, 215, 230, 246, 294, 308*
Price Mural, *178*
Provo, *123–129*

Q
Quarry Exhibit Hall, *188–189*

R
Radio, *312*
Rafting, *24, 110, 147, 186, 189–190, 299*
tours, *349*
Rainbow Bridge National Monument, *336*
Rainbow Point, *226, 232–233*
Ranger programs, *203, 218–219, 233–234, 281–282, 298*
Red Butte Garden and Arboretum, *55*
Red Canyon Lodge ☒ , *193*
Red Canyon Visitor Center, *191*
Red Iguana ✕ , *68*
Red Mountain Resort ☒ ,*257*
Religion, *19, 32, 41, 47*

Restaurants, 11, 26–27, 344–345
Ride with a Ranger Shuttle Tours, 219
Rio Grande Depot, 50
River expeditions, 283, 290, 317–318, 328, 331
Rock climbing, 110, 127, 287, 304
Rodeos, 255
Roosevelt, 181–183
Rosenbruch Wildlife Museum, 253

S

Sabaku Sushi ✕ , 320
Safety concerns, 347–348
St. George, 252–258
St. George Art Museum, 253
St. George Dinosaur Discovery Site at Johnson Farm, 254
St. George Tabernacle, 254
St. George Temple, 253
St. Regis Deer Valley ⊡ , 119
Saloman Center at the Junction, 145
Salt Lake City, 14, 35–94
Capitol Hill and the Avenues, 38, 50–53
downtown, 37–38, 48–50
East Side and University of Utah, 38, 53–57
exploring, 42–59
Great Salt Lake, 38–39, 57–59
lodging, 73–77, 85–86, 90
nightlife and the arts, 78–80, 86, 91
North of, 14
restaurants, 46–47, 53, 62–65, 68–73, 89–90, 92–93
side trips, 82–94
Temple Square, 37, 43, 46–48
tours, 41–42
transportation, 40–41
visitor information, 42, 47–48
Wasatch Front, 39
Salt Lake City Main Library, 49
Salt Lake City Sports Complex, 61
Salt Lake Temple, 43
San Rafael Swell, 178–179
Sand Island Recreation Site, 330
Savor the Summit, 102–103
Scenic flights, 186
Scott M. Matheson Wetlands Preserve, 312–313
Sego Canyon Rock Art Panels, 326, 328

Seven Peaks Water Park, 125
Shafer Trail, 296
Sheep Creek Canyon Geological Area, 192
Sherald's ✕ , 180
Shooting Star Saloon ✕ , 154
Shopping
Dinosaurland and Eastern Utah, 188
Moab and Southeastern Utah, 324, 330
North of Salt Lake City, 150–151, 166–167
Park City and the Southern Wasatch, 122–123, 129, 132
Salt Lake City, 81–82, 93
Southwestern Utah, 257–258, 259, 264, 268, 270–271
Skiing, 19, 25
North of Salt Lake City, 153, 170
Park City and the Southern Wasatch, 106, 110–113, 130–131
Salt Lake City, 62, 83, 85, 88–89
Southwestern Utah, 250–251
tours, 349–350
Skydiving, 318
Skyline Arch, 281
Snow Canyon State Park, 253–254
Snow tubing, 113
Snowbird Ski and Summer Resort, 86, 87, 88–89
Snowboarding, 25, 110–113, 250–251
Snowmobiling, 113, 154
Soccer, 62
Soldier Hollow, 134
Sorrel River Ranch ⊡ , 323
South of Salt Lake City, 97, 123–136
Southern Wasatch. ⇨ *See* Park City and the Southern Wasatch
Southeastern Utah. ⇨ *See* Moab and Southeastern Utah
Southwestern Utah, 241–272
Itineraries, 244
lodging, 246, 249–250, 251, 256–257, 259, 262, 263–264, 268, 269
nightlife and the arts, 270
restaurants, 245, 248–249, 251, 255–256, 258–259, 262, 263, 266, 267–268, 269
tours, 265–266, 268, 270
transportation, 245

visitor information, 246, 248, 253, 261, 265
Spirit Goat (shop), 167
Spirit Lake Scenic Backway, 192
Sports and outdoor activities, 20-25
Arches National Park, 282–287
Bryce Canyon National Park, 234–238
Canyonlands National Park, 298–304
Capitol Reef National Park, 203–207
Dinosaurland and Eastern Utah, 179, 182, 185–186, 189–190, 192–193, 194
Moab and Southeastern Utah, 313–318, 328, 331, 336
North of Salt Lake City, 146–147, 152–154, 157, 162–164, 168–170
Park City and the Southern Wasatch, 106–113, 125–127, 130–131, 134–135
Salt Lake City and environs, 59–62, 83, 85, 87–89, 92
Southwestern Utah, 248, 250–251, 254–255, 257, 263, 267, 269
Zion National Park, 219–223
Springdale, 258–259
Stein Erikson Lodge ⊡ , 119
Stokes Nature Center, 161, 163
Sugar House Business District, 56
Sugar House Park, 56
Summerhill Suites by Marriott ⊡ , 166
Sundance Film Festival, 19, 40, 103, 132
Sundance Resort, 129–132
Sundance Resort ⊡ , 131
Sunrise Point, 233
Swaner Preserve & EcoCenter, 105–106
Swett Ranch, 192
Swimming, 223
Symbols, 11

T

Tabernacle, 43
Taxes, 348
Taxis, 41
Temple Square, 37, 43, 46–48
Thanksgiving Point, 93
This Is the Place Heritage Park, 56
Time, 348

Timing the visit, *18*
Timpanogos Cave National Monument, *94*
Tipping, *348*
Tony Caputo's Market and Deli ✕, *69*
Torrey, *270–272*
Tour operators, *348–350*
Bryce Canyon National Park, 234, 237–238
Canyonlands National Park, 298
Dinosaurland and Eastern Utah, 186, 189–190
Moab and Southeastern Utah, 316–318
North of Salt Lake City, 161
Park City and the Southern Wasatch, 113
Salt Lake City, 41–42
Southwestern Utah, 265–266, 268, 270
Zion National Park, 219
Tracy Aviary, *56–57*
Trail of the Ancients, *330*
Train travel, *40–41, 142, 278, 294, 342*
Transportation, *338–342.* ⇨ *See Also under specific cities and areas*
Treehouse Museum, *146*
Trip insurance, *350*
Trolley Square, *57*

U

U.S. *89, 243, 259–264*
Uinta Basin (Dinosaurland), *173, 181–194*
Uintah and Ouray Reservation, *182*
Uintah County Heritage Museum, *185*

Under-the-Rim Trail, *226*
Union Pacific Building, *50*
Union Station (Ogden), *145*
Upheaval Dome, *297*
Upper Ogden Valley, *151–154*
Upper Provo Falls, *194*
Utah Arts Festival, *40*
Utah Cowboy & Western Heritage Museum, *145*
Utah Field House of Natural History State Park, *185*
Utah Museum of Fine Arts, *57*
Utah Olympic Oval, *61*
Utah Olympic Park, *105*
Utah Shakespearean Festival, *247*
Utah State Capitol, *51, 52–53*
Utah State Railroad Museum, *145*
Utah State University, *160*
Utah's Dixie, *243, 246–259*

V

Vernal, *183–188*
Vernal Brewing Company ✕, *187*
Visitor information, *350.*⇨ *See also under specific cities and areas*

W

Wahso Asian Grill ✕, *117*
Wasatch Mountain State Park, *133–134*
Washington School House 🏨, *120*
Waterpocket Fold, *203*
Weather, *18, 97–98, 114, 140, 174, 198–199, 212–213, 228, 243–244, 276, 292, 307*
Weeping Rock, *218*

Western Legends Roundup, *261*
Wildlife preserves
Bear River Migratory Bird Refuge, 156
Ouray National Wildlife Refuge, 181–182
Scott M. Matheson Wetlands Preserve, 312–313
Willard Bay State Park, *157*
Windows, The *274, 281*
Winter sports, *223, 238*
Wooden Shoe Arch, *297*
Wolfe Ranch, *279*
Worthington Gallery, *259*

Y

Yovimpa Point, *226, 232–233*

Z

Zion Canyon Field Institute, *218*
Zion Human History Museum, *216–217, 218*
Zion Lodge, *217*
Zion-Mount Carmel Highway and Tunnels, *216*
Zion National Park, *16, 34, 209–224*
camping, 224
itineraries, 213–214
lodging, 215, 224
permits, 214–215
plants and wildlife, 213
restaurants, 215, 223–224
scenic drives, 216
tours, 219
transportation, 214
visitor information, 215–216
Zoos, *55*

PHOTO CREDITS

Front cover: Ioseba Egibar/age fotostock [Description: Arches National Park]. 1,Steve Greenwood/Visit Salt Lake City. 2, SCPhotos / Alamy. 4, Courtesy of Deer Valley Resort. 5 (top), Utah Office of Tourism. 5 (bottom), Maridav / Shutterstock. 6 (top left), Utah Office of Tourism/Steve Greenwood. 6 (top right), Courtesy of Natural History Museum of Utah. 6 (bottom right), Michael Runkel Utah / Alamy. 6 (bottom left), Johnnya123 | Dreamstime.com. 7 (top), Douglas Pulsipher/Visit Salt Lake City. 7 (bottom), Greg Gard / Alamy. 8 (top left), Ian Dagnall / Alamy. 8 (top right), Sharron Schiefelbein / age fotostock. 8 (bottom), imageBROKER / Alamy 13, imageBROKER / Alamy . 15 (left), Johnny Adolphson / Shutterstock 17 (left), NPS 17 (right), Jacom Stephens/Avid Creative, Inc./iStockphoto. 20, Saro17/iStockphoto. 21 (left), Avid Creative, Inc./iStockphoto. 21 (right), Larry Hansen/iStockphoto. 22, Sportstock / Shutterstock. 23, Daniel Kourey/iStockphoto 24, Utah Office of Tourism/Western River Expeditions. 33, David Underwood (RH Sales) 35, Sashabuzko | Dreamstime.com . 95, Scott Markewitz / Alamy. 137, Lee Foster / Alamy. 171, Jim West / Alamy. 195, Dinhhang | Dreamstime.com. 196 (top), Jacom Stephens/Avid Creative, Inc./iStockphoto. 196 (center and bottom), Frank Jensen/Utah Office of Tourism. 209, tusharkoley / Shutterstock. 210 (both) and 211, pdphoto.org [Public Domain] 225, ozoptimist / Shutterstock. 226 (all), Public Domain. 241, Michael Just / age fotostock. 273, John A Davis / Shutterstock. 274 (all), NPS. 289, Sierralara / Shutterstock . 290, (all) and 291, NPS. 305, Sportstock / Shutterstock. Back cover (from left to right): CampPhoto/iStockphoto; photo.ua / Shutterstock; Johnny Adolphson/Shutterstock. Spine: JanBer405/iStockphoto.

About Our Writers: All photos are courtesy of the writers except for the following: John Blodgett, courtesy of Tom Darnall; Lisa Church, courtesy of Kelly Thornton.

NOTES

Fodor's UTAH

Publisher: Amanda D'Acierno, *Senior Vice President*

Editorial: Arabella Bowen, *Editor in Chief*; Linda Cabasin, *Editorial Director*

Design: Tina Malaney, *Associate Art Director*; Chie Ushio, *Senior Designer*; Randy Glance, *Production Designer*

Photography: Jennifer Arnow, *Senior Photo Editor*; Mary Robnett, *Photo Researcher*

Production: Linda Schmidt, *Managing Editor*; Evangelos Vasilakis, *Associate Managing Editor*; Angela L. McLean, *Senior Production Manager*

Maps: Rebecca Baer, *Senior Map Editor*; David Lindroth, Inc. and Ed Jacobus, *Cartographers*

Sales: Jacqueline Lebow, *Sales Director*

Marketing & Publicity: Heather Dalton, *Marketing Director*; Katherine Punia, *Publicity Director*

Business & Operations: Susan Livingston, *Vice President, Strategic Business Planning*; Sue Daulton, *Vice President, Operations*

Fodors.com: Megan Bell, *Executive Director, Revenue & Business Development*; Yasmin Marinaro, *Senior Director, Marketing & Partnerships*

Copyright © 2015 by Fodor's Travel, a division of Random House LLC

Editors: Salwa Jabado, Penny Phenix

Writers: John Blodgett, Lisa Church, Kellee Katagi, Amanda Knoles, Caitlin E. Martz, Steve Pastorino

Production Editor: Carolyn Roth

5th Edition

ISBN 978-1-101-87926-9

ISSN 1547–870X

SPECIAL SALES

This book is available at special discounts for bulk purchases for sales promotions or premiums. For more information, e-mail specialmarkets@penguinrandomhouse.com

PRINTED IN THE UNITED STATES OF AMERICA

10 9 8 7 6 5 4 3 2 1

ABOUT OUR WRITERS

Writer **John Blodgett** moved to Utah three times in 16 years and still visits often. He's explored almost every corner of the Beehive State, but has a particular passion for the south's silent canyons and wide-open lands. He also became a better skier schussing Utah's famous powder. Currently based in Southern California, he has written for *Utah Business, Salt Lake Magazine, Utah Homes & Garden, Salt Lake City Weekly,* and *Catalyst*; and is a former magazine editor, newspaper reporter, and photojournalist. He updated the chapters on Capitol Reef, Zion, Bryce Canyon, Arches, and Canyonlands national parks.

Lisa Church is a freelance writer and photographer based in Moab, Utah. She is also the editor of the *Times-Independent,* Moab's hometown newspaper for more than 100 years. With roots in the South and the Midwest, Church has made her home in Moab for the past 20 years. Her work has appeared in a variety of newspapers and magazines, including the *Salt Lake Tribune, High Country News,* and *Mother Jones.* Lisa updated the Moab and Southeastern Utah chapter.

Kellee Katagi grew up exploring the American West, and the only thing that changed when she became an adult is that, as a writer and editor, she now gets paid for doing it. Katagi lives in Colorado, where she enjoys mountain excursions with her husband, Wes, and three grade-school-age budding adventurers. When she's not playing, she's usually writing about travel, sports, fitness, health, and food in all its glorious forms. She has written previously for *Fodor's Colorado* and *National Parks* guides, and, as a former managing editor of *SKI* magazine, discovered the wonders of Utah's slopes and wilderness. She updated this book's Dinosaurland and Eastern Utah chapter.

Native Texan **Amanda Knoles** first visited Utah on vacation. Her love of the mountains inspired her to move to Salt Lake City a few years later. North of Salt Lake City and southwestern Utah are two of her favorite getaways, and she updated those chapters for this book. Amanda previously contributed to four editions of *Fodor's San Diego.* She has written travel guides to Los Angeles and Las Vegas and frequently writes about cities throughout the United States for Chamber of Commerce publications. During her seven years as managing editor for a travel book publisher, she helped produce guides to a variety of domestic and international destinations.

Caitlin E. Martz is a Park City–based snow sport enthusiast who originally moved here for one winter season . . . six years ago. Hailing from Southern California, Caitlin considers skiing Utah's famous powder trumps anything else and was lucky enough to find a public relations career in Utah that allows her to enjoy everything the state has to offer. Travel and the outdoors take up her spare time. Caitlin updated the Park City and Southern Wasatch and Salt Lake City chapters.

Steve Pastorino is a Bay Area–based sports executive who loves to travel and write in his spare time. He has written extensively for Fodor's about Utah, and a half-dozen Western national parks from Arches to Yellowstone to Zion. He and his wife Teri have three children who fortunately have inherited their parents' love of travel. He updated Experience Utah and Travel Smart for this edition.